D0354855

Dramatic Literature for Children:
A Century In Review

Second Edition

Edited with Introduction & Essays by
Roger L. Bedard

Anchorage Press Plays, Inc.
Woodstock, Illinois
www.applays.com

Anchorage Press Plays, Inc.
PO Box 2901
Louisville, KY 40202-2901 USA
www.applays.com

Library of Congress number
2005930992

ISBN 978-087602-038-8
ISBN 0-87602-038-4

To

Parker and Sophie
...and all the "Little Bears"

PREFACE TO THE SECOND EDITION

In editing this second edition, almost two decades after the first, I have made many changes, including the selection of plays and the content of the introductory essays. I omitted several plays included in the first edition and added others, both to reflect my current perspectives on the development of the field and to extend this survey through the twentieth century. I also revised the introductory essay and the essays preceding each play to bring the material up-to-date.

What an interesting experience to revisit this anthology after so many years! When I assembled the first edition, I approached the work with a certainty and a sense of mission possessed only by a young professor, fresh from graduate school. I am pleased to report that this certainty has been tempered with age, experience, and the rewarding interaction with several generations of graduate students. The history of theatre for children offers a rich and complex artistic, social, and cultural mosaic. In creating this anthology, and in selecting fourteen plays to reflect over one hundred years of development in the field, I am aware that I am offering a particular construct of that history. But I offer this narrative in the hope that it illuminates some of the important issues in the development of dramatic literature for children.

RLB, May 2005

ACKNOWLEDGEMENTS

Many people have contributed to the completion of this second edition. I am personally and professionally enriched through my interaction with scores of theatre artists across the country, who have dedicated themselves to bringing quality theatre to young audiences. By inviting this professor into your play development projects and your theatres, you have greatly expanded my knowledge, understanding, and love for the field.

I wish also to thank the graduate students with whom I have worked over the years, many of whom are now working in theatres and schools across the country. You keep me thinking every day!

And thank you CJ!

TABLE OF CONTENTS

Preface

THE CENTURY IN REVIEW

Early Historical Contexts

Young people have attended the theatre and participated in drama and theatre activities, both purposefully and casually, since the beginnings of theatre in western civilization. Although histories often do not tell the story, educators have used theatre and drama throughout much of our recorded history; and, over that same time, a large percentage of theatre audiences have also included young people along with adults, but with little special attention paid. At other times in our history, particularly beginning in the last century, theatre artists have focused specifically on the needs and interests of children, creating plays and theatre events specific to young audiences. Therein rests the focus of this book.

Any consideration of the history of dramatic literature for children in the United States must move through multiple issues that impact the subject, including:

1) the practical, ideological, and aesthetic differences between literature created for playground, classroom, and theatrical uses;

2) long-held prejudices in the theatre world that privilege the work of "professionals" over that of "amateurs," while at the same time valuing theatre created for adults over that focused on children;

4) issues of canonicity that have preserved and elevated some texts while dismissing others; and

5) ever-changing cultural and societal views of children and childhood.

This anthology includes a selection of plays (with commentary) that were written to be produced *for* young audiences throughout the twentieth century, with specific attention to those works that I find reflective of particular issues or trends in the field. Thus, given the issues noted above, and the many activities of the theatre

1

for youth field (theatre education, recreational drama, amateur youth theatre, professional theatre, etc.), I offer a relatively narrow narrative through a broadly diverse subject. But in the telling, I hope to clarify some of these same issues and confusions.

Several factors specific to the twentieth century figure prominently in this narrative, including: the creation and sustenance of a tradition of professional theatre artists working specifically for young audiences, the wider dissemination of plays for children through professional networks and through publication, and the contemporary views of children and childhood that in many ways more clearly differentiate between adult and child than the views of centuries past.

Historical Precedents

There exists today a wide selection of plays written to be performed for young audiences. Although this dynamic field continues to redefine itself in terms of form, style, and subject matter, it owes much of its definition to historical precedents, some of which I wish to consider briefly.

Lowell Swortzell, writing in 1969, asserts that "the first known play expressly intended for youngsters," appeared "[s]ome time between 1553 and 1558." This play, written by an "anonymous dramatist," was entitled, *A New Interlude for Children to Play, Named Jack Juggler, both Witty and Very Pleasant.*[1] Jonathan Levy and Floraine Kay, writing in 1996, trace historical vestiges of drama with and for young people to European Jesuit schools of this same mid-sixteenth century period.[2]

Various forms of theatre with and for young people undoubtedly occurred prior to that time—in education and in communities, if not the theatres—even though the historical footprints remain hidden. Indeed, Plato, writing over 2000 years ago, warns of the pernicious effects of the presentation of bad poetry (including drama) on the education of young people:

> And shall we just carelessly allow children to hear

2

any casual tales which may be devised by casual persons, and to receive into their minds ideas for the most part the very opposite of those which we should wish them to have when they grow up?[3]

In addition to the protectionist ethos explicit in that statement, it also suggests the pervasiveness of the practice.

Contemporary general theatre history texts make little or no mention of theatre activity *for* children prior to modern times. In most instances, this omission occurred because for much of recorded history anyone beyond the age of a biologically dependent infant was generally considered little different from an adult. But certainly young people were a part of the audiences of much of the diverse theatre activity that occurred throughout the course of western theatre history. From the strolling storytellers, to the rag-tag troupes performing in town squares, from the community religious and secular dramas of the Middle Ages, to the *commedia* players in sixteenth and seventeenth century Europe, young people viewed the theatre. The exceptions to this came when theatre became more formalized. For example, whenever the theatre moved indoors, into royal courtrooms or to formal theatres, issues of accessibility often precluded the attendance of young people.

Drama situated in education, including storytelling and other forms of mimesis, as suggested early on by Plato, provides both the clearest historical through line of drama activities with young people, as well as an early legacy of published children's plays. From the virtually non-existent historical evidence of the nature, purpose, and context of *Jack Juggler* in the late sixteenth century, we can trace lines of activity to the well-documented dramatic activity with young people of the late eighteenth and early nineteenth centuries. During this period, under the pervasive influence of the philosophies of Locke and Rousseau, parents and teachers used dramatic play as a tool in the proper moral education of young people, and this resulted in the publication of numerous such plays throughout Europe and the United States. Among the more widely disseminated were the works of French

3

educator, Madame La Comtesse de Genlis–particularly her *Theatre d'education a l'usage de la jeunesse,* a collection of plays designed for moral and spiritual education.[4] Jonathan Levy, in his *Gymnasium of the Imagination,* has chronicled the work of several European and American playwright/educators from this period, including Hannah More, Arnaud Berquin, Maria Edgeworth, and Anna Jameson.[5]

Colonial Traditions in the United States

Theatre and young people in colonial United States mirrored the activities found elsewhere in the world. One can find, for example, many instances of the protectionist ethos that arose from the fear of the commingling of young people and the theatre. In 1762, when the Governor of New Hampshire refused a license to performers, the petition against the theatre read, in part, that plays "would be of very pernicious consequences, not only to the morals of the young people, (even if there should be no immoral exhibitions) by dissipating their minds, and giving them an idle turn of attachment to pleasure and amusement, with other ill effects. . . ."[6] Community leaders at a 1768 Society of Friends meeting in Philadelphia warned the gathering to be "especially mindful of the youth" that they not be "captivated by the ensnaring diversion of the . . . Stage Plays . . . intended to be exhibited in and near the city."[7]

Historical accounts of the theatre of Colonial America assume a theatre designed for adults. In the pre-revolution years theatre companies performed with makeshift arrangements in taverns, town halls, and in a very few theatres. Each playing situation, in turn, influenced the class, age, and gender of the audience; and as the American theatre in the nineteenth century moved into formal theatre spaces in the large cities, and presented traditional classical repertoires, it also became more restricted, by economics, if not by class. Yet, these factors did not always preclude the attendance of children. For example, an 1809 account from an audience member at a production starring noted child actor, Master Payne, acknowledges "a knot of youngsters . . . sitting together." Of

4

course he also notes that "some of . . . [them] were not particularly interested in what was going on before them."[8]

As early American professional theatre artists showed no interest in young audiences, educators quickly filled this void, explicitly acknowledging the utility of using theatre in the moral education of young people. Note the publication in 1798 of Charles Stearns' *Dramatic Dialogues for the Use of the Schools*.[9] A century after the publication of the book, educators acknowledged both the "pioneer" nature of this text and, more importantly, cited its widespread use.[10]

Stearns, on his significant authority as an eighteenth century minister and school headmaster, enthusiastically promotes the use of moral dialogues in school exhibitions, noting that, when properly "managed," performances of dialogues can "be productive of a most innocent and rational amusement, and not only improve the outward carriage of the students, but implant the most useful morals in them, and in the minds of their friends, who attend their performances."[11]

Within this moral context drama-in-education, manifested primarily in the form of dialogues and informal home and community children's plays, became widespread throughout the nineteenth century. Levy and Mahard, in their "Preliminary Checklist of Early Printed Plays in English, 1780–1855," list over five hundred published plays "written to be performed by or for children."[12] With the exception of the occasional "grand allegorical pantomime spectacle," the vast majority of these plays were written for school or home use. This underscores both society's endorsement of this "proper" use of the drama in the home and the schools and the parallel lack of such activity in the professional theatre of the time. As Levy notes, "Historians will probably never know the true extent of theatrical activity in American schools between the end of the eighteenth century and the middle of the nineteenth, for performances and recitations of one kind or another were simply too common to be taken special note of."[13]

The Professional Theatre and Young People: Initial Stirrings

Popular theatre activities in the first half of the nineteenth century looked much different than the theatre of today, and as one historian notes, "[c]ommon people did not just join the audiences. They dominated them."[14] A theatre event of the time might have included a melodrama or a freely altered version of a Shakespeare play (purged of "vulgarity" and "blemishes"), an equestrian act, and entertainment between acts by jugglers, acrobats, trained animals, and assorted "freaks." Each play generally had an explicit message (sentimentality, nationalism, democracy) reinforcing traditional moral values. This "common" theatre also spawned the creation of large theatre structures, like the Bowery Theatre (1826) in New York, which held an audience of four throusand people.[15] The circus soon followed this popular entertainment, as by the 1830s traveling exhibitions of such things as bears and tigers, claiming to be educational in nature, combined with equestrians and acrobats to offer circus-like entertainment.[16] Given the widespread popularity of these offerings, young people certainly availed themselves of this entertainment, although the commercial theatre did not offer much fare specifically for children until the later half of the nineteenth century.

Popular melodramas such as *Uncle Tom's Cabin* and *Rip Van Winkle* also toured extensively throughout the country in the nineteenth century, firmly establishing the popularity of a dramatic form that included spectacle, clearly defined good and bad characters, and explicit moralizing—all attributes that became fundamental to the emerging repertoire designed for children.

Throughout the last part of the nineteenth century, theatregoing adults and children also patronized a new addition to the New York professional stage: adaptations of British pantomimes. Although still presented in England today, primarily as holiday family entertainment, these spectacular entertainments have not appeared on the US commercial stage much beyond the beginning of the twentieth century. The pantomime grew from centuries old traditions of British popular entertainment, many of which did not translate well to eighteenth century U.S. popular culture. Pantomimes on the New York stage varied in form and content in terms of their target audiences. Some tended more toward burlesque, and thus were definitely targeted to adult audiences; others, often billed as "Spectacles" or "Extravaganzas," attempted to appeal to audiences of all ages and, often, specifically to children. Regardless of their design, most pantomimes presented traditional fairytale characters and stories amid lavish visual spectacle. While U.S. audiences were probably somewhat put off by the many conventions peculiar to this British form, the spectacle undoubtedly enthralled old and young alike.

Between 1878 and 1903 at least ten pantomime-like productions appeared on the New York stage, including such titles as *Cinderella* (1878), *The Crystal Slipper* (1888), *Aladdin* (1895), and *Little Red Riding Hood* (1900).[17] An 1896 production of *Jack and the Beanstalk* was specifically described as a "nursery play" presented "in the manner of the English Christmas Pantomime."[18]

Historian and theorist Constance D'Arcy Mackay, writing in 1915, asserted that "the first professional play designed for children" in this country was the stage adaptation of Frances H. Burnett's popular children's story, *Little Lord Fauntleroy*, presented in New York in 1888.[19] While the issue of "firsts" remains problematic from historical perspectives, this production stands out because of its ability to attract significant New York press coverage and thus establish high profile precedents for theatre for young people in the professional/commercial theatre. The *New York Herald*, for example, offered a headline that read: "*Little Lord Fauntlerory* Makes a Big Hit at the Broadway."[20]

The celebrated production of *Little Lord Fauntleroy* grew out of a timely convergence of talents and opportunities: Burnett was then a well-known children's book author and also an emerging professional playwright (for adults); the wide popularity of the Fauntleroy story preceded the play; the casting of child stars (who would play the lead character) helped draw audiences to the New York stage; and the popularity of circuses and other popular entertainments in New York suggested the commercial viability of theatre for children.

An earlier production of Burnett's *Editha's Burglar* proved an important impetus to the staging of *Fauntleroy* and to Burnett's later success with *The Little Princess*. In 1887 eight-year-old Elsie Leslie, who, as a four-year-old, had played Meenie in Joseph Jefferson's *Rip Van Winkle*, appeared to critical acclaim as Editha in the New York production of *Editha's Burglar*, and she followed that with her role as Fauntleroy. Soon the practice of placing young actors in leading roles so dominated the American stage that, in 1889, editors of the *New York Times* decried "the 'Fauntleroy' craze . . . [that] threatens to precipitate on the American theatre a swarm of young 'stars' to the number of which there would seem to be no limit."[21]

The commercial success of *Fauntleroy* quickly spawned other New York productions designed for children, including a well-publicized dramatization of Mark Twain's *The Prince and The Pauper*, which also capitalized on a popular story, a noted author, and the use of child actors.[22]

Counting revivals of these plays and others, at least one play for children generally appeared in a Broadway theatre each year for the three decades following the premier of *Fauntleroy*. In some years, such as 1899, 1913, and 1918, as many as four different children's plays were presented. Thus theatre took its place among an increasingly diverse array of commercial entertainment available for children at the beginning of the twentieth century. According to historian Laura Salazar, "[d]uring Easter week in 1900, an adult in New York had the choice of amusing a child at seven different shows recommended by the *New York Times*," including *Jack and the Giant*, *Rip Van Winkle*, *Buffalo Bill's Wild West Show*, and an array of other circus-like events.[23]

The success of children's plays on the commercial stage during this time stemmed from many issues, including the escapist sentimentality presented and the faddish appeal of the child actors. The following programs notes from the *The Little Princess*, hail the play as the success of the year, offering this explanation:

> In noting the unusual unanimity of the press and public in praising and patronizing *The Little Princess*, it is worth while to speculate on the reason. Perhaps it is because the play offers no problem. There is presented just a plain old view of right and wrong-doing without romantic attachments. The story is dainty, true to life, and thoroughly interesting in a straight-forward human way. In it Mrs. Burnett has incorporated sweetness, pathos and humor. It is all simple, but it has its complications; not the complications arising from the misunderstandings which are the ordinary conventions of the stage, but emotional complications of the most delicate order. . . .[24]

While these "entertainments" may have, as Salazar notes, "provided charming escapism," the theatre activities available for young people at this time, including the plays aimed specifically at child and family audiences, did little to create a viable repertoire of new plays for children. Most plays commercially produced during this time were based on popular children's books or fairytales. This reliance on known and marketable material obviously met the monetary needs of the commercial stage; but it also set a precedent, and, for many decades after, playwrights rarely used original subjects for their children's plays.

Frances H. Burnett became the most-produced playwright for children of this time. She adapted three of her children's stories for the stage, and one of them, *The Little Princess*, is still produced today in various adaptations. Other notable commercial productions from this period include *Snow White and the Seven Dwarfs*, by Jessie Braham White, *Alice in Wonderland*, by Alice Gerstenberg, and *Treasure Island*, by Jules Eckard Goodman.

James M. Barrie's *Peter Pan,* one of the most widely known children's plays of the twentieth century, opened in New York in 1905. This play, which has remained popular in revival after revival throughout the century, has also been seen in several film and television adaptations. *Peter Pan* typifies many of the complex identity issues endemic to this "first" generation of professional theatre for young audiences. Situated within an explicitly commercial world, the play attracted audiences by capitalizing on a number of factors, few of which bore any direct relationship to the needs and/or interests of the potential children in the audience. First, while the play was not written explicitly for young audiences, the story of the longing for never-ending youth and the presence of youthful protagonists easily helped it tap into the then increasingly accessible family market. Additionally, the play initially succeeded primarily as a star vehicle for Maude Adams, who had played the role with acclaim in the London production. That she was playing a male role, in the British tradition of the so-called "Breeches" parts, only added to the allure. The combination of these factors helped the play secure audiences of all ages, while it also claimed an identity as a play for children.

Plays of interest to family audiences also grew out of the work of Stuart Walker and his Portmanteau Theatre Company, organized in 1916. Concentrating on adaptations of well-known literature, Walker wrote such plays as *The Birthday of the Infanta*, *Six Who Pass While the Lentils Boil*, and *Jonathan Makes a Wish*. The Portmanteau Theatre operated on the fringes of the commercial theatre world, touring fully staged professional productions to settlement houses and other neighborhood centers.[25]

Records suggest that by about 1920 the popularity of professional, commercial plays for children had diminished, as such activity virtually ceased on the New York stage. For several decades after this time, the only professional productions of children's plays presented in New York consisted of limited revivals of the few plays available, such as *Peter Pan* and *The Little Princess*.

Theatre as Social Work

This late nineteenth century commercial theatre activity in New York appeared amidst significant cultural shifts in the United States;

and out of this grew a different picture of children and childhood than that fostered in the early republic. After the Civil War, large-scale industrialization brought the decline of agrarian communities, the growth of cities, the displacement of large numbers of both black and white southerners, and a significant influx of immigrants from western Europe into the growing urban centers. This urbanization exacerbated issues of social and economic class and strained the existing legal and social systems of these cities; and the resulting culture wars challenged many long held views of the relationship between parent and child.

In 1875 Elbridge T. Gerry founded the New York Society for the Prevention of Cruelty to Children (SPCC), an organization that quickly expanded throughout the country. Formed in response to what was seen as the widespread physical and emotional abuse of children (often in the workplace, and often at the hands of or with the knowledge of their parents) the SPCC was but one manifestation of the emerging idea of a necessary civic responsibility for the well-being of children. As children became seen less as just "property" of their parents, and more as "innocents" that needed societal "protection," social welfare and legal issues came to the forefront, resulting in the widespread enactment of child labor and compulsory education laws.

During what has come to be known as the Progressive Movement (c.1890–1920), social activists, particularly those based in the larger cities, expressed increasing alarm at what they saw as profound dangers to the nations' youth. The Progressive Movement was dominated by two sometimes conflicting impulses: humanitarianism and the desire for social control.[26] This widespread movement sought to maintain "American values" and middle-class ideals amidst the onslaught of immigration and the class stratification exacerbated by industrialization and urbanization. Issues of race, class, and ethnicity often defined the battle lines of these culture wars.

Out of this complex context grew a number of organizations to serve and to mold youth, from the rigid organization of the

Boy Scouts (established in the U.S. in 1912) to the supervision fostered by the Playground Association of America (founded in 1906).[27] The settlement houses became one of the most dominant players in this social movement. Created essentially as social service agencies, the settlement houses typically served inner city neighborhoods, which often included immigrant populations as well as the poor and indigent. Jane Addams established the most famous of these, Hull-House, in Chicago in 1889; and by 1910 there were over four hundred settlement houses in existence in cities throughout the country.[28] Hull-House programs, as with many of the settlement houses, included a variety of social service programs; but their drama and theatre programs became among the more visible and influential of the services offered for adults and young people. As Addams notes:

> . . . long before the five-cent theatre was even heard of, we had accumulated much testimony as to the power of the drama, and we would have been dull indeed if we had not availed ourselves of the use of the play at Hull-House, not only as an agent of recreation and education, but as a vehicle of self-expression for the teeming young life all about us.[29]

Motivated by her own experience of viewing the Passion Play at Oberammergau, Addams vigorously pursued in this drama work what she saw as: "the stage, as a reconstructing and reorganizing agent of accepted moral truths."[30]

Other notable settlement house drama programs of the time include those at the Henry Street Settlement, established in New York in 1893 by Lillian Wald, and the Children's Educational Theatre, created by Alice Minnie Herts Heniger in 1903, as a part of the Educational Alliance, a New York Settlement House serving Russian and Polish Jewish immigrants. Historian Nellie McCaslin describes the Children's Educational Theatre as "the first organized theatre for children in this country."[31] While the Children's Educational Theatre became a popular neighborhood institution, neither this group nor other settlement house children's theatre programs exerted influence in expanding the repertoire of plays available for young audiences. Plays produced by the Educational Theatre (and the other settlements) primarily included previous successes from the commercial stage, such as *The Little Princess*, *The Prince and the Pauper*, and *Little Lord Fauntleroy*.[32]

The settlement houses, often based in communities with diverse ethnic populations, used drama primarily as a means of instilling perceived "universal values" of those who ran the organizations; but occasionally such organizations celebrated that diversity through the arts. For example, Karamu House, founded in Cleveland in 1915, focused primarily on theatre, storytelling, and the arts as reflected in the families of the community, who were, at various times, of Jewish, Syrian, Italian, and African heritage.[33]

The practice of children's theatre as social work received a significant, long-term boost with the establishment of the Junior League in New York in 1901. This organization grew quickly; and by 1921 The Association of Junior Leagues of America (AJLA) was formed to unite the thirty leagues then in existence, covering most of the major cities in the country.[34] The Junior League was formed to provide an outlet for wealthy young women (debutants) to serve their communities prior to taking on the responsibilities of home and family. As these young women traveled to the settlement houses, they translated their social work into what they knew: the arts. Before long, many leagues were presenting plays for child audiences. As early as 1912 the Boston League presented seventeen performances of *Aladdin*; and, within the next few years, the Chicago and New York groups also presented children's plays.[35]

In 1924 the members of the Chicago League voted to make theatre their "main work," and the group quickly progressed from an organization that occasionally presented "a little fairy play, requiring the simplest of arrangements," to one that set as its major social work agenda the production of a season of plays for young audiences.[36] While no other league embraced children's theatre as completely as the Chicago League, according to one history

13

of the Junior League, "children's theatre in one form or another was the pet project of nearly every 1920s Junior League."[37] This commitment to children's theatre continued to grow until mid-century, and AJLA set up a national Play Bureau through which they launched a number of programs to promote the development of children's theatre. These included: 1) hiring theatre-trained staff to work with the local leagues to improve the quality of their children's theatre work; 2) organizing national children's theatre conferences and regional "institutes" as resources for the local leagues; and 3) establishing a manuscript play library to encourage the dissemination of plays suitable for production by the leagues.

In 1940–1941 Junior Leagues presented 1,679 children's theatre performances to audiences totaling almost 600,000 young people. The number of productions waned considerably during World War II, and the AJLA thereafter gradually diverted their focus from children's theatre to their many other social work pursuits; yet a significant number of leagues then began to sponsor professional children's theatre companies rather than produce theatre themselves. In 1955–1956 Leagues presented over five thousand children's theatre performances, including league presentations and also then including sponsored professional groups.[38]

As early as 1924 Leagues were holding contests for new children's plays.[39] Beginning in 1928 Samuel French, Inc. agreed to publish some of the winning plays of annual AJLA contests; and, in 1946, Dramatic Publishing issued eight plays from the Junior League library. In 1947 AJLA began its own publishing by releasing some of its manuscripts in mimeographed form.[40] AJLA continued the practice of licensing children's theatre productions until 1971.[41]

The Junior League stands as one of the significant forces in the development of dramatic literature for children in this country through the middle of the twentieth century. This organization strove to be a resource for high quality children's plays and an agent for the playwrights. They carefully screened their play library holdings and insisted upon the payment of royalties for the production of their plays. Yet, few notable plays resulted from these efforts. Rather, the League, focusing on social work goals, developed a body of work that increased the repertoire, quantitatively, but also narrowed the repertoire in form and content. They generally offered only plays with familiar fairy and folktale titles, and the plays all required small casts and minimal technical requirements. They also favored plays that could easily be toured and could be presented by casts of women, thus particularly foregrounding plays with animal characters. In spite of their best intentions, the plays that resulted from this work did not move much beyond the 1915 idea of "putting on a simple fairy play with the simplest of scenic requirements."

The children's-theatre-as-social-work movement took a different turn after the work of the leagues; and, in the latter part of the century, this manifested itself through plays written to warn young people of the various evils confronting them in society. During this time many producers (and funders) saw theatre as a way to teach *explicitly,* resulting in a barrage of plays dealing with a variety of social concerns, including sexual abuse, teen pregnancy, substance abuse, and teen suicide. This movement, like the settlement house work and the League plays that preceded it, added few if any lasting plays to the repertoire. But these explicit "issue" plays graphically illustrate yet another dimension of the often-perceived role of dramatic literature for children in the past century: to teach.

Community and Recreational Children's Theatre

Constance D'Arcy Mackay, who promoted amateur theatre production, advocated the use of drama in recreation in her 1915 book, *How to Produce Children's Plays.*[42] She also compiled four volumes of her own dramatizations of legends and folktales for use by amateur groups: *House of the Heart and Other Plays, Silver Thread and Other Plays, Patriotic plays and Pageants for Young People,* and *Forest Princess and Other Masques.*[43]

The Drama League of America offered a similar perspective of children's plays in a bibliography published in 1915. This list focuses explicitly on plays that reflect children's theatre as a "popular branch of recreation" and an "important branch of education." [44]

Although few writers had shown an interest in writings plays for the professional children's theatre of the time, this recreational emphasis spurred the creation of scores of new plays. Many of these writers had little interest in the theatre and much interest in playground activities, and thus the body of literature offered more promise as "playtime" activities than theatre events. Such plays typically present moralistic stories that sacrifice character and plot development to simplistic situations to be enacted by children. Anthologies from the period with such titles as *Child's Book of Holiday Plays, Household Plays for Young People, Industrial Plays for Young People,* and *Red Letter Day Plays,* accurately reflect this trend in the development of dramatic literature for children.[45]

Montrose Moses, editor of three anthologies of children's plays, described the status of the development of dramatic literature for children in the early 1920s:

> The paucity of children's plays continues; yet the schoolroom, the club, the recreation groups still make their insistent demands. And where there is the demand, there is the supply. . . . Teachers are frantically teaching educational dramatics. Little bodies are being swathed in Dennison paper, little arms are being stretched in Dalcroze eurythmics, little minds are being crammed with innocuous dialogue. Wrong kinds of books are being written, demonstrating easy methods of play production, by Professors of Athletics, who know nothing whatsoever about the theatre, and recommend rules for acting that are totally absurd. Those who write children's plays have in mind all the limitations of a child's ability. . . .
>
> These educational requirements are having a devastating effect on the dramatic output, and the editor has oftentimes been discouraged by the seeming

indifference on the part of the writers of children's plays to attempt anything of an artistic nature.[46]

The rapidly growing Little Theatre movement also influenced the growth and development of plays for children during the 1920s and 1930s. Beginning with a network of three theatres established in 1911–1912, this movement grew so that by 1917 it included over fifty theatres throughout the country. While these theatres offered diverse programming, a survey taken in 1928 showed that over half of the "outstanding" community-based theatres in this country produced plays for young audiences.[47]

The dominance of recreational drama at the time severely restricted producers seeking plays for aesthetic rather than recreational values. Since amateur groups had neither the status nor the financial resources to attract professional writers to create new children's plays, they too relied heavily on the plays previously developed for the commercial stage. Favorites on this circuit included *The Little Princess* and Jessie Braham White's *Snow White and the Seven Dwarfs*. During this time, A.A. Milne, the author of the popular Pooh books, also supplied two new plays to this repertoire: *Make Believe* and *Toad of Toad Hall*. These, plus whatever fairytale adaptations the producers could secure, became the mainstay of the Little Theatre programs.

New Playwrights Emerge

During the 1920s and the 1930s children's theatre producers supported little innovation as they quickly recognized the profits to be earned from titles recognized by the adults who bought the tickets for the young people. As a consequence the development of the literature stalled between the economic considerations, which discouraged the professionals and inhibited the amateurs, and the recreation movement, which spawned a different form of literature. But slowly a new generation of trained playwrights turned their attention to the child audience with a seriousness of artistic purpose seldom evidenced in the field to that time.

In 1915 Alice Gerstenberg presented her *Alice in Wonderland* on the New York stage, and at the time she reportedly was surprised at the number of young people in attendance. In 1921 Gerstenberg led the Chicago Junior League in its ground-breaking work in children's theatre. Commenting on this work several years later, Gerstenberg noted:

> From its inception the theatre for children was intended to rank credibly with those many little art theatres which have become a significant and vital part of the dramatic life of all countries today. . . . Those executive few chosen as leaders must inform themselves as to what has been going on in the world in the history of drama for the last quarter of a century and link their theatre credibility to the best of the day. . . .

> The Junior League Children's Theatre must stand for more than charity, for more than the fun of play and self expression; it has a spiritual obligation toward the grown-up audience of the future.[48]

Noted children's playwright Charlotte Chorpenning first turned her attention to writing plays for children in 1928, when asked by Winifred Ward, then her colleague at Northwestern University, to write a play for Ward's Evanston Children's Theatre.[49] Chorpenning's own career up to that time provided her with unique preparation for this job. Beginning as an English teacher decades before, Chorpenning developed an interest in play writing. This led to specialized study with George Pierce Baker in 1913, and a short career as a professional playwright (for adults). Chorpenning subsequently became involved in community drama, after which she was hired by Neva Boyd, of the Recreation Training School of Chicago, to train social workers and playground leaders in the use of drama. This work led to an appointment in the school of sociology at Northwestern and her interaction with Ward.

Chorpenning subsequently served (from 1932-1952) as director of children's theatre at the Goodman Theatre, then located at the Art Institute of Chicago. During this period Chorpenning wrote over forty children's plays and collaborated on several others. She also taught play writing, advised scores of fledgling Chicago playwrights, and conducted play writing workshops across the country. Playwrights who took her courses included Madge Miller, Nora MacAlvay, Martha B. King, Geraldine B. Siks, and Rosemary Musil. Each of the writers subsequently published at least one play for children.

Once Chorpenning's work and reputation spread, she influenced the field in ways both invigorating and limiting. Producers looked to her plays to bolster their predictable seasons, while some playwrights looked to her work for standards and even formulas that they might apply to their own writing.

Although not all of the playwrights of the time were Chorpenning's students, most of the plays written at this time echo her techniques. She wrote plays and taught playwriting much in the style taught her by George Pierce Baker. Emphasizing formal structure and clearly defined characters and action, she created sometimes elaborate, and always melodramatic, "well-made" plays, each with explicit moralistic perspectives. Most of her plays are dramatizations of familiar fairy and folktales, written in a realistic style. Yet they reflect a theatrical sophistication and seriousness of purpose much beyond that seen in the "simple fairy plays" of the Junior League; and, they caught the attention of amateur and professional producers and several publishers. Because her plays were produced widely, she exerted significant influence in defining a mid-century aesthetic for the field. Among her more popular works at that time were: *The Emperor's New Clothes, Rumpelstiltskin, The Sleeping Beauty, Jack and the Beanstalk,* and *Hansel and Gretel.*

Organizing The Children's Theatre Movement

In 1944 Winifred Ward convened a meeting at Northwestern University of children's theatre practitioners from around the country to unify the work under some sort of national organization. Electing to align themselves as the Children's Theatre Committee of the American Educational Theatre Association (AETA), this group brought together teachers, professors, recreation leaders, and representatives from junior leagues to promote drama and theatre with and for young people. This advocacy group quickly became active in all manner of projects related to these objectives, including promoting the writing of "quality" plays for young audiences.[50]

In 1949 a "Children's Scripts Evaluation Committee" of AETA published a list of sixty-one "recommended" full length plays for children.[51]   This list, divided among "Fairy Tale Plays," "Favorite Story Plays," and "Historical Plays," reflects both the quantitative growth in the literature to that time as well as the narrow parameters of that growth. This list also clearly indicates the firm grip that certain dominant perspectives (in the style of Chorpenning's work) held on the field. The categories preclude any plays based on original stories; and most all of the recommended plays fit what was becoming the standard form: no more than one hour in length; simple, melodramatic characters and situations, with a male protagonist; and a lighthearted story with an unambiguous, happy ending.

Some of the then more popular of the recommended plays included: *Aladdin and the Wonderful Lamp* (Norris), *The Elves and the Shoemaker* (MacAlvay), *The Emperor's New Clothes* (Chorpenning), *Jack and the Beanstalk* (Chorpenning), *The Land of the Dragon* (Miller), *Peter, Peter, Pumpkin Eater* (King), and *Rumpelstiltskin* (Chorpenning). This list also includes the ever present successes from the professional theatre: *Snow White and the Seven Dwarfs* (White), *Peter Pan* (Barrie), and *The Little Princess* (Burnett).

Children's Radio Drama

Beginning in the 1920s radio emerged as the most important and ubiquitous source of entertainment for young and old alike; and, just as the country plunged into the Great Depression, radio brought free entertainment into homes across the nation. In 1936 more than twenty-three million homes contained radios; and children of the time listened to an average of six hours per week of programming, primarily to dramatic programs.[52] In prior years, the popularity of motion pictures with young people had caused many groups and organizations (such as the settlement houses) to position themselves explicitly as protectors of youth against these new forms of representation. These social crusaders found that the "traditional" children's plays presented a safe and simplistic morality appropriate, if not important, for the young people of the time. Yet the popularity of dramas produced on radio presented an even more ubiquitous and insidious threat to this normalizing ethos. The following code of ethics for children's programming adopted by the National Association of Broadcasters in 1928 (revised in 1935 and 1939) gives voice to the protective ideologies that governed society's view of the potential difficulties with radio drama, and, implicitly, children's drama as a whole. The code states:

> ... the programs should reflect respect for parents, adult authority, law and order, clean living, high morals, fair play and honorable behavior. Such programs should not contain sequences involving horror or torture or use of the supernatural or superstitious or any other material which might reasonably be regarded as likely to overstimulate the child listener, or be prejudicial to sound character development.[53]

Radio programmers of the time offered a variety of dramatic programs specifically for young people, and, of course, young people also listened to programs designed for adult listeners. The popular children's radio dramas (many of them serials) included such titles as: *Buck Rogers*, *Bobby Benson*, *Let's Pretend*, *Jack Armstrong*, and *Little Orphan Annie*.[54]

Let's Pretend, a popular radio program focusing on dramatizations of fiction and fairy tales, played from 1930 to 1954. The history of this show, including the commercial sponsorship by Cream of Wheat (1943–1952) and the recording of six record albums of the show (1946–1947), demonstrates the significant economic and social influence radio had on the lives of young people.[55]

Radio drama, in its way, offered innovation to the children's dramatic form through a wide range of original stories, contemporary child protagonists, and realistic settings. The children's theatre field of the time did not always mimic that innovation, content instead to sustain itself on the traditional fairy and folktale repertoire.

The Professionals Return

From the 1920s through the 1950s the New York commercial theatre continued offering the occasional homage to the family audience, but neither this venue nor the wider professional adult theatre provided much impetus for the development of new plays for young audiences. Yet, at least two distinct professional children's theatre groups operated during this time, keeping the hope of professional children's theatre alive.

In 1923 Clare Tree Major began her Clare Tree Major Children's Theatre, which lasted almost thirty years. This theatre group first played in theatres in New York, and then toured to the schools. Major developed a unique partnership with the English teachers in some of the schools, planning her repertoire to align with the schools' curricula, thus building audiences for her group. Ultimately Major sent several toured companies out each year, playing in schools across the country. While the work of this company provided an alternative to such amateur groups as the local leagues, the fact that they were professional did not necessarily ensure quality; nor did the work of this group expand the canon of available plays. Major herself wrote most of the plays produced, compiling a repertoire of over fifty-seven children's plays. Consistent with the trends of other organizations, Major primarily wrote and produced plays based on fairytales or popular stories. Few other theatre organizations produced these works.[56]

A second organization, The Federal Theatre Project (FTP), operating from 1935 until 1939, supported and developed professional theatre groups across the country, including groups specifically performing for child audiences. Organized by the federal government as one part of the Works Progress Administration, the Federal Theatre Project was created to provide gainful employment for qualified artists who were then on "relief." According to one historian, the group had a grand vision for children's theatre:

> Federal Theatre officials dreamed of a nationwide network of children's theatres established in every large city and extending into every town and hamlet. Performances would reach thousands, perhaps millions, of children never touched before by live theatre. Entertainment and education would go hand-in-hand, as child audiences learned about various cultures and participated vicariously in problem solving. . . . With government subsidy, the Federal Children's Theatre would not be subject to economic pitfalls of commercial children's theatre. The Federal Theatre, therefore, represented the first serious attempt by theatre professionals to create a theatre for children on a scale large enough to reach the thousands of children who had never seen a play.[57]

The Federal Theatre established children's theatre units (adults performing for young people) in New York City, Los Angeles, and Cleveland. In addition, at least thirteen other Federal Theatre groups performed children's theatre on a regular basis. The FTP also sponsored Black theatre troupes, many of which also presented theatre for children. While these segregated troupes reflected the racially polarized communities of the time, the Black troupes offered a different racial perspective to child audiences by presenting black actors on the stage in the roles of sympathetic protagonists.

The FTP conducted surveys and consulted experts in theatre

and education to inform the selection, creation, and style of presentation for their plays for young people. This, reportedly, led them to lessen the emphasis on entertainment and to "place the greater emphasis on the educational."[58] The FTP produced a wide range of children's plays during its brief existence. The plays included some from the popular repertoire, such as Chorpenning's *The Emperor's New Clothes*, as well as some new creations, such as Yasha Frank's *Pinocchio*, and a play called *Flight*, created in the "living newspaper" format popularized by the FTP. Yet, according to historian Lowell Swortzell, the FTP "children's theatre repertory was dominated by plays drawn from fairy and folktales and by dramatizations of famous stories and novels." The "most performed" of these included: *Aladdin, Cinderella, Hansel and Gretel, Jack and the Beanstalk, Snow White,* and *The Emperor's New Clothes.*[59]

In May 1937 the New York troupe premiered Oscar Saul's *Revolt of the Beavers,* perhaps the most famous, or infamous, children's play produced by the FTP. Opening in the midst of growing conflict between the FTP and the Congress, the play presented an allegorical tale of worker beavers struggling against their leader. After *New York Times* theatre critic Brooks Atkinson published a review of the production under the headline "Mother Goose Marx,"[60] the political struggle of FTP reached a crisis point, and two years later (1939) Congress eliminated all funding for the Federal Theatre.[61]

Ultimately Congress closed the FTP because they were convinced that the theatre organization was a center of communist activities, and they did not exclude the children's theatre troupes and activities from this condemnation. The promise of a national theatre thus died in the breakup of the often untenable relationship between artists and government funding, playing out a dispute repeated many times since then, on both local and national levels. The FTP existed only from 1935 until 1939; yet, from many perspectives, this group injected a vitality into the children's theatre field that had long-term implications in the development of the field. The FTP introduced professional theatre artists to the idea of performing for young audiences; and they produced children's shows, particularly in the larger cities, with the same serious commitment to the art form that they approached all of their theatre projects.

The work of the FTP sometimes created strong political reverberations as it played out amid a society slowly recovering from a massive economic depression and embroiled by international politics that would ultimately lead to world war. Thus the ideological dimensions present in all theatre became even more strident and explicit in some of the FTP children's theatre, particularly when read within the context of the politics of the time. Theatre for children historically reflects dominant ideologies as a useful tool for education and or social work. For the theatre artists of the FTP, the "emphasis on the educational" in the children's theatre did not always translate into support for dominant political ideologies, and, in this time of political unrest, the FTP was silenced for this perceived subversive behaviour.

"Boomers" Arrive

After World War II, the large numbers of soldiers suddenly returning to domestic life radically transformed mid-century society and culture. These young veterans used the financial support of the "GI Bill" to pursue college educations in numbers far surpassing preceding generations. They also spurred a cultural shift to the suburbs as they married and started families. The resulting "baby boom," beginning in the late 1940s, not only literally increased the numbers of young people in the U.S. population, it also introduced a growing leisure class with an increased focus on families, children and childrearing, schools and education. Guided by widely popular self-help books, such as Benjamin Spock's *The Common Sense Book of Baby and Child Care*,[62] modern concepts of parenting as a learned skill gained credence at home, and the development of comprehensive schools to train well-rounded citizens of the future became increasingly important throughout society. Sociologists describe the young people of this period as the healthiest, best-fed, best-housed generation to that time; but, notably, in this racially segregated society, this description applied primarily to those living in the middle-class, white suburbs.[63]

The values of the suburbs of the 1950s found reinforcement in the programs offered on television, the newest entertainment medium to enter the home. Popular television shows of the time offered countless images of upper-middle-class, white, nuclear families, anchored by domesticated women, looking after docile and benignly mischievous children. The most popular shows included: *Ozzie and Harriet, Father Knows Best*, and *The Donna Reed Show*. Additionally, television introduced the children to *The Howdy Doody Show, Kukla, Fran, and Ollie*, and endless cartoon fare. Critics cite *Walt Disney's Mickey Mouse Club* as ushering in the "modern" era of children's television.[64] There, young audiences found cartoons and serialized dramas with young protagonists, along with young performers (The Mouseketeers) extolling the virtues of the new theme park, Disneyland.

This narrow worldview of the 1950s, coupled with the ideal of tightly disciplined family structures, provided a fertile context for traditional forms of theatre and drama for young people (particularly in the schools and playgrounds). But this prosperous and complacent post-war society suffered a significant culture shock in October 1957, with Russia's launch of Sputnik. When Russia launched this artificial satellite, the world's first to orbit the earth, they initiated a decades-long "space race" and a cultural/political face-off that heightened the communism-vs-democracy debate in a way that many believed threatened the very existence of the United States "way of life."[65] This struggle, which dominated nearly three decades of American politics and education, caused a strident national reordering of political and educational priorities, effectively moving arts and arts education to a second place behind science and technology in school systems throughout the country.

Nonprofit, Professional Theatre for Young Audiences

Amid the major cultural transitions of this "cold war," the traditions of educational and recreational drama persisted, and a revitalized professional children's theatre movement gradually developed a substantial, ongoing presence in the children's theatre field. The generation of parents and schools in mid-century, overseeing the largest generation of young people in U.S. history, proved a ready audience for the developing professional theatre scene.

This generation of professional children's theatres differed markedly from their commercial predecessors. Most of the new theatres were organized as nonprofit corporations, dedicated to the ongoing production of children's theatre, in contrast to the typical commercial ventures focused on the economic gains from a particular production. This innovation brought a long-term commitment to children's theatre production within each organization, a commitment that often provided the spark for experiments in production style and the creation of new plays. Such theatres also provided extended employment to a company of artists, who, with this promise of security, worked for organizational stability, assessing audiences and the resources of the field, and then often sought innovation in the repertoire of literature.

Some initial mid-century endeavors in professional children's theatre began on the fringes of the commercial theatre in New York. In 1947 a group of professional actors, led by Monte Meacham, created the Children's World Theatre in New York, which initially played at the Barbizon Theatre and later toured throughout the East Coast. This troupe was strongly influenced by Charlotte Chorpenning's work, and in their initial season the Children's World Theatre produced four of her plays.[66]

The Paper Bag Players, created in New York in 1958, illustrate the range of mid-century children's theatre literature. The "Bags," as they are known, developed their own sketches centered on the use of paper bags and boxes for all of their props. This group still performs today under the leadership of one of the founders, Judith Martin.[67]

In the early 1960s the Ford Foundation took the lead in supporting the development of community-based arts organizations; and in 1965 Congress established the National Endowment for the Arts (NEA), which provided a means of federal support for arts organizations across the country. The NEA, in turn, helped support a network of state and local arts agencies. Out of these influences and the growing commitment to theatre grew a vibrant professional regional theatre movement, including professional children's theatres.

The development of professional regional children's theatres owes much to the legacy left by the Association of Junior Leagues of America. In mid-century, children's theatres originally created by Junior League groups were already operating in several eastern cities. These included (listed by founding date):

> 1931, Nashville Children's Theatre (TN)
>
> 1938, Lexington Children's Theatre (KY)
>
> 1947, Birmingham Children's Theatre (AL)
>
> 1949, Emmy Gifford Children's Theatre, currently
> Omaha Theatre Company for Young
> People (NB)[68]

As the Junior League changed the nature of its commitment and support of children's theatre, and in concert with the growing regional theatre movement, all of these theatres had, by the 1980s, come under professional artistic and managerial leadership. By that time they all functioned as fully professional theatre organizations, producing annual seasons of plays for young audiences.

In addition to those theatres founded by Leagues, many other professional children's theatres began at this time, including some that now rank as the largest and/or most influential in the contemporary scene. These include (listed by founding date):

> 1961, The Children's Theatre Company of Minneapolis
> (MN)
>
> 1961, TheatreworksUSA (New York City) formerly,
> Performing Arts Repertory Theatre

1973, Metro Theater Company (St. Louis, MO)
formerly, Metro Theater Circus

1975, Seattle Children's Theatre (WA)

1975, Theatre IV (Richmond, VA)

1976, ArtReach Touring Theatre (Cincinnati, OH),
now operated by Theatre IV

1977, Childsplay, Inc (Tempe, AZ)

1978, The Coterie Theatre (Kansas City, MO)

1984, Dallas Children's Theatre (TX)

1987, First Stage (Milwaukee, WI) [69]

Professional theatres for young audiences now exist in most large cities in this country, and, additionally, many professional troupes tour extensively in all areas of the country. These theatres, individually, and as a group, brought an important new level of artistic innovation (in the literature and in production) to the children's theatre field.

Many of the contributions professional theatre organizations made to the development of the literature are unique to specific organizations in terms of programs or projects; but, considered as a whole, these theatres have greatly expanded the quality and diversity of the literature through:

1) Supporting playwrights and the development of new work through commissions, workshops, and staged readings

2) Commissioning play adaptations of noted children's books, including those by such authors as Dr. Suess (Theodor Geisel), Tomi De Paola, Judith Viorst, Maurice Sendak, C.S. Lewis and many others;

3) Collaborating with other theatre, dance, and performance art specialists to create innovative performance pieces that challenge traditional children's theatre forms;

4) Creating partnerships and exchanges with theatres throughout the world that introduce U.S. theatre artists to different views of theatre for young people;

5) Involving the wider professional theatre community in developing and producing plays for young audiences; and, perhaps most important of all,

6) Encouraging the work of playwrights by providing a steady, competitive market for new plays for children, including those plays that explore different themes, styles, and forms.

Some professional theatres, such as TheatreworksUSA, focus primarily on touring, which generally dictates productions with small casts, running times of about one hour to fit within the school schedules, and minimal technical requirements. Others, such as Minneapolis Children's Theatre and Seattle Children's Theatre focus more on productions staged in their fully equipped theatres, and thus produce and develop plays with fewer of these restrictions. Some theatres, such as Metro Theater Company, often produce original, ensemble-created work.

The development of these companies spanned significant cultural eras in the US, and their work likewise reflects changing perspectives of both children and childhood and the art of theatre for young people. The post-war prosperity and baby boom era, through the Sputnik era and the cold war of the early 1960s, supported a dominant cultural ethos advocating clear-cut values of right and wrong and traditional gender roles amid a generally racially segregated and conservative society. During this time, the Chorpenning style dramas offered parents a useful tool in reinforcing singular codes of behavior, and provided theatres recognizable and marketable products.

Until mid-century, most children's plays offered escape into fantasy worlds of fairytale and myth. While many of these plays presented stories that told of serious threats to protagonists, these were always worked out satisfactorily and clearly, and the style of the works appropriately distanced young audience members so that they would not personalize the protagonists' troubles. This changed significantly as the literature matured amidst the societal turmoil of the 1960s and 1970s, brought by a new generation of playwrights, nurtured in the professional theatre and influenced by the overt politics of the time.

The complex cultural wars of the 1960s and 1970s, ignited by anger over the escalation of the war in Vietnam, resulted in widespread questioning of the values and the authoritarian structures that nurtured the baby boom generation. The civil rights struggles and the renewed women's movement reflected an increased focus on the idea of society as a collection of unique individuals, each reflecting personal perspectives, rather than a society defined by singular and universal goals and ideals.

The adult theatre of the 1960s and 1970s developed many responses to the political and social turmoil. These ranged from the Black Theatre movement to Guerilla Theatre, from anti-war plays to environmental theatre. But regardless of the political focus, these theatre movements all advocated a theatre of immediacy, one that offered theatregoers a vivid image of themselves within their current realities. While playwrights and producers saw much of the frankness of these theatre movements as well beyond the scope of theatre for children, they slowly began to move the field beyond the increasingly anachronistic fairytale forms and subjects to a more realistic look at contemporary young people. And they took baby steps, indeed, responding to a market that first must address the concerns and preferences of parents and teachers, before necessarily considering the needs and interests of young audiences.

International influences figured prominently in the gradual modernization of the literature, as exchanges, festivals, and publications brought international work to the attention of U.S. producers. The ideologically explicit work of Berlin's Grips Theatre was translated and published by Jack Zipes in 1967 as *Political Plays for Children*.[70] Sweden's Unga Klara Theatre caught the attention of the international children's theatre community in 1975 with a bold production entitled *Media's Children*, wherein a realistic story of the effects of divorce on young people is juxtaposed against the classical story of the struggles between Medea and Jason. This play particularly challenged American stereotypes through its frank language and discussion of sexuality.[71] In addition, Theatre-In-Education (TIE) companies, which developed throughout England and Ireland, offered models of interactive theatre interrogating contemporary political concerns.

While the political and economic realities of U.S. children's theatre in the 1960s precluded the widespread production of plays that diverged greatly from the traditional fare, playwrights slowly began to introduce more sophisticated literature for more demanding audiences. These plays presented child protagonists based in a contemporary reality, who embodied realistic complexities and the ambiguities of actual youth. Playwrights also began to introduce more serious issues and/or themes and stories, made more sophisticated by the "reality" of their protagonists. For example, in Joanna Kraus's *The Ice Wolf* (1964) the protagonist must deal with the difficult consequences of her desire for revenge; Suzan Zeder's *Step on a Crack* (1974) introduces the character Ellie, who grapples with the problems brought by a new stepmother in her life; while Aurand Harris's *The Arkansaw Bear (1980)* treats the sadness and questioning of a young girl whose beloved grandfather dies.

In a speech delivered in 1982, Moses Goldberg, at that time the Producing Director of Stage One: The Louisville Children's Theatre, observed the then dynamic changes in the field brought by the professional theatres, noting that "as fast as the world is changing, the field [children's theatre] is changing too." The network of sophisticated professional theatres was slowly expanding the horizons of the field, making it, as Goldberg noted, "respectable to be a professional artist who works for young audiences." [72]

The Publishers and Canonization

Writing in 1980, playwright Joseph Robinette, reporting on an informal poll of publishing houses, noted that the most-often performed children's plays of the time included: *Androcles and the Lion* (Harris), *Step on a Crack* (Zeder), *Gollywhoppers* (Atkin), *Winnie-the-Pooh* (Sergel/Milne) and *Velveteen Rabbit* (Grecian/ Williams), among others.[73] While this list reflects both the old and the new in the repertoire of the 1980s, it bears interrogation as a list, in and of itself. In 1980, the major publishing houses of plays for young audiences at that time, Anchorage Press, New Plays, and Dramatic Publishing, listed "126, 39, and 102 children's plays respectively." At that time the publishers reportedly received a total of over five hundred scripts for consideration yearly, and they ultimately published less than one percent of those submissions.[74] These publishers thus functioned as important gatekeepers, bringing definition to the field through the plays they published. Every new play written and produced at a theatre challenges this definition, but unless that play is ultimately published, and thereby "kept alive," it fails to sustain a place in the field and a voice in defining the repertoire.

Samuel French, Inc, established in 1830, pioneered the concept of providing published scripts to producing groups. Together with Dramatic Publishing, established in 1885, they purveyed a limited number of plays for young people throughout the first decades of the century. French published most of the few commercial successes of the time, such as *Peter Pan*, *Little Princess*, and *Snow White and the Seven Dwarfs*, and also published some plays from contests held by the Junior League (AJLA). During this time the children's theatre field was known much more for the pageants and the home and school dramas offered in separate published anthologies explicitly for home or school use.

In 1935 Sara Spencer started The Children's Theatre Press (now called Anchorage Press Plays), because she believed the children's theatre field suffered from the larger commercial publishers handling a limited repertoire of children's plays. Spencer started with four plays: *Jack and the Beanstalk*, by Charlotte Chorpenning; *The Christmas Nightingale*, by Eric P. Kelly and dramatized by Phyllis Groff; *Rip Van Winkle*, by Grace Dorcas Ruthenburg; and her own adaptation of *Tom Sawyer*.[75]

Spencer began her publishing house within the context of her work as a director of the Charleston Children's Theatre (operated by the Junior League). She also sought advice from Helenka Adamowska, Junior League children's theatre consultant. While she was thus embedded in particular perspectives of children's theatre, she saw the Press as a way of raising the standards of the field by attracting good playwrights through paying royalties for each production. According to Spencer:

> If a play is worth giving for welfare children, it should be worth giving for privileged children. If it is worth giving to privileged children, it is worth being paid for. And my aim in life is to encourage more and more formal, paid productions. That is why I started my Press.[76]

Given its kinship to drama in the playgrounds and the classrooms, theatre for children in this country has only slowly developed as a separate, professional artistic field. Yet its identity remains closely aligned with the financial realities of what plays producers can sell to parents and schools, the primary gatekeepers to a child's theatregoing experience; and the plays with the most potential for production get published. This system favors known titles: traditional fairy and folktales, plays based on popular children's books, or plays based in the popular culture of television and movies. While this does not preclude quality, it does inhibit innovation.

Many professional theatres address these publishing limitations, in part by working directly with playwrights to produce their work and then to share these plays from theatre to theatre. Some theatres has also begun to publish plays they have developed in their theatres. For example, Seattle Children's Theatre and the Children's Theatre

Company of Minneapolis have recently formed a partnership called Plays for Young Audiences (PYA) to market production rights for over fifty such plays. PYA includes such diverse works as: *Tales of a Fourth Grade Nothing* (from the book by Judy Blume, adapted by Bruce Mason), *Alice's Adventures in Wonderland* (by Deborah Frockt), *Frankenstein* (by Thomas Olson, from the Shelly book), and *The Little Match Girl* (by John Donahue).[77]

The wide range of subject matter and style represented by the productions of the largest TYA companies has greatly expanded the literature of the field and encouraged a new generation of professional playwrights to work for child audiences. But the sustaining face of the field comes from the published plays, that small percentage of all plays written that publishers offer to producers.

National New Play Development Programs

In addition to widespread development work and commissioning on the part of the professional theatres, other organizations and groups also support playwrights in this work.

ASSITEJ/USA, the national service organization for professional TYA, supports national festivals and symposia, many of which focus on the examination of new plays. In 1984 ASSITEJ/USA began the publication of *Outstanding Plays for Young Audiences*, an international bibliography of new plays for young people. This bibliography publishes titles and information about new work nominated by the various international centers of ASSITEJ. In 2002 the US center selected the following US plays for inclusion in this bibliography: *Black Butterfly, Jaguar Girl, Piñata Woman, and Other Superhero Girls Like Me*, created by Luis Alfaro and Lisa Peterson, based on the writings of Alma Cervantes, Sandra C. Muñoz, and Marisela Norte; *Lilly's Purple Plastic Purse*, by Kevin Kling, based on books by Kevin Henkes; *Salt and Pepper*, by José Cruz González; *Tomato Plant Girl*, by Wesley Middleton; and *The Wrestling Season*, by Laurie Brooks.[78]

The American Alliance for Theatre and Education (a direct

35

descendant of the committee formed by Winifred Ward in 1944) conducts ongoing playwright support activities, including, "The Unpublished Play Reading Project" (to publicize notable unpublished plays); informal play readings at national conferences; annual awards for playwrights; and juried awards for published plays.

In 1981 Professor Dorothy Webb, from Indiana University/ Purdue University at Indianapolis, held the first of what has become a biennial national children's play development symposia, now called the Bonderman Symposium. This event includes week-long development workshops for four to five plays, selected from submissions solicited nationally. Staged readings are held in conjunction with workshops and discussions focused on issues of writing plays for young audiences. Numerous plays have moved into the national repertoire from this symposium, including: *Selkie*, by Laurie Brooks, *Amber Waves*, by James Still, *The Ghost of the River House*, by Max Bush, *The Riddling Child (Liza and the Riddling Cave)*, by John Urquhart, and *The Music Lesson*, by Tammy Ryan.[79]

In 1991 a similar biennial program, called New Visions/New Voices (NV/NV), began at the Kennedy Center for the Performing Arts in Washington DC.[80] To participate in NV/NV, theatres submit proposals with names of a team of artists, a script sample, scenario, or treatment, and they verify a commitment to future development of the work. Six to eight teams participate in five-day development workshops; and staged readings of the resulting work are conducted before a national conference of theatre artists and educators. Prominent plays developed at NV/NV include: *The Yellow Boat*, by David Saar; *Afternoon of the Elves*, by Y York; *The Wrestling Season*, by Laurie Brooks; *Black Butterfly, Jaguar Girl, and Other Super Hero Girls, Like Me; Columba*, by Alma Cervantes, Sandra C. Muñoz, and Marisela Norte; *The Highest Heaven*, by José Cruz González, and *Alicia and Wonder Tierra* (working title: "I Can't Eat Goat Head") by Sylvia Gonzalez S.

Diversity Issues

Throughout much of the history of this field, teachers and social workers have used dramatic literature for children to reinforce values and behavior based on perspectives that seldom accommodated any diversity amidst their audiences or participants. The narrative histories of this activity acknowledge this diversity only in the reality of its exclusion or suppression. In the early years of the republic, young people of "privilege" attended schools and sometimes attended the theatre. This "privilege," defined by economics and race, excluded large segments of the population, particularly American Indian, African American, and Mexican American youth. The social workers of the next decades, while often working with diverse populations, explicitly reinforced the norms of the dominant, upper-class, white society, through the plays they presented and the participatory dramas they led. Likewise, the commercial children's theatre of the late nineteenth century spoke in a narrow voice to a select few. This only began to change, and very slowly, with the beginning of the nonprofit professional theatre movement in the 1970s. As theatre artists began to focus more specifically on the interests and needs of their child audiences, and as our society became less segregated, economically and socially, drama for young people began to reflect, as well as speak to, more diverse voices; but it is an ongoing journey and struggle.

In 1993 Professor Susan Pearson-Davis, of the University of New Mexico, conducted an important study assessing the racial and ethnic diversity of the children's theatre and creative drama fields at that time. As Pearson-Davis notes:

> When I began my travels, I expected and hoped to find flourishing drama and theatre programs that brought young people from different ethnic backgrounds together to make and view drama about culturally-specific and intercultural issues. I found very few. [81]

Citing the dominance of "mainstream theatre and education communities," Pearson-Davis concluded "that although some voices and faces of color are beginning to be heard and seen in the field, there is still a long way to go. . . .[and] too little is being done that utilizes creative drama and theatre in truly multicultural ways or as a tool for multicultural awareness, understanding, and education."[82]

In the years since Pearson-Davis's study the most significant strides in creating diverse dramatic literature for children stem from development projects of some of the larger professional theatre companies, many of which have focused specifically on voices of multiple cultures. These programs and others, such a New Visions/New Voices, are slowly introducing into the canon plays and playwrights that write from and about racial and ethnic perspectives that more truly reflect the diversity of contemporary audiences; but the fulfillment of this task stands as a significant and crucial challenge to the field.

The Contemporary Field

In 1984, in the first edition of this book, I wrote:

> The development of the literature has lagged behind the stylistic, formalistic, and thematic innovations of the American theatre as a whole; but the last thirty years in particular have seen the introduction of new perspectives that hold promise for the future growth of the field. The repertoire of plays has grown larger; the stylistic and thematic parameters have widened; and the market for new plays continues to expand.[83]

From my current perspective, over twenty years later, the field has, in multiple ways, met that "promise" of artistic maturity. Ben Cameron, the Executive Director of Theatre Communications Group, recently editorialized in *American Theatre*, that "theatre for young audiences is among the most exciting, innovative, powerful, unapologetic artistic work in our field [theatre, as a whole] today"[84] This same magazine included cover headlines declaring: "The New Face of Theatre for Youth" and "These days no subject is Taboo."

The contemporary repertoire still includes an almost intractable core of traditional fairy and folktale plays, but many of those stories have been revisited by contemporary playwrights, who have created more theatrically sophisticated and interesting versions. In addition, a wide range of new plays, offering alternatives in style, form, and subject matter, balance this traditional core. Contemporary producers have at their disposal a wide and diverse range of dramatic literature, much of which honors the intelligence and sophistication, as well as the joys, cares, and concerns of children. The field indeed has made significant progress toward plays that, in the words of Montrose Moses in 1926, "are written as all good plays are written—according to laws that make of drama an art."[85]

Notes

1 "Children's Drama," *The Reader's Encyclopedia of World Drama*, ed. John Gassner and Edward Quinn (New York: Thomas Y. Crowell Co., 1969), 125.

2 Jonathan Levy and Floraine Kay, "The Use of the Drama in the Jesuit Schools, 1551–1773," *Youth Theatre Journal* 10 (1996): 56–66.

3 Plato, *The Republic*, Trans. Benjamin Jowett (Oxford: Clarendon Press, 1921), 377.

4 Numerous English translations of this work appeared in the eighteenth century, including *Theatre of Education Translated from the French of the Countess de Genlis. . . . In Four Volumes* (London: T. Cadell and P. Emsley, and T. Durham), 1781.

5 (NY: Greenwood Press, 1992).

6 Quoted in George B. Bryan, *American Theatrical Regulation 1607–1900: Conspectus and Texts* (Metuchen, NJ: Scarecrow, 1993), 27.

7 Society of Friends (Philadelphia Monthly Meeting), "Advice and Caution from the Monthly Meeting of Friends, the Twenty-Third Day of the Ninth Month, 1768," *To Our Friends and Brethren, in Religious Profession with Us* (Philadelphia: D. Hall and W. Sellers, [1768]). Microform, *Early American Imprints*, First Series, no. 41824.

8 William Wood, *Personal Recollections of the Stage* (Philadelphia: Henry Carey Baird, 1855), as quoted in Martha Mahard, "1750–1810." *Theatre in the United States: A Documentary History Volume I: 1750–1915 Theatre in the Colonies and the United States* (Cambridge: Cambridge UP,1996), 41.

9 (Leonminster, MA: John Prentis and Co.).

[10] *Proceedings in observance of the one hundred and fiftieth anniversary of the organization of the first church in Lincoln, Massachusetts, August 21 and September 4, 1898* (Cambridge: The University Press, 1899), 71–72. As quoted in Jonathan Levy, "The Dramatic Dialogues of Charles Stearns: An Appreciation," *Spotlight on the Child Studies in the History of American Children's Theatre*, eds. Roger L. Bedard and C. John Tolch (Westport, CT: Greenwood Press, 1989), 11.

[11] "Introduction," *Dramatic Dialogues for the Use of Schools* (Leonminster, MA: John Prentis and Co., 1798), 7.

[12] Jonathan Levy and Martha Mahard, "Preliminary Checklist of Early Printed Children's Plays in English, 1780–1855," *Performing Art Resources Vol. 12 Topical Bibliographies of the American Theatre,* ed. Barbara Naomi Cohen-Stratyner (New York: Theatre Library Association, 1987), 2.

[13] "The Dramatic Dialogues of Charles Stearns: An Appreciation," 5.

[14] Robert C. Toll, *On With the Show* (New York: Oxford UP, 1976), 7.

[15] Toll, 9–10.

[16] Toll, 52–55.

[17] Reviews from *New York Times* in the years mentioned.

[18] Edward A. Dithmar, "Jack and the Beanstalk," *New York Times,* November 8, 1896, II: 11.

[19] Constance D'Arcy Mackay, *How to Produce Children's Plays* (New York: H. Holt and Company, 1915), 15.

[20] "On Many Stages," *New York Herald,* December 4, 1888: 6.

[21] "Children of the Stage," *New York Times*, June 16,1889: 16.

[22] "The Prince and the Pauper," *Evening Post*, January 21, 1890: 6.

23 Laura Gardner Salazar, "Theatre for Young Audiences in New York City, 1900–1910: A Heritage of Jolly Productions," *Spotlight on the Child Studies in the History of American Children's Theatre*, eds. Roger L. Bedard and C. John Tolch (NY: Greenwood Press, 1989), 25.

24 Program for the Dillingham production of *The Little Princess*, Criterion Theatre, New York, January 14, 1903.

25 Stuart Walker, *Portmanteau Plays*, ed Edward Bierstadt (Cincinnati: Stewart and Kidd Co., 1917).

26 Ronald D. Cohen. "Child Saving and Progressivism, 1885–1915," *American Childhood: A Research Guide and Historical Handbook*, eds. Joseph M. Hawes and N. Ray Hiner (Westport, CT.: Greenwood Press, 1985), 273–309.

27 Cohen, 292.

28 Victoria Bissel Brown, "Introduction: Jane Addams Constructs Herself and Hull-House," ed. Victoria Bissel Brown, *Twenty Years at Hull-House with Autobiographical Notes by Jane Addams* (Boston: Bedford/St. Martins, 1999), 19.

29 *Twenty Years at Hull-House*, 186.

30 *Twenty Years at Hull-House*, 188.

31 Nellie McCaslin, *Historical Guide to Children's Theatre in America* (New York: Greenwood Press, 1987), 98.

32 Alice Minnie Herts Heniger, *The Children's Educational Theatre* (New York: Harper & Brothers, 1911).

33 Noerena Abookire and Jennifer Scott McNair, "Children's Theatre Activities at Karamu House, 1915–1975," *Spotlight on the Child Studies in the History of American Children's Theatre*, eds. Roger L. Bedard and C. John Tolch (NY: Greenwood Press, 1989), 69–85.

34 Janet Gordon and Diana Reische, *The Volunteer Powerhouse*

(New York: Rutledge Press, 1982).

[35] *A Handbook for Children's Theatre* (New York: Association of Junior Leagues of America, 1942), 7.

[36] *A Handbook for Children's Theatre*, 7.

[37] Gordon and Reische, 75.

[38] Uncatalogued lists and statistics found in AJLA Archives, New York City.

[39] *Junior League Bulletin*, 10.9 (June 1924): 43.

[40] "League Council on Community Arts," Minutes from meeting held September 8, 1947, 3, AJLA Archives, New York City.

[41] George Latshaw, Letter to "All Junior League Children's Theatre Chairmen." February 26, 1971, AJLA Archives, New York City.

[42] (New York: Holt, 1915).

[43] All published by Holt Co., New York, in 1909, 1910, 1911, and 1916, respectively.

[44] Kate Oglebay, ed., *Plays for Children* (New York: The Drama League, 1915), 3.

[45] Kate Oglebay and Marjorie Seligman, eds., *Plays for Children: A Selected List,* 3rd ed. (New York: Wilson, 1920), 10–21.

[46] Montrose Moses, ed., *Another Treasury of Plays for Children* (Boston: Little Brown & Co., 1926), 604–605.

[47] Kenneth Macgowan, *Footlights Across America* (1929; rpt. New York: Kraus, 1969), 359–365.

[48] "Children's Theatres," *Junior League Bulletin*, 13.5 (March 1927): 29.

[49] For details about Chorpenning's life and work, see Roger L. Bedard, *The Life and Work of Charlotte Chorpenning*, diss., U. of Kansas, 1979.

[50] The current American Alliance for Theatre and Education descended directly from this committee.

[51] Louise C. Horton, ed., *Handbook for Children's Theatre Directors* (Cincinnati: National Thespian Society, 1949), 22–23.

[52] Marilyn Lawrence Boemer, *The Children's Hour Radio Programs for Children, 1929–1956* (Metuchen, NJ: The Scarecrow Press, 1989), 5, 8–9.

[53] H.B. Summers, *A Thirty Year History of Programs Carried on National Radio Networks in the United States: 1926–1956* (New York: Arno Press, 1971), 12.

[54] Boemer, 8–9.

[55] Arthur Anderson, *Let's Pretend: A History of Radio's Best Loved Children's Show by a Long Time Cast Member* (Jefferson, NC: McFarland & Co., 1994).

[56] Michael Gamble, *Clare Tree Major: Children's Theatre, 1923–1954*. Diss., NY University, 1976.

[57] Doreen B. Heard, "Children's Theatre in the Federal Theatre Project," *Spotlight on the Child: Studies in the History of American Children's Theatre*, eds., Roger L. Bedard and C. John Tolch (New York: Greenwood Press, 1989), 7.

[58] Hallie Flanagan, "Brief: Containing Detailed Answers to Charges Made by Witnesses Who Appeared Before the Special Committee to Investigate Un-American Activities, House of Representatives," August 1938, 97. As quoted in Lowell Swortzell, ed., *Six Plays for Young People From the Federal Theatre Project (1936–1939),* (New York: Greenwood Press, 1986), 10.

[59] Swortzell, *Six Plays*, 11.

[60] Brooks Atkinson, *"The Revolt of the Beavers* or Mother Goose Marx, Under WPA Auspices,"* New York Times*, May 21, 1937.

[61] For detailed accounts of the FTP see Jane DeHart Mathews, *The Federal Theatre 1935–1939 Plays, Relief, Politics* (Princeton: Princeton UP, 1967) and Hallie Flanagan, *Arena* (New York: Duell, Sloan and Pierce, 1940).

[62] (New York: Duell, Sloan and Pearce, 1946).

[63] Charles A. Strickland and Andrew M. Ambrose, "The Baby Boom, Prosperity, and the Changing Worlds of Children, 1945-1963," *American Childhood: A Research Guide and Historical Handbook*, eds., Joseph M. Hawes and N. Ray Hiner (Westport, CT.: Greenwood Press, 1985), 533–585.

[64] Cy Schneider, *Children's Television The Art The Business and How it Works* (Lincolnwood, IL: NTC Business Books, 1967), 47–55.

[65] Roger D. Launius, "Sputnik and the Origins of the Space Age," January 30, 2004 <http://www.hq.nasa.gov/office/pao/History/sputnik.

[66] Roger L. Bedard, *The Life and Work of Charlotte B. Chorpenning*, Diss. University of Kansas, 1979, 111.

[67] "About Us," January 30, 2004, http://www.paperbagplayers.org.

[68] Roger L. Bedard, "Junior League Children's Theatre: Debutants Take the Stage," *Spotlight on the Child: Studies in the History of American Children's Theatre*, eds., Roger L. Bedard and C. John Tolch (New York: Greenwood Press, 1989), 47.

[69] *Marquee 2003–2004* (Nashville: ASSITEJ/USA, 2003).

[70] (St. Louis: Telos Press, 1967).

71 Per Lysander and Suzanne Osten, *Medea's Children*, trans., Ann-Charlotte Harvey (Rowayton, CT: New Plays, 1985).

72 "American Children's Theatre in the '80s," *Children's Theatre Review*, 31.4 (1982): 13-16.

73 Joseph Robinette, "Publishers Discuss Needs for Children's Theatre Scripts," *Children's Theatre Review*, 29.1 (1980): 15–16.

74 Robinette, 15.

75 Katherine Krzys, "Sara Spencer: Publisher, Advocate and Visionary," *Spotlight on the Child: Studies in the History of American Children's Theatre*, eds., Roger L. Bedard and C. John Tolch (New York: Greenwood Press, 1989), 141.

76 Sara Spencer, Letter to Helenka Adamowska, September 13, 1935. As Quoted in Krzys, 141.

77 "Plays for Young Audiences," April 25, 2005, http://www.playsforyoungaudiences.org.

78 *Outstanding Plays for Young Audiences International Bibliography Volume 7* (Nashville, TN: ASSITEJ/USA, 2002).

79 Dorothy Webb, "Symposia Finalists and Semi-Finalists," manuscript sent to author, February 5, 2004.

80 "New Visions/New Voices," January 19, 2004, http://www.kennedy-center.org/education/nvnvlist.html.

81 Susan Pearson-Davis, "Cultural Diversity in Children's Theatre and Creative Drama," *Youth Theatre Journal*, 7.3 (1993): 16.

82 Davis, 16.

83 p. 16.

[84] Ben Cameron, "Transformations," *American Theatre*, 17.4 (Apr. 2000): 6.

[85] *Another Treasury of Plays for Children* (Boston: Little Brown & Co., 1926), 608.

THE
LITTLE PRINCESS

A play for children and grown-up children
in three acts

by
Frances Hodgson Burnett

The story of the little princess, as told in both book and play form, remains one of the most popular children's stories of the twentieth century. It first appeared in *St. Nicholas* magazine in the late 1880s, and in 1905 was published in a single edition, entitled *A Little Princess*. In the interim Burnett wrote a dramatized version, ultimately performed and published as *The Little Princess*. First produced in England, the play opened in New York in 1903, and it has appeared in countless revivals since that time. Child star, Shirley Temple, was featured in a noted movie version of the story in 1939, and the story has subsequently been presented in various stage, movie, and television versions.

The play presents the melodramatic story of Sara Crewe, a romantic thirteen-year-old, who, through no fault of her own, suffers a literal and dramatic reversal of fortunes, only to be rescued in the end and restored to her former state. Consistent with the melodramatic form, Burnett created one-dimensional characters, a transparent and predictable plot structure, and unabashedly sentimental situations.

The dominant themes and ideas of the play grow from the dictates of the melodramatic form—namely, that good *will* triumph over evil. In the case of this play, the good (Sara) is very good, and the evil, Miss Minchin, is unrelentingly bad, but not so evil as to risk upsetting a youthful, sentimental audience. Act one shows Sara in a pleasant situation that changes quickly when the greedy and duplicitous Miss Minchin discovers that Sara's family fortune has been lost. The second act reveals Sara's unfortunate new role as an abused servant in the household. The conflict between Sara and Minchin heightens, and with each confrontation Sara's circumstances become increasingly difficult. Act three appropriately presents a series of remarkable coincidences that cause Sara to be reunited with a family friend who assures her that her family fortune is intact. Miss Minchin is then rebuked for her behavior, and the audience is shown that, with her friends and her fortune restored, Sara will live "happily ever after." True to melodrama, Sara embodies kindness and generosity, even when mistreated; and she consistently demonstrates her faith in the goodness of the people around her, until she is rescued in the end.

By today's standards, the structure and story, designed to elicit a strong emotional response from the audience, appear trite and overly sentimental. But the play is little different from much of the theatre of that time, and the romanticized style of the play easily embraces the simplistic dialogue and predictable situations. The play offered turn-of-the-century audiences a Victorian Cinderella story, with the evil stepmother character realized through Miss Minchin, the greedy school mistress, and the prince character shown through the friendly neighbor who saves Sara from her deprived situation. With this play Burnett offers parents, and their children, very proper Victorian attitudes about culture and class, children and childhood, respect for adults, proper behavior, and, most importantly, humility.

In contrast with many more contemporary children's plays, Burnett gives her youthful protagonist little agency. Then prevailing cultural perspectives often posited children as little more than "property" of their parents or guardians; and in the dramatic world that Burnett creates, the characters reflect that ethos. The "action" of the play (the restoration of Sara's situation) comes from adults, rather than young people; and Sara's "goodness" stems not from her ingenuity and cleverness, but rather from her unfailing cheerfulness in the face of her abuse. While Sara's "inaction" is problematic from a dramatic perspective, the pathos of the story and the complete reversal remain consistent with the melodrama form.

Burnett creates this audience empathy more with her skillful use of exaggerated sentimentality than with realistic detail. The New York audiences of 1903, not yet influenced by the naturalism of the European stage, saw Sara as a character neither distanced by the trappings of a fairytale nor diminished by the spectacle of a Pantomime. But from modern perspectives, even though the work has a realistic veneer, the improbable action, the obvious machinations of plot structure, and the generalized view of the Victorian world make the play more akin to a fairytale than to modern realism.

The popularity of *The Little Princess* throughout the century reflects, in part, the importance of melodrama in popular entertainment. This play stands as prototype—in form and style, if not subject matter—of what came to be considered proper children's theatre through much of the last one hundred years. Playwrights in succeeding decades did not so much imitate the story of *The Little Princess,* as they copied the form of the play. Yet, because of Burnett's particular skill with melodrama, this play, in performance, can still delight contemporary audiences through its style, its evocations of period, and its charming characters.

FRANCES HODGSON BURNETT (1849–1924) emigrated from England to the United States in 1865, and shortly thereafter began her formal writing career. In 1873 Hodgson married S.M. Burnett, a physician who also gained considerable prominence in his field.

Burnett's first literary success, *That Lass o' Lowries,* appeared as a serial in *Scribner's Monthly* from August 1876 through May 1877, and was issued separately in 1879. By 1886, with the publication of *Little Lord Fauntleroy,* Burnett had a large critical and popular following.

Burnett wrote over forty novels and several plays. The plays include works for children and adults. Particular favorites with child audiences include: *Little Lord Fauntleroy, Rackety Packety House*, and *The Little Princess.*

THE
LITTLE PRINCESS

by
Frances Hodgson Burnett

Characters

SARA

MISS MINCHIN

BECKY

LOTTIE

LAVINIA

JANET

NORA

JESSIE

MAZIE

LILLY

DONALD

ERMENGARDE

AMELIA

MRS. CARMICHAEL

RAM DASS

BARROW

CARRISFORD

JAMES [SERVANT]

EMMA

BLANCHE

NED

CARMICHAEL

ACT I

SCENE: *A large schoolroom at Miss Minchin's boarding school. Central window with view of snow street. Fireplace with fire lighted. On the walls four bracket-lamps and four maps. A green carpet. In front window a platform on which there is a blackboard easel. The room contains a large table, a sofa above fireplace, a piano with bench behind it, and several chairs. Lace curtains behind central window curtains for Ermengarde.*

At the rise of curtain: JESSIE at piano; extra Children, Lilly and others in ring. LAVINIA and one of the girls sitting. AMELIA up stage. JESSIE plays a waltz; Children dance, singing, "One, Two, Three, Four."

CHILDREN *(singing):* One, two, three, four. *(All around the other way; change dance)* One, two, three, four. *(Repeat)*

AMELIA *(breaking in upon the noise):* Stop, stop, children; do stop. I only wanted to try the music before the company came. *(Children stop and get into lines.)* Let me look at you all.
(LAVINIA crossing) Don't poke your head forward. Please turn out your toes. *(Lilly has crossed to right.)* Lilly, your sash is untied. Let me tie it for you. *(Does so)* You know Miss Minchin —

LAVINIA: Huh! Huh!

AMELIA: I will be very angry if there is any rude or unladylike conduct this afternoon. The lady and gentleman who live across the street in number 46 are coming in to see you. They have a very large family — nearly all old enough to go to a genteel school. That's why dear Sara is giving you this party.

LAVINIA: Dear Sara ... huh!

AMELIA: Now, Lavinia, what do you mean by that?

LAVINIA: Oh, nothing, Miss Amelia.

ERMENGARDE: Oh, she did it because she's jealous of Sara.

LAVINIA: I didn't.

ERMENGARDE: You did.

LAVINIA: I didn't.

ERMENGARDE: Did

LAVINIA: Didn't! *(This ad lib. three times.)*

ERMENGARDE: Did

AMELIA *(coming between them):* Stop. I never saw such rude conduct. *(LAVINIA laughs)* You are a spiteful child, Lavinia. I believe you *are* jealous. It's very nice indeed of Sara to give you all this party on her birthday. It's not every child who cares about her school-fellows. And she has not looked at one of her beautiful presents yet because she wanted you to have the pleasure of seeing them unpacked. *(Children crowd around her.)*

CHILDREN: Ah ... ! *(Dance around her)*

ERMENGARDE: Are they going to be unpacked here?

CHILDREN: Yes, yes, yes!

LAVINIA *(sarcastically):* Did her papa send them all from India, Miss Amelia?

LILLY: Did he?

AMELIA *(grandly):* Most of them came from Paris.

CHILDREN: Oh ... ! Paris.

AMELIA: There is a doll that was ordered months ago.

CHILDREN: Oh, a doll!

AMELIA: And a whole trunk full of things like a real young lady.

LOTTIE *(jumping up and down):* Are we going to see them right this minute?

AMELIA: Miss Minchin said they might be brought in after you had tried the new waltz.

LOTTIE: Tra-la-la! *(Dancing)*

AMELIA: I am going to tell her you have finished. *(Laughter)* Now do be nice and quiet when I leave you. *(ERMENGARDE*

swings LOTTIE around) Lottie, don't rumple your new sash. One of you big girls look after her. *(LOTTIE picks up pillow from sofa, ready to throw at LAVINIA)* Now do *(at door)* be quiet.
(Exit. As AMELIA exits, ERMENGARDE runs up to door. Children, except LAVINIA, form picture on platform.)

ERMENGARDE: It's all right girls. She's gone.
(LOTTIE throws pillow at LAVINIA and runs, with LAVINIA in pursuit. ERMENGARDE runs to LOTTIE's rescue.)

LOTTIE *(as LAVINIA catches her and drags her):* Ermy, Ermy. Oh! Oh!
(ERMENGARDE catches LOTTIE's other hand and drags her away from LAVINIA; other Children watch)

CHILDREN: Now.
(JESSIE playing piano. Children begin to do "ring around" again, laughing and chattering the while.)

LAVINIA: I wish you children wouldn't make so much noise. Jessie, stop playing that silly polka.

CHILDREN: No, no, go on, Jessie, go on.
(LOTTIE runs over and pushes LAVINIA twice; falls the second time — hurts her knee.)

LOTTIE: Oh! Ah! Oh!

LAVINIA: I never saw such rough things. I wish Miss Minchin would come in and catch you.

LOTTIE: I guess it's all right.

BLANCHE: You girls think you are so big. You always try to stop the fun. Jessie, go on. *(Piano begins again.)* We're not going to stop, just because you want to talk.

ERMENGARDE: I'm going to be the leader.
(JESSIE stops playing suddenly.)

CHILDREN: What's the matter?

JESSIE: Oh girls! Ermengarde has thrown all the music into the piano.

*(Girls crowd around her, and take music out of piano.
ERMENGARDE is laughing.)*

LAVINIA: You'd stop fast enough if it was the Princess Sara talking.

ERMENGARDE: Oh, we all *like* Sara. *We're* not jealous of her.

CHILDREN: *(Exclamations of assent; playing "London Bridge")*

LAVINIA: Oh, of course you like Sara, just because she's the rich girl of the school and the show pupil. There's nothing so very grand in having a father who lives in India, even if he *is* in the army.
(JESSIE plays.)

LOTTIE: At any rate he's killed *tigers,* and he sends Sara the most beautiful presents!
(Pulls LAVINIA's hair)

LILLY: And he's told Miss Minchin that she can have *anything* she wants.

ERMENGARDE: She's cleverer than any of us. My father says he'd give thousands of pounds if I were as clever as she is. She actually *likes* to read books. I can't bear them.

LAVINIA *(contemptuously):* We all know that.

ERMENGARDE: Well, if I am the stupidest girl in the school, Sara's the nicest. You don't see Sara walking with her friends and saying spiteful things.
*(Bell rings off. CHILDREN run into straight lines.
ERMENGARDE to blackboard and draws a cat. LAVINIA up stage.)*

CHILDREN: Miss Minchin's coming. Miss Minchin's coming!

LAVINIA: Yes, and leading Sara by the hand as if she were a "Little Princess."

ERMENGARDE *(pointing to board):* That old cat, Miss Minchin
(CHILDREN laugh. Enter MISS MINCHIN, leading Sara,

followed by JAMES, WILLIAM, EMMA, and BECKY.
SERVANTS carry presents.)

MISS MINCHIN *(sweeping grandly down):* Silence, young
ladies ... James, place the box *(doll)* on the table and remove
the lid. William, place yours there *(Trunk)*. Emma, put yours
on the table *(Nine books)*. Becky, put yours on the floor.
(BECKY looks at the CHILDREN.) Becky, it is not your place
to look at the young ladies. You forget yourself. *(Waving
servants off)* Now you may leave us.
*(Exeunt servants. BECKY starts to follow them. Sara stops
her.)*

SARA: Ah, please, Miss Minchin, mayn't Becky stay?

MISS MINCHIN: Becky — my dearest Sara—

SARA: I want her because I'm sure she would so like to see the
doll. She's a little girl, you know.

MISS MINCHIN *(amazed):* My dear Sara — Becky is the
scullery-maid. Scullery-maids are not little girls — at least
they ought not to be.

SARA: But Becky *is,* you know.

MISS MINCHIN: I'm sorry to hear it.

SARA: But I don't believe she can help it. And I know she would
enjoy herself so. *(Crosses to MISS MINCHIN)* Please let her
stay — because it's my birthday.
(BECKY backs into the corner in mingled terror and delight.)

MISS MINCHIN *(dignified):* Well, as you ask it as a birthday
favour — she may stay.

SARA: Thank you.

MISS MINCHIN: Rebecca, thank Miss Sara for her great
kindness.

BECKY *(comes forward, making little charity curtseys, words
tumbling over each other):* Oh, if you please, Miss — thank
you, Miss. I am that grateful, Miss. I did want to see the
doll, Miss — that — that bad. I thank you, Miss. *(Sara nods*

happily to BECKY, who bobs to MISS MINCHIN.) And thank you, Ma'am, for letting me take the liberty.

MISS MINCHIN: Go stand over there. *(Pointing grandly to corner)* Not too near the young ladies. *(BECKY backs into corner, rolls down sleeves, etc.)* Now, young ladies, I have a few words to say to you. *(Sweeping grandly up to platform)* You are aware, young ladies, that dear Sara is thirteen years old to-day.

CHILDREN: Yes, Miss Minchin.

MISS MINCHIN: There are a few of you here who have also been thirteen years old, but Sara's birthdays are different from most little girls' birthdays.

CHILDREN: Yes, Miss Minchin.

MISS MINCHIN: When she is older she will be heiress to a large fortune which it will be her duty to spend in a meritorious manner.

ERMENGARDE: No, Miss Minchin — I mean yes, Miss Minchin.

MISS MINCHIN: When her papa, Captain Crewe, brought her from India and gave her into my care, he said to me, in a jesting manner, "I'm afraid she will be very rich, Miss Minchin."

CHILDREN: Oh! — Ah! — Oh!

MISS MINCHIN: My reply was, "Her education at my seminary, Captain Crewe, shall be such as will fit her to adorn the largest fortune." *(LOTTIE sniffs loudly)* Lottie, do not sniff. Use your pocket handkerchief. *(ERMENGARDE wipes LOTTIE's nose. LOTTIE sniffs again. Miss Minchin coughs LOTTIE down.)* Sara has become my most accomplished pupil. Her French and her dancing are a credit to the seminary. Her manners — which have caused you all to call her Princess Sara— are perfect. Her amiability she exhibits by giving you this party. I hope you appreciate her generosity. I wish you to express your appreciation by saying aloud, all together, "Thank you, Sara."

ALL: Thank you, Sara.

ERMENGARDE *(alone):* Thank you, Sara.

BECKY: I thank you, Miss.

SARA: I thank *you* for coming to my party. And you
(Retires)

MISS MINCHIN: Very pretty indeed, Sara! That is what a real
princess does when the populace applauds. I have one thing
more to say. The visitors coming are the father and mother
of a large family. I wish you to conduct yourselves in such
a manner as will cause them to observe that elegance of
deportment can be acquired at Miss Minchin's seminary.
(ERMENGARDE poses in corner) I will now go back to the
drawing-room until they arrive. Sara, you may show your
presents.
(Exits. ERMENGARDE imitates her walk.)

ERMENGARDE: Sara, you may show your presents!

AMELIA *(coming out from behind):* Ermengarde——

ERMENGARDE: Oh! Miss— *(AMELIA crosses to door)* Amelia
please forgive me — I did — didn't —
*(Exit AMELIA. Children laugh and flock around the boxes on
table, etc.)*

SARA *(getting chair from piano):* She caught you that time,
Ermy. *(Getting on chair behind table)* Which shall we look at
first? *(Picking up books)* These are books, I know.
(Trying to untie them)

CHILDREN: Oh — books
(Disgusted)

ERMENGARD *(aghast):* Does your papa send you *books* for
a birthday present? He's as bad as mine. Don't open them,
Sara.

SARA *(laughing):* But I like them the best — never mind

though. This is the doll. (*Uncovering long wooden box*) I'll open that first.

(*Stands doll upon its feet. Doll is on a metal stand.*)

CHILDREN: Oh! — Ah! — Oh!

LILLY: Isn't she a beauty?

(*BECKY gets stool from above door and stands on it to see doll.*)

JESSIE: She's almost as big as Lottie.

LOTTIE (*dancing down*): Tra-la-la.

LILLY: She's dressed for the theater. See her magnificent opera-cloak.

(*LAVINIA does not get on floor.*)

ERMENGARDE: She has an opera-glass in her hand.

SARA: So she has. (*Getting down*) Here's her trunk. Let us open that and looks at her things; Ermy, you open the other.

(*Takes trunk with JESSIE down stage; opens it. Ermy takes other one with help of JESSIE and opens it too. Children crowd around trunks, sit on floor, looking at the clothes. BECKY looks on from behind*) Here is the key.

CHILDREN: Oh!

SARA: This is full of lace collars and silk stockings and kerchiefs. Here's a jewel-case with a necklace and a tiara of diamonds. Put them on her, Lilly. All of her underclothes. Ah, look.

(*Showing.*)

ERMENGARDE: Here's a velvet coat trimmed with chinchilla, and one lined with ermine, and muffs. Oh, what darling dresses! A pale cloth, trimmed with sable, and a long coat. (*LOTTIE takes coat and puts it on*) A pink, covered with white little buttons, and a white tulle dress, and dresses, dresses, dresses!

SARA: And here are hats, and hats, and hats. Becky, can you see?

(*Rises.*)

BECKY: Oh, yes, Miss, and it's like 'eaven.
(Falls off stool backwards.)

SARA *(rises):* She is a lovely doll. *(Looking at doll)* Suppose she understands human talk, and feels proud of being admired.

LAVINIA: You are always *supposing* things, Sara.

SARA: I know I am — I like it. There's nothing so nice as supposing. It's almost like being a fairy. If you suppose anything hard enough, it seems as if it were real. Have you never done it?

LAVINIA *(contemptuously):* No — of course not — it's ridiculous.

SARA: Is it? Well, it makes you happy at any rate. *(LAVINIA turns away;changing her tone)* Suppose we finish looking at the doll's things when we have more time. Becky will put them back in the trunk.
(LOTTIE goes up to doll, to see tiara.)

BECKY *(comes forward quickly — shyly):* Me, Miss? Yes, Miss. Thank you, Miss, for letting me touch them. *(Down on knees, wiping hands)* Oh — my — they are beautiful.

LAVINIA *(at table, catching LOTTIE touching doll):* Get down this minute. That's not for babies to touch.
(Takes her.)

LOTTIE *(crying):* I'm not a baby — I'm not — Sar-a, Sar-a — oh!

JESSIE: There now, you've made her cry — the spoiled thing.

SARA *(runs to LOTTIE; kneeling):* Now, Lottie! *(Puts her on side)* Lottie, dear, you mustn't cry.

LOTTIE *(howling):* I don't want to stay in a nasty school with nasty girls.

SARA *(to LAVINIA and JESSIE):* You ought not to have scolded her. She's such a little thing. And you know she's only at boarding-school because she hasn't any mother.
(Children sympathetically. JESSIE to door.)

LOTTIE *(wailing):* I haven't any mamma.

JESSIE: If she doesn't stop, Miss Minchin will hear her.
(ERMENGARDE gets tiara from doll.)

LILLY: And she'll be so cross that she may stop the party. Do
stop, Lottie darling. I'll give you a penny.

LOTTIE: Don't want your old penny.

ERMENGARDE: Yes, do stop, and I'll give you anything.
(Offering box.)

LOTTIE: She called me a baby. *(Crying.)*

SARA *(petting her):* But you will be a baby if you cry, Lottie,
pet. There, there.

LOTTIE: I haven't any mamma.

SARA *(cheerfully):* Yes, you have, darling. Don't you know we
said Sara'd be your mamma. Don't you want Sara to be your
mamma? *(LOTTIE stops crying)* See. *(Rising and giving doll
to LOTTIE)* I'll lend you my doll to hold while I tell you that
story I promised you.

LILLY: Oh, do tell us a story, Sara.
(Puts doll on chair.)

JESSIE: Oh, yes, do.

CHILDREN: Oh!

SARA: I may not have time to finish it before the company
comes — but I'll tell you the end some other time.
(LOTTIE takes doll to chair.)

LAVINIA: That's always the way, Princess Sara! *(Passionately)*
Nasty little spoilt beast. I should like to *slap* her.

SARA *(firing up):* I should like to slap you too. But I don't want
to slap you — at least I both *want* to slap you and should *like*
to slap you.

CHILDREN *(in group, interested in fight):* Oh, Oh!

SARA: We are not little gutter children. We are old enough to
know better.

LAVINIA: Oh, we are *princesses, I* believe — or at least one of us is — Jessie told me you often pretended to yourself that you were a princess.

SARA *(getting control of herself):* It's true. Sometimes I do pretend I'm a princess. I pretend I am a princess so that I can try to behave like one.

CHILDREN: Ah!

ERMENGARDE: You *are* queer, Sara, but you're nice.
(Hugs her)

SARA: I know I'm queer, and I try to be nice. Shall I begin the story?

CHILDREN *(ad lib.):* Story. Oh, oh! Yes, yes, begin, Sara, do.

SARA: I'm going to turn all the lights out. It's always so much nicer to tell a story by firelight.
(Turns out brackets with switch above fireplace; gets on sofa for story. All the children sit, except LAVINIA, who stands near the piano. Children on the floor in front of the sofa. ERMENGARDE goes up to the window and pulls curtains apart and makes up in them for ghost.)

LILLY: It's such fun to sit in the dark.

SARA: Once upon a time

ERMENGARDE *(from behind curtain):* Woo-o-oo

JESSIE: What's that?

SARA: It's nothing but the wind. Once upon a time

ERMENGARDE *(coming down in curtains):* Whoo-oo-oo-oopee
(Frightens Children. SARA turns on lights. Children scream and get up; fall on ERMENGARDE and take curtain off her. Laugh)

CHILDREN: Oh, it's Ermengarde.

LILLY: Begin again, Sara!
(SARA turns out lights.)

ALL: Yes.

SARA *(all seated as before, — SARA on sofa):* Once upon a time —long ago — there lived on the edge of a deep, deep forest a little girl and her grandmother.

LILLY: Was she pretty?

SARA: She was so fair and sweet that people called her Snowflower. She had no relations in the world but her old grandmother, Dame Frostyface.

JESSIE: Was she a nice old woman?

SARA: She was always nice to Snowflower. They lived together in a little cottage thatched with reeds. Tall trees sheltered it, daisies grew thick about the door, and swallows built in the eaves.

CHILDREN: Oh, Lottie!

LILLY: What a nice place!

SARA: One sunny morning Dame Frostyface said, "My child, I am going on a long journey, and I cannot take you with me, and I will tell you what to do when you feel lonely. You know that carved oak chair I sit in by the fire. Well, lay your head on the velvet cushions and say, 'Chair of my grandmother, tell me a story,' and it will tell you one."

CHILDREN: Oh!

SARA: "And if you want to travel anywhere, just seat yourself in it, and say, 'Chair of my grandmother, take me where I want to go'."

ERMENGARDE: Oh, I wish I had a chair like that.

LOTTIE: Oh, go on, Sara.

CHILDREN: Do go on.

ERMENGARDE: And so

LOTTIE: And so

SARA: And so Dame Frostyface went away. And every day Snowflower baked herself a barley cake, *and every night the chair told her a beautiful new story.*

66

ERMENGARDE: If it had been my chair, I should have told it to take me to the King's Palace.

SARA: That is what happened — but listen. The time passed on, but Dame Frostyface did not come back for such a long time that Snowflower thought she would go and find her.

LOTTIE: Did she find her?

SARA: Wait and listen. One day she jumped into the chair and said, "Chair of my grandmother, take me the way she went." And the chair gave a creak and began to move out of the cottage and into the forest where all the birds were singing.

ERMENGARDE: How I *wish* I could have gone with her.

SARA: And the chair went on, and on, and on — like a coach and six.

LOTTIE: How far did it go?

SARA: It traveled through the forest and through the ferns, and over the velvet moss — it traveled one day, and two days, and three days — and on the fourth day

LILLY: What did it do?

SARA (*slowly*): It came to an open place in the forest where a hundred workmen were felling trees and a hundred wagons were carrying them away to the King's Palace.

ERMENGARDE: Was the King giving a ball?

SARA: He was giving seven of them. Seven days' feasting to celebrate the birthday of his daughter, the Princess Greedalend.

LOTTIE: Did he invite Snowflower?

SARA: Listen. The chair marched up to the palace, and all the people ran after it. And the King heard of it, and the lords and ladies crowded to see it, and when the Princess heard it was a chair that could tell stories she cried until the King sent an order to the little girl to come and make it tell her one.

LOTTIE: Did she go in?

LILLY: Oh, how lovely.

SARA: The chair marched in a grave and courtly manner up the grand staircase and into the palace hall. The King sat on an ivory throne in a robe of purple velvet, stiff with flowers of gold. The Queen sat on his right hand in a mantle clasped with pearls, and the Princess wore a robe of gold sewn with diamonds.

LILLY: Oh, what splendid clothes!

SARA: But Snowflower had little bare feet, and nothing but a clean, coarse linen dress. She got off the chair and made a curtsey to the grand company. Then she laid her head on the cushion, and said, "Chair of my grandmother, tell me a story," and a clear, silvery voice came out from the old velvet cushion, and said, "Listen to the story of the Christmas Cuckoo."
(Door-bell peals)

ALL *(jumping up from floor and sofa, forming two lines, in readiness for the visitors):* Miss Minchin is coming — Miss Minchin is coming.
(Enter MISS MINCHIN, followed by AMELIA. BECKY under table.)

MISS MINCHIN: What are you naughty children doing in the dark? Amelia, turn up the lights immediately. *(She does so with switch above fireplace)* How dare you?

SARA: I beg pardon, Miss Minchin. It was all my fault. I was telling them a story, and I like to tell them in the firelight.

MISS MINCHIN *(changing):* Oh, it was you, Sara! That is a different matter. I can always trust you.

LAVINIA *(aside):* Yes, of course, if it's the Princess Sara, it's a different matter.

MISS MINCHIN *(speaking off to MRS. CARMICHAEL):* Won't you come in, Mrs. Carmichael?
(Enter MRS. CARMICHAEL followed by DONALD, MAZIE, NORA, and JANET in a line, DONALD has mother's skirt in his hand, playing horse; three children are dressed for the

street. They follow their mother to a sofa and sit down.)

MISS MINCHIN: She is *(referring to SARA)* such a clever child. Such an imagination. She amuses the children by the hour with her wonderful story-telling.

MRS. CARMICHAEL: She has a clever little face. *(ERMENGARDE offers to make friends with DONALD, who fights her into her corner.)*

MISS MINCHIN: Won't you sit here, Mrs. Carmichael? *(Indicating sofa)*

MRS. CARMICHAEL: I hope I won't disturb the dancing if I am obliged to leave you suddenly.

MISS MINCHIN: You will not disturb us, although we shall, of course, be very sorry.

MRS. CARMICHAEL: Mr. Carmichael has just had bad news from an important client in India. The poor man has suddenly lost all his money and is on his way to England, very ill indeed.

MISS MINCHIN: How distressing!

MRS. CARMICHAEL: Mr. Carmichael may be called away at any moment. He said he would send a servant for me if he received a summons to go. If it comes I shall be obliged to run away at once. The children wanted so much to see the dancing that I did not like to disappoint them.

MISS MINCHIN: Sara, my dear, come here. *(Aside to Mrs. Carmichael)* Her mother died when she was born. Her father is a most distinguished young officer — very rich, fortunately. *(To SARA)* Shake hands with Mrs. Carmichael. *(SARA does so. To MRS. CARMICHAEL)* Sara is thirteen years old to-day, Mrs. Carmichael, and is giving a party to her schoolfellows. She is always doing things to give her friends pleasure.

MRS. CARMICHAEL *(motherly woman, pats SARA's hand)*. She looks like a kind little girl. *(LOTTIE brings doll over to sofa and shows it to the Carmichael children.)* I'm sure my children would like to hear her tell stories. They love stories, and some day you must come and tell them one.

(Turns and sees doll) Oh, what a splendid doll! Is it yours?

MISS MINCHIN *(grandly):* Her papa ordered it in Paris. Its wardrobe was made by a fashionable dressmaker. Nothing is too superb for the child.

LOTTIE *(to SARA):* Sara, may that little boy hold your doll?

SARA: Yes, dear.

(LOTTIE takes doll to DONALD, who boxes it away from him, boy fashion.)

LOTTIE *(taking doll out of harm's way):* He's one of the large family across the street — the ones you make up stories about.

MRS. CARMICHAEL *(good-naturedly):* Do you make up stories about *us?*

SARA: I hope you won't mind. I can see your house out of my window, and there are so many of you, and you all look so happy together, that I like to pretend I know you all. I *suppose* things about you.

LILLY *(the CHILDREN have been standing in two lines listening to all this):* She has made up names for all of you.

MRS. CARMICHAEL: Has she? What are they?

SARA: They are only pretended names — perhaps you'll think they're silly.

MRS. CARMICHAEL: No, I shall not. What do you call us?

LOTTIE *(solemnly):* You are Mrs. and Mister Mont-mor-ency.

MRS. CARMICHAEL *(laughing):* What a grand name! And what do you call the children?

SARA *(shyly but smiling):* The little boy in the lace cap is Ethelbert Beaucham Montmorency — and the *second* baby is Violette Cholmondeley Montmorency, and the little boy with the fat brown legs and socks is Sidney Cecil Vivienne

Montmorency.

LOTTIE *(interrupting and dancing):* Then there's Lillian Evangeline — and Guy Clarence — and Maude — Marion — and Veronia Eustacia — and Claude Audrey Harold Hector.
(Laughs and goes into corner)

MRS. CARMICHAEL: You romantic little thing!

SARA *(apologetically):* I shouldn't have *supposed* so much about you if you hadn't all looked so happy together. *My* papa is a soldier in India, you know, and my mamma died when I was a baby. So I like to look at children who have mammas and papas.

MRS. CARMICHAEL *(kissing SARA):* You poor little dear, — Miss Minchin *must* let you come and have tea with us.

MISS MINCHIN: Certainly, certainly. Sara will be delighted. Now, young ladies, you may begin the entertainment Sara has prepared for Mrs. Carmichael.
(Enter MAID)

MAID: A gentleman would like to see you, Ma'm. He says he comes from Messrs. Barrow & Skipworth.

MISS MINCHIN: The lawyers? *(Annoyed)* What can he want? I cannot be disturbed at present. Ask him to wait.

MAID: And if you please, Ma'm, a note for Mrs. Carmichael. *(Delivers same to MRS. CARMICHAEL, who rises to receive it, and goes down stage. Exit MAID.)*

MRS. CARMICHAEL: A note for me?
(Takes it. Opens note)

MISS MINCHIN: Not bad news, I hope?

MRS. CARMICHAEL: Very bad, I am afraid. My husband's client, poor Mr. Carrisford, has just landed, dangerously ill. Much worse. Mr. Carmichael wants me to go and see him at once. I am sorry to run away like this. It has all been charming. Thank you for asking us. Come, children. Say good afternoon. Papa needs us. *(Shaking hands with MISS*

MINCHIN) Your school is delightful.
(Exit MRS. CARMICHAEL and CHILDREN in same order as entrance, DONALD driving his mother as before.)

DONALD: Geddap — whoa — go along.

ALL: Good-bye. Good afternoon, etc.

MISS AMELIA: What a pity she was obliged to leave so soon.

MISS MINCHIN: She was evidently very much pleased.

MAID *(entering):* Will you see the gentleman from Messrs. Barrow & Skipworth, Ma'am?

MISS AMELIA *(meekly):* The children's refreshments are laid in your parlour, sister. Could you see him in here while the children have their cake and sherry and negus?

MISS MINCHIN: Yes. *(To CHILDREN)* Now, young ladies, you must go and enjoy the nice things Sara has provided for you. *(CHILDREN all troop out.)*

CHILDREN: Cake and sherry and negus.

MISS MINCHIN *(to SERVANT):* Bring the gentleman in here. *(Exit SERVANT. Enter BARROW, ushered on by SERVANT. BARROW is a middle-aged, high-class lawyer, well dressed.)*

MAID: Mr. Barrow, Ma'am.
(Exit MAID)

MISS MINCHIN: Good evening, sir. Be seated. *(Indicating sofa)* Of the legal firm of Barrow & Skipworth, I believe?

BARROW: Yes, Barrow, representing the late Captain Crewe, of the—

MISS MINCHIN *(startled):* The late Captain Crewe? You don't mean to say that Captain Crewe is

BARROW *(sits on sofa.):* Dead, Madam, dead of jungle fever.

MISS MINCHIN *(shocked):* It seems impossible. How shocking! How sudden!

BARROW: It was sudden. The firm thought that you should be told at once, as his child is in your care.

MISS MINCHIN: Very right and proper. Poor Captain Crewe! Poor little orphaned Sara! *(Handkerchief to her eyes)* She will need my care more than ever.

BARROW: She will indeed, Madam.

MISS MINCHIN: What do you mean?

BARROW: That, as she has apparently no relations to take charge of her, she is fortunate in having such a friend as yourself.

MISS MINCHIN: Most certainly. An heiress to so large a fortune — for I believe it is a very large fortune? *(BARROW clears throat significantly. MISS MINCHIN takes him up sharply)* What do you mean? You certainly mean something. What is it?

BARROW: She has *no* fortune, Madam, large or small. She is left without a penny.

MISS MINCHIN: Without a penny! It's impossible. Captain Crewe was a rich man.

BARROW: Ah! *Was,* — that's it, Madam, he *was.*

MISS MINCHIN *(leaning forward excitedly):* You don't mean he has lost his money? Lost it?

BARROW: Every penny of it. That young man had too much money. He didn't know what to do with it, so he let a speculating friend — a very dear friend — *(sarcastically)* play ducks and drakes with it. The friend was mad on the subject of a high diamond mine — put all his own money into it —all of Captain Crewe's — the mine proved a failure — the dear friend — the very dear friend — ran away. Captain Crewe was already stricken with fever when the news came — the shock was too much for him. He died delirious. *(Rises)* Ruined.

MISS MINCHIN: Do you mean to tell me that he has left *nothing?* That Sara will have no fortune — that the child is a *beggar* — that she's left on my hands a little pauper instead of an heiress?

BARROW: She is certainly left a beggar — and she is certainly left on your hands, Ma'am.

MISS MINCHIN *(rising):* It's monstrous. She's in my drawing-room, at this moment, dressed in a pink silk gown and lace petticoats, giving a party at my expense.

BARROW: She's certainly giving it at your expense, Ma'am, if she's giving it. Barrow & Skipworth are not responsible for anything. Captain Crewe died without paying our last bill, and it was a considerable one.

MISS MINCHIN: That is what happened to me. I was always so sure of his payments that I have been to all sorts of expenses since his last check came. I actually paid the bill for that ridiculous doll and all its ridiculous fantastic wardrobe. The child was to have *anything* she wanted. She has a carriage and a pony and a maid, and I've paid for all of them.

BARROW: You hadn't better pay for anything more unless you want to make presents to the young lady. She has *not a brass farthing to call her own.*

MISS MINCHIN: But what am I to do?

BARROW: There isn't anything to do, Ma'am. Captain Crewe is dead. The child is left a pauper. Nobody is responsible for her but you.

MISS MINCHIN: I'm not responsible for her. I refuse to be made responsible for her.

BARROW: I have nothing to do with that, Ma'am. I only know that Barrow & Skipworth are not responsible.
(Bows and turns to go)

MISS MINCHIN: But you cannot go like that and leave her on my hands, — I won't have it. I have been cheated; I have been swindled; I'll turn her out into the streets.

BARROW *(impersonally):* *I* wouldn't, Madam, if I were you; you can if you like, but I wouldn't. Bad for the school — ugly story to get about. Pay you better to keep her as a sort of charity pupil.

MISS MINCHIN: This is infamous. I'll do nothing of the sort.

BARROW: She might teach the little ones, run errands, and that sort of thing.

MISS MINCHIN: Ah, you want to foist her off on me. I won't have her foisted off on me.

BARROW: Just as you please, Madam. The matter is entirely in your hands. Good evening. Very sorry the thing has happened, of course. Unpleasant for all parties. Good evening.
(Exit. Children off stage singing)

CHILDREN *(singing):* "Here we go round the mulberry bush, the mulberry bush, the mulberry bush, — here we go round the mulberry bush, so early in the morning."
(MISS MINCHIN stands a moment glaring after BARROW. Then she starts toward door. Stops as AMELIA enters)

AMELIA: What's the matter, sister?

MISS MINCHIN *(fiercely and hoarsely):* Where is Sara Crewe?

AMELIA *(astonished):* Sara? Why, she's with the children in your room.

MISS MINCHIN: Has she a black frock in her sumptuous wardrobe?

AMELIA *(stammering):* Why — what — she has only an old black velvet one that is much too small for her — it is too short for her to wear.

MISS MINCHIN: Go tell her to take off that preposterous pink silk gown, and put the black one on, whether it is too short or not. She is done with finery.

AMELIA: Sister, what can have happened?

MISS MINCHIN: Captain Crewe is dead.

AMELIA: Oh!

MISS MINCHIN: He died without a penny.

AMELIA: Oh!

MISS MINCHIN: That spoilt, pampered, fanciful child is left a pauper on my hands.

AMELIA: Oh! Oh!

MISS MINCHIN: Hundreds of pounds have I spent on nonsense for her — hundreds of pounds — I shall never see a penny of it.

CHILDREN *(outside).* Ha, ha, ha!
(Applause)

MISS MINCHIN: Go, put a stop to that ridiculous party of hers. Go and make her change her frock.

AMELIA *(gapes and stares):* M-must I go and tell her now?

MISS MINCHIN *(fiercely):* This moment. Don't stand there staring like a goose. Go.
(Exit AMELIA)

CHILDREN *(singing):* "Here we go round the mulberry bush."

MISS MINCHIN: Hundreds of pounds! I never hesitated at the cost of anything. Princess Sara, indeed! The child has been pampered as if she had been a queen. *(Loud sniffles from BECKY under table)* What's that?

BECKY *(coming from under table):* If you please, Ma'am. *(Sobs)* It's me, Ma'am. I hadn't ought to, but I hid under the table when you came in, and I heard.

MISS MINCHIN: You impudent child!

BECKY *(sobs frequently):* Oh, please 'm, I dare say you'll give we warnin', but I'm sorry for poor Miss Sara — she is such a kind young lady, Ma'am.

MISS MINCHIN: Leave the room.

BECKY: Yes, 'm, I will, 'm, but I just wanted to arst you — Miss Sara's been such a rich young lady — 'm — she's been waited on and — poor — and what'll she do, Ma'am, without no maid? If — if — oh, please, would you let me wait on her after I'm done my pots and kettles? I'd do them so quick

— if you'd let me wait on her — now she's so poor — or — poor little Miss Sara — Ma'am — that was called a princess.

MISS MINCHIN: No, certainly not. She'll wait on herself and on other people too. *(Stamping foot)* Leave the room this instant — or you — leave this place.

BECKY *(at door, turns):* Wouldn't you?

MISS MINCHIN *(in pantomime, says "Go." Exit BECKY. Fiercely).* Wait on her! No, she will not be waited on. *(Enter SARA, with doll in arms, in black dress)* Come here. *(Sara advances a little.)* Put down that doll. You will have no time for dolls in the future.

SARA: She was the last thing my papa gave me before he died.

MISS MINCHIN: He did not pay for her, at any rate. I paid for her.

SARA *(crossing to chair and putting doll on it):* Then she is your doll, not mine.

MISS MINCHIN: Of course she is my doll. *(Crossing to table)* Everything that you have is mine. For a whole year I've been spending money on all sorts of ridiculously extravagant things for you and I shall never be paid for one of them. I've been robbed, robbed, robbed!

SARA *(turning from doll, suddenly and strongly):* My papa did not mean to rob you — he did not — he did not!

MISS MINCHIN: Whether he meant to do it or not, he did it — and here I am left with you on my hands. Do you understand?

SARA: Yes, I understand, — Miss Amelia told me. *(Kneels, covering face with arms, in doll's lap, and bursting into tears)* My papa is dead — my papa is dead!

MISS MINCHIN: Stop crying. I sent for you to talk to you, and I have no time to waste. *(SARA sobs.)* Stop crying, do you hear? *(Pause until SARA rises and faces MISS MINCHIN.)* You are not a princess any longer. Remember that. You have no friends. You have no money. You have no one to take care of you. Your pony and carriage will be sold at once. Your maid will be sent away. You'll wear your plainest and oldest frocks. Your extravagant ones are no longer suited for your station. You're like Becky — you will have to work for your living.

SARA: If you tell me what to do, I'll do it.

MISS MINCHIN: You will be obliged to do it whether you like it or not. If I do not choose to keep you out of charity, you have no home but the street.

SARA *(sobbing): I* know that.

MISS MINCHIN: Then listen to what I say. If you work hard, and try to make yourself useful, I may let you stay here. You are a sharp child, and pick up things readily. You speak French very well, and you can help with the younger children.

SARA: Yes, I can help with the little ones. I like them and they like me.

MISS MINCHIN: Don't talk nonsense about people liking you. You will have more to do than to teach the little ones. You will run errands and help in the kitchen as well as in the schoolroom. If you don't please me you will be sent away. Now go. *(Sara crosses to door to go.)* Stop, don't you intend to thank me?

SARA: What for?

MISS MINCHIN: For my kindness to you — for my kindness in giving you a home.

SARA *(wildly):* You're *not* kind, you are *not* kind!

MISS MINCHIN: Leave the room instantly. *(SARA starts to go.)* Stop. *(SARA stops.)* You are not to go to the bedroom you used to sleep in.

SARA: Where must I go?

MISS MINCHIN: In future you will occupy the garret next to Becky's — under the roof.

SARA: The garret, next to Becky's, where the rats are?

MISS MINCHIN: Rubbish! There are no rats there.
(Crossing to door)

SARA *(following to chair):* There are. Oh, Miss Minchin, there are! Sometimes Becky can hardly sleep at all. She says that in the garret next to hers they run about all night.

MISS MINCHIN: Whether there are rats or not, you will sleep there. Leave the room.
(Exit MISS MINCHIN. Door opens)

LOTTIE *(outside):* Sara! *(Enters)* Sara! *(Embraces SARA who is on her knees)* The big girls say your papa is dead, like my mamma; they say you haven't any papa. Haven't you any papa?

SARA: No, I haven't, Lottie; no, I haven't.

LOTTIE: You said you'd be my mamma. I'll be your papa, Sara! Let Lottie be your papa.

SARA: Oh, Lottie, love me; please, Lottie, love me — love me.

CURTAIN

ACT II

SCENE: *A garret under the roof at Miss Minchin's; rake roof with garret window, outside of which are showing housetops with snow on them. There are rat holes around. A bed, covered with old blanket, sheet, and old coverlet, badly torn. A table with bench behind it. Chairs, an armchair, and a four-legged stool above fireplace. A wash-stand with pitcher, bowl, soap-dish, and mug. An old trunk. A candle in stick unlighted.*

At the rise of curtain: Wind off stage; window opens and snow flutters through. Stage in semi-darkness. Broken pane in window.

RAM DASS appears on platform back of window, with dark lantern. He raises window, examines room from platform with light, then beckons GUEST to follow him. Enter GUEST on platform, also carrying lantern.

GUEST *(kneeling beside RAM DASS):* You saw the child go out?

RAM DASS: Yes, Sahib. *(GUEST lets himself down by table through window)* She has been sent out upon an errand.

GUEST: And no one ever enters here, but herself? You are sure?

RAM DASS: Sure, Sahib.

GUEST: Then we are safe for a few moments. We must look about and plan quickly. You have sharp ears; stand near the door. If you hear a sound on the stairs, we must bolt through the window.

RAM DASS *(going to door):* Yes, Sahib.
(Stands listening)

GUEST: What a place to keep a child in! *(Going to fire)* No fire — no sign of one. *(Crosses to bed)* Blanket thin, sheet miserable. We must alter this.

RAM DASS *(at door):* When first my master thought of this plan, it made him smile, and he has not smiled for many days. He said: "The poor child will think a magician has worked a spell."

GUEST *(back of table, making notes):* She will indeed. It's a curious plan, but the Sahib is a sick man and lonely. Now listen, Ram Dass. You lascars can be as silent as ghosts. Can you, with the other three to help you, steal in through that window, and do what your master wishes, and make no sound?

RAM DASS: Yes, Sahib, Ram Dass can do it. He knows well how to make no sound at all.

GUEST: Will it be safer to do it while she is out upon some errand, or at night when she is asleep?

RAM DASS: At night when she sleeps. Children sleep soundly,

80

even the unhappy ones.

GUEST: As Mr. Carrisford's house is next door, you and I can bring the things across the roof together. Yes, yes, the window is wide enough to allow them to pass through.

RAM DASS: Shall it be done tonight?

GUEST: Yes. Everything is ready, — the measurements are correct. What's that?

RAM DASS *(at door):* On the staircase two flights below. It is the child herself returning.

GUEST: Here — through here, quickly.
(Exit through window)

RAM DASS *(in window):* Yes, Ram Dass will do this thing tonight.
(Exit. Enter SARA, shabbily dressed, wet, and tired; she closes door and stands a second leaning against it; looks about the room, out of breath and exhausted with climbing up stairs.)

SARA: I thought I should never get back, never, never. *(To table. Lights candle)* How miserable it looks and how tired I am. *(Takes hat and shawl and puts them on chair)* They are wet as though they'd fallen in a pond. *(Coming down to armchair; sits in same)* I've been sent out on errands ten times since breakfast. I'm cold — I'm wet — I'm as hungry as a wolf. *(Wind. Rats squeak. Sara has dropped head in lap on square stool. Hears rats, looks up. Wind howls during this pause)* What a noise my rats are making; they must have heard me come in. *(1st rat runs on)* Oh, there's Melchisedek. Poor thing, he's come to ask for crumbs. *(Puts hand into pocket to hunt for crumbs and turns it out)* Are you hungry too, poor Melchisedek. I'm sorry, I haven't one crumb left. Go home, Melchisedek, and tell your wife that there was nothing in my pocket. She's not as hungry as I am. *(1st rat off under bed)* Good night. Poor thing. *(Crosses back to armchair, drops into chair, and takes Emily in her arms)* Do you hear, Emily, why don't you say something?

Sometimes I'm sure you could, if you tried. You are the only relation I have in the world. Why don't you try? Do you hear? I've walked a thousand miles to-day, — errands and errands, and errands and errands. Errands for the cook, errands for Miss Amelia — and for Miss Minchin — and even for the girls — I had to go for pencils for Lavinia. *(Outburst)* Everybody sends me errands. And because I came in late they wouldn't give me any supper. I'm so hungry I could almost eat you. *(Wind, Passionately)* Do you hear? *(Pause, and breaks out again)* You are nothing but a doll, doll, doll — you are stuffed with sawdust — you never had a heart. *(Throws Emily on stool and cries. Picks her up; sets her in chair, sits on stool, elbows on knees, and gazes at her relentingly)* You can't help being a doll, I suppose, any more than good-natured Ermengarde can help being stupid. I oughtn't have slapped you. You were *born* a doll — perhaps you do your sawdust best. *(Knock on door)* I wonder who it is. *(Rises hesitating)* Lottie is in bed and poor Becky was crying when I came through the kitchen. The cook was in a passion and she couldn't get away. *(Opens door, sees LOTTIE alarmed, surprised. Enter LOTTIE in nightgown, hugging a birthday doll. Wind)* Oh, Lottie, you oughtn't to come here so late. Miss Minchin would be so cross if she caught you. What do you want, darling?

LOTTIE *(who has run to SARA and is clinging to her):* I want you, mamma, Sara! Oh, I had such an ugly dream, and I got frightened

SARA *(leads her to armchair, and takes her up in lap):* I'll hug you a minute, Lottie, but you mustn't stay, — it's too cold.

LOTTIE: Hug me and kiss me like a real mamma — Sara, it was such an ugly dream

SARA *(hugs her.):* Are you better now darling?

LOTTIE: Yes. You are such a comfty hugger, Sara — *(Sits up cheerfully, and sees doll on ottoman)* There's Emily. She's not so pretty as Arabella, is she?

SARA: No, but she's the only relation I've got in the world. My papa gave her to me when he brought me to Miss Minchin's, six years ago.

LOTTIE *(putting her doll beside Emily):* There, Emily, Lady Arabella has come to see you. *(To SARA)* Have you seen your rat lately, mamma Sara?

SARA: Yes — poor Melchisedek — he came out to-night to beg for crumbs, and I hadn't any for him. But there, Lottie dear, you must not stay in the cold. *(Coaxing her)* You won't have any more ugly dreams — for Sara will keep thinking good dreams for you after you've gone back to bye-lows, — you must run back now, like a sweet Lottie.

LOTTIE: Oh, but Sara, I like to stay with you. I like your old garret and Emily and the rat.
(Wind and snow)

SARA: But listen to the wind. See the snow coming through the broken window. You mustn't stay here in your little nightie. I'll take you to the top of the stairs and you must go back to bed.

LOTTIE: But mayn't I say my seven times to you before I go? I have to say it to Miss Amelia in the morning. May I sit here on your bed — *(does so)* and say it?

SARA *(kneeling in front of LOTTIE):* Well, you can say it to me once.

LOTTIE *(singsong):* Seven times one are seven —
Seven times two are fourteen —
Seven times three are twenty-one —
Seven times four are forty-eight —

SARA *(caressingly):* Oh, no, Lottie, not forty-eight.

LOTTIE *(anxiously):* Not forty-eight

SARA *(suggestively):* Not forty-eight

LOTTIE *(catching at straws):* Not forty-eight — then — it's sume-ty other eight.

SARA *(encouragingly):* Seven times one are seven —
Seven times two are fourteen —

LOTTIE *(drawing hope):* Seven times three are twenty-one —
(Excited haste) Seven times four are twenty-eight

SARA *(hugs and kisses her):* Yes, that's it — go on.

LOTTIE *(much cheered — singsong):*

Seven times five are thirty-five,
Seven times six are forty-two,
Seven times seven are forty-nine —
Seven times eight are fifty-six —
(Slowing up)
Seven times — nine — seven times — seven times
ni — nine — seven times nine are — *(Despairingly)*

Oh, Sara, seven times nine is such a hard one.

SARA *(slow, suggestively):*

Seven times nine — are — si — si —
Seven times nine are six —

LOTTIE *(catching her up with a shout of glee):* Sixty-three
— seven times nine are sixty-three —
(Rattles off with triumphant glee and ease)
Seven times ten are seventy —
Seven times eleven are seventy-seven and
Seven times twelve are eighty-four.

SARA *(hugs her):* That's beautiful — all you have to remember
is seven fours are twenty-eight and seven nines are sixty-
three. Now we must go, pet.
*(Sets LOTTIE down, giving her doll — leads her out of
room door. Garret left empty for few minutes, then cautious
knock — outside. Door is opened by ERMENGARDE who
at first looks around edge cautiously and enters. Wind.
ERMENGARDE has pile of books under arm, is dressed in
nightgown, with bare feet, and has hair done in curl papers.)*

ERMENGARDE: I wonder where she's gone. *(Rats squeak.
ERMENGARDE screams, runs and jumps on bed.)* Oh, these

rats — oh — *(ad lib. — Rat comes out from behind wash-stand, stops. ERMENGARDE drops slipper)* Oh, Melchy — *(to rat)* please go way — oh, do go way — and let me get my slipper, — there's a good Melchy — *(As rat moves)* I'll give you a bun to-morrow. *(Rat runs off. ERMENGARDE, out of bed, hops across floor to get her slipper, and sinks in chair, sighing. She puts on slipper.)* I wonder where she's gone. I wonder if that nasty cook has sent her out in all the snow and slush. *(Rises and sees hat and shawl on chair)* No, she's not gone out — there are her hat and shawl, — they are dripping wet. It's a shame. *(Puts books on table)* These came to-day from my papa. He wants me to read every one of them, and he'll ask me questions about them when he sees me. It's awful. *(Impatiently)* I'm not clever like Sara. I'd as soon take castor-oil as read them, and if I did read them, I couldn't remember what's in them. *(Drops books on floor)* I was born stupid. *(Wind. Rises from chair)* I wish Sara would come. *(Goes to bed)* What a horrible little bed. She must nearly freeze to death on these cold nights. Oh, it is a shame. She's treated worse than poor little Becky, the scullery maid. *(Rat heard squeaking. ERMENGARDE screams again, runs to chair, and hides feet under her in terror)* I wish she'd come. *(Enter SARA)* Sara!

SARA: I didn't know you were coming here to-night, Ermengarde.

ERMENGARDE: I crept out of my room after the other girls were asleep. Papa has sent me some more books, Sara! *(Dejectedly pointing to table and books on floor)* There they are.

SARA *(delightedly):* Oh, has he? *(Runs to books, and sits on floor. Looks at titles on books, opens them)* How beautiful. Carlyle's "French Revolution." I have *so* wanted to read that!

ERMENGARDE: I haven't. And papa will be so cross if I don't. He'll want me to know all about it when I go home for the holidays. What shall I do?

SARA *(excited):* Look here, Ermengarde. If you'll lend me these books, I'll read them, and tell you everything that's in them afterwards, and I'll tell it so that you'll remember it too.

ERMENGARDE: Oh, Sara, Sara, do you think you could?

SARA: I know I can. The little A, B, C children always remember what I tell them.

ERMENGARDE *(pause):* Sara, if you'll do that, and make me *remember,* I'll — I'll give you some of my pocket-money.

SARA: I don't want your money, Ermy, I want your books. *(Holds them tight in arms)* I want them!

ERMENGARDE: Take them then, — you're welcome. I wish I wanted them.

SARA *(cheerfully):* Well, that's all right. I'm so glad. *(Puts books on floor beside her)* Now let's tell each other things. How are you getting on with your French lessons?

ERMENGARDE: Ever so much better since I began to come up into your garret, and you began to teach me.

SARA: I am glad. *(Looks around room)* The garret would be rather nice if it wasn't so very dreadful. *(Laughs)* It's a good place to pretend in.

ERMENGARDE *(eagerly):* What do you pretend, Sara?

SARA: Well, generally I pretend it is the Bastille, and I'm kept a prisoner here like Doctor Manette in "A Tale of Two Cities."

ERMENGARDE *(interested):* And what else?

SARA: I pretend I have been here for years — and years and years — and years — and everyone has forgotten all about me, and Miss Minchin is the jailer. And I pretend that there's another prisoner in the next cell, — that's Becky, you know, — I've told her about it — and I knock on the wall to make her hear, and she knocks like this, — you know. *(Knocks three times on wall; listens a moment)* She's not there; if she were she'd knock back. Ah!

ERMENGARDE: Ah, it's just like a story.

SARA: It is a story; everything is a story — you're a story, I'm a

story, Miss Minchin's a story.
(Rats squeak.)

ERMENGARDE *(gets on stool and screams.):* Ah, there are the rats again. Are you never afraid of the rats, Sara?

SARA *(on floor):* Not now. I was at first, but now they're a part of the story. There were always rats in prisons, and the prisoners tamed them with crumbs. That is how I tamed Melchisedek and his wife. *(Calls rats)* Come on, Melchy dear, come, nice Melchy.

ERMENGARDE *(stumbles):* Oh, don't call them out; come back, Sara. Tell me some more stories — they are so nice. *(They resume former positions.)*

SARA: Well, I tell myself stories about the people who live in the other houses in the square. The *large* family, you know.

ERMENGARDE *(seated on stool):* Did Miss Minchin ever let you go there to tea?

SARA *(shakes head):* No, she said visits were not suited to my station.

ERMENGARDE: Old — cat

SARA: But I watch them out of the garret window there. When I stand on the table under it, I can see all up and down the street. That's how I got to know the lascar and the monkey.

ERMENGARDE: What lascar and what monkey?

SARA: The lascar is the Indian gentleman's servant, and the monkey is the Indian gentleman's monkey.

ERMENGARDE: Where do they live?

SARA: They live next door. He is the rich gentleman who is always ill — *(Stops and listens)* Didn't you hear something at the window?

ERMENGARDE *(frightened):* Yes.

SARA *(gets up and goes to window):* There's nothing there. *(Laughs)* Perhaps Melchisedek and his wife are having a party under the roof. The lascar lives in the next garret, and the monkey lives with him — one day the monkey ran away and came in through my window, and the lascar had to come after him.

ERMENGARDE: What, that black Indian man in the white turban, Sara? Did he really come in here?

SARA: Yes, and he took the monkey back. I like him and he likes me. I remember enough Hindustani to talk to him a little, — so now he salaams to me when he sees me. Like this *(Salaams, stops, and listens again)* I'm sure there's something at the window; it sounds like a cat trying to get in. *(Goes to window. ERMENGARDE stumbles. Turns from window, pleased)* Suppose it was the monkey who had got away again. Oh, suppose it was *(Tiptoes to window, lifts it and looks out)* It is the monkey.

ERMENGARDE *(crossing to end of table)*: He lost his way and saw the light. Are you going to let him in, Sara?

SARA *(on table)*: Yes, it's too cold for monkeys to be out — they are delicate. I'll coax him in. He's quite close; how he shivers. He's so cold — he's quite *tame. (Coaxingly)* Come along, monkey darling, I won't hurt you. *(Takes monkey through window — jumps down.)*

ERMENGARDE *(Sara crosses to end of table, and sits. ERMENGARDE back of table)*: Oh, Sara, how funny he is — aren't you afraid he'll bite you?

SARA: Oh, no — nice monkey, nice monkey. Oh, I do *love* little animal things. Oh, you queer little darling.

ERMENGARDE *(sits to right of table.)*: He looks like a very ugly baby.

SARA: I'm glad he's not a baby. His mother couldn't be proud of him — and no one would *dare* to say he was like any of his relations. I do like you — perhaps he's sorry he's so ugly and it's always on his mind. I wonder if he has a mind?

ERMENGARDE: What are you going to do with him?

SARA: I must take him back to the Indian gentleman. But I am sorry. Oh, the company *you would* be to a person in a garret!

ERMENGARDE: Shall we take him back to-night?

SARA: It is too late to-night. I must keep you here, monkey my love, but I'll be kind to you.

ERMENGARDE: Where will he sleep?

SARA *(looks around).* Oh, I know — that cupboard —— *(Gets up, crosses to cupboard, and opens door)* See, I can make a bed for him here. I'll give him one of my pillows to lie on, and cover him with my blanket. *(Crosses to bed)*

ERMENGARDE: But you'll be so cold.

SARA: But I'm used to being cold and he isn't. I wasn't born in a tropical forest. Let's make his bed now and see if he likes it. *(Takes pillow from bed)* You bring the blanket. *(ERMENGARDE takes blanket.)* Yes, monkey, pet lamb, you shall have nice bye-lows and go rock-a-bye baby.

ERMENGARDE: What?

SARA: I mean rock-a-bye monkey *(Makes bed in closet)* And Sara will take you back home to your family. *(Noise outside, of BECKY coming upstairs.)*

ERMENGARDE *(frightened):* What's that?

SARA: It's only Becky coming up to bed.

MISS MINCHIN *(outside door):* Rebecca, Rebecca!

SARA: What, — Miss Minchin, — she might come up. *(ERMENGARDE looking wildly about the room, suddenly tucks nightgown around her and rolls under bed. SARA hurriedly shuts monkey up in cupboard.)*

MISS MINCHIN *(outside):* Remember, Rebecca, you get up at five in the morning.

BECKY*(outside):* Yes, mum, thank 'e, mum *(MISS MINCHIN heard outside, descending steps. SARA to bed and lifts cover so ERMENGARDE can get out from under it.)*

SARA: Come out, — it's all right. She's gone to bed herself.

ERMENGARDE *(sees she's gone — crawling out):* What if she caught us?
(Three knocks heard from BECKY)

SARA *(disappointedly):* Oh, that means — "the cook would not give me the cold potatoes."

ERMENGARDE: Cold potatoes — were they to feed the rats with?

SARA: They were to feed me with. *(Little laugh.*
ERMENGARDE amazed) You know how nice cold potatoes are — if you pretend they are something quite different — and put salt on — that is — if you are hungry.

ERMENGARDE *(aghast):* Sara — Sara — are you ever hungry enough for cold potatoes?

SARA: Yes, I am. I am so hungry now that I could eat — I could eat Miss Minchin if she were different — but she'd have to be very different.

ERMENGARDE: She wouldn't be different enough if you'd put pepper on her as well as salt — Sara — *(suddenly)* I've just thought of something splendid. *(Inspirited)* I've just thought of something splendid!

SARA: What is it?

ERMENGARDE *(excited hurry):* This very afternoon, I had a box full of good things sent me. My aunt sent it. I haven't touched it. It's got cakes in it — and little meat pies and jam tarts and buns and red currant wine, and figs and raisins and chocolates. I'll creep back to my room and get it this minute. And we'll eat it now.

SARA *(clutches ERMENGARDE's arm):* Oh, it makes me faint to hear it. You are good, Ermy. *(Hug)* Do you think you *could?*

ERMENGARDE: I know I could.

SARA: Don't make a noise.

ERMENGARDE *(runs to door, peeps out, then back to SARA):* The lights are out. Miss Minchin turned out the gas when she went down. I can creep and creep, and no one will hear me. *(Dance)*

SARA: Ermy, let's pretend — let's pretend it's a party — and oh, *won't* you invite the prisoner in the next cell?

ERMENGARDE *(delighted):* Yes, yes, let's knock on the wall now, — the jailer won't hear.

SARA *(goes to wall and knocks once):* That means "Prisoner, the jailer has made his last rounds and we can talk." *(They both listen until two knocks are heard in response)* That means "Are you sure it is safe?" *(Knocks three times herself)* That means "Quite sure, I heard the iron gates clang and the key turn in the lock." *(BECKY knocks four times.)* That means "Is it safe for me to come to you through the secret passage we have dug under the wall?" *(Knocks smartly one knock — and then two — separated by pause)* That means — "Quite safe — come." *(Knock at door is heard)* Here she comes. *(Opens door. BECKY enters. She starts at sight of ERMENGARDE.)* Don't be frightened, Becky. *(Catching BECKY, who tries to run off)* Miss Ermengarde is our friend; she asked you to come in here, because she's going to bring a box of good things up here.

BECKY: To eat, Miss *(Bursting in)* Things that's good to eat?

SARA: Yes, and we're going to pretend a party.

ERMENGARDE: And you shall have all you want to eat
(All dance and exclaim. BECKY stops them by)

BECKY: Sh —
(Points down)

ERMENGARDE: Oh, that old cat, Miss Minchin — but there's Magus and Brazil nuts and lots of good things

BECKY: Ow 'ev'nly.
(ERMENGARDE drops shawl.)

SARA: Ermy, you go for the box and we will set the table.

91

(Puts ERMENGARDE out of the door.)

BECKY: Oh, Miss — oh, Miss, I know it's you that asked her to let me come. It makes me cry to think of it.

SARA *(cheerfully, embracing her):* No, no, you mustn't cry. We must make haste and set the table. What can we put on it? *(Sees red shawl)* Here's her shawl — I know she won't mind. It will make such a nice red table-cloth. *(Picks it up and spreads it on table with BECKY's help)* What next? Oh! *(Clasps hands delightedly)* I know, I'll look for something in my old trunk, that I used to have when I was a princess. *(Runs to trunk, opens it and rummages in it. Stops and sees BECKY)* Becky, do you know what a banquet is?

BECKY: No, Miss, is it something to be 'et, or something to be wore?

SARA *(sitting by trunk):* It's a magnificent feast. Kings have them, and Queens, and Lord Mayors. We are going to have one. Now begin to pretend just as hard as ever you can — and straighten the richly embroidered table-cloth.
(Sara turns to trunk again, as BECKY straightens tablecloth. BECKY then stands, squeezing her eyes tight shut, clenching her hands and holding her breath. SARA takes package of handkerchiefs from trunk, rises to go to table, sees BECKY and laughs.)

SARA: What are you doing, BECKY?

BECKY *(opening her eyes and catching her breath):* I was pretending, Miss. It takes a good bit of strength.

SARA: Yes, it does — just at first. But it doesn't take so much when you get used to it. I'm used to it. Now what do you suppose these are?

BECKY *(delighted):* They looks like 'ankerchiefs, Miss, but I know they ain't

SARA: No, they are not. They are plates and napkins. Gold and silver plates and richly embroidered napkins — to match the tablecloth. These are the plates and these are the napkins.

(Giving each bundle to BECKY separately)

You must not take the napkins for the plates, or the plates for the napkins, Becky.

BECKY: Lor', no, Miss. They ain't nothin' like each other.

SARA: No, they're not. If you pretend hard enough. *(Steps back)* Don't they look nice?

BECKY: Jest lovely, Miss. Particular them gold and silver plates.

SARA: Yes, but the embroidery on the napkins is beautiful; nuns did it in a convent in Spain. *(Suddenly)* Oh, Becky, I forgot to tell you. This isn't the Bastille now.

BECKY *(eagerly):* Ain't it, Miss? Lor' now, what has it turned into?

SARA *(grandly):* It's a marble hall.

BECKY: A marble hall? I say

SARA: Yes, it's a marble hall in a palace — it's a banquet hall.

BECKY *(looking around room, opening eyes wide):* A banket hall!

SARA: No, — a banquet hall — that window opens into the vast conservatory where the tropical plants grow — *(Suddenly)* Oh, that reminds me of flowers. We ought to have some flowers.

BECKY: Oh, yes, Miss, we ought to have some flowers.

SARA: Where can we get flowers from? Oh, the trunk again *(Runs to trunk, tumbles out the contents; drags out old summer hat with flowers on it)* Here they are *(Tears flowers off hat)* What shall we put them in? *(Looks about and sees wash-stand)* Becky, there's something that looks like a toothbrush mug — but it isn't. It's a crystal flagon — bring it here.
(BECKY brings it — SARA arranges flowers in it.)

BECKY: There you are, Miss, a Christmas Dragon. There's something else there, Miss, that looks like a soap dish — but it ain't. Shall I get it?

SARA *(nods "Yes".):* Yes.
(BECKY brings it.)

SARA *(takes it from BECKY):* It's a gold epergne encrusted with gems. *(Wreathes flowers about it)* Oh, Becky, Becky. *(They both gaze with delight. BECKY clutches her lips with one hand and lifts them up and down)* Now if we had something for bonbon dishes — there, I remember — I saw something this minute. The darling old trunk. *(Crosses to it)* It's like a fairy. *(Takes out bundle of wool, wrapped in scarlet and white tissue paper. Goes back of table, tears off paper and twists into shapes of little dishes)*

BECKY: Ah, Miss Sara, this 'ere Blanket Hall — I mean Banket 'all, and all them golden gems — ain't them beautiful? *(SARA puts candle on table from mantel shelf. Enter ERMENGARDE with hamper of goodies. She starts back with exclamations of joy.)*

ERMENGARDE: Oh, Sara, you are the cleverest girl I ever saw

SARA: Isn't it nice? They are things out of my old trunk.

ERMENGARDE: And here's the hamper *(Sets it on chair)* You take the things out, Sara. You'll make them look nice.

BECKY: Yes, Miss, you take them out — I don't dast trust myself.

SARA: Thank you *(Looks in box)* What a lovely cake. *(Takes out same and puts it on table)* And mince pie — a chicken patty — and grapes — and oranges — and plum buns with sugar on — and crystallized fruit in an angel box and chocolate caramels.

BECKY: Chocolate camels
(Arranging the goodies, etc., until table is quite decorated.)

SARA: There.

ERMENGARDE: It's like a real party.

BECKY: It's like a Queen's table.

ERMENGARDE *(sudden thought):* Sara, do you ever pretend you are a princess now?
(BECKY puts basket on bed, and chairs at table.)

SARA: Oh, yes, I have to pretend it all the time. It helps me to be polite to people when they are rude to me. I'm a princess in rags and tatters, but I'm a princess inside.

ERMENGARDE *(suddenly):* I'll tell you what, Sara. Pretend you are a princess now, and that you are giving a banquet.

SARA: But it is your banquet — you must be the Princess, Ermy. We'll be your maids of honour.

ERMENGARDE: Oh, I can't — I'm too stupid — and I don't know how — *you* be her.

BECKY: Yes, Miss — go on, you be her.

SARA: Well, if you want me to —— *(Pause, — then suddenly)* But I've thought of something else *(Goes to fireplace)* Yes, there is a lot of paper and rubbish left in here. If we light it, it will blaze up for a few minutes, and we can pretend it's a real fire. If we only had more paper.

ERMENGARDE *(with sudden inspiration, running to books):* I know — books.

SARA: No, no, don't tear the books, Ermy.

ERMENGARDE *(pause, then quickly):* The curl papers then. *(Runs to SARA kneels before fire. Sara pulls papers off Ermy's head)* Oh, oh, they hurt.

SARA: By the time it stops blazing we shall forget it's not being real. *(Strikes light on box, starts fire. The three girls before it)* Doesn't it look real? Now we will begin the party *(From behind table)* Oh, girls — this — *(paper off a cake)* shall be my crown, and this my sceptre. *(Making spill of paper)* Advance, fair damsels, and be seated at the banquet table *(SARA sings)* Tra-la-la — tra-la-la *(Beats time with paper)* Take each other's hand and advance *(BECKY not knowing how)* No, no; Ermy, show Becky how, you know — show Becky. *(Sings again)* Tra-la-la —— *(BECKY and*

ERMENGARDE join hands and dance to music. BECKY falls over books. Finally at end of strain both are in chairs, — all sit together) My noble father, the King, who is absent on a long journey, has commanded me to feast you. *(Addressing air)* What ho, there *(Looking into mid-air, ERMY and BECKY look puzzled, not understanding)* Minstrels, strike up with your viols and your bassoons. *(ERMENGARDE and BECKY look puzzled. SARA explains to them, resuming her natural manner)* Princes always have minstrels at the feast. Pretend there's a minstrel gallery up there. *(Points up toward audience)* What ho there — strike
(ERMENGARDE and BECKY stare at her in rapture, then jump to feet. Imitate trombone, humming "Johnny, get your hair cut." At end of song they sit.) Now we will begin.

> Close your eyes tight now and fancy
> How Grandmother looked when a girl,
> With soft dimpled cheek and manners so sweet,
> With her powder, patches and curl.
> Suppose I pretend I am like her
> With her quaint, dainty ways, at a ball, —
> See the dance she is in — 'tis about to begin;
> Can you fancy scene, costumes and all?
> Suppose you were all at this old-fashioned ball,
> Suppose, suppose, suppose
> Here's what you would see if you could be
> Her guest at a dance of '73.
> Suppose in a far-off country,
> In the days of long ago,
> You've entered the gate at the time of a fete
> In a garden of Tokyo.
> Can you see the Japanese maidens
> With their dainty figures so small,
> See the dance they are in — it's about to begin.
> Can you fancy scene, flowers and all?
> Suppose you are hid in Snowflower's chair,
> Suppose, suppose, suppose,
> See their black heads bow low as they dance to
> and fro?

These quaint little geishas of Tokyo?
Suppose in the fairies' country,
Where the moss makes a carpet green
Out under the trees with their rustling leaves
At the Court of the Elfin Queen,
You could hide yourself in a tree-top
And peep into Hazel Brush Hall,
See the dance they are in — 'tis about to begin.
See the Brownies, moonbeams and all?
Suppose you are there, unseen to the stare,
Suppose, suppose, suppose,
Here's what you would see if you could be
A visiting sprite in the top of a tree.

(Door is thrown violently open. Enter MISS MINCHIN. ERMY dives under table. BECKY cowers with cake in hand; afterwards puts cake back on table. SARA stands behind table with crown on.)

MISS MINCHIN: What does this mean?

ERMENGARDE *(under table):* It's a party.

MISS MINCHIN *(to BECKY):* You audacious creature. You leave the house in the morning.

BECKY: Yes, mum.

ERMENGARDE: Don't send her away, please. My aunt sent me a box full of good things

BECKY: Yes, mum — an' we're only just 'avin' a party.

MISS MINCHIN *(witheringly):* So I see, with the Princess Sara at the head of the table. *(Turns on SARA)* This is your doing, I know — Ermengarde would have never thought of such a thing. You decorated the table, I suppose, with this rubbish. *(To BECKY)* Go back to your garret. *(BECKY crosses, steals off, face in apron.)*

MISS MINCHIN *(to ERMENGARDE):* Ermengarde, put those things in the hamper. *(To SARA)* As for you, I will attend to you to-morrow. You shall have neither breakfast, dinner nor supper!

SARA: I've neither dinner nor supper to-day, Miss Minchin.

MISS MINCHIN: Then all the better. You will have something to remember. Don't look at me like that. *(Sara has not taken her eyes from MISS MINCHIN. To ERMENGARDE, after seeing her books on floor — SARA front of table)* Ermengarde, you have brought your beautiful new books into this dirty garret; pick them up and go back to bed. You will stay there all to-morrow, and I shall write to your papa. What would he say, if he knew where you are tonight?

ERMENGARDE: I don't know, Miss Minchin.

MISS MINCHIN: Take that hamper.

ERMENGARDE: Yes, Miss Minchin. *(Does so. Exits, turning at door)* Cat *(Noise heard of her falling down stairs.)*

MISS MINCHIN *(turning on SARA fiercely):* What are you thinking of — why do you stare at me in that fashion?

SARA *(quietly):* I was wondering.

MISS MINCHIN: What?

SARA *(not pertly but sadly and quietly):* I was wondering what *my* papa would say if he knew where I am tonight.

MISS MINCHIN *(threateningly):* You insolent minx, how dare you! I will leave you to wonder. Go to bed at once. *(Exits)*

SARA *(left alone, takes up EMILY, sits on ottoman):* There isn't any party left, Emily — there isn't any princess — there's nothing left but the prisoner in the Bastille. *(Head down and cries softly)* I won't cry. *(To table with EMILY)* I'll go to bed and sleep. I can't pretend any more to-night. *(Blows out candle)* I wish I could. *(Going to bed)* I'll go to sleep and perhaps a dream will come to pretend for me — *(Takes off shoes — in bed)* I'll suppose a little to make it easier. Suppose there was a bright fire in that grate — with lots of little dancing flames — suppose there was a soft rug on the floor and that was a comfortable chair — and suppose the attic was furnished in lovely colours. *(Voice becomes dreamy)* And suppose there was a little table by the fire with a little

hot supper on it — and suppose this was a beautiful soft
bed with white sheets and fleecy blankets and large downy
pillows — suppose — sup-p-ose — sup-po-se *(Falls asleep)*

*(RAM DASS appears at window with three lascars. He
carries one dark lantern. Surveys the room, sees Sara asleep,
raises window, enters with others, and without noise makes
the trick change, bringing everything through window. First,
three men help RAM DASS to clear away the old furniture.
After furniture is cleared, Indian stuff is brought on and
placed. At end of change three lamps are brought on. RAM
DASS lays fire in grate and, before lighting same, stands
with lighted taper in front of grate which is signal for other
lascars to light their lamps. Discovered, three lascars
standing by their respective lamps with folded arms. RAM
DASS then takes books from tray on table, puts them on
cushions, and exits through window.)*

*(SARA wakes slowly, sees the wonderful change and is
bewildered.)*

SARA: What a nice dream. I feel quite warm. *(Stretches out
arms, feels blanket dreamily)* I don't want to wake up —
(Trying to sleep) Oh, I am awakening. *(Opens eyes, sees
everything — thinks she is dreaming)* I have not wakened.
I'm dreaming yet. *(Looks around smiling, bewildered but
waking)* It does not melt away, — it stays. I never had such
a dream before. *(Pushes bedclothes aside, puts feet on floor,
smiling)* I am dreaming, I'm getting out of bed. *(Closes eyes
as she gets out, as if to prolong dream; then opens eyes)* I'm
dreaming, it stays real — I'm dreaming, it feels real. *(Moves
forward, staring about her)* It's bewitched, or I'm bewitched.
(Words hurrying themselves) I only think I see it all. But
if I can only keep on thinking it, I don't care, I don't care.
(Sudden outburst of emotion. Sees fire and runs to it) A fire,
a little supper. *(Kneels at fire — hands before it)* A fire I only
dreamed wouldn't be hot. *(Jumping up, sees dressing-gown*

and slippers) A dressing-gown! *(Holding it to face, then putting it on)* It is real — it is, it must be. It's warm, it's soft. *(Puts feet in slippers, cries out)* Slippers — they are real too. They are real, it's all real. I am not — I am not dreaming. *(Sees books on cushions. Runs to them)* Books, books *(Opens one, turns over leaves rapidly)* Some one has written something. Oh, what is it? *(Runs to lamp. Reads aloud)* "To the little girl in the garret from a friend." *(Clasping book to her breast, grabs up EMILY and hugs her)* Oh Emily, oh papa —— *(Kneels)* Papa, I have a friend, I have a friend!

CURTAIN

ACT III

SCENE. *Mr. Carrisford's study in house next door to Miss Minchin's Seminary for Young Ladies. Room handsomely furnished. Window looks out on winter street. Chairs, bric-a-brac cabinet, curtains, with soft cushions on window seat, lady's writing-desk, fireplace and fire-dogs. A table with books on it, and a big armchair nearby. Oriental rugs on floor with a tiger's head rug for Donald. Large sofa beside baby grand piano. Noah's ark with animals in it.*

At the rise of curtain: Door opens. Enter RAM DASS, followed by DONALD, MAZIE, NORA, and JANET CARMICHAEL. RAM DASS stands up stage. DONALD with a whoop sits on tiger's head. MAZIE and NORA to piano, to play with toys in ark.

JANET: Please tell Mr. Carrisford we can wait as long as he likes. We'll go away if he doesn't want us. We're only come to cheer him up a little.

RAM DASS: The Sahib will be glad. I go.
(Exits)

DONALD: I'll sit here on the tiger's head. Gee up — gee up — gee up! I'm on the tiger's head.

100

JANET: Now, Donald, you must *remember.* Mr. Carrisford has been very ill, and when you come to cheer up a person who is ill you don't cheer him up at the top of your voice.

DONALD *(riding tiger's head):* Well, I can cheer him up better when I'm sitting on the tiger's head than I can on a chair. Gee up
(Falls off)

JANET: You can sit there, if you'll be quiet. *(Crosses and sits in chair)* Mr. Carrisford is very anxious to-day. He is waiting for papa to come back from Paris. Mamma said we might help pass the time for him — because he likes us when we're quiet. *(At piano with animals)* I'm going to be quiet.

MAZIE *(with her):* So am I.

DONALD *(riding tiger boisterously):* We'll all be as quiet as mice.

JANET *(to him):* Mice don't make a noise like that.

DONALD: A whole lot of mice might. A thousand mice might.

JANET *(severely):* I don't believe fifty thousand mice might. And we have to be as quiet as one mouse, I'm the oldest and I'm responsible.
(MAZIE gets down from the piano, and pushes DONALD off tiger's head on the floor. He retaliates by pushing her off on the floor.)

MAZIE: Oh, Donald, you are rough!

DONALD: You pushed me off, I pushed you off.
(Sits on tiger again)

JANET *(arranges pillows.):* Now, that will be ready for him when Ram Dass brings him in, poor thing. *(Leans head on hands on table)* Oh dear, I wish papa would come. I do hope he will say he has found the lost little girl.

DONALD: Yes.

NORA: Perhaps he will bring her back from Paris.

DONALD: I wish he would. She could tell us about when her

papa shot this tiger in India. Mr. Carrisford said Captain Crewe shot it.

MAZIE: I want her to be found because I want to play with her

NORA: I want her to be found because I'm sorry for her.

JANET: I'm sorry for her. Perhaps she's a poor little beggar in the streets. She has no father and no mother, and Mr. Carrisford does not know where she is. He only thinks she was sent to a boarding-school in Paris.
(DONALD throws animals into ark.)

CHILDREN: Oh, ah, Donald!

NORA: Papa has been to ever so many schools to look for her.

MAZIE: But he could never find her.

JANET: But he went to Paris on Thursday because he heard of a school where there was a little girl whose papa died in India. If he doesn't find her this time, he says he shall not know what to do.
(DONALD bangs the piano.)

JANET AND MAZIE: Oh, Donald, Donald!

NORA: Oh, I wish it was time for him to come. *(To window)* Perhaps she is cold and miserable somewhere. And all the while, Mr. Carrisford wants her so much.

MAZIE *(tearfully):* Perhaps she's out in the wet in bare feet and torn frock. It makes me want to cry.

DONALD *(taking stage manfully):* I say, if papa doesn't bring her back from Paris, let's all go and look for her, — every one of us. Let's go to the park and stand at the gate, and every time we see a little girl let's ask her what her name is.

JANET *(desperately):* We can't let her stay lost and be poor always when she ought to be so rich and live in such a beautiful house. I can't bear it.
(Door opens. Enter CARRISFORD and RAM DASS. They cross to armchair.)

CHILDREN *(when they see him):* Oh, Mr. Carrisford, there you are! Oh, how do you do.

(Running to him and leading him down)

CARRISFORD: How do you do, my dears; it's very good of you to come and see me.

CHILDREN: Oh, no!

NORA: We like to come.

JANET *(who has fixed pillows for CARRISFORD):* Mamma said we might come and see you on our way from the party.

MAZIE: We wanted to show you our party frocks.

DONALD: We're not going to make a noise.
   (Blows whistle)

CARRISFORD: Oh, dear me, let me see — how smart you all are. Let me look at you.
   (DONALD struts, showing coat and pants.)

DONALD: Would you like to see the back?
   (Showing it)

NORA: Mamma lent me her locket.

MAZIE *(showing frock):* Mine is quite a new frock.

DONALD: I have four pockets. *(Showing them)* One, two three *(Loses fourth; suddenly finds it)* Ah, four.

CARRISFORD: I have only two.

DONALD: Oh, ho, he has only two!

JANET: Do you think you are any better, Mr. Carrisford?

CARRISFORD: I'm afraid not, Janet. I'm anxious and it isn't good for me. I shall be better if your papa brings me good news. Ram Dass, you may go.
   (Exit RAM DASS)

NORA: He won't be long now. When he comes from Paris, he always comes in the afternoon.

DONALD: I say, I'll go to the window and watch for the cab. Mazie, you come and watch too.

JANET: Mr. Carrisford, do you think he will come back and say he found the lost little girl?

CARRISFORD: I hope so, Janet, I hope so. I shall be very unhappy if he does not.

NORA: Do you think that perhaps she is so poor that she is begging in the streets this very minute — while we are waiting for her to be found?

CARRISFORD *(startled and miserable):* I hope not — I hope not — Heaven knows what she may be doing. That is what makes me so miserable.

DONALD *(shouts from window):* Here's a cab, here's a cab

ALL: Oh

DONALD: I believe it's going to stop here. *(CARRISFORD rises, partly turns up stage. NORA and JANET rise)* Oh, no, it isn't and there's only a fat old lady in it with a blue bonnet on. *(CARRISFORD sinks back into chair.)*

JANET: Oh, Donald, you must be careful.

DONALD: I was careful. It was a cab. The cabman looked at this house when the umbrella was poked out.

CARRISFORD *(pats JANET's hand.):* You are a nice little girl, Janet. Thank you.

JANET *(kneels beside him.):* I wish I could cheer you up until papa does come — but when anyone feels ill perhaps cheering up is too loud.

CARRISFORD: Oh, no, no

JANET: May we talk about the little girl?

CARRISFORD: I don't think I can talk about anything else just now.

NORA: We like her very much. We call her the little lost Princess.

CARRISFORD: Do you, — why?

JANET: Because she will be so rich when she is found that she will be quite like a little princess. Is it true that her papa gave all of his money to one of his friends to spend in a mine that had diamonds in it — and then his friend thought he had lost all and ran away because he felt as if he was a robber?

NORA: But he wasn't really, you know!

CARRISFORD: No, he wasn't really. The mine turned out well after all. But it was too late. Captain Crewe was dead. If he had lived he and his little girl would have been very rich indeed

JANET: I'm sorry for the friend.

CARRISFORD: Are you?

JANET: I can't help it.

CARRISFORD: I am sorry for him too. *I* am the friend, Janet.

JANET: Oh, de-ar *Poor* Mr. Carrisford.

NORA: Oh, papa must find her!

JANET: Yes, he must find her!

DONALD (*from window, dancing up and down in seat \with MAZIE*) Here he is. Here he is.

ALL: Oh, ah

CARRISFORD (*trying to rise*): I wish I could get up, but it's no use, I cannot, I cannot
(*NORA and JANET to window*)

JANET (*coming down*): But there isn't any little girl.
(*Enter RAM DASS*)

RAM DASS: Sahib, Mr. Carmichael is at the door.

ALL: May we go?

CARRISFORD: Yes, yes, go, go
(*CHILDREN exeunt running, followed by RAM DASS.*)

CARMICHAEL (*outside*): No, no, children. Not now —

CHILDREN: Daddy, daddy

CHARMICHAEL: Not now, — you can come in after I have talked with Mr. Carrisford. Go away and play with Ram Dass.

CHILDREN: All right!
(Enter Carmichael.)

CARRISFORD *(shaking hands):* I am glad to see you — very glad. Pray sit down. What news do you bring?

CHARMICHAEL *(sits.):* No good news, I am sorry to say. I went to the school in Paris and saw the little girl. But she is not the child you are searching for.

CARRISFORD: Then the search must begin all over again.

CARMICHAEL: I'm afraid so.

CARRISFORD: Have you any new suggestions to make?

CARMICHAEL: Well, perhaps. Are you quite sure the child was put in school in Paris?

CARRISFORD: My dear fellow, I am sure of *nothing.*

CARMICHAEL: But you thought the school was in Paris?

CARRISFORD: Because her mother was a French woman, and had wished that the child should be educated in Paris. It seemed only likely that she should be there.

CHARMICHAEL: I assure you I have searched the schools in Paris thoroughly. The journey I have just returned from was really my last hope.

CARRISFORD: Carmichael, I must find her, — I shall never get well until I do find her and give her the fortune the mine has made. It is hers, and she, poor child, may he begging in the streets. Poor Crewe put into the scheme every penny he owned, and he died thinking I had ruined him.

CARMICHAEL: You were not yourself at the time. You were stricken with brain fever two days after you left the place — remember that.

106

CARRISFORD: Yes, and when I returned to consciousness, poor Crewe was dead.

CARMICHAEL: You did not remember the child; you did not speak of her for months.

CARRISFORD: No, I had forgotten, and now I shall never remember.

CARMICHAEL: Come, come. We shall find her yet.
(Rises.)

CARRISFORD: We will find her if we search every city in Europe. Help me to find her.
(Shake hands)

CARMICHAEL: We *will* find her. As you say — if she is alive she is *somewhere*. We have searched the schools in Paris. Let us try London.

CARRISFORD: There are schools enough in London. By the way, there is one next door.

CARMICHAEL: Then we will begin there. We cannot begin nearer than next door.

CARRISFORD: There's a child there who interests me. But she is not a pupil. *(Enter RAM DASS)* She is a little forlorn creature as unlike poor Crewe as a child could be. Well, Ram Dass?

RAM DASS: Sahib, the child, she herself has come — the child the Sahib felt pity for. She brings back the monkey who had again run away to her garret. I have asked that she remain. It was my thought that it would please the Sahib to see and speak with her.

CARMICHAEL: Who is she?

CARRISFORD: God knows. She is the child I spoke of.
(To RAM DASS)
Yes, yes, I should like to see her.
(CHILDREN enter, except DONALD, crying and dancing with joy.)

JANET: Mr. Carrisford, Mr. Carrisford, papa, papa, the little girl, she's the little girl we saw at the school

CARMICHAEL and CARRISFORD: At the school?

NORA: She was quite a rich little girl in a beautiful frock.

MAZIE: And now she's poor and thin and ragged — at least almost ragged.
(Enter MRS. CARMICHAEL)

MRS. CARMICHAEL: My dears, my dears, what are you talking about — all at once?

JANET: It's the little girl who made up names about us — and now she's quite poor and shabby.

MAZIE: She brought the monkey back.

DONALD *(runs on — joining clamour):* I say, I say, she won't come in, she won't come in, — I want her to come in! She talked Indian to Ram Dass, but she won't come in.
(During this he jumps behind MR. CARRISFORD, pulls his bath robe — is taken away by his father.)

CARRISFORD *(to RAM DASS):* She spoke Hindustani?

RAM DASS: Yes, Sahib, a few words.

CARRISFORD: Ask her to come here. *(Exit RAM DASS)*

CARMICHAEL *(to CARRISFORD):* You must compose yourself. Remember your weakness. The fact that the child knows a little Hindustani may mean nothing. Don't prepare yourself for another disappointment.

CARRISFORD: No, no.

CARMICHAEL *(to DONALD):* Here, you young rascal.
(Spanking. Enter SARA with monkey in arm)

MRS. CARMICHAEL: I believe it is the same child, but I should not have known her.

SARA: Your monkey got away again. He came to my garret window and I took him in last night. I would have brought him back if it had not been so late. I knew you were ill and might not like to be disturbed.

CARRISFORD: That was very thoughtful of you.

SARA: Shall I give him to the lascar?

CARRISFORD: How do you know he is a lascar?

SARA: Oh, I know lascars. I was born in India.

CARRISFORD *(excited):* Were you? *(Holds out his hand)* Come here. *(To RAM DASS)* Ram Dass, take the monkey away. *(Exit RAM DASS with monkey. To SARA)* Come, you live next door, do you not?

SARA: Yes, sir, I live at Miss Minchin's.

CARRISFORD: She keeps a boarding-school. But you are not a pupil, are you?

SARA: I don't know what I am.

CARRISFORD: Why not?

SARA: At first I was a pupil and a parlour-boarder, but now

CARRISFORD: What now?

SARA: I sleep in the garret next to the scullery-maid. I run errands for the cook and I teach the little ones their lessons.

MRS. CARMICHAEL *(to MR. CARMICHAEL):* Poor little thing.

CARRISFORD *(gestures to CARMICHAEL as if agitation was too much for him):* Question her, Carmichael, – I cannot.

CARMICHAEL: What do you mean by "at first," my child?

SARA *(turning to him):* When I was first taken there by papa

CARMICHAEL: Where is your father?

SARA: My papa died. He lost all his money, and there was none left for me, and so

CARRISFORD: Carmichael!

CARMICHAEL *(pantomime with wife):* And so — you were sent up into the garret and made a little drudge? That's about it, isn't it?

SARA: There was no one to take care of me. I belong to nobody.

CARRISFORD (breaking in): How — how — did your father lose his money?

SARA: He didn't lose it himself. He had a friend he was very fond of — he was very fond of him — it was his friend who took his money. I don't know how. (To CARMICHAEL) I don't understand. (To CARRISFORD) He trusted his friend too much.

CARRISFORD (agitated): But the friend might not have meant to do harm. It might have happened through a mistake.

SARA: But the *suffering* was just as bad for my papa. It killed him.

CARRISFORD (faints): Carmichael!
(Confusion. CARMICHAEL goes to CARRISFORD. SARA stands before them, bewildered; she picks up shawl and starts to go.)

SARA: I think I had better go.

CARRISFORD (recovering): Stay. What was your father's name?

SARA: His name was Ralph Crewe.

CARRISFORD: Oh

SARA: Captain Crewe — perhaps you knew him. He died in India

CARRISFORD: Yes, yes, yes — Carmichael, it is the child!

SARA (looking from CARRISFORD to CARMICHAEL, trembling): What does he mean? What child am I?

CARRISFORD: I was your father's friend — he loved me — he trusted me — if he had lived he would have known — but now (Sinks back)

MRS. CARMICHAEL (to SARA): My dear little girl. My poor little girl! (CHILDREN start to go to SARA; JANET stops them.)

110

SARA: Did he know my papa? Was *he* the wicked friend? Oh, do tell me!

MRS. CARMICHAEL: He was not wicked, my dear; he did not really lose your papa's money — he only thought he had lost it — he was ill — and when he got well — your poor papa was dead, and he didn't know where to find you.

SARA: And I was at Miss Minchin's all the time.

MRS. CARMICHAEL: Yes, he saw you pass by, and he was *sorry* for you, and he told Ram Dass to climb through your attic window and try to make you comfortable.

SARA *(joyfully):* Did Ram Dass bring the things, — did he tell Ram Dass to do it? Did he make the dream that came true?

MRS. CARMICHAEL: Yes —yes — my dear — he did. He is kind and good, and was sorry for you.

SARA *(going to CARRISFORD):* You sent the things to me — the beautiful things — the beautiful, beautiful things — you sent them?

CARRISFORD: Yes — poor dear child — I did.

SARA: Then it is you who are *my friend. (Kneels to CARRISFORD)*

SERVANT *(outside):* Pardon me, Madam, but Mr. Carrisford is not well enough to see visitors.

MISS MINCHIN *(partly off stage):* I am sorry *(enters door)* to disturb Mr. Carrisford, but I must see him at once. I have explanations to make. *(Meeting CHARMICHAEL)* I am Miss Minchin, the proprietress of *"The Young Ladies' Seminary"* next door.

CARMICHAEL: So you are Miss Minchin?

MISS MINCHIN: I am, sir.

CARMICHAEL: In that case you have arrived at the right time.

MISS MINCHIN: I have come to explain that an insolent charity pupil of mine has intruded here without my knowledge *(Sees SARA.)*

CARRISFORD *(to SARA):* There, there, it's all right.

MISS MINCHIN: You are here still — the forwardness of such conduct — *(indignantly)* go home at once — you shall be severely punished! Go home at once, at once!
(SARA rises and starts to go.)

JANET: Oh, please don't let her go.

ALL CHILDREN *(going to MR. CARRISFORD):* Oh, please don't let her go!

CARRISFORD: No, no — she is not going.

ALL CHILDREN: Ah! *(CHILDREN back to sofa)*

MISS MINCHIN: Not going?

CARRISFORD: No, Miss Minchin. She is not going *home* — if you give your house that name. Her home for the future will be with me.

MISS MINCHIN: With *you,* with *you,* — what does this mean?

CARRISFORD: That she is done with you, Madam, — with you and her misery and her garret.

MISS MINCHIN: I am dumbfounded. Such insults. *(To SARA)* This is your doing — come back to the school at once.
(Starts forward as though to take her)

CARMICHAEL *(coming down):* That will do, Miss Minchin.

MISS MINCHIN *(violently):* Not do? How dare you interfere! *(To CARRISFORD)* How dare *you?* She shall go back if I have to call in the police.

CARRISFORD: The lady is too violent for me, Carmichael, — please explain to her.

CARMICHAEL: I am Mr. Carrisford's lawyer, Madam. Mr. Carrisford was an intimate friend of the late Captain Crewe — the fortune which Captain Crewe supposed he had lost is in the hands of Mr. Carrisford.

MISS MINCHIN *(startled):* The fortune — Sara's fortune? *(Turns, and stares aghast at SARA)*

CARMICHAEL: It will be Sara's fortune — it is Sara's fortune now.

MISS MINCHIN (*to CARMICHAEL*): Captain Crewe left her in my charge. She must return to it until she is of age. The law will interfere in my behalf.

CARMICHAEL: No, the law will not, Miss Minchin. Captain Crewe constituted Mr. Carrisford her guardian long ago. If Sara herself wishes to return to you, I dare say he would not refuse her. But that rests with Sara.

MISS MINCHIN: Then I appeal to Sara. *(To SARA)* I have not spoiled you, perhaps, but I have always been very fond of you.

SARA: Have you, Miss Minchin? I did not know that.

MISS MINCHIN: Yes. Will you not do your duty to your poor papa and come home with me?

SARA *(steps forward)*: No, I will not. *You* know why I will not go home with you, Miss Minchin, you know.
(This spoken quietly, steadily, and politely, looking squarely at her.)

MISS MINCHIN *(spitefully)*: Then you will never see your little companions again, — Ermengarde and Lottie.

CARMICHAEL: Oh, yes, she will, she will see any one she wishes in her guardian's house.
(MISS MINCHIN goes wrathfully to CARMICHAEL.)

CARRISFORD: Ram Dass — show this lady out. *(MISS MINCHIN makes for CARRISFORD)* That is all, Miss Minchin — your bill will be paid.
(MISS MINCHIN looks around and, putting shawl over head, exits. DONALD whistles.)

CHILDREN *(delightedly)*: Good-bye.

(RAM DASS follows her off.)

SARA *(goes toward CARRISFORD drawing in breath; shuts eyes and then opens them wide with wondering expression,*

113

like waking from dream of night before): I — I — did not wake up from the other — last — night — that was real. I shall not wake up from *this,* shall I?

CARRISFORD: No, no, you shall never wake up again to anything that is not happiness.

SARA: But there was another little girl — she was as lonely and cold and hungry as I was — *could* you save her too?

CARRISFORD: Yes, indeed: Who was she?

SARA: Her name is Becky — she is the scullery-maid. She has no one but me, and she will miss me so. She was the prisoner in the next cell.

CARRISFORD: You shall take care of her — Carmichael — *(who turns)* will bring back to us the prisoner in the next cell.

CHILDREN *(rushing around her):* You're found — you're found, — we are so glad you're found! *(All joyfully)*

SARA: I didn't know I was lost, and now I'm found I can't quite believe it.

MRS. CARMICHAEL: What shall we do to make her feel that her troubles are over and that she may be happy as she used to be?

DONALD: I say, you said you would tell us a story. Tell us one now.

SARA: Shall I?

ALL: Yes, oh, yes, a story.

SARA: Just as I used to?

CHILDREN: Just as you used to.

SARA: Well, — once upon a time, long, long ago — there lived a little Princess

CURTAIN

THE
BIRTHDAY OF THE INFANTA

Based on a story by Oscar Wilde

by
Stuart Walker

Stuart Walker first produced *The Birthday of the Infanta* in Binghampton, NY, in November 1916 and subsequently in New York City the following month. By 1916 the number of professional children's theatre productions on the New York stage had diminished markedly, probably in part because of the diffusion of the commercial market by children's theatre in amateur and recreational settings. Previously, New York audiences had seen successful professional productions of numerous children's plays, including Burnett's *The Little Princess*, James M. Barrie's *Peter Pan*, Alice Gerstenberg's *Alice in Wonderland*, and Jessie Braham White's *Snow White and the Seven Dwarfs*.

Stuart Walker started his Portmanteau Theatre as an alternative to the frankly commercial Broadway theatre. He served as producer, director, and playwright for this group, working to realize the goal of bringing quality theatre to *family* audiences. His plays thus deviated markedly from the sentimental melodramas then prevalent on the New York stage. The Portmanteau Theatre traveled complete with its own portable proscenium, and presented its repertoire in theatres, community centers, and settlement houses.

The Birthday of the Infanta, the most noted of the plays of this relatively short-lived group, offers a glimpse of a kind of sophisticated theatre for young people that only gradually became more prevalent as the field developed throughout the century. The play, based on a short story by Oscar Wilde, presents multidimensional child characters, a serious story, and the death of a sympathetic character, all of which are revealed in a moving, non-melodramatic form.

In the description of the setting offered at the beginning of the play, Walker describes a "grim stone arch" framing a "brilliant sky." Therein he subtly embodies important aspects of the world of the play, a world of harsh contrasts. *The Birthday of the Infanta* is more a play of character than a play of action in that it does not offer a suspenseful plot structure or an explicit conflict between characters. Instead, the play presents characters in conflict with the persons they wish to be and the personas that their culture imposes on them.

At the opening of the play we see the Infanta, the young daughter of the King of Spain; she is a thirteen-year-old child who is forced to act as an adult. The Infanta struggles with the friction caused by her desire for freedom to experience her childhood in opposition to the strictures placed on her by her royal position. By the end of the play we see an unsettling resolution to this personal conflict in her simplistic and cynical perspective of life, when, upon hearing that the Fantastic has died of a broken heart, she scornfully declares: "For the future, let those who come to play with me have no hearts."

The Fantastic, the major focus of the play, mirrors in vivid detail the internal conflicts briefly sketched in the Infanta. His gnarled body creates a repulsive, and, to some people, laughable, image; yet these grotesque features stand in contrast to the gentle, naïve, and romantic personality of the child inside. The play focuses first on this duality, and second on his complete inability to reconcile the two. While the Infanta survives through adopting a precarious balance in the lack of feeling, the Fantastic cannot adjust to his internal struggle. The reality of his physical being, coupled with the knowledge of just why he is a source of laughter, completely overpowers his gentle soul.

The story of the play unfolds amid the context of death. During the course of the play we hear of the King who mourns his dead wife, we meet the Chamberlain who reminisces about his dead son, and we hear of the uncle who "wishes" the Infanta "were dead." Even the passing of the Infanta's childhood becomes complete in her final, bitter tirade against the Fantastic who dared to die. The sentimentality in the play diminishes with the dialogue and the Fantastic's gradual and moving death. That this death corresponds with the Fantastic's self-knowledge adds to the irony and pathos of the situation.

The importance of this work rests both in the play itself and the spirit with which it was presented. The play presents a serious subject that, although distanced in time and place from audiences of the day, unfolds in an honest and forthright manner. While the characters are romanticized, the play does not present a romantic view of the world. Unlike the happy-ever-after ending of *The Little Princess*, the Fantastic dies at the end of the play, and the Infanta is driven deeper into her unhappy world. This is harsh material, unaltered for family or child audiences.

Although *The Birthday of the Infanta* stands as a bit of an anomaly in the history of dramatic literature for children in this country, it did not die with the Portmanteau Theatre Company. While fairy tale adaptations have dominated the field throughout much of the last century, sporadic productions of this play stand as a testimony to a small but constant interest in serious plays for young audiences.

Other plays of note written by Walker and performed by the Portmanteau Theatre Company include *Six Who Pass While the Lentils Boil*, *Jonathan Makes a Wish*, and *Seventeen*.

Stuart Armstrong Walker (1880-1941) was born in Augusta, Kentucky, and educated at the University of Cincinnati (BS, 1903) and the American Academy of Dramatic Art. After working as an actor and stage manager for David Belasco, Walker established The Portmanteau Theatre Company in 1915. This group played primarily at two theatres in New York and then toured throughout the Midwestern United States.

Walker abandoned this project in 1917, and subsequently directed the Indianapolis Repertory Company (1917-1923) and the Cincinnati Repertory Company (1923-1931). Walker then embarked on a successful career as a film director and producer, for which he is best known as the director of *Great Expectations (1934)* for Universal Pictures.

THE
BIRTHDAY OF THE INFANTA

by
Stuart Walker

From the book Portmanteau Adaptations
by Stuart Walker

THE BIRTHDAY OF THE INFANTA

Characters

THE INFANTA OF SPAIN

THE DUCHESS OF ALBUQUERQUE

THE COUNT OF TIERRA-NUEVA

THE CHAMBERLAIN

THE FANTASTIC

A MOORISH PAGE

ANOTHER PAGE

Setting

THE SCENE IS THE ROYAL BALCONY

OVERLOOKING A GARDEN. THE TIME IS THE

SIXTEENTH CENTURY.

The opening of the curtains discloses a balcony overlooking a garden. The grim stone arch frames a brilliant sky. Gay flowers and a few white roses cover the railing. A bit of gaudy awning which can be lowered over the arch flutters in the breeze. At the right is a large mirror so draped that the dull, black hangings can be lowered to cover the mirror entirely. The hangings are of velvet, powdered with suns and stars. At the left similar hangings adorn a doorway. There are rich floor coverings and several formal chairs.

A Moorish attendant in black and yellow livery enters and arranges the chairs, and stands at attention.

The Infanta enters, followed by the Duchess of Albuquerque. The Infanta is dressed in gray brocade, very, very stiff and stately. She is small, with reddish hair and a settled air of self-possession and formality. Occasionally her eyes twinkle and her feet suggest her childishness; but she soon recovers herself under the watchful eye of the Camerera, and she never really forgets that she is the Infanta of Spain.

The Infanta bows, if the slight inclination of her head can be called bowing, to the Moorish attendant. The Duchess also inclines her head and stands in the doorway.

INFANTA: I would be alone.

DUCHESS: Your Highness —

INFANTA: I would be alone.
   (The DUCHESS turns in the doorway and speaks to those behind her.)

DUCHESS: Her highness would be alone. *(Then to the INFANTA)* This is unheard of.

INFANTA: My birthday is rare enough to be almost unheard of, your Grace of Albuquerque. I would be alone on my birthday — and I'm going to be alone! *(Then to the attendant)* You may go! ... But wait. *(She stands admiringly before the mirror)* Hold back the curtain. *(The attendant lifts the curtain. She preens herself.)* Why do I not look so well in my

121

own suite? See how wonderful this is here. Look at the gold in my hair.

DUCHESS: That is vanity, your Highness.

INFANTA: Can I not admire myself on my birthday? Have I so many birthdays that I must live them as I live every other day?

DUCHESS: What is wickedness on other days is also wickedness on your birthday.

INFANTA *(taking a white rose from the balustrade and trying it in her hair and at her waist):* See — see — I like it here. *(The DUCHESS, outraged, speaks to the attendant.)*

DUCHESS: You may go.

INFANTA: No, no — stay — draw the curtains across the mirror!

DUCHESS: What will your father: say? *(The INFANTA is quite beside her little self.)*

INFANTA: Draw the curtains across the mirror and hide me from myself as those curtains hide my dead mother's room!

DUCHESS: Please —

INFANTA: I have spoken, your Grace. The curtains are to be drawn. We shall have no mirror to-day. *(The attendant closes the curtain.)*

INFANTA: You may go! *(The attendant exits. The INFANTA goes to the balustrade and looks into the gardens below. The DUCHESS, quite at a loss of what to do, finally crosses to the Infanta.)*

DUCHESS: Your Highness, I am compelled to remonstrate with you. What will his Majesty, your father, say?

INFANTA: My father will say nothing. He does not seem to care.

DUCHESS: Oh — Oh — Oh —

INFANTA: And my uncle wishes that I were dead. ... No one cares. I have to be a queen all the time, and I can never be a

122

little girl like the little girl I saw in Valladolid. She just played ... and no one corrected her every moment.

DUCHESS: You play with the finest dolls in the world.

INFANTA: I do not have mud like hers!

DUCHESS: Mud!

INFANTA: I'd like to smear my face!

DUCHESS: Oh!

INFANTA: And I'd like to climb a tree!

DUCHESS: Oh, your Highness, you fill me with horror! You forget that you are the daughter of a king!

INFANTA: Well, it's my birthday body. and I'm tired of being a wooden body.
(She seats herself most unmajestically on the footstool.)

DUCHESS: Such wickedness! I shall have to call the Grand Inquisitor. There is a devil in you!

INFANTA: Call him! I'll rumple my hair at him.

DUCHESS: He'll forbid you to enjoy your birthday.

INFANTA: What is it for my birthday — the same old story.

DUCHESS *(mysteriously):* Who knows?

INFANTA *(not so surely):* When I was ten, they had dancing in the garden, but I could not go amongst the little girls. They played and I looked on.

DUCHESS: An Infanta of the house of Aragon must not play with children.

INFANTA: And when I was eleven they had dancing in the garden and a shaggy bear and some Barbary apes; but I could only sit here. I couldn't touch the bear, even when he smiled at me. And when one of the apes climbed to this balustrade, you drew me away.

DUCHESS: Such animals are very dangerous, your Highness.

INFANTA: I do not care. I do not want to be an Infanta.

DUCHESS: You are the daughter of Ferdinand, by grace of God, King of Spain!

INFANTA: Will my father come to me to-day? And will he smile?

DUCHESS: This is all for you alone.

INFANTA: Will not my sad father then come to me to-day? And will he not smile?

DUCHESS: He will see you after the surprise.

INFANTA: A surprise?

DUCHESS: Yes, your Highness.

INFANTA: What is it?

DUCHESS: I cannot tell.

INFANTA: If I guess?

DUCHESS: Perhaps.

INFANTA: It's hobby-horses!

DUCHESS: No. *(They almost forget their royalty.)*

INFANTA: It's an African juggler with two green and gold snakes in a red basket.

DUCHESS: No.

INFANTA: In a blue basket?

DUCHESS: No.

INFANTA *(ecstatically):* Three snakes?

DUCHESS: Not at all.

INFANTA *(dully):* Is it a sermon by the Grand Inquisitor?

DUCHESS: No.

INFANTA *(with new hope):* Is it a troupe of Egyptians with tambourines and zithers?

DUCHESS: No.

INFANTA: Is it something I've never seen before?

DUCHESS: Never in the palace.

INFANTA *(screaming):* It's a fantastic!

DUCHESS: Who knows?

INFANTA: Oh, it's a fantastic. It's a fantastic!
(She dances about.)

DUCHESS: Your Highness forgets herself.

INFANTA: It's a fantastic! It's a fantastic! *(She suddenly regains her poise.)* Where is my cousin, the Count of Tierra-Nueva? I shall tell him that I am to be entertained on my birthday by a fantastic And I shall let him come here to see it.
(The Moorish attendant steps inside the door and holds the curtain aside.)

INFANTA: Your Grace, inform the Chamberlain that I shall have the fantastic dance for me in my balcony. The sun in the garden hurts my eyes. Besides, I want to touch his back.
(She goes out, every inch a queen.)

DUCHESS: She has guessed. Tell the Chamberlain to send the fantastic here.

ATTENDANT: The fantastic is waiting in the ante-chamber, your Grace. *(The DUCHESS exits after the INFANTA. The Attendant crosses to ante-chamber.)*

ATTENDANT: Her Grace, the Duchess of Albuquerque, bids you enter. Inform the Chamberlain that her Highness, the Infanta, is ready for the dance.
(The FANTASTIC and an Attendant enter. The Fantastic is a hunchback, with a huge mane of black hair and a bright face that shows no trace of beauty, but great light and wonder. The Fantastic looks about the balcony. It is all so strange to him. As he goes about touching the things in the place the Attendant follows him closely, watching him with eagle eyes. As the boy nears the mirror and lays his hand upon the black velvet hangings the Attendant steps in front of him and prevents his opening the curtains. The little boy then sits — a very small, misshapen little creature — on the steps of the

balcony. The CHAMBERLAIN enters. He is a middle-aged man, with some tenderness left in his somewhat immobile face, and when he addresses the little boy there is a note of pathos that is almost indefinable.)

CHAMBERLAIN: Little grotesque, you are to see the King's daughter!

FANTASTIC *(almost overcome):* Where is she?

CHAMBERLAIN: Come now, you must not be afraid.

FANTASTIC: I have never seen a king's daughter.

CHAMBERLAIN: You must smile.

FANTASTIC: Is she very big — and all bright and shiny?

CHAMBERLAIN: Smile! You did not have such a long face yesterday. That is why we bought you.

FANTASTIC: Will she smile upon me?

CHAMBERLAIN: You must make her smile.

FANTASTIC: Will she beat me if I do not make her smile?

CHAMBERLAIN: You shall be beaten if you displease her. This is her Highness's birthday. And you are to dance for her to make her happy.

FANTASTIC: I have never danced for a king's daughter before.

CHAMBERLAIN: You must dance bravely before her as you danced when we found you in the woods yesterday.

FANTASTIC: I am afraid of the King's daughter.

CHAMBERLAIN: We cannot have fear on the Infanta's birthday. We must have happiness.

FANTASTIC: I wish my father had not sold me.

CHAMBERLAIN: Your father was very poor, and he wanted you to make the Infanta happy.

FANTASTIC: My father did not care for me.

CHAMBERLAIN: You shall make the Infanta happy.

FANTASTIC: If you had a son would you sell him?

CHAMBERLAIN: You were sold to the Infanta.

FANTASTIC: Have you a son?

CHAMBERLAIN: No.

FANTASTIC: My Father had seven sons.

CHAMBERLAIN: I had a little boy once.

FANTASTIC: And did you sell him?

CHAMBERLAIN: No. He went away ... He died.

FANTASTIC: Could he make the Infanta smile?

CHAMBERLAIN: I think he could.

FANTASTIC: Did he dance for her?

CHAMBERLAIN: No, he rode a hobby-horse in the mock bull fight.

FANTASTIC: What is a hobby-horse?

CHAMBERLAIN: A hobby-horse is a make-believe horse — like the stick that you ride through the woods.

FANTASTIC: Oh, can't I ride a hobby-horse in a bull fight?

CHAMBERLAIN: Some time ... If you make the Infanta happy on her birthday I'll give you a hobby-horse.

FANTASTIC: Can I ride it to-day — for her?

CHAMBERLAIN: No. You'll have to dance for her.

FANTASTIC: Is she terrible?

CHAMBERLAIN: Not if you are good.

FANTASTIC: I think — I'm afraid.

CHAMBERLAIN: Afraid? You were not afraid of the woods.

FANTASTIC: They would not hurt me. I did not have to make them smile.

CHAMBERLAIN: What will you do when you see the Infanta?

FANTASTIC: I don't know. That man who dressed me up said I

must smile and bow. My smile was very funny, he said, and my bow was funnier. I didn't try to be funny.

CHAMBERLAIN: Some boys are funny even when they don't try to be.

FANTASTIC: I don't feel funny. I just feel happy, and when I am happy people laugh ... Did she smile upon your son when he rode the hobby-horse?

CHAMBERLAIN: She threw a rose to him.

FANTASTIC: Do you think she'll throw a rose to me? I like roses ... Am I like your son?

CHAMBERLAIN: My son was tall.

FANTASTIC: I would be tall and strong, too; but I broke my back, and my brothers say I am very crooked ... I do not know ... I am not as strong as they are, but I can dance and sometimes I sing, too ... I make up my songs as I go along. And they are good songs, too, I know, because I've heard them.

CHAMBERLAIN: How did you hear them, Señor Merry-Face?

FANTASTIC: Some one sang them back to me.

CHAMBERLAIN: A little girl, perhaps?

FANTASTIC: Some one ... When I sang in the valley she would mock me.

CHAMBERLAIN: Who was it? ... Tell me.

FANTASTIC: It was Echo.

CHAMBERLAIN: Echo? And does she live near your house?

FANTASTIC: She lives in the hills — and sometimes she used to come into the woods when it was very still.

CHAMBERLAIN: Did you ever see Echo?

FANTASTIC: No. You can't see her ... You can only hear her.

CHAMBERLAIN: Would you like to see her?

FANTASTIC: I always wonder if Echo might not mock my face as she mocks my voice?

CHAMBERLAIN: Who knows?

FANTASTIC: I go into the hills and I sing a song and then Echo sings back to me — just as I sing ... But when I go into the woods Echo doesn't stand in front of me — just as I look.

CHAMBERLAIN: Haven't you ever seen yourself?

FANTASTIC: No, but I would like to. I always make people happy when they look at me. They always laugh. Would I laugh if Echo mocked my face?

CHAMBERLAIN: I do not know.

FANTASTIC: Am I really happy looking?

CHAMBERLAIN: You are a fantastic.

FANTASTIC: That sounds happy.

CHAMBERLAIN: I hope it always will be.

FANTASTIC: Have you ever seen yourself?

CHAMBERLAIN: Yes.

FANTASTIC: Did your son see himself?

CHAMBERLAIN: Yes.

FANTASTIC: Where?

CHAMBERLAIN: In a mirror.

FANTASTIC: Is that Echo's other name?

CHAMBERLAIN: Yes.

FANTASTIC: Can I see myself sometime?

CHAMBERLAIN: Yes.

FANTASTIC: I'll sing, too.
    (The ATTENDANT enters.)

ATTENDANT: Her Royal Majesty, the Infanta of Spain!
    (The FANTASTIC is very much frightened.)

CHAMBERLAIN: Go behind the door there ... Wait ... Be brave ... Smile. ... And do not speak until you are asked to.
(The INFANTA enters sedately, followed by the DUCHESS and the COUNT of Tierra-Nueva, an unpleasant-looking boy of sixteen. The CHAMBERLAIN bows very low and kisses the Infanta's stiffly preferred hand.)

INFANTA *(regally):* My lord Chamberlain, this is our royal birthday, and in accord with the wish of our father, the King of Spain, we are to be entertained with some mirthful sport *(suddenly a little girl)* — and I know what it is. It's a fantastic.

CHAMBERLAIN: Your Highness, it is the pleasure of the Chamberlain to His Majesty, your father, the King of Spain, to offer my felicitations this day on which God has deigned to send happiness and good fortune to Spain in your royal person. His Majesty the King through me desired to surprise you with mirth this day.

INFANTA: Is our royal father well? And does he smile to-day?

CHAMBERLAIN: His Majesty does not smile, your Highness. He cannot smile in his great grief.

INFANTA: Let the surprise be brought to us. But I guessed what it was! ... It must be very ugly and very crooked and very, very funny to look at — or we shall be highly displeased.
(She settles into her royal place and takes on a manner. The FANTASTIC, having been summoned by the page, barely enters the door. The INFANTA, looking royally straight before her, does not turn her head. After a moment)

INFANTA: Well?

CHAMBERLAIN: Here is the surprise, your Highness.
(The FANTASTIC is the picture of grotesque misery. He looks first at the CHAMBERLAIN and then at the INFANTA. Finally she turns to him, and he tries a timid smile and an awkward bow. The INFANTA claps her little hands and laughs in sheer delight. The FANTASTIC looks desperately at the CHAMBERLAIN.)

INFANTA: Go on ... Isn't he funny!

CHAMBERLAIN (to Fantastic): Bow again and then begin to dance.

FANTASTIC *(joyfully):* She is only a little girl, and I've made her happy!

CHAMBERLAIN: What will you dance, Señor Merry-Face?

FANTASTIC: I'll dance the one I made up and no one ever saw or heard it except Echo. It's the dance of the autumn leaf. I'll show you what the autumn leaves do and I'll tell you what they say.

INFANTA: How do you know, you comic little beast?

FANTASTIC: I know because I live in the woods, up in the hills, and I dance with the leaves — and I have two pet woodpigeons.

INFANTA: Where is the music?

FANTASTIC: I sing — it's happier that way.

INFANTA: Dance! Dance!

(The FANTASTIC bows in an absurdly grotesque way — his idea of stateliness and grace.)

INFANTA: I've never seen such a monstrous fantastic.

COUNT: We must touch his back before he goes — for good luck.
(The FANTASTIC begins to sing and dance The Song of the Autumn Leaf.)

FANTASTIC *(singing):*

> **All summer long**
> **I cling to the tree,**
> **Merrily, merrily!**
> **The winds play and play,**
> **But I cling to the tree,**
> **Merrily, merrily!**
> **The summer sun**

Is hot and gold.
Cheerily, cheerily.
But I hang on
In the August heat,
Wearily, wearily!
I am not free,
For I have to hang
Wearily, wearily!
Until autumn frosts
Release my grasp,
Cheerily, cheerily!
Then I'm free,
All crumpled and brown
Merrily, merrily!
I roll and I blow
Up and around,
Merrily, merrily!
All crumpled and brown
In my autumn coat,
I dance in the wind,
I hide in the rain,
Dancing and blowing

And waiting for winter,
Cheerily, cheerily,
Merrily, merrily,
Wearily, wearily.

(He falls like a dead leaf on to the floor. The INFANTA is delighted.)

INFANTA: I'm going to throw him a rose!

DUCHESS: Your Highness!

INFANTA: See — like the Court ladies to Caffarelli, the treble. *(The FANTASTIC has risen and bowed in his grotesque way. The INFANTA tosses the rose to him. He takes it up and, bowing absurdly, presses it to his lips.)*

DUCHESS *(who has never smiled):* Your Highness, you must prepare for your birthday feast.

132

THE BIRTHDAY OF THE INFANTA

INFANTA: Oh, let him dance again! The same dance!

DUCHESS: Think of the birthday feast, your Highness. Your father, the King of Spain; your uncle, the Grand Inquisitor; the noble children.

INFANTA: Once more!

DUCHESS: Your Highness, you must see the huge birthday cake with your initials on it in painted sugar — and a silver flag ...

INFANTA: Very well. He can dance again after my siesta. ... My cousin, I trust that you will see the next dance.

COUNT: I'll ride a hobby-horse and he'll be the bull. It will be very funny with such a funny bull.
(He kisses her hand and exits the opposite way.

The INFANTA, followed by the DUCHESS, exits, and as she goes she looks once more at the FANTASTIC and breaks into a laugh. The FANTASTIC is delighted and stands looking after her.)

CHAMBERLAIN: Come!

FANTASTIC *(putting out his hand):* I think she liked me.

CHAMBERLAIN: The Infanta of Spain is the daughter of the King of Spain. You have made her smile. Come!
(They go out. The ATTENDANT crosses and closes the awning. He draws the curtains from the mirror and preens himself a bit, looking now and then until he disappears.

A sunbeam coming through the fluttering awning, strikes the mirror, and reflects on to the tessellated floor.

There is a short intermezzo. Far-a-way harps and violins echo the Fantastic's little song.

The FANTASTIC enters furtively, looking about. He takes the rose from his bosom.)

FANTASTIC: I think I'll ask her to come away with me when I've finished my dance.
(He crosses to her door and listens. Then smiles and skips a step or two. He sees the sunbeam through the awning and

133

goes to it. He again takes the rose from his coat and holds it in the sunlight. Again he dances to the door and listens, then turns facing the mirror for the first time. He breaks into a smile, but first hides the rose hastily. He waves his hand.)

FANTASTIC: Good morrow! ... You are very funny! ... You are very crooked! ... Don't look that way! ... Why do you frown at me? ... Can't you talk? ... You only move your lips. ... Oh, you funny little boy! *(He puts his hands on his sides and breaks into a great laugh)*

FANTASTIC: If you could see yourself, you'd laugh still more. *(He makes a mocking bow and breaks into shouts. He plays before the mirror. The mockery is too clever.)*

FANTASTIC: You mock me, you little beast! ... Stop it! Speak to me ... You make me afraid ... Like night in the forest. *(He has never known anything like this. He is in turn enraged, terrified. He runs forward and puts out his hand. He rubs his hand over the face of the mirror and the cold, hard surface mystifies him. He brushes the hair from his eyes. He makes faces. He retreats. He looks about the room. He sees everything repeated in the mirror — the awning, the chairs, the sunbeam on the floor.)*

FANTASTIC *(calling):* Echo!
(He strains for an answer. He hides behind a chair. He makes a plan.)

FANTASTIC: I know, miserable little monster. You shan't mock me. *(He takes the rose from his coat.)*

FANTASTIC: She gave me this rose. It is the only one in the world ... She gave it to me — to me.
*(He emerges from behind the chair and holds out the rose. With a dry sob he shrinks away and, fascinated, stares at the mirror. He compares the rose, petal by petal, terror and rage rising in him. **He** kisses it and presses it to his heart. Suddenly he rushes to the mirror with a cry. He touches the glass again, then with a cry of despair he hurls himself sobbing on the floor. Once more he looks upon the picture*

134

and then, covering his face with his hands, he crawls away like a wounded animal, lies moaning in the shadows and beating the ground with his impotent hands. The INFANTA enters, followed by the COUNT. At the sight of the FANTASTIC the INFANTA stops and breaks into a laugh.)

INFANTA: His dancing was funny, but his acting is funnier still. Indeed he is almost as good as the puppets.
(His sobs grow fainter and fainter. He drags himself toward the door, trying to hide his face. Then with a sudden gasp he clutches his side and falls back across the step and lies quite still. The INFANTA waits a moment.)

INFANTA: That is capital; it would make even my father, the King of Spain, smile ... But now you must dance for me:
Cheerily, cheerily!
Merrily, merrily!
Wearily, wearily!

COUNT: Yes, you must get up and dance and then we'll have a bull fight and I'll kill you.
(The FANTASTIC does not answer.)

INFANTA *(stamping her foot):* My funny little fantastic is sulking. You must wake him up and tell him to dance for me.

COUNT: You must dance, little monster, you must dance. The Infanta of Spain and the Indies wishes to be amused. *(Then to a PAGE)* A whipping master should be sent for.
(The PAGE goes out.)

COUNT: Let's touch his back *(as the children touch his hump)* and make a wish.

INFANTA: I *wish* he would dance.
(Enter the CHAMBERLAIN and the DUCHESS.)

DUCHESS: Your Highness!

INFANTA: Make him dance or I shall have him flogged.
(The CHAMBERLAIN rushes to the body. He kneels. Feels the heart — sees the sunbeam and the exposed mirror —

shrugs his shoulders — rises.)

CHAMBERLAIN: Mi bella Princess, your funny little fantastic will never dance again.

INFANTA *(laughing):* But why will he not dance again?

CHAMBERLAIN: Because his heart is broken.

INFANTA *(thinks a moment, then frowns):* For the future let those who come to play with me have no hearts.
(She passes out, not deigning to look back, every inch the queen — the disappointed, lonely, shut-in little queen.

The others follow her properly according to rank; but the CHAMBERLAIN, remembering a little boy who would ride hobby-horses no more in mock bull fights, returns and throws the Infanta's mantilla over the little warped body. It is a moment of glory. The CHAMBERLAIN again starts to follow his Mistress; but memory is stronger than etiquette. He goes to the FANTASTIC and takes up the little hand which clutches something precious. He opens the fingers and finds the rose. He holds it out and lets the petals flutter to the floor. That is all.)

THE CURTAINS CLOSE

THE
GHOST OF MR. PENNY

by
Rosemary Musil

The premiere production of this play was given
in March, 1939, by the Children's Theatre of Evanston,
Illinois, under the direction of Miss Winifred Ward.

During the 1920s and the 1930s children's theatre production became more prevalent in amateur and community theatre venues than in professional theatres. This, in turn, influenced the nature of the plays written and published. Much of the literature of the time reflects an influence from community youth theatre programs—that is, programs that cast large numbers of young people as performers in their plays and thus necessitate large numbers of youthful roles. The plays of Rosemary Musil typify this movement.

Throughout the middle of the last century, *The Ghost of Mr. Penny* remained the most popular of Musil's works, particularly among amateur theatre producers. This play differs greatly from the melodramatic fairytales, and its realistic style owes more to the influence of then popular radio dramas than it does to the prevailing traditions in children's theatre. Musil borrows from melodrama and the well-made play form, and she adds liberal doses of sentiment and comedy in the portrayal of lifelike children placed in a recognizable world.

The Ghost of Mr. Penny presents the story of Sally, who is about to be sent to an "orphan asylum" because of the illness of her guardian. While playing in an abandoned house, Sally and her friends stumble upon Bill, a good-natured drifter, who serves as the adult agent for the young people, and represents the "good guys" in the conflict. The action begins with the discovery of a picture, which suggests that Sally might be the heir of the Penny fortune, and thus may not have to go to the asylum after all. Meanwhile, Mr. Jenkins, a distant relative of Mr. Penny, appears on the scene to claim the estate.

Much of the story depends on events that happened prior to the beginning of the play. This, and the many characters that figure prominently in the action, necessitates copious exposition in act one. Musil delivers this exposition through lengthy conversations between the characters, so that the entire act, much like radio drama, takes on the qualities of a narrative wherein the story is told more than presented.

The elaborate exposition provides some justification for the odd assortment of characters that are thrown together in act two. The setting, the supposedly haunted Penny mansion, provides a useful site for a series of situations where the characters frighten one another, and then come to suspect the presence of an actual ghost. This action in the mansion, almost the high point in the play, has little to do with Sally's situation. The children go to the house to search for a "hidden treasure." They fully expect to confront a ghost, and these fears precipitate the ensuing antics. Because this threat is only imagined, the audience may delight in the situation rather than fear for the well-being of the characters. During the chaos of the situation, Sally inadvertently discovers her birth certificate (although she does not know what it is), and uses it to fill a hole in her shoes. The characters later discover this important document at the most appropriate dramatic moment in the next act.

The third act returns to the setting and style of act one, and here Musil resorts to the more obvious techniques of melodrama. Mr. Jenkins threatens to prevail, until Bill discovers the birth certificate and verifies Sally's claim to the fortune. In true melodrama form, Mr. Jenkins gets his just punishment, while the play ends with the implication that Sally will live happily ever after.

Musil does not overemphasize either the sentimentality or the melodrama in the work. In contrast to Sara Crewe, whom Miss Minchin badly mistreats, nothing bad happens to Sally. The story creates tension through the threat to send Sally to an orphanage. The "villain," Mr. Jenkins, appears more inept than mean, and he never directly threatens to harm Sally as he tries to obtain the fortune for himself. The emotional involvement in melodrama usually comes from empathy with characters in a difficult situation, but, here, Sally is rescued from only the threat of a bad situation. Also Musil reduces the tension by so foreshadowing the reversal of action that little suspense arises, thus minimizing another significant attribute of melodrama.

Viewed from contemporary perspectives, the play appears naïve and simplistic, as it includes limited characterizations, implausible situations, and a contrived denouement. But the youthful characters are rambunctious, inquisitive, and even a little mischievous as they question Bill's veracity and as they challenge adult authority by sneaking into the haunted house. In a manner reminiscent of the detective/mystery stories long popular in children's literature, the children involve themselves in an adventure. While Musil found it necessary to have an adult unravel the mystery, she places the children in the center of the action and creates several potentially entertaining situations, particularly those in the "haunted" house.

First produced in 1939, and thus contextualized by a culture gradually moving out of the Great Depression and embroiled in international politics that would ultimately lead to World War II, the play offered audiences a lighthearted, escapist adventure, with little danger and several pleasant surprises. In that era, Bill (the drifter character) evoked none of the suspicion a stranger might to a contemporary group of young people; and the pleasure of play evoked by the story suggests a view of children and childhood embodied by innocence and insulated from the larger problems of the day.

Rosemary Musil was born in Dearborn, Missouri, in 1903. She received a degree in Fine Arts at Horner Institute in Kansas City; and she also studied at the State University of Central Missouri.

Musil subsequently moved to Chicago, Illinois, where she met Winifred Ward. With Ward's encouragement, Musil wrote more than seventeen plays, most of which were presented by Ward's Children's Theatre of Evanston.

Musil was instrumental in organizing a children's theatre organization in Elmhurst, Illinois, and served as its director for over twenty-six years. Her writings include TV scripts, pageants, and traditional plays—four of which were published by Anchorage Press. In 1975, Musil was awarded the Chorpenning Cup by the Children's Theatre Association of America, for her achievements as a playwright.

In addition to *The Ghost of Mr. Penny*, Musil's published plays include *Seven Little Rebels, Five Little Peppers,* and *Mystery at the Old Fort.*

Rosemary Musil, at the age of one-hundred and one, was honored by a Resolution of the Missouri State Senate in April 2004.

THE
GHOST OF MR. PENNY

by
Rosemary Musil

144

THE GHOST OF MR. PENNY

To
SKIPPY and his pals

THE GHOST OF MR. PENNY

Characters

BILL,
a tramp, good-natured, easy-going, lovable.

LEWIS,
twelve years old, whose ambition is to be a "tough guy"

TOMMY,
his friend and pupil.

SALLY,
their playmate, a gallant and spirited girl.

ELLEN,
another playmate, rather prim and cautious.

PHINEAS,
an awkward boy of eighteen or so.

MR. JENKINS,
a fussy little middle-aged man.

MR. SIMMONS,
Ellen's father, and the neighborhood policeman.

Setting

ACT ONE:
The abandoned coach-house of the old Penny estate, late one afternoon in autumn.

ACT TWO:
The living room of the old Penny house, after dark, that evening.

ACT THREE: The coach-house, the next morning.

THE GHOST OF MR. PENNY

ACT ONE

SCENE: *The abandoned coachhouse of an old estate. There are
three openings in the set — the outside door up right
center, the wooden casement window up left center, and a
door down left which leads into the harness room. There is a
manger filled with straw at right.*

*The room looks dusty and neglected. Just below the window
is a gas plate with boxes piled high upon it, and the plate
itself protected by an oil-cloth. A rickety old table occupies
the center of the stage, and there are two matching chairs
piled up against the door, which is locked and barred. An old
rusty lantern hangs over the manger.*

*At the rise of the curtain, the stage is empty, but outside the
window, someone can be heard approaching. The window
swings open, revealing a man with a battered felt hat set on
the back of his head.*

*Bill is evidently a sailor of sorts, for he wears part of a sailor
costume. He is big and athletic-looking, though lazy, and
in his prime of life. He may be thirty-five or forty-five. It is
hard to tell, for he enjoys life, and his sense of humor and
kindliness have kept him young. He is neat, in spite of the
battered felt hat, and a two days' growth of beard. He opens
the window cautiously, looks inside, and expresses his delight
in a long, low whistle.*

*He throws a leg over the sill, steps onto the boxes, and
into the room. He is carrying some provisions tied up in
a bandana handkerchief. He pushes the window to, and
looks about him with pleasure, giving out a big sigh of
contentment. Then he begins a more detailed
examination of the premises.*

*He peeps into the harness-room, finding everything to his
taste. Then he crosses to center, and tries the table for dust,
testing it with a gingerly finger. He brushes his hands off with
elaborate care, then spotting the manger at right, he crosses
and punches the straw to test it for bedding.*

147

*It all suits him down to a T, and he begins to make
preparations for a formal supper. Taking a handful of straw,
he dusts the table efficiently, then unstacks the two chairs,
and dusts them, arranging them at the table, as for a banquet.
Then, spying the oil-cloth, he pulls it out and spreads it over
the table, straightening it daintily. He puts his bandana on
the table and opens it up, taking out spoon, knife, and fork.
Placing these carefully, he casts a critical eye over the whole,
and decides something is missing. Then he snaps his fingers
and springs out the window, returning almost instantly with a
handful of goldenrod, which he crams down into the neck of
an old bottle which is found among the boxes and debris.*

*Surveying his handiwork with pride, Bill beams happily, and
draws a can from his bandana. Then he pulls a can-opener
from his pocket, and starts to tackle the can. The can-opener
offers difficulties, and Bill is still trying to make it work,
when a voice is heard outside calling, and he stops to listen
attentively.*

TOMMY *(outside):* Lewis! Hey Lewie! I shot you. You're dead!
Leeeewie!
*(The voice grows fainter, but a scuffling at the window warns
BILL, who hastily puts the can-opener in his pocket, gathers
up his things, and piles into the manger. The window opens
as he does so, and LEWIS, a little boy about twelve, climbs
in, carrying a home-made shotgun. He squats down beside
the table, waiting. The voice of his pursuer comes closer.)*

Lewie! ... Leewwie! Quit your hidin' and come on back here!
You're dead! ... Lew ... I bet I know where you're hidin' at!
*(TOMMY climbs up on a box from outside, opens the window
and crawls in. He is about the same age and size of LEWIS,
and carries a toy pistol.)*

LEWIS: Bang! Bang! ... I got ya! *(He runs out from behind the
table.)*

TOMMY: Ah, you did not. I got you outside by the house. You
were dead before you came in here!

148

LEWIS: I was not. You just got me in the shoulder.
(SALLY "yoo-hoos" from back in the deep yard surrounding the coachhouse.)

SALLY *(offstage)*: Leeeewis! ... Tommieeee! Hey, Tommy, I want to play too!

LEWIS: It's Sally! Quick, shut the window! We don't want any ole girl playing in here.
(The boys slam the window shut, and pull the bar across it.)

SALLY *(at the window):* Tommy Tommy Higgins! ... I saw you slam this window. Open it up. I want to play in the coachhouse too.

TOMMY: Ah, go away.

LEWIS: We're playin' G-Men. Girls can't be G-rnen.

SALLY: I'll be a G-woman then.
(The boys think this remark terribly funny. They go off into gales of derisive laughter.)

BOYS: Ha, ha, ha! She'll be a G-woman. Silly old girls think they can be G-women.

SALLY *(outside):* I've got as much right in there as you have.

TOMMY: Ah, go cook a radish!
(Overcome with this brilliant retort, the boys howl with laughter and slap each other on the back.)

SALLY: You open this window! The coachhouse doesn't belong to you.

LEWIS: It doesn't belong to you either.

SALLY: Well, anyway, you let me in!

TOMMY *(whispering):* Don't answer, and maybe she'll go away.

SALLY: You let me in, or I'll — I'll bust the door down!

TOMMY: She'll bust the door down! Ha! Ha! That's good!

TOMMY: Ho! Ha! Ole door's got about a million bolts in it, I reckon, but she's gonta bust it in! That's good!

SALLY: All right. I'll show you.

(SALLY throws her weight against the door. The boys are surprised at her attempt.)

TOMMY: She's tryin' it!

LEWIS: Of all the silly ...
(The rusty old door, weak in the hinges, suddenly gives way, and SALLY falls headlong upon it, into the coachhouse. For a moment, no one can speak, so surprised are they. Then SALLY gets up slowly, rubbing certain parts.)

SALLY: Gee, I did it!

TOMMY: Gosh!

LEWIS: She busted the door in!

SALLY: I told you I would.
(The boys examine the door. SALLY smoothes her dress and hair.)

TOMMY: Look, the hinges were rusty and they busted right off!

LEWIS: Yeah ... Hey, hadn't we better set up the door.
(SALLY has taken off her shoe and is hopping about trying to find the paper she lost out of it.)

TOMMY: I say we had. What if somebody saw it busted in! Come on, Sally, help us put the door back.

SALLY: Wait a minute, I've got to find the paper out of my shoe.

LEWIS: Paper out of your shoe?

SALLY: Yes, there's a hole in the sole, and I'll ruin my stocking if I don't keep a paper in it.

LEWIS *(picking up folded paper)*: This it?

SALLY: Yes ... Thanks *(She sits on chair and puts paper back in shoe.)* Now! ... Do you think we can pick it up?

TOMMY: Grab hold of here and shove it as you raise it; *(The children set the door up, and wonder of wonders, it jams into the doorway and stands by itself.)* Gee! It sticks by itself!

SALLY: Careful, it might fall down!
(The children hold their hands out for a minute, then breathe

easier as they see it is going to stand.)

LEWIS: Nope, she really sticks ... Can't even tell it was knocked down!

SALLY: We'd better get away, in case the wind blows it over, or something! *(They back off and turn to the table, leaning on it, and SALLY sits in one of the chairs.)*

TOMMY *(examining the table suddenly):* Hey look!

SALLY: What?

TOMMY: There's oil cloth on the table!

LEWIS: Gee, yes, and the chairs are drawn up too, just like somebody had put them there! I never noticed that before!

SALLY: Do you suppose somebody's been here besides us?

LEWIS: Who could have?

TOMMY: Maybe it was the ghost!

SALLY: The ghost!

LEWIS *(derisively):* What ghost?

TOMMY *(lowering his voice and looking about him):* The ghost of Mr. Penny!

SALLY: Of all the silly things! There isn't any such thing as ghosts!

LEWIS: I don't know. They say the big house is haunted.

TOMMY: Yeah, and old Mr. Penny's ghost walks up and down the steps at night, looking for his little boy that shot himself accidentally with a gun!

SALLY: Oh, that's too silly for words! Mr. Penny isn't even dead!

TOMMY: No? Then where is he?

SALLY: Nobody knows. After his little boy shot himself, Mrs. Penny died from shock, and Mr. Penny just wandered away and went to sea.

TOMMY: Well, people have seen his ghost wandering about the big house at night, so he must be dead!

SALLY: The idea! If there'd been a ghost wandering around old Mr. Herman would have seen him, wouldn't he? And Mr. Herman says Mr. Penny isn't dead and that he's coming back some day. That's the reason he stays on there in the big house, waiting for Mr. Penny to come back!

LEWIS: If Mr. Herman saw that ole ghost wanderin' around, he'd have him arrested fer trespassin'!

SALLY: Shh! Somebody's calling!
(Children listen.)

ELLEN *(outside window):* Sally, are you in there?

SALLY: It's Ellen! *(Opens window.)* Hello, Ellen, come on in!

ELLEN*(standing at the window):* I don't want to climb in the window. I'll get my dress dirty *(superiorly).*

LEWIS *(mischievously):* Then why don't you come in by the door?

ELLEN: Is the door open?

LEWIS: Sure it is! Sally came in that way!

ELLEN: Well for pity sakes, why didn't you say so, Sally?

SALLY: Oh, but Ellen you—
(ELLEN starts to turn toward the door, and Lewis puts his hand over SALLY's mouth to keep her from telling.)

LEWIS: Just push against the door real hard!

SALLY *(jerking free from LEWIS):* Don't you do it, Ellen!
(LEWIS grabs her again and keeps her from talking.)

ELLEN: Well, I guess I can do it if you did, Sally Andrews!
(ELLEN pushes, the door falls in, and the boys howl with laughter. ELLEN is mad as a wet pussy cat, and SALLY runs to her solicitously to help her up.)

ELLEN: You think you are funny, don't you, Lewis Bleck?

LEWIS *(laughing):* No! I think you are!

SALLY: I tried to tell you, Ellen!

ELLEN: Well, I came over here to tell you something exciting,

but if you're going to act mean—
(She starts out the door, but SALLY brings her back.)

SALLY: Oh, don't pay any attention to the old boys, Ellen!

LEWIS *(helping TOMMY lift the door back into place):* Sure, we're sorry. What's doing?

TOMMY: Did your father capture a bandit or somethin'?

ELLEN: No. Mr. Herman's dead!

CHILDREN: Mr. Herman!

SALLY: Oh, when did it happen?

ELLEN: Sometime yesterday, I guess. My mamma went over to the big house at supper time to take him some hot soup, and he was lying on the table. He'd had a heart attack. He'd been writing, the papers were scattered all over. ... Mamma went over and swept them up in the fireplace!

SALLY: For goodness sake!

TOMMY: Gee!

LEWIS: Poor old Mr. Herman can't have us arrested for trespassin' now, I reckon!

ELLEN: And that isn't the worst of it!

SALLY: No?

ELLEN: My mother went back over there late last night, intending to burn the papers she'd swept up in the fireplace ... and she ... *(her voice breaks with the weight of her horrible tale)* she took my father's flashlight and went into the old house, and right away ... right away ... *(her voice breaks again).*

TOMMY: Yeah, go on!

ELLEN: She saw it!

SALLY: What?

ELLEN: The ghost, of course!

SALLY: Ah, that's silly!

ELLEN: Yes? Well, maybe you think my mamma would tell a story. Maybe you think ...

TOMMY: Gosh, Ellen, what was it like?

ELLEN: It was a kind of head hanging in space, and pink cheeks, and purple ...

LEWIS: Whiskers!

ELLEN: Whiskers ... er ... *(The spell is broken, the children laugh at ELLEN's story.)* It did not! It had whiskers, though ... and a purple tie!

LEWIS: A pink ghost with purple whiskers! Ha, ha! *(Children laugh at her, and ELLEN is angry.)*

ELLEN: All right, smarties, laugh all you please, but I guess my mamma knows what she saw. She was too scared to even burn the papers!

SALLY: Poor Mr. Herman. All these years, he's kept that house open, waiting for Mr. Penny to come back. And now—he's dead.

LEWIS: Gosh, it gives me the creeps.

TOMMY: Let's don't think about it. Let's play G-men. You girls go away now. We want to play G-men.

SALLY: We'll be G-women, and play too.

LEWIS: Of all the silly — there isn't any such thing as G-women!
(Disgustedly) G-women!

TOMMY: Why don't we play Secret Service? They got girls in that.

SALLY: Sure! Let's do!

LEWIS: Ah, we don't want to play with girls!
(He throws his gun down on the table, and looks disgusted.)

ELLEN: You'd better treat Sally nice, 'cause she's got to go to the orphan's asylum tomorrow, and you won't get a chance to play with her any more.

(The children all look at SALLY pityingly. SALLY is serious, too.)

LEWIS: Gee, Sally, do you haff to go tomorrow?

SALLY: I — I reckon so.

TOMMY: Gee, Sally, I'm sure sorry.

SALLY *(rallying and attempting to make light of it):* Oh, it's ... it's just a temporary arrangement. Uncle Jim says ... I'm just going to stay long enough for Uncle Jim to get well, then he's going to get me back again. Besides, it really isn't an orphan asylum, Ellen ... It's a boarding house for children, and it's got swings and slides, and everything.
(The children are sad, they love Sally.)

TOMMY *(impulsively):* Here, you can have my gun, Sally.

LEWIS: Mine too.

SALLY *(lighthearted once more, for she has learned to take her troubles a step at a time):* Thanks ... but what will Ellen do?

ELLEN *(airily):* Oh, I could have a real gun if I wanted it!

TOMMY: Gee, Ellen, you mean your father's policeman's gun?

SALLY: Ellen, you wouldn't!

ELLEN: I could if I wanted to. I saw where he keeps it, last night!

LEWIS: Gosh, is it loaded?

ELLEN: Of course. Policemen always keep their guns loaded.

TOMMY: Gee! Go get it, Ellen!

ELLEN: All right, wait here a minute!
(She turns and goes to the window to climb out of it, but the tramp can not stand by now. He hurries out of the stall, crosses quickly to the window, shuts it and bars the way.)

BILL: Oh, no! No, no, Princess! Don't do it!
(The children scream, and scramble together in a heap downstage at left.) Guns is bad medicine fer children ... er anybody fer that matter!

ELLEN: Who—who are you?

TOMMY: You'd better let us out of here!

LEWIS: Yeah, her father's a policeman.

ELLEN: And he'll arrest you for trespassing!

BILL: Aw, shucks! Don't be afraid of me ... I wouldn't hurt no one, and I like kids! I wouldn't 'a let you know I was here, but shucks, I couldn't stand by and let the Princess here get her pappy's loaded gun ... Why, you kids might of shot each other! That would have been awful!

ELLEN: You were hiding in there! *(pointing to the stall)*

BILL: Aw, now!

TOMMY: Yes, and you'd better get out of here!

BILL: Aw, shucks, I'm not a goin' to hurt nothin' er nobody; I wasn't goin' t' stay long nohow. I'll go now if you say so. But, listen, kids, about guns — guns don't do nobody any good ever! Not even grown up people, let alone kids!

LEWIS: Yeah? Well, I'll bet they do G-men some good!

BILL: G-men? Why, they don't even use 'em most of the time!

TOMMY: Aw, like fun they don't!
(The boys have forgotten to be afraid, and come out and speak boldly with the gentle Bill.)

BILL: Naw, they don't. They use their brains to catch crooks! Take this here feller at the head of the G-men ... you know what he says?

LEWIS: What?
(The children relax perfectly now, grouping themselves about Bill who is at the table.)

BILL: Well, he says only cowards use guns ... you know, people who are afraid! And he never uses a gun 'ceptin' in self-defense, 'cause he's seen so many cowardly people dependin' on guns to make 'em brave, that he's downright ashamed t' have a gun!

LEWIS: Honest?

BILL: Sure, that's what he says ... and me, I never like guns! I don't even like to see kids play with toy guns, 'cause I've seen too much grief they've cause in the world.

TOMMY: You mean like in wars?

BILL: Sure, and in peace times too. So don't ever fool with your pappy's loaded gun, Princess. Why, didn't that poor little Penny boy get killed playin' with his pappy's gun? Just like you were goin' t' do!
(SALLY looks at him and catches her breath in sudden excitement. Maybe this tramp is Mr. Penny come back!)

SALLY: Why! How did you know that?

BILL *(unconsciously contributing to her thought):* Oh, I know a lot of things that would surprise you!

ELLEN: You're just a tramp, that's all, and you can't boss us around! I'll tell my father ... he's a policeman, and he'll have you—

BILL *(patiently):* Yeah, I know ... arrested fer trespassin' ... but first we got to sort of figure out which one of us is trespassin', ain't we?

ELLEN: Which one of us? Why, you are, of course!

BILL: Well, that depends. Now this here coachhouse don't belong to you kids, does it?

ELLEN: It doesn't belong to you either! It belongs to Mr. Penny, only he's dead!

SALLY *(quickly):* No, he isn't dead, either!

BILL *(amused):* Now, you see there? You don't know much about it after all, do you? Why, for all you know, maybe I own the place!

SALLY: Oh! Oh, are you ...

ELLEN: Own the place! Why, you're just a tramp!

TOMMY: Are you?

BILL: Am I what?

TOMMY: Just a tramp like Ellen says?

BILL: Me a tramp? Shucks, Matey, I'm a sailor!

TOMMY: A sailor?

SALLY (*suddenly sure of herself*): Of course he is!
(*BILL looks at her surprised.*)

ELLEN: Oh, what do you know about it? If you aren't a tramp,
why were you hidin' over there in the manger?

BILL: I just stopped in the manger there to take a little siesta!

LEWIS: A what?

BILL: Siesta! You know ... a beauty nap. I was kinda tired when I
got off the train this morning, so ...

ELLEN: I knew it! You're just a tramp that comes off of freight
trains. My papa's arrested them plenty of times. He'll arrest
you, too!

BILL: Aw now, Princess!

SALLY: Her name's Ellen.

BILL: Is it now? She's the very spittin' image of a Princess I once
knowed in the South Sea islands, time I got wrecked off the
coast of Singapore.

TOMMY: Gee, are you a sailor sure enough?

BILL: Me a sailor? Why shucks, Matey, look here!
(*He rolls up his sleeve, and the children crowd about him,
even ELLEN.*)

TOMMY: Gee! Look at the tattoos!

BILL: Look at this here one.
(*He doubles up his fist and the lady on his arm dances,*)

LEWIS: Look! The lady's dancin'!

TOMMY: Yes, sir! Boy, look at her go!

BILL: And look at this here one!

(*Rolls up other sleeve and displays arm.*)

TOMMY: Gee, look at the swell snake.

LEWIS: Have you really been shipwrecked?

BILL: Shipwrecked? He asks me have I been shipwrecked! Why Matey, I've been shipwrecked more times than you got fingers er toes! Why, man and boy I sailed the six seas fer ...

ELLEN *(triumphantly):* I knew you weren't a sailor?

BILL: Huh?

ELLEN: You said you'd sailed the six seas ... they're seven! I learned that in geography!

BILL: Yeah, but hadn't you heard? One of 'em died.

ELLEN: Which one?

BILL: Ain't you never heard of the dead sea?
(Rest of children laugh at ELLEN's angry face.)

TOMMY: Ha, ha! ... I get it. They're seven seas, but one of 'em is the dead sea ... so that leaves six!

ELLEN: I don't think it's funny at all. I don't believe you ever saw the sea!

BILL: What? Me not saw the sea? Why Princess!

SALLY *(slyly looking at BILL as she tries out this next remark on him):* Mr. Penny was a sailor! Did you know him?

BILL: Sure, I know all about him. His little boy got shot, and his wife died, and he went away and never came back ... at least not up to now.
(BILL loves children, and he plays their game, talking seriously to them, and giving them the courtesy of answering all their questions in detail. But this answer to SALLY is just about perfect to confirm her suspicions that BILL is Mr. Penny himself.)

SALLY: I knew you'd know? *(She smiles knowingly at BILL, who looks at her a little puzzled.)*

ELLEN: I'll bet when my father sees you, you'll get out of here mighty quick!

BILL: Aw now Princess, you wouldn't give me away, would you?

I haven't hurt nothin' ...

ELLEN: You're a trespasser and —

SALLY: He is not!

ELLEN: He is too! Anybody that is on property that don't belong to them is a tres—

SALLY: Well, this property belongs to him!
(She tosses her head triumphantly. The children and BILL look at her in amazement.)

ELLEN: Have you gone crazy?

SALLY: Certainly not. This man you've been calling a tramp is just Mr. Penny come back, that's all! *(Airily)*

LEWIS and TOMMY: Mr. Penny come back??

SALLY: Of course he is! Don't you see? He's a sailor, isn't he? Well, Mr. Penny was a sailor, too, after he ran away! Mr. Herman said so!

LEWIS: Gee!

SALLY: And he knows all about the little boy shooting himself with a gun.

TOMMY: Gosh!

(The boys look at the dazed BILL in awe. BILL looks a little uncomfortable. He doesn't want to sail under false colors, but he doesn't want to let SALLY down. He finally decides she is just tormenting Ellen, and so he backs her up as best he can without deliberately committing himself.)

ELLEN: Well, that's just about the silliest thing you ever made up, Sally Andrews! He looks like Mr. Penny, doesn't he? Sneaking around the coachhouse and hidin' in the hay!

TOMMY: Yes, if he's Mr. Penny, why didn't he go right to the big house, and walk in the front door?

SALLY: How you talk? Suppose your wife and little boy had died in that house years ago, and you had gone away trying to forget your troubles. And then you came back, after years of

160

wandering, and found that your faithful old servant had just died there too. Would you feel like bouncing right up to the front door, and walkin' in just like a—a heathen?

TOMMY: Well — maybe not. But —

SALLY: Think of it! (*She uncorks her fertile imagination, and fairly revels in her fanciful tale of the heart-broken Mr. Penny. The boys are immensely impressed. BILL has to put his hands over his mouth, To keep from laughing. ELLEN is about to explode with growing indignation.*)

Poor Mr. Penny! Too grief-stricken with memories, he hides out here in the coachhouse, unable to go back and return to the—(*She reaches for the proper expression, then comes through with a flourish.*) the scene of his former triumph!

ELLEN (*snorting in her disgust*): If that isn't about the ... You got that out of one of your Uncle Jim's books, Sally Andrews! (*She takes BILL in her confidence, so disgusted is she that she forgets he is an enemy.*)

She's always making things like that up! Her uncle writes stories and she's got too big an imagination!

SALLY: I have not!

ELLEN: You have so! I guess even my mother said so! Talking about going to a boarding school for children ... when everybody knows it's just a plain old orphan asylum!

SALLY (*yelling*): It is too a boarding house for children!

ELLEN: It is not! My mamma said so!
(*SALLY begins to cry, and BILL takes a hand.*)

BILL: Here, here. (*He soothes Sally.*) Of course it's a — boarding house. (*He puts his arms about her protectingly and she sobs against him.*)

SALLY: It's got swings and slides and little tents!

BILL: Of course it has, and anybody says it hasn't is crazy! Don't you pay any attention to the Princess here. She just wound up

161

her tongue and let it fly!

ELLEN: I did not! I'm telling the truth. ... She even makes it up when she says Mr. Andrews is her Uncle Jim. He's not really her Uncle!

SALLY: He is too my Uncle Jim!

ELLEN: He is not! He found you on his doorstep when you were a little baby. He's no relation of yours at all! *(To BILL)* And now he's sick and has to go to a sanitorium and Sally has to go to a —

BILL *(glaring):* WHERE?

ELLEN *(backing away frightened):* To a — a boarding house!

BILL: That's better!

SALLY: It's only for a short time, Mr. Penny, and when Uncle Jim is well again he'll write more stories and—

BILL: And he'll make so much money that you'll have a big red automobile and silk dresses and servants and —

SALLY *(happy right away when someone can play her own game):* And ice cream every day!

BILL: You bet! With chocolate sauce!

SALLY: And nuts!

ELLEN *(under her breath):* Nuts is right!

SALLY: But you're rich already, aren't you, Mr. Penny?

BILL: Who? Me?

ELLEN: He looks it!

SALLY: Of course! You've got the big house and all the furniture, and the land is VERY valuable!

BILL: You don't say!

LEWIS: Yeah, and I heard you had money hid in the big house too, Mr. Penny.

TOMMY: Yeah, everybody talks about that. Did you hide some money in the big house, Mr. Penny?

BILL: Why, I — er ...
(He looks at SALLY for a ewe, but she seems just as interested as the boys, and BILL hesitates about lying.)

MR. JENKINS *(outside with PHINEAS)*: Now stand back, Phineas, my boy, while I try to open the door. These keys may not work in this rusty lock without a great deal of pushing and pulling. *(The children and BILL get to their feet, electrified motionless for a second. Then they all scamper with one accord to safety.)*

TOMMY: Gosh, somebody's coming!

SALLY: They'll find we busted the door down!

LEWIS: Hide in the harness room, quick!
(The children hide in the harness room, and BILL scoots back into his stall.)

PHINEAS *(outside)*: Maybe I'd better haul off and give it a kind of running push when you put the key in the lock.

MR. JENKINS: Yes, yes, Phineas , that's a good idea!
(Phineas makes a flying tackle against the door, and comes down with it to the floor with a bang. Shocked and surprised, he stares up at MR. JENKINS with mouth wide open.)

PHINEAS: The door fell down;

MR. JENKINS *(sarcastically)*: Do tell!

PHINEAS: Guess I don't know my own strength! *(Gets up stiffly and sets the door against the wall.)* I'm awfully sorry, Mr. Jenkins ... I didn't go to do it!

MR. JENKINS: Well, no matter now! We haven't time for apologies!
(MR. JENKINS is a fussy, prissy little nervous man, never smiling and easily annoyed. PHINEAS is a tall, overgrown boy of eighteen who takes himself quite seriously, though he is not very bright. He is quite important to himself, but good-natured too.)

Hummmm! *(He inspects the table.)* This place looks as if it had been occupied recently.

PHINEAS *(knowingly):* It's those kids. They play in here lots of times. They come in at the window.

MR. JENKINS: Dear, dear. Something will have to be done about that. I can't have children running all over my property!

PHINEAS: Is the property all yours now, Jenkins?

MR. JENKINS *(inspecting the gas plate):* Oh yes. I am the closest of kin, and the property will all come to me. My, my! Such gross negligence! The gas is still turned on.

PHINEAS: What kin are you?
(MR. JENKINS is peering into the manger. He starts, draws back, thinks he saw something. He looks again, then decides he is mistaken.)

MR. JENKINS: Eh — eh — what's that?

PHINEAS: I said — what kin are you?

MR. JENKINS: Oh! Mr. Penny was my brother-in-law.

PHINEAS: Brother-in-law, eh?

MR. JENKINS: That's right!
(MR. JENKINS is prissing around, examining chairs, tables, and peering into corners. PHINEAS, with his hat pushed back on his head, is lounging against the wall, conversationally inclined.)

PHINEAS: If you're Mr. Penny's brother-in-law, why didn't you turn up here a long time ago, when he first disappeared?

MR. JENKINS: I live a good piece away from this town, Phineas, and I did not keep in touch with the Pennys, and until last night, nobody ever troubled to inform me that the Penny family was all dead.

PHINEAS: Well, they do say that Mr. Penny himself ain't dead.

MR. JENKINS: Nonsense!

PHINEAS: Old Mr. Herman always thought Mr. Penny would come back.

MR. JENKINS: That's ridiculous. It's been established by law that he died at sea in a shipwreck. What's in here, Phineas? *(He has his hand on the knob of the harness-room door.)*

PHINEAS: There's an old carriage and some harness. That's all. *(There is a loud scuffling sound, as the children scurry about to find a better hiding place.)*

MR. JENKINS *(terrified):* I heard a noise in there!

PHINEAS *(listens, then nods his head knowingly.)*: Yeah — rats. There's lots of 'em out here in the coachhouse.

MR. JENKINS: Oh my! Oh my! How terribly embarrassing! I have a phobia about rats.

PHINEAS: A what?

MR. JENKINS: A phobia.

PHINEAS: Oh, a fobula. Is it a kind of trap?

MR. JENKINS: Is what a kind of trap?

PHINEAS: That fobula thing you said you had fer rats.

MR. JENKINS: Certainly not! A phobia is a — well, it's a fear! I'm afraid of rats, if you want to know. Well — *(looking about)* I don't see anything more here—

PHINEAS: Say, Jenkins, if you're Mr. Penny's brother-in-law, why, I reckon you might want to keep this. It's a picture I found this morning up at the big house, when I was goin' around with them lawyer fellers.

MR. JENKINS: A picture?

PHINEAS: Yep. It was throwed away, in the old fireplace, in the living room. I thought nobody'd want it, and the lady was kinda purty —

MR. JENKINS: Why, this is a picture of my brother-in-law and his family. There's Penny with his little boy, just as I knew him. And there's his wife and — why, whose baby is this in the picture?

PHINEAS: I wouldn't know. I didn't even know who the lady was, but she looked so purty. But then you bein' a relation, I reckon it's only right you should have it.

MR. JENKINS *(thinking aloud, and suddenly very much upset):* He didn't have another child. He just had a little boy. The one that shot himself with the gun. *(Sharply:)* Phineas!

PHINEAS *(jumps):* Uh huh?

MR. JENKINS: Phineas, did anyone ever say my brother-in-law had another baby?

PHINEAS: Heck, nobody round here even knew Mr. Penny 'ceptin' maybe Jim Andrews.

MR. JENKINS: Jim Andrews?

PHINEAS: Yeah, he lives back in the woods, and when Mr. Penny built his house Jim was the only one lived hereabouts. It was the Andrews that found the baby on their doorstep, you know, just 'bout the time Mr. Penny left.

MR. JENKINS *(angrily, and with great suspicion that all is not well):* Confound it, Phineas, I don't know anything about this neighborhood. I told you I haven't heard of my brother-in-law these past fifteen years ... Now out with it ... what about this baby left on a doorstep? When did it happen?

PHINEAS: About ten years ago, I reckon, Sally's ten years old now.

MR. JENKINS: Sally? You mean this baby that was found on the doorstep is still around here?

PHINEAS: Yep. Sure, she's Sally ... Sally Andrews, they call her ... Only she won't be around here long. She's going to an orphan asylum tomorrow.

MR. JENKINS *(relieved):* She is? Then this Andrews fellow must be dead.

PHINEAS: Nope, but he's sick, and Sally ain't got nobody to stay with 'cause Jim has to go to the sanitarium.

MR. JENKINS *(to himself):* What luck!

PHINEAS: Yeah. Bad luck, ain't it?

MR. JENKINS: Eh? Oh, yes, yes, of course. Very sad.

PHINEAS: Yep, you bet. Everybody likes little Sally.
(There is a loud scuffling noise here. Mr. Jenkins is petrified with fear. Uttering a little scream he drops the picture in his hand, and flees. PHINEAS looks at him in astonishment, and goes after him, talking reassuringly. As PHINEAS stands in the doorway, his back to the audience, an arm reaches out of the manger, and picks up the picture MR. JENKINS has just dropped.) Hey, Jenkins. It's just rats.

MR. JENKINS *(from outside, peering in gingerly):* Are — are they gone?

PHINEAS: Well, not very far, I reckon. But rats won't hurt you. Rats is fun.

MR. JENKINS *(shuddering):* Fun? Ugh! Phineas, I dropped that picture over there somewhere. You bring it along, and let's get out of here.

PHINEAS *(looking around):* Where'd you drop it?

MR. JENKINS: Why, I don't know. Isn't it there?

PHINEAS: Don't see it anywhere.

MR. JENKINS: I was standing right there by the manger. It couldn't have gone far.

PHINEAS: Well, don't that beat all! Reckon the rats could have got it?

MR. JENKINS: Phineas! Don't mention it!

PHINEAS: I've known 'em to get away with bigger things than that. If you say so, I'll look for their nest, and find it.

MR. JENKINS: No, no! Let them have the picture! So long as it's out of the way, I don't care what happens to it.

PHINEAS: It's kind of a shame. The lady was so purty.

MR. JENKINS: Phineas, there wasn't anything else in that fireplace, was there?

PHINEAS: There's lots of papers and things stuck back in there.

MR. JENKINS: Papers! We'll have to get them out of there!

PHINEAS: Oh, no sir! Them lawyers said absolutely nothing was to be taken off the place.

MR. JENKINS: But the place is mine, Phineas. I've got a right to dispose of my own property.

PHINEAS: Yes, sir. But I got instructions to keep everything just like it is, 'til the lawyers are through with it.

MR. JENKINS: But those old papers, Phineas . It's dangerous to keep things like that around. Why, anything might happen!

PHINEAS: Anything! Tain't likely, is it?

MR. JENKINS: Why, with those old papers scattered around in the fireplace, mice or rats might get in, and somehow start a fire. And that old house would go up, just like that.

PHINEAS: Gee, I never thought of that! They've hired me to keep watch there tonight, and I wouldn't like to get burned up!

MR. JENKINS: Phineas, you take my advice, and burn those papers, before they catch fire.

PHINEAS: Oh, I'd be scared to, Jenkins. Them lawyers said —

MR. JENKINS: Phineas, you burn those papers, and I'll give you five dollars.

PHINEAS: But them lawyers said — five dollars!

MR. JENKINS: That's what I said.

PHINEAS: What fer?

MR. JENKINS: Why, for burning the papers.

PHINEAS: Five dollars fer burnin' some papers?

MR. JENKINS: Yes. It's worth that much to me to see the property protected.

PHINEAS: But what if those lawyer fellers finds out?

MR. JENKINS: Don't worry. They won't find out. I won't tell them. And I'm sure you won't.

PHINEAS: Jenkins, tell you what. I couldn't take the responsibility of burning them papers myself. But — fer five dollars I'll let you into the house tonight, since it's your own property, and you can burn them yourself.

MR. JENKINS: That's a very good idea, Phineas .

PHINEAS *(putting out his hand, importantly):* It's a deal!

MR. JENKINS *(looking down at his hand in astonishment):* A what?

PHINEAS: A deal. Put her there, Jenkins!

MR. JENKINS: Oh! Yes, indeed.
(PHINEAS pumps his hand down with a bang, and MR. JENKINS groans.)

PHINEAS: Yes, sir. It's a deal.

MR. JENKINS: Let's get away from here. Do you think you can set up that door, Phineas, 'til it can be fixed?

PHINEAS: Yep, sure. You go on out. I'll take it like this, and—
(He turns about with the door, pulling it up to the opening with him outside. As he tries to put it in place, his long foot gets caught in it. He picks it up again, and comes back into the coachhouse with it. This time, his hands get caught, as he tries to fix it up into the frame. Finally, he succeeds in propping it upright, but then finds himself inside the coach house, instead of outside. He gives up, and climbs out the window. When he is safely gone BILL climbs out of the manger, looks through the crack in the door, then takes the picture downstage, to examine it with great eagerness. He looks from it to the harness room, where SALLY is. The door of the harness room opens cautiously, and TOMMY peeps out.)

TOMMY: They gone?

BILL *(startled, hastily puts the picture in an inner pocket):* Huh? Oh, sure. Sure they've gone. You can come out now.

TOMMY *(to LEWIS, behind him):* They've gone. Tell the girls.

LEWIS: Hey, you all can come out now.
(The four children appear, somewhat the worse for hay, cobwebs, etc.)

SALLY: Whew! That was a close call. It's a good thing he was afraid of rats.

LEWIS: Rats nothin'! That was Tommy rollin' all over the bottom of the carriage.

TOMMY: Yeah, you'd have wriggled too, if somebody's foot had been in your mouth.

ELLEN: Now I know you're not Mr. Penny, or you wouldn't have run and hid.

TOMMY: Yeah, that was strange!

SALLY: Why so? You don't think he wants to meet people around here yet, do you?

ELLEN: Of course not. They'd arrest him for trespassing.

SALLY: Trespassing? When he owns all this property, and has all that money?

ELLEN *(scornfully):* What money?

SALLY: The money that's hidden in the big house.

ELLEN: Well, if he's got money there, why don't he go and get it, 'stead of hiding out here in a barn? I don't think there's any money hidden in the house at all. And you're not Mr. Penny either. You're just a tramp!

SALLY: He is too Mr. Penny! Aren't you, Mr. Penny?

BILL *(uncomfortable):* Well, you see, I —
(He hardly knows what to say.)

ELLEN: If you're Mr. Penny, where's your key to the big house?

BILL: The key?

ELLEN: Certainly. If you own the house, you must have a key to it, haven't you?
(BILL looks at SALLY blankly, but she only encourages him to produce.)

170

SALLY: Go on, Mr. Penny. Show her the key.

BILL: Well, now, you know — a key's a mighty easy thing to
lose.

ELLEN *(triumphantly):* Aha!

SALLY: Oh, but you wouldn't lose that key, Mr. Penny. I bet it's
right in your pocket.
*(She plunges her hand into his coat pocket, and brings out
the can opener.)* There! Now what do you say!
(The children cluster around to look at it closely.)

ELLEN *(skeptically):* It's a very funny key.

SALLY: Well, it's a very funny door!

BILL *(weak with relief):* My, my! I don't see how you do it,
lassie.

TOMMY: Gosh! The key to the big house! Will it really open the
big house, Mr. Penny?

BILL *(broadly):* Why, sure!

ELLEN: Like fun it will! Come on up to the big house, and let's
see you try it!

SALLY: Ellen, don't you have any feelings at all? If you don't, I
do. Mr. Penny, I'm so sorry about all the troubles you've had,
and I know you haven't got the heart to go near the big house
yet, or meet any people. But you'll feel better in a little while.
And in the meantime, you can just stay right here in the quiet,
and we won't breathe a word.

LEWIS: Sure you can. And if Ellen looks like she's going to tell
her father, I'll bop her one.

TOMMY: And if you want anything, why just tell us. We'll fix
you up.

BILL: Well, now, that's real thoughtful of you.

SALLY: Is there anything you want, Mr. Penny?

BILL *(fingering the picture, and looking furtively from it to
Sally):* Well, — yes. There is something I want. But it's up at

171

the big house and I don't much like—

SALLY: Is it something we can get for you, Mr. Penny?

BILL: Well — yes. I reckon you could. But —

TOMMY: I bet I know what it is! The hidden money!

SALLY: The treasure? Oh, Mr. Penny, is it? How wonderful!

LEWIS: Sure, we can get that for you, Mr. Penny — if you'll just tell us where it is.

BILL: Now here, hold on. I didn't say I wanted any hidden money, did I?

TOMMY: No, but you do, don't you?

BILL: I didn't even say there was any hidden money there, did I?

SALLY: No. But there is, isn't there?

BILL: Lassie, there may be. And there may not be. I didn't put any there myself, but it's quite likely Mr. Herman did. And as far as I'm concerned, you're perfectly welcome to look for it.

LEWIS: Let's do!

SALLY: All right, we will! We'll go tonight!

BILL: Listen lassie. You be careful. There'll be a night watchman there tonight. Named Phineas.

ELLEN: Yes. My father is hiring Phineas to guard the place.

TOMMY: Oh pooh! Who's afraid of Phineas? Anybody could get by Phineas.

BILL: Anybody?

LEWIS: Yeah. Anybody. Why, you could get by Phineas yourself, if you wanted to.

BILL: You think I could?

TOMMY: Why, sure. Phineas is scared of his own shadow.

LEWIS: If he saw you coming, he'd hide.

SALLY: Well, just the same — we won't risk it. We'll go early, before Phineas gets there.

ELLEN: We'll have to go before eight o'clock then. Phineas gets there at eight.

SALLY: Oh, Ellen, you do believe he is Mr. Penny now, don't you?

ELLEN: I didn't say so.

SALLY: But you're going!

LEWIS: Sure, she's afraid she'll miss out on something.

BILL: How'll you get in?

SALLY *(holding up the can opener):* We've got your key!

BILL *(uneasily):* Ellen here says it won't work.

ELLEN: I just said *maybe* it wouldn't work.

SALLY: Well, it will work!

TOMMY: Even if it won't — there's the pantry window!

BILL: What about the pantry window?

LEWIS: The catch is broken. We'll get in, all right.

BILL: Well — yes. It looks like there's a way to get in, all right.

SALLY: And when we do, Mr. Penny, what is it you want us to get for you?

BILL: Oh, never mind, Sally girl. It — it's not important.

SALLY: Are you sure? We'd be glad to get it for you.

BILL: No, don't bother. Just forget it.

SALLY: Oh. Well, I wish we could do something for you, Mr. Penny.

BILL: Aw, don't worry about me. I'll be all right.

PHINEAS *(outside the window):* Hey, you kids in there? You gotta get out. Open the window.

SALLY: It's Phineas!

BILL *(making for the manger):* Don't tell on me, will you?

LEWIS: Of course not.

SALLY: Let's tell Phineas about the ghost!

TOMMY: Let's do! He'll be scared polka-dotted.

PHINEAS *(outside):* I know you're in there now. Open up this window, or I'll get old man Simmons.

LEWIS: Aw, keep your shirt on, Sill. We're a'comin'.

(Waiting until BILL is well concealed, he opens the window.)

PHINEAS: Well, it's about time. You kids can't play in here any more. I made a deal with old man Jenkins to keep you out of here.

LEWIS: Say, Phineas, did you see the ghost when you were in the big house this afternoon?

PHINEAS: Now come on you kids, 'cause I ... huh! Ghost?

LEWIS: Sure ... The Ghost of old Mr. Penny.

TOMMY: Yeah, it's got pink cheeks and purple whiskers.
(Boys snicker.)

PHINEAS: Aw, you're just tryin' t' scare me.

ELLEN: I guess my mamma wouldn't tell a story!

PHINEAS: Who? Old lady Simmons? Did she see it?

ELLEN: She certainly did! She went in there to burn the papers in the fireplace, and —

PHINEAS: Yeah, I know!

ELLEN: Well, she saw it. It was a kind of pink face with white whiskers and a purple tie!

PHINEAS *(impressively):* Gosh!

SALLY: If I were you, Phineas, I sure wouldn't sleep in that old house tonight.

PHINEAS *(impressed):* Gosh, no. You're right. I'll ... say! *(suddenly catching on)* How'd you know I was goin' t' sleep there t'night? *(SALLY puts her hands over her mouth realizing she's made a slip.)* Huh, I see now! You kids were tryin' t' scare me so's you could play 'round there and

174

nobody 'ud bother you! Well, you can't now, see? Now come on and git outta here . . . come on!

TOMMY: Put us out!

LEWIS: Yeah!

PHINEAS: Don't you think I can't!

TOMMY: You got to catch us first!
(Round and round the table they go, the boys laughing. PHINEAS muttering. The door falls down. PHINEAS trips over it and falls flat. The boys laugh and run out. PHINEAS gets up grumbling, shakes his fist after the kids, rubs his hips, and sets the door back up as before.)

PHINEAS: Those crazy kids, tryin' t' scare a feller outta a deal just when he's gettin' in the money. ... Hope ole man Jenkins don't go charging me fer the door! I didn't go to do it! I'm jest too strong!

CURTAIN

ACT TWO

SCENE: *The living room of the old Penny house. The room is long and narrow, and furnished in late Victorian gingerbread fashion. Downstage right is the front door of the house, leading out of doors. Up left is the first flight of a stairway leading to the upper regions of the house, and down left is the fireplace, containing the fateful scraps of paper. Equally spaced across the back are two high old-fashioned windows, hung with faded draperies. Between them a Victorian sofa sits against the wall and directly over it hangs an old chroma of a man with a white beard and pink cheeks. Down right from the sofa is a table with a comfortable chair beside it, and there is another chair near the fireplace. All the furniture, is covered with big white sheets for protection, which gives a rather ghostly effect. Two old swords are crossed over the fireplace, and the andirons, fire-screen, poker and broom are on the hearth.*

The stage is quiet for a moment, then the children's voices are heard approaching.

TOMMY *(outside):* Hey, Sally, have you got the key?

SALLY *(outside):* I don't need it. Look, the door's not locked! *(She opens the door wide, and the four children are seen standing together on the threshold, all peering into the room.)*

TOMMY: Gee, I wonder if old Phineas is here already.

LEWIS: It isn't eight yet.

ELLEN: Go see, Sally.

SALLY: Well, don't push me! *(SALLY enters on tip-toe, flashing her light about cautiously. The white sheets over the furniture, and the ghostly moonlight through the back windows, give all the children a thrill.)* No, he's not here. Come on in. *(The children enter, almost holding their breath. Their lights are directed straight ahead at first, and the light all goes one way.)*

TOMMY: Gee, look!

ELLEN: I — I think I'm going home!

SALLY: Oh Ellen, they're just white sheets.

ELLEN: But the ghost!

SALLY: Now in the first place there aren't any ghosts, and if they were, you said yourself, they don't come out 'til midnight ... and it's only eight o'clock!

TOMMY: Just the same, I'm a-gonta go kinda slow! *(The children are in the room well up front now, flashing their lights about. Suddenly ELLEN's light falls on the picture of the old man hanging above the sofa. She utters a shriek and dashes for the door. The boys hear and dash with her. In the doorway they fight to get through all at once, and are stuck tightly.)* Let me outta here!

ELLEN: Oh! Oh!

176

LEWIS: Get outta my way!

SALLY: Stop it! What's the matter?

ELLEN: The ghost! I saw the ghost!

SALLY: Where?

ELLEN: Up there!

SALLY: On the wall? *(She flashes her light on the picture.)* You mean that thing?

ELLEN *(reassured):* Oh!

SALLY: It's just a picture of an old man!

ELLEN: But it had pink cheeks and a purple tie, and ...

SALLY: Yes, and that's what your mother saw when she came in here the other night, too. There aren't any such things as ghosts!

TOMMY: Of all the silly fraid-cats!

LEWIS: Yeah, you did your share of runnin', boy!

TOMMY: Aw, she hollered so loud she scared me!

SALLY: Look, there's the fireplace!

LEWIS: Gee, and look at the old swords, would you! *(Their lights on the fireplace reveal the trash within, and the crossed swords above the mantel. Lewis quickly sets his light upon the mantel and pulls up a chair, climbs up and gets the swords down.)*

TOMMY: Are they swell, though! Real swords!

SALLY: You haven't any right to take them down, Lewis. Leave them alone.

LEWIS: Aw, we just want to see what they're like. Here, Tommy!

TOMMY: Yeah, we won't hurt 'em. I'm Robin Hood! Look! *(He brandishes his sword.)*

LEWIS: Robin Hood nothin' ...He had a bow. *(He jumps down and assumes a ferocious pose.)* Out of me way, you land lubbers ... Captain John Silver speaks!

TOMMY: Yeah! Treasure Island!

(He begins to stomp about the room, brandishing his sword and chanting in rhythm with his step)

> **Fifteen men on a dead man's chest!**
> **Yo-ho-ho and a bottle of rum!**

(Lewis runs to him, puts his hand on his shoulder and joins the chanting and stomping.)

BOYS: **Drink and the devil have done for the rest!**
Yo-ho-ho and a bottle of rum! (SALLY is delighted.)

SALLY: Oh, come on, Ellen! We're all pirates hunting buried treasure!

ALL: (They line up with hands on each other's shoulders and *in big hoarse voices stomp about the room and repeat the chant.)*

> **Fifteen men on a dead man's chest!**
> **Yo-ho-ho and a bottle of rum!**
> **Drink and the devil have done for the rest!**
> **Yo-ho-ho and a bottle of rum!**

ELLEN: But where's the treasure?

SALLY: Yes, we'd better hurry and find it before old Phineas gets here. Put the swords up, boys, and let's go get it.

LEWIS: Where?

SALLY: Where what?

LEWIS: Where'll we go find it?

TOMMY: Where do you hide money in houses, Sally?

SALLY: In books, there's usually a map to guide you.

ELLEN *(sarcastically)*: Now wouldn't you just imagine Mr. Herman would have made a map and left it around?

TOMMY: Aw, he might, to show Mr. Penny where to look.

SALLY: Oh, the fireplace? They nearly always hide things in fireplaces. *(The children turn to the littered fireplace.)*

TOMMY: There's enough junk here! What's this thing? *(He picks*

178

up a piece of paper and reads): "To whom it may concern ...

ELLEN: Oh, I know what that is! *(She takes it from TOMMY, casually looks at it, then tosses it aside.)* It's a reference. We had them in grammar and they always start out, "To whom it may concern..."

SALLY: Look, could this be a map? *(She has a rectangular piece of crumpled paper. The children all inspect it).*

LEWIS: Oh, that's the thing they have in hospitals where babies are born. My mom has one in my baby book. Those are the baby's footprints, and see, there's the baby's name and the doctor and nurse and—

ELLEN: Well, for goodness sakes, did we come here to read or find money? We've got to hurry! *(She takes it and tosses it aside.)*

SALLY: Wait a minute. *(She stops, picks up the paper and folds it.)* I've got to have some more paper for my shoe. *(She sticks the paper in, tries the shoe, finds it's too thin, and picks up the letter also which had been tossed aside. All this time TOMMY has been poring over a blueprint he has found.)*

TOMMY: Hey, is this thing a map? Look, it's got drawings of floors and things.

LEWIS: Naw, that's a blueprint to a house!

ELLEN: Oh, there's nothing but trash here, let's look somewhere else!

TOMMY: Look, here's something on the back! *(Children crowd around.)* It's a drawing of some stairs, with a little arrow leading up it...

SALLY: Do you suppose that means to go up the stairs? Maybe it is a map!

LEWIS: Yeah, and see that little box like thing at the head of those three flights of stairs? Know what that is?

TOMMY: Sure, that's the little cupola up on top of the house!

SALLY: Oh, do you suppose the money's hid up there?

ELLEN: Why not? That would be the best place for it.

TOMMY: Come on, let's get goin'! Up the stairs, me hearties!
(He still has his sword, which he brandishes.)

SALLY *(catching the spirit of the thing):* Men — up yon hill, a treasure awaits us. Fall in!

ALL: **Fifteen men on a dead man's chest,**
       Yo-ho-ho, and a bottle of rum!
       Drink and the devil have done for the rest,
       Yo-ho-ho, and a bottle of rum!

(They line up as before, and start up the stairs, chanting and stomping. As they disappear from view, another light wavers across the stage, and BILL comes in cautiously, carrying the old lantern that he found in the stable. He goes quickly to the fireplace and begins searching. Suddenly he hears two people approaching the house. He gathers up the trash on the hearth quickly and stuffs it down his shirt, then hides behind the chair at the fireplace.

Enter: PHINEAS and OFFICER SIMMONS. The policeman is carrying a lantern type flashlight. Mr. SIMMONS' entrance is brisk and cheerful, but PHINEAS takes one look at the ghostly place and his knees begin to tremble.)

SIMMONS: Well, here you are, Phineas ... See, there's a soft sofa you can sleep on if you want to. The lawyers won't care. They just want somebody in the place until they ... hey, what's the matter with you?

PHINEAS: Th-hose white things! ! ! !

SIMMONS: You mean these sheets? *(He picks one off the chair and puts it back again.)* Don't be silly. They're just to cover the furniture to keep it from getting dirty. Mrs. Simmons put them on when she cleaned up yesterday.

PHINEAS: They sure look like ghosts or something.

SIMMONS: Well, they're not. They're just sheets! Well, Phineas , as I said, make yourself comfortable, I've got a beat to patrol, so I'll be going. Good night!

PHINEAS: Hey, Mr. Simmons!

SIMMONS: Yes?

PHINEAS: Did — did you ... er ... did you ever hear of ghosts with pink whiskers?

SIMMONS: Ghosts with pink whiskers? Ha, ha! That's good, yes sir! Well, good night, Phineas !
(He leaves and PHINEAS stares dumbly for a minute, then streaks after him.)

PHINEAS: But Mr. Simmons, Mr. Simmons! *(He realizes the policeman is gone.)* Gosh! *(Phineas stands uncertain for a moment, then takes the lantern off the mantel where the policeman has placed it, and walking on tip-toe, as if he were treading egg-shells, he looks under every sheet. His method of doing this is to give a quick look behind him just as he takes the sheet in hand, then to stoop and glance quickly with the lantern. He looks under everything, coming to Bill's chair last of all. He is startled for a moment, as he seems to see something. His knees tremble, then cautiously and very slowly he starts around the chair. As he comes, BILL slides around it behind him. PHINEAS makes a complete circle around the chair, without catching sight of Bill, and while he stops to scratch his head, BILL seizes the opportunity to glide behind the fire screen. PHINEAS reverses direction and goes around the chair again. Then, greatly relieved, he mops his perspiring brow.)*

Whew! For a moment there, I thought I saw sumepun!
(He takes the lantern now, and inspects the sofa.)

Well, the bed's soft. That's somepun!

(He puts the lantern on the table near the sofa, unlaces his shoes and drops them to the floor with a thump. While he is absorbed in this task, BILL picks up the fire screen, and holding it for a shield, glides up towards the back window. PHINEAS does not notice at first, but when he does, his

hair simply stands on end. He makes a dive for the table, and waits for the roof to fall. BILL peeps out above the fire screen, but ducks back as PHINEAS peeps out above the table. Finally PHINEAS emerges, quaking. The fire screen is quietly behaving itself by the window. PHINEAS looks it over from a safe distance.)

Funny! I thought that thing was over in front of the fireplace. *(He starts to lie down again on the sofa, but then decides to make provision for easy escape, if necessary. He makes sure the outside door is unlocked, places the table right nearby the sofa, and pantomimes his intention to dive under the sheet-covered table, scoot it over to the door, and crawl out, in case of trouble. As he starts to lie down again, the searchlight in his hand flashes on the awful picture! With a yell, he makes for the table, bumps his head, and sits on the floor moaning. Then he sees it is just a picture, and is disgusted with himself.)*

Dern them kids! Tellin' me about ghosts. *(He puts the light on the table and lies down determinedly on the sofa again. But he is no sooner settled than there is a loud thump above him, and the picture falls down on the couch, right on PHINEAS' feet. He jumps up, yells, dives under the table, then sees it is only the picture. He climbs out sheepishly.)*

Doggone the doggone old picture. The wire's busted! *(He throws it onto the floor by the door)* Stay there on the floor, you crazy old mutt. They oughtta have things like that in the museum — or the zoo. — He looks like an old walrus, with that —

(He freezes upright on the sofa in a listening position. The children are heard descending the stairs, chanting their pirate tune in deep, awful tones. PHINEAS is too paralyzed to move. Slowly, and with quaking knees, he makes for the table, and gets under it.)

It's them! It's the ghosts! They've come to get me! Oh! Oh! *(With trembling fingers, he puts up a hand, and draws the flashlight under the table with him. Then he walks the table*

182

toward the outer door, but bumps into the chair at right.
Confused, he turns the table around, and starts the other
way. He stops right in the children's line of march, and as the
children enter the room, he can go no further. BILL arranges
his fire screen to look as innocent as possible.)

CHILDREN *(entering):*

> **Fifteen men on a dead man's chest,**
> **Yo-ho-ho, and a bottle of rum!**
> **Drink and the devil have done for the rest,**
> **Yo-ho-ho, and a bottle of rum!**

(TOMMY, leading the march, and coming up to the table,
pretends it is an enemy blocking their path. He draws his
sword and cries out in a hoarse voice.)

TOMMY: So, ye traitorous dog! Ye will seek to block me path,
  eh? Take that, and that — *(hitting his sword on the table as if*
  he were cutting his enemy) and ... *(He stops and the children*
  stare in horror. The table is walking! PHINEAS walks it
  over to the doorway, sneaks out from underneath and runs
  outside ... but the children, naturally, do not see his escape.
  They think it must be the work of the ghost! They scream and
  bunch together downstage at left.)

ELLEN: It's the ghost!

SALLY: The table's walkin'!

TOMMY: Oh! Oh!

LEWIS: Help!

ELLEN: I wish I was home!

TOMMY: Me — me too!

SALLY: We've got to get out of here!

LEWIS: We can't! It's in the way.

ELLEN: Isn't there a back door?

TOMMY: It'ud be locked.

ELLEN: Oh dear!

SALLY: Maybe there wasn't anybody under the table! Maybe the table just scooted when Tommy hit it.

LEWIS: Is — is somebody under there?
(Pause while children listen breathlessly for an answer.)

SALLY: That's what it was! The table just slid when Tommy kinda pushed it with his sword. We—we're sillies to be so scared! *(She isn't as brave as she sounds. She's trying to bolster up their courage.)*

TOMMY: Yeah ... I'll bet you're afraid to look.

ELLEN: Oh, don't! It might be something awwwwwful!

LEWIS: Go on, Sally, you're not afraid!

SALLY: Of course I'm not! *(She is, though; her knees are shaking.)*

TOMMY: Let's see you do it then.

SALLY: All right! *(But she makes no move, just stares fascinated at the table. TOMMY gives her a shove toward it. She draws back.)* Don't! Stop shoving me! I'm going!
(Cautiously, she slides a step at a time nearer to the table ... then with lightning speed, she snatches the cloth off and runs back with it to the group. Once there, she stoops, looks under the table and is reassured.) There! I told you there was no one there! *(She takes the sheet back and puts it on the table with assurance. The children look, and are reassured. TOMMY swaggers about.)*

TOMMY: Shucks, I knew it all the time! I was just trying to scare' the rest of you!

LEWIS: Oh yeah? Boy, you're sure a good actor!

ELLEN: Yes, but what was it doing in the middle of the floor?

SALLY: What was it doing? Why, what does any table ... *(She stops, remembering the table wasn't there at first.)*

LEWIS: It wasn't there when we came in! Somebody's been here!

SALLY: Yes it was! *(Affirming it to make it so, but as she looks at*

184

the others, she's not sure either.) Or wasn't it?

ELLEN: It was not!

TOMMY: Are you s-s-s-s-sure?

ELLEN: Of course I'm sure!
(She flashes her light to the picture, and sees it is gone from the wall.) It — it's gone!

LEWIS: What's gone?

ELLEN: Him! The ghost! ... I'm getting out of here!

TOMMY: Me too!

SALLY: But we haven't found the treasure yet.

TOMMY: You can have the whole blame treasure, for all I care.

ELLEN: There isn't any treasure, Sally Andrews. And Mr. Penny is dead! And that man in the coachhouse is just a tramp! And I'm going to tell my father about him the first thing in the morning. *(At this, the fire-screen topples slightly, then falls over with a crash. The children all scream at once, and ELLEN and TOMMY fly out the door. LEWIS follows close behind, and SALLY after him. BILL, looking quite lost without his screen, slips behind the drapery at the window. SALLY on her way to the door, stumbles into the picture.)*

SALLY: Lewis! Lewis, come back here. Look what I found.

LEWIS *(poking a wary head in):* What?

SALLY: Remember when you and Tommy fell up there on the floor, when you were in that bedroom upstairs?

LEWIS: Yeah.

SALLY: Well, your fall jarred this old picture, and broke the wire. See, here it is. There aren't any such things as ghosts, honest there aren't. Uncle Jim says there's a reason for everything.

LEWIS: Yeah — but what about that table?

SALLY: Oh, that was nothing. It was —

LEWIS: Oh yeah? And what about that noise

SALLY *(suddenly terrified):* Lewis! Lewis, look!

LEWIS: What is it?

SALLY *(pointing to PHINEAS' shoes, peeping out from under the sheeted couch):* There's a man under there! *(Lewis just gives one big gulp, and starts for the door. SALLY grabs him.)* Lewis, don't you dare go and leave me!

LEWIS: Hang on, then.

SALLY: Lewis, let's capture him! We're two to one.

LEWIS: We haven't any weapons.

SALLY: Here's your sword. And I'll hit him with the picture. *(They stand quaking, but armed, and challenge the invisible figure.)* Come on out of there, you!

LEWIS: We g-got you c-c-covered! *(Nothing happens. The feet do not move. SALLY and LEWIS look at each other.)*

SALLY *(suddenly, in a terrified whisper):* Lewis! Maybe it's a dead man! *(LEWIS yells, drops the sword instantly, and breaks away. The sword, in falling, strikes one of the shoes, knocking it over, and SALLY calls LEWIS back.)* Lewis, it's only a pair of shoes!

LEWIS: Shoes? Whose shoes?

BOTH CHILDREN *(suddenly remembering):* Phineas ! It's Phineas ' shoes!

SALLY: Of course! Lewis, you know what?

LEWIS: What?

SALLY: I'll bet — *(she giggles)* I'll bet old Phineas was down here when we were upstairs!

LEWIS: Golly! I'll bet he was! ... Oh! and it was him under the table!

SALLY: Yes. Remember how we came down yelling about "dead men"? I'll bet old Phineas thought we were ghosts!

LEWIS: Yeah, and when Tommy hit the table with his sword ...

SALLY *(she is giggling fit to kill):* He ran! Ha, ha, ha!

186

LEWIS *(laughing):* Boy, that's it! Ha, ha! I'll bet old Phineas thought a herd of elephants were after him! Gee, we were silly to get so scared.

SALLY: Uncle Jim says there's nothing to ever be scared of!

LEWIS: I wish he was here. I'll bet he could think of places to look for the treasure. Where do they hide treasure in your Uncle Jim's books?

SALLY: Oh, in fireplaces and ...

LEWIS: We looked there.

SALLY: And in hollow panels ... Oh, we could do that!

LEWIS: What?

SALLY: Knock on the walls with something to see if any of them are hollow. Come on, we'll try it. Here's the poker, and I'll take this thing ... *(She hands LEWIS the poker and she takes a little broom used to sweep the fireplace.)*

LEWIS: How do you do it?

SALLY: You just knock ... like this *(she knocks)* ... and listen to see if it's hollow. It'll kinda echo if it's a hollow panel.

LEWIS: We ought to do it all over ... upstairs too.

SALLY: All right ... come on, we'll start upstairs, then try down here next.
(SALLY and LEWIS go up the stairs, knocking on the walls as they go. As the sound gets fainter and fainter, BILL creeps out from behind the draperies, and comes down to the table. He pulls the papers out of his shirt, and starts to look through them, but he hears someone coming. He scoops up the papers, and starts to dodge behind the chair. A voice calls softly outside the door.)

MR. JENKINS *(outside):* Phineas! Phineas, my boy — are you in there? *(BILL recognizes the voice, and suddenly decides to hide in the chair. He climbs under the sheet, and covers himself and the chair completely. MR. JENKINS enters cautiously, flashing his light about.)*

Phineas! I say, Phineas, where are you?
(He looks all about, but the only trace he finds of PHINEAS is the shoes, which he picks up and puts on the table.)

That's strange!

(He picks up the fallen portrait, and props it against the chair where BILL is hidden. Then he crosses directly to the fireplace. Just as he stoops to look for the papers there, BILL knocks over the picture with a crash. MR. JENKINS straightens up, frozen with fright. When he finally nerves himself to look around, and sees only the fallen picture, he is vastly relieved, and puts his hand over his heart, to stop its racing. Then he bends to the fireplace again. Suddenly, from upstairs, is heard a dull, rhythmic pounding. MR. JENKINS raises his head and listens, stricken dumb with fright. Then he rises silently, and with a minimum of wasted effort, makes his way toward the door. When he gets as far as BILL's chair, the pounding suddenly stops, and MR. JENKINS, holding his heart again, sinks into the chair with relief. Immediately, BILL folds his sheeted arms about him gently. MR. JENKINS looks at the arms about him, and begins to tremble. His eyes pop out, his mouth hangs open, and slowly he slides off onto the floor. Quickly picking himself up, he scurries out, squeaking like a frightened mouse. BILL follows, waving his sheet about like a ghost. Then, sure that JENKINS is gone, he takes the sheet off, and laughs to himself.)

BILL: Nice work, Bill, me jolly old ghost.
(He starts to spread the sheet back on the chair, but stops when he hears more voices coming.) Oh! Oh!
(Again he sits in the chair, and pulls the sheet over it. MR. SIMMONS appears at the door, followed somewhat shakily by PHINEAS)

SIMMONS: Fine night watchman you are! The next time I get you a job, you'll know it! Seeing ghosts! Why, Phineas, I'm ashamed of you! *(PHINEAS comes in cautiously, peering about.)* Well, now that we're here, where's the ghost?

PHINEAS *(doggedly):* They come down the stairs, and they

had clubs and things ... First they tried to bean me with the picture, and then they ganged up on me ... I hit 'em this way and that way *(he shadow boxes)* but they was too many fer me!

SIMMONS: Oh yeah? Well, there's not even a mouse in here now! How do you account for that? Now, what am I going to do with you? I promised the lawyers this place would be protected tonight.

PHINEAS: Maybe you'd like to do it, Mr. Simmons. *(Hopefully)* The bed's nice and soft!

SIMMONS: Just like your head! The idea of a grown man seeing ghosts!

PHINEAS: I didn't see 'em ... I heard 'em!

SIMMONS: Now if you had been a woman ... my wife, for instance ... I'd understand this silliness ... but a grown man!

PHINEAS: I tell you they come down the stairs ... they had clubs...

SIMMONS: Yes, and just now you said you didn't even see them. Now Phineas, you just had a nightmare, that's all. You go on back there and forget all about it. *(He waves his hand toward the sofa. PHINEAS is almost convinced. He goes over to the sofa and sits on it, looking up at MR. SIMMONS, almost persuaded.)*

PHINEAS: You think I could a' dreamed it?

SIMMONS: Of course you did!

PHINEAS *(laughing shakily):* Well — m-maybe I did.

SIMMONS: Now you just lie back down there and stop having nightmares. I've got a beat to patrol tonight, boy, I can't play nursemaid to an eighteen-year-old fraid-cat.

PHINEAS: Sure, sure, I know. I'm sorry, Simmons. Them crazy kids just got me jittery, I reckon. And then the picture dropping off the wall and —

SIMMONS: Of course! You just heard the wind. See the table's right where you left it. The sheet's on it, and everything.

PHINEAS *(grinning sheepishly):* Sure, sure.

SIMMONS: All right now. Go to sleep and forget it. So long!
(He goes out.)

PHINEAS *(waving his hand airily):* So long, Simmons ... Gosh,
I sure am ashamed of myself, I am. *(All at once, he looks
under the couch and notices his shoes are missing.)* Where's
my shoes? My shoes! Hey Simmons! Simm— *(But on his
way to the door, he finds his shoes sitting peacefully on
the table. His new confidence is decidedly shaken by his
discovery.)* I don't care what Simmons says, I ain't a-goin' to
sleep again. I'll set right down in this chair, where I can see
if any gho—*(He sits on BILL, and at once realizes something
is wrong. He lets a feeble ejaculation escape from him, but he
cannot move.)* Whoa-ho-ho—

BILL *(putting his arms about PHINEAS):* Comfortable, dearie?

PHINEAS *(galvanized):* Wahoo! Let me outta here! Simmons!
Hey, Simmons!

SIMMONS *(answering outside):* Now what?

PHINEAS *(outside):* They're back!

SIMMONS: Who's back?

PHINEAS: The ghosts! Inside!
*(SALLY and LEWIS are heard continuing their rhythmic
pounding as they come down the steps. BILL, stranded
center stage, realizes there is only one thing to do, to escape
discovery. Throwing the sheet over the chair, he springs
quickly to the window up left, throws it open, and vanishes.
The pounding grows louder — and nearer — as SIMMONS
rushes inside, with PHINEAS in his wake.)* Look! The
window! *(Mr. Simmons rushes to the window, and looks out.)*

Listen! *(Mr. Simmons whirls around from the window, and
listens intently to the pounding. PHINEAS, shaking and
trembling, slides over to the door, takes one quick look
behind him, and runs for all he's worth. MR. SIMMONS*

locks the window quickly, draws his gun, and slips behind the chair, where he can command the stairway. The knocks come closer and closer, as SALLY and LEWIS come down the steps. Finally, the pounding ceases, and they come into the room. With a shock MR. SIMMONS recognizes the ghosts.)

SALLY: It's no use, I reckon, Lewis. We've tapped all over.

LEWIS: I guess we might as well give up.
(MR. SIMMONS rises up behind the chair, and both children shriek, and cling together.)

SIMMONS: Sally! What are you and Lewis doing here?

SALLY: Gee, Mr. Simmons, you scared us!

LEWIS: Boy! I never did think I'd be so glad to see a policeman!

SIMMONS: What are you two doing in this old house? Don't you know you could be arrested for prowling around in old houses like this? How did you get in?

LEWIS: Oh, we had a key.

SIMMONS: A key? Let's see it.

SALLY: Here it is. Only we didn't have to use it, because the door was already open. *(SIMMONS looks at the can opener, and grins, spreading his feet wide apart. He looks down at SALLY, amused in spite of himself.)*

SIMMONS: Sally, you're some girl!

SALLY: Am I, Mr. Simmons?

SIMMONS: Yeah, but you be careful, or that imagination of yours will get you into trouble.

SALLY: But that is the key, isn't it? Of course the door was open, but —

SIMMONS: Yes, I left the door open — for Phineas ... This is a can opener!

LEWIS: A can opener! *(He looks at SALLY.)* And you said that guy was Mr. Penny, eh?

SALLY: Oh, Lewis, really and truly — he is!

SIMMONS: Now, Lewis, you ought to know better than to believe Sally's stories. You know she's always making up things.

SALLY: But Mr. Simmons, really and truly —

SIMMONS *(laughing):* Now, now, now! Don't go tryin' any of your stories on me! You've scared the liver out of Poor Phineas. Now I don't have any night watchman for this house. Come on, get out of here. You two got to go to bed! *(He shoos them out the door, inserts the key in the lock, then turns and flashes his light all about the place.)* Well, ghostie, if you're in here — you'll stay in! *(The key is heard turning in the lock as —*

CURTAIN

ACT THREE

SETTING: *The old coachhouse, same as Act One. There is a faint snoring at the rise of the curtain, to indicate that Bill is asleep in the manger. Outside Sally is calling.*

SALLY: Mr. Penny! Mr. Penny! *(Snoring stops.)* Mr. Penny! It's Sally! Please let me in. I have something to tell you!

BILL: Eh? What's that? Who is it? Sally?

SALLY: Yes, open the window, please, Mr. Penny. I've got something to tell you. It's important.

BILL: Sure ... sure, just a minute ... *(He hurries out of the stall, suspenders dangling about his hips, his shoes and shirt off. He is so sleepy that at first he doesn't realize he's not presentable. He hurries across the stage, then remembers as he looks at his dangling suspenders.)*

Oh! *(To SALLY)* Hey, Princess, wait just a minute, won't you? I got to perform my morning ablutions.

SALLY: You got to do what?

BILL: Got to get dressed ... Won't take but a minute, though. Can you wait?

SALLY: Oh! Yes, I'll wait but hurry, won't you?

BILL: Sure ... sure ... *(He slips on his shirt, pulls his middy tie over his head already knotted, then puts on his shoes.)* Won't take but just a minute! Almost through now! *(He knots his other shoe.)* There! Now I'm ready! *(He crosses the floor, opens the window, and just as SALLY gets up to come through, thinks of something else and closes it again quickly.)* Oh! 'Scuse me, I forgot something! Just a minute! Just a minute! *(He dances on tiptoe hurrying over to the gas plate where he has a can of water and an old plate. He pours some water out in the pan, dips in fingertips cautiously, makes a circle about both his eyes, and his mouth ... puts his fingers in and shakes them ... then dries it all on a bandana out of his pocket. Then he takes out a mirror and pocket comb from his pocket and combs the straw out of his hair.)*

SALLY: Are you hurrying, Mr. Penny?

BILL: Sure, sure! I'm almost through ... There! *(He puts mirror and comb back in his pocket, turns to the window, opens it with a great flourish.)* Good mornin' to you, Princess. You're an early riser!

SALLY: Oh, Mr. Penny, I had to come early because there's not much time! *(She climbs in over the window sill. She is still carrying the blueprint they found the night before.)* Uncle Jim and I are going away this morning.

BILL: Gee, Princess, I'm awful sorry.

SALLY: I wanted to show you this. Is this a map?

BILL: This? *(He takes the blue print, and looks at it.)*

SALLY: I thought maybe that was a map pointing to the treasure that Mr. Herman hid for you. But we looked all over the house, Mr. Penny, and we didn't find it.

BILL: Yeah. I know.

SALLY: You know?

BILL: Yeah. I — I went in too.

SALLY: Oh, did you, Mr. Penny?

BILL *(very uncomfortable):* Sally.

SALLY: Yes, Mr. Penny?

BILL: Don't call me Mr. Penny.

SALLY: But why not, Mr. Penny?

BILL: *(worried):* Sally ... you — you didn't really think I was Mr. Penny, did you?

SALLY *(horrified):* Think you were Mr. Penny?

BILL: Naw. You were just foolin' that little smarty Ellen, weren't you?

SALLY: But you said you were Mr. Penny. And you gave us the key —

BILL: Now, now, now!

SALLY *(she knows what he means):* Yes, but you — well, anyhow, when I said you were Mr. Penny, you let me think it.

BILL: Listen here, Sally. Yesterday when you kids were here, I thought you were just — well, kinda stringin' that Ellen along by makin' out I was the Mr. Penny feller. Remember, I never said I was him. Not once. I don't tell lies. But you got such a big imagination — and you seemed to like to pretend so well — that I didn't think it'd do no harm to help you put one over on the kids.

SALLY: But if you're not Mr. Penny, who are you?

BILL: Aw, Sally, I'm just an old sailor, like I said. I'm on my way to the East coast to catch a ship. I don't amount to much, but I'm not a bad feller. Looky here, Sally, I got something to show you.

SALLY: What?

BILL *(taking out the picture):* See this here picture?

SALLY: Why, it's a picture of a man and his wife and little boy and baby, isn't it?

194

BILL: That man is Mr. Penny. And that lady is his wife. And that's his little boy and girl baby.

SALLY: But Mr. Penny didn't have a girl baby did he?

BILL: Yes, Sally. I think maybe he did.

SALLY *(puzzled):* But —

BILL: Look at that lady in the picture, Sally.

SALLY: She's pretty. She has an awful sweet smile. She looks kind of like somebody I've seen somewhere.

BILL: I reckon she does. She's the very spittin' image of you!

SALLY: Me?

BILL: Here, hold this. *(He hands her his pocket mirror.)* Now look, when I pile your hair up on your head like this — see?

SALLY: I do look like her!

BILL: Sure you do. And Sally, I got a big imagination too, and — you know what I think?

SALLY: What?

BILL: I think the baby in this picture is you!

SALLY: Me?

BILL: Um hum.

SALLY: You mean — I'm Mr. Penny's little girl, and the lady is —

BILL: I think so.

SALLY: Oh, that would be wonderful!

BILL: And I'll tell you something else. Listen. That brother-in-law of Mr. Penny's — this Jenkins guy — he thinks you're the little Penny girl too. And he is afraid all this property would go to you instead of him. So last night, he fixed it all up with Phineas to burn any possible proof that this baby was ever born.

SALLY: Why, the meany!

BILL: But I went up to the big house last night to try to get those papers before he did.

SALLY: Did you find them?

BILL: I got all the papers there were, Sally — but no proofs. And with out proofs — we can't do a thing.

SALLY: Oh!

BILL: I'm awful sorry, honey.

SALLY *(trying not to show her disappointment):* Oh, that's all right. Thank you for trying, Mr. — Mr. —

BILL: Just call me Bill, Sally.

SALLY: Mr. Bill.

BILL: Even if you're not the little Penny girl, you're my idea of one swell girl!

SALLY *(through her tears):* Thank you, Mr. Bill.

BILL *(to keep from crying himself):* Sally girl, I gotta be goin'. First thing you know, they'll lockin' me up for trespassin', and if I don't get that train outta here this afternoon, I'll miss my boat. *(While he is talking, he is putting things back where he found them — shoving the table back, covering up the gas plate, getting his bundle out of the manger. SALLY watches him dolefully.)*

SALLY: I wish you were going to stay here, Mr. Bill.

BILL: Me, with my disposition? Don't try to fool me. Well ... *(He looks about him.)* I guess things are just like I found 'em so I better be sayin' good bye. It sure was nice knowin' you, Sally. *(He stands there a little awkwardly, his whole heart aching for her disappointment.)*

SALLY: Yes, it's been nice knowing you too, Mr. Pen — Mr. Bill.

BILL: Gosh, honey, I wish I had some money. Do you have to go to that — er — boarding house?

SALLY: I'm afraid so, Mr. Bill. They're coming for Uncle Jim and me this morning.

BILL: Gosh! *(He gets out his handkerchief and blows his nose*

196

lustily. Then realizing there is nothing more he can do for her, he squares his shoulders and starts for the window.) Well, good bye, honey. Keep your chin up.

SALLY: Good bye, Mr. Bill. *(BILL swings his foot over the window ledge, but he stops and looks back. The pause is fatal. SALLY flings herself at him, sobbing wildly.)* Oh, Mr. Bill, don't go! Don't go!

BILL *(holding her close):* Now, now, Sally girl.

SALLY: It's not a boarding house, Mr. Bill. It's an orphan asylum. And I'm so scared Uncle Jim won't get well.

BILL: Aw now, honey ... Gosh! Look what you got me doing.

SALLY: What?

BILL: Bawlin' like a big overgrown calf after his mammy, that's what!

SALLY: You mean crying? I guess maybe it was my fault. I guess I just sort of hated to see you go, I guess.

BILL: Sure, that's what's the matter with me too, I guess. Here. Blow. *(He holds his handkerchief to her nose. SALLY blows her nose hard.)* Now. The storm's all over, isn't it? *(SALLY nods.)* All right, let's see the sunshine come out. *(SALLY smiles.)* There now, that's more like it. That's fine! *(SALLY steps back, and as she does so, she reaches for her offending shoe.)*

SALLY: *(taking the shoe off):* Oh!

BILL: What's the matter now?

SALLY: My other shoe's got a hole in it now, and I haven't any paper to put in it.

BILL: Say, I can fix shoes!

SALLY: Doesn't it cost a lot of money?

BILL: Doesn't cost a cent. Here, give 'em to me. I can make some soles to fit inside 'em, out of tree bark.

SALLY *(taking them off and handing them to him):* But have you got time?

BILL: Sure, and I'll take time, by golly. I wish my knife was sharper.

SALLY: There's a grind stone out there, around the corner of the coachhouse.

BILL: Is there now? Well, whaddya know? Here, hold my bag, and I'll just find me some soft tree bark, and —
(He is out of the window, and SALLY climbs up after him.)

SALLY *(calling after him):* There's an old mallet there, too, you can use for a hammer. I'll show you.

BILL *(from outside):* No, you just stay there, lassie. You'll catch cold without your shoes. I'll find it.

SALLY: It's around the corner, by the rain barrel.
(SALLY sits in the window ledge, cheerfully humming a tune. All at once, she stiffens in alarm, as she sees the enemy approaching. She tries to warn Bill.)

Mr. Bill! Mr. Bill! *(But BILL is out of sight, and out of earshot. SALLY wrings her hands helplessly.)*

MR. JENKINS *(at a distance):* I see you! I see you, you little scamp! *(SALLY leaps inside the room, and bars the window. She stands there uncertainly for a moment, then notices Bill's bandana in her hand, and shoves it down her dress. It bulges out ludicrously, and she tries to pat it down, but failing to conceal it, she sits up close to the table, so it will not show. She shuts her eyes tightly and prays)* Please don't let him find Mr. Bill! Please don't let him find Mr. Bill!
(Meanwhile, MR. JENKINS has reached the door of the coachhouse. He speaks to the policeman outside.)

I saw one of those children climb in here, officer. It's trespassing, that's what it is! Tres—
(The door suddenly falls down, and MR. JENKINS with it.)

SIMMONS *(helping him up):* Don't be in such a hurry, Jenkins.

MR. JENKINS: Confound that door! There! *(He points to SALLY dramatically.)* There she is!

SIMMONS: Yes, I see her. Well, Sally, I seem to find you in all sorts of unexpected places, lately.

MR. JENKINS: Well, ask her where that tramp is.

SIMMONS: Where is he, Sally?

SALLY: Where is who?

MR. JENKINS: You know who we mean!

SIMMONS: Ellen told us about him, Sally. That fellow who went around here yesterday calling himself Mr. Penny. Has he gone?

SALLY: Oh! Yes, he — he's not here any more.

MR. JENKINS: I don't believe her. He's hiding in there! *(He crosses swiftly to the harness room, and throws open the door.)* Come out of there, you! *(Nothing happens.)* He isn't there ... I know! The manager! That's where I heard that noise yesterday when — *(He darts over to the manger, and grabs up the hay.)* I've found you! I've got you! I've — he's not there!

SALLY: I told you he wasn't here.

MR. JENKINS *(pointing to SALLY):* She knows where he is! Arrest her!

SIMMONS: Now, Jenkins, keep your shirt on. Sally, this property belongs to Mr. Jenkins here now, and you'll have to stay out of it, understand?

SALLY: Y-yes sir.

SIMMONS: All right now, Sally. Come on and clear out.

MR. JENKINS: She ought to be arrested, and put under lock and key.

SIMMONS: Never mind, Jenkins. You won't have to worry about SALLY any more. She's going away today. Come on, Sally.

MR. JENKINS: I'll board this place up. That's what I'll do.

SIMMONS *(as SALLY sits still):* Sally, didn't you hear me? I said come on.

SALLY: I — I can't.

SIMMONS: You can't? Why not?

SALLY: I — I haven't got any shoes on.

SIMMONS: Where are they?

SALLY: They — they got mud on 'em, and Phineas took 'em off to clean 'em. *(Mr. Simmons stares at her in amazement. Outside, BILL begins to hammer. The two men look at each other, and JENKINS rushes toward the harness room.)*

MR. JENKINS: He's in here. *(But he looks in and sees nothing. To SIMMONS):* Didn't you hear that, too? *(SALLY is kicking the table.)*

SALLY: You mean this? Like I was swinging my feet?

MR. JENKINS *(annoyed):* Oh! Then don't do it!

SIMMONS: How long is Phineas going to be, Sally?

SALLY: Oh, he'll be back in a minute. You don't have to wait, Mr. Simmons, I'll leave here just as soon as I get my shoes.

SIMMONS *(suddenly suspicious of SALLY):* I think maybe I'd better wait. *(BILL starts working the grindstone industriously outside, and the noise penetrates the room. The men are alert, and instantly SALLY begins a buzzing noise with her teeth.)*

SALLY: Bzzz! I'm a bee! Bzzz! Bzzz! *(The men say nothing, but look at each other understandingly, and rush into the harness room together. SALLY springs up and runs to the window, calling softly.)* Mr. Bill! Mr. Bill! *(The two men rush out, and she jumps away from the window, guiltily.)*

MR. JENKINS: That tramp's still around here, and she knows where he is!

SIMMONS: Sally, you mustn't protect this tramp. If you know where he is, say so.

MR. JENKINS: What's that inside her dress? What's that inside her —

SIMMONS *(disgustedly):* The tramp, no doubt! Sally, honey,

what's this all about? What have you there?

SALLY: It's — it's just some old things we — we —
(At this moment, BILL lets out a wild war whoop, and comes bounding through the window, everything else temporarily forgotten. MR. JENKINS grabs him by the collar, but BILL doesn't even see him. He shakes him off as he would a flea, and JENKINS staggers back, protesting.)

BILL: Sally! Sally honey! I've found a real treasure! Look what I found in your shoes!

SALLY: Oh, Mr. Bill, why didn't you stay hidden?

BILL: Look, Sally, you're rich!

MR. JENKINS: It's the tramp, and he's gone crazy. *(To SIMMONS)* Do something quick!

SIMMONS *(collaring BILL):* Come on, you. We've been looking for you.

BILL: Hey, hold on a minute. Listen, Officer, that feller's a crook!

MR. JENKINS: Why, you—you—how dare you call me names, you—

BILL: Because I got the goods on you, that's why.

MR. JENKINS: Officer, lock him up. He's a tramp, and a dangerous character.

SIMMONS: Yeah? *(To BILL)* And what's your side of the story?

BILL: Listen, Officer. Yesterday I came in here to rest a bit before I continued my journey, and —

MR. JENKINS: See, he admits it. He's been trespassing on my property. Why do you stand there —

SIMMONS: Just a minute, Jenkins. *(To BILL)* Go on.

BILL: Well, this feller came in here with a guy named Phineas, and Phineas had this here picture. It's a picture of Mr. Penny and his wife and little boy — and baby.

SIMMONS: Baby? I didn't know he had a baby.

BILL: Neither did anybody else, it seems like. But there it is.

SIMMONS: But then, in that case —

MR. JENKINS *(indignantly):* He didn't have a baby! That picture is a forgery! Officer, would you take the word of a tramp against mine?

BILL: You don't have to take my word. Those papers there prove it, in black and white!

MR. JENKINS: Those papers? You stole them out of the house, you rascal! *(He makes a lunge toward SALLY, to seize the papers, but MR. SIMMONS intercepts and takes the papers himself.)*

SIMMONS: Now hold on here, Jenkins. These papers came out of the big house, you say?

BILL: Yes, they did! This here's the footprints and birth notice of a baby girl born the time of Sally here, and read this!

SIMMONS *(looking at it):* It's a letter written by — written by Mr. Herman, Penny's old servant that just died.

BILL: And this Jenkins offered Phineas five dollars to let him into the house last night, so that he could burn those papers. Because they prove that Sally there is heir to the whole Penny estate!

MR. JENKINS: That's not true! I'm the heir to this estate. He's made this all up. Give me those papers! *(He grabs the papers out of MR. SIMMONS' hand, and tears them. BILL makes a dive for him, brings him to the ground, wrenches the papers away and gives them to MR. SIMMONS. Then he sits on MR. JENKINS.)*

BILL: Here now, read it.

MR. JENKINS: Get off of me! You're killing me!

BILL: Well, I ain't yet, but if you don't keep still —
(He swings his fist. MR. JENKINS subsides, and MR. SIMMONS sits at the table and reads the letter, with SALLY at his side.)

SIMMONS *(reading):* "To whom it may concern: Feeling at last that my master will never return home, and afraid this heart attack will be my last ... " He was having a heart attack when he wrote this letter! He died of a heart attack!

BILL: Go on.

SIMMONS *(reading):* " ... will be my last, I am writing this letter to tell the real story of this tragic household." *(SIMMONS reads slowly, and with many significant pauses, as if this revelation were too much for him to digest in a hurry.)* "This picture, taken after the birth of the baby girl, shows the baby of whom I alone know the fate. Her name is Nancy Bell Penny, and she has been raised by a neighbor, Jim Andrews, and is now called Sally Andrews" ... Sally!

BILL: Sure. Sure, I told you! This Herman feller put her on Mr. Andrews' doorstep when Mr. Penny left, because her mother was dead, and he didn't know what to do with her. It tells it there in the letter. And that other thing is her birth certificate and everything to prove it.

MR. JENKINS: It's not so! It's a frame-up! Let me up from here!

SIMMONS *(eyeing MR. JENKINS coldly):* If it's not so, then why did you try to destroy these papers?

MR. JENKINS: It's a frame-up, I tell you! Let me up, you ruffian! You're stuffing the breath out of me! You're going to kill me!

BILL *(spitting on his fist significantly):* That's not a bad idea!

SIMMONS: Sally, the little Penny girl! I can't get over it! It — it's fantastic!

SALLY: Mr. Simmons, does it mean that — that I own the house and property?

SIMMONS: Well, I just guess you do, honey! Why, Sally — er —Nancy, maybe I should say — you're rich! Do you realize that? Rich!

SALLY: And then I won't have to go to the orphan asylum?

SIMMONS *(laughing):* Orphan asylum? I should say not! Why, you can build one, if you like.

SALLY: But will Uncle Jim have to go away?

SIMMONS: You just bet he won't! We'll go tell him about it right away. You can have doctors and nurses, and get him well in no time!

SALLY: Oh, Mr. Bill!
(She throws herself down on BILL's lap, sobbing in her happiness. MR. JENKINS gives a grunt, and cries out at the extra weight.)

MR. JENKINS *(panting):* Officer, you get me up from here before they kill me. I demand my rights!

SIMMONS *(squinting down at him significantly):* Oh, yes, your rights! Well, you let him up, Bill — and give him his rights!

BILL *(understanding):* Sure, if you say so, Officer. Jump up, honey. I gotta give him his rights. *(As JENKINS rises to his feet, BILL plants a good solid kick in his pants. MR. JENKINS squeals.)*

SIMMONS: Now, that's your first right. And when I get you down at the police station, and tell the Chief about you, you crooked swindler, you're going to get some more rights that belong to you. Come along now, march outta here.
(He takes him out by the collar, MR. JENKINS protesting feebly all the while. SALLY throws herself into Bill's arms.)

SALLY: Mr. Bill! Oh, Mr. Bill!

BILL: Shhh! *(He pushes her away gently, then putting his finger to his lips for silence, tip-toes over to the door, and looks anxiously after the departing men.)*

SALLY *(whispering):* What is it?

BILL *(whispering back):* They forgot to arrest me!

SALLY: Oh!

BILL *(wiping his forehead with relief, and sitting weakly at the table):* They forgot me! Whew! I just have to make that boat this week.

SALLY *(sitting on his knee):* But Mr. Bill, you don't now.

BILL: No?

SALLY: Of course not! I'm rich now and I got all this big house and everything, and you can stay with uncle Jim and me!

BILL: And what 'ud I be doin' t' pass the time away?

SALLY: Oh! *(thinking)* Well, you could fix my shoes!

BILL: No, Sally girl, it wouldn't work! I gotta get back t' a ship! I been sailin' too long t' sprout land legs at my age! *(Gets up and gets his bandana.)*

SALLY: But you will come back, won't you?

BILL: Well, I tell you, Princess, I never like t' make promises like that! A seaman's life is kinda at the mercy of a ship, you know, an'...

SALLY: Oh, but you got to come back!

BILL: Well, sir, I tell you what! Remember that story about Cinderella and how the prince got back t' Cinderella?

SALLY: Of course; he kept her slipper and ... Oh! *(She grabs up her shoes off the table where BILL laid them and shoves them in his hand.)* Take both of them, Mr. Bill, and then you'll be sure to come back!

BILL: You bet I will! I reckon I can't fail now! *(Sticks them in his pocket.)* It's all set then! I'll come back soon as my ship gets in ... long about next Christmas time, I reckon. *(Moves toward door.)*

SALLY: That will be wonderful! I'll hang up a stocking for you!

BILL: All right now ... Don't say goodbye then ... cause goodbye means forever!

SALLY: What'll I say, then, Mr. Bill?

BILL: They's a French name fer saying goodbye fer just a short time. You say "Over the river," see? *(Stoops and kisses her on the cheek. She hugs him tightly.)* Well, "Over the river." *(With a wave of his hand, he's gone out the door. SALLY runs to the door and stands there waving.)*

SALLY: Over the river, Mr. Bill ... Over the river 'til next Christmas!

CURTAIN

RUMPELSTILTSKIN

dramatized by
Charlotte Chorpenning

From 1913–1915, Charlotte Barrows Chorpenning studied play writing with Professor George Pierce Baker and participated in his noted Workshop 47 at Radcliffe College in Cambridge, Massachusetts. During this period Chorpenning actively pursued a career in the professional theatre as a playwright for adult audiences. One of her plays, *The Sheepman* (which included in the cast a then unknown Spencer Tracey) received a professional production. But this play closed "out-of-town" after receiving harsh critical reviews; and Chorpenning's interest in a career in the adult theatre apparently waned considerably with that experience.

Chorpenning subsequently returned to Minnesota to teach and work with her first love, community drama; and, after establishing a national reputation in that field, she moved to Chicago and became an important part of the progressive social work movement blossoming in the playgrounds of the city. A later appointment to the faculty at Northwestern University caused Chorpenning to share an office with Winifred Ward, who, in turn, introduced Chorpenning to children's theatre. After writing a few successful children's plays for Ward's Children's Theatre of Evanston, Chorpenning accepted a position as director of children's theatre at the Goodman Theatre in Chicago, then a highly-regarded professional theatre training school affiliated with the Chicago Art Institute. Chorpenning worked at the Goodman from 1932 until 1952, and during this period she wrote more than fifty plays for children, at least thirty of which were published. Through her writing, her play writing classes, and her national advocacy for "good" children's plays, Chorpenning became the most influential and prolific children's playwright of the period.

All but a handful of Chorpenning's plays are dramatizations of well-known fairy or folktales. This speaks to the then common perception of the nature of children's theatre, as well as Chorpenning's need to produce familiar titles at the Goodman to help with ticket sales.

Rumpelstiltskin reflects both the craft and style taught by Baker, and the context within which the play was first produced at the Goodman Theatre. Chorpenning wrote her plays with the knowledge that they would receive full productions within the Goodman production season. This translated into large, skilled (conservatory student) casts, elaborate costumes, and sometimes complex scenic requirements—characteristics which all suit the fairytale genre and the story of *Rumpelstiltskin* well.

The play includes three acts, typical of the well-made play form. In the first act Chorpenning clearly sets out the dramatic question: will Rumpelstiltskin succeed in bargaining with a queen to secure her baby, so that he might ultimately "rule the hearts of men"? The second act offers a series of complications that raise suspense, as the daughter is first pressured by the King to spin more gold and then by Rumpelstiltskin to strike increasingly difficult bargains to escape the King's wrath. The third act offers the crisis scene of the action, wherein the suspense rises as Rumpelstiltskin almost succeeds in winning the child, only to be defeated by the daughter. Chorpenning then, after answering the dramatic question posed at the end of act one, quickly ends the play with a tableau of the Queen holding her infant son, while Rumpelstiltskin flies into a rage and disintegrates in a wild tantrum.

The play requires significant exposition to explain the two worlds of the play, to reveal the various agendas of the many characters, and to develop the major throughline. Chorpenning uses the complications between pairs of characters, such as Rumpelstiltskin and Mother Hulda, King and Son, and Miller and Wife, to flesh out necessary expository details, as well as to embellish the major dramatic action. Liberal doses of humorous business mute the seriousness of the overall action. Notably, Chorpenning takes the threatening edge off of Rumpelstiltskin, the antagonist/villain, by exaggerating his tantrums and vanity, causing the audience to laugh at him more than fear him.

Chorpenning's plays were produced widely during this period, and playwrights also imitated her subject matter and style. Yet, Chorpenning's training and experience as a playwright, coupled with her penchant for wordy, expository dramas, presented many producers and imitators significantly different production challenges than the ubiquitous fairy plays of the Junior League and other groups. The tasks of creating the necessary scenic magic, of delivering long speeches of exposition in a believable manner, and of bringing life to relatively complex characters with alternately comic and tragic traits, often fell beyond the abilities of the amateur groups who presented these plays. As a result, although Chorpenning set the mid-century standard for children's plays in tone, style, and subject matter, it is likely that few places beyond the Goodman Theatre fully realized her vision of theatre for young audiences.

While seldom produced today, Chorpenning's plays brought a seriousness of purpose and a theatrical sophistication to the field that was rare at that time. Beyond the rather self conscious style of *Rumpelstiltskin* and the stilted dialogue, the play offers the opportunity for creating an entertaining theatre event very much in the style of mid–century children's theatre production.

Charlotte Barrows Chorpenning (1872–1955) first worked as a high school teacher in Columbus, OH. She then taught at Wolfe Hall in Denver, CO (1901–1904) and Winona (Minnesota) Normal School (1904–1921). In 1913 she took a leave from her teaching to study play writing with George Pierce Baker.

Beginning in 1921, Chorpenning worked at the Recreation Training School in Chicago, which led to a position in the School of Speech at Northwestern University in 1927. At that time Chorpenning began writing plays for children, and she then served as director of children's theatre at the Goodman Theatre in Chicago from 1932 until her retirement in 1952. Chorpenning wrote over fifty plays for children. The most popular of these include *Rumpelstiltskin*, *The Emperor's New Clothes*, *Jack and the Beanstalk*, and *The Sleeping Beauty*.

RUMPLESTILTSKIN

dramatized by
Charlotte Chorpenning

212

RUMPLESTILTSKIN

Characters (in the order of their appearance)

RUMPELSTILTSKIN

MOTHER HULDA

MILLER'S DAUGHTER

MILLER'S WIFE

MILLER

GOTHOL

INGERT

KING

KING'S SON

KAREN

NURSE

TWO LADIES IN WAITING

PAGES

Setting

ACT ONE:
Scene 1.   At the Edge of the World.
Scene 2.   In the Queen's garden.

ACT TWO:
The Queen's spinning-room, the next morning.

ACT THREE:
Same as Act One, a year later.

THE SCENE

The settings for this play may be very simple, or they may be elaborated to varying degrees.

It may be given on small stages by closing the curtain between the scenes on the hill and those in the garden in Acts One and Three. This cuts out Rumpel's looking down at the scenes in the garden, which is interesting but not essential. In this case, the curtains begin to close on Rumpelstilskin's "Boil scarlet and gold, etc." The dialogue goes on behind the curtains while the pot is swiftly removed and the Miller's Daughter enters.
They open almost instantly to show her standing looking around in wonder. She speaks as soon as she can be seen by the whole audience, identifying the scene as the garden by her line.—"How sweet the air is in the King's garden—", and the scene continues without break. In the same way, at the end of the garden scene, the curtains close on the Miller and his Wife strutting off, and Rumpelstilskin's "Ho, ho, ho!" is heard behind them, continuing after the curtains open again. The changes in the third act are handled in the same fashion.

If drapes are used, these entrances are taken care of simply by openings through which the actors enter, letting them fall together again behind them. If flats are preferred, the decoration must be of such that the same ones can serve as background for both the hill and the garden, and the entrances are through wings, as it makes too long a wait to unlash and lash flats. Continuity is more important than elaboration of the set.

If equipment permits dimming and bringing up the lights as the curtains close and open, it will add to the effect, but it is not necessary. No lighting which delays the opening of the curtain is worth while, but if a change in tone on the two sets can be achieved without any delay, it adds to the charm.

If it is desired to go further in indicating the settings, cutouts of bushes, rocks and so on can be added to the hill, and bits of wall and flowers can be painted on the background set and concealed by the cutouts when the scene is the hill; or a throne, or other cutouts can be brought in, during the change. This should only be done when there can be a large enough crew to make the changes with great speed, however. There should be almost one 'worker to each movable piece, and careful "traffic routing" so there is no interference of movements.

If the stage is large enough to show the garden and the hill at once, as was done at the initial production at the Goodman Theatre in Chicago, the hill is on a platform at the back of the stage, as high above the garden as the proscenium permits. There are steps leading up to it on either side, and some sort of background, either sky or foliage or rocks, etc. Again, the pot is the only essential. Mother Hulda can come up the steps, or from the back. The garden is separated from it by a wall which is high enough to conceal the construction of the hill. This hill may be regular platforms, or boxes, or even, as has been done once at least successfully, large tables set together and blocked so they can't slip. A gauze between the hill and the garden is effective but not necessary. The decoration of both scenes, in this case, can be made as complete as desired, since it involves no loss of time between the scenes. It is very effective, but again, not necessary, to have the lights dim out on the hill and up on the garden etc. as the scene changes location.

In Act Two, the only essentials are Rumpelstilskin's little door, an entrance to the palace, and the doors to the three rooms to be filled with straw. If the play is done in drapes, these doors can be merely openings in the drapes which are held back to show the straw and the gold. This will mean that the straw is put in by one while the other holds the drapes, and that two people hold back the drapes when the King discovers the gold, but this will require little if any change in the lines.

The change from straw into gold is accomplished by fastening to some support set back of the drapes a piece of cloth to which enough straw has been glued to give the impression that it goes on back. It can be so slanted on the down stage side that the Miller and his Wife can throw their straw up and beyond it, pushing and prodding as if the room would barely hold this last armful. While the drapes are closed, the first cloth can be changed for one in which the straw has been well sprayed with gold radiator paint. If a strong amber light is thrown on it from above or from the two sides between the straw and the drapes, the effect will be heightened, but this is not necessary.

If the play is done in flats, the three doors can of course be built into the flats. It is effective to have each door a little larger than the last. The little door can be so painted into the set as not to show until it is opened. The door to the palace can be as simple or as ornate as the designer wishes, to match the tone of the other acts.

The lighting can be perfectly simple. The play offers opportunity for very interesting lighting effects, but none are essential. Even Rumpelstilskin's magic over the wheel when it spins is effective with merely his dancing, or if the actor does not dance, with his motions. The wheel may be made to turn either by electric connection, or by an invisible cord, worked by hand by some one oft stage.

COSTUMES

Costumes may be of any period or nationality which removes them from the modern. The folk-tale from which the play is made is German, but there are variants in many countries. The English variant is Tom Tit Tot, and any early English costumes are suitable. For that matter purely original costumes, controlled by nothing but the designer's imagination, are perfectly in order.

PROPERTIES

RUMPELSTILTSKIN'S POT: This should be large enough to be impressive from a distance. If a large pot is not available, it can be a cutout, of wall board or corrugated pasteboard. Lights behind it, to shine up on Rumpelstilskin when he leans over it, and to change color according to his spells, add to the effect.

216

BAG OF FLOUR: This gift which the Miller brings should be not too large a bag, of some fantastic color or decoration.

TWO PIES: The Miller's Wife brings pies of size large enough to seem large from the front.

THREE SPINDLES: Wound with threads of different colors— one blue, one green, one vivid pink. These also should be larger than actual size. String, colored, serves for thread.

GIFTS FOR EXCHANGE: Chain of metal and jewels for the King's Son. Chain of flowers for the Miller's Daughter. Ring of gold and jewels for the King's Son. Ring of plaited grass for the Miller's Daughter.

STRAW: For the Pages to bring, and for the Miller and his Wife to thrust through the three doors.

SPINNING WHEEL: This may be a genuine spinning wheel, if one is available, or a fantastic one may be made, all that is needed being a frame of the general shape of a spinning wheel and a cutout wheel of wall board, or pasteboard, or some old wheel covered and painted. The important thing is that it can be made to whirl apparently without human hands.

TRAY OF FLOWERS: For the Page to bring to the Miller's Daughter, including three noticeable ones which Rumpel afterward asks for.

THE SHADOW OF THE TREE ON THE GRASS: If there is no window, as will be the case if the play is done in drapes, something, such as an hour glass, large enough so that the audience can see the sand running, or at least see the top which shows the sand getting lower and lower is used. This top can be made of a large glass bowl, and the sand can be a colored powder, so it shows from a distance. The amount needed is easily timed, during rehearsal. The lower part of the hourglass can be glass, or opaque as desired In case there is a window, and it is desired to have the shadow's movement show, for suspense, it can be thrown on a wall through the window. If left to the imagination, all that is needed is to have the actor go to the window to report on it.

SWORDS FOR THE KING'S SON AND THE PAGES: If these actors do not know fencing and there is no one to teach them, a physical conflict can be substituted.

CRADLE: The cradle should be decorated, and regal. If it is desired to have Rumpelstilskin stamp through it, in his final rage, the bottom can be made of paper.

FLOWERS FOR THE KING'S SON: In Act I, probably on the bench where he can pick them up.

BABY FOR RUMPELSTILTSKIN TO LIFT FROM THE CRADLE: This may be a large doll, or merely a bundle, wrapped in fine garments. If the doll is used, care must be taken to keep it well covered, so its immobility will not spoil the illusion.

FRAGMENTS OF RUMPELSTILTSKIN: To be thrown into the air after Rumpelstilskin leaps off the edge of the world. If it is possible to have a trap, and have him stamp himself into the ground and out of sight, instead of flying to pieces, his end will be nearer the story. In that case the opening to the trap must be hidden during the earlier scene, he can work down steps, shouting and waving his hands as he goes. The trap should be closed from below after he disappears and whatever hides the opening—e.g., a piece of furniture—should be moved by the Queen, looking for him and showing no opening. In that case the lines about flying to pieces should be replaced by line about stamping himself into the ground.

THE MUSIC

The author intends Rumpelstiltskin's little rhymes, and the lovely, poetic words of the Miller's Daughter, to be chanted rhymically and tunefully, arising from the actor's own imagination. There should be no actual form or melody to the songs of either character. They are called "songs" in the script, because they have lilt and rhythm, and they are the voices of two souls.

The dance between the Prince and the Miller's Daughter should be a stately court dance, such as a minuet, or pavanne, for which appropriate music is usually provided by phonograph, offstage.

This play was given its premiere production at the Goodman Memorial Theatre, of Chicago, under the direction of the author, Charlotte B. Chorpenning.

ACT ONE

SCENE: *On the Edge of the World.*

At the back, for some width — (enough for Rupel's dancing) — is a level considerably higher than the forestage. Rumpel is circling his pot and chanting.

RUMPLE *(Dancing around pot)*:

> **Today I brew, tomorrow I bake.**
> **I stamp my foot, and the world doth shake.**
> **And no one knows from whence I came,**
> **Or that Rumpelstilskin is my name.**
> **Oh, show me east, and show me west.**
> **Till I find the child that suits me best.**
> **Show me north and show me south —**

(During this, a woman's tall figure comes up over the edge of the world; she watches him. Her eyes twinkle, and she laughs silently, but at this point, she shakes her head, and taps him on the shoulder sharply. He stops chanting, and backs away from her. He is afraid of her.)

MOTHER HULDA: Rumpeelstiltskin —

RUMPEL: Eh-h?

MOTHER HULDA: What are you doing:

RUMPEL: I am boiling my pot.

MOTHER HULDA: What are you doing that for?

RUMPEL: It is showing me this place and that in the world.

MOTHER HULDA: Now, now, now! Why do you want to see this place and that?

RUMPEL: I am looking for something to put in my pot.

MOTHER HULDA: Something new?

RUMPEL: Yes.

MOTHER HULDA: Something different?

RUMPEL: Yes.

220

MOTHER HULDA: What?

RUMPEL: Something.

MOTHER HULDA: What? ... Stand still. Look at me. Straight into my eyes. What do you want to put in your pot?

RUMPEL: A baby. A King's baby.

MOTHER HULDA: A King's baby!

RUMPEL: Then, you see, when I boil my pot, I can rule the thoughts of men.

MOTHER HULDA: Why do you want to rule the thoughts of men?

RUMPEL: I want to make an end of them: I want the whole world to myself.

MOTHER HULDA: You told me that before.

RUMPEL: I know it.

MOTHER HULDA: Haven't I given you every power you asked for?

RUMPEL: Yes.

MOTHER HULDA: Why don't you use them?

RUMPEL: When I stamp my foot, the earth shakes, and hurls all men's work to the ground. But they only build it up again.

MOTHER HULDA: That isn't the only thing I let you do.

RUMPEL: When I blow my breath, and my pot sends hot winds to burn men's crops in the field, or cold ones to freeze them in the ground, or floods to wash them away, they only plant the field again: There's something I've found out.

MOTHER HULDA: What?

RUMPEL: You can never make an end of men by sending them trouble. They only learn things from it.

MOTHER HULDA: I knew that all the time. That is why I let you try it.

RUMPEL: But if I can rule their thoughts, I can fill them as full of greed as a night is full of dark when there are no stars. Then they will make an end of each other.

MOTHER HULDA: For once you've found out something important.

RUMPEL: A King's child. A little King's son! *(He runs to the pot and flings something into it. It flames up.)* Today I brew —

MOTHER HULDA: Now, now!

RUMPEL (continuing): ... Tomorrow I bake —

MOTHER HULDA: I didn't say you could.

RUMPEL *(continuing)*: Show me a King's son I can take —

MOTHER HULDA *(following him and giving him a spank)*: Stop it!

RUMPEL: For nobody knows from whence I came — *(MOTHER HULDA snatches him away from the pot by the seat of his trousers.)*

MOTHER HULDA: Rumpelstiltskin! You bad little thing! I didn't say you could put a King's son in your pot.

RUMPEL: I wasn't. I was only making it show me palaces and King's gardens, where a queen might be walking with her baby.

MOTHER HULDA: However would you get the baby if the pot did show one?

RUMPEL: That's easy: I have only to go three times around my pot backward, and my little door will open onto any place in the world I tell it to. When it is dark, and the world is asleep, I can go through my door and steal the baby away.

MOTHER HULDA: Nothing of the sort! If you want your pot to make men greedy, you must bargain for the baby.

RUMPEL: Bargain? Queens don't bargain their babies away.

MOTHER HULDA: You must get a queen to give you her child in exchange for gold.

RUMPEL: No mother in the world would do that.

MOTHER HULDA: Then you can never make men quite greedy enough to make an end of each other.

RUMPEL: There might be one. Or maybe I can trick one into it: I'll keep looking. May I keep looking?

MOTHER HULDA: Oh, yes. You may look. *(RUMPEL skips to his pot, and flings something in.)*

RUMPEL:

> **Today I brew, tomorrow I bake,**
> **I search the earth for a child to take.**
> **And nobody knows from whence I came,**
> **Or that Rumpelstiltskin is my name.**
> **Boil scarlet and gold, and show me a hall**
> **Where queens and princes dance at a ball.**
> **Boil —**

MOTHER HULDA: You'll never see a baby at a ball.

RUMPEL: That's so. I'll change.

> **Boil green, and show me a garden fair,**
> **Where a queen walks soft in fragrant air —**

(The lights, green at first, then sunny daylight, come up on the garden below. The Miller's Daughter is discovered. She has just slipped through the gate, and stands drinking the fragrant air, her hand lifted in wonder. She is in brilliant peasant holiday dress.)

That's not a queen.

MOTHER HULDA: Sh-h-h! The pot knows.

DAUGHTER: How sweet the air is in a King's garden: But the sun has no more gold than at my father's mill.

RUMPEL: It's just a Miller's daughter.

MOTHER HULDA: Wait a while:

(Rumpel settles dozen to listen. The Miller's Wife, who has peered in at the gate from the beginning of the Daughter's speech, thrusts her head farther in.)

WIFE: What are you doing, Daughter.

DAUGHTER: I just tried to see through the gate, and it came open, so I came in.

MILLER *(following his WIFE in)* : You will get us all killed.

DAUGHTER: I can't help going in when a gate opens. Something seems to call to me — "Find out!" ... It's wonderful here.

WIFE: No one is allowed to enter the King's garden unless a servant opens the gate.

DAUGHTER: But there wasn't any servant.

WIFE: You'd better knock now.

MILLER: I'll knock very loud.

WIFE: No, don't go way back to the gate. Knock here at the palace.

MILLER *(knocks timidly at palace)*: Do you hear anybody?

WIFE: Not yet.

MILLER and WIFE *(going out the gate, to Daughter)*: Come out! Come back!

DAUGHTER: It's silly to pretend I'm out when I'm in.

WIFE *(entering to pull at her)*: What will happen to us?

DAUGHTER: Don't cry.
(The MILLER comes in a step, too, to hustle them both out. The gate is closed tightly from outside. Ingert, a courtier, enters and crosses to the gate. He throws the gate open. The MILLER and his WIFE and DAUGHTER enter.)

INGERT: Who are you who come knocking so loudly on the gate of the King's garden?

MILLER: I am the Miller who grinds the King's grain. I have brought a gift of fine new flour to the King. You can't find flour like it anywhere.

WIFE: And I am the Miller's wife. I have brought a gift of fine pies made from our flour. You will never taste such pies in the world.

INGERT: And who is this pretty maid.

DAUGHTER: I am the Miller's daughter, sir.

INGERT: What have you brought?

DAUGHTER: Nothing. I have nothing good enough.

WIFE: I bade you bring a spindle of your fine spinning.

DAUGHTER: It is not perfect enough for a King.

WIFE: It is better than the work of any maiden in this valley.

MILLER *(to Ingert)*: There is no one who can spin as our daughter can.

WIFE: She is the cleverest lass. You can't think!

DAUGHTER *(ashamed)*: I'm not really clever, sir. My parents only think I am.

INGERT: But can you spin at all.

DAUGHTER: Of course, sir. All the girls are taught to do that. But my thread is not as smooth and fine as the thread I can see in my mind. Nothing but the best one can think of is good enough for a King.

MILLER: She spins perfect thread.

DAUGHTER: Oh no! I should have to sit all day at my wheel, and think of nothing else, to do that. And I like too well to walk in the forest and the fields. Then when I am spinning, I shut my eyes and remember how the clouds turned the brook to silver, and the sun turned the grain in the field to gold, and I pretend the whirr of my wheel is music, and I sing. The world spins, and I spin. I spin flax into thread for the King to use. The clouds spin the brook into silver for the moon to walk on. The sun spins straw into gold. And knots come into my threads because I am not watching. I am a very bad spinner.

INGERT: All the same, I think the King would like a gift of your spinning, and to hear your song about turning straw into gold.

Send your daughter to fetch some of her work, Miller. I will tell the King you are here with your gifts.
(INGERT exits.)

DAUGHTER: Now see what you have done. My spinning is only like everyone else's and I must show it to the King.

MILLER: Go quickly, quickly! The King will come out to us soon. You are ordered to bring your work to the King. My daughter is called by the King!

WIFE: Run like a fox, daughter. Tell everyone as you go — "The King sent for my spinning!"

DAUGHTER *(going)*: I should be ashamed to tell it.

WIFE *(calling after her)*: Don't let your feet touch the ground. Hurry! Haste!

MILLER *(looking out the gate after her)*: She goes like an arrow. Oh, what a daughter we have! No one can come near her swiftness.

WIFE: How her feet twinkle in the grasses.

MILLER: If she keeps on like that, she will meet herself going when she comes back.

WIFE: I never heard of that.

MILLER: Our daughter can do it if anyone can.

WIFE: The King himself wishes to see her spinning! What will the neighbors say to that? Ah — get down. The King is coming!
(The KING enters. They kneel, holding out their gifts, as the KING enters. The KING is an old man, greed written on every line of him. He is preceded by INGERT and GOTHOL, two courtiers, and followed by his SON, and daughter, KAREN, and her lady-in-waiting. All are excited and looking eagerly around, except the King's SON, who is skeptical of what he has heard.)

MILLER: Your Majesty, here is the flour from my fine new wheat —

WIFE: And two pies made out of it —

KING *(waving their gifts aside)*: Yes, yes. You are good subjects. But where is the wonderful spinner Ingert told me about:

MILLER: That is our daughter.

WIFE: She is the most wonderful girl in the world.

KING: Is it she who sang of spinning straw into gold:

WIFE: Oh, yes, King. She sings more sweetly than a nightingale!

MILLER: No one in the village has a voice like hers. The birds in the forest gather to listen to her.

KING: Straw into gold! Straw is easy to get. I will fill a room with it. Gothol, fill the three secret rooms with straw.

GOTHOL and INGERT: Straw! ... Straw!

KING: Why not? Haste! If she can do what you say, she shall marry my son, and be queen of the land. Straw into gold! Gold! Gold! What a wife for you, son!

SON: Nay, King, my father, this cannot be true.

KING: Why not? Why not: All my life I have wanted more gold. I have looked for ways to make more and more. No end to more! Now I have found it. No long digging by a thousand men. No hours of waiting while it is cooked and heated in a crucible. A maid who can spin straw into gold. Where is she? Fetch her to me! She shall come to dwell in the palace, straightway. There is not her like in the land!

WIFE *(to MILLER)*: Even the King says there is not her like. Wait till the neighbors hear that!

MILLER: Our daughter will dwell in the palace!

WIFE: She is going to be queen!

KAREN: Surely, good Miller's wife, your daughter is not as wonderful as all this —

WIFE: She is most beautiful, and most kind and gentle —

KAREN: But her spinning —

227

MILLER: Nothing like it has ever come off a wheel.

WIFE: It is as fine as a spider's web when she wants it to be. And she makes her threads of this color and that —

SON: But Ingert said she told him sometimes it knotted —

MILLER: She is so modest. She never believes anything fine about herself.

WIFE: Don't ask her what she can do. She will say no, to everything. But there is nothing she cannot do! If you could taste the cakes she bakes! If you could sip the ale she brews, or see her planting a furrow in the spring. Everything grows that she has to do with. Everything she makes is perfect. It isn't only her spinning. She can weave, and sew a seam, and — and she can dance like birch leaves in the wind, and sing like a brook, or a thrush —

SON: Ah, yes, but can she spin gold?

MILLER: She can spin anything! You should see her at the wheel —

SON (*seeing her approach*): Ah-h-h-h —
(They all turn to the gate. The DAUGHTER enters, carrying spindles of colored threads. She looks around taken aback by the splendid court folk. After a scrutiny of the company, she goes to the King's SON, and kneels with grace, but simply.)

DAUGHTER: They bade me bring my most fine-spun thread to the King.

SON: I am not the King. I am the King's son.

KING: I am the King.
(The DAUGHTER kneels again, after gazing at him in manifest disappointment and surprise, and lays her spindles at his feet, as she speaks.)

DAUGHTER: Here is the best of my work, your Majesty. The best is not worthy a King.

KING: Where is the gold one?

DAUGHTER: It is not beautiful enough to bring. The gold thread

228

is never bright enough to please me. I want it to be bright like the sun, and it never is. But this spindle-full is the color of the sky. And this one has the green of leaves in April, when the sun falls through them. And this is like wild roses, along the wayside. All the threads have rough spots, where I fell a-dreaming. But they are brave colors.

KING: Yes, yes. The colors do very well. But it's the gold one I want.

DAUGHTER: I made a bad choice, then. I'm sorry, King. Shall I fetch the gold spindle?

KING: Never mind now. You can make plenty more, can't you?

DAUGHTER: Yes, King. There is plenty of color left in the pot, and plenty of flax on the distaff.

KING: What's that? What do you mean?

WIFE: She means she can have the gold thread spun very quickly, if you want many more spindles-ful.

KING: Good. Get up ! It is not fitting that you should kneel to me now, for I have a surprise for you. You are going to marry my son, and dwell in the palace.
(The MILLER and his WIFE gurgle with delight, in spite of themselves.)

WIFE: Thank the King, Daughter. Don't gape like that.

MILLER: You are honored. Show your manners. Say "Thank you, King."

DAUGHTER: The King's son will be King some day.

KING: That day will come soon enough. 1 am an old man, and the crown is heavy on my head. Now that I have all the gold I want, I shall pass the crown on to my son. The day you are wed, he shall be King, and you shall be Queen.

DAUGHTER: But I am just a miller's daughter. I don't know how to be Queen.

KAREN: I will teach you. You please me. You shall be my sister.

DAUGHTER: Then 1 am not afraid.

KING: Son, take the chain from your neck, and the ring from your finger, and exchange betrothal rights with this maid.

SON: Miller's daughter, take my chain and give me yours, as has been done as a sign of betrothal by King's sons in our line, from the early days. *(WIFE pulls at DAUGHTER's skirt, and she kneels. The King's SON puts his chain on her.)* It shall be a token and a bond between us.

DAUGHTER *(lifting her flower chain off)*: This is only field flowers I gathered on my way here.

SON: They please me more than gold and jewels.

DAUGHTER: But tomorrow they will be dry and dead.

SON: Tomorrow you shall make me another. And every tomorrow after. Take my ring and give me yours, as has been done in token of betrothal by King's sons in our line, from early days.

DAUGHTER: Mine is only plaited grass.

SON: I shall keep it as long as you keep mine. The rings are a token between us also.

KING: Karen, lead her in. And give her garments such as my son's betrothed shall wear.

SON: I will lead her. Karen may come too.
(INGERT, KAREN, DAUGHTER, and SON go off. The pages, headed by GOTHOL, enter, bearing armsful of straw. They are disdainful and amazed as they go toward the palace.)

KING: That's not enough.

GOTHOL: There is no more at the threshing place, your Majesty.

KING: Miller! Get all the pages and fetch all the straw from the field and mill. Fetch it to the Queen's spinning room. Have you straw enough to fill a room?

WIFE and MILLER: Yes! Oh, yes!

KING: Could you fill two rooms?

WIFE and MILLER: Yes, of course! Oh, yes!

KING: Here are three doors. They open into three rooms for storing the Queen's spinning. Fill those rooms full. I will order them emptied of all else this instant. Three roomfuls of straw! I shall have gold enough.
(KING exits.)

MILLER: The King has ordered all our straw for the palace!

WIFE: We shall be carrying straw under the moon, and in the white dawn.

MILLER: We shall be going in and out of the palace as if we were at home there!

WIFE: Husband! After this night, we shall be as much at home in the palace as in our own mill.

MILLER: Of course! For our daughter is to be Queen.

WIFE: I always told you she was not like other girls.

MILLER: It is good we spoke up for her. She would never speak up for herself: She is so modest.

WIFE: Without her mother and father, she would not be where she is today.

MILLER: I always knew she would come to something great, but to be the bride of the King's son, I never thought of.

WIFE: It will go beyond that, too. Some day, she will hold a little King's son in her arms.

MILLER: She will really be the mother of a little King's son!

WIFE: We have done this for her.

MILLER: It is our work.

WIFE: Come. Let us begin our trips to the palace before the neighbors are off the streets:
(MILLER and WIFE exeunt.)

RUMPELSTILTSKIN *(laughing with glee, on his high perch)*: Ho, ho! Ho-ho-o-o-o! *(He rises and throws something into the pot, circling. The lights change as he sings, coming up on him, and down on the garden scene.)*

> **Boil, purple and blue, and dim and grey.**
> **The garden shall fade and fade away.**
> **And nobody knows from whence I came.**
> **Or that Rumpelstiltskin is my name!**

(He is so full of triumph and self-importance that he shouts his name louder and louder.)

> **Rumpelstiltskin! R-u-m-p-e-l-s-t-i-l-t-s-k-i-n!**
> **RUMPELSTILTSKIN!**

MOTHER HULDA: Now, now, now!

RUMPEL: It is my name.

MOTHER HULDA: Why do you shout it so loud?

RUMPEL: I can't help it. I feel like it.

MOTHER HULDA: Suppose someone hears you?

RUMPEL: How could that happen?   No one ever comes to the edge of the world. They are all afraid.

MOTHER HULDA: Now, now! Didn't I say, when I gave you this place, that if anyone in the rest of the world was brave enough, he could get here? *(RUMPEL sulks away from her.)* Why don't you answer me?

RUMPEL: I'm not listening.

MOTHER HULDA: Yes, you are. Why don't you answer?

RUMPEL: I don't like to think about it.

MOTHER HULDA *(giving him a spank)*: Tell me what I said.

RUMPEL: I've forgotten.

MOTHER HULDA: Nothing of the sort!

RUMPEL: I've forgotten:
(MOTHER HULDA catches him by the seat of the trousers, and sets him down.)

MOTHER HULDA: Rumpelstiltskin, you bad little thing! Tell me what I said.

RUMPEL: You said anyone in the world who was brave enough

could come here.

MOTHER HULDA: And what else did I say?

RUMPEL: Nothing!

MOTHER HULDA: Now, now, now, now! What else did I say?

RUMPEL: Nothing!

MOTHER HULDA: What?

RUMPEL: You didn't say anything at all.

MOTHER HULDA: Sit still! Look at me: I am going to say it
   again.

RUMPEL: No, no, no, no!

MOTHER HULDA: Come back.

RUMPEL: I don't want to hear it.

MOTHER HULDA: Why not?

RUMPEL: I don't like it to be true.

MOTHER HULDA: I will do it whether you remember it or not.
   So you'd better stop shouting our name to the sky: You'd
   better even stop singing about it. Someone might come this
   way.
   *(He sulks away from her, muttering. A thought strikes him. He
   points a finger at her, laughing immoderately.)*

RUMPEL: Ho, ho! Ha, ha!

MOTHER HULDA: What are you laughing at?

RUMPEL: You.

MOTHER HULDA: Take care. Take care.

RUMPEL: I know a joke on you.

MOTHER HULDA: Are you sure ?

RUMPEL: You think someone will find out my name, and there
   isn't going to be anyone left in the world to find out. I know
   how I can get a King's son to put in my pot, and get the
   whole world to myself.

MOTHER HULDA: Now! What will you do to get a King's son for your pot?

RUMPEL: Something!

MOTHER HULDA: What ?

RUMPEL: Something.

MOTHER HULDA *(goes to him)*: You must tell me.

RUMPEL: Will you let me do it?

MOTHER HULDA: If I think best.

RUMPEL: The Miller's daughter thinks she is going to be Queen.

MOTHER HULDA: Yes.

RUMPEL: The King ordered a roomful of straw to be carried into the palace.

MOTHER HULDA: Yes.

RUMPEL: The King thinks the Miller's daughter can spin all that into gold.

MOTHER HULDA: I know.

RUMPEL: She can't.

MOTHER HULDA: Of course not.

RUMPEL: What will the King do when he finds out she can't?

MOTHER HULDA: I suppose he will order her put to death.

RUMPEL: Ho! I will go down there and make a bargain with her: I will offer to turn the straw into gold for her, if she will give me the first child born to her when she is Queen. ... I must make haste. *(Rumpel runs to circle the pot, singing:)*
>**Three times backward round my pot.**
>**Then I'll be where I am not.**
>**Three times backward —**

MOTHER HULDA: Now, now! I didn't say you could go down now.

RUMPEL: Three times backward round my pot —

MOTHER HULDA: Stop it!

RUMPEL: Then I'll be where I am not.

MOTHER HULDA: Do not take another step: *(RUMPEL slinks down, but obeys.)* There is no use in going down to the palace until I give you the rule.

RUMPEL: I know it already.

MOTHER HULDA: What do you know already

RUMPEL: The rule for turning straw into gold.

MOTHER HULDA: Oh? What is it:

RUMPEL: Before I can make gold out of straw, I must get the one I do it for to give me something that was dug from deep under the ground, and something that sprang from the soil.

MOTHER HULDA: That is right.

RUMPEL: Well! The gold in the chain which the King's son put on the Miller's daughter was dug from deep in the ground. And the flowers in the chain she gave him sprang from the soil. So there ! I can bargain to turn her straw into gold for the chains. Then I can do it, can't I?

MOTHER HULDA: That will give you the chains. But it will not give you the King's child. *(RUMPEL mutters, very sulky.)* Will it? *(RUMPEL turns his back.)* What is the rule for that? *(RUMPEL folds together, more sulky than ever.)* Oh, well, if you know already, you don't need me to tell you. *(She starts off. RUMPEL is up like a shot, obstructing her way.)*

RUMPEL: I don't know it: Tell me. Will you tell me?

MOTHER HULDA: Oh yes, I'll tell you: Sit down: Before you can spin straw into gold, in exchange for a Queen's child, you must make two other bargains with her.

RUMPEL: Why must I bargain twice?

MOTHER HULDA: Because once isn't enough.

RUMPEL: Well, what bargains must I make?

MOTHER HULDA: Twice you must get her to bargain away

something else she loves — something that was given to her by another, as a token and a bond between them.

RUMPEL: Twice?

MOTHER HULDA: Twice.

RUMPEL: Once she might do it without thinking. But she'd never do it twice. Let me spin the gold for one bargain.

MOTHER HULDA: Nothing of the sort. It must be twice.

RUMPEL: Perhaps she would rather bargain than die! I'll go down and try. May I go down and try?

MOTHER HULDA: Oh yes, you may try.

RUMPEL:
> **Three times backward round my pot,**
> **Then I'll be where I am not.**
> **Three times backward, and my door**
> **Will be where there was none before.**
> **Three times backward, here I go**
> **To bargain with a Queen below!**
(He leaps down and out of sight.)

CURTAIN

ACT TWO

SCENE: *The Queen's spinning room. On one side, three doors, growing larger from downstage to back.*

WIFE: To think that I have spent, the whole night before my daughter's wedding carrying straw!

MILLER *(Throwing his onto the top of the heap)*: This is the last of it. The room won't hold another load. There! That is the end of what I brought.

WIFE: This will be the end of mine.

MILLER: Don't try to take so much at once.

WIFE: Don't you hear the bells: They are calling people to see our daughter made Queen. I must be tidied up in time to go into the church.

MILLER: It will be quicker to make two of it.

WIFE: One is enough.
(She is carried across the room by her efforts.)

MILLER: Now, if you made two loads —

WIFE: One is enough.

MILLER: I am the father of the most wonderful girl in the world, and I say it would be quicker to make two.

WIFE: I am her mother, and I say, one is enough.

MILLER: I say two is better — And my daughter can spin straw into gold !
(He turns to the wheel with a wide gesture, but stops short. He gulps and stands staring at the wheel. He touches the straw on the spindle. His jaw drops.WIFE goes to the door and succeeds finally in getting her load to stay on, and with some difficulty steers herself to the straw pile. She makes a number of preparatory swings of her shoulders, and then pitches the straw up onto the pile. It comes back into her face. She gasps and whirls, looking quickly to see if her husband has caught her, but seeing him engrossed in the wheel, recovers her dignity, gathers up the straw, and gets it onto the pile. She tries to shut the door on it, and has plenty of difficulties, the straw falling out every time she tries it, but eventually gets it shut. The bells stop toward the end of this.)

WIFE: What are you doing over there?

MILLER: I'm looking at this wheel.

WIFE: It's just a spinning wheel.

MILLER: Yes. It's large, but it would spin.

WIFE: This room is made for it. The King called this the Queen's spinning room.

MILLER: It will be our daughter's spinning room.

WIFE: Yes, for she is to be queen.

MILLER: And this will be her wheel.

WIFE: That's why it is so fine. It is a queen's wheel.

MILLER: The King has put straw on the distaff.

WIFE: I didn't notice that:
(They look at each other, and then away.)

MILLER: Of course our daughter can spin more beautifully than anyone — but what if the King should say to her —"Sit right here and spin this very straw into gold for me."

WIFE *(touching it)*: It's just ordinary straw.

MILLER: Yes. It's strange.

WIFE: What is strange?

MILLER: That we didn't think of that before.

WIFE: Spinning straw into gold has such a beautiful sound. It seemed as if she could. I felt sure she could. The feeling rose right up in me.

MILLER: Aye, I felt that way too. But I was only thinking of how wonderful she was. I wasn't thinking about a wheel you could touch, with straw from the harvest field on the distaff.

WIFE: No, that seems different, somehow.

MILLER: It would be terrible if we brought our daughter harm.

WIFE: I would rather die.

MILLER: I can't bear to look at it.

WIFE: No, it spoils everything. Anyway she will be queen. She can do as she likes.

MILLER: Why, yes, of course! Queens needn't spin at all if they don't wish!

WIFE: And the King is pleased with her. He wouldn't let her out of his sight.

MILLER: Is there anyone who isn't pleased with her' Didn't the King's son smile on her, and lead her in himself? And the

238

King's daughter called her sister in the first breath. There never was a girl like that! To be made queen all of a sudden!

WIFE: O, what a daughter we have!

MILLER: She will make the King forget all about spinning straw into gold.

WIFE: I wouldn't be surprised if she could spin straw into gold, if she set her mind to it.

MILLER: She's clever enough: She'd find a way.

WIFE: And then how the people will worship her!

MILLER: There will be shouting and trumpets, and flowers flung under her feet every time she goes abroad.

WIFE: What will the neighbors say then?
(A PAGE enters, bearing a tray or basket piled with field flowers. The King's SON follows, with GOTHOL and INGERT. MILLER bows, and WIFE curtsies.)

SON: Gothol, tell the Miller's daughter I have brought fresh flowers for the chain.

WIFE: Do you remember us, King's son? It is our daughter who will become your queen.

MILLER: We are her parents.

WIFE: She is our daughter. Is it almost time to set out for the wedding? I heard the bells calling just now.

SON: Those were the bells to call the people from the country, and the far edges of the town. There will be bells again before we set out from the palace.

MILLER: Yesterday we came in our holiday togs, but the night's work for the King has put dust in our hair and down our necks. Do you think there will be time for us to go back to the mill and make ourselves fresh?

WIFE: It would never do for us to be a shame to our daughter.

SON: There is no need for you to go back to your mill. Follow this gentleman. Ingert, call one of the serving men to attend

the Miller and make him fresh for the wedding. And call one
of the serving-women to wait on the Miller's wife.
(INGERT leads the way off. They follow in ecstasy.)

MILLER: We are to be tended by the servants in the palace.

WIFE: Why not? Is not our daughter to be over them all?
*(GOTHOL enters, with KAREN leading in the Miller's
DAUGHTER. She is beautifully clad in satin, trimmed with
a border of jewels, and wears the chain the King's SON put
on her in Act One. She is radiant with joy. She makes a court
curtsey to the King's SON, doing it carefully with delight as
she rises from it, clapping her hands. He has bowed to her at
the same time. KAREN sets the head-dress and the long train
on the bench.)*

DAUGHTER: You see, I have learned how to bow to a king
already! Of course it wasn't perfect. I suppose it never will
be. I am only a girl of the common folk. But I am not afraid
to be queen any more, King's son. Shall I tell you why?

SON: Yes. Tell me why.

DAUGHTER: Yesterday, I was afraid. At the very thought of it,
my heart beat like a wild bird. Karen tried to teach me how to
walk like a queen, and how to dance your way, in the palace,
instead of our way on the green. And I grew more frightened
all the time. At night, when they left me alone in the great
queen's room, I couldn't sleep. I sat at the window, and saw
the moon climb up the sky, and over it, and down again. And
I said to myself: "The moon looks down on all the folk who
will call me Queen. And all at once, I seemed to see them all,
and hear them. There were so many who were sad, and so
many very poor, and so many crying out for someone wise
enough to tell them what to do, that tears fell on my hand,
and I called out loud to the night. If only I could help them!
And all of a sudden a thought came like a song into my mind.
I will be queen, and I can. And when I thought about all that,
it seemed quite easy to walk like a queen. Yes, and to dance
like one, too! If there were music, I would show you how
easy it is. *(Music is heard.)*

SON: There is music. Have them play for us, Gothol.
(They dance. She stops in the middle of a strain.)

DAUGHTER: Here I am, so full of joy in being queen, I forgot you wanted me to weave you another chain.

SON: Here are the flowers, ready.

DAUGHTER *(putting her face to them)*: They are from my fields! The dew is on them still.

SON: I gathered them myself. *(He takes out three or four.)* Use any but these. These I climbed high to gather. They are to fasten your bride's head-dress.

KAREN: It is custom to fasten that with a great jewel from the royal treasure-room, brother.

SON: Which will you have, Miller's daughter: A costly jewel from the treasure-room or my gift of flowers?

DAUGHTER: I will take your flowers. A jewel from the king's treasure room is only a sign of riches. Flowers you climbed high to gather are a sign of kindness.

SON: I am glad you choose them. All my life, I have imagined a queen who would choose like that.

DAUGHTER *(working on the chain)*: I will measure your chain by this.
(She touches the gold chain she wears. The KING enters, with retinue. MILLER and WIFE follow all.)

SON: You will have to make your chain small. The King has come to tell us to set out.

KING: It is not time to set out yet. Before we do that, I must have proof of this maiden's skill in spinning:.

DAUGHTER: I told you there are often knots in my thread.
(KING throws open the first door.)

KING: How long will you need to spin this into gold:

DAUGHTER *(to KING)*: I do not understand your jest.

KING: I am not jesting. In the night, I thought to myself: "Her father said she could spin straw into gold, and her mother, too. But parents' word is not always the one to listen to. I will see it done with my own eyes."

DAUGHTER: Straw into gold Why should anyone wish to do such a thing? Straw is for the comfort of beasts, to bed them soft and warm, and for helping the soil in our fields when it is turned under the furrow. Who would waste it, giving it the hardness of gold?

KING: What trick are you trying on me now?   You want to keep your gold to yourself, is that it?

DAUGHTER: I have no gold.

KING: I do not believe you. I will not believe you. I have set my heart on the gold you spin, and I will not give it up. Begin, now. Spin!

DAUGHTER: I cannot.

KING: To the wheel. There is straw ready, on the distaff.

DAUGHTER: Give me flax, and I will spin you thread, ordinary thread. That is all the spinning I know.

KING: I will not hear such words! They tear me to pieces! Give me gold — a roomful of gold. Your father said you could. Your mother praised you for it. They brought straw all night long, for your spinning. Begin!

DAUGHTER: Nay, but King —

KING: Do not say nay. Do not dare say "Nay"! Spin!

DAUGHTER: That would be to work a wonder. I am a simple girl from the mill. I cannot work wonders.

KING: Your mother said you could. Your father boasted about it. I believed them, and I will not be robbed of my belief. Gold out of straw. All night I dreamed about it. I have built my hopes high on it. You shall bring them true, or die. Spin! *(General outcry.)* Be quiet! All! Spin, or I will have you put to death!

SON: No!

242

DAUGHTER *(to parents)*: I cannot ... Look what you have done now.

MILLER: Try, Daughter. Try. Surely you can find some way.

WIFE: See, there's the wheel! Spin! Do not stand there so dull and blank. Try! Only try! Find a way! I cannot bear to see you stand like that. I could never look in the face of the sun or the moon, if things go like this. You cannot die! Take courage. You must live. Live!

MILLER: There must be a way. Don't despair like that. You break our hearts. We cannot live without you. Find a way! Find it. Find it!

KING: Let her alone. Maid, will you spin that straw into gold, or die?

WIFE *(kneeling to KING)*: Do not punish her for our words. Our tongues went fast. Forgive us. Do not harm our child.

KING: If you deceived your King—

MILLER: We did not mean to deceive you, King. We said only what we felt.

KING: What you said, she must pay for. I will not eat my heart out with bitter disappointment. I will have gold. Rooms full of it! *(Opens a casement window.)* Come here *(DAUGHTER goes to him. He points out the window.)* I will give you till the shadow of that tree touches this door, to spin this straw on the distaff into gold. If you do it, the bells shall ring for your wedding, and you shall be queen. If you do not, you shall be put to death, and the bells shall toll for your funeral.

SON *(to DAUGHTER)*: Do not tremble so. My father shall not do this to you.

KING: Are you my son?

SON: I have been dutiful all my life. But I will not see this thing done.

KING: I am old, but I have not given over my crown to you.

SON: For all that, you shall not harm this maid.

KING: Let her keep the promise that was made for her, and she shall come to honor, and not harm.

SON: You heard her say that she cannot. Are you mad, to command such a thing?

KING: I may be mad, but I am King. Miller's daughter, the sun's rays are moving on the grass. I shall wait beyond that door. When you have spun this much straw into gold, knock on the door. That much will prove your parents did not lie. If there is no knock before the time is up, I shall send guards to lead you to your death.

SON: I forbid it.

KING: You will forbid the King's guards to do my will?

SON: They shall not lay a hand on her.

KING: You will be King. If you would rule, you must first obey. I bid you to go to the dungeon room and wait, alone, till this maid spins, or dies.

SON: I will not leave her side.

KING: Take his sword from him, Ingert, Gothol.

INGERT: Two against one?

KING: Do not harm him. Take his sword. *(They fight.)* You use your sword as a King's son should. Yet if two can't take you, twenty can.

SON: They will have to slay me first.

KING: Not a hair of your head shall be harmed, if it takes a hundred men.

SON: A thousand men cannot take me alive.

KING: This maid has turned your heart from me. But know this. If you lift your sword against my guard, you lift it against her. She shall pay with her life without waiting to spin, if you defy me.

DAUGHTER: Go, King's son, for my sake. Go, and let me spin the gold.

SON: Can you spin gold?

DAUGHTER: Let me try.

SON: That I must know. For her sake I will do your bidding, King, my father, if you give me your word to let me know whether the gold is spun before you order her death.

KING: You shall know. *(SON goes, under guard.)* So you can spin it, after all!

DAUGHTER: No. It was to save him I said it. I cannot spin straw into anything at all. Believe me.

KING: We shall see. And do not trust to my son's help. I gave my word to tell him. Not to set him free. The bolts shall be drawn on the dungeon room. He shall not come forth till I have the gold. Or your life. Spin!

PARENTS: Have mercy!

KING: Let her spin!
(The PARENTS go out, the KING after them. The DAUGHTER stands an instant, then gathers up some flowers and buries her face in them, weeping. RUMPEL pushes open the little door, and comes out. He dances around her silently in delight before he speaks.)

RUMPEL: Why do you weep ?

DAUGHTER: Oh! ... Who are you?

RUMPEL: Someone.

DAUGHTER: Who?

RUMPEL: Someone who wonders why such a pretty maid should weep.

DAUGHTER: I must spin straw into gold, or be put to death. I do not even know how to begin.

RUMPEL: What will you give me to spin all that into gold before the sun on the wall moves the breath of a hair?

DAUGHTER: No one can spin straw into gold.

RUMPEL: I can.

245

DAUGHTER: Oh, will you?

RUMPEL: If you give me what I ask.

DAUGHTER: What do you ask?

RUMPEL: Something!

DAUGHTER: What?

RUMPEL: Two things.

DAUGHTER: What are they?

RUMPEL: Will you give them to me?

DAUGHTER: Tell me what they are, and I can answer.
(RUMPEL skips and rubs his hands together, then comes close to her, touching the chain she wears.)

RUMPEL: This.

DAUGHTER: No! I cannot give you that. The King's son put it around my neck for a betrothal token.

RUMPEL *(dancing to touch the flowers the King's SON chose for her headdress)*: And this.

DAUGHTER: I can't give you that, either. The King's son climbed high to gather those, as a sign of kindness.

RUMPEL *(sulking, cross-legged on the floor)*: Very well.

DAUGHTER: I'll give you jewels far finer than those.

RUMPEL: I do not want jewels.

DAUGHTER: But I can't give you my betrothal chain.

RUMPEL: Very well.

DAUGHTER: Here are other flowers, just as beautiful.

RUMPEL: I do not want other flowers.

DAUGHTER: But how can I give you the gift the King's son brought me?

RUMPEL: Very well:
(DAUGHTER weeps. RUMPEL peeps at her. The sun on the wall is moving.)

DAUGHTER: I do not want to die!

RUMPEL: Give me what 1 ask, and you need not die.

DAUGHTER: Why will you not take other flowers?

RUMPEL: I want those.

DAUGHTER: But they are the only ones that matter to me.

RUMPEL: Very well.

DAUGHTER: I will give you jewels far finer than any you ever saw.

RUMPEL: I want the chain.

DAUGHTER: But it's the dearest thing in the world to me, for the sake of the one who gave it to me.

RUMPEL: Very well.
(*She weeps. He watches, rocking back and forth.*)

DAUGHTER: What shall I do?

RUMPEL: Give me the chain!   Give me the flowers!   And the straw will be gold in the wink of an eye.

DAUGHTER: I cannot give you those.
(*RUMPEL stamps his foot, and shakes his arms and fists, running abound and jumping up and down in rage, squeaking and chittering in jury. When the gust of temper passes:*)

RUMPEL: Don't put me in a temper. I shall fly to pieces.

DAUGHTER: I only said I can't.
(*RUMPEL repeats the outbreak worse.*)

RUMPEL: I can't stand this ... Good bye!

DAUGHTER: Don't go.

RUMPEL (*cocking his head on one side*): Will you give me what I ask?

DAUGHTER (*fingering chain, touching flowers*): Whatever shall I do?

RUMPEL: The sun is moving very fast.

DAUGHTER (*runs to the window and looks out*): It is almost to the door.

RUMPEL: Shall I spin the straw into gold?

DAUGHTER: Yes!

RUMPEL: My bargain?

DAUGHTER: Yes!

RUMPEL: Shall I have the chain, and the three small flowers?

DAUGHTER: Yes, yes! Only haste!
(RUMPEL dances up to the wheel, chuckling and capering on the way. He dances around it; turning spinning movements into magic. Lights flash, and the wheel whirls faster and faster. He suddenly holds quiet, as if listening intently.)

RUMPEL: It is done!　　*(He prances to the door, and opens it.)*
Look and see:
(DAUGHTER is overwhelmed at the mass of shining gold.)

DAUGHTER: It is really true!

RUMPEL: Is not that worth a chain, and few field flowers?

DAUGHTER: Alas, what will the King's son say? I have given away his tokens.
(RUMPEL begins to prance about her, his eyes on her hand, chuckling and squeaking.)

RUMPEL: This is once.

DAUGHTER: What are you thinking of?

RUMPEL: I am thinking of twice.

DAUGHTER: Twice? What do you mean? Twice as much gold? It would please the King.

RUMPEL: I will turn more straw into gold. For something.

DAUGHTER: For what?

RUMPEL: Something.

DAUGHTER: What?

RUMPEL *(darting and touching her ring)* : That!

DAUGHTER: My ring? No! That is the last of the things the

King's son gave me. I will not part with that.

RUMPEL: Another room full of gold. Twice as large!

DAUGHTER: All the gold in the world is not worth this.

RUMPEL: *(stamping his foot. It sticks in the floor, but he gets it out.)*: I want the ring!

DAUGHTER: You shan't have it.

RUMPEL *(stamping his foot so hard, it sticks again.)*: The chain is no good to me without it.

DAUGHTER: Then give it back to me.

RUMPEL *(gets his foot free, and wheedles)*: Give me the ring, Miller's daughter. Give me the ring for double the gold. Make a bargain. Queen. Much gold for a silly ring.

DAUGHTER: Do not call it silly. The King's son gave it to me as a token, and he lies in a locked room for my sake.

RUMPEL: Give me your token for gold — for a world full of gold. Bargain with me, Miller's daughter. Bargain with me, Queen.

DAUGHTER: I have said no. Go away! I am tired of you. The King will come soon. *(DAUGHTER runs to look out of the window.)*

RUMPEL: Give the ring first.

DAUGHTER: I will never give it to you. The sun is touching. It is time. Go away from here. Go away, and never come back.

RUMPEL: Very well. *(He opens the little door.)*

KING *(off stage)*: Go in and take her.
(Guards strike on the door.)

RUMPEL *(sticking his head through the little door)*: If you tell anyone I spun the gold, it will turn back to straw.
(He whisks the door shut, as guards enter, letting the KING come between them. KAREN follows.)

KING: Gold! It is true! Gold! Yellow gold! See it shine! *(He rushes to touch it, to take a bit in his hands, Reeling its weight, and tapping to hear the sound of it.)* All this is out of straw from the fields. What a wonderful girl. You shall be queen this hour. Every day, you shall spin again. Karen, bid them set the bells ringing.

DAUGHTER: Nay, King! Nay Karen! Do not start the bells till I explain. I cannot spin gold every day, King. This is all the gold I can ever spin, ever in all my life.

KING: What?

DAUGHTER: I haven't skill to do it again.

KING: If you can do it once, you can do it twice.

DAUGHTER: No. I cannot do it again. You do not believe me, but I cannot.

KING: That is what you said before.

DAUGHTER: If I could, I would.

KING *(throwing open the second door)*: Perhaps you would rather die than do it again? We shall see. You shall spin this before you take a step toward the church. You shall spin it before my son comes out of the dungeon. You shall spin it before the sun moves to here, or those two shall put you to death. *(He stalks off, motioning for the guards to go ahead.)*

KAREN *(stops to whisper to DAUGHTER)*: Do it for my brother's sake.*(KAREN follows after her father.)*

DAUGHTER: I wish I hadn't sent the little spinning man away. *(She tries to open the little door.)* How did he get out of there? *(She knocks on the door.)* Little man! *(There is no response. She goes to the pile of flowers.)* I will finish the chain for the King's son. *(She works a bit, her tears coming faster. She puts it aside, and runs to look out of the window.)* How fast the sun moves! *(She goes back to the chain.)* This is like one of those he chose for me. I will try to fasten them together in the chain for my bride's head-dress. And this is another. And this. I will put them together. Will he know I was thinking of him, when he sees it after they have put me to death, I wonder? ... I shall never be queen now.

(She sobs bitterly, her face in her hands. RUMPEL peeps out, and then skips around her silently. He peers at the rings on her hand, chuckling to himself, and finally darts a finger out to touch it.)

RUMPEL: Why are you weeping so bitterly?

DAUGHTER: The King has ordered me to turn more straw into gold, all that room full. Will you do it again?

RUMPEL: Will you give me the ring?

DAUGHTER: It is better to let you have this ring, than to have him lie in a dungeon. He would not want me to die for a ring. I will give it to you.

RUMPEL: I must have one thing more.

DAUGHTER: Whatever it is, I must give it to you.
(RUMPEL takes the flower chain she was working on, and puts it over his head. Then he dances to the third door.)

RUMPEL: How much is there this time?

DAUGHTER: That is not the right door.

RUMPEL: There is straw in here.

DAUGHTER *(opening second door)*: This is the room he bade me spin.

RUMPEL: There is no use in spinning this one room full: The King will only order you to spin this other.

DAUGHTER: That is true! The more gold he has, the more he wants. It will surely end in his putting me to death.

RUMPEL: What will you give me to spin all that into gold, too?

DAUGHTER: After all, the King may not order this one.

RUMPEL: But if he does, what will you give me?

DAUGHTER: I have nothing left to give.

RUMPEL: Then give me a promise.

DAUGHTER: Promise?

RUMPEL: Something!

DAUGHTER: What?

RUMPEL: Something.

DAUGHTER: What?

RUMPEL: Something!

DAUGHTER: Tell me quickly. The sun has a very little way to go.

RUMPEL: Promise me the first child born to you when you are Queen.

DAUGHTER: That isn't likely ever to happen.

RUMPEL: Will you promise me?

DAUGHTER: If the King orders me to spin this great room full, will you come and spin it?

RUMPEL: If you will give me that promise.

DAUGHTER: I will give it: Begin on this, or there will not be time.
(RUMPEL dances joyfully around the wheel, as before, except that the lights and sounds are more brilliant. He stops and listens, as before.)

RUMPEL: It is done:
(She opens the door to the second room. The straw is gold. Then opens the door to the last room. It is still straw.)

DAUGHTER: You will not forget about this room full?

RUMPEL: I will not forget.

DAUGHTER: But how will you know whether he orders it or not? You may be far away.

RUMPEL: I shall know.
(The door is flung open. RUMPEL leaps into the door of the last room, closing the door after him. The KING enters, with the GUARDS and KAREN. The door of the second room is open, showing the shining gold. KAREN runs to throw her arms around the DAUGHTER. The Miller's WIFE has also entered. Voices off. DAUGHTER runs to meet the KING at

252

railing.)

DAUGHTER: It is all finished, King. Call your son.

KING: You did it, then!

MILLER: She is saved!

WIFE: I told you she would find a way. My darling, my daughter, my wonderful child!

DAUGHTER: Now will you set him free? Your son?

KING: Suppose, my clever lass, you do just one thing more, before I do that. Here is one more room full of straw. Why not just spin it into gold before we start to the church?

DAUGHTER: I will make a bargain with you. King. I will spin this one more room full into gold, if you will promise never to ask me to spin gold again.

KING: That's a poor bargain, Miller's daughter.

DAUGHTER: Why should I go on making gold all my life? Look at all there is here.

KAREN: You can never use it all, even now.

DAUGHTER: And if you will let this be the end, I'll make all this room full more.

KING: But tomorrow —

DAUGHTER: No, I will not do any more tomorrow. I will not go on spinning straw all my life.

MILLER: Hush, daughter! Don't anger the King.

WIFE: He will think of putting you to death again.

DAUGHTER: Well, if I must do this or die, I may as well die today as after awhile. So if it is your will that I should be put to death, King, let it be now. Then you will never have gold for this straw. You will lose it all.

KING: It would make a great deal. Well, then, turn all this gold, as you did the rest, and I will never ask you to spin again.

DAUGHTER: Leave me alone a little while. It will not take long.

KING: This is a wonderful thing you do. I should like to see it happen.

MILLER and WIFE: Yes, yes, let us watch.

DAUGHTER: No: I could not do it if I were watched.

MILLER: Hear her. The most modest maid. Come, daughter! Sit at the wheel.

WIFE: What a sight it will be. Our daughter, spinning straw into gold!

KING: That is right. Take her to the wheel.

MILLER: Come, modest one: Don't make your father push you so.

KING: Come. The King himself will lead you.

DAUGHTER: I must be alone.

KAREN: Don't be afraid of our eyes. Sit down, now, and begin.
(They push her onto the stool, and stand back, expectant.)

WIFE: Put your hand on the wheel:
(WIFE lifts it herself, in spite of the DAUGHTER's shrinking away from her. The wheel starts to turn at the touch of her foot, and the lights play. They stand amazed, and ecstatic. While the wheel is spinning, noise is heard in the hall without. Shouts, clash of swords, etc.)

SON *(off stage)*: Out of my way!

INGERT *(as he comes flying in)*: He lights like a hundred—
(INGERT is overcome by the sight of the wheel. GOTHOL and SON enter immediately after him, fighting. Both are halted by what they see. DAUGHTER goes to SON with cry of joy.)

DAUGHTER: You are safe!

(Cry from all, as she leaves the wheel.)

KING: Stay at your spinning!

DAUGHTER: I forgot —
(DAUGHTER goes back to the wheel. It runs down.)

254

WIFE: Why do you stop!

DAUGHTER: It stops when it is done.

KING: It can't be done as soon as this, can it?

DAUGHTER *(breathless)*: I don't know.
  (The third door is opened.)

KING: How foolish you would have been to die! You shall be served as never queen was served before. There has never been your equal among queens. Gold! Gold! Gold!

MILLER *(at second door)*: Our daughter did it!

WIFE *(at first door)*: It is her work!

SON *(to DAUGHTER)*: I don't know how you have done this, but you are more wonderful than any of them know.

DAUGHTER: I am not wonderful. They only think I am.

SON: Now you are more wonderful than ever ... Where is my chain?

DAUGHTER: I bargained for the gold with it. Are you angry?

SON: You are my queen. What does a chain matter? ... The people are waiting, King. Shall we set forth?

(They go out in procession, the bells pealing. The last door opens stealthily. RUMPLE comes out, and skips joyfully about.)

RUMPEL:

> **For a million years I brew and bake.**
> **I stamp my foot, and the world doth shake.**
> **And nobody knows from whence I came,**
> **Or that Rumpelstiltskin is my name.**
>
> **For a million years, I bake and brew.**
> **I blow my breath, and the winds blow too.**
> **And nobody knows from whence I came,**
> **Or that Rumpelstiltskin is my name.**

For one year more, I brew and bake,
And then I shall a King's son take,
And nobody'll know from whence I came,
Or that Rumpelstiltskin is my name!

CURTAIN

ACT THREE

SCENE 1: *In the King's garden, a year later. Rumpelstiltskin is nowhere visible. The Edge of the World is dim and unobtrusive, above. The Miller's Daughter, now the Queen, is seated beside the royal cradle, gazing in still delight on her baby son. The nurse also sits near, singing. The Pages, Miller, Wife, the King, the King's son, Karen, Gothol, Ingert, and the ladies-in-waiting are all watching the child. Ingert is accompanying the Nurse on his guitar. It is a tableau, all eyes bent on the child in adoration.*

DAUGHTER: He is sound asleep. *(To the PAGES:)* Carry him over there, where the light is soft and dim.

WIFE: We will carry him.

KING: No, He shall be carried by the King himself.

MILLER: He is our grandson.

KING: So is he mine:
(The three near the cradle.)

WIFE: A little King's son! And our daughter is his mother. Look! A smile passed over his face just then! He is dreaming. What a wonder-child, to dream, when he is so tiny and so small!

MILLER: He is not small. He grows like grain that was sown in the moon. See how round his arm is! He will be the strongest man in the whole kingdom, in his day! That little arm will lift a mill-stone as if it were a bit of thistle-down, bye and bye.

WIFE: He will have nothing at all to do with mill-stones! He will be King over wide lands. Oh, daughter, what a child you have

256

brought into this world!

KING: See, his little ringers curl around my big one, even in his sleep.

MILLER: So will they around mine.

KING: My great, tall son was like this once. I had forgotten that. My mind was so full of gold.

NURSE: You'll awaken him, between you.

DAUGHTER: Yes, let him sleep

MILLER: We will carry him in.

DAUGHTER: The attendants will do it better.

WIFE: No, they will not be as careful as we.

MILLER: You lift your end too high.

WIFE: No, yours is too low.

KING: Neither of you hold it level. This is how it should be.

NURSE: He is stirring, with all your fuss.

DAUGHTER: You are more careful, but they are more steady.

WIFE: We do it for love.

DAUGHTER: Yes, but they know how.

KING: We are spoiling his sleep. Gothol, Ingert, take him. *(PAGES lift the cradle. Very slowly they move, toward the palace door, to music.)*

DAUGHTER: Do not take him from my sight: Leave the cradle here, by the steps. *(Exeunt all but SON and DAUGHTER.)* How happy they are to have a baby in the palace.

SON: The old King, my father, even forgets his gold, to wonder at him.

DAUGHTER: No one is as happy as I! To please them all in the court, I go quiet and like a Queen. But if I did what I feel like doing, my feet wouldn't touch the ground for joy. Hark! They are dancing by the mill.

SON: They are safe within, all of them. We will please no one but ourselves.

(He swings her up. They do this, laughing. She runs to baby.)

DAUGHTER: It's good you don't see how wild we are! That is because we are mad with joy about you, little King's son. Are you warm enough? Do you think he should have just a little more to cover him?

SON *(lifting flowers from the bench)*: Use these.

DAUGHTER: No I am weaving these for you.

SON: The fields are purple and white with bloom outside the gate. I'll bring him some.
(SON goes. DAUGHTER settles down to weave the rest of the almost-finished flower chain. RUMPEL pushes open the little door, and enters. He moves noiselessly to her. He sits beside her, watching her intently, smiling triumphantly. She rises to look at the baby. Turning back, she sees RUMPEL. She screams.)

DAUGHTER: Who are you? *(RUMPEL laughs silently, his eyes unwavering.)* What—what do you want? *(RUMPEL laughs.)* Oh, go away! I didn't think it would ever happen.

RUMPEL: I have come for my bargain.

DAUGHTER: That was so long ago. It couldn't still be true. I had forgotten all about it.

RUMPEL: Things do not end because you forget them. Fetch the baby,

DAUGHTER: Oh, no! I can't give you my baby!

RUMPEL: There's no use in saying that. This was not a common bargain, such as men make and break. It was made with me! I did what cannot be done: I turned straw into gold. I can do more! I can stamp my foot, and the earth will shake, and this whole place will fall on your head and break your baby into bits.

DAUGHTER: I didn't know that.

RUMPEL: Very well! Fetch the child.

258

DAUGHTER: He can't do without his mother. He is too little.

RUMPEL: It won't be long he'll need you.

DAUGHTER: What do you mean to do with him?

RUMPEL: Something.

DAUGHTER: Oh, what?

RUMPEL: Something.

DAUGHTER: Will you be good to him?

RUMPEL: Never mind.

DAUGHTER: You have some terrible plan in your mind. I can tell by the sound of your voice. I can tell by the way you laugh. I can tell by the way you walk.

RUMPEL: You must keep your bargain, for all that.

DAUGHTER: I will give you back your gold! I will give you everything I have. The young King, my husband, will give you broad lands and heaped-up treasure.

RUMPEL: I'd rather have a living thing than all the gold in the earth and stars. *(He stamps.)* Come. I have waited long enough.

DAUGHTER: Don't take him from me.

RUMPEL: Fetch him!

DAUGHTER: Take me, instead. Do anything you want to me. Flog me, torture me, kill me, tear me to pieces! Only let my little son stay safe with his Father. Go away and let him be. Go away. Go away!

RUMPEL: Don't do that! Don't do it any more. It upsets me.

DAUGHTER *(exhausted)*: Go away —

RUMPEL: Don't do it! It makes me want to say — "You can keep your child."

DAUGHTER: Say it! Say it!

RUMPEL: No, no, no, no, no, no, no! I only want to say it; I don't want to do it! Don't look at me. I don't like to

259

feel like this.

DAUGHTER: You feel sorry. You will have mercy. You will not take him away.

RUMPEL: Yes, I will! Don't look at me!
(RUMPEL covers his eyes and jumps up and down.)

DAUGHTER: I am looking at you. I shall keep looking at you till you promise me: Look! Look! *(She kneels and stretches out her arms.)* Make me a promise. Say you will leave me my little King's son. Little man! Little spinning man! I don't know your name: I don't know what to call you —

RUMPEL *(laughs when she says she doesn't know his name, then uncovers his eyes)*: I will make you a promise.

DAUGHTER: Yes —

RUMPEL: I have the strangest name in the world. I give you three guesses. Three times three guesses. If you can tell me my name, I will not make you keep your bargain.

DAUGHTER: Three times three guesses!

RUMPEL: Now I feel the way I like to feel.

DAUGHTER: Now let me see. I have heard of the three kings who journeyed over mountains and deserts from very far away. Their names were strange. Never have I heard of them in these parts. But which, I wonder, is the strangest?

RUMPEL: Why not try them, one at a time? You have plenty of guesses more.

DAUGHTER: So I have. Well, are you called Casper?

RUMPEL: That is not my name.

DAUGHTER: Are you called Melchior?

RUMPEL: That is not my name.

DAUGHTER: Are you called Balthazar?

RUMPEL: That is not my name! Go on! Guess some more, Miller's daughter. Guess some more, Queen.

DAUGHTER: You must give me time to think. I was wrong to waste my guesses without thinking.

RUMPEL: I didn't say I'd give you time. Come, what is my name?

DAUGHTER: I must ask my husband, the young King, for help. I must ask Karen, and my ladies, and my father, and all of them. You will not deny me time for that! *(RUMPEL turns his back.)* I am begging you.

RUMPEL: Very well. Ask your husband. And his sister, and all the fine folks in the palace—*(He stamps.)* You have been too slow. I hear someone coming! Give me the baby! *(He starts for it. She blocks him, as the young King's voice, singing, draws near. RUMPEL whips out his little door. DAUGHTER runs to meet the SON.)*

DAUGHTER: Will you help me!

SON *(puts the chain on)*: Help you? How?

DAUGHTER: You must think. Think hard! What is the strangest name you know? *(SON laughs)* Don't laugh! Tell me! It must be a very strange name.

SON: What is the matter, little Queen? You are frightened: Why do you cling to me so?

DAUGHTER: You must not ask me questions. You must tell me names. Quick, now. You have been about the world. What is the strangest name you have ever heard?

SON: In far-away places, 1 have heard many names that sounded strange to me. But they did not sound strange to those who used them. I suppose a name isn't really strange unless it sounds so to those who use it.

DAUGHTER: Still, you must have heard one that sounded queer to you.

SON: Not after I thought about it. One name is as good an another,

DAUGHTER: Then call my father and mother, and Ingert and

261

Gothol. They go about among the people. They will surely know names to tell me.

SON: Whatever you wish, little Queen.

DAUGHTER: Don't leave me alone!

SON: Shall I not fetch the others?

DAUGHTER: Call them! Stand here and call.

SON: Ingert! ... Bring the Miller and his Wife, and Gothol, into the garden.

DAUGHTER: They mustn't ask me why.

SON: I'll see to that. Now laugh a little. I do not like to see you sober and afraid.

DAUGHTER: I can't laugh yet.

WIFE *(entering, followed by the others)*: What do you want?

SON: We are trying to think of strange names. Whoever can think of the strangest name will have a reward. Now, Gothol. Speak.

GOTHOL: Well, once, when I was journeying in a land where alligators blinked on the banks of the streams, and parrots flew in twos high in the sky, I met a man named after a river, and the river's name was: Pappaloappaloapam.

DAUGHTER: Poppaloappalo — what comes next?

MILLER: Pappaloappaloappaloappaloppale —

INGERT: No, no, no: Pappaloappaloapam.

MILLER: Why do you cut me short?

INGERT: Because it is time you stopped.

MILLER: What ground have you for saying such a thing?

INGERT: Enough is enough. More is too much.

MILLER: Why should you say "enough" to me? What have you done in this world? I have brought a daughter up to be Queen, and not a Queen like other Queens, either, but one who has spun straw into gold! And one who is the mother of a little King's son whose like is not to be found in the land!

WIFE: What do you say about that?

DAUGHTER: Oh, hush, Father!   Hush —

MILLER: Do you say hush to me, Daughter? Do you take sides against us, who have set you so high? Was it not your mother and I who told the King you could make gold out of straw?

WIFE: And wasn't it that very thing that brought about all the rest?

DAUGHTER: Ah, yes, Alas!

MILLER: Would your little son be sleeping in a royal cradle now, if we had not told the King how wonderful you were? And now you say hush to us, and side with Ingert.

DAUGHTER: No, no, no, Father! I do not side with anyone. I want more names, that's all. Ingert!   It is your turn.

INGERT: Well, when I was wandering in our own village the other day, I heard one man say to another, "Now that the Miller's daughter is Queen, I suppose he lines his stomach with fine wines and roasted meats. And just then the Miller passed by, and the man said —"There goes Roast-Ribs now." I call that a very strange name: Roast-Ribs.

MILLER: Are you making a laughing-stock of me?

DAUGHTER: Roast-Ribs! That is surely a strange name.

MILLER: Before my own daughter!

WIFE: Will you laugh at your own father, child?

DAUGHTER: It is a funny name.

MILLER: Roast-Ribs! What do you mean by calling me that?

INGERT: I called you nothing: I was only saying what I heard. I suppose, perhaps, the man who said it meant you looked as if your ribs were padded well with roasted meats.

WIFE: And what if they are?   It's well enough he has some weight to him: What sort of job would he make, running a mill and grinding meal for a kingdom, if he were a reed blown in the wind, like you. You pipestem!

MILLER: You yardstick!

WIFE: Are you the father of a Queen ! You —You —

MILLER: Are you the grandsire of a King's son?

WIFE: You sheepshanks!

DAUGHTER: Sheepshanks!

WIFE: You spindleshanks!

DAUGHTER: Spindleshanks! Oh, these are the very strangest names I ever heard! You shall all have rewards, for one name is as strange as another. Take them in, and let them choose each a jewel from my casket.

SON: Lead the way, Spindleshanks. Come, Roast-Ribs.

(They go. Rumpel enters behind their backs, and is sitting grinning at the Daughter when she turns around.)

RUMPEL: Pappaloapappaloapam! Pooh!

DAUGHTER: That isn't one of my guesses.

RUMPEL: Pipestem ! Pooh !

DAUGHTER: I didn't guess that, either.

RUMPEL: Well, what is my name?

DAUGHTER: Is it Roast-Ribs?

RUMPEL: No! It is not Roast-Ribs.

DAUGHTER: Is it Sheepshanks!

RUMPEL: No! It is not Sheepshanks.

DAUGHTER: Is it Spindleshanks?

RUMPEL: No, it is not Spindleshanks! Guess again! What is my name? What is my name? What is it? What is it? What is it?

DAUGHTER: Keep still! I can't guess so soon. I have only three guesses left.

RUMPEL: A thousand guesses would be no better. Nobody

knows from. whence I came. Nobody's ever heard my name.

DAUGHTER: Not even where you live?

RUMPEL: Nobody ever comes there!

DAUGHTER: Where is it:

RUMPEL: Somewhere.

DAUGHTER: Oh, tell me where!

RUMPEL: Somewhere.

DAUGHTER: Which way is it from here?

RUMPEL: There is a long way, and a short way. If you go east till you come west, or west till you come east, that is the long way. If you go round and round, and say the right words, the door is where you want it. That is the short way.

DAUGHTER: What are the right words?

RUMPEL: Never mind.

DAUGHTER: Do you know them?

RUMPEL: Yes.

DAUGHTER: Who else knows them?

RUMPEL: No one.

DAUGHTER: How long does the long way take from here and back?

RUMPEL: Half a year, and a day besides.

DAUGHTER: How long does the short way take?

RUMPLE (*wheeling*): Like that.

DAUGHTER: Can nobody but you go the short way to where you live?

RUMPEL: Not unless I leave the door open.

DAUGHTER: What door?

RUMPEL: Never mind.

DAUGHTER: Tell me what door you could leave open.

RUMPEL: It doesn't matter, because I never will. And even if I should, you wouldn't come, because you'd be afraid.

DAUGHTER: What should I be afraid of?

RUMPEL: As soon as you put a finger, or a hair of your head through the door, you'd feel a wild wind. If you went on, it would whirl you round and round, till you came to a high hill, and on it a little house. And before the house a fire burning, and around the fire, you'd see me dancing and maybe shouting my name to the sky and the air.

DAUGHTER: Why do you shout your name?

RUMPEL: Because nobody knows it, and I feel full of myself.

DAUGHTER: Let me see — let me see —

RUMPEL: Now, Mrs. Queen, what is my name?

DAUGHTER: Let me see —

RUMPEL: It's no good hunting in your mind for it. You've never heard it.

DAUGHTER: I'm not.

RUMPEL: Yes you are. You are thinking up names.

DAUGHTER: No, I'm thinking up ways to make you feel sorry for me again.

RUMPEL *(stamping his foot)*: I won't feel sorry for you again.

DAUGHTER *(seizing his hand)*: I will make you. My tears are on your hand.

RUMPEL: No, no, no, no! I will not give up the child! I won't! I won't!

DAUGHTER: That isn't what I'm asking you to do.

RUMPEL: What is it you are asking?

DAUGHTER: Only a little more time.

RUMPEL: I've given you twice already.

DAUGHTER: But I must have more. Your name is very hard to find. I didn't know at first it would be so hard: I must have a long time.

RUMPEL: What's the use of that? You'll never find my name:
And when that time is up, you'll come crying and praying
and going on your knees again.

DAUGHTER: No. Give me half a year and a day besides, and
I'll never ask for time again.

RUMPEL: In half a year and a day besides you'll promise to give
me your child without any fuss?

DAUGHTER: If I don't find out your name.

RUMPEL: You won't drop tears on my hand?

DAUGHTER: I'll keep all my tears in my heart.

RUMPEL: Your eyes won't look at me so I'll want to give him
up?

DAUGHTER: I'll shut my eyes.

RUMPEL: You won't tremble and shake and kneel at my feet?

DAUGHTER: I will stand like a Queen.

RUMPEL: No! I shall know how you feel, for all that, and I shall
feel queer. You must come to meet me as if I were the young
King your husband, and say "Here you are again."

DAUGHTER: I will come like that, if you will give me half a
year and a day besides.

RUMPEL: Very well! Cover your eyes. I am going away. For
half a year and one more day, I am going away, I am going
away!

DAUGHTER: Are you gone?

RUMPEL *(opening the door)*: Not yet.

DAUGHTER: I am going to look.

RUMPEL: No!

DAUGHTER: I can't keep from looking much longer. *(RUMPEL
scrambles through backward. He thrusts his face out, and is
about to speak, when she lowers her arm.)* I will look when

I count five. *(RUMPEL pulls the door to, but shuts it on his finger. He opens it in a temper, making faces at it.)* One, two, three, four, five—*(As she reaches five, he shuts the door. It does not go quite shut. She sees it move, or she would not know it.)* Are you gone? He has left it open. That must be the short way. *(She puts out a hand to open it more, hesitates, then goes ahead, She thrusts her hand in a little way, cries out.)* Oh-h-h! Shall I leave my baby here? Suppose I never come back. No. I'll try the long way first. *(Runs to palace door.)* Gothol! Ingert! 1 must have all the strange names in the whole world. Ingert, ask in every town and hamlet, on the top of every hill, and in the hollow of every valley. And ask among the palm trees and orange groves. And Gothol, you must go east until you come west, and Ingert, go west until you come east. In half a year and one day more, you must be back with names for me. *(They bow, and go.)* Half a year and one day more.

(The curtain closes, but open immediately on the same scene. It is dark in the King's garden below. RUMPEL, on the Edge of the World. is circling his pot and singing.)

RUMPLE:
> **Today I bake, tomorrow I brew.**
> **And half a year is almost through.**
> **My name, my name, I shout and shout.**
> **For no one's here to find it out.**

(RUMPEL leaps from one side to the other, and front, shouting "Rumpelstiltskin'" He breaks into laughter, so hard that he fairly rolls.)

Now it is time to blow up my fire. Burn, fire burn. Boil, pot, boil. The half year is up. In only one day more I shall bring you something. Something new! Something different! *(MOTHER HULDA appears as he bends over the fire.)*

MOTHER HULDA: So you haven't learned not to shout your name? *(He scrambles away from her, still afraid of her. Then he recovers himself.)*

RUMPEL: I will shout my name if I want to. Rumpelstiltskin!

I feel like shouting it, because I have won my bargain. I am the head of everything. I can do as I like in the world. I shall make an end of men. I have a little King's son to put in my pot.

MOTHER HULDA: Where is he? *(RUMPEL turns his back.)* Where is he?

RUMPEL: He is in the Queen's garden, *(recovering spirit.)* He's waiting for me. I gave the Queen time. But now the time is. up.

MOTHER HULDA: Why did you give the Queen time

RUMPEL: Because.

MOTHER HULDA: Why?

RUMPEL: Because, because, because!!!!!

MOTHER HULDA: Why?

RUMPEL *(stamping)*: I don't want to tell.

MOTHER HULDA: Take care. One day you will stamp too hard.

RUMPEL: I will stamp when I feel like it. I feel like it when you say I must tell why I gave the Queen time.

MOTHER HULDA: Then tell, and have it over with. Come ... come .... come!

RUMPEL *(spitting)*: I felt sorry for her.

MOTHER HULDA: Ah ...

RUMPEL: I couldn't take the baby when I felt sorry for her. The feeling stopped me from it *(Brightening)*: I bargained with her for half a year and one day more, that she couldn't make me feel sorry when I came again.

MOTHER HULDA: But you did feel sorry for her.

RUMPEL: I don't any more: I never will again.

MOTHER HULDA: You might.

RUMPEL: No! *(RUMPEL stamps so hard that his foot sticks. He has a hard time getting it free. He feels very sheepish, his*

269

eyes sideways on MOTHER HULDA. When he gets free, his swagger returns.) I have forgotten how it feels to be sorry.

MOTHER HULDA: Perhaps you will remember it when you go to take the baby away from its mother.

RUMPEL *(flying into fury)*: No, no, no, no, no, no, no, no!

MOTHER HULDA: Now, now, now. What did I tell you about getting into a temper?

RUMPEL: Nothing.

MOTHER HULDA: Yes I did.

RUMPEL: I've forgotten.

MOTHER HULDA: No you haven't. Look at me! *(He starts to cower, as before, but recovers.)* I am going to tell you again.

RUMPEL: I don't care if you do, I don't believe it.

MOTHER HULDA: It is just as true when you don't believe it, as when you do. I said if you let your temper get the best of you, you will fly to pieces. *(RUMPEL struggles between his defiance and his awe of her, then bursts out laughing, pointing at her.)* Rumpelstiltskin, you bad little thing. Why do you laugh at me?

RUMPEL: You said I would fly to pieces. I've been in lots of tempers. I've been in frightful tempers, and I never flew to pieces in my life. I don't care about you. I don't care about anything. I will shout my name if I want. I will be just as mad as I please. I will never be sorry again. I will laugh when I take the King's son from his mother. I will put him in my pot, and make an end of men! *(He laughs in triumph.)*

MOTHER HULDA: Very well. Only be sure you do not make an end of yourself, instead.

RUMPEL: I won't listen to you any more. I don't like to hear the things you say. I'd rather hear myself. I'd rather feel full of myself, and shout my name to the sky.

MOTHER HULDA *(going)*: Very well.
  (RUMPEL flies to shout after her, then to the other side,

270

then front.)

RUMPEL: Rumpelstiltskin!   R-u-m-p-e-1-s-t-i-l-t-s-k-i-n!
    RUMPELSTILTSKIN!   *(He circles he pot, singing)*
>   **Boil, purple and red and gold and green,**
>   **Boil every color that ever was seen.**
>   **For something different, something new,**
>   **This very same hour I'm bringing to you.**
>   **For soon my bargain I shall win.**
>   **For my name is —**

(During this, INGERT on one side, and GOTHOL on the other, have come, wandering, up the lull. They see each other, and make signs of silence. At the word "name," each takes an eager step forward, and this calls RUMPEL's attention to them. He sees the nearest first.)

What are you doing on my hill?

GOTHOL: I was coming east through the woods of the world, and I heard a great shout, and I followed it up, and I found myself here —

INGERT: I was coming west over the wastes of the world, and I heard a shout, and I followed it here —

RUMPEL: What was the word you heard? —
    (They are on the edge of recalling it, but finally give it up.)

INGERT: Why — it was —

GOTHOL: Oh yes. Ah ... it was — let me see —

INGERT: I don't remember.

GOTHOL: Nor I. It was a word I had never heard before. Was it you who shouted?

RUMPEL: Yes.

GOTHOL: What did you say?

RUMPEL: Something.

INGERT: To whom were you shouting?

RUMPEL: Nobody.

INGERT: What a strange little man. What is your name?

GOTHOL: What are you called?
  (RUMPEL laughs some more.)

INGERT: You do not seem to know who we are. We are from the King's court.

GOTHOL: Men do not laugh when we ask them questions.
  (RUMPEL laughs more.) What is your name?

RUMPEL: I won't tell you.

INGERT: You had better tell us. The Queen sent us.

RUMPEL: What for?

INGERT: To find out all the strange names we could, to tell her.

RUMPEL: You will never tell her mine! I don't want her to know it.

GOTHOL: It doesn't matter what you want. Make an end of this nonsense. Tell us your name.

RUMPEL *(stamping)*: No!

INGERT: You might as well, first as last. We shall make you before we go.

RUMPEL *(in a temper, flies first at one, then at the other)*: Get off my hill! Get off my hill!

INGERT: Mind your manners, and tell us your name.

RUMPEL: Go away! *(GOTHOL takes him and lifts him on one arm, holding him horizontally.)*

GOTHOL: What is your name?

RUMPEL: Stand at the edge of the hill, where you came up, and I will sing you a song about my name.
  (GOTHOL and INGERT go to the edge of the hill. RUMPEL circles his pot backwards.)
  Three times backward round my pot,
  Then you shall be where you are not —

INGERT: You said you'd tell us your name.

RUMPEL: It's at the end of the song.
Three times backward, and a door
Shall open where you were before.

INGERT: I feel strange.

GOTHOL: He's working a spell on us.

RUMPEL: Three times backward.

GOTHOL: Stop!

INGERT: Stop!

RUMPEL: There you go!

GOTHOL: Hold him!

RUMPEL: Whirling to your place below! *(They are caught by the spell at once, and whirl and disappear. RUMPEL dances and smirks, full of airs. He puts his hands to his mouth, and calls his name down after each, in a tiny voice.)* Rumpelstiltskin ... RUMPELSTILTSKIN! ... I wonder what the little Queen will say to them ... I'll look *(He runs to his pot.)*
Boil green, and show me the garden fair,
Where the Queen walks in the fragrant air.
For nobody knows from whence I came,
Or that *(whispers)* **Rumpelstiltskin** *(loud)* **is my name.**
(The lights come up on the garden. DAUGHTER, entering from the palace, is listening. RUMPEL's voice now sounds far away. He runs to look down on the edge of the hill.)

SON *(entering from the palace)*: What are you doing all alone in the garden, little Queen?

DAUGHTER: I am looking for Gothol and Ingert. It is past time for Ingert and Gothol to return. I must have a name. I must have one! *(The little door flies open, and INGERT whirls out, then GOTHOL. Both are dazed, and look about in teror.)* Did you find it? *(They nod gasping.)* The hill on the edge of the world? *(They nod.)*

GOTHOL: As I passed through the woods at the edge of the world, I came to a high hill, and on it was a little house. And before the house burned a fire, and round the fire danced a comical little man. and he hopped on one foot and sang. Just as he came to his name, he saw us, and he drove us away.

INGERT: He put a spell on us, and we knew nothing till we were here.

DAUGHTER: Why didn't you get his name?

INGERT: He would not tell it.

DAUGHTER: You must go back, at once, and get it.

GOTHOL: No. Queen, no. I can never go there again.

INGERT: You had better send us to our death.

GOTHOL: Do not send me up that hill.

SON: I will go for you, little Queen. Tell me the way.

GOTHOL: Do not let the young King go! He will never come back.

SON: You came back again, afraid! But I am not afraid.

DAUGHTER: You must not go. I do not want you to go. Rise, Gothol. Think nothing more about it. Go in, all of you! *(RUMPEL laughs, gets up, stretches, yawns, curls on steps: To the SON:)* Call the others, to sit by my son. I wish to walk in my field, as I used to. *(SON goes into palace, to summon ladies-in-waiting. DAUGHTER crosses to cradle, for a loving look at her baby.)* I am going to save you, little King's son. I am going to find the name myself. *(The LADIES enter from the palace.)* Do not leave his side until I am here again. Promise me to stay fast.

FIRST LADY: We will stay fast!
(DAUGHTER runs to the door, pulls it open, shrinks away.)

DAUGHTER: Watch him carefully:
(She gives a muffled cry as she goes out the door. The LADIES do not see her go.)

FIRST LADY: I wish we did not have to stay in this garden. There is dancing down by the mill.

SECOND LADY: If we could slip away, we could dance to their music. *(INGERT and GOTHOL enter.)* Oh, Ingert, will you do something for me?

INGERT: Say what I can do, and it is done.

SECOND LADY: Stay with the King's son, while we run to the mill and back.

INGERT: If that will please you.

FIRST LADY: It will.

SECOND LADY: You must not leave him till we come again.

FIRST LADY: Promise to stay fast.

INGERT: We will stay fast.
(FIRST and SECOND LADY exeunt.)

GOTHOL: What do you think draws them away with so much laughter?

INGERT: I'd like to follow and find out.
(KAREN enters.)

KAREN *(to BABY)*: Is he well covered?

INGERT *(at a nudge from GOTHOL)*: Princess Karen, will you sit beside the little King's son, while we stroll to the mill and back?

KAREN: Very gladly. Do not be long.

GOTHOL *(at exit)*: You will not leave him till we come again?

KAREN: I will not leave.

INGERT: You promise to stay fast?

KAREN: I will stay fast. *(INGERT and GOTHOL exeunt.)* I wonder what goes on they wish so much to see? I'd like to follow them and find out. *(The KING enters.)*

KING: Is he awake?

KAREN: King, my father, will you stay with the baby while I go to the mill and back?

KING: Take as long as you like.

275

KAREN: You will not leave his side. You will stay fast?

KING: I will stay fast: *(She goes.)* She runs off with a will: I wonder what draws her down to the mill. I'd like to follow her and find out. *(MILLER and his WIFE enter.)* Miller, will you and your wife stay with our grandson here, while I go over the hill to your mill?

MILLER: Go as soon as you like.

KING: You must not leave his side an instant.

WIFE: Do you tell me how to care for my daughter's child?

KING: You must stay fast.

WIFE: Who should stay as fast as we?
(The KING goes.)

MILLER: Why do you think the King goes to our mill?

WIFE: There is dancing on the grass there: It is likely he has gone to hear how the people praise his little grandson.

MILLER: It would be that.

WIFE: All the neighbors will be saying fine things of the child.

MILLER: It would be good to hear them.

WIFE: It wiuld not take long to get there and back.

MILLER: The child is safe in the garden here.

WIFE: No one can enter from without, except by knocking at the gate.

MILLER: We will not be gone but a short while.

WIFE: We will hasten our steps:
(They go. The DAUGHTER climbs up the hillside of the edge of the world, above. RUMPEL is fast asleep. She looks about in fear and amazement.)

DAUGHTER: There is no one here.
(RUMPEL stretches and yawns. DAUGHTER leaps soundlessly back out of sight. RUMPEL goes to the edge of the hill, front, and looks down into the garden.)

276

RUMPEL: Aha! Now is the time! *(He circles the pot, singing.)*
> **Today I brew, tomorrow I bake,**
> **And now I shall the King's child take.**
> **For nobody knows from whence I came,**
> **Or that —**

(RUMPEL burns his finger, and hops around shaking it and sucking it. He returns to the pot and sings again.)
> **For nobody knows from whence I came,**
> **Or that RUMPELSTILTSKIN is my name!**
> **Three times backward round my pot,**
> **Then I shall be where I am not.**
> **Three times backward, and my door**
> **Will open where was none before.**
> **Three times backward, here I go,**
> **To fetch the baby from below!**

(He whirls down. DAUGHTER runs to look after him, when he is well out of sight.)

DAUGHTER: What shall I do?
(She returns and mimics RUMPEL's charm. It works. She cries out, and disappears. Just as she does so, RUMPEL is seen coming through the door, looking at the baby in the cradle. He claps his hands and hops with satisfaction. He lifts the baby and starts to the little door, but stops at the sound of people approaching, leaps back, alert. The voices offstage grow stronger. RUMPEL disappears with the baby.)

FIRST LADY *(entering)*: Are you sure it was Ingert you saw?

SECOND LADY: And Gothol with him!

FIRST LADY: It is true! They are not here!

SECOND LADY: The child is alone!

FIRST LADY: What will the Queen say: *(FIRST LADY runs to the cradle and gives a scream of terror! The others rush over.)* He is gone!

SECOND LADY: No, no! He can't be!
(They rush about, looking. One lifts the cradle, looking behind. One rushes to the palace door.)

277

FIRST LADY *(Going in)*: Maybe someone carried him in!

GOTHOL *(offstage)*: Are you sure it was Karen you saw?

INGERT: There could be no mistake: Hasten! Make haste!
   (They stop with relief as they enter.)

FIRST LADY: We left the child with you.

SECOND LADY: You promised to stay fast. And now he is
   gone!

FIRST LADY *(entering)* : He is nowhere within.

KAREN *(offstage)*: Is someone there? ... Oh, thank Heaven! He
   is not alone.

GOTHOL *(to KAREN)*: We left the child with you.

INGERT: You promised to stay fast.

BOTH: And now the child is gone.

KAREN *(to cradle)*: Gone?   Gone!

KING *(offstage)*: Miller ... Ah! The child is not alone.

KAREN: King, my father, I left the child with you.

KING: Well? Well? Get up! Why are you like this?

KAREN: You promised to stay fast.

KING: Why do you weep Why do you cry out? Where is my
   grandchild??? Speak! Speak! *(He strides to the cradle.)*

KAREN: Now he is gone!

KING: Gone!

MILLER *(offstage)* : Run!   Run!   You stayed too long.

WIFE: It was you who wouldn't come.

BOTH: It was you. It was not I!

KING *(as they enter)*: You! YOU!   YOU!   I left the child with
   you!

MILLER: Why do you shout at us? What has come to pass?

WIFE: King!

KING: The child is gone! Gone!

EVERYONE *(to the appropriate person)*: You promised to stay fast. And now the child is gone!
(The DAUGHTER has entered by the little door, unseen because she was covered by the crowd. She breaks through them.)

DAUGHTER: What do you say? *(Silence. She looks into their faces, turns to the cradle. They all turn away. She is silent and still.)* I am too late! *(They move toward her. She motions them away.)* Where is the young King, my husband:

KAREN: I will tell him you have returned.
(They all go in, leading her motionless. She covers her face with her hands. RUMPEL appears, grinning, the baby in his arms. He prances around her. Finally he laughs aloud. She looks up and cries out, then remembers her bargain.)

DAUGHTER: Oh-h-h-h ! ... Well, here you are again.
(RUMPEL swaggers to lay the child in the cradle.)

RUMPEL: Guess your guess, Mrs. Queen. What is my name?

DAUGHTER: Is it—Henry?

RUMPEL: Ho! Ho! Ho! That is not my name.

DAUGHTER: Is it—John?

RUMPEL: Ho! Ho! Ho! That is not my name.

DAUGHTER: Is it—is it, perhaps—RUMPELSTILTSKIN?
(He flies into a terrible rage, stamping, screaming, spitting, and running about the stage. Finally, he stamps with one foot in the cradle. The bottom goes through, and he has a fun out time getting tree of it, rushing, screaming through his little door, up his hill, stamps himself off at the edge, flying to pieces as he does so. This is of course done with dummy arms and legs, wig and cap, trunk, etc. DAUGHTER clasps her baby close.)

CURTAIN

REYNARD THE FOX

Adapted from *Gestes de Renart le Goupil*

by
Arthur Fauquez

translation by
Marie-Louise Roelants

Beginning mid-century, writers slowly began to respond to the needs and interests of increasingly sophisticated and discriminating audiences, nurtured on television and children's movies. The Chorpenning-style fairytale dramas still comprised the bulk of the theatre repertoire, but the maturation of a new generation of playwrights and a renewed interest in professional theatre production stimulated further development of the literature; and slowly new types of plays caught producers' attention to meet these needs.

The repertoires of children's theatres from others countries became an important new source of plays as publishers, particularly Sara Spencer of The Children's Theatre Press, broadened their offerings by translating and publishing works from abroad. *Reynard the Fox*, by Belgian playwright Arthur Fauquez, is one of the most significant plays that Spencer imported and published during this period.

This play ostensibly presents the anecdotal story of a group of animals in a forest, which suggests that the play is no more innovative than the popular fairy and folk plays. In this play, however, Fauquez uses a well-conceived view of the human world to create a sophisticated satire on human greed and hypocrisy. The play offers an interesting story, unique characters, an unpredictable plot structure, and a delightfully provocative look at human foibles and weaknesses.

The cunning, mischievous, and loveable Reynard (the fox), occupies center stage in this play, as his unscrupulous pranks have the animal kingdom in an uproar. Reynard's sometimes vicious trickery, which precipitates successive conflicts between himself and the other characters of the forest society, defines the basic throughline of the play; but the ramifications of this action, made real through the detailed characterizations, extend far beyond the resolution of these conflicts. Reynard repeatedly harasses the other animals until, totally exasperated, they band together to plot his downfall. When they finally catch Reynard in the act of one of his pranks, Noble the Lion, King of the forest, declares that if Reynard commits more than twenty-four pranks in the next year he will be hanged. Subsequently, Reynard, seemingly oblivious to his own fate, tricks first one character and then another by appealing to their own less-than-upright behavior.

The animal characters, as cleverly drawn as any found in dramatic literature for children, effectively embody their respective animal types, while at the same time reflecting human behavior. This, in turn, reveals a large chorus of human frailties, including: Brun, the greedy bear, who readily compromises himself for the promise of fresh honey; Noble, the lion, whose vanity makes him an easy target for Reynard's manipulation; and Tiecelin, the crow, whose shrill impudence raises the ire of the animal community.

Fauquez uses these characters to create a world without clear-cut villains and heros, or easily recognized right and wrong. He endows each character with both moral strengths and weakness, and he pushes each character slightly toward selfish or antisocial behavior when it serves his or her own needs. This world becomes even more complex when Reynard, nominally the protagonist in the play, serves as an antagonist in the action. His practical jokes keep the world in constant turmoil, but the success of these pranks depends on the foolishness and complicity of the victims.

Reynard operates as a rogue hero: he lives on the fringes of accepted moral behavior, but his sense of exuberance, his cleverness, and his insights into human behavior transcend his lack of scruples. When the other animals fail to capture Reynard in the end, the audience happily cheers his escape, but remains reticent to argue in his defense. Reynard is sometimes cynical, sometimes untruthful, and sometimes mean; but he is always lifelike and believable. Unlike many rogue characters in literature, Fauquez provides little justification in the play for Reynard's antisocial behavior. Fauquez thus creates a lifelike world, not an idealized one.

At one point Tiecelin, the Crow, commenting on a plan to gain revenge against Reynard, declares: "as far as being fair, certainly not. Honest—even less so. But as for being smart—ha ha!" With this statement Fauquez does not suggest that we favor "smart" behavior over "honest" behavior. Instead, he leaves such moralizing to the audience. He also supports these thematic elements with a plot structure that deviates from the predictable well-made play form. Rather than build the action melodramatically, Fauquez focuses more on individual episodes, with each standing as a microcosm of the play as a whole. And in the end the audience is left to decide who wins, and if that victory is, by any standards, just.

It is important to note that this is a play of ideas, as much as it is a play of action. There are very few children's plays written before this time that offer anything more than moralistic stories wherein "right" is clearly defined, and wherein the ideologically correct "right" proudly prevails. This play stands in marked contrast to that ideological simplicity. With its sophisticated story line, this play assumes a child audience capable of discerning and understanding complexity and grappling with moral ambiguity.

Arthur Fauquez was born in Antwerp, Belgium, in 1912. Before his retirement he worked for many years as a businessman in Brussels. Working closely with his wife, Fauquez wrote over seventy plays. These include twenty-five children's plays, two plays for adults, plus puppet plays, radio serials, and short television plays. Three of his children's plays have been translated and published in the United States: *Reynard the Fox, Don Quixote of La Mancha,* and *The Man Who Killed Time.*

REYNARD THE FOX

by
Arthur Fauquez

translated by
Marie-Louise Roelants

REYNARD THE FOX

Characters

TIECELIN, THE CROW

REVEREND EPINARD, THE HEDGEHOG

BRUN, THE BEAR

NOBLE, THE LION

YSENGRIN, THE WOLF

REYNARD, THE FOX

LENDORE, THE MARMOT

Setting

THE ENTIRE PLAY TAKES PLACE IN THE HEART OF THE FOREST.

Scene 1. Spring

Scene 2. Summer

Scene 3. Autumn

Scene 4. Winter

PROLOGUE

(Tiecelin, perched in the crotch of a tree, practicing.)

TIECELIN: Caw! *(Higher)* Caw! *(Higher)* Caw!
(BRUN enters, patch over one eye, his arm in a sling.)

BRUN: Stop that infernal racket!

TIECELIN: Caw! *(Higher)* Caw!

BRUN: Stop!

TIECELIN: You are interrupting my practice, Seigneur Brun. Caw!

BRUN: Stop this instant, and summon the King!

TIECELIN: *(notices him.)* The King? Good heavens, what has happened to you? Have you been caught in a bramble bush? Ha, ha, ha!

BRUN: Enough of your insolence! Call the King at once!

TIECELIN: Lord Bear, I am the King's Registrar. If you wish an audience with the King, you must state your reason to me.

BRUN: I have been beaten, do you hear? Look at me!

TIECELIN: Ha, ha, ha!

BRUN: I have been beaten, and it is all the fault of Reynard the Fox!

TIECELIN: Reynard did this to the mighty Bear?

BRUN: He tricked me. I want the King to punish him.

TIECELIN: Oh, if it was only one of Reynard's tricks —

BRUN: But look at me!

TIECELIN: I am. Ha, ha, ha!
(YSEGRIN limps in, on a crutch, his head bandaged.)

YSEGRIN: Sound the trumpets

TIECELIN: Baron Ysengrin!

BRUN: You, too?

TIECELIN: What a pair! Ha, ha, ha!

288

YSEGRIN: One more caw from you, Crow, and I'll wring your scrawny neck. Summon the King!

TIECELIN: The king is not to be called just because you stubbed your toe.

YSEGRIN: Stubbed my toe? I have been attacked by dogs. Look at me!

TIECELIN: Yes, I see. Ha, ha, ha!

BRUN: Who has done this to you?

YSEGRIN: It is all the doing of Reynard the Fox!

BRUN: Gr-r-r-r!

TIECELIN: Reynard did this to the powerful Wolf?

YSEGRIN: He tricked me.

BRUN: Me, too.

BOTH: Summon the King!

TIECELIN: *(climbs down.)* Gentlemen, if I were to summon the King every time Reynard played a trick, he would soon appoint a new Registrar.

YSEGRIN: But this is not to be borne!

BRUN: I intend to accuse Reynard in court.

YSEGRIN: Yes. We'll bring him to trial.

BRUN: And we shall demand his punishment.

YSEGRIN: I shall demand his hanging.

TIECELIN: Hanging?

BRUN: Yes! We have had enough of his tricks.

YSEGRIN: We are going to get rid of the Fox!

TIECELIN: If you have been unable to get rid of him in the field, how do you expect to get rid of him in Court?

BRUN: The King will do us justice.

YSEGRIN: Bring us to the King!

TIECELIN: Gentlemen, I am a man of law, and I will give

you my best legal advice. Go home and lick your wounds. Reynard will trick you in Court, just as he has tricked you in the field. You have no evidence.

BRUN: Evidence? What of my black eye? And my arm?

YSEGRIN: Look at my lame leg. And my head!

TIECELIN: Yes, ha, ha, ha! What a picture! Now you will excuse me. I must return to my practicing.
(He climbs up.)

BRUN: You miserable Crow! The King shall hear of your insolence!

YSEGRIN: If you had a little more meat on your bones, I should have a nice fat crow's wing for my supper!

TIECELIN: Caw!

BRUN: Save us from that deafening noise!
(Exit, holding his ears.)

TIECELIN: Caw!

YSEGRIN: Take care, Crow, that the Fox does not trick you.
(Exit, limping. REYNARD enters, unseen by TIECELIN.)

TIECELIN: Ho, ho, ho! The Fox trick me? What a joke! I am too smart for that. Caw! Caw! Caw!

REYNARD: *(groaning with pain)* Oh-h-h-h-h!

TIECELIN: Can I never practice in peace? Caw-w-w-w — Good Heavens, it is the Fox himself!

REYNARD: *(weakly)* Tiecelin, my friend — Oh-h-h-h!

TIECELIN: What is your tale of woe? Do you wish to summon the King too?

REYNARD: No. I wish only to die in peace.

TIECELIN: To die?

REYNARD: Tiecelin, I have been poisoned.

TIECELIN: Poisoned?

REYNARD: Oh-h-h-h! It was an oyster I found. Sing me one

of your sweetest songs, so that I may die with your music in my ears.

TIECELIN: You are not serious?

REYNARD: Sing, my good fellow.

TIECELIN: Like this? Caw-w-w-w-!

REYNARD: Thanks, old friend.
(He gasps, then falls quiet.)

TIECELIN: Reynard? Reynard! Don't act the sleeping beauty. I know you. You are only faking. Oh, very well. I will rouse you. Caw! Caw! Caw! Not a wince. Not a quiver. He is very smart. Reynard? Is he really faking? *(He climbs down to look.)* My word, he sleeps like the dead. I can't even see him breathe. Good Heavens, he isn't breathing! Could he really be dead! What a release, Lord, if this is so! *(He moves REYNARD's tail, which drops back, limp.)* But how could he be dead? This is too much to hope. He said an oyster. It is possible. *(He pokes the Fox with a long stick. REYNARD rolls over, a dead weight.)* It's true! Brun! Ysengrin! No, I am the one who found him. It will win me the gratitude of the whole kingdom if I hint that I am a tiny bit responsible for this — oh, just a very tiny bit — just enough to make them think I am the one who liberated the world from this rascal. I should be hailed as a hero. I shall have my portrait painted in triumphant attire, crushing my vanquished enemy, and I shall sell his skin for a fur.
(He rests his foot upon REYNARD, in a conqueror's pose.)

REYNARD: *(grasping his ankle)*   Dear Tiecelin!

TIECELIN: Help! Help! He is not dead!

REYNARD: You had better learn, dear friend, never to sell Reynard's skin before you have killed him.

TIECELIN: What I said about it was only in fun. I — I only wanted to give you a laugh.

REYNARD: Well, you see, you succeeded. I am laughing. I am laughing with all my teeth, which in a few moments are going to gobble you up.

TIECELIN: You are not going to kill me like a simple chicken?

REYNARD: Why not?

TIECELIN: I am the Royal Registrar. And besides I am your friend.

REYNARD: Yes?

TIECELIN: Only a minute ago, I saved you from a Court trial.

REYNARD: I am very grateful, believe me. And because of that I'll swallow you in one gulp, without chewing.

TIECELIN: Let me go!

REYNARD: *(plucking a feather from TIECELIN's tail)* And moreover, I'll keep this to remember you by.

TIECELIN: Aie! You have ruined my beautiful tail!

REYNARD: Never mind, Tiecelin. You will not be needing it any more.

TIECELIN: Oh-h-h, you monster! I am going to be eaten, and I can see no escape.

REYNARD: None whatever.

TIECELIN: Then at least grant my last wish. If I have to be eaten, don't just gobble me down like a piece of cheese. Treat me as a delicacy, and prepare your stomach for this feast.

REYNARD: My stomach is always prepared.

TIECELIN: Oh, no. To enjoy a dainty morsel fully, it is necessary to warm your stomach and your head — like this.
(He rubs his stomach and his head.)

REYNARD: Why your head?

TIECELIN: To eat intelligently.

REYNARD: And why your stomach?

TIECELIN: To warm your appetite.

REYNARD: It is an odd method.

TIECELIN: But it works, I assure you.

REYNARD: Like this?
(He lets go of TIECELIN, to rub head and stomach.)

TIECELIN: Oh, harder than that.

REYNARD: It certainly does warm me up.

TIECELIN: *(clambering up to his perch)* The best way to digest well is to eat nothing.

REYNARD: Why, Tiecelin!

TIECELIN: You savage! Did you think I was going to let you eat me for lunch?

REYNARD: Eat you for lunch? I would have to be starving.

TIECELIN: I am going to denounce you to the King.

REYNARD: *(laughing)* Oh. Tiecelin, you take yourself so seriously.

TIECELIN: The King also will take me seriously. Trumpets!
(Trumpets.)

REYNARD: Caw! Caw! Caw! *(Mimicking)* Oh, Tiecelin, sing me one last song before I die. *(Exit, laughing. Returns immediately.)* By the way, keep this to remember me by. *(Tosses feather. Exit.)*

TIECELIN: My feather! Monster! Thief! Cannibal! *(He climbs down to retrieve the feather.)* My beautiful feather! But this is evidence. Now we have him! Brun! Ysengrin! Bring the fox to trial! I have the evidence! Trumpets!
(Trumpets. EPINARD enters quietly.)

EPINARD: My dear fellow, what are the trumpets all about?

TIECELIN: Reverend Epinard. Stand there. I am about to make a proclamation. Trumpets! *(Trumpets.)* We, Tiecelin, the Crow, Royal Registrar, announce a great Court of Justice meeting, to put on trial the most infamous of all criminals, His Majesty's Own Knight — *(Drum roll.)* Reynard the Fox!

EPINARD: Reynard, on trial? But will you explain —

TIECELIN: One moment. Whoever wishes to accuse the Fox is requested to give his name to the Registrar. I am the Registrar. Trumpets! *(Trumpets.)*

EPINARD: What is this all about?

TIECELIN: It means. Reverend, that we are at last going to put Reynard on trial, and punish him for his misdeeds. Don't you yourself have some complaint to make against the Fox?

EPINARD: I?

TIECELIN: Yes, you. Has your religious robe protected you from his tricks?

EPINARD: Oh, no. Only last week, he got a duck-egg away from me.

TIECELIN: Well, then. You will lodge a charge against him?

EPINARD: Ahem! I should not wish it made public how I — ah — came by the duck-egg.

TIECELIN: As you wish. Sit over there. Here come two who will testify. *(EPINARD sits and reads in his Bible. BRUN and YSEGRIN enter.)*

YSEGRIN: You are bringing him to trial?

TIECELIN: I have the evidence.

BRUN: Where is the King?
(NOBLE the LION enters, majestically, theatrically.)

NOBLE: Since when do the trumpets not greet my arrival?

TIECELIN: *(bowing)* Sire — your Majesty — I think — I thought — Trum — Trumpets! *(Trumpets.)*

NOBLE: Let my arrival be announced to the Court.

TIECELIN: Yes, Sire. Trumpets! *(Trumpets.)* Gentlemen, the King! *(All bow, as NOBLE seats himself.)*

NOBLE: I declare the Court of Justice open. Now, Tiecelin, why have you assembled us all in Court?

TIECELIN: To hear charges against your Majesty's Knight, Sir Reynard the Fox.

NOBLE: Reynard? What charges?

YSEGRIN: I have been attacked!

BRUN: I have been beaten!

TIECELIN: My very life has been threatened!

NOBLE: Brun! Ysengrin! Where have you received these terrible injuries? Have you been fighting again?

BRUN: Sire, it is Reynard!

YSEGRIN: We are the victims of Reynard's trickery!

TIECELIN: This is Reynard's doing!

NOBLE: If this is true, Reynard is a dangerous criminal indeed. Bring him in.

TIECELIN: But your Majesty —

BRUN: We do not require his presence to recite his crimes.

YSEGRIN: We can tell you —

NOBLE: Where is Reynard?

TIECELIN: Knight Reynard thinks — he does not know — actually, I think he thinks —

NOBLE: Enough thinking. Where is Reynard?

TIECELIN: He th — I mean, he believes — your Majesty, I will have him brought before you.

NOBLE: Let this insolent character be called at once.

TIECELIN: Y-y-yes, Sire. S-s-s-sir Reynard the Fox! Trumpets! *(Trumpets, resembling a hunter's call, ending with a drum roll. During this fanfare, each animal makes his own preparation for REYNARD's entrance, reflecting his attitude toward this dangerous criminal.)*

YSEGRIN: Here comes the villain! *(REYNARD enters, smiling, confident. Bows to the King.)*

NOBLE: I greet you, Knight Reynard.

REYNARD: Good evening, Sire.

NOBLE: Just answer our questions.

REYNARD: Allow me, Sire, to wish that this day may not go by without being the best one of your life.

NOBLE: Quiet. We have assembled the High Court of Justice, for the express purpose of putting you on trial.

REYNARD: On trial? Me? The most devoted and faithful of all your subjects? But why, Sire? What have I done to be tried for?

NOBLE: You shall know this very minute. Tiecelin, announce the first accuser.

TIECELIN: Master Ysengrin the Wolf.

NOBLE: We are listening, Ysengrin.

YSEGRIN: I accuse —

REYNARD: Cousin Ysengrin, you, my accuser?

YSEGRIN: I accuse! Do you deny that you led me into a farm-yard under the pretext of showing me a flock of nice, plump ducks?

REYNARD: Not at all. I did show you a flock of nice, plump ducks, Cousin. Is that a crime?

YSEGRIN: And do you deny that you fastened me in, and roused the dogs, so that I was so cruelly bitten, I barely escaped alive?

REYNARD: Oh, my dear Cousin, is that how you suffered those grievous wounds? Those dreadful dogs!

NOBLE: So you admit luring him into a trap where he almost lost his life?

REYNARD: Oh, no. Excuse me, Sire. I only took him to the farm-yard to show him nice, plump ducks, as he says. But when he saw them, he began to drool and slobber and lick his lips at the sight, and even started to chase them. I could not stay for this. I fled, and cried out for help. Was it my fault if the gate shut behind me, and locked Ysengrin in with the dogs?

296

NOBLE: If the story is as you tell it —

YSEGRIN: Allow me —

NOBLE: And I am inclined to believe you — the Marshal Ysengrin is as guilty as you are, and by the same token, deserves the same punishment. It is up to you, Lord Wolf, to fix Reynard's fate, since the fate shall be yours also. What punishment would you suggest?

YSEGRIN: Ah — uh — in that case — yes, in that case, I think it is better — and wiser — not to punish Reynard.

REYNARD: Thanks, dear Cousin, for your generous intervention.

NOBLE: This case is settled. Who is next, Tiecelin?

TIECELIN: Seigneur Brun.

BRUN: I accuse!

REYNARD: You, my Uncle?

BRUN: Be quiet!

NOBLE: We are listening, Seigneur Brun.

BRUN: Your Majesty, I was taking a peaceful nap under an apple tree, when this creature —

REYNARD: Uncle.

BRUN: This mongrel —

REYNARD: Uncle.

BRUN: This rascal —

REYNARD: Uncle!

BRUN: For Heaven's sake, will you let me speak?

NOBLE: Proceed, Seigneur Brun.

BRUN: I was only sleeping, your Majesty, doing no harm to anyone —

REYNARD: He means, Sire, he was resting, after a large lunch. He had just stripped the apple tree, bare.

BRUN: It is not true! But this scoundrel found me there, and screamed for the farmer. Can you deny it?

REYNARD: No, not at all. I thought he was stricken. Sire. His belly was swollen till it looked like a barrel. I cried out in my grief. Could I help it if the farmer heard me? Uncle Brun heard me too, and tried to run away, but he was so full of apples, he couldn't even get to his feet.

BRUN: This is slander! He yelped for the farmer, your Majesty, and the farmer attacked me with a pitchfork. Before I could move from the spot, he gave me a black eye and four loose teeth, not to mention the hair and skin I lost in the fray.

NOBLE: If you had stolen his apples, Brun, it seems to me the punishment you received was justified. What do you think?

BRUN: I think — I think it was a very high price to pay for a few apples.

NOBLE: Forget it. Next one.

TIECELIN: The next one is myself: Master Tiecelin the Crow, Man of Law, and Royal Registrar.

NOBLE: What is your complaint against Reynard?

TIECELIN: I accuse!

REYNARD: Come, now.

TIECELIN: Yes! I accuse Reynard of trying, just a minute ago, to twist my neck and gobble me up, as simply as if I had been a chicken.

NOBLE: This is more serious. What have you to reply, Master Reynard?

REYNARD: One thing only. Look at this piteous carcass, and judge for yourself, Sire. Who would wish to gobble him up, skinny and emaciated as he is? And even if I did, am I any more guilty in this matter than my Cousin Ysengrin?

YSEGRIN: I protest!

REYNARD: Or my Uncle Brun?

BRUN: I deny it!

REYNARD: Or the cat, the dog, the sparrow, the vulture — or you yourself, Sire Lion, our very beloved King, as well? *(Laughter.)*

NOBLE: Silence! *(Nobody laughs any more.)* Tiecelin, you over-estimate yourself. None of us wishes to eat crow.

TIECELIN: Reynard did. And here is the evidence. He pulled out one of my tail-feathers — this very feather.

REYNARD: Pouf! The wind plucks your feathers all the time.

TIECELIN: The wind! *(General laughter.)*

NOBLE: Let's file this ridiculous case. Has anybody else any complaints against Reynard?

TIECELIN: Yes! The Reverend Epinard! *(He prods Epinard, who has appeared immersed in the Bible.)*

EPINARD: Uh? Yes?

NOBLE: We are listening, Reverend Epinard?

EPINARD: You are listening to me? This doesn't happen every day. *(He opens his Bible, and prepares to preach.)*

NOBLE: What charge do you wish to lodge against the red-haired Fox?

EPINARD: I?

TIECELIN: Remember — that duck-egg.

EPINARD: Duck-eggs?

NOBLE: Look now, Reverend, has the Fox ever tried to harm you?

EPINARD: He wouldn't dare, Sire. My quills, you see.

NOBLE: If you have nothing to say, sit down. Is there any other accuser?

TIECELIN: Yes, Sire. There are countless ones. But they are not present.

NOBLE: Where are they?

TIECELIN: They are dead, Sire.

NOBLE: Dead?

TIECELIN: Yes, Sire. The rooster Chanticler, and his four hens. The drake, Halbran-des-Mares, and his three ducks. The guinea-fowl, Hupette. The turkey, Gloussard. And thousands of other winged creatures. All have met death and burial in the stomach of Reynard the Fox. Let's hang him, Sire.

YSEGRIN: Let's hang him upside down!

BRUN: Yes, he must hang!

NOBLE: This is a harsh judgement. Knight Reynard, can you think of any reason against it?

REYNARD: As many reasons as you have subjects, Sire. Doesn't my cousin Ysengrin himself devour innocent lambs and peaceful sheep? Doesn't my Uncle Brun treat himself to the honey he robs from the bees? Doesn't the Registrar Tiecelin eat the wheat and the grapes he steals from men? And you yourself, Sire, didn't you only yesterday have a gentle kid and half a deer for your supper!

YSEGRIN: We must hang him!

BRUN: Hang him!

TIECELIN: Hang him at once!

NOBLE: Do you hear?

REYNARD: I hear, Sire, and I don't worry too much, because I know there is more wisdom under a great King's crown than in the little brains of his courtiers. A very great King can forgive when need be.

NOBLE: A very great King can forgive when need be.

REYNARD: Mighty and gallant Majesty, I trust my fate to your hands.

NOBLE: I am a very great King, Reynard.

REYNARD: Without question, Sire.

NOBLE: You shall not hang.

REYNARD: Thank you, Sire.

TIECELIN: This is insane!

NOBLE: Who said that?

YSEGRIN: Sire, it is a mistake.

NOBLE: I pray you —

BRUN: If you will allow me, Sire —

NOBLE: I allow nothing! Silence, everybody, and let me render my sentence. You will not hang, Master Reynard. I grant you mercy for one more year.

TIECELIN: Mercy for one more year?

NOBLE: But this will be your last chance. In that year a record will be kept of your every crime.

BRUN: Of what use is a record, if he is left free to continue his crimes?

NOBLE: Twenty-four crimes we shall forgive you, without punishment.

YSEGRIN: Twenty-four crimes?

TIECELIN: Sire, this is preposterous!

NOBLE: Silence! We are all sinners, and hope for forgiveness. We shall forgive you twenty-four times.

REYNARD: You are a gracious King, Sire.

NOBLE: But take care. One crime more than twenty-four, and you shall be punished without mercy.

REYNARD: I understand, Sire.

NOBLE: One year from now, we shall hold court on this case again, and examine your record. Now you are free. Remember under what conditions.

REYNARD: Sire, you shall hear no further complaints from your humblest, most respectful servant, Reynard.

NOBLE: All right. Go.

REYNARD: I leave, Sire, broken-hearted to have earned the

displeasure of so many esteemed friends. *(Exit.)*

TIECELIN: Your Majesty, how can you —

YSEGRIN: Sire, this is madness!

BRUN: You have turned loose the greatest scoundrel in the kingdom!

TIECELIN: Who can keep track of all his crimes?

NOBLE: You will.

TIECELIN: I?

NOBLE: Yes. You are the Royal Registrar. I appoint you to keep a record book, and enter into it any crimes committed by Reynard.

TIECELIN: Thank you, your Majesty. It will give me pleasure.

NOBLE: I am very pleased with my judgement — stern, fair, but still merciful. Now, let each of you go peacefully back home, and recall my great justice.

TIECELIN: Trumpets! *(Trumpets.)*

YSEGRIN: Hail to thee, Sire, Lion. *(Aside)* What folly to let Reynard go free! *(Exit.)*

BRUN: Hail, Sire. *(Aside)* How foolish to forgive that redhair! *(Exit.)*

NOBLE: You see, everybody is satisfied with my judgement. I am well satisfied myself. Good night, Tiecelin. *(Exit.)*

TIECELIN: Good night, Sire. *(Aside)* What a blunder, to leave that rascal at large! *(He goes to pinch Epinard's arm.)*

EPINARD: Eh? Yes?

TIECELIN: It is all over, Reverend.

EPINARD: Yes, yes, I see. Moreover, it was very interesting. Very interesting indeed.

TIECELIN: I must say, you showed little interest in the cause of justice.

EPINARD: The cause of justice?

TIECELIN: Yes. Why didn't you tell the King about that duck-egg?

EPINARD: My dear fellow, I should not wish to earn Reynard's ill-will. The time might come when I should need Reynard on my side. Good night. *(Exit.)*

TIECELIN: Good night, good night? How can I ever have another good night, after this? Reynard will make short work of me, if I give him the chance. My feathers rise with fear at the very thought. *(LENDORE enters, half-asleep, pillow under her arm, bumps into TIECELIN, who freezes with terror.)* He has got me, already! Reynard?

LENDORE: What do you say?

TIECELIN: What? It is you? Lendore?

LENDORE: It's me.

TIECELIN: Why didn't you say something?

LENDORE: You didn't ask me anything?

TIECELIN: The Marmot. And I thought you were Reynard.

LENDORE: You didn't look at me very well.

TIECELIN: Where are you going?

LENDORE: To Reynard's trial. Is it here?

TIECELIN: The trial is over.

LENDORE: Already? I must have fallen asleep on my way.

TIECELIN: As usual.

LENDORE: How did it go?

TIECELIN: That rascal Reynard went scot-free, for a year!

LENDORE: Good!

TIECELIN: What is more, he is allowed to commit twenty-four crimes, without punishment.

LENDORE: Twenty-four? That will not take him long.

TIECELIN: But one crime more than twenty-four, and he shall hang! And I am appointed to keep the record.

LENDORE: The record?

TIECELIN: Yes. I am not the Royal Registrar for nothing. The King has appointed me to keep account of all his crimes. I shall make a book of them.

LENDORE: It's amazing how sleepy I still feel.

TIECELIN: Go to sleep, then. I intend to keep my eyes open, for the whole year.

LENDORE: *(settles to sleep, against a tree.)* Good night.

TIECELIN: It will be easy to accumulate twenty-five counts against him in a year. Ha, ha! I'll put an end to him, with my record-book.

END OF PROLOGUE

SCENE ONE — SPRINGTIME

(LENDORE enters, yawning. REYNARD bounds in.)

REYNARD: Ah, Lendore! You have come out of your shelter. Spring is truly here.

LENDORE: Is it?

REYNARD: Melted is the cold snow that kept my feet wet all winter.

LENDORE: So it is.

REYNARD: Gone is the bitter frost that kept the burrows closed.

LENDORE: Ah, yes.

REYNARD: Quiet is the freezing wind that pinched my nose.

LENDORE: Excuse me. I don't hear any quiet.

REYNARD: Welcome, Spring — welcome to you, who brings back the innocent young rabbit, and the tender birdies, not to mention the dainty little chickens.

LENDORE: Go somewhere else to sing your Spring Song, Reynard. I need a nap. *(Sleeps. YSEGRIN enters, quietly.)*

304

REYNARD: *(at the overlook.)* Ah, look, Lendore. See the fine rooster in the farm-yard over there. I see you, Seigneur Coincoin. I have given you all winter to get fat, and now I am saving a place for you in my bag.

YSEGRIN: So! You are up to your old tricks, Reynard.

REYNARD: Cousin Ysengrin! You always tip-toe.

YSEGRIN: Naturally.

REYNARD: I was just — ah — admiring the spring.

YSEGRIN: You were just plotting to gobble up that rooster. I heard you.

REYNARD: I have always admired your ears Ysengrin.

YSEGRIN: Just dare to attack that rooster. The King shall hear of it.

REYNARD: Very well, Cousin. I leave Seigneur Coincoin to you. Happy hunting! *(Exit.)*

YSEGRIN: Happy hunting, indeed. That wily Fox would beat me to the farm-yard, if I let him. *(LENDORE stirs.)* Ah! Perhaps I won't have to go as far as the farm-yard.
(Drooling, he quietly creeps up on her, with obvious intentions. REYNARD returns.)

REYNARD: Ah, Cousin, you have found what you want without hunting?

YSEGRIN: What brings you back here?

REYNARD: To do you a good turn, Cousin. I have found you a hunting companion. Here comes our Noble King. *(NOBLE enters, with zest and majesty.)* Your servant, Sire.

YSEGRIN: The Marmot, Sire. The Marmot. She sleeps.

NOBLE: Lendore, indeed. She has come out of her shelter. This is the herald of spring.

YSEGRIN: As you say, your Majesty.

NOBLE: Ysengrin, we have had to keep under cover all winter. Now I feel like hunting. Come and join me.

YSENGRIN: I am honored, Sire. And — ah — Reynard?

NOBLE: Reynard has given up hunting for a year. Let's go. *(Exit.)*

YSEGRIN: I am coming, Sire. *(To REYNARD)* You — you schemer! *(To NOBLE, off)* I come! *(Exit.)*

REYNARD: *(laughs)* Happy hunting, Cousin. *(To LENDORE)* Lendore, Lendore, wake up.

LENDORE: Eh? What? What do you say?

REYNARD: Wake up. It is not wise to sleep when the hunting season is open.

LENDORE: I am a Marmot. It is the nature of a Marmot to sleep, any time.

REYNARD: Find yourself a private spot, then: And don't trust Ysengrin.

LENDORE: I don't trust anybody, Reynard — not even you.

REYNARD: Lendore.

LENDORE: All the same — I like you.

REYNARD: Thanks, old friend.

LENDORE: By the way, don't sit there. It is a bumble-bee nest. *(Exit.)*

REYNARD: A bumble-bee nest? Fortunately she warns me. Ah, and here comes my Uncle Brun. What a heaven-sent opportunity to play a joke on him! But if the King should find out, there would be one of my twenty-four chances gone. Shall I do it? Yes! It is too good a chance to miss. *(BRUN enters, out of sorts.)* Good morning, Uncle. Still grumbling?

BRUN: Leave me in peace.

REYNARD: That is just what I offer you. Let's make peace, and forget our little misunderstandings. As a token of good faith, I offer you some fair honey-cakes left by the bees. What do you think of that?

BRUN: I think it is another of your fabrications.

REYNARD: How unfortunate I am! My uncle himself doubts my sincerity.

BRUN: I don't believe a word. Where are those honey-cakes?

REYNARD: Why show them to you, since you don't believe there are any?

BRUN: And why, if they exist, don't you eat them yourself?

REYNARD: I am on probation for a year, Brun. It would count against me if I should rob the bees. Heigh-ho! Since you don't care for it, the honey will be lost to everyone. *(He makes a subtle move toward the bumble-bee nest.)*

BRUN: *(to himself)* So there they are.

REYNARD: It's a shame.

BRUN: Yes. Too bad, isn't it? Well, I am off.

REYNARD: So am I. Good bye, Uncle.

BRUN: Goodbye. *(Neither makes a move to go.)* Aren't you leaving?

REYNARD: Oh, certainly. And you?

BRUN: Me, too. So good bye.
(He pretends to leave.)

REYNARD: *(Pretending to leave also.)* Good bye.

BRUN: *(Comes back and finds himself in front of REYNARD.)* I have lost something.

REYNARD: Can I help you look for it?

BRUN: Stupid of me. I left it at home. Good bye. *(Exit.)*

REYNARD: Good bye, Uncle.
(Exit, but hides himself. BRUN comes back.)

BRUN: *(Rushes to bumble-bee nest.)* Honey! That fool thought I was going to leave honey here to spoil! *(He puts his paw in the nest, withdraws it quickly.)* Bumble bees! The traitor! *(Bumble-bees come out in swarms and pursue him. Music. The flight of the bumble-bees can be suggested by light spots.)* Ah! Go away! My nose! Leave me alone! Ouch! My

tail! A-h-h! It stings! My ears! Oh! Ah! It stings! Help, Help!
(TIECELIN enters.)

TIECELIN: Seigneur Brun! What is the matter?

BRUN: Out of my way, Crow! Ouch! My neck!

TIECELIN: Are you hurt?

BRUN: Am I hurt? I am eaten up! Aie! My leg! Stop blocking
me! Oh, it stings! It stings!
*(He runs off, followed by the bumble-bees. TIECELIN,
pushed about, and stricken by fear, takes refuge on a tree.
REYNARD is convulsed.)*

TIECELIN: Has he lost his mind?

REYNARD: Oh, no. He always acts that way, when the bees are
after him.

TIECELIN: Well, he needn't be so rude about it. He nearly made
me crush my Camembert.

REYNARD: *(nostrils wide open.)* Camembert? Ah, Master
Crow, that cheese looks delicious. Will you give me a taste?

TIECELIN: No. I went to too much trouble to get it.

REYNARD: But cheese is bad for your voice. A singer should
never eat cheese.

TIECELIN: Nonsense. It has never harmed me in the least.

REYNARD: Nevertheless, a fine voice should not be abused. If
you were unable to sing anymore, the animal kingdom would
lose its best tenor.

TIECELIN: Do you think so? *(Crows.)* Do you really think so?

REYNARD: Sing, Tiecelin. Sing, and listen yourself.
(TIECELIN crows awfully.) Ah! Very good, though a little
low. I thought you could sing higher than that. *(TIECELIN
croaks more shrilly.)* Better. One note higher ... Ah! ... More
... Louder ... Higher ... Splendid! ... Go on! ... Higher! ... You
are almost there! Keep on! ... More! ... Now you have it!
(TIECELIN drops his cheese.) And I have it too!

TIECELIN: My cheese!

REYNARD: Don't worry. It is in good hands.

TIECELIN: Give it back to me.

REYNARD: Come and get it.

TIECELIN: I know you.

REYNARD: We will share the cheese like brothers.

TIECELIN: If I come down, you will gobble me up first, and you
will eat the cheese for dessert.

REYNARD: No, no. Come.

TIECELIN: Cheese robber!

REYNARD: What a wonderful aroma!

TIECELIN: Rob — you like the smell?

REYNARD: Heavenly!

TIECELIN: When you close your eyes, you find the smell even
better.

REYNARD: What's that?

TIECELIN: To get the full, rich, luscious flavour of a Camembert
cheese, it is necessary to shut out all other senses, and enjoy
it with your nose alone. Your nostrils are much more sensitive
when your eyes are closed.

REYNARD: Is this possible? *(He closes his eyes and sniffs.)* You
are right. It is unbelievably richer.

TIECELIN: *(Taking advantage of the chance to climb down.)*
Cheese robber!

REYNARD: Tiecelin —

TIECELIN: This will go into my book!

REYNARD: Your book? What book?

TIECELIN: Aha! The King has appointed me to keep a record of
all your doings in a book. This will make a fine beginning.

REYNARD: Indeed.

TIECELIN: Keep on, Master Fox. The book will soon be full. Crime Number One! Reynard stole my cheese! Cheese robber! Cheese robber! Cheese robber! *(Exit.)*

REYNARD: So, he is keeping a book! And on the very first day of spring, I have managed to spend one of my twenty-four chances, and get it recorded in the book. Oh, what a stupid, bungling Fox I am! That tattle-tale will cry the news aloud, all through the forest. I'd better get rid of the evidence. *(He hides cheese, as NOBLE enters, followed by YSEGRIN.)*

NOBLE: Did you see a pheasant fly over?

REYNARD: No Sire, but I can guide your Majesty toward some very attractive turkeys.

YSEGRIN: Oh, no. You are out of this hunt, remember.

REYNARD: I am talking about big, fat turkeys.

NOBLE: We can hardly afford to let such a chance go by, Ysengrin.

YSEGRIN: But Sire, Reynard has given up hunting for a year. You said so yourself.

NOBLE: I think— ahem — we may make an exception this time.

REYNARD: This way, Sire. *(Bows low. NOBLE and YSEGRIN exeunt.)* Let's hope that Tiecelin will not find his cheese until I get back. *(Exit. Music. Ballet-mime for the hunt. NOBLE, YSEGRIN, and REYNARD chasing a turkey around the stage and off. NOBLE in the lead, graceful but heavy; YSEGRIN lumbering along behind, eager but clumsy; REYNARD nimbly outstripping both. The chase carries them offstage. LENDORE enters.)*

LENDORE: *(Crossing, pillow under her arm.)* Impossible to sleep with this infernal music. *(Exit. The ballet ends with the entrance of REYNARD, who carries a turkey with head hanging limp. NOBLE and YSEGRIN follow.)*

NOBLE: Bravo!

YSEGRIN: You caught it right under my nose!

REYNARD: It is a matter of skill, Cousin.

NOBLE: Anyhow, now we must share.

REYNARD: *(Throwing the turkey at NOBLE's feet.)* Let's share, by all means.

NOBLE: You, my dear Ysengrin, may decide about each one's share.

YSEGRIN: In my opinion, it is fitting, first of all, to set aside the claim of this redhair, who had no right to be hunting anyway. The head, the neck, and one wing will be enough for me — and one leg. It is only right that you, being the King, should take all the other pieces.

NOBLE: *(Boxing his ears.)* You don't have the first instinct of a sportsman. *(To REYNARD.)* And you, how would you divide it?

REYNARD: It is easy. Take first what pleases you, Sire — the body and legs, for instance. Her Majesty Lioness the Queen, shall have the wings and the head. Your son, the Cub, will gladly practice on the neck, I'm sure. Ysengrin seems to have too much trouble with his teeth to eat anything. And when it conies to me, I don't really feel hungry.

NOBLE: This is what I should call a fine division. Who taught you to divide so fairly?

REYNARD: My Fox's wisdom, Sire — and most of all, the sight of your royal fist on Ysengrin's ears.

NOBLE: I congratulate you. As for you, Seigneur Wolf, take a lesson from Reynard. Well, good bye, my friends. Thank you for your company in the hunt. *(Exit, taking turkey.)*

YSEGRIN: Take a lesson — take a lesson from Reynard! Ah-h-h-h! I don't know what keeps me from giving you the beating of your life, you scheming, mealy-mouthed rascal!

REYNARD: Is that not better than to have your jaw crushed under the Lion's paw?

YSEGRIN: I am mad. Oh, I am good and mad!

REYNARD: Cheer up. We don't lose much in this settlement. The turkey was so old that the King, the Queen, and the Cub face the risk of breaking their teeth on it. Anyway, I see a much better dinner coming than the King's.

YSEGRIN: Epinard?

REYNARD: Yes, the Reverend, carrying a wonderful ham! It will be ours.

YSEGRIN: Beware the quills.

REYNARD: Don't worry about the quills. Hide there, and be on the watch. I'll get Epinard to lay the ham down near your hiding place. You pick it up and wait for me. Afterward we shall divide it.

YSEGRIN: Agreed. *(He hides.)*

REYNARD: *(Waiting for EPINARD's entrance.)* Now is the moment, Oh, miserable fox that I am! *(EPINARD enters, carrying ham.)* Shall I never be able to do anything but bad deeds? With the help of Heaven, let me find a holy man to hear my confession, and absolve me of my sins!

EPINARD: My son.

REYNARD: Reverend. Did you hear me?

EPINARD: Yes, my son.

REYNARD: I will go to Hades, won't I?

EPINARD: The one who repents will not go to Hades.

REYNARD: Ah, but I repent. I repent.

EPINARD: Very well, my son.

REYNARD: Heavens, what do I see?

EPINARD: What do you see?

REYNARD: It has gotten me again.

EPINARD: What has gotten you again?

REYNARD: My terrible sin of greediness. Ah, how wretched am I! The very sight of your ham makes me forget my pledge.

EPINARD: Be calm, my son. Be calm.

REYNARD: It is impossible, Reverend, as long as that splendid ham remains before my eyes. I shall be unable not to covet it.

EPINARD: My goodness! Have some will power.

REYNARD: It is Satan. It is Satan who tempts me. "Get thee behind me, Satan." Take that ham away from my sight, Reverend, and pray for me. *(EPINARD puts his ham down.)* Take it away from my nostrils — farther — still farther, so that its wonderful aroma will not tempt my nose any more.

EPINARD: *(Puts the ham down near YSEGRIN's hiding place.)* Kneel, my son, my dear Reynard. Kneel. I will pray for you. *(YSEGRIN seizes the ham, takes a bite, makes his escape. REYNARD, seeing this, cries out involuntarily.)*

REYNARD: Aie! Wait for me, you thief! *(Recovers himself.)* Excuse me, Reverend. Save the prayer for another time. Right now I have — ah — other business. *(Exit hurriedly, in pursuit of YSEGRIN.)*

EPINARD: *(Discovering his loss.)* Pig! Rascal! Robber! My ham! My ham! *(Exit. In the distance are heard the joined cries of TIECLIN —"Cheese Robber!" — and of EPINARD— "My ham!" — NOBLE enters.)*

NOBLE: This morning the forest is full of strange sounds. Don't I hear someone claiming a ham? And somewhere, this side, someone else shouting "Cheese Robber"? That joker Reynard must not be far away. Ham? Cheese? It is strange, but I fancy my royal nose thrills under the odor of a very near Camembert. *(He searches, and discovers the cheese.)* Ha! But I am not mistaken. By jove, my royal nose is still in its prime. Ah, this suits me admirably. It makes up for that skimpy breakfast I had, eating that tough old turkey. *(He eats the cheese.)* It is truly fit for a King.

TIECELIN: *(Offstage, drawing nearer.)* Cheese robber! Cheese robber! *(NOBLE gulps down the last of the cheese hurriedly. TIECLIN enters.)* Sire, my cheese.

NOBLE: What cheese?

TIECELIN: My Camembert.

NOBLE: So it was your cheese that — ah — which is missing?
    (BRUN enters, shaking off REYNARD behind him.)

BRUN: Don't give me any of your sweet talk. I am stung all over.

TIECELIN: He stole it!

NOBLE: Who? Brun?

TIECELIN: No, Sire, Reynard.

NOBLE: Reynard, did you steal his wheeze?

REYNARD: Wheeze, Sire? No, Sire, I did not wheeze.

TIECELIN: Cheese robber! Cheese robber!

REYNARD: I did not wheeze. Nor did I hear anyone else
    wheeze, nor sneeze, nor queaze, nor —

TIECELIN: Cheese robber!

REYNARD: Oh, cheese? Tiecelin has lost a cheese?

TIECELIN: Your Majesty will do me justice. He has stolen my
    Camembert.

REYNARD: Oh, what slander!

TIECELIN: Punish that thief.

REYNARD: Your Majesty, this Crow is insane. Had I stolen
    his cheese, I should have eaten it at once, and you would be
    able to smell it. Uncle Brim, be good enough to smell my
    moustache.

BRUN: You stay away from me.

REYNARD: But smell, and tell us all. Do you detect the very
    strong odor of a Camembert cheese?

BRUN: *(Sniffing)* I wouldn't put it past you, you honey-fibber
    — but to tell the truth, I smell nothing at all on your breath.

TIECELIN: You have taken it away from me!

REYNARD: After all, the simplest way would be to ask everyone

314

to submit to the test, would it not!

NOBLE: Do you think this necessary?

TIECELIN: I insist! I insist!

BRUN: It seems logical to me. So smell.

TIECELIN: *(Smelling BRUN's breath.)* You smell more like a honey-robber.

BRUN: It is my natural fragrance.

REYNARD: You, Sire?

NOBLE: Although my royal eminence places me above all suspicion, I submit to your insulting request.

TIECELIN: *(Smelling NOBLE's breath.)* Sire! Sire! One would almost think —

NOBLE: What would one think?

TIECELIN: If I weren't afraid of hurting your Majesty's feelings, I should say — it's funny, but it smells more or less like —

NOBLE: More or less like what?

TIECELIN: Like Camembert.

NOBLE: This exceeds the limits. Get out of here, and go fast. Let me not set eyes on you any more today, or it might be costly for you.

TIECELIN: But —

NOBLE: Get out, I say!

TEICELIN: Very well, then.*(Exit).*

BRUN: What a fool!

TIECELIN *(Offstage.)* Cheese robber! Cheese robber!

REYNARD: He has a one-track mind.

BRUN: How absurd to think that your Majesty's moustache might smell like cheese!

NOBLE: Sniff yourself, Seigneur Brun, and give us your opinion, sincerely and honestly.

BRUN: *(Sniffing.)* Uh — ah—

NOBLE: Well?

BRUN: I don't believe I am mistaken, Sire, when I say that your moustache does have an odor.

NOBLE: What odor, I pray you?

BRUN: A very delicate perfume — ah — yes, very similar to the roses.

NOBLE: So that is your honesty! Lies and hypocrisy! Out of my sight. Bear without conscience!

BRUN: Well, then — *(Exit hastily.)*

NOBLE: It is your turn, Reynard. What do you smell?

REYNARD: To tell the truth, Sire, I don't smell anything today. I have a cold in my head.

NOBLE: This is a cold that comes at a convenient time for you, doesn't it?

REYNARD: Yes, Sire.

EPINARD: *(In the distance.)* My ham! I claim my ham!

REYNARD: Sire, allow me to retire, and nurse my cold.

TIECELIN: *(In the distance, on the other side.)* Cheese robber! Cheese robber!

NOBLE: You are quite right. Let's both retire and nurse our colds. *(Exeunt. EPINARD enters.)*

EPINARD: My ham!
  (TIECELIN enters.)

TIECELIN: My cheese!
  (BRUN enters.)

BRUN: I am stung all over!
  (YSEGRIN enters.)

YSEGRIN: I am in the King's bad graces!

BRUN: So am I!

TIECELIN: So am I!

YSEGRIN: Whose fault is it?

TIECELIN: It is Reynard!

EPINARD: Reynard!

BRUN: Reynard!

TIECELIN: It is all the fault of that rascal Reynard!

EPINARD: Tiecelin, put all this down in your book against him.

TIECELIN: Don't worry. It shall go into my book, all right. H'm, h'm! We can almost be glad. This will make three crimes on the very first day. Ha, ha!

END OF SCENE ONE

SCENE TWO — SUMMER
(Appropriate music. REYNARD is hidden behind a tree. LENDORE and EPINAARD enter from opposite sides, both very thirsty, both looking for the spring. They collide.)

LENDORE: Oh, it's you?

EPINARD: As you see. Don't you think it's terribly hot?

LENDORE: Yes. Are you looking for the spring?

EPINARD: Where is it?

LENDORE: The hole is there, but the water doesn't flow any more. The brook has disappeared in the sand, the pond is dried up, and the fish, turned upside down, die in the sun.

EPINARD: May Heaven save us, dear Lendore! It is a dreadful summer. *(YSEGRIN enters, brushes them aside.)*

YSEGRIN: Out of the way, both of you! *(EPINARD bristles. LENDORE puts pillow on her head.)* Where is the spring? Who emptied the spring? You?

LENDORE: Certainly not. It is the sun.

YSEGRIN: I want a drink. Where is the water?

EPINARD: In the ground.

317

YSEGRIN: It must come out. I want it to gush, as it did before. Come out of your hole, water. I want a drink.

EPINARD: Don't shout so. Water doesn't hear. Each of us must be patient under our sufferings.

YSEGRIN: Don't preach your sermons to me. Go somewhere else. *(He pushes EPINARD, stings himself.)* Thunderation!

EPINARD: As you wish. *(Exits calmly.)*

LENDORE: He who plays with needles gets stung.

YSEGRIN: You think this is funny.
(YSEGRIN strikes at LENDORE, who pushes her pillow into his muzzle, and hurries off. YSEGRIN fights alone with the pillow, as BRUN enters, carrying a wooden bucket. He sets the bucket down, to watch YSEGRIN in astonishment.)

BRUN: Here, don't upset my bucket!

YSEGRIN: What bucket? *(He throws the pillow down, and rushes to the bucket, kneeling in front of it.)*

BRUN: *(Tumbles him down with a push.)* Don't touch!

YSEGRIN: Just a gulp.

BRUN: No.

YSEGRIN: I am thirsty.

BRUN: So am I.

YSEGRIN: I beg you.

BRUN: No.

YSEGRIN: One drop.

BRUN: No.

YSEGRIN: Only let me dip the tip of my tongue.

BRUN: No! *(He pushes YSEGRIN back violently. YSEGRIN tumbles down and rolls close to a tree, behind which REYNARD is hidden. BRUN drinks noisily. REYNARD whispers a few secret words to YSEGRIN, who then gets up and pretends to depart.)* Good bye, my nephew.

YSEGRIN: Good bye. *(He stops and pretends to gather honey, which he eats with delight.)*

BRUN: *(Stops drinking to watch YSEGRIN, then puts his bucket down and draws near.)* Is it honey? *(REYNARD picks up the bucket and disappears.)* It is most probably honey?

YSEGRIN: No. I was just licking the wind. *(Exit, in pursuit of REYNARD. BRUN rushes for honey, finds none.)*

BRUN: He *was* just licking the wind. *(Looks for his bucket.)* Ysengrin! Robber! Ysengrin! My bucket! *(Exit in pursuit. REYNARD returns, drains the bucket, puts it back in place, then leaves. YSEGRIN re-enters, rushes to the bucket, finds it empty.)*

YSEGRIN: Scoundrel!
(BRUN rushes in.)

BRUN: Give me that!

YSEGRIN: It is empty.

BRUN: *(Beating him.)* I'll teach you to rob your Uncle.

YSEGRIN: Uncle! Ouch! ... Ouch! ... I haven't — it isn't — oh, it is —

BRUN: Don't cross my path again, or you'll get twice as much. *(Exit. REYNARD returns.)*

REYNARD: Well? Do you have colic from drinking too much?

YSEGRIN: I have been beaten — through your fault. I am going to give you your share.

REYNARD: You are mistaken.

YSEGRIN: You have emptied the bucket, to the last drop.

REYNARD: Ah no! Is it my fault if there is a hole in the bucket?

YSEGRIN: Where?

REYNARD: Look!
(He puts the bucket on YSEGRIN's head.)

YSEGRIN: Remove the bucket! I am smothering! Reynard, where are you?

319

REYNARD: I am here.

YSEGRIN: Get me out of this bucket at once!

REYNARD: Eat your way out. Remember, you ate Epinard's ham, all by yourself. *(Exit quietly)*

YSEGRIN: I'll strangle you! I'll pull out every hair of your moustache! I'll report this to Tiecelin to put in his book! *(NOBLE and BRUN enter.)*

BRUN: You see, Sire, the spring is dry.

NOBLE: Ah-h-h, yes.

BRUN: But I had the foresight to have back a bucket of water.

NOBLE: *(Panting.)* Where is it?

BRUN: That is what I am trying to tell you, Sire. I was tricked out of it.

NOBLE: Bah! Brun, I'm so thirsty I could drink the ocean.

BRUN: Drink the ocean?

NOBLE: I'd be willing to wager I could drink the ocean to the last drop.

YSEGRIN: *(Grapples with the King.)* Ah, villain, there you are!

NOBLE: *(Throwing him back so hard, it shakes the bucket.)* This will teach you to respect your King!

YSEGRIN: King? Oh, forgive me, Sire. I cannot see your Majesty.

NOBLE: Even if invisible, our Majesty is to be respected.

YSEGRIN: Take this bucket off my head, and I'll explain.

NOBLE: Quite unnecessary, I understand. *(Exit.)*

YSEGRIN: Sire, I didn't rob Seigneur Brun. He jabbers a great deal lately.

BRUN: I, jabber?
(Gives him a mighty blow, and exits.)

YSEGRIN: Sire — your Majesty — will nobody help me?
(LENDORE enters to pick up her pillow, notices WOLF. She

320

knocks at the bucket discreetly.) Who is there?

LENDORE: It's me, Lendore the Marmot, sir. And you, under the bucket, who are you?

YSEGRIN: I am the poor Ysengrin. For Heaven's sake, liberate me.

LENDORE: Promise first not to try to gobble me up again?

YSEGRIN: I promise anything, my sweet Lendore. I swear it a hundred times, a thousand times, if you wish. But remove this bucket. It is smothering me.

LENDORE: Don't move.
(She pulls the bucket.)

YSEGRIN: You are pulling my ears off!

LENDORE: I have to.

YSEGRIN: *(Free, at last.)* You did hurt me!

LENDORE: It was unavoidable.

YSEGRIN: You deserve a thrashing.

LENDORE: Don't forget you swore —

YSEGRIN: Away with promises! Here is your reward.
(Trying to kick her, he misses, kicks the bucket instead. LENDORE runs away. YSEGRIN, in pain, hops on one foot. TIECELIN enters.) Oh I am in a rage — a rage — a rage!

TIECELIN: What is the matter with you? Have you lost one leg?

YSEGRIN: It is all the fault of that bounder Reynard!

TIECELIN: *(Eager, pencil poised.)* Reynard? What did he do? Tell me at once. I will put it in my book.

YSEGRIN: Your book? Your book? That for your book!
(He strikes the book from TIECELIN's hand.)

TIECELIN: *(Retrieving his book.)* Here, have a care!

YSEGRIN: Of what use is your everlasting book?

TIECELIN: It is a record of all his crimes, to bring against him at the trial.

321

YSEGRIN: Winter will be over before the trial. Are we to put up with his trickery till then!

TIECELIN: It is the King's judgement.

YSEGRIN: I want to deal with him now — right now!

TIECELIN: I, too. But how?

YSEGRIN: O, leave me in peace. I am lame for life!

TIECELIN: All the same, you needn't treat my book so lightly. This is legal evidence, sanctioned by the King. And it is getting full. He hasn't many chances left. If all else fails, this will bring him to account in the end. *(Exit.)*

YSEGRIN: Prattling Crow! *(REYNARD enters, but finding YSEGRIN alone, conceals himself.)* It all goes back to the King's judgment. Leaving that Fox free for a year, to commit twenty-four crimes without punishment. *(Enter BRUN.)* Uncle Brun!

BRUN: Don't speak to me, you water-thief!

YSEGRIN: But I beg you, listen to me. It was not I who emptied your bucket.

BRUN: Not you? Who, then?

YSEGRIN: It was Reynard.

BRUN: Reynard?

YSEGRIN: I swear it.

BRUN: Reynard, who drained my bucket dry?

YSEGRIN: And then stuck it on my head, and caused me to get a beating.

BRUN: The King shall hear of this!

YSEGRIN: Of what use is that! It was the King who set him free for a year, to perpetrate such tricks.

BRUN: And the year is not half over.

YSEGRIN: Exactly.

BRUN: It is not to be borne! We must put an end to this Fox.

YSEGRIN: If we are to get rid of the Fox, we must first get the King out of the way.

BRUN: The King is a fool. If I were King, now —

YSEGRIN: Or I —

BRUN: Why not?

YSEGRIN: Eh?

BRUN: Why should the Lion be King?

YSEGRIN: He always has been.

BRUN: Do you know any document that gives the title of King of the animals to the Lion?

YSEGRIN: All the school books say so.

BRUN: I know a way to topple him off his throne.

YSEGRIN: What way?

BRUN: Listen. This afternoon, His Majesty declared several times that he could drink the entire ocean, to the last drop.

YSEGRIN: That was only to express how thirsty he was.

BRUN: Of course. But what would happen if we should challenge him?

YSEGRIN: He would naturally be most embarrassed. I don't see how he could very well drink the ocean dry.

BRUN: Well, then! Do you think the animal kingdom will accept a King who is unable to keep his word?

YSEGRIN: No!

BRUN: No! Certainly not! We shall demand his abdication.

YSEGRIN: And take the throne ourselves!

BRUN: Tonight, my friend, we shall be Kings.

YSEGRIN: And we shall make an end of that rascal Reynard. Go and get him. I will gather the Court.

BRUN: Reynard has played his last trick.
    (*Exit.*)

YSEGRIN: And that for you, Master Reynard. Trumpets!
(Trumpets. REYNARD appears in the open, pretending to answer the trumpet call.)

REYNARD: Cousin, what is going on?

YSEGRIN: You'll see. Trumpets!
(Trumpets. TIECELIN enters.)

TIECELIN: Why are you calling a meeting when it is so hot? It must be most important.
(Trumpets. Enter LENDORE.)

YSEGRIN: It certainly is. Trumpets!

LENDORE: There, there. Everybody has heard you. What is the matter now?

YSEGRIN: The King has made a very audacious boast, and he wants everybody present to see how he keeps it.
(NOBLE sweeps in, escorted by BRUN.)

NOBLE: What is all this congregation for?

TIECELIN: The trumpets have called us to Assembly. I, as Royal Registrar, demand to know the business before the Court.

BRUN: You shall know it now. Sire, the animal kingdom, whose beloved sovereign you are, wishes to know if it possible for your Majesty to keep a promise made by you this afternoon.

NOBLE: Why, certainly.

BRUN: Would you be willing to put your throne at stake?

NOBLE: Of course I would. I always keep my promises. What did I promise?

BRUN: To drink the ocean, Sire.

NOBLE: Ha, ha! It is true I made that statement, I was so thirsty.

YSEGRIN: The achievement you are going to perform thrills all your people, Sire.

NOBLE: You didn't take me seriously, I hope?

BRUN: We know your Majesty is capable of accomplishing the greatest feats.

NOBLE: But you know very well —

YSEGRIN: Your people are looking forward to it, Sire.

BRUN: Gentlemen, your highly esteemed sovereign will, in a moment, lead you to the beach, and show you how, when one is a very great King, one can achieve things that would be impossible for his subjects.

YSEGRIN: His Majesty is going to drink the ocean.

BRUN: You will see how the strength of your sovereign, his bravery, his keen intelligence, his wit, and his determination will give him the power to drink the whole ocean. Our great King, gentlemen, is about to swallow the ocean. Sire, the ocean is waiting.

NOBLE: Did I actually say that I would drink the ocean?

BRUN: Indeed you did, Sire — to the last drop.

NOBLE: Did I say that?

BRUN: Those were your very words, Sire.

NOBLE: But — but I shall drown!

BRUN: Does your Majesty mean you cannot keep your promise?

NOBLE: I — ah —

YSEGRIN: A King always keeps his promises.

NOBLE: But it was only in jest —

REYNARD: Ah — your Majesty. Gentlemen.

YSEGRIN: You stay out of this.

REYNARD: Did the King also say that he would drink the water of all the rivers that flow into the ocean?

BRUN: Is this any business of yours?

NOBLE: No. I did not.

REYNARD: In that case, my dear Brun, will you stop all the rivers of the world, dam their flow, and prevent them from pouring their waters into his Majesty's soup? After you have done this, I'm sure his Majesty will gladly drink what is left.

BRUN: Stop up all the rivers of the world?

NOBLE: Exactly.

BRUN: How can anyone do that?

NOBLE: When you are able to do that, I will drink up all the waters of the ocean, to the last drop.
(General laughter.)

REYNARD: Bravo, Sire. It is easy to see that we have a wise King. Don't you agree, Cousin Ysengrin?

YSEGRIN: It is easy to see that the King has a clever counsellor.

BRUN: Counsellor? This redhair? Your Majesty, this is an outrage, that you should be taken in by this rogue!

NOBLE: Rogue? Are you referring to my trusted knight, Sir Reynard the Fox? Guard your tongue, Seigneur Bear.

BRUN: Only today he tricked me out of a bucket of water.
(TIECELIN writes busily.)

YSEGRIN: And then he inverted the bucket on my head, and caused me to get a beating.
(TIECELIN writes this down too.)

NOBLE: *(To BRUN.)* You dare to complain to me, when you have just tried to cheat me out of my throne? *(To YSEGRIN.)* And you, who just this afternoon, without provocation, assaulted your King? Let me not hear another word from either one of you. Come, Reynard. A rain is coming up. Let us seek shelter.
(EPINARD rushes in.)

EPINARD: Sire! I beg — a matter of utmost importance!

BRUN: Save your important matters for the pulpit, Reverend.

EPINARD: Sire, give me leave to —

NOBLE: In good time, Reverend.

EPINARD: Your Majesty, it cannot wait. Does no one realize that a very serious danger threatens us all?

NOBLE: What danger can be greater than this wicked plot to

over-throw my throne?

EPINARD: Men, Sire.

LENDORE: Men? *(The very word draws them together, in a tight little knot, glancing fearfully toward the overlook.)*

EPINARD: Sire, I have just come from the farm. The farmer has his hunting dogs out on a leash, training them to pick up our scent.

NOBLE: How do you know this?

EPINARD: He led the dogs first to the hen-yard, where Reynard was careless enough to leave some tracks. Then he took them to the marshes where I — ahem! — paid a brief call on some ducks recently. When I left, he was heading toward the pig-pen, where the dogs will easily pick up the trail of Seigneur Brun.

BRUN: The dickens!

EPINARD: From there, he will take them to the sheep-fold, where the smell of Wolf is very strong.

YSEGRIN: Oh, no!

EPINARD: Next they will go to the wheat field, where the Crow dropped a feather on his last visit.

TIECELIN: Aie!

EPINARD: And finally they will make for the pasture, where the Lion has left his traces.

NOBLE: Is this true?

EPINARD: Send Tiecelin to see.

NOBLE: Tiecelin, to the farm!

TIECELIN: A-a-a-alone, Sire?

NOBLE: Have we anybody else with wings?

TIECELIN: Y-y-yes, Sire. I mean — no, Sire.

NOBLE: Quickly!

TIECELIN: I — I'm going, Sire.

(Exit slowly, with obvious reluctance.)

EPINARD: Your Majesty, this is no time for nonsense. I know those farmers down there. They are all united in plotting our destruction. They want our bodies; the pelt of Seigneur Brun; Reynard's fur; Tiecelin's feathers; Ysengrin's skin and teeth; yours, Sire; my quills — and Heaven knows what else. Fall is coming, when all men go hunting for game. The dogs have our scent. Men are polishing up their weapons, oiling their rifles, filling their cartridges, sharpening their knives. It will be a fearful period for those of our kind. I make it my duty, Sire, to warn you that if we wish to survive, we must all band together against the common enemy — Man.

REYNARD: That, Reverend, is one of your very best sermons.

NOBLE: You agree, then?

REYNARD: Oh, unquestionably, your Majesty. Alone, we are each of us weak and vulnerable. United, we could resist the hunters and their dogs.

NOBLE: But how can we unite?

REYNARD: Ah! That, Sire, is the question.

NOBLE: It is always the question. I am going to require each of you to take an oath.

EPINARD: Excellent, Sire.

NOBLE: And I will expect you to be bound by this oath, no matter what the emergency.

YSEGRIN: Never fear, Sire. You can depend on us.

NOBLE: Hold out your right hands. Now, repeat after me. All for one. One for all.

ALL: All for one. One for all.
(Low, distant rumble of thunder. All are frozen.)

YSEGRIN: Listen!
(TIECELIN, flies in, terrified.)

TIECELIN: Did you hear that?

YSEGRIN: It's gunfire.

BRUN: The hunters! The hunters are after us!

LENDORE: Merciful heavens! Already?

TIECELIN: Hunters? That is cannon!

YSEGRIN: They've brought in the Army!

BRUN: The Army? Soldiers?

TIECELIN: The soldiers are coming!

LENDORE: E-e-e-ek!

REYNARD: It is only thunder, Sire.

BRUN: Thunder? *(Violent cracks, as the storm breaks.)* Sire, this redhair doesn't know the difference between gunfire and thunder.

YSEGRIN: It is the hunters!

TIECELIN: It is the soldiers!

REYNARD: Gentlemen, calm yourselves. It is simply thunder.

NOBLE: Hunters, soldiers, or thunder — I am taking no chances. Excuse me, gentlemen. *(Exit, hurriedly.)*

TIECELIN: Your Majesty! Wait for me! *(TIECELIN, BRUN, and YSEGRIN collide in their scramble to run for safety.)*

BRUN: Out of my way, Crow!
(TIECELLIN exits in a panic.)

YSEGRIN: No you don't. Me first! *(Exit.)*

LENDORE: Where is everybody going?

BRUN: It is the hunters! Save yourself! *(Exit, on the run.)*

LENDORE: The hunters? Oh, help me!
(Clings fearfully to EPINARD as he rushes past, on his way to the overlook.)

EPINARD: Help you? Each one help himself!

LENDORE: But we just promised — All for one. One for all.

REYNARD: Only when convenient, Lendore.

EPINARD: Ah! You were right, Reynard. It was only thunder, after all. And here comes the rain.

LENDORE: Rain?

REYNARD: Yes, Lendore. Use your pillow for an umbrella.

EPINARD: These thunder-showers bring out the snails. You understand? I must be on the watch for them. *(Exit hastily.)*

REYNARD: Of course, Reverend.

LENDORE: But the Reverend is the one who said we must unite.

REYNARD: Ah, yes, Lendore. And yet, you see, at the first thunder-stroke, he goes off in his own interest, like everybody else.

LENDORE: But suppose it *had* been the hunters

REYNARD: You and I would have been left to meet them, alone.

LENDORE: *(Hastening out)* Heavens! Not me! *(Exit.)*

REYNARD: Then it is Reynard alone against the hunters. Let them come! Even the rain is on my side. It will wash away my tracks, so the dogs can no longer pick up my trail. Let it rain! Ha, ha! It is a good joke on Man!

END OF SCENE TWO

SCENE THREE — AUTUMN

(Music. Sounds of gaiety and merriment from the distant vineyard. EPINARD stands at the overlook, peering off toward the farm. LENDORE enters cautiously, carrying a basket.)

LENDORE: Greetings, Reverend. Is it safe to gather my supplies here?

EPINARD: For the present. Men are still busy celebrating.

LENDORE: Blessed be God who created the autumn.

EPINARD: It is the harvest season, my dear Lendore. You can see the wine-growers' dance from here. Men are full of joy, for the grapes are ripe.

LENDORE: So are the pears and apples, and the nuts and acorns. They will make a good crop to fill my attic.

EPINARD: As long as men are dancing, we are safe. But as soon as the harvest is over, they will take down their guns, call their dogs, and sound the horn. Then our only salvation will be to flee into the heart of the forest, and hide. May Heaven help us when they blow the horn!

LENDORE: Yes. Well, meanwhile, give me a hand in gathering my provisions. *(They start out, but encounter BRUN coming in.)*

BRUN: Do you have to take up the whole path?

LENDORE: No, but I wish you would watch where you step. You just crushed a chestnut. *(Exit.)*

BRUN: You and your chestnuts! I have an appointment with the Royal Registrar.

EPINARD: Don't venture out into the open. Men are about.

BRUN: Men?

EPINARD: You can see them from there. *(Exit. BRUN goes to the overlook. TIECELIN enters.)*

TIECELIN: The Royal Register is not accustomed to be kept waiting, Master Brun.

BRUN: Look — Men!

TIECELIN: *(Looking.)* It is the wine-growers' dance.

BRUN: Don't let them see you.

TIECELIN: Do you take me for a dunce?
(YSEGRIN enters.)

YSEGRIN: Brun! Tiecelin! I have been looking for you.

TIECELIN: Men are dancing, Ysengrin.

YSEGRIN: Men?

BRUN: They are celebrating the harvest.

TIECELIN: Don't show yourself. From now on, we shall have to stay under cover.

YSEGRIN: I will not be hedged into this forest all winter with that rascally Fox!

BRUN: Nor I!

TIECELIN: Gentlemen, take heart. Do you know how many counts I have accumulated against him in my book? Twenty-two!

YSEGRIN: But the year is only half over!

BRUN: Are we to suffer through the fall and winter, without any respite from his tricks?

TIECELIN: Do you have anything else to suggest?

YSEGRIN: Yes!

BRUN: Eh?

YSEGRIN: I have a new plan to dispose of the Fox!

BRUN: Now?

YSEGRIN: Now!

BRUN: Without waiting for Tiecelin's book to fill up?

YSEGRIN: Without waiting one more day.

BRUN and TIECELIN: We are listening.

YSEGRIN: Suppose I should convince the King that the lower classes — the pheasants, the ducks, geese, turkeys, chickens, rabbits, pigeons and mice — have chosen me as their defender, and have charged me to challenge Reynard to a duel.

BRUN: Yes?

YSEGRIN: If you two should back me up, with all the prestige of your position, the King would not be in position to refuse the fight, and I should make a quick end to the redhair. You know me.

BRUN: Good! Eh, Tiecelin?

TIECELIN: Why didn't you think of this sooner? You could have saved me a lot of trouble.

BRUN: We'll help you. But if you give that Fox half a chance, he will turn the tables. I want all the chances to be on your side.

YSEGRIN: The chances *are* on my side. I am the best swordsman in the kingdom.

BRUN: Nevertheless, I shall provide the swords. Reynard's will be so skillfully made, that it will break at the first stroke.

YSEGRIN: I can win without such trickery.

BRUN: Some caution is necessary, my dear nephew. Follow my advice, and Reynard will be out of our way soon. I will go to fix the swords. You inform the King. *(Exit.)*

YSEGRIN: Do I need this treachery? Am I not stronger and braver than Reynard?

TIECELIN: You are, and without flattery, Siegneur Wolf. But nobody is as tricky as he is.

YSEGRIN: Tiecelin, you are a man of law. Give me your advice. Do you think it is honest and fair to allot him a faked weapon?

TIECELIN: As for being fair, certainly not. Honest — even less so. But as for being smart — ha, ha!

YSEGRIN: Do you think so?

TIECELIN: A trick is just what that Fox deserves!

YSEGRIN: But this one will cost him his skin.

TIECELIN: Isn't that what you wish? Besides, so do I.

YSEGRIN: Then consider it done. You may throw away your book, Tiecelin.

TIECELIN: Throw away my book? This book is going into history! Throw away my book, indeed!

YSEGRIN: As you wish. But we shall make an end of Reynard without it. I am going to arrange this matter with the King. As for you, not a word about this. *(Exit.)*

333

TIECELIN: Count on me, Seigneur. This time Reynard shall definitely be punished.
(EPINARD enters.)

EPINARD: Who is going to punish Reynard? You?

TIECELIN: That, Reverend, is a secret. I promised —

EPINARD: Oh, very well. I don't insist.
(Goes to the overlook to watch the wine-growers' dance.)

TIECELIN: Reverend —

EPINARD: Still dancing. Did you call me?

TIECELIN: If I told you that secret —

EPINARD: That wouldn't be very proper, would it? ... I am listening.

TIECELIN: Ysengrin is going to challenge Reynard to a duel.

EPINARD: Is that a secret?

TIECELIN: No, but what is one — and it is this I beg you to keep secret — is that Reynard's sword will be faked.

EPINARD: Faked?

TIECELIN: It will break in two, at the first stroke.

EPINARD: That is certainly not fair, but it is fitting.

TIECELIN: Do you think so, too?

EPINARD: That scamp has tricked me out of a ham, and a duck-egg. He doesn't deserve any better.

TIECELIN: I couldn't agree with you more. *(Trumpet off.)* The King is calling me. *(He starts out.)* Not a word. It is a secret. *(Exit.)*

EPINARD: *(Alone.)* It was bound to turn out this way. Reynard has so often fooled the rest of us. Now it is his turn to be fooled.
(Enter LENDORE.)

LENDORE: See how much I have gathered?

EPINARD: We gather what we sow, and I pity — yes, I deeply

334

pity the one who has sown bad seed.

LENDORE: Who has sown bad seed?

EPINARD: Reynard.

LENDORE: Has Reynard been planting seeds?

EPINARD: He has spread the spirit of trickery among the animals, and he will be destroyed by trickery.

LENDORE: Is someone going to destroy Reynard?

EPINARD: Ysengrin is calling for a duel with him.

LENDORE: The Wolf is strong, of course, but Reynard is shrewd.

EPINARD: He cannot escape this time. In fact, my dear Lendore, I will tell you — but for Goodness' sake, don't repeat it to anyone. Reynard will soon meet his end, for his sword will be faked. It will break in two at the first stroke.

LENDORE: Oh, no!

EPINARD: It is a secret, Lendore. Don't tell anybody. *(Exit.)*

LENDORE: It is wrong just the same. Oh! They all agreed we should unite against Men — and that was right. But we should also unite against those who fake swords.
(Enter REYNARD.)

REYNARD: Who fakes swords?

LENDORE: Reynard, I will tell you, because foul play is wrong.

REYNARD: Foul play?

LENDORE: Ysengrin is going to challenge you to a duel.

REYNARD: Ho! I am equal to that kind of trap.

LENDORE: That is not all. They will provide you with a faked sword. It will break in two at the first stroke. Ysengrin will kill you.

REYNARD: That remains to be seen.

TIECELIN: *(Offstage.)* Reynard! Reynard the Redhair! Where ar you?

REYNARD: Here comes the messenger of death. Leave me, Lendore— and thanks, old friend.

LENDORE: Don't forget. It is a secret. *(Exit.)*

TIECELIN: *(Offstage)* Reynard the Redhead!

REYNARD: What do you want with me?
    (TIECELIN enters.)

TIECELIN: Stay where you are. Trumpets! *(Trumpets.)* Royal message! By order of the King — stay there! His Majesty Noble the Lion — don't move! We, Tiecelin the Crow, Royal Registrar — stop — request the Knight Reynard to hold himself at the disposal of the King, in order to meet in a duel the accuser, Ysengrin the Wolf, Marshall of the Court, and defender of the lower class. Let it be known! Signed, Noble the Lion, King of the animals. Trumpets! *(Trumpets.)*

REYNARD: Is that all? Pouf, it is not much. Tell your master that Reynard is ready.
    (NOBLE enters.)

NOBLE: Come, Tiecelin, if we have to have this duel, let's get it over. Sound the call.

TIECELIN: Yes, Sire. Trumpets! *(Trumpets. The offstage festival gaiety dies away.)*

REYNARD: Hail, oh Noble Sire Lion, the wisest and bravest among us all.

NOBLE: Greetings, Knight Reynard. You already know the reason for my royal call.

REYNARD: I know, Sire.
    (YSEGRIN enters.)

YSEGRIN: I humbly greet your Royal Majesty.

NOBLE: Greetings, Seigneur Ysengrin.
    (EPINARD enters.)

EPINARD: God keep you, gentlemen.

NOBLE: Knight Reynard, Marshall Ysengrin has been chosen the champion of the lower class, and I am compelled — against

336

my will, believe me — to grant him the duel he calls for. As
weapon, your Cousin has chosen the sword.
(Enter BRUN, with two swords.)

BRUN: Here are the weapons, Sire.

NOBLE: You have the choice, Ysengrin.
(BRUN openly hands YSEGRIN the sword prepared for him.)

YSEGRIN: *(Pretending to select.)* I'll take this one, the shorter.

BRUN: Here is yours, Reynard.

REYNARD: *(Takes the sword without looking at it.)* Your
Majesty, I cannot accept this weapon.

BRUN: Why not?

YSEGRIN: What does this mean?

NOBLE: Do you refuse to fight?

REYNARD: I am not a champion, your Majesty. I am unworthy
to fight Ysengrin with a sword. *(He breaks the sword across
his knee.)*

NOBLE: What do you mean?

REYNARD: Sire, Ysengrin represents the lower classes,
and fights as their champion. I am defending nobody but
myself, a poor Fox. I will be satisfied with a Fox's weapon.
Attendant! *(LENDORE enters, carrying a stick.)* Here, Sire,
is my weapon.

NOBLE: This is not customary, but I don't think the Marshall
will object?

YSEGRIN: I agree. But under the circumstances, I require the
use of a shield.

NOBLE: Granted.
(BRUN brings a heavy iron shield.)

REYNARD: My shield!
(LENDORE hands him her pillow.)

NOBLE: Do you expect to fight in this attire?

REYNARD: It is good enough for me, Sire.

337

NOBLE: As you wish, though I think this whole thing is absurd. Gentlemen, take your places. The fight will start when I give the signal, after three trumpet calls. It is strictly forbidden for anyone to interfere in the fight. On guard, Knights, and let the noblest be victorious!

ALL: Let the noblest be victorious!

TIECELIN: Trumpets! *(Trumpets. The opponents eye each other.)* Trumpets! *(Trumpets. Each one raises his shield and gets ready.)* Trumpets! *(Trumpets.)*

NOBLE: Go!

> *(Music. Ballet-mime. Long duel, during which REYNARD's cunning is matched against YSEGRIN's strength. REYNARD uses the pillow as much as the stick. YSEGRIN gets nervous and loses his balance. Any impulse on the part of spectators to take YSEGRIN's side is sternly frowned down by the King. After several phases, REYNARD, with a masterful pillow blow, tumbles YSEGRIN to the ground. Immediately he puts his foot on YSEGRIN's shield, as a token of victory, and greets the King with his stick. YSEGRIN, taking advantage of this moment of inattention, lifts his shield violently, throwing REYNARD down, and making him drop his stick and pillow. YSEGRIN leaps up and puts his foot on REYNARD's chest, threatening him with his sword.)*

BRUN: *(Quickly.)* Ysengrin is the winner!

NOBLE: But only a moment ago —

EPINARD: Heaven has judged.

TIECELIN: His Majesty will declare Ysengrin the winner!

NOBLE: *(Reluctantly.)* Seigneur Ysengrin, I proclaim you Reynard's conqueror. His life belongs to you.

YSEGRIN: I want him to hang. But first of all, I want him humiliated in front of all — to beg forgiveness for his crimes. After that, he shall die.

REYNARD: Oh, Ysengrin, you are truly generous, to give me the opportunity to confess my sins, and beg forgiveness. Let me confess privately to each of you, and ask your blessing.

NOBLE: Granted, my poor Reynard. Come, gentlemen, let us make it possible for Reynard to unburden his conscience.

BRUN: That Fox will find a way to escape, if we give him such a chance.

NOBLE: If you are afraid of that, Seigneur Brun, you may keep watch on the east side, and Ysengrin will guard the west. I myself will take care of the north.

EPINARD: *(Indicating the auditorium.)* Do you wish me to watch the south?

NOBLE: It is not necessary, Reverend. The forest is impenetrable, this side. Who will be the first to hear your confession?

REYNARD: Lendore, if you will allow it.

NOBLE: Granted. Let's go, gentlemen. And keep watch.
(All leave, except LENDORE and REYNARD.)

LENDORE: My poor Reynard.

REYNARD: *(On his knees.)* Draw nearer, Lendore, and receive my confession. *(Whispers.)* Look as stern as you can, and open your ears.

LENDORE: *(Loudly.)* Go on, wretched scoundrel. Unload your conscience, and don't dally.

REYNARD: *(Whispering.)* You must get me out of this fix.

LENDORE: All the roads of escape are guarded.

REYNARD: If I cannot run away, we must make *them* do it. Go out and find a loud instrument somewhere, to make a big noise. Imitate the barking of dogs. Make a monstrous uproar. If you can make them think the hunters are here, they will run away? Do you understand?

LENDORE: You can count on me.

REYNARD: Give me your blessing, good and loud, for their benefit. Thanks, old friend, and don't fall asleep on your way.

Hurry back!

LENDORE: One for all, all for one. *(Exit.)*

REYNARD: Next, Ysengrin.
   (YSEGRIN approaches.)

YSEGRIN: Well, Master Joker. Are you expecting to receive our
   pardon?

REYNARD: Ysengrin, I acknowledge that I fully deserve the fate
   that lies in store for me.

YSEGRIN: Oh, yes?

REYNARD: Yes. And besides, if I had to lose, I'm glad to lose to
   so brave an adversary.

YSEGRIN: Enough hypocrisy!

REYNARD: I don't want to leave this world without proving that
   I hold no grudge against you for your victory. A short while
   ago, I spotted an easy and very appetizing prey. How would
   you like to benefit from it, since I shall not be here any more?

YSEGRIN: Is this your confession?

REYNARD: How would you feel about a plump hen?

YSEGRIN: Easy to catch?

REYNARD: Child's play. Every night she takes a walk right
   here, looking for her rooster. Just hide over there when
   twilight comes, imitate the rooster's cry, and the hen will
   come to you trustingly. You can make short work of her, if
   you strike her down with a heavy stick. Hit well and hit hard,
   for she is tough to kill, they say. That hen. Cousin, ought to
   be worth your benediction.

YSEGRIN: Yes. Pax vobiscum. *(Exit.)*

REYNARD: Next, Uncle Brun.
   (Enter BRUN.)

BRUN: Not hanged yet?

REYNARD: In good time, Uncle.

BRUN: I shall not be sorry for it.

REYNARD: I will not beg your pardon, for I have done you too much wrong, but let me be remembered for one last good turn. Would you like a good meal?

BRUN: Is it another bumble-bee's nest?

REYNARD: Don't talk so loudly. It is a wonderful rooster. Each night, he strolls right here, looking for his hen. Just hide over there, and imitate her cackling to lure the rooster. It will be child's play for you to strike him down with a heavy stick. Hit well and hit hard, for he is tough to kill, they say.

BRUN: Is this not a new trap?

REYNARD: Uncle! How can you think I would play you a trick at the moment I am going to die? No. I wish you good appetite, and ask your blessing.

BRUN: Go in peace. And may the rope be quickly ready, so you may go soon. *(Exit.)*

REYNARD: Thank you, Uncle. Don't forget. Over there, when twilight comes. *(To himself.)* What the dickens can be keeping Lendore? *(Aloud.)* Next, Sire.
(NOBLE enters.)

NOBLE: Reynard, I was maneuvered into this, and now I am powerless to help you.

REYNARD: Rest easy, Sire. I attach no blame to you. Let me only take this last chance to thank you, Sire, for your many kindnesses —

NOBLE: Oh, Reynard, how am I to do without you?

REYNARD: I am only a wicked Fox, Sire.

NOBLE: You are the only honest rogue among us. Why did you let yourself in for this? Don't you know they will not rest until they have your life? See, here is Brun, with the rope.
(BRUN enters, with tying-rope.)

BRUN: Sire, the time has come to tie him up.

REYNARD: *(To himself.)* And still Lendore has not come back.
(The company re-gathers on stage. BRUN ties

341

REYNARD's hands.)

YSEGRIN: *(Brings hanging-rope, flings it over tree-limb.)* Next. You, Reynard.

REYNARD: *(Tied.)* Here I am. May God have mercy on me, a miserable Fox, who was led by demons to the most dreadful crimes.

BRUN: Hang him quick, and let us forget about it.

REYNARD: But where is Lendore?

BRUN: She is gone.

REYNARD: I would like to hug her one more time.

YSEGRIN: Don't let us wait any longer, Sire.

REYNARD: May I not see her once more?

BRUN: Can't you see he is only trying to gain time?

REYNARD: She was my true friend.

BRUN: Ah, well, let's put an end to this.

TIECELIN: Hang him!
(YSEGRIN pulls the rope, experimentally. At this moment, there is the sound of a hunting-horn.)

BRUN: Men!

EPINARD: *(Rushing to look.)* They have stopped dancing?
(An outbreak of dog-barks, offstage.)

YSEGRIN: Dogs!

BRUN: On the chase!
(A dramatic explosion of rapid-fire, staccato bangs.)

EPINARD: It is the hunt!

NOBLE: The hunt is on: Take cover!
(NOBLE flees.)

TIECELIN: Escape if you can! *(Exit, flying. General flight.)*

YSEGRIN: *(Holding REYNARD's hanging-rope.)* Wait! Wait! We must hang him!

BRUN: Come! Do you wish to get pulled apart by dogs? *(Exit.)*

YSEGRIN: *(Torn, he starts off, hesitates.)* But — *(Another burst of rapid-fire bangs, accompanied by barking.)* Farewell, Master Reynard. The dogs will take care of you. *(Exit.)*

REYNARD: *(Alone.)* Lendore was a true friend.
(LENDORE enters, beating a saucepan, blowing a hunting-horn, and barking.)

LENDORE: Woof! Woof! Bow-wow! Bow-wow! *(She laughs.)* Ha, ha, ha! I never saw them run so fast!

REYNARD: Thanks, my dear. It was high time.

LENDORE: *(Releasing him from the rope, and untying his bonds.)* You'll never know the trouble I had to find this horn, and this saucepan.

REYNARD: My good friend, I must be off.

LENDORE: Where will you go?

REYNARD: I will have to make for the outer edge of the woods.

LENDORE: *(Concerned.)* But that is where the men do their hunting.

REYNARD: If I can elude this pack of rascals, I can surely stay out of the reach of men.

LENDORE: Take care, Reynard.

REYNARD: I will need a little time to get away. If you will be good enough to keep up the music a few moments —

LENDORE: Oh, gladly!

REYNARD: Good bye, old friend.
(LENDORE gleefully beats, blows, and barks, though her barking turns a little plaintive, as she watches REYNARD go. As she goes out the opposite side, her noise retreats, and soon gives way to the renewed sounds of celebration in the distant vineyard. Lights dim slowly, leaving the empty stage in twilight. Cautiously, TIECLIN peers around a bush, then creeps in.)

TIECELIN: *(Alone.)* The rope is empty. Reynard is gone. But where is the hunt? *(Music and laughter from the vineyard, TIECLIN runs to look.)* They are dancing again. Ah-h-h! It was all a hoax! There were no hunters. There were no horns. There were no dogs. There was only noise. Reynard has fooled us once again. Oh, that wily Fox! He has out-tricked Ysengrin. He has out-tricked Brun. But he will not out-trick me. I still have my book. And this will make his twenty-third crime! *(Exits. A moment of music. Night falls. Semi-darkness with light background, so that the following scene may be played in silhouette. YSEGRIN enters, right side, with stick.)*

YSEGRIN: This is the place where Reynard told me to look for that hen. Kikikiki —
(BRUN enters, left side, armed with club.)

BRUN: Cluck, cluck, cluck —

YSEGRIN: Kikiriki —
(They advance slowly toward each other.)

BRUN: Hold still, you rooster!

YSEGRIN: Rooster? How dare you call me a rooster! Take that, you miserable hen!

BRUN: Hen? Is this a hen stroke? *(They fight in earnest, and quickly discover each other at the same time.)* Ysengrin! So you want to fight, do you?

YSEGRIN: Brun! What are you beating me for?

BRUN: *(Chasing him.)* I'll show you what a beating is.

YSEGRIN: *(Fleeing.)* Help! Help!
(From the distant vineyard comes a burst of laughter.)

END OF SCENE THREE

SCENE IV — WINTER

(Music. Wind. In the distance the howling of the WOLF can beheard. Stage lights come up slowly. TIECELIN, shivering,

is stamping his feet. BRUN enters, muffled up in his fur.)

TIECELIN: It is winter, Master Brun.

BRUN: You don't have to tell me.

TIECELIN: Here we are, huddled together in a tight little circle, with fortifications all around us. We don't even have any place to run, to keep warm.

BRUN: Hug yourself with your feathers.

TIECELIN: I have tried that, but my feathers are cold, too. And the frost has made the ground so hard that it doesn't provide food any more. I am hungry, Seigneur Brun, and I am not the only one. Listen to the Wolf. What bitter cold! The pool is covered with ice, and even my tongue is frozen, and stiff as a stick.

BRUN: If you kept your mouth shut, this wouldn't happen.

TIECELIN: I would gladly shut it on some food, wouldn't you? *(LENDORE crosses slowly, pillow under her arm, overwhelmed with sleep.)* Where are you going?

LENDORE: To sleep.
(NOBLE enters, overcome by a comic cough.)

NOBLE: Find me a doctor. Promise him a fourth, even half of my kingdom, but let him release me from this awful cough.

TIECELIN: A doctor? Where are we to find a doctor?

BRUN: We are holed up here like fugitives.

TIECELIN: Beyond the barricade, hunting dogs are waiting to pounce on us.

BRUN: And behind them are the hunters with their guns.

TIECELIN: None of us dares to stick our nose beyond the barricade.

NOBLE: But this is a matter of life or death.

TIECELIN: Your Majesty only has a bad cold.

NOBLE: Bad cold? Your King is dying of pneumonia, and there is no one here to lift a finger. Oh, where is Reynard!

TIECELIN: Reynard? The redhair!

NOBLE: Yes. Oh, my good Reynard, if you were only here!

BRUN: He'd better not show his face around here.

NOBLE: Find him. Search the kingdom!

TIECELIN: Outside the barricade, where the dogs are lurking?

NOBLE: Even to the edge of the forest!

BRUN: The edge of the forest, where men are waiting with their guns?

TIECELIN: Would you have us risk our lives?

NOBLE: Yes! Bring me Reynard.

TIECELIN: Your Majesty, Reynard is in hiding. He would not dare to come.

BRUN: He knows a hanging is waiting for him.

NOBLE: Tell him I will forgive him everything, if he will only come back.
(LENDORE exits quietly, but purposefully.)

BRUN: Forgive him?

TIECELIN: Forgive him all the crimes he has committed against us?

BRUN: Forgive him this rope?

TIECELIN: It is beyond your power, Sire. My book is full of indictments against him — twenty-four, to be exact.

NOBLE: Then I am doomed. Only Reynard can find a way to save me.
(YSEGRIN enters, starving, violent.)

YSEGRIN: Give me something to eat — no matter what, but something.

NOBLE: I am sick, Ysengrin.

YSEGRIN: And I am hungry, Sire.

TIECELIN: Be patient, Sire. Don't die yet. When good weather returns, you will be well again.

NOBLE: I shall not last that long, my friends. My kingdom! Who will save my kingdom?

BRUN and YSEGRIN: *(At the same time.)* I! Me!

TIECELIN: Gentlemen.

YSEGRIN: *(Pushing BRUN back.)* *I* can take your place, Sire. Don't be afraid to die.

BRUN: *(Elbowing YSEGRIN away.)* I can do it, Sire. You may trust me.

TIECELIN: Don't die, your Majesty, or these two will kill each other to take possession of your throne.

NOBLE: Death is inexorable, my friends. There is only one who can help your poor, unfortunate King, and he is not here. *(Outbreak of savage barking.)* Listen!

BRUN: It is the dogs!

YSEGRIN: The dogs have broken through!

TIECELIN: The hunters have found us!

BRUN: They are coming!

YSEGRIN: We are trapped!

NOBLE: *(Struggling weakly to his feet.)* My friends, gather round me. We shall die together.
(Cowering together in a close huddle, they await the enemy's approach. LENDORE enters, followed by REYNARD, disguised as a Minstrel.)

LENDORE: Your Majesty —

NOBLE: Lendore!

TIECELIN: Lendore? It is not the hunters?

LENDORE: Hunters? It is only a poor Minstrel I found hiding beneath the barricade, to escape the dogs. I thought he might be able to help you.

BRUN: If he led the dogs to our stronghold, we are all done for.

TIECELIN: How did you get by the hunters?

REYNARD: *(Minstrel accent.)* Perdone, Señor. I no understanda very well.

YSEGRIN: Who are you, who plays the guitar while our King is dying?

BRUN: Cease your music, vagrant.

REYNARD: No de musique? Porque?

TIECELIN: The King is dying.

NOBLE: Let him approach. Who are you?

REYNARD: Un troubadour, from Andalusia d'Espagne, my gran Señor.

NOBLE: Can you play and sing?

REYNARD: Si. Very good player and singer. And very good doctor, too.

NOBLE: What? You are a doctor? Can you cure my pneumonia?

REYNARD: Si, Señor. I can cure anychosa.

BRUN: Beware. He is a spy.

REYNARD: I can save el gran Señor.

YSEGRIN: Get away.

REYNARD: I can kill la pneumonia, just like that — crac!

NOBLE: Do you really have a remedy?

REYNARD: Si, Señor, un gran remedia.

NOBLE: Relieve me of this cough, and you shall become my prime minister.

BRUN: Allow me, Sire —

NOBLE: I have spoken.

YSEGRIN: What remedy do you recommend?

REYNARD: *(Showing a bottle.)* Esta boteilla, gran Señor. Vino. Good vino. Vino grandissimo to kill la pneumonia.

NOBLE: Give it to me.

REYNARD: Ma, que, but it is not enough by itself. Needa still some otrechosa.

NOBLE: Some other things, such as what?

REYNARD: *(Makes gesture of pulling his moustache.)* Some chosa like this, but bigger, moocha bigger.

NOBLE: A big moustache?

REYNARD: Moustachio, si, yes. Yes, moustachio! Like that! *(Points to BRUN.)*

BRUN: My moustache?

REYNARD: Si, Señor. Si. Gracias.

NOBLE: Has it got to be cut?

REYNARD: Cut? Si, yes. That is of the most importance. It goes in la pocha — *(Shows his leather pouch.)* — and then on la cabeza, there. *(Indicates the King's head.)*

NOBLE: Brun, your moustache.

BRUN: But Sire, it is impossible.

NOBLE: *(Stern.)* Your moustache.

BRUN: I shall be disgraced.

NOBLE: It is your King's life,

YSEGRIN: You cannot refuse, my dear Brun.

REYNARD: *(Scissors ready.)* Cut?

BRUN: Sire?

NOBLE: I am waiting.

YSEGRIN: Go ahead, troubadour.
(REYNARD cuts off half of BRUN's moustache.)

BRUN: Let Heaven be the witness of my disgrace!

NOBLE: It is for your King's welfare, Seigneur Brun.

REYNARD: It is truly un gran moustachio, Señor the Majesty. Half will be enough. No cut la otre. No wish to rob the fat senor.

BRUN: But Sire, I look ridiculous.

349

NOBLE: You will wear the half-moustache in remembrance of your self-sacrifice.

REYNARD: *(Putting moustache in his pouch.)* Ah, that is good, so far. But gran senor, that is not all.

NOBLE: You need something else? What is it?

REYNARD: A ball of white fur.

NOBLE: White fur?

REYNARD: Si. Oh, a very little ball. Perhaps no more than that. *(Points to YSEGRIN's ears, which are lined with white.)*

YSEGRIN: My ears? Oh, no! *(Frantically seeks a means of escape.)*

REYNARD: Not the ears, señor. Only the white lining of them.

NOBLE: How lucky! Use your scissors, troubadour.

YSEGRIN: But Sire, I need my ear-linings!

BRUN: You cannot refuse, my dear Ysengrin.

NOBLE: This is for your King.

YSEGRIN: I shall never be the same!

NOBLE: Go ahead, Minstrel.

YSEGRIN: My ears! My ears!

REYNARD: *(Cutting.)* If the senor would only stand still — I do not wish to hurt the señor.

YSEGRIN: Ouch! He is taking my whole ear, Sire! Tell him to — Ouch!

REYNARD: Ah! Since the señor is so unhappy to lose a little bit of fur, we may content ourselves with this one piece. *(The ear he has trimmed has lost its erectness, hangs down ludicrously over one eye. The other ear stands up.)*

YSEGRIN: But my ears will not match!

REYNARD: Small matter. We do not wish to ask too great a sacrifice of the señor.

YSEGRIN: I am lop-sided!

350

NOBLE: In the service of your King, Seigneur Wolf. You are sure you have enough white fur for the remedy, troubadour?

REYNARD: Oh, si, gran Señor.

NOBLE: And now do you need anything else?

REYNARD: Only one otrechosa, Sire.

NOBLE: And what is that?

REYNARD: We must have three black feathers.
    (TIECELIN starts creeping out.)

NOBLE: Tiecelin!

TIECELIN: You c-c-called me, Sire?

REYNARD: Ma, que, such beautiful, glossy black feathers!

NOBLE: Tiecelin, we have need of some feathers.

TIECELIN: But I have no feathers to spare, Sire.

REYNARD: Ah, si, si. On this side, too short. In front, too soft. On this side, the colour is not true. But ah, the back is just right. *(He seizes TIECELIN by the tail feathers.)*

TIECELIN: Sire! He would not take my tail!

NOBLE: Do you find there what you require, troubadour?

REYNARD: Ah, si, si, Señor the Majesty.

TIECELIN: Help! Help! My beautiful tail!

YSEGRIN: Your tail is no better than my ear, Tiecelin.

BRUN: Or than my moustache.

REYNARD: *(Plucking.)* One!

TIECELIN: Aie!

NOBLE: It is for your King's life, Tiecelin.

REYNARD: Two!

TIECELIN: Aie!

YSEGRIN: At least you will not be one-sided.

REYNARD: Three!

TIECELIN: Aie! Oh, I am so undressed! Sire, I shall take my death of cold. *(He does indeed look odd, with his stub tail.)*

REYNARD: *(Placing feathers in the pouch.)* 1 regret any inconvenience this may cause the little señor. Now, your Majesty, all is ready. Gran señor. On la cabeza. There. *(He places the pouch inside NOBLE's crown.)*

NOBLE: Are you sure this will cure me?

REYNARD: Oh, very sure, gran señor.

NOBLE: And if your remedy doesn't work?

REYNARD: Then we shall have to resort to extreme measures. But let us hope for the best.

NOBLE: No extreme measures. This will cure me. I can feel it. Give me that bottle.

REYNARD: Ah, si. This is the wine that gives life.

NOBLE: The moustache, what is it for?

REYNARD: Strength. It is the strength of the fat senor.

NOBLE: And the fur?

REYNARD: Warmth. It will dissolve the cough.

NOBLE: And the feathers?

REYNARD: It is a cover, to hold the strength and the warmth in. With the wine, it will spread through the body, and give new life. Drink.
(NOBLE drinks. All watch with suspense.)

TIECELIN: How does your Majesty feel?

NOBLE: To tell the truth, I don't feel any difference.

REYNARD: Ah, then, we shall have to use the last resort. For this I shall need three needles.

NOBLE *(Alarmed):* Needles? What for?

YSEGRIN: Needles? The Reverend!

BRUN: Of course. Epinard.

TIECELIN: I'll fetch him. *(Exit.)*

NOBLE: What are these needles for?

REYNARD: Ah, Señor the Majesty is so very fortunate, to have such willing subjects to supply every need.

NOBLE: But what do you propose to do with these needles?
(TIECELIN returns with EPINARD.)

EPINARD: Peace be with you, Master Troubadour.

REYNARD: Ah, si. I can see that he has needles to spare.

EPINARD: *(Bristling.)* Needles? What is this about needles?

NOBLE: That is what I want to know.

REYNARD: We wish to request a small favour of you, Reverend, with your permission.

YSEGRIN: With or without your permission, his Majesty desires you to give up three needles to this troubadour here.

EPINARD: But my needles are my protection!

BRUN: Don't be stingy. You have plenty of them.
(REYNARD has circled him, and selected three choice needles, between his ears.)

EPINARD: But your Majesty, I am not — Ow! Have some respect for my — Ow! Will you give me a chance to — Ow! Oh, I am unfrocked!

TIECELIN: It is for your King, Reverend.

REYNARD: Here are three needles, gran señor — nice and long and sharp.

NOBLE: Wait! I demand to know what you intend to do with these needles.

REYNARD: Why, if the first remedia has not cured you, it will be necessary to bleed you, Señor the Majesty.

NOBLE: Oh, no!

REYNARD: First in the arm —

NOBLE: Wait!

REYNARD: Then in the leg —

NOBLE: Stop!

REYNARD: And then, of course, in the — ah — underneath the — ah —

NOBLE: Enough! It is not necessary. I feel better now.

REYNARD: Ah, the remedia is taking effect?

NOBLE: I feel perfectly well. Throw those needles away.

REYNARD: My congratulations, Sire. The King is saved, gentlemen.

ALL: Long live the King!

NOBLE: Thank you. As for you, troubadour, I wish to reward you.

YSEGRIN: Are you going to make him your prime minister?

NOBLE: Did I say that?

BRUN: It is impossible, Sire. A Minstrel — a guitar-player —

NOBLE: Did I really promise it?

TIECELIN: According to law, Sire, a stranger cannot hold office in the animal kingdom.

NOBLE: Ah! You hear, Troubadour. The law prevents it.

REYNARD: The gran Señor is cured, that is good. The povre Minstrel is not minister, that is also good. I ask only the gift of your royal favour in the country of los animalos.

NOBLE: Granted. Take this.

YSEGRIN: Your ring, Sire!

BRUN: The King's diamond!

TIECELIN: It is worth a million at least.

NOBLE: Is this too high a price for my life?

TIECELIN: No, indeed, indeed.

NOBLE: This ring will be the token of my royal protection. Whenever you show it to anyone in my kingdom, help and assistance will be granted you.

354

REYNARD: The señor is gran, gran como la luna. I am his servitor.

NOBLE: Do you wish anything else?

REYNARD: Only la pocha, there.

BRUN: My moustache!

NOBLE: Half of your moustache.

YSEGRIN: My ear!

NOBLE: The lining of one ear.

TIECELIN: My tail!

NOBLE: Three paltry feathers.

EPINARD: *(As REYNARD tucks his quills into the pouch.)* My quills!

NOBLE: We wish you good luck, Minstrel.

REYNARD: Gracias, Señor the Majesty. Now I must go.

BRUN: Go? Out there?

TIECELIN: Sire, if he so much as snaps a twig going through the barricade, the dogs will be upon us in a flash.

REYNARD: Ma, que, Señors, the dogs will be upon me, not you. But have no fear, Majesty. I know how to escape the dogs.

NOBLE: Just the same, it would seem only wise for us all to take cover, until you are safely away. Follow me, gentlemen. Good bye, my good fellow.

REYNARD: The gran señor is good also. Viva, olle the gran Señor. And gracias for the so beautiful ring.
(NOBLE exits, followed by BRUN, YSEGRIN, and EPINARD. TIECELIN pretends to follow, but lags behind, as REYNARD prepares to leave. LENDORE has fallen asleep.)

TIECELIN: One moment, my friend.

REYNARD: The little Señor said "my friend."

TIECELIN: I said "One moment." It is customary, in cases of audience with the King, to leave an expression of your thanks with me.

REYNARD: Ma, que, I did not know.

TIECELIN: Doubtless you do not know that I am the King's Registrar, and that I regulate, manage, and organize everything in the animal kingdom.

REYNARD: Hombre, que, I thought the gran Señor King did it all.

TIECELIN: He does what I command. When I say "Here comes the King," he comes. I say "The King sits down." He sits down. The King drinks." He drinks. "The King gets up." He gets up. He can do nothing without my order. Without me there would be no King of the animals any more.

REYNARD: Ha, que, how about that! The little señor is a very important persona. It is a pity that he had to sacrifice his so beautiful tail plumage to the King's health.

TIECELIN: It is nothing less than a disgrace.

REYNARD: Ah, yes. Your costume is now a little lacking in dignity for a so important persona. Wait! I have a chosa in la pocha, to make him look more gran. Look. Would the señor do me the great honour to accept this, in place of the feathers he has lost? *(He takes out three peacock feathers.)*

TIECELIN: They are peacock feathers, aren't they?

REYNARD: Si. The feathers del peacock. The very marvelosa bird que outshines the sun a hundred times, in his brilliance.

TIECELIN: He is a very beautiful bird indeed, but he is stupid.

REYNARD: Ma, que. but this is the tail, not the head. The little senor with the plumage del peacock, and his own gran intelligencio, will make the greatest bird of all, the very gran Phoenix of the occupantos of these woods.

TIECELIN: Do you think so?

REYNARD: Que, it is the truth. It is the thanks del troubadour to the gran persona del little señor.

TIECELIN: I accept the very humble present you give me. Now

you may go.

REYNARD: Ah, si. Adios, señor.

TIECELIN: Take care, as you leave, not to draw the attention of the dogs.

REYNARD: Trust me, señor. Servitor, gran Phoenix. Servitor. *(Pretends to leave, but conceals himself on one side. Lendore stirs on the other side.)*

TIECELIN: *(Listens tensely a few moments, for any possible disturbance caused by Minstrel's departure.)* Ah, he is safely away. *(Not noticing LENDORE, he adorns himself with the peacock feathers.)* I can feel myself becoming very beautiful, very beautiful indeed. The King is far behind me when it comes to grace, charm, bearing, and elegance. I am really a Phoenix. The Minstrel said so. When the others see me, they will say "Look at the Crow!" And they will be green with envy. They will say "Look at the Crow!" And the echoes of the forest will endlessly repeat — "Look at the Crow!" "Look at the Crow!"

REYNARD: *(Echoing.)* Oh!... Oh!... Oh!... Oh!

TIECELIN: How beautiful, beautiful, beautiful. How very beautiful!
More beautiful than the Wolf, more beautiful even than the Lion. *(Shouts.)* More beautiful than the King!

REYNARD: *(Echoing.)* ... Ing! ... Ing! ... Ing! ... Hee — hee —-hee!
(LENDORE takes it up, and the echo gradually changes into a laughter which is curiously prolonged.)

LENDORE: Hee — hee — hee — Hi — hi — hi —

TIECELIN: *(At first taken aback, stops and wonders.)* What? Hush, Echo.

REYNARD: Ho — ho — ho — ho —

LENDORE: Ho — ho — ho — ho —

TIECELIN: Instead of laughing, look at the Crow!

REYNARD: Ho — ho — ho — ho —

LENDORE: Ho — ho — ho — ho —

TIECELIN: *(In a rage.)* Are you almost through?

REYNARD: Hou — hou — hou — hou —

LENDORE: Hoo — hoo — hoc — hoo —

TIECELIN: You laugh at me?

REYNARD and LENDORE: Hee — hee — hee — hee — *(The laughter seems to come from everywhere at once.)* Ha — ha — ha — ha! Hee — hee — hee — hee! Look at the Crow! Ho — ho — ho! How beautiful is he! Hee — hee — hee! Ho — ho — ho! Ha — ha — ha! Hohoho! Hahaha! Hihihi! Hohohohahahahihi! Hohohohahahahihi!
(In shame TIECELIN divests himself of the peacock feathers, but the laughter continues to grow in volume.)

TIECELIN: *(Finally manages to top the laughter.)* Enough! Stop!
(REYNARD stops, but LENDORE, unaware of danger, continues, convulsed with genuine laughter.) There is more to this than echoes. *(Creeping quietly across he discovers and seizes LENDORE.)* Lendore! You were making fun of me!

LENDORE: I — Oh, Tiecelin, you were oh, so funny!

TIECELIN: Nobody is going to laugh at me, and live to tell it.

LENDORE: H — H — H — Stop! You are strangling me.

TIECELIN: *(Choking her.)* I am going to do more than that. I amgoing to feed you to the Wolf!

LENDORE: *(Struggling in his grasp.)* H-h-help! H-h-h-help!
(REYNARD steps out of hiding, discarding his cape.)

REYNARD: Let her go.

TIECELIN: *(Frozen.)* I have surely heard that voice before.

REYNARD: Ma, que, Señor, your costume is a little lacking in dignity —

TIECELIN: *(Trying shamefully to cover up his stub tail.)*

Reynard! It is you!

REYNARD: At your service, Tiecelin.

TIECELIN: You, the Minstrel! I might have known it.

REYNARD: *(Placing peacock feathers at his tail and mimicking TIECELIN.)* Am I not beautiful? The most beautiful of all? Am I not the great Phoenix of the deep woods?

TIECELIN: You will pay for this. It is your last trick. Everybody! Come! It is Reynard! It is his twenty-fifth crime! Trumpets! Trumpets!

REYNARD: Am I not splendid? Am I not the best-looking, the most intelligent —
(Trumpets. At the sound, REYNARD breaks off short.)

TIECELIN: Everybody come! It is Reynard! Trumpets!
(REYNARD runs desperately in all directions, seeking an escape. Trumpets.) Twenty-fifth crime! Trumpets!
(Trumpets.)

VOICES: *(Off.)* Reynard! Twenty-fifth crime!
(The Epilogue follows immediately, without break.)

END OF SCENE FOUR

EPILOGUE

TIECELIN: By order of the King, his Majesty Noble the Lion —

REYNARD: All right. I know what is coming next. *(He tries to leave at right, but encounters NOBLE, entering, and has to bow.)* Sire.

NOBLE: Reynard.
(REYNARD tries to leave at left, but BRUN and YSEGRIN enter there.)

REYNARD: Uncle Brun. Cousin Ysengrin.

BRUN: The rope is still in place.

YSEGRIN: We have kept it waiting for you.

REYNARD: I am in no hurry.

NOBLE: This time, Reynard, you have put the noose around your own neck.

LENDORE: Why did you let yourself get caught? Oh, Reynard, I cannot watch this! *(Exit. EPINARD enters.)*

EPINARD: What brings on this new disturbance? Ah, it is you, Reynard. You must be out of your mind.

NOBLE: Gentlemen.

TIECELIN: The King is about to speak. Trumpets! *(Trumpets.)*

NOBLE: We are now at the end of the year of mercy granted to Reynard the Fox. What are the grievances charged against him now?

TIECELIN: A book full, your Majesty. Twenty-five crimes. *(He reads.)* The Knight Reynard, called Reynard the redhair, is accused —

NOBLE: Never mind, Tiecelin. You have all witnessed Reynard's misdeeds. So you will judge if he deserves to hang, or if he should be granted mercy. How do you feel about it?

YSEGRIN: I demand his hanging.

TIECELIN: He must hang!

BRUN: Hang him!

EPINARD: May Heaven forgive me, let him hang.

NOBLE: You hear, Reynard?

REYNARD: Nevertheless, your Majesty, I have the right to present my defense, I presume?

YSEGRIN: There is no defense.

TIECELIN: He has committed twenty-five crimes.

NOBLE: Have you any defender?

REYNARD: Yes, your Majesty.

NOBLE: Who is it?

REYNARD: You yourself, Sire.

NOBLE: I?

REYNARD: Doesn't this ring remind you of anything. *(Minstrel accent.)* The gran Señor has lost la pneumonia. El troubadour has cured the gran Señor.

NOBLE: So, it was you?

REYNARD: It was me, Sire, at your service.
(All the animals cry out with rage.)

BRUN: He has cut off half my moustache!

YSEGRIN: My ear!

EPINARD: My quills!

TIECELINS *(Writing furiously)*: My feathers! And all this is going in the book!

BRUN: The bumble-bees have stung me all over!

EPINARD: He made away with my ham!

NOBLE: An end to this! Stop! Enough! Silence!

TIECELIN: Let the King speak. *(But the silence is broken by the sound of a hunting-horn, off-stage. LENDORE flies in, frantic.)*

LENDORE: The hunters! The hunters are coming! *(The hunting horn is repeated from a different direction, and again from another. Everyone is electrified.)* They are closing in, from all sides of the woods!

BRUN: This has happened once before.

YSEGRIN: Is this rascal going to escape us again?

TIECELIN: The rope is ready.

BRUN: Let's not wait any longer. Hang him!
(Genuine rifle shots off-stage.)

EPINARD: This is no joke!

NOBLE: We are caught! *(All make a grand rush for the left. The fanfare breaks out on that side, with renewed vigor.)* Tiecelin, go and see what is going on.

TIECELIN: B-b-b-but —

NOBLE: Go and see, I tell you.

EPINARD: It is no use, Sire. We are surrounded.

LENDORE: *(At right.)* There are more than twenty.

YSEGRIN: *(At back)*: They are coming this way, too.

BRUN: *(At left.)* And this way.

NOBLE: This time, my friends, we shall not escape the men. Let
each one of you show your courage, and defend your life at a
high price.

TIECELIN: Sire, I wish you a very gallant death. As for me, I
have wings. Allow me to make use of them.
(Exit. His flight is hailed by shouts and rifle shots.)

BRUN: There goes our brave Phoenix.

YSEGRIN: What shall we do with the prisoner?

NOBLE: We are all prisoners, Seigneur Ysengrin.

REYNARD: I can save you, Sire.

BRUN: Don't listen to him. He is only trying to escape.

NOBLE: How can you save us?

REYNARD: Don't move from here. Stay under cover. I will go
out of the woods. The fortifications will hold them until I can
get out.

YSEGRIN: You see, he is only trying to get away.

REYNARD: I will let the hunters see me, willingly, in the open.
The dogs will jump for me, and follow my tracks, and the
men will follow them. I will lead them out of the woods, to
the other end of the plain.

NOBLE: You will lose your life doing that.

REYNARD: It is possible — but it will save yours.

NOBLE: Release him. May Heaven help you!

REYNARD: Farewell, Sire. Farewell, my friends.
(He takes time to choose his exit point with care, then leaps

362

out, to be greeted by furious dog-barking, men's shouts, and rifle shots. Ballet-mime, as the animals left onstage follow the progress of the chase. The cries, the barks, the shots, and the horn-calls intermingle. Cries and yells, close at first — "The fox! The fox! Loose the dogs! Shoot! Shoot!" By some means, possibly by amplifying, there should be a noticeable difference between the human voices and the animal voices. At first the animals huddle together, frozen with terror, silent, distressed, listening intently. As the offstage sounds retreat, they relax enough to register their fear, stopping up their ears, covering their heads, running for shelter, cowering under rocks, bushes, stumps. Eventually the noises fade away in the distance, indicating that REYNARD is leading the chase far away. They begin to express their relief, and then their absolute joy, as the hunt moves further away, leaping with elation, embracing each other, dancing in triumph.)

LENDORE: *(Hopping up and down.)* He has done it! He has done it! *(One last, distant, terribly final shot, then a distressing silence.)* Oh, no!
(All are suddenly sobered.)

BRUN: And so, Sire, this is the end of Reynard.

EPINARD: May Heaven welcome his soul.

YSEGRIN: And the hunters his skin.

LENDORE *(Who has rushed to the overlook.)* He is nowhere in sight.

YSEGRIN: Of course not. The dogs have got him.

NOBLE: He could outrun the dogs.

BRUN: But not the bullets, Sire.

YSEGRIN: The hunters have saved us the trouble of hanging him.
(TIECELIN returns, very cocky and proud.)

BRUN: Ah! Now that the danger is over, our valiant Crow returns.

TIECELIN: Sire, you are saved.

363

NOBLE: Where do you come from?

TIECELIN: From a tree. Sire. When I left here, I risked thousands of rifle shots — and look. Not a scratch.

LENDORE: Have you seen Reynard?

TIECELIN: He is dead. I saw him fall, covered with blood, and crawl under a hazelnut bush.

LENDORE: No!

NOBLE: The brave fellow!

TIECELIN: The dogs will catch up with him shortly. But they will find him dead. So will the hunters. I am the only one who saw his end.

YSEGRIN: Oh, stop your bragging. Reynard is dead, and that is all that matters.

LENDORE: *(Weeping.)* Poor redhair!

BRUN: We finally got rid of him.

EPINARD: Since he is gone, let him rest in peace.

NOBLE: At least he died like a hero — not by hanging.
(REYNARD staggers in, tattered, exhausted, faltering, exaggerating his condition dramatically.)

REYNARD: Sire, my King —

TIECELIN: *(Hastily scrambling up his tree.)* What! You are not dead?

REYNARD: I ... fulfilled ... my promise — *(He staggers.)*

NOBLE: Yes, good fellow. You have our undying gratitude.

LENDORE: Are you wounded?

REYNARD: No, it is nothing ... no, nothing — *(He collapses.)*

LENDORE: Reynard!

EPINARD: This time, Sire, beyond any doubt, he is really gone.

YSEGRIN: So much the better.

TIECELIN: Beware. He has more than one trick up his sleeve.

BRUN: Oh, no. Look. *(He lifts one leg, which falls back limply.)*

TIECELIN: He did that to me once before. *(But he ventures down from his perch, nevertheless.)*

EPINARD: *(Lifts one arm, which falls back, lifeless.)* He has undoubtedly passed away.

YSEGRIN: *(Lifts the tail, which falls back, a dead weight.)* There is no doubt indeed.

LENDORE: *(Sobbing.)* He was so good.

EPINARD: He was a rogue.

LENDORE: So witty.

YSEGRIN: He was a scoundrel.

LENDORE: So clever.

BRUN: He was a villain.

LENDORE: So full of fun.

TIECELIN: He was a cheese robber!

EPINARD: A ham robber!

BRUN: A moustache robber!

YSEGRIN: An ear robber!

TIECELIN: A tail robber!

EPINARD: A quill robber!

TIECELIN: And it is all down in my book. See, my book? Here are all his crimes.

NOBLE: Yes — and here is he. We live, because of him. Give me your book, Tiecelin. Let the accusations against him be buried with Reynard. *(He tears out pages, letting them fall on REYNARD.)*

TIECELIN: My book! My book!
(Silence. REYNARD stirs.)

REYNARD: What gentle winds have blown this soft covering over my poor body? Ah, it is my noble King. *(He gathers loose pages and tears them across.)* What a relief it is to know that your royal person is safe from the hunters! *(He rises.)*

BRUN: He lives!

LENDORE: Reynard, my friend!

YSEGRIN: He is alive!

TIECELIN: My book! My book!

REYNARD: Ah, you are concerned about your book, Tiecelin? Allow me to return it to you — at least part of it. And a part for you, Uncle Brun. And some for you, Ysengrin. *(Gaily he pelts them all with torn fragments. TIECELIN, driven to despair by this desecration, scrambles out frantically, trying to gather them up.)*

BRUN: Sire, he lives — and there goes all the evidence against him.

REYNARD: Indeed. Then we shall have no use for this grim thing. Let us use it for a gayer purpose. *(He snatches down the hanging-rope, jumps rope for a few steps.)* Come, my faithful friend Lendore, it is a moment to rejoice. If you will hold this end, perhaps the Reverend will be good enough to hold the other?

TIECELIN: *(Picking up torn pages.)*   My book! My book!

YSEGRIN: Sire, he is free to start his crimes all over again.

NOBLE: Reynard, you are really a very bad fellow.

REYNARD: I know, Sire. We all have a little bad in us, don't we? Reverend, can't you turn a little faster?

EPINARD: Reynard, you have not changed one bit.

REYNARD: Faster, Lendore. Sire, won't you join me?
(He takes NOBLE's hand, and leads him into the game.)

LENDORE: Reynard is alive! *(And as the rope twirls faster, all take up the refrain.)*

BRUN: *(Grumpy.)* Reynard is alive.

YSEGRIN: *(Bitter.)* Reynard is alive.

EPINARD: *(Resigned.)* Reynard is alive.

TIECELIN: *(In tears with frustration.)* My book! My book!

NOBLE: *(Amused.)* Reynard is alive!

LENDORE: *(Joyful.)* Reynard is alive!

REYNARD: *(Triumphant.)* Reynard is alive!

THE END

ANDROCLES
AND THE LION

by
Aurand Harris

A play for the young based on the
Italian tale of "Androcles and the Lion"
and written in the style of the Italian
Commedia dell'arte.

Aurand Harris's dramatization of this familiar fable premiered in New York in 1963, a time when professional theatre artists were beginning to turn their attention once again to young audiences. Throughout the 1960s and 1970s they developed an extensive network of new professional children's theatre organizations across the country. This regional theatre movement created a demand for scripts that spoke to child audiences in a more sophisticated theatrical manner than the literature popular with the amateur theatres in the 1940s and 1950s. Harris's *Androcles and the Lion* met that need, and it subsequently became one of the most popular plays of the next three decades. The play reflects none of the limiting preconceptions of theatre for children of the previous decades; instead, in language and style, Harris offers farce, one of the oldest, most difficult to produce, and most popular of theatre forms.

Prior to the premier of Harris's adaptation of the Androcles fable, George Bernard Shaw's 1912 play of the same name remained the best-known dramatic version of this story. But other than sharing the same title, these plays differ markedly. Shaw reportedly wrote his *Androcles and the Lion* as a reaction to what he saw as the condescension to young people in Barrie's *Peter Pan*. Shaw expands the lion and slave fable into a polemical discussion of Christianity and martyrdom. While Shaw's play has received periodic productions (some for child audiences), it never became as popular as Harris's dramatization. Although these plays are based on the same fable, Harris tells the story with flamboyant action and theatricality, while Shaw offers restrained intellectual discussion; where Harris offers the sometimes outrageous physical conventions of farce, Shaw uses discourse to underscore the moral issues of the fable.

Harris tells the slave and lion fable as a play-within-a-play, ostensibly performed by a traveling *commedia dell' arte* troupe. Harris thus turns the explicit moralizing and predictable melodrama of children's theatre on their heads by theatricalizing them in the *commedia* form. The *commedia* troupes of the sixteenth century traveled through much of Europe performing scenarios based on the comic business of stock characters. In some instances, performers predetermined the dialogue and directions for the *lazzi* (slapstick comedy routines), but the plays generally had at least the appearance of improvisation as the troupes altered the plays to suit particular audiences. The *commedia* plays emphasized witty repartee, broad, physical humor, and fast-paced, fluid action—all of which describe Harris's *Androcles and the Lion*.

To accommodate the stock characters and the *commedia* style, Harris significantly altered the fable. Harris fits the servant character, often the center of *commedia* scenarios, into the slave role in the play; and he has the actor who delivers the prologue fill the role of the lion. All of the other characters in the play (the foolish young lovers, the braggart warrior, and the miserly old man) are taken from the *commedia* tradition; and, where appropriate, Harris added scenes to the fable so that these characters can play out their typical *lazzi*. The interaction of the characters thus becomes as important a part of the play as the story of the slave and the lion.

The original fable offers a pointed moral. Shaw elected to use this moral as the basis for an extended argument; Harris chose to use the moral as the basis for a farcical anecdote. The spirit of *commedia* humor dictates a presentational performance style and a close actor/audience relationship. From the introduction of the characters in Harris's play, through the narrated exposition and comic asides, the characters invite the audience to join them in poking fun at themselves and their world. When a character has to consult the scenario to find his place in the action, this reminds the audience they are in the theatre. When Androcles "hides" behind a non-existent tree, the audiences freely allows him that convention, as the zany world of farce creates its own logic.

Harris relies heavily on the dialogue for humor and to establish the appropriate sense of style. The melodic language, which includes various combinations of rhythm and rhyme, humorously contrasts the seriousness with which each character pursues her/his goal. In some instances, Harris intersperses rhymed couplets with long lists of rhyming words. He also uses multiple rhymes within a single speech, as well as sometimes having one character's line complete the rhyme scheme begun in another character's line. Some lines flow easily; while others have a deliberate halting effect, and they end humorously with a seemingly forced rhyme. Harris uses these techniques with a skillful unpredictability, and he invites the audience to laugh at the artifice of the writing as well as the nonsense of the action in the play.

Buffoonery and slapstick humor, as befitting the *commedia* style, abound in all of the characters and situations of the play. The frenzied chase scenes, the exaggerated proclamations of love, and the ridiculous behavior of the inept soldier are all a part of the language of farce.

Given the importance of farce in the history of the theatre, it is surprising that very few farces have been written specifically for child audiences. Many children's plays include broad physical humor, but most often simply as a device to make the protagonist appear foolish at the point of his/her downfall, and then only as a small part of a more serious world. *Androcles and the Lion* includes the ubiquitous one-dimensional characters and predictable plot structure, but Harris makes conscious theatrical use of these elements in crafting his play. While it is a good play for children, in the true tradition of farce, this play speaks to all ages in terms that are timeless in their simplicity and hilarious in their execution.

Aurand Harris (1915–1996) was born in Jamesport, Missouri, on July 4, 1915. He attended the University of Kansas City (AB 1936), Northwestern University (MA 1939), and Columbia University. He worked for many years as a teacher at Grace Church School in New York, in addition to serving short terms as playwright-in-residence at several universities throughout the country. He received the Chorpenning Cup from the Children's Theatre Association of America in 1967, in honor of his work as a playwright for young audiences.

Throughout the later decades of the twentieth century Harris was the most prolific and most-produced playwright for children. His plays range from original works, such as *The Arkansaw Bear*, to adaptations of traditional stories, such as *The Brave Little Tailor*. Harris died in New York City in 1996.

A more complete summary of Harris's life and work can be found in *Six Plays for Children by Aurand Harris, with biography and play analysis by Coleman Jennings* (Austin TX: University of Texas Press, 1977).

ANDROCLES
AND THE LION

by
Aurand Harris

376

ANDROCLES AND THE LION

Characters

ANDROCLES

PANTALONE

ISABELLA

LELIO

CAPTAIN

LION AND PROLOGUE

Setting

THE IMPROVISED STAGE OF A COMMEDIA

DELL'ARTE TROUPE OF STROLLING PLAYERS.

SIXTEENTH CENTURY, ITALY.

THE PLAY IS IN TWO PARTS.

The following is a copy of the programme of the first performance of ANDROCLES AND THE LION, presented at the Forty-First Street Theatre in New York City, 7 December, 1963:

Expore, Inc. Presents

Stan Raiff's Production of

ANDROCLES AND THE LION

A Play With Music in the Style of Commedia dell'Arte

by
AURAND HARRIS

Directed by Stan Raiff

Musical Score	*Choreography*	*Costumes and Settings*
Glenn Mack	Beverly Schmidt	Richard Rummonds

ANDROCLES .... Joseph Barnaba
LION .... Richard Sanders
PANTALONE .... Leonard Josenhans
CAPTAIN .... Eric Tavares
ISABELA .... Jacqueline Coslow
LELIO .... Christopher McCall

Assistant Director: Montgomery Davis

ANDROCLES AND THE LION

For

Stan Raiff

who first produced and directed

ANDROCLES AND THE LION

379

MUSIC NOTE

The music for *Androcles and the Lion* covers a wide range of styles. In order to enhance the character of the Commedia dell'arte form of the play, we chose to begin and end *Androcles* with music that is reminiscent of the early Renaissance.

Thus, the Overture, Finale, and some of the incidental music utilize rythmic modes, short melodic fragments built from modal scales, and improvised percussion sounds executed by the players, on such instruments as hand drums, bells, and cymbals.

As each of the players is introduced, he is given a musical theme, to help emphasize his character in the play. Some of this material is then used in the songs.

The songs are simple, and were composed with the playwright's co-operation. Their purpose is to bring out the dramaitc quality of various situations. They range from a work-song for Androcles, to a lament for Isabella, and a mock funeral march as the Captain and the Miser march Androcles into the pit.

There is also a chorus for everyone to sing. This, and the Lion's song, which end the first act, invite audience participation.

— Glenn R. Mack
New York City

ACT ONE

(The curtains open on a bare stage with the cyclorama lighted in many colors. There is lively music and the Performers enter, playing cymbals, flute, bells, and drums. They are a Commedia dell'arte group.

Arlequin, dressed in his traditional bright patches, leads the parade. Next is Lelio and Isabella, the romantic forever young lovers. Next is Pantalone, the comic old miser. Next is the Captain, the strutting, brassing soldier. And last is the Prologue who wears a robe and who later plays the Lion.

After a short introductory dance, they line up at the footlights, a colorful troupe of comic players.)

PROLOGUE:

Welcome!
Short, glad, tall,
Big, sad, small,
Welcome all!
(Actors wave and pantomime "Hello".)

We are a troupe of strolling players,
With masks, bells, and sword,
(Actors hold up masks, ring bells, and wave sword.)

A group of comic portrayers
Who will act out upon the boards
A play for you to see —
A favorite tale of Italy,
Which tells how a friend was won
By a kindness that was done.
Our play is — "Androcles and the Lion."
(Actors beat cymbals, ring bells.)

The players are: Arlequin —
(ARLEQUIN steps forward.)

Who will be Androcles, a slave.
(ARLEQUIN bows, steps back, and

381

PANTALONE steps forward.)

Pantalone, stingy and old.
Who thinks only of his gold.
(PANTALONE holds up a bag of gold, bows, steps back; and ISABELLA and LELIO step forward and pose romantically.)

Isabella and Lelio, two lovers
Whose hearts are pierced by Cupid's dart.
(They bow, step hack, and CAPTAIN marches forward.)

It is the bragging Captain's lot
To complicate the plot.
(CAPTAIN waves his wooden sword, bows, and steps back.)

There is one more in our cast —
The Lion! He, you will see last.
Set the stage —
(Actors quickly set up small painted curtain backdrop.)

Drape the curtains — raise the platform stand!
Here we will make a magic circle —
Take you to a magic land —
Where love is sung, noble words are spoken,
Good deeds triumph, and evil plots are broken.
(Holds up a long scroll).

Our story is written on this scroll which I hold.
What happens in every scene here is told.
(Hangs scroll on proscenium arch at L.)

Before we start, I will hang it on a hook
So if someone forgets his part
And has the need, he may have a look
And then proceed.
All the words in action or in song
We will make up as we go along.
All is ready! Players, stand within.
(Actors take places behind curtain).

For now I bow and say — the play — begins!
(He bows.)

In ancient Rome our scene is laid,
Where the Emperor ruled and all obeyed.
(Points to curtain which is painted with a street in the middle and with a house on either side.)

A street you see, two chariots wide,
With a stately house on either side.
In one lives Pantalone — rich, stingy, sour,
(PANTALONE leans out the window-flap on the house at R. and scowls.)

Who counts and recounts his gold every hour.
(PANTALONE disappears.)

With him lives his niece, Isabella, who each day
(ISABELLA leans out the window.)

Looks lovingly — longingly — across the way
(LELIO leans out the window of the house at L.)

At the other house, where Lelio lives, a noble sir, who looks
across lovingly — longingly — at her.
(LELIO sighs loudly. Isabella sighs musically, and they both disappear. Androcles enters from R., around the backdrop with broom.)

And all the while Androcles toils each day.
A slave has no choice but to obey.
(Prologue exits at R.)

ANDROCLES *(Music. He sweeps comically, in front of the door, over the door, then down the "street" to footlights. SINGS)*:
> **Up with the sun**
> **My day begins.**
> **Wake my nose,**
> **Shake my toes,**
> **Hop and never stop.**
> **No, never stop until I —**
> **Off to the butcher's,**
> **Then to the baker's**
> **To and from the sandalmaker's.**
> **Hop and never stop.**

> **No, never stop until I —**
> **Spaghetti prepare**
> **With sauce to please her.**
> **Dust with care**
> **The bust of Caesar.**
> **Hop and never stop.**
> **No, Never stop until I — drop.**

Some masters, they say, are kind and good. But mine ...! He cheats and he beats — he's a miser. Never a kind word does he say, but shouts, "Be about it!" And hits you a whack on the back to make sure. I'm *always* hungry. He believes in under eating. I'm fed every day with a beating. I sleep on the floor by the door to keep the robbers away. My clothes are patched and drafty because my master is stingy, and cruel, and crafty! When — oh when will there ever be a Roman Holiday for me!

(SINGS):

> **Will my fortune always be,**
> **Always be such drudgery?**
> **Will hope ever be in my horoscope?**
> **Oh, when will I be free?**

PANTALONE (*Enters around R. of backdrop, counting money)*: ... twenty-two, twenty-three, twenty-four, twenty-five ... *(ANDROCLES creeps up behind him, and playing a trick, taps PANTALONE on the back with broom.)*

PANTALONE: Who is there?

ANDROCLES: Androcles.

PANTALONE: Be about it! Be off! Go! Collect my rents for the day. Everyone shall pay. *(ANDROCLES starts R.)* Lock the windows tight. Bolt the doors. *(ANDROCLES starts L.)* My stool! Bring me my stool. *(ANDROCLES exits R.)* *Lazy* stupid fool! There will be no supper for you tonight. Oh, I will be buried a poor man yet — without a coin to put in my mouth to pay for ferrying me across the River Styx. *(ANDROCLES runs in R. with stool.)* My stool!

ANDROCLES *(Places stool behind PANTALONE and pushes him down on it roughly. PANTALONE gasps in surprise):* Yes, my master.

PANTALONE: Go! Collect my rents. Make them pay. Bring me — my gold. Away!

ANDROCLES: Yes, oh master. I run!
(He starts "running" to L. at top speed, then stops, looks back impishly, and then slowly walks.)

PANTALONE *(Brings out bag and starts counting):* Twenty-six, twenty-seven, twenty-eight, twenty-nine, thirty ...

ISABELLA *(At the same time, she leans out the window, calls, stopping ANDROCLES):* Androcles ... Androcles! *(He runs to her U.R. She gives him a letter).* For Lelio. Run! *(ANDROCLES nods and smiles, pantomimes "running" to painted house on curtain at L., pantomimes knocking. There is music during the letter scene).*

LELIO *(Appears at his window, takes letter):* Isabella! *(Androcles smiles and nods. Lelio gives him a letter. Androcles "runs" to Isabella who takes letter.)*

ISABELLA: Admired!
(Gives ANDROCLES another letter. He "runs" with leaps and sighs to LELIO who takes it.)

LELIO: Adored!
(He gives ANDROCLES another letter. He "runs" enjoying the romance, to ISABELLA who takes it.)

ISABELLA: Bewitched!
(She gives him another letter — they are the same three sheets of parchment passed back and forth — which he delivers. This action is continued with a letter to each lover, and with ANDROCLES "running" faster and faster between them).

LELIO: Bewildered!

ANDROCLES: And she has a dowry. The gold her father left her.
("Runs" to ISABELLA with letter.)

ISABELLA: Enraptured!

LELIO: Inflamed!

ISABELLA: Endeared!
(Holds letter.)

LELIO: My dear!
(Holds letter.)

ANDROCLES: My feet!
(ANDROCLES sinks exhausted to ground. ISABELLA and LELIO disappear behind the window flaps. Music stops.)

PANTALONE *(Picks up the dialogue with his action, which has been continuous):* One hundred three, one hundred four, one hundred five, one hundred six ... *(Bites a coin to make sure.)* one hundred seven ... one hundred ...

LELIO *(Enters from L., around backdrop):* Signer Pantalone.

PANTALONE *(Jumps from stool in fear):* Someone is here!

LELIO: A word with you, I pray.

PANTALONE *(Nervously hides money):* What — what do you wish to say?

LELIO: I come to speak of love. I come to sing of love! *(Reads romantically from a scroll he takes from his belt.)* "To Isabella."

PANTALONE: My niece?

LELIO: "Oh, lovely, lovely, lovely, lovely flower,
Growing lovelier, lovelier, lovelier every hour ...
Shower me your petals of love, oh Isabella,
I stand outside — with no umbrella."
Signer, I ask you for Isabella. I ask you for her hand in marriage.

PANTALONE: Marry — Isabella?

LELIO *(Reads again.):* "My life, my heart, revolve about her,
Alas, I cannot live without her."

PANTALONE *(Happy at the prospect):* You will support her?

LELIO: I ask you — give me, Isabella. *(PANTALONE nods gladly.)* Give us your blessing. *(PANTALONE nods eagerly and raises his hand).* Give her — her dowry.

PANTALONE *(Freezes)*: Money!

LELIO: The gold her father left her.

PANTALONE: Gold! It is mine — to keep for her.

LELIO: But hers when she marries.

PANTALONE: How did he find out? No. She shall not marry you. Never! Part with my gold! Help! Androcles! *(ANDROCLES runs to him.)*

LELIO: Part with Isabella? Help! Androcles! *(ANDROCLES, between them, runs from one to the other as their suffering increases.)*

PANTALONE: My heart is pounding.

LELIO: My heart is broken.

PANTALONE: Quick! Attend!

LELIO: Lend!

PANTALONE: Send!

LELIO: Befriend!

ANDROCLES *(To LELIO)*: There is hope.

PANTALONE: I am ill.

LELIO: Amend!

ANDROCLES *(To LELIO)*: Elope!

PANTALONE: I have a chill!

LELIO *(Elated with the solution)*: Transcend! *(Exits around L. of backdrop)*

PANTALONE: I will take a pill! *(Exits around R. of backdrop)*

ANDROCLES *(To audience)*: The end! *(Comes to footlights and SINGS)*

They are my masters and I obey.
But who am I? I often say.
"Androcles!" They ring.
"Androcles!" I bring.
But who am I?
A name — I am a name they call,
Only a name — that's all.
(Speaks simply and touchingly).

My father's name was Androcles. We lived on a farm by the
sea, Free to be in the sun — to work the land — to be a man.
One day when my father was away, a ship came in the bay.
"Pirates," my mother cried. I helped her and my sisters hide,
but I was caught and brought to Rome — and sold — for
twenty pieces of gold. I thought I would run away! But when
they catch a slave they decree a holiday. The Emperor and
everyone comes to watch the fun of seeing a run-away slave
being beaten and eaten by a wild beast. Personally I don't
feel like being the meal for a beast. So I stay ... just a name ...
(SINGS).

"Androcles!" They ring.
"Androcles!" I bring.
But who am I?
If I were free
Who would I be?
Maybe ... maybe ...
A doctor with a degree,
A poet, a priest, a sculptor, a scholar,
A senator — emperor with a golden collar!
I want to be free
So I can find — me.

PANTALONE *(Calls off, then enters U.R.):* Androcles!
Androcles!

ANDROCLES: You see what I mean.

PANTALONE: Androcles!

ANDROCLES: Yes, my master.

388

PANTALONE: Quick! Answer the bell. Someone is at the gate. *(ANDROCLES picks up stool and crosses to R.)* Then come to me in the garden by the wall. *(Holds up a second bag of gold, different colors from the first)* I am going to bury — to plant — this bag of — stones.

ANDROCLES: Plant a bag of stones?

PANTALONE: Be off! To the gate! *(Androcles exits D.R. PANTALONE holds up bag, schemingly)* Ah, inside this bag are *golden* stones! It is Isabella's dowry. *(There is a loud crashing of wood off R. announcing the entrance of the Captain.)* Who is at the gate? I have forgot. *(Hurries to scroll hanging by the proscenium arch, reads — announcing in a loud voice)* "The Captain enters!"

CAPTAIN *(He struts in D.R. wooden sword in hand. His voice is as loud as his look is fierce.):* Who sends for the bravest soldier in Rome? Who calls for the boldest Captain in Italy?

PANTALONE: I — Pantalone. *(Goes to him, speaks confidentially)* I will pay you well — *(Looks away. It breaks his heart.)* — in gold — *(Then anxiously, Androcles peeks in at R.)* to guard my niece. I have learned today she wishes to marry. You are to keep her lover away. Stand under her window. Station yourself at the door. Isabella is to be kept a prisoner forever more.
(No reaction from Captain)

ANDROCLES: A prisoner? She will be a slave — like me.

PANTALONE: What do you say?

CAPTAIN *(pompously):* I say — she who is inside is not outside.

ANDROCLES *(To audience):* I say — no one should be held a slave. This is treachery! *(Exits U.R. around backdrop.)*

CAPTAIN *(Struts):* I have guarded the royal Emperor. I have guarded the sacred temple. I can guard one niece — with one eye shut.
(Shuts one eyes and marches L.)

PANTALONE: No, no. The house is over there. *(Points R.)* And

that is her window.
(ISABELLA leans out of window.)

CAPTAIN: Someone is there! Death to him when he tastes my sword! *(Advances with sword waving).*

PANTALONE: No. No! It is she! *(Whispering)* It is — Isabella.

ISABELLA *(SINGS happily)*:
>**Oh, yellow moon**
>**Mellow moon**
>**In the tree,**
>**Look and see**
>**If my lover**
>**Waits for me.**

PANTALONE *(Softly):* Keep watch. Keep guard. She must not meet her lover.
(CAPTAIN salutes, clicks his heels, turns and with thundering steps starts to march. ANDROCLES slips in from around backdrop U.L. and listens.)

Sh!
(CAPTAIN marches with high, silent steps to window and stands at attention. PANTALONE speaks to audience.)

I must go to the garden! In this bag is the gold her father left her. I gave my oath to *keep* it — for her. To keep it safely — and for me. I will bury it deep, deep in the ground. Never to be found. *(He hurries off D.L.)*

ANDROCLES *(To audience):* More trickery that's wrong. The gold belongs to Isabella.

ISABELLA *(Aware someone is outside):* Lelio?

CAPTAIN *(Laughs):* Ha ha ha — no.

ISABELLA: Oh!

CAPTAIN: I am the Captain!

ISABELLA: Oh?

CAPTAIN: I guard your door. You cannot come or go.

ISABELLA: Oh.

CAPTAIN: Do not despair. I will keep you company. Observe how handsome I am — fifty women swooned today.

ISABELLA *(Calls softly)*: Lelio ...?

CAPTAIN: Know how brave I am — on my way to the barber two dragons I slew!

ISABELLA: Lelio?

CAPTAIN: Hear what a scholar I am — I say, "He who is sleeping is not awake."

ISABELLA: Lelio-o-o-o. *(Cries daintily. CAPTAIN makes a sweeping bow to her.)* No! *(She disappears, letting the flap fall.)*

CAPTAIN: She sighs. *(Louder crying of musical "o's" is heard).* She cries. Ah, another heart is mine! *Fifty-one* women have swooned today! *(Poses heroically)*

ANDROCLES: I must do something! She cannot be put in bondage. No one should be. Everyone should be free. But how — *(Beams with an idea, looks at scroll by proscenium arch and points)*. Ah, look and see!
(He quickly reads scroll at side.)
> Oh lonely moon,
> Only moon,
> Do you sigh,
> Do you cry
> For your lover
> As — as I?

ANDROCLES: Yes, here is the plan I need! *(Clasps hands and looks up in prayer.)* Oh, gods of the temple, please give me the courage to succeed. *(Makes a grand bow to CAPTAIN)* Signor Captain! *(CAPTAIN jumps).* It is said you are so fierce the sun stops when you frown.

CAPTAIN: That is true. *(Makes a frightening frown, turns, and frightens ANDROCLES)*

ANDROCLES: And that the tide goes out whenever you sneeze.

CAPTAIN: That is true. *(Screws up his face comically, puffs up and up his chest, then sneezes)* A-a-a-achew!

ANDROCLES *(Circling in front of CAPTAIN, going to R. toward window):* Ah, brave and mighty Captain, I shake before you. *(Bows, back to audience, shaking.)*

CAPTAIN: Yesterday I swam five hundred leagues.

ANDROCLES: I heard you swam one thousand.

CAPTAIN: One thousand leagues I swam into the sea.

ANDROCLES: I heard it was the ocean.

CAPTAIN: The ocean! To meet a ship —

ANDROCLES: A fleet of ships.

CAPTAIN: To meet a fleet of ships!
(CAPTAIN suddenly huffs and puffs as he starts pantomiming how he swam in the ocean, his arms pulling with great effort.)

ANDROCLES *(At the same time, whispers to ISABELLA)*: I have a plan to set you free, listen — carefully. *(Whispers, pointing to Captain. Pantomimes dropping handkerchief and fanning himself.)*

CAPTAIN *(Suddenly starts coughing and waving his arms)*: Help! Help! I am drowning! Drowning!

ANDROCLES *(Rushes to him, hits him on back)*: Save him. Throw out a rope. Man overboard!

CAPTAIN *(Sighs in relief, then dramatically continues with his adventure)*: I was saved by a school of mermaids — beautiful creatures — and all of them swooned over me.

ANDROCLES: Then you swam on and on —

ANDROCLES *(Pushing him to exit):* And on —

ANDROCLES *(Pushing him to exit):* And on —

CAPTAIN: And on —

ANDROCLES: And on —

CAPTAIN: And on —

(Exits L. "swimming")

ANDROCLES *(Quickly speaks to ISABELLA)*: Do as I say and you can escape. We will trick the Captain. Wave your handkerchief. Get his attention. Then say the night is so warm — fan yourself. As he becomes warmer, he will shed his cap and hat and sword — and you will put them on. You will be the Captain.

ISABELLA: I?

ANDROCLES *(On his knees):* Try.

ISABELLA: The Captain's cape and hat will cover me, and I will be free to go — to Lelio.

CAPTAIN *(Re-enters at L.):* After I had sunk the fleet of ships —

ANDROCLES: And brought the treasure back.

CAPTAIN: Treasure?

ANDROCLES: You awoke.

CAPTAIN: Awoke?

ANDROCLES: And found — it was but a dream.
(ISABELLA waves her handkerchief, then drops it coyly. CAPTAIN sees it and smiles seductively.)

CAPTAIN: Ah! She signals for me to approach. Signora — your servant. *(ANDROCLES, behind him, motions for ISABELLA to begin the trick.)*

ISABELLA *(Accepts handkerchief with a nod.)*: The night is so warm. The air is so still, so stifling. There is no breeze.

CAPTAIN: I will command the wind to blow a gale.

ISABELLA: The heat is so oppressive.

CAPTAIN: I will command the wind to blow a hurricane!

ANDROCLES: My nose is toasting.

CAPTAIN: I will call the wind to blow a blizzard!

ANDROCLES: My ears are roasting.

ISABELLA: The heat is baking.

393

(CAPTAIN, between them, looks at each one as each speaks. CAPTAIN becomes warmer and warmer. The dialogue builds slowly so the power of suggestion can take the desired effect on the CAPTAIN).

ANDROCLES: Sweltering.

ISABELLA: Smoldering.

ANDROCLES: Simmering!

ISABELLA: Seething.
  (CAPTAIN begins to fan himself.)

ANDROCLES: Stewing!

ISABELLA: Parching!

ANDROCLES: Scalding!

ISABELLA: Singeing!
  (CAPTAIN takes off his hat, which ANDROCLES takes, as CAPTAIN mops his brow.)

ANDROCLES: Scorching!

ISABELLA: Smoking!

ANDROCLES: Sizzling!

ISABELLA: Blistering!
  (CAPTAIN, growing warmer and warmer, removes his cape and sword which ANDROCLES takes.)

ANDROCLES: Broiling!

ISABELLA: Burning!

ANDROCLES: Blazing!

ISABELLA: Flaming!

CAPTAIN: Help! I am on fire! Blazing! Flaming! I am on fire!
  (CAPTAIN goes in a circle, flapping his arms, puffing for air, fanning, hopping and crying, "Fire! Fire!" At the same time, ANDROCLES quickly gives hat, cape, sword to ISABELLA.)

ANDROCLES *(Comes to CAPTAIN, who is slowing down):*
  Throw on water! Throw on water!

CAPTAIN *(Stops, dazed):* Where am I?
(ISABELLA dressed in CAPTAIN's hat, cape, and sword, marches from R. and imitates CAPTAIN with comic exaggeration.)

ANDROCLES *(Salutes her):* Signor Captain! What is your philosophy for the day?

ISABELLA *(Poses and speaks in low loud voice):* I say — he who is outside — is not inside.

ANDROCLES: Yes, my Captain.

CAPTAIN: Captain?

ISABELLA: I am off to fight a duel. Fifty-four I slew today. Fifty more I will fight — tonight!

ANDROCLES: Yes, my Captain.

CAPTAIN: Captain? Captain! I am the Captain.
(They pay no attention to him).

ANDROCLES: Your horse is waiting. *(Pantomimes holding a horse)* Your horse is here. Mount, O Captain, and ride away. *(ISABELLA pantomimes sitting on a horse, holding reins.)*

CAPTAIN: I am the Captain!

ISABELLA: Did you hear the wind blow?

CAPTAIN: I am the Captain!

ANDROCLES *(Listening and ignoring CAPTAIN):* No.

ISABELLA: I will ride a thousand leagues —

ANDROCLES: Two thousand —

ISABELLA: Three —

CAPTAIN: I am the Captain!

ISABELLA: Is that a shadow — there?
(Points sword at CAPTAIN)

ANDROCLES: A shadow ... ? *(Takes sword and slashes the air, making CAPTAIN retreat fearfully.)* No one is here ... or there ... or anywhere.

CAPTAIN *(Almost crying):* But I am the Captain.

ANDROCLES: To horse! Away — to the woods.

ISABELLA: To the woods!

ANDROCLES: But first, a bag of stones — by the garden wall, yours to take before you go.

ISABELLA: And then — to Lelio!

ANDROCLES: Yes, my Captain.

CAPTAIN *(Crying comically):* But I am the Captain. Look at me. Listen to me.

ISABELLA: To the woods! *(Starts pantomiming riding off L.)* Ride, gallop, trot, zoom!

ANDROCLES: Hop, skip — jump over the moon! *(They "ride" off U.L.)*

CAPTAIN *(Crying):* But I ... I am the Captain. *(Then horrified)* If that is the Captain — then — who — who am I?

PANTALONE *(Enters D.L.):* Captain ... Captain.

CAPTAIN: Some one calls. Oh, Pantalone ... Pantalone! Can you see me? *(Waves his hands in front of PANTALONE, then shouts in his ear)* Can you hear me?

PANTALONE: Yes.

CAPTAIN: Am I ... I here?

PANTALONE *(Peers at him):* Yes.

CAPTAIN: Ah, I live. I breathe again. *(Breathes vigorously)* I am the Captain. *(Struts)* Look on my hat and shudder. Look at my cape and shiver. Feel my sword — *(Realizes he has no hat, cape, or sword)* It is gone! Ah, your slave took it. Androcles! It was a trick of his. After him!

PANTALONE: My slave? Ha, ha, a trick on you.

CAPTAIN: And another one dressed in my clothes!

PANTALONE *(Laughing, stops immediately)*: Another one?

CAPTAIN: One who came from your house.

PANTALONE: From my house? *(Runs to house U.R., then turns)* Isabella!

CAPTAIN: Ha, ha, a trick on you.

PANTALONE *(In a rage)*: Fool, stupid, simpleton! You have set Isabella free!

CAPTAIN: I let Isabella free?

PANTALONE: Fathead, saphead, noodlehead! It was she who left the house in disguise — and is off to meet her lover. Stop them! Which way? Which way?

CAPTAIN: He said — *(Thinks, which is difficult)* to the woods!

PANTALONE: Bonehead, woodenhead, block head! Quick! Save her! Before she is wed! To the woods!
(Starts R.)

CAPTAIN: He said — *(Thinks)* first, take a bag of stones by the wall.

PANTALONE: A bag of stones — the gold! Muttonhead, pumpkin head, cabbage head! To the garden! Before he finds it. *(Starts to L. as CAPTAIN starts R.)* Forget Isabella. Save the gold! *(PANTALONE exits D.L. CAPTAIN salutes and marches after him. Lights may dim slightly. There is music as the Wall enters D.R. and crosses to C. Wall is an actor (LION) with a painted "wall" hanging on his back and short enough to show his feet. The back of his head is masked by a large flower peeping over the wall. He stands at C. feet apart, back to audience. He puts down a bag of gold and then puts a rock over it. ANDROCLES, followed by ISABELLA, tiptoes in U.L. They circle around to D.R. ANDROCLES starts feeling for the wall.)*

ANDROCLES: The gold is buried — by the wall — *(Flower on the wall nods vigorously),* buried under a stone — *(Flower nods again).* Look — feel — find a stone — a stone — a stone — *(WALL stomps his foot, then puts foot on top of stone, but ANDROCLES passes by it.)*

ISABELLA *(Wall again taps foot and points it towards stone.*

397

ISABELLA *sees stone and points to it)*: A stone!

ANDROCLES: Ah, I see it! Pray that this will be it! *(Slowly lifts stone)* Behold! *(Holds up bag)* A bag of gold! *(Jumps up, sings and dances)* We've found it! We've found it! We've found the gold! Yours to keep! To have! To hold!

ISABELLA: Sh!

ANDROCLES: You are free — go! Off to Lelio, who implores you — adores you. Quick, do not hesitate. Run — before it is too late.

ISABELLA: Thank you. Some day may you be set free, too. *(Kisses her fingers and touches his nose with it).* Good bye. *(Exits D.L.)*

ANDROCLES *(Thrilled that she has touched him)*: Fly — arrivederci. *(Sees he has the gold)* Wait! The gold! Isabella forgot the gold! Isabella! Isabella! *(He exits after her D.L. At the same time, PANTALONE, followed by CAPTAIN, tip-toes in U.L., circling D.R. where they stop).*

PANTALONE *(Peering and groping):* It is so dark I cannot see.

CAPTAIN *(Also peering and groping):* Wait ... wait for me.

PANTALONE: The gold — by the wall — under a stone — find — find —

CAPTAIN: You look in front. I'll look behind.

PANTALONE *(He turns R. CAPTAIN turns L. Each peers and steps in the opposite direction on each word.):* Search — scratch — dig around it.

CAPTAIN *(Still peering, they now step backwards toward each other on each word.):* Feel — touch — crouch — *(They bump into each other from the back.)*

PANTALONE: Ouch!

CAPTAIN *(Grabs and holds PANTALONE's foot.):* I've found it! I've found it!

PANTALONE: Knucklehead of soot! You've found my foot! *(Kicks free and creeps toward C.)* Here ... there ... oh, where

398

... where is my gold? The stone ... the stone ... where has it flown? Quick ... on your knees ... search ... find ... use your nose ... and not to sneeze. *(He and CAPTAIN, on their knees, comically search frantically.)* Pat ... pound ... comb ... the ground ... chase ... race ... find the place. *(He finds stone)* I have found it! Ah, to gods in prayer I kneel. The stone is here. My gold is back. *(Reaches between feet of WALL, then freezes in panic.)* What do I feel? There is no sack! *(Rises in a frenzy)* I have been robbed! Thieves! The gold is gone!

CAPTAIN *(Rises):* It was the slave who took it! Androcles!

PANTALONE: He is a robber. He is a thief! He will pay for this — with his life!

CAPTAIN: I will find him ... bind him ... bend ... make an end of him!

PANTALONE: He has run away! To the woods! Catch him! Hold! *(CAPTAIN stomps to R.)* To the woods! Before his tracks are cold. *(CAPTAIN stomps to L.)* Follow! Follow! My bag of gold! *(PANTALONE exits D.L. CAPTAIN salutes and follows him. WALL picks up stone, then he pulls the street scene curtain to one side, revealing another curtain behind it and painted like a forest. Over his shoulder, back still to audience, WALL announces, "The forest," and exits quickly at R. Chase music begins. ISABELLA and LELIO run in from L. look about.)*

ISABELLA: The forest paths will guide us.

LELIO: The forest trees will hide us.
(They exit D.R. around the backdrop.)

ANDROCLES *(Runs in from L.):* Isabella! Lelio! I cannot find you. You have left the gold behind you.
(Exits off U.R. around backdrop)

CAPTAIN *(Enters D.L.):* After them! I say — follow me! This way! *(Exits U.R. behind backdrop)*

PANTALONE *(Enters, wheezing, trying to keep up, from L.):* We are near him. I can hear him — and my gold.

(PANTALONE exits U.R. around the backdrop. ISABELLA and LELIO run in U.L. from behind the backdrop, start to R. but suddenly stop frightened at what they see offstage R.)

ISABELLA: Oh, what do I see?

LELIO: It is a — quick! We must flee!
(ISABELLA and LELIO exit U.R. behind the backdrop.)

CAPTAIN *(Enters U.L. around the backdrop, starts to R.):* This way! This way! Follow me! Onward to — (Stops horrified at what he sees off-stage R.) What is that behind a tree? It is a — Oh, no! We must never meet. The order is — retreat! *(CAPTAIN runs off U.R. behind backdrop. PANTALONE enters U.L. around the backdrop.)*

PANTALONE: Find him. Fetch him. Catch him. My gold has run way. *(Stops and looks off-stage R)* What is that? Can that be he? *(Starts to call)* Andro— No! It is a — Help! It's a lion — coming after me! *(There is a loud roar off R. PANTALONE sinks to his knees and quickly walking on his knees, exits L. Music of Lion's song.)*

LION *(Enters at R. a most appealing creature, he dances to C. and SINGS):*
> **Have you roared today,**
> **Told the world today how you feel?**
> **If you're down at the heel**
> **Or need to put over a deal,**
> **Happy or sad**
> **Tearful or glad**
> **Sunny or mad,**
> **It's a great way**
> **To show the world how you feel!**
> **Without saying a single word**
> **Your meaning is heard,**
> **"Good morning" is dull,**
> **But a roar is musical!**
> **Happy or sad**
> **Tearful or glad**

> **It's a great way**
> **To show the world how you feel!**

(He gives a satisfied low roar, then looks about and speaks.)

The sun is up. It is another day — *(Yawns)* to sleep. Hear all! The King speaks. No birds are allowed over my cave — chirping and burping. No animals are allowed near my cave — growling and howling. Silence in the woods. The King is going to sleep. *(Actors off-stage imitate animal sounds, loud buzzing, barking, etc. Or actors may in simple disguise with masks enter as animals, dance and make sounds.)* Silence! *(All noise and motion stops.)* The King says, "Silence." *(Noise and motion increases, Lion becomes angry, puffs up and roars like thunder, stalking about in all directions).* R-r-r-r-r-roar! *(There is absolute silence. If actors are on stage, they run off.)* You see—
(SINGS)

> **A roar's a great way**
> **To show the world how you feel!**

(He roars and exits majestically into cave — a split in the painted backdrop).

ANDROCLES *(Enters from around backdrop U.R. He runs to C. He looks anxiously to R. and to L. and calls softly.):* Isabella ... ? Lelio ... ? They are lost in the woods. *I* am lost in the woods. I have run this way — I have run that way — I have run — *(A terrible thought strikes him.)* I have run — away! I am a run-away slave! No! *(Calls desperately)* Isabella! Lelio! Where will I go? My master will hunt me. He will track me down. He will take me back. I will be thrown to the wild beasts! *(Sees bag he holds)* The gold — my master will say I stole it. A run-away slave — and a thief! No, I was only trying to help. *(Calls)* Isabella! Help *me*, Lelio.

PANTALONE *(Off L. loudly):* Oh, beat the bushes. Beat the ground. Find my slave. Find my gold!

ANDROCLES: My master! What shall I do? Where shall I go? Hide — *(Runs behind imaginary tree R.)* Behind a tree — *(Runs to imaginary bush U.L.)* Under a bush — he can see.

(Points at cave) What is that? Ah, a cave! I will hide — inside the cave and pray he never finds me. *(Quickly he goes into cave, gives a loud "Oh!," and quickly backs out again.)* It is someone's house.

CAPTAIN *(Off)*: Follow me. I say — this way!

ANDROCLES *(Knocks at cave in desperation):* Please! Please may I come in? I am —

PANTALONE *(Off):* I think — I hear him!

ANDROCLES: I am — in danger.
(ANDROCLES quickly goes into cave. PANTALONE enters U.L. followed by CAPTAIN. They are in hot pursuit.)

PANTALONE *(Crosses to R.):* My gold! Find the slave. Bind him! Bring him to me.

CAPTAIN *(Circles D.C.):* I will look in every brook and nook and hollow tree!

PANTALONE: Fetch — catch my gold! *(Exits D.R.)*

CAPTAIN: Follow me!
(He exits D.L. From inside the cave, a long loud roar is heard, and ANDROCLES calls, "Help!" Another and louder roar is heard. ANDROCLES runs out of cave to D.L. and cries "Help ... help!" LION runs out of cave to D.R. and roars.)

ANDROCLES: It is a lion!

LION: It is a man! He will try to beat me.

ANDROCLES: He will try to eat me. *(They eye each other. LION springs at ANDROCLES with a roar. ANDROCLES backs away.)* I am sorry I disturbed you. *(LION roars. ANDROCLES holds up bag.)* I — I will have to hit you if you come closer.

LION: Hit — hit until he kills — that is man.

ANDROCLES: Leap — eat — that is a lion. *(LION roars and then leaps on him. ANDROCLES struggles and fights, but soon he is held in a lion-hug.)* Help! Help!

402

(LION roars. ANDROCLES gets his arm free and bangs LION on the back with bag of gold. LION roars with surprise and releases ANDROCLES. ANDROCLES, thinking he is free, starts off, but LION holds on to his pants. ANDROCLES, at arm's length, runs in one spot. ANDROCLES gets loose, turns, lowers his head and charges, butting into LION's stomach. LION roars. ANDROCLES runs to L. and hides behind imaginary tree. LION, angry, roars and slowly starts to creep up on him. ANDROCLES looks around "tree," one side, then the other, shaking with fearful expectation. LION springs at him in front of "tree." ANDROCLES leaps and runs back of "tree." LION turns and runs after him. ANDROCLES tries to escape, running in figure-eights around the two "trees." They stop, each facing opposite directions, and start backing toward each other. ANDROCLES turns, sees LION, jumps, then cautiously tip toes toward him and kicks the bent over approaching LION. LION roars and circles. ANDROCLES laughs at his trick. LION comes up behind him and grabs him, holding ANDROCLES around the waist and lifting him off the ground. ANDROCLES kicks helplessly. LION throws ANDROCLES on ground. LION, above him, roars, raises his paw, and gives a crushing blow. But ANDROCLES rolls over and the paw hits the ground. LION immediately roars and waves his paw in pain. ANDROCLES cautiously slides away and is ready to run. He looks back at LION who, with tearful sob-roars, is licking and waving his paw.)

ANDROCLES: He is hurt. I can run away. *(He starts, but stops when LION sobs.)* He is in pain. Someone should help. No one is here. No one but one — I — am here. *(LION roars in frustration. ANDROCLES turns away in fear. LION sobs sadly. ANDROCLES looks back at him).* If I go — I maybe can be free! If I stay — *(LION growls at him),* he may take a bite out of me! *(ANDROCLES starts to leave. LION sobs. Throughout the scene the LION "talks" in grunts and groans almost like a person in answering and reacting to ANDROCLES. ANDROCLES stops.)*

When someone needs your help, you can't run away. *(Trying to be brave, he turns to LION, opens his mouth, but can say nothing.)* I wonder what you say — to a lion? *(LION sobs appealingly.)* Signor — *(LION looks at him. ANDROCLES is afraid.)* My name is Androcles. *(LION roars, looks at his paw and roars louder.)* Have you — have you hurt your paw? *(LION grunts and nods).* If you — will sit still — I will try to help you. *(LION roars defiantly. ANDROCLES backs away.)* Wait! If we succeed, we will need to — cooperate! *(LION looks at him suspiciously and grunts.)*

You don't trust me — *(LION roars),* and I don't trust you. But someone must take the first step — greet the other, or we will never meet each other. *(Cautiously ANDROCLES takes a step sideways, facing audience. LION cautiously takes a step sideways, facing audience.)* That is a beginning — *(LION roars. ANDROCLES holds his neck.)* But what will be the ending? *(Each raises a leg and takes another sideways step toward each other).* I don't want to hurt you. I want to help you. *(He slowly holds out his hand. LION "talks" and slowly shows him his paw.)*

It's a thorn. You have a thorn stuck in your paw. *(LION breaks the tension, crying with the thought of it and waving his injured paw.)* I know it hurts. *(Talks slowly as if explaining to a small child)* Once I stepped on a thorn. My father pulled it out. *(LION grunts and reacts with interest.)* My father —on the farm—by the sea. I will pull it out for you— as my father did—for me. *(LION grunts undecidedly, then slowly offers his paw. ANDROCLES nervously reaches for it.)* It — it may hurt a little. *(LION draws back and roars in protest).* I thought a lion was brave — not afraid of anything. *(Lion stops, then grunts in agreement and with great bravery thrusts out his paw.)* Now — hold still — brace yourself. *(LION begins to tremble violently.)* Get ready — *(LION shakes more).* One — *(LION shakes both of them).* Two — *(LION cries and tries to pull away. ANDROCLES is stern, with pointed finger).* Don't move about! *(LION tries to obey, meekly.)* Three! *(LION steps backwards.)* It's out!

LION *(Looks at his paw, looks at ANDROCLES, then roars joyfully and hops about. SINGS):*
> **Let me roar today**
> **Let me say today**
> **We feel great!**
> **Celebrate!**
> **Exhilarate!**
> **Congratulate!**
> **It's a great way**
> **To show the world how you feel.**

ANDROCLES *(LION rubs against ANDROCLES and purrs softly. ANDROCLES, being tickled by LION's rubbing, giggles and pets him):* You — you are welcome.

LION *(To audience):* He looks tired. I will get a rock.
(Quickly picks up a rock off R and holds it high)

ANDROCLES: He is going to crush me! *(He starts to defend himself, but LION shakes his head and grunts, and shows ANDROCLES that he should sit.)* For me? *(Lion nods, trying to talk, and dusts the rock with his tail).* He wants *me* to sit. *(Lion, delighted, grabs Androcles to help him and seats him roughly).* Thank you.

LION *(To audience):* He looks hungry. *(Roars, shows teeth, and chews).*

ANDROCLES: He is going to eat me! *(LION shakes his head and "talks," points to ANDROCLES and indicates from his mouth down into his stomach.)* He wants *me* to eat. *(LION agrees joyfully.)* I am hungry. I am always hungry.

LION *(Thinking):* What was for breakfast today? A man's skull in the cave — his liver down by the river — *(Embarrassed at what he has thought).* Oh, I beg your pardon.
(Roars with a new idea, motions ANDROCLES to watch. LION hums and purrs lightly as he comically pantomimes picking fruit from a tree and eating and spitting out the seeds.)

ANDROCLES: Fruit! *(LION, encouraged, purrs happily and hops about pantomiming filling a basket with berries from bushes.)* Berries! *(LION, elated with his success, buzzes loudly and dances in ballet fashion like a bee.)* What? *(LION buzzes and dances bigger.)* Honey from the bee! *(LION agrees loudly.)* Oh, that will be a banquet for me.

LION *(Speaks to audience):* A new twist in history! Man and beast will feast together. Celebrate! Sit — wait! I'll be back with cherries and berries for you — and a bone or two, before you can roar — *e pluribus unum!*
(Roars happily and exits R.)

ANDROCLES *(Sits alone on rock, looks around, smiles, and speaks quietly):* I am sitting down. I am being served. I am being treated like a person. I — I have a friend. This is what it is like to be free. To be — maybe —
(SINGS)

> **Maybe**
> **A doctor with a degree,**
> **A poet, a priest, a sculptor, a scholar,**
> **A senator — emperor with a golden collar!**
> **want to be free**
> **So I can find — me.**

PANTALONE *(Off):* Hun — hunt — search and find my slave. Find my gold!

ANDROCLES: My master has come. My freedom has gone.

PANTALONE *(Off R.):* Ah, his footprints are on the ground! I have found him!

ANDROCLES *(Calls quickly):* Oh, Lion, I must be off before we have fed. I must run — or it is off with my head! *(He starts D.L. but sees CAPTAIN.)* Oh! The Captain! Where will I hide? In the cave! *(Quickly hides in cave.)*

CAPTAIN *(Enters L .with fishing net and a slap-stick.):* Beware slave, wherever you are. I shall leap and keep and capture you. In this net — I will get you. *(Holds net out ready.)*

PANTALONE *(Enters R. peering at the ground, crosses to L.):* His footprints are on the ground. Toe-heel, heel-toe. This is the way his footsteps go.

CAPTAIN *(To audience):* The trap is set.

PANTALONE: Lead on — lead me to him.

CAPTAIN: Ha, caught in the net!
(Throws net over PANTALONE who has walked into it.)

PANTALONE: Help! Help!

CAPTAIN: You stole my hat!
(Hits PANTALONE over the head with slap-stick.)

PANTALONE: Oh!

CAPTAIN: My sword. *(Hits him again.)*

PANTALONE: No!

CAPTAIN: My cape? *(Hits him again).*

PANTALONE: Let me loose!

CAPTAIN: What?

PANTALONE: You squawking goose!

CAPTAIN: Who speaks?

PANTALONE *(Pulling off the net):* I — Pantalone.

CAPTAIN: Pantalone? Oh, it was my mistake.

PANTALONE: It was my head!

CAPTAIN: Where is the slave? The runaway? Where is Androcles?

PANTALONE: He is — with my gold.

CAPTAIN *(Struts):* I will drag him back to Rome. The Emperor will honor me — decree a holiday — so all can see the slave fight a wild and hungry beast. And after the fun is done and the slave is eaten, all will cheer the Captain of the Year.

PANTALONE: Before you count your cheers, you have to catch one slave — Androcles!

CAPTAIN *(They start searching, a step on each word. Captain circles to L. and upstage. Pantalone circles to R. and upstage.)*: Search.

PANTALONE: Seek.

CAPTAIN: Track.

PANTALONE: Trail.

CAPTAIN: Use your eyes.

PANTALONE: Scrutinize!

CAPTAIN *(Stops):* Think — if you were a slave ... ?

PANTALONE: I?

CAPTAIN: Where would you hide?

PANTALONE: Inside.

CAPTAIN *(Sees and points):* A cave! *(They tip-toe to entrance, hold net ready, whisper excitedly)* Clap him.

PANTALONE: Trap him.

CAPTAIN *(Nothing happens):* The problem is — how to get him to come out.

PANTALONE: Poke him?

CAPTIAN: Smoke him?

PANTALONE: I have a great idea! You will call him in a voice like Isabella.

CAPTAIN: I — I speak like Isabella?

PANTALONE: You will cry for help in a soft sweet voice. He will think you are her. He will come to Isabella.

CAPTAIN *(In high voice, comically):* Help! Oh, help me! I am Isabella *(They look at cave entrance).* I heard —

PANTALONE: Something stirred.

CAPTAIN *(Falsetto again):* Andro-o-cles. Come out, ple-e-ese. *(They look at cave and excitedly hold net ready.)* Ready.

PANTALONE: Steady. *(ANDROCLES, behind backdrop, roars*

— long and loud!) It is a lion in the cave!
(Runs D.R. and hides behind a "tree")

CAPTAIN: *(ANDROCLES roars again, up and down the scale, louder and louder. Even the backdrop shakes. CAPTAIN jumps and runs to PANTOLONE and hides behind him.)* It is *two* lions in the cave! *(They stand shaking with fright.)*

ANDROCLES *(Peeks out of cave, then comes out.):* They have gone. Ran away from a noise. I have learned that a roar is a mighty thing. No wonder a lion is a king. *(He enjoys another roar.)*

PANTALONE *(Still hiding):* We are undone!

CAPTAIN: Run! Crawl!

PANTALONE: I cannot move at all. *(ANDROCLES roars again with joy.)* I have an idea. You — you will call in a voice like a lion. He will think you are another lion — a brother.

CAPTAIN: I — roar like a lion?

PANTALONE: Our only chance is to answer back.
(CAPTAIN gulps, and then roars).

ANDROCLES: *(He is startled. He hides behind "tree" at L.)* It is another lion. *(PANTALONE, helping, gives a roar.)* It is two lions! *(With an idea, he roars back)* Ro-o-o-hello.

CAPTAIN *(He and PANTALONE look at each other in surprise. CAPTAIN answers):* Ro-o-o-hello.

ANDROCLES *(Now ANDROCLES looks surprised):* Ro-o-o-lovely-da-a-ay.

CAPTAIN *(He and PANTALONE look at each other and nod, pleased with their success):* Ro-o-o-have-you-seen—ro-o-o-ar-a-runaway slave?
(ANDROCLES is startled, then he peeks around "tree".)

PANTALONE: Named-Andro— *(CAPTAIN nudges him to roar)* —roar—cles?

ANDROCLES: It is my master and the Captain. They have come

for me. *(He roars loudly.)* Ro-o-oar-he-went—roar-r-r-r-that-away.

CAPTAIN *(They nod):* Ro-o-o-thank-you.
(He and PANTALONE start to tip-toe off R.)

ANDROCLES *(Too confident):* Ro—o-ar. You are welcome.

PANTALONE: It is his voice. It is my slave, Androcles.

CAPTAIN: It is another trick of his.

PANTALONE: Nab him.

CAPTAIN: Grab him. *(They start back to get him.)*

ANDROCLES *(Unaware he has been discovered, continues to roar gaily.):* Ro-o-ar. Goodbye. Ro-o-o-ar. Happy eating.

PANTALONE *(Confronts ANDROCLES on R.):* Eat, cheat, thief! I will beat you!
(ANDROCLES turns to L. and walks into net held by CAPTAIN.)

CAPTAIN: Slide, glide, inside. I have you tied!
(ANDROCLES is caught in the net over his head.)

PANTALONE *(Grabs his bag of gold.):* My gold!

CAPTAIN: My captive!

ANDROCLES: Help! Help!

CAPTAIN: You stole my hat! *(Hits ANDROCLES over the head with slap-stick)* You stole my sword! *(Hits him).* You stole my cape! *(Hits him).* This time you will not escape.

PANTALONE *(Takes stick from CAPTAIN and swings it.):* Robber, Traitor. Thief! Let me hit him. *(PANTALONE, in the mix-up, hits CAPTAIN several times on his head.)*

CAPTAIN: Help! *(He drops the rope of the net.)*

ANDROCLES *(Runs to R):* Help!

PANTALONE: Help! He is running away!

CAPTAIN *(Quickly catches ANDROCLES and holds the rope.):* Back to Rome. To the Emperor you will be delivered!

PANTALONE: Into the pit you will be thrown.

CAPTAIN: Where the wild beasts will claw, gnaw, and chew you! *(They start to lead him off, marching — CAPTAIN, ANDROCLES, and last PANTALONE.)* Munch!

PANTALONE: Crunch!

ANDROCLES: I will be eaten for lunch! Help! Lion! Signor Lion, set me free. Come and rescue me! Oh, woods echo my cry for help. Echo so the Lion will know I am in trouble. Roar — roar with me. Echo from tree to tree! *(He roars and the Ushers — and the children — help him roar, as he is led off L.)* Roar! Roar!

LION: *(He leaps in at R and roars)* Someone roars for help? Androcles! *(Off, ANDROCLES cries "Help!")* He calls for help.
(SINGS).

> **Oh, roar and say**
> **Shout out without delay,**
> **Which way, which way, which way?**
> **Oh, roar me a clue,**
> **Roar me two.**
> **I have to know**
>
> **Which way to go before I start.**
> **Oh, roar, please,**
> **An-dro-cles.**
> **Give a sigh,**
> **Give a cry,**
> **Signify!**
>
> **I'll sniff — I'll whiff-**
> **Smell (Sniffs) — Tell (Sniffs)**
> **Fe, fi, fo, fum.**
> **Here —**
> *(Shouts)*: I come!
> *(He exits L.)*

ISABELLA *(She and LELIO run in from R.):* Oh, Androcles, what has happened to you?

411

LELIO *(To audience):* That you will see in Act Two. Now
— we must bow and say, "Our play is half done." This is the
end of Act One.
(They bow.)

THE CURTAINS CLOSE.

A short intermission.

*(Or if played without an intermission, omit the last speech of
Lelio's and continue with his first speech in Act Two.)*

ACT TWO

*(Music: Reprise of "Oh, Roar and Say." The curtains open.
The scene is the same. Isabella and Lelio stand in C. Music
dims out.)*

ISABELLA: Androcles. What has happened to you?

LELIO: I heard his voice, calling in the woods.

ISABELLA: He has followed us to bring the gold — my dowry
which I left behind. *(Calls)* Androcles?

LELIO: Androcles!
*(LION roars as he enters U.R. He sees the lovers and
watches.)*

ISABELLA: It is a lion!

LELIO: Do not fear.

ISABELLA: Androcles is alone — unarmed. What if he should
meet a lion! Androcles! Androcles!

LELIO: Androcles!

LION: Someone else roars "Androcles." I will stay and hear who
is here.
(LION hides his head behind the small rock).

ISABELLA: Androcles! Androcles!

LELIO: We are alone. *(LION's head pops up behind rock.)* Together. It is time to speak — to sing of love! *(He turns aside, takes scroll from belt.)*

ISABELLA *(Not looking at him):* Please, speak no prepared speech, but sing true words that spring freely from your heart.

LELIO *(Looks surprised, glances again at scroll, then SINGS):*
Oh, lovely, lovely flower,
Growing lovelier every hour,
Shower on me, petals of love, Isabella —
(LION, enjoying the music, nods his head in rhythm).

ISABELLA: So unrehearsed — so sincere.

LELIO *(SINGS):*
My life, my heart revolve about you.
Say yes, I cannot live without you.
(LION, unable to refrain, lifts his head and roars musically on LELIO's last note — unnoticed by the lovers — then hides his head behind the rock.)

ISABELLA: Oh, Lelio —
(Turns to him and speaks or SINGS)
My answer is — can't you guess?
Yes, yes, yes, yes, yes!

LELIO *(In ecstacy):*
Oh, woods abound with joyous sound!
Melodies sing in the trees —
(Music sound. LION raises up and listens to R.)
Bells ring in the breeze —
(Music sound. LION stands up and listens to L.)
Let the lute of the lily lying in the pond —
(Music sound. LION stands and begins to move his arms like an orchestra conductor).
Let the flute of the firefly's fluttering wand —
(Music sound. LION motions to R.)
And let the flight of the nightingale —
(Music sound. LION motions L)

Harmonize!
(Music sounds blend together. LION holds up paw ready to begin directing an orchestra.)
The moment we will immortalize!
(Music of all sounds play a folk dance. LION leads, dramatically, the unseen musicians. ISABELLA and LELIO do a short dance. At the conclusion, they hold their pose and LION bows to audience.)

ISABELLA *(Points to ground.):* Look! Footprints — boots and sandals.

LELIO *(Examines them.):* The Captain's boots — Pantalone's sandals. The Captain and Pantalone were here — following us — following Androcles.

ISABELLA: His cry was for help. He ran away. He is — a runaway slave! And they have found him —

LELIO: Bound him —

ISABELLA: Taken him back to Rome.

LELIO: To the pit!

ISABELLA: We must stop them.

LELIO: If we can.

ISABELLA: We must help him.

LELIO: All we can.

LION *(Jumps on rock heroically.):* And — we can! *(Roars)*

ISABELLA: Help!

LELIO: Run! *(Lovers run off D.R.)*

LION: Lead the way. I will follow you. To Androcles! To — the rescue! *(Lion roars, picks up rock, and runs off D.R. Chase music begins — repeated. But the running is reversed, going around in the opposite direction. Lovers enter from U.R. and run across. At C. they look back, "Oh!" and exit U.L. behind backdrop. Lion runs in U.R. At C, roars, and exits U.L. behind backdrop. Lovers enter U.R. from behind backdrop, running faster. At C. they look back in great fright, "OH!"*

and exit U.L. behind backdrop. LION follows. At C, roars majestically, and shouts: "Andr-roar-cles! Here we come!" LION exits after lovers. Lovers enter U.R. from around backdrop. LELIO pulls the curtain of the woods scene back to L. showing the street scene again. Chase music dims out.)

LELIO *(Breathless):* Safe at home — I hope. What does the scroll say?

ISABELLA *(Reads scroll on proscenium arch):* The next scene is — a street in Rome.

LELIO: Ah, we can stay.

ISABELLA *(Reads, announcing):* "The Captain enters."
(Clashing of slap-stick is heard off L. ISABELLA runs to C.)
He will find us here.

LELIO: Do not fear. We will hide — behind a mask. Quick! We will hide behind another face, and re-appear in the Market Place. *(They exit R.)*

CAPTAIN *(Enters at L.):* Make way, make way for the hero of the day! Bow, salute, kneel and gaze upon the hero. Raise your voice with praise for the hero. The hero passes by. The hero is — I!
(LELIO and ISABELLA enter R. Each holds a long, sad begger man's mask on a stick in front of his face. They walk and act and speak like beggars.)

LELIO: Help the poor. Help the blind.

ISABELLA: Alms for the cripple. Alms for the old.

CAPTAIN: Away beggars! The emperor comes this way. It is a holiday!

LELIO: What Senator has died? What battle have we won?

CAPTAIN: None! We celebrate today the capture of a runaway.

ISABELLA: A slave?

(They look at each other and speak without their masks and at the same time, the CAPTAIN speaks. They all say together, "Androcles!").

CAPTAIN: Today all Rome will celebrate! A wild beast was caught outside the wall, clawing the gate as if he could not wait to come into the City. Now in the pit the beast is locked and barred, waiting to be released — waiting to eat a juicy feast.

LELIO and ISABELLA: *(They nod to each other and say)* Androcles!

CAPTAIN: Ah, what a sporting sight to see — a fight — man eaten by a beast. Then I, who caught the slave, will appear. Women will swoon, men will cheer, and I will be crowned the hero of the year! *(Shouts rapidly and marches quickly)* Hep, hep, ho! Step, step, high. Hail the hero. I, I, I! *(Exits R.)*

ISABELLA *(They take their masks away.)*: Poor, poor Androcles.

LELIO: We must try and save him. Quick, before it is too late. We will go to the Arena—

ISABELLA: Yes!

LELIO: We will go to the Royal Box! Implore the Emperor with our plea!

ISABELLA: Yes!

LELIO: For only he by royal decree can save — our Androcles. *(LELIO and ISABELLA run off L. There is music. CAPTAIN, leading ANDROCLES by the rope, and PANTALONE following, marches in from R. As they march, they SING.)*

PANTALONE and CAPTAIN:
Off to the pit we three. Who will be left?

ANDROCLES:
Just me.

PANTALONE and CAPTAIN:
Who will be left alone, shaking in every bone?

PANTALONE:
Just —

CAPTAIN:
Just —

416

ANDROCLES:
> **Me!**

CAPTAIN and PANTALONE:
> **Off to the pit we three. Who will be left?**

ANDROCLES:
> **Just me.**

CAPTAIN and PANTALONE:
> **Who will the animal meet? Who will the animal eat?**

PANTALONE:
> **Just —**

CAPTAIN:
> **Just—**

ANDROCLES *(Shouts):* Just a minute! I want to be an absentee! *(Music ends as he speaks.)* I want to be free — to be just me!

CAPTAIN: To the Arena! Forward march! *(Music: Reprise of Introductory Music of Act One. CAPTAIN, ANDROCLES, and PANTALONE march across the front of the stage or across down in the orchestra pit. At the same time, LELIO and ISABELLA, disguised with masks, dance in U.L. carrying colorful banners, one in each hand, and on stands. They set the banners down in a semi-circle in front of the backdrop to indicate the Arena. They dance off as the music stops, and the three marchers arrive in the middle of the scene.)*

CAPTAIN: Halt! We are at the Arena! The slave will step forward.

PANTALONE: Step forward.

ANDROCLES: Step forward. *(Frightened, he steps forward.)*

CAPTAIN: The slave's head will be covered. *(He holds out left hand to ANDROCLES, who holds out left hand to PANTALONE.)*

PANTALONE: Covered.
> *(He gives a cloth sack to ANDROCLES, who gives it to*

CAPTAIN, *who puts it over ANDROCLES' head.)*

CAPTAIN *(Trumpets sound):* The Emperor's chariot draws near. *(Trumpets)* The Emperor will soon appear. *(Trumpets)* The Emperor is here! *(A royal banner is extended from the side D.L., indicating the Royal Box.)* Bow!

PANTALONE: Now! *(CAPTAIN and PANTALONE bow low toward Royal Box, facing D.L. ANDROCLES groping with his head covered, turns and bows facing R.)* Turn around! *(ANDROCLES turns around)* To the ground! *(ANDROCLES bows to ground).*

CAPTAIN: Most noble Emperor — *(Pushes ANDROCLES' head down, making him bow)* Most honored Emperor — *(Pushes ANDROCLES, who keeps bobbing up, down again)* Most imperial Emperor — *(Pushes ANDROCLES down again. He stays down.)* The guilty slave stands before you. Stand! *(ANDROCLES quickly straightens up.)* As punishment for a slave who runs away, he will today fight a wild beast in the Arena for all Rome to see. *(ANDROCLES shakes his head under the sack.)* He will battle for his life — to survive. There will be but one winner — the one who is left alive. *(ANDROCLES, courageously, draws his fist and is ready to strike. CAPTAIN, growing more eloquent, begins to strut.)* I have fought and slain a hundred wild beasts. *(ANDROCLES, visualizing the animals, starts hitting the air.)* With fiery eyes, with knashing teeth, they charged at me. Fight! The crowd cried, fight! *(ANDROCLES, ready, starts to fight, hitting wildly for his life, hitting the CAPTAIN who is near and whom he cannot see.)* Help! Stop! I am not the wild beast. *(At a safe distance, he regains his bravery.)* I — I am the Captain, the boldest, bravest fighter in Rome — in all Italy! Go — stand at the side. Appear when you hear the trumpets blow. *(CAPTAIN points to L. ANDROCLES starts to R.)* No. The other way!

ANDROCLES: *(He turns and starts to L. Loud trumpets blow. He stops, faces R., ready to fight.)* The trumpets! Now?

PANTALONE: No! *(ANDROCLES, groping, exits U.L.*

PANTALONE bows to Royal Box.) Most Imperial Emperor, I am Pantalone, Master of the slave. From me he ran away. From me he stole. I am told you plan to reward me for this holiday with a bag of gold.

CAPTAIN: I tracked and captured him. I am sure you will confer a title of bravery on me. *(Trumpets blow).*

ANDROCLES *(Enters U.L., ready to fight):* The trumpets! Now?

CAPTAIN: No! *(ANDROCLES turns and exits.)* Ah, the Emperor waves. It is the signal. Open the gates. Let the wild beast in!

PANTALONE: Let the entertainment begin!
(CAPTAIN and PANTALONE quickly go D.R. where they stand. Drum rolls are heard. Then loud roars are heard off U.R. LION, roaring, angrily stalks in from U.R.)

LION: Barred — locked — caged! I am — outraged!
(Roars and paces menacingly)

PANTALONE: What a big lion! I am glad he is below.

CAPTAIN: I could conquer him with one blow.

LION: Captured! Held in captivity! Robbed of my liberty! Only man would think of it. Only man would sink to it. Man — man — little — two legged — tailless thing. Beware man, I am a King! *(Roars).* The first man I meet I — will eat! *(Trumpets blow.)*

ANDROCLES *(Enters, head still covered.):* The trumpets! Now?

LION *(Sees him):* Ah, a man! A chew or two and a bone to pick. *(Roars)*

ANDROCLES *(Frightened and groping):* Oh! I am not alone. I must get out quick.

(Drum starts beating in rhythm to the fight, ANDROCLES starts walking, then running, the LION after him. The chase is a dance mime, fast, comic, with surprises and suspense. It ends with LION holding ANDROCLES in his clutches.)

LION: Caught! Held! *(Shakes ANDROCLES like a rag doll)* Flip

— flop. I will start eating at the top!
(Takes off ANDROCLES' head covering)

ANDROCLES: No hope ever to be free. This is the end of me!
(LION looks at ANDROCLES, is surprised and roars questioningly. ANDROCLES, frightened, freezes, then slowly feels his neck, his face and nose. He looks at LION and he is surprised. LION tries to "talk".) You? *(LION nods and roars, pantomimes pulling out a thorn from his paw, and points to ANDROCLES who nods.)* Me. *(LION "talks" and points to himself.)* You! *(LION nods and roars happily.)* Signor Lion! *(LION "talks" and roars, and they embrace each other joyfully.)*

PANTALONE: Let the fight begin! Beat him!
(LION stops and looks at PANTALONE.)

CAPTAIN: The Emperor waits to see who wins. Eat him!

ANDROCLES: He is my master — who bought me. He is the Captain — who caught me.

LION: Slave makers! Taker of men! I will beat you! I will eat you! *(Roars and starts to C.)*

PANTALONE: Help! The lion is looking at me. Draw your sword! *(Hides behind the CAPTAIN)*

CAPTAIN *(Shaking):* I am afraid his blood will rust my blade.

PANTALONE: Show you can do what you say — slay him with one blow!

CAPTAIN: I suddenly remember — I have to go! *(Starts off R. At the same time, LION leaps with a roar and attacks the two.)*

PANTALONE: Help! Guards! Save, attend me!

CAPTAIN: Help! Somebody defend me! *(There is an exciting and comic scramble, with LION finally grabbing each by the collar and hitting their heads together. Then he holds each out at arms length.)*

LION: Listen and learn a lesson: only a coward steals and holds a man. *(Roars. Shakes PANTALONE)* Only a thief buys

420

and sells a man. And no one — can — own another man! *(Roars).* The world was made for all — equally. Nod your heads if you agree. *(LION shakes them and makes their heads nod violently. Then he releases them, and the two drop to the ground.)* The vote is "Yes"— unanimously! *(Trumpets sound. Off-stage voices shout, from R. and L. and from the back of the auditorium: "Kill the lion. The lion is loose. Club him. Stone him. Kill the lion. Kill! Kill! etc." CAPTAIN and PANTALONE crawl to R. Hands appear off R. and L. shaking clubs and spears. This is a tense moment. The Arena has turned against the lion. LION is frightened. He crouches by ANDROCLES who stands heroically by him.)*

ANDROCLES: Stop! Stop! Hold your spears and stones and clubs. Do not kill the lion. You see — he is not an enemy. He remembers me and a kindness which I did for him. Today that kindness he has returned. He did not eat my head, which would have been the end. Instead — he is — my friend. *(He offers his hand to LION. LION takes it. Music begins and the two start to waltz together. PANTALONE and CAPTAIN crouch and watch in amazement. Hands and weapons disappear from the sides at R. and L. ANDROCLES and LION waltz bigger, funnier, and happier. Trumpets sound. Music and dancing stops. LELIO enters D.L. by royal banner.)*

LELIO: The Emperor has spoken. His words will be heard. *(All bow low toward the Box as LELIO holds up a royal scroll.)* The Emperor is amazed, astounded, and astonished — with delight — at this sudden sight. A fight unlike any in history. Indeed it is a mystery. Two enemies — man and lion — dancing hand in hand! To honor this unique occasion, the Emperor has issued this command: today shall be, not one for fighting, but of dance and revelry! *(Trumpets play and people cheer.)* The Emperor gives to the Master of the slave —

PANTALONE: That is I, Pantalone. How much gold does he give?

LELIO: The Emperor gives this order: *you* will give twenty

pieces of gold to Androcles.

ANDROCLES: To me!

LELIO: A sum he has well earned.

PANTALONE: Give twenty pieces of gold! Oh, I shall die a poor man. No. No! *(LION starts toward him and growls loudly).* Yes — yes, I will pay. *(Quickly takes a bag from pocket and begins counting).* One — two — three —

LELIO: Furthermore: the Emperor decrees to the Captain who caught the slave —

CAPTAIN: Ah, what honor does the Emperor give to me?

LELIO: You will command a Roman Legion in a distant land. You will sail to the Isle of Britain where even the boldest man must fight to keep alive, where it is so dangerous only the bravest survive.

CAPTAIN *(Shaking violently):* Danger? Fight? Me?

LELIO: Because of your boasted bravery.

CAPTAIN: I would prefer to stay, please. A cold climate makes me sneeze. *(LION starts and roars loudly.)* I will go. *(LION follows him roaring).* I am going! I am gone!

LELIO: And to me — the Emperor has given me the lovely, lovely Isabella — *(ISABELLA enters D.L.)* and has blessed our marriage which soon will be.

ISABELLA: For me the Emperor decreed, Pantalone shall pay without delay my dowry which he holds for me.

PANTALONE: Pay more gold! Oh, no — no! *(LION roars at him loudly.)* Yes — yes. I will pay. It is here, my dear.

LELIO: And finally: *(Trumpets blow)* The Emperor has ruled that both lion and slave today have won a victory unequalled in history. So — both lion and slave are hereby — set free!

ANDROCLES: Free? I am free.

LION: The way the world should be!

ANDROCLES: Free — to find my family — to work the best I

can — to raise my head — to be a man. To find out — who I am!

(Music. They all SING.)

ALL:
    Let us roar today,
    Let us say today
    We feel great.
    Celebrate!
    Exhilarate!
    Congratulate!

PANTALONE and CAPTAIN *(Dejected):*
    We don't feel great.

ALL:
    It's a great way
    To show the world how you feel.
    When in need — find a friend.
    Laws will read — have a friend.
    We feel great.
    Don't eat, but meet.
    Why wait, make a friend.
    Extend!
    Do your part, make a start.
    Roar today. Show the world today,
    It's a great way
    To show the world how you feel.

(All the actors bow, then ANDROCLES comes forward).

ANDROCLES: Our story is told. The lovers are joined in happiness. The bragger and miser are undone. And a friend was won by kindness. Our masks and bells and curtains we put away for another day. And we go our way — a group of strolling players. We say —

LION *(Points at audience.):* Be sure you roar today!

ALL: Arreviderci!
    (They all bow low and the music swells.)

THE CURTAINS CLOSE.
423

THE
ICE WOLF

by
Joanna Halpert Kraus

A TALE OF THE ESKIMOS

A play for young people in three acts

A small number of plays, written around mid–century, gradually expanded the scope of the repertoire of plays for children. Prominent among them was *The Ice Wolf,* by Joanna H. Kraus. This play stands tall in the company of plays such as *Reynard the Fox* and *Androcles and the Lion,* but it also stands out as perhaps the "bravest" of these works. While each of these plays offers a refreshing theatrical sophistication, and each offers interesting and believable fictive worlds, *The Ice Wolf* pursues serious ideas in an uncompromising manner rarely seen in dramatic literature for children prior to this time.

In the story of the play, Anatou, the protagonist, is born into the Eskimo culture with fair skin and light hair. Because of these differences, the people of her village fear her, and they make her the scapegoat for all of their problems. The play follows Anatou's entire life, from birth to death: as she grows up amid the suspicions of the villagers, as she is forced to flee, as she petitions the Wood God to transform her into a Wolf, as she succumbs to her desire for revenge, and as she dies trying to save her friend. The play presents a serious story of prejudice, revenge, death, and redemption, which is played out in a world where "the spirits and the Shaman ruled."

The Ice Wolf operates on many levels simultaneously. On one level the audience sees a realistic portrayal of Anatou, a young girl who must deal with her real-life feelings of anger, fear, and the desire for revenge. This character also functions on a quasi-mythological level, as she freely interacts with animals and with the gods, and she undergoes a transformation from a human to a wolf. While focusing on Anatou's life, the play offers a larger view of a time and a culture, and the primal fears that ruled that culture. As *Androcles and the Lion* presents an exaggerated view of the foibles of human nature, *The Ice Wolf* presents an intense view of Anatou's ritualistic life struggles.

Kraus reveals the story through a series of episodes, each of which she frames by remarks from the storyteller, who guides the audience through the events and sets the appropriate mood for each scene. In this way Kraus moves the action forward rapidly, allowing the audience glimpses of only the climactic moments in Anatou's life. In one sense, this appropriately generalizes the tale; but the simple truthfulness of the conflict (Anatou's anguish at her persecution because she is different) provides a meaningful particularity to the play.

The play contains two separate parts, almost two separate plays, which Kraus reconciles in the end. The first part focuses on Anatou's struggle with the villagers. This external, almost melodramatic, conflict places Anatou in opposition to a clearly defined antagonist, represented by the chorus of villagers. Anatou offers the voice of reason in this struggle, but she loses this fight, and is driven from the village. Anatou's exile into the forest concludes the first part of the play, which is left unresolved and made secondary to Anatou's conflict within herself. From this point in the play, as Anatou wrestles with her consuming passion for revenge, Kraus draws her somewhat like a classic tragic character who becomes responsible for her own downfall.

The persecuted victim becomes the persecutor as Anatou, now in the form of a wolf, kills one of the humans. Anatou gradually becomes aware that her actions are driven by her "thick coat of hate," but by then the villagers are rising up against her once again. However, Wood God assures Anatou that if she can show that her "heart is empty of all its hate and cruelty" her "spirit will not die." Kraus brings together the two worlds of the play in the final scene where Anatou gives her life to save her human friend, and the play ends with a vision of Anatou's spirit rising above the repentant villagers.

Anatou kills, and Anatou dies. While the fact of her death grows logically from the action of the play, it is neither the end of the play nor the major thematic element of the story. Like many heroes in dramatic literature for children, Anatou reflects qualities of the innocent victim; yet the play also offers the complexity of a sympathetic protagonist who must take some responsibility for the tragic happenings in the play. Through her suffering Anatou redeems herself, and she also stands as a symbol of salvation for the people of the village, who also realize they were wrong.

Kraus writes in the idiom of folktale, but with a contemporary resonance. She distances the time and place of the characters and action to soften the harsh action in the play. Yet, she invests Anatou with realistic qualities with which contemporary audiences can empathize. Traditional fairy and folktale protagonists often are passive individuals that overcome their difficulties through the intervention of another person. In *The Ice Wolf* Anatou petitions the Wood God to help her, but he tells her clearly that she must take the responsibility for her own actions in order to solve the problem. Anatou grows to a nearly heroic stature, not because of her deeds, but because of her growth of mind and spirit.

The Ice Wolf has retained a consistent place in the repertoire throughout the last forty years, attesting to the important resonance of serious plays in the development of the literature.

Joanna H. Kraus is an award-winning playwright of fifteen published scripts that are widely produced throughout the United States, Canada, England, and Australia. She currently has an ongoing column on children's books in the *Contra Costa Times*, and also writes reviews for the *Rossmoor News* and *Downeast Coastal Press*.

She is Professor Emeritus of Theatre and former Graduate Coordinator of the Interdisciplinary Arts for Children program, State University of New York College at Brockport. She received the 1995 Special Achievement Award from the New York State Theatre Education Association. She is a member of the Dramatists Guild, the American Alliance for Theatre and Education and the Society of Children's Book Writers and Illustrators.

THE
ICE WOLF

by
Joanna H. Kraus

THE ICE WOLF

Characters

STORYTELLER

ANATOU,
A girl born to Eskimo parents. Her skin is pale and her hair blond; a phenomenon in the village.

KARVIK, her Father

ARNARQIK, her Mother

TARTO, her best friend, a village boy

KIVIOG, Tarto's Father

ATATA, an old man of the village but a good hunter

SHIKIKANAQ, a village girl

MOTOMIAK, a village boy

VILLAGER 1, a woman

VILLAGER 2, a man

WOOD GOD, the God of the Forest

A BEAVER

A FOX

AN ERMINE

Setting

The entire action of the play takes place in a small isolated Eskimo village, Little Whale River, and the forest, a few days inland. It is located in the Hudson Bay area of Canada.

The time is long before the missionaries established their settlements, long before white man had been seen, a time when the spirits and the Shaman, or the Wise Man, ruled.

431

PROLOGUE

It is the end of January. In the foreground we see an expanse of white spread out. It is broken in a few places by hillocks which rise up like seal's heads from the plains. There is an atmosphere of cold beauty and awesome space.

The Storyteller *enters on the apron of the stage. He is dressed, as all the Eskimos, in the attire of the Hudson Bay Eskimos, but somehow there is the quality about him of excitement. He is no ordinary hunter.*

STORYTELLER:

Far beyond the world you know —
Of sun, rushing rivers, and trees
Is the Northland
Where the winter snow is gray,
There is no sound of birds
Nothing but the stillness of space
Of endless snow
And endless cold.
There, the child Anatou was born
In the village of Little Whale River
It was small, beside the sea
But the search for food never ended.
(Lights up on igloo, Eskimos in circle, one beating drum, chanting)

Aja, I remember. It was one of the coldest nights of the year, so cold the dog team had buried themselves in the snow.

ATATA: And the seal-oil lamps trembled before the Great North Wind.

KARVIK: Just before dawn, when the baby came, Karvik had to go out and repair their home. His fingers seemed to freeze at once. Never had there been such a storm in Little Whale River. *(Lights up on KARVIK cutting a snow block and fitting it into dome)*

ARNARQIK: Inside Arnarqik sewed the caribou skins she had chewed. She was making new clothes for Karvik. Only once

432

did she dare look at the small child beside her wrapped in skins. It was strangely still, strangely quiet. It was unlike any child Arnarqik had ever seen.

STORYTELLER: Atata was by the seal's breathing hole ... *(Lights up on ATATA crouched by breathing hole, poised, ready with harpoon)* ... waiting ... waiting ... waiting until the seal came up for air. For days there had been no food in Little Whale River. He thought the birth of a new child might bring him luck! Then ... he struck with his harpoon!

(ATATA harpoons seal.)

ATATA: Aja, Nuliayuk, now everyone will eat!

STORYTELLER: He took the choice bit of meat, the seal's liver to return to the seal goddess, Nuliayuk. The Shaman, the wise man, had told him to do this so she would feast on it and then remember to send more seals to the hunters of Little Whale River. Atata rushed back. Now there was something to celebrate. A new child, a fresh caught seal. There would be drum chants and dancing and stories in the long white night. *(Drum Chants begin. They break off abruptly)* But there was no singing or dancing.

KARVIK: It was long ago ...

ARNARQIK: Just about this time.

STORYTELLER: It was a pale dawn ...

ATATA: Like this one ...

STORYTELLER: When Anatou was born.

ACT I, SCENE I

The interior of Karvik and Arnarqik's home in Little Whale River. Masses of thick, heavy caribou skins are spread about. Seal-Oil lamps, made of soapstone, light the home.

At rise, the sound of Eskimo dogs howling. A strong wind is blowing. Villagers come in from all sides dressed in their habitual furs. They crawl through the passageway and lights come up in the interior of the igloo. Karvik and Arnarqik are seated. Their new child is beside Arnarqik on a caribou skin not visible from the entrance.

KARVIK: Welcome! Welcome all of you!

VILLAGER 2: Aja! Your first child. Of course we'd come. *(To others)* We must sing many songs to welcome it.

KIVIOG: And if it's a man child, Karvik will already have made him a harpoon, and a whip.

VILLAGER 1: By the next moon he will be able to use them. Wait and see!
(They laugh.)

VILLAGER 2: Good, he can hunt a seal with us this winter and the caribou next fall. If he's as good a hunter as Karvik, we'll get twice as much.

KIVIOG: And he'll be a companion for my son, Tarto, born under the moon.
(They all laugh except KARVIK and ARNARQIK who are strangely quiet.)

VILLAGER 1: Karvik! Arnarqik! You are silent. Show us the man child. We've come a long way to see him. *(ARNARQIK moves slowly.)*

ARNARQIK: It is a girl child ... but we are glad.

KARVIK: She will be good.

ARNARQIK: It is true. There is joy in feeling new life come to the great world.

VILLAGER 1: A girl! Ah-ah. That means more care.

VILLAGER 2: And more attention.

KIVIOG: She cannot hunt.

VILLAGERS *(Politely):* But let us see her anyway.
(ARNARQIK moves away troubled, then points to the caribou skin.)

ARNARQIK: There, look for yourself.
> *(KARVIK has turned away. VILLAGERS crowd around the child, move back abruptly, and whirl on KARVIK and ARNARQIK.)*

VILLAGER 1 *(In low horror):* Her hair is white!

VILLAGER 2: Her face is pale.

KIVIOG: She cannot be an Eskimo.

VILLAGER 1: She cannot be one of us!

KARVIK: Of course she is. Her hair will get darker. Wait.

VILLAGER 2: But her face. Look at it. No Eskimo child was ever born as pale as that.

VILLAGER 1: She's a devil.

ARNARQIK: No!

VILLAGER 1: She will not live one moon.

ARNARQIK: She will live.

VILLAGER 1: She will bring bad luck.

ARNARQIK: She's only a baby.

KIVIOG: Put her out in the snow now, before she turns the gods against us.

VILLAGER 2: And our stomachs shrink.

VILLAGER 1: And our dishes are empty.

VILLAGER 2: It's happened before. We all know it. Get rid of the child before it's too late.

KIVIOG: She will offend Nuliayuk, the goddess of the seals. Nuliayuk will stay at the bottom of the sea, and keep the seals beside her, and we will all go hungry. Put the child out into the snow or we will die of famine!

ARNARQIK: No! She will be a good Eskimo.

VILLAGER 2: Then let her grow up in another village. We don't want her here.

KIVIOG: She doesn't look like us. She won't think like us.

VILLAGER 1: She doesn't belong here.

KARVIK: Then where does she belong? Where should she go?

VILLAGER 1: Put her out in the snow.
(Starts to grab her)

ARNARQIK: No! No! No, I can't. Don't you understand? She is our child.

VILLAGER 2: Then leave our village in peace. Don't anger the spirits of Little Whale River.

KARVIK: But this is our village and you are our people. How can we leave it? Wait! She will be like the others. You'll see. She'll sew and cook just as well as any Eskimo girl. Better! Arnarqik will teach her.

KIVIOG *(Holds up his hands.):* Very well. We will watch and wait. Perhaps you are right, and we will see her hair and cheeks grow darker. But we have no gifts or good wishes to welcome a white-faced child — a white-faced girl child! *(VILLAGERS exit. ARNARQIK tries to run after them.)*

ARNARQIK: Come back! Wait! Please wait. Don't go yet. Oh, Karvik, what will we do?

KARVIK *(Slowly):* Her hair should be as dark as the raven's wing.

ARNARQIK: It is as white as the caribou's belly. Karvik, what if they are right? She is different. Karvik, why is her hair pale? Why doesn't she cry? She is so still! It's not natural.

KARVIK: She is frightened already. The Fair One will have a hard journey. *(Looks out the passageway)* Arnarqik, the villagers spoke wisely. *(Looks for a long time at his wife)* She would never know. It would not hurt her in the snow now.

ARNARQIK: No, Karvik! You mustn't ask me to.

KARVIK: But if we leave, will the next village think she looks more like an Eskimo?

ARNARQIK *(Shakes her head.):* No, she is Anatou, the Fair One — she will not change. But I will teach her, Karvik. She will be a good Eskimo girl!

KARVIK: But will they ever think she is like the others?

ARNARQIK: Yes. Yes. Of course they will. Let us stay here.
Who knows what is beyond the snow?

KARVIK: Then we must be strong. We must teach Anatou to be
strong. Only then will our home be her home and our friends
her friends. It won't be easy, Arnarqik.
(ARNARQIK is beside the baby.)

ARNARQIK: Oh Karvik, I couldn't leave her. Not like that!
(Abruptly she changes.) Look, Karvik ... she is smiling.
(Picks her up) Oh, Karvik, we mustn't let them hurt her. We
must protect her.

KARVIK: Sing, Arnarqik, sing the morning song. Bring Anatou
luck. She will have a hard journey.

ARNARQIK: *(Sits, sings or chants)*
> **I rise up from rest**
> **Moving swiftly as the raven's wing**
> **I rise up to greet the day**
> **Wo-wa**
> **My face is turned from dark of night**
> **My gaze toward the dawn**
> **Toward the whitening dawn.**

(Lights fade)

STORYTELLER: But her hair did not grow dark as the raven's
wing. Instead, each day she grew fairer. They called her the
"different one," and when the blinding snow swept across
the North or when the hunters returned with empty sleds, the
villagers whispered, "It's Anatou. She's the one."

ACT I, SCENE 2

*The village. Tarto, Shikikanaq and Motomiak are playing an
Eskimo game, a combination of Hide-and-Seek and Touch.
Motomiak is just dashing for the goal pursued by Shikikanaq.*

Tarto is at the goal watching and laughing.

TARTO: Hurry up, Motomiak. She's right behind you. Shikikanaq is right behind you!
(MOTOMIAK turns to look, still running. ANATOU enters. She sees the race but moves out of the way too late and they collide. MOTOMIAK falls and SHIKIKANAQ tags him)

SHIKIKANAQ: There! I won!

MOTOMIAK: That wasn't fair. You made me lose the game, Anatou. I've never lost before — not to a girl! See what you made me do. Clumsy!

ANATOU: I'm sorry. I tried to get out of the way. I didn't see you in time.

SHIKIKANAQ *(Whispering):* You better not say anything more, Motomiak, or Anatou will put a spell on you — the way she did the seals.

TARTO: What are you talking about? You know that isn't true.

ANATOU: Oh, I'm sorry I spoiled your game, Motomiak, but couldn't you start again?

SHIKIKANAQ: No. I won. Tarto saw. Didn't you, Tarto?
(He nods).

MOTOMIAK: Beside, we don't want to play in front of a freak.
(ANATOU gasps)

TARTO: Who's a freak?

MOTOMIAK: She is. The whole village says so.

ANATOU *(Furious):* No, I'm not! I'm an Eskimo just like you.

SHIKIKANAQ *(Doubtfully):* Ohh

MOTOMIAK: Well, her face is different enough.
(ANATOU touches it.)

TARTO: Why, what's wrong with it? It has two eyes, a nose and a mouth just like everyone else's.

SHIKIKANAQ: But it's white, Tarto — like snow. I bet if you put her in the sun she'll melt and that's why she stays inside

438

all the time.

TARTO: You're just jealous because she's prettier than you, Shikikanaq.

ANATOU: Stop it. Stop it, all of you. *(She is crying.)* Leave me alone. *(Starts to go)*

TARTO *(Furious):* Now see what you've done. If she were made of snow, Shikikanaq, she couldn't cry. *(Crosses to her)* Come on, Anatou. They didn't mean it. Please come back. *(To others)* Let's have another game — all four of us.

SHIKIKANAQ: Well ... all right ... if she'll tell us why she looks that way.

TARTO *(Sharply):* What way?

SHIKIKANAQ: I mean her eyes and her hair. They're such funny colors. There must be a reason.

ANATOU *(Desperate):* I don't know. Each time you've asked me I said I didn't know.

SHIKIKANAQ: I bet if you asked your mother and father they'd know. It must be something terrible or they'd tell you.

MOTOMIAK: Maybe the wood god from the forest put a spell on an animal and sent it back here. No one else in Little Whale River looks like you. Maybe that's why you look so funny. They say he has the power to make an animal appear like a human.

SHIKIKANAQ: And he can make people look like animals too ... just by saying a spell! My father says that's why no Eskimo should go into the forest.

ANATOU: No! No! It's not true. I'm just like you are!

MOTOMIAK: Then, maybe, some devil spirit looked at you and it took all the color away.

SHIKIKANAQ: Yes, that's it. And why do you always sit inside and sew?

ANATOU *(Lying):* There's a lot of work. It has to get done.

439

TARTO *(Quickly):* She can sew better than any woman in the whole village! Show them, Anatou.
(He points to her dress which is carefully and beautifully stitched. Shikikanaq examines it.)

SHIKIKANAQ: It is beautiful. There aren't any mistakes at all.

ANATOU *(Can't believe her praise.):* My mother taught me and she is very good and careful.

SHIKIKANAQ: Can you make anything else?

ANATOU: Two snows ago, I made warm boots for my father. Very special boots and he's worn them ever since.

MOTOMIAK: Then how come he's lost in the snow right now, if the boots you made were so special.

ANATOU: He went to look for food. Both my mother and father did. That's all I know.

MOTOMIAK: There's barely any food left in the village. For three days the hunters have returned with empty sleds.

ANATOU: Famine is everywhere. Not just here. I heard my father say so before he left. That is why he said he was going far away to look.

MOTOMIAK: You made those boots your father wore. I bet you put a charm on them. Shikikanaq and I saw you talking to them once and blowing on them.

ANATOU: No! That's not true. I was cleaning them.

MOTOMIAK: But you were talking too, you were putting a charm on them, weren't you?

ANATOU: Don't you see? If I did have any magic powers, I'd bring them back. They're my parents. I love them. They're the only ones who've been good to me. *(Softly)* I couldn't stay in Little Whale River if it weren't for them.

SHIKIKANAQ *(Cruelly):* Well, they're gone now. So you can go too.

ANATOU: What do you mean? They're coming back. I know they are.

440

MOTOMIAK: Maybe. But my father says you killed your own parents.

ANATOU *(With a cry):* No!

TARTO *(Challenging him and pinning his arm back):* Take that back or else!

MOTOMIAK *(Stubbornly):* That's what my father said.

TARTO *(Knocking him down):* Well, he's wrong.

(A fight starts. SHIKIKANAQ shrieks and ANATOU watches horrified. Three villagers rush in.)

SHIKIKANAQ *(Quickly):* She started it. It's all her fault. Anatou's fault!

KIVIOG *(To ANATOU):* Get away from our children. *(VILLAGER 2 has separated the boys.)*

TARTO: Anatou wasn't doing anything.

KIVIOG: Be still!

VILLAGER 1: She's brought nothing but trouble since the day she was born.

TARTO *(To KIVIOG):* But it's not fair, Father, she ...

KIVIOG: Silence! For days we have searched for Karvik and Arnarqik. They are good people. Karvik was the best hunter we had. But no man can fight off charmed boots.

VILLAGER 2: No wonder they got lost in the blizzard.

VILLAGER 1: Look at her. She doesn't care her parents are gone.

ANATOU *(Suddenly):* I don't understand. Do you mean they're ... dead? *(KIVIOG nods.)* How can you be sure?

KIVIOG: If they haven't frozen, they have starved. We cannot find them anywhere.

VILLAGER 1: You're to blame. You and your witchcraft.

VILLAGER 2: Look, she doesn't even care.

ANATOU: Don't you think I want them here? Don't you think

441

the fire is colder without my mother's face and lonesome without my father's singing? They went to look for food ... for all of us. I'm hungry too ... just like the rest of you.

VILLAGER 1: Then why do you anger the Seal Goddess? We used to have days of feasting.

VILLAGER 2: Pots boiling ...

KIVIOG: But since the same day you were born, the hunters have had to work twice as hard — twice as hard for the same amount!

VILLAGER 2: We used to thank the Seal Goddess, bow down to her and give her seal liver. Now there is none to give her and she is angry — at the bottom of the sea. Our harpoons break in our hands.

ANATOU: It is the bitter cold.

VILLAGER 2: Why is there blizzard after blizzard if the gods aren't angry?

VILLAGER 1: Why is there a famine if the gods aren't angry.

KIVIOG: It's your fault.

VILLAGER 2: You're to blame.

KIVIOG: We have kept silent for the sake of Karvik and Arnarqik, but now they are no longer here.

VILLAGER 1: They took care of you and see what it brought them to!

ANATOU (Sobbing): But I am all alone too.

VILLAGER 2: There is no more to eat.

VILLAGER 1: No oil to burn.

VILLAGER 2: We fear sickness.

KIVIOG: And the souls of the dead.

VILLAGER 1: The souls of animals and men.

VILLAGER 2: We know the spirits of the earth and the air are angry with us.

442

ANATOU: What am I to do? What do you want of me?

KIVIOG: Leave here. Leave us!

ANATOU: But I haven't done anything. Where will I go? I'll never find my way alone.

KIVIOG: If you stay, you will get no help or protection from us, Anatou. From now on, find your own food and eat with the dogs. No one else will eat with you.

VILLAGER 2: And from now on, speak to yourself. No one else will listen. *(Adults start off.)*

VILLAGER 1: Go home, children, all of you. Go home quickly.

KIVIOG: Don't talk to that one. That one is evil. Leave her alone. *(They leave. ANATOU has turned away. TARTO looks back before exiting but she doesn't see it. ANATOU sinks down, unable to bear it.)*

ANATOU: It isn't true! I loved my parents. Even Tarto believed them. He didn't say a word — he didn't even say good-bye. Oh, Moon God, is there nothing I can do.
(She is crying. TARTO reappears, puts his hand out to touch her hair, then in fear withdraws it.)

TARTO *(Gently):* What are you going to do? Where will you go?

ANATOU *(Jerks her head abruptly but doesn't turn around.):* All right! All right! I'm leaving. Are you satisfied now?

TARTO: But it's me, Anatou — Tarto. I want to say good-by.

ANATOU *(Turns around.):* Tarto, you came back!

TARTO: But I can't stay. If they catch me ... I'll ... I'll get into trouble. I brought you some food Anatou. It's just a little, but I thought ...

ANATOU: Thank you, Tarto. *(Suddenly she takes off an amulet that she is wearing.)* Tarto, you're the only friend I have now. I want you to keep this to remember me. The Shaman gave it to my mother before I was born. It's to bring good luck, but it was really always meant for a boy child, not a girl. *(He takes it.)* Tarto, I wish I had something special to give you, but it's all I have.

TARTO: Then it is special, Anatou. I'll always keep it. I won't
forget you. I promise. And when I am older, Anatou, I'll
harpoon my own seal. I'll be the best hunter in the village
and the men will do anything I say because I'll know all the
hiding places of the seals. Then they'll listen to me and ...
(Breaks off and slowly asks what he has always wondered)
Anatou, why is your hair so light?

ANATOU *(Pierced by the question):* Tarto, why is the sky gray
in the winter? I don't know. All I want is to be like the others,
to play with you and sing with you, and I want to see my
mother and father again. I love them. Do you believe me?
(He nods.) I want to be friends with the villagers, but they
won't let me. You're the only one who tries to understand.
I used to wake up and say, "Today will be different." My
mother said, "Anatou, every day is the beginning of some
new wonderful thing." But it wasn't true! Each day ended the
same way and each dawn I was frightened again. And then
today ... today it was the worst of all.

TARTO: I'm sorry, Anatou.

ANATOU: Tarto, you were brave to come back here. You know
they'll be angry if they find you here.

TARTO: I know.

ANATOU: You will be a fine hunter, Tarto ... the finest of the
whole village one day. Tarto, why did you come back?

TARTO: I am your friend, Anatou. I always will be even if ...

ANATOU: Even if what, Tarto?

TARTO: Anatou, listen. My father said ... that ... well, he said...
(Gulps) ... He said you put spells on the seals so they couldn't
come out of the water. Anatou, couldn't you say another spell
so we could all eat? Then it would be all right again, Anatou.

ANATOU *(Horrified):* Do you believe that, Tarto?

TARTO *(Miserably):* Well, first I said it wasn't true! But today ...

ANATOU: Tarto, listen. There's nothing I can do. I can't make a spell like a shaman, like the wise man. I'm hungry, too, just like you. Even if I wanted to, there is nothing I can do.

TARTO *(Slowly):* Don't you want to? Don't you want to help us, Anatou?

ANATOU: Don't you believe me either, Tarto? Doesn't anyone? I'm not any different. I don't have any magic powers. I'm just like anyone else.

TARTO: Your skin is white, mine is brown. Your hair is pale like the dawn, mine is dark like the night. *(He is colder now.)* You're not like anyone I've seen. *(A long pause)*

ANATOU: I've never heard you say that before. Everyone else, but you! You never seemed to care. You made up for all the others.
(Sound of Eskimo dogs)

TARTO *(Uncomfortably):* I have to go, Anatou ... it's late. What will you do?

ANATOU *(With a horrible realization):* I know I can't stay here now. Tarto, when you lose everything at once, your choice has been made. You can only follow it.

TARTO: But where will you go? What will you do?

ANATOU *(Pauses, making difficult decision):* The forest, Tarto. It's only a few days from here. I've heard about it from the old men and the Shaman.

TARTO *(Impulsively):* But you can't. Don't you know about it? It's a place of whispers in the night, of strange whines. They say the trees are living beings but they can't speak. It's not safe for an Eskimo to spend a night in the forest. What if the Wood God changes you into a wolf or another animal?

ANATOU *(Slowly):* Yes ... what if he changes me into a wolf?

TARTO *(Continuing without hearing her):* It's dark and mysterious, Anatou. It's a place where Eskimos never go.

ANATOU: But, don't you see? That's just why. There is no place else! *(Pauses)* Maybe the Wood God won't care if my hair is pale ... like the dawn!

ACT II, SCENE 1

Outside the forest at night. Late March. The opening of this scene is mimed and the audience sees Anatou's silhouette.

STORYTELLER: Anatou ran. It was dark and frightening. The only sound she heard was the wind whipping the snow around her. *(ANATOU drops from exhaustion. She is crying but she must continue.)*

ANATOU: Where shall I go?

STORYTELLER: No one could hear her cry. There was no one but the wind. Anatou knew if she stopped too long she would freeze in the fierce cold. Then suddenly she saw the place where no one had ever been.
(Part of the forest appears stage right. ANATOU stops stage left.)

ANATOU: The forest! I remember the old men used to tell each other tales by the fire. What did they say? No Eskimo must ever go into the forest. You must never spend the night there. But that's where the Wood God lives. *(She starts to move toward the forest.)* I must go. I must ask him. *(Rest of forest scrim appears as ANATOU runs first to stage right, then to stage left, stopping at center stage. Exhausted, she sinks to the ground. She is trembling with fear and slowly rises to her knees. Softly)* Wood God! *(Louder)* Wood God! *(Looks all around her)* Wood God ... help me.
(The WOOD GOD enters. He appears, as the spirits are reputed to, in the shape of an animal. He has chosen the shape of an awesome owl which is white in color.)

WOOD GOD: Who dares to come into my forest where the wind and snow cry into the darkness?

ANATOU *(Draws back.):* Are you the Wood God?

WOOD GOD: I am! And will be till the end of time! Who said you could enter my forest?

ANATOU *(Terrified):* No one.

WOOD GOD: Where do you come from?

ANATOU: I come from Little Whale River.

WOOD GOD: Are you an Eskimo? *(She nods.)* Then why did you come here? Don't you know no Eskimo comes into the middle of the forest and dares to disturb my sleep? Leave my kingdom now and be glad you still have your life.

ANATOU *(Pleading):* No! You don't understand. Please don't send me away. *(Crying. The Wood God comes closer and as he approaches, moonlight shines around them both.)*

WOOD GOD: Ah-ah. Even in the darkness your hair shines. Is it the moon, child?

ANATOU *(Desperate):* Wood God. Wood God, can't you see? Even hidden here it shines and glitters. If I were to crawl into a cave it would be the same .

WOOD GOD *(Lifts her face and peers into it.):* Your face is as pale as ice. *(Softer)* And your eyes are red from crying. *(Shakes his head)* That's too bad. It means you're human.

ANATOU: I am an Eskimo. But they don't believe me. Nobody does. Help me. Wood God, help me!

WOOD GOD: How can I help you? Are you hungry, child? Is that why you came here?

ANATOU *(Nods.):* We all are ... no one has eaten in days. But it is not my fault ... they blame me because my hair shines, because it isn't like the raven's wing. But I am hungry too. I can't go any further ... I can't.

WOOD GOD: We have no food to give you child. You must leave. Your people will be worried. *(He starts to exit.)*

ANATOU: Wait! Wait and hear me, Wood God. It is not food I want. It is not food that made me wake the great spirit of the

Wood God.

WOOD GOD: What then?

ANATOU *(Slowly):* I want what only your powers can grant. But first, Wood God, hear my story.

WOOD GOD: Begin. Quickly, child. You mustn't savor what tastes bitter.

ANATOU: Aja. It is true. You do see much.

WOOD GOD: Begin from the beginning; when you were born.

ANATOU: Even though I was a girl, my parents were happy, or at least they seemed to be. Even though I couldn't hunt ... even though ... even though I was different.

WOOD GOD: Why? You have two arms, two legs, and a face with two eyes and a mouth.

ANATOU: But a face that people were afraid of and hair that grew lighter instead of darker. They named me Anatou, the Fair One.

WOOD GOD: So you are Anatou. Then not all the spirits of the earth and air can help you. You are as you are.

ANATOU: But you can help me, Wood God. Please. You must.

WOOD GOD: Go home, fair child. I can do nothing. I cannot turn your pale hair to the dark of the night or your fair skin brown. I cannot teach them to like you. You must do that yourself. Go home to your parents. Go home where you belong.

ANATOU *(Blurts out):* I can't. They'll kill me if I do.

WOOD GOD *(Puzzled):* Who will? Your parents, too?

ANATOU: No, they are spirits now. They were the only good people I ever knew. I did love them, Wood God. Some people say that I am a witch and that I cursed my parents, that the Seal Goddess is angry with me. They say that is why there is no food. But it isn't true, Wood God! It isn't true!

WOOD GOD: My power would only hurt you, Anatou. You are

young. Go back.

ANATOU: I've heard you can make a seal seem like a man or a girl seem like a wolf. Is that true?

WOOD GOD: I can.

ANATOU: Then, Wood God ...

WOOD GOD *(Interrupts.):* Think Anatou. Is it so terrible to be an Eskimo girl, to learn to laugh and sing, or sew or cook.

ANATOU: Wood God, my father and mother taught me to sew and cook, but not to laugh and sing. I don't know what that is.

WOOD GOD: But what about the villagers?

ANATOU: They only taught me one thing — to hate. When my parents were gone, they wanted me to eat in the passageway with the dogs. They would not give me a skin to sew. Everywhere I went they turned away. *(Softly)* Even Tarto.

WOOD GOD: Tarto?

ANATOU: My best friend.

WOOD GOD: Where is he?

ANATOU: Wood God, they all say I'm planning evil, and now even Tarto thinks so, too. Wood God, Wood God, there are more ways of killing than with a harpoon!

WOOD GOD *(Pauses before he speaks.):* What do you wish, Anatou?

ANATOU: I don't want to be human any more. It hurts too much. I want you to turn me into a wolf. Then they'll be afraid of me. Then they'll leave me alone.

WOOD GOD: Think, Anatou, think! An animal cannot ...

ANATOU: Is a wolf's face white like mine?

WOOD GOD: You know it is not.

ANATOU: Then quickly change me into a beast.

WOOD GOD: An animal is hungry.

ANATOU: I am used to that.

WOOD GOD: He tears with his teeth to eat. A wolf is alone.

ANATOU: I am alone now.

WOOD GOD: Anatou, there is no return. What if you miss your village?

ANATOU: Miss them! When you take a thorn out of an animal's paw, does it miss it? When you fill an empty stomach, does it miss the ache? When you cannot remember pain, do you miss the tears? What would I miss, Wood God, but all of these things.

WOOD GOD: Once it is done, you cannot change your mind.

ANATOU: I will not want to.

WOOD GOD: You will never be an Eskimo girl again, not until you are about to die. Not 'till then. Are you sure? Are you sure, Anatou?

ANATOU: Will I forget everything? I want to forget everything. Now.

WOOD GOD: No, Anatou. Not at first. As time goes by, you'll forget more and more and only remember your life here.

ANATOU: No! I want to forget everything now. Everything, Wood God. I want to forget I was ever Anatou, the Fair One.

WOOD GOD: But you can't escape pain, Anatou. Even a wolf can't escape that. *(She pauses to think, she looks up. He watches her closely.)* Are you ready?

ANATOU: Yes. *(Suddenly frightened)* Wood God, will it hurt much?

WOOD GOD: Listen to my words. Hear them well. *(Lifts his arms so it appears as though his spirit, in the shape of a white owl, were commanding the universe. Drum beat begins)*
Come spirits of earth and sky.
Rise through the snow.
Speed over the ice.
Encircle this child in a coat of thick fur.

(Three forest animals appear — a fox, a beaver and an ermine — and form a circle around Anatou.)

FOX: Night protect it.

BEAVER: Forest watch it.

ERMINE: Nothing harm it.

WOOD GOD: As long as it remembers ...

FOX: As long as it remembers ...

BEAVER: As long as it remembers ...

WOOD GOD: To stay in the forest far from man.

ERMINE: Far from man.

FOX *(Echoes):* ... from man. *(There is more dancing. Animals close in. Their movements become more intense, then with a cry, they disappear and we see the wolf)*

FOX: It is done!

ERMINE: Now you are a wolf!

BEAVER: A wolf!

(This should not be a realistic representation, but rather done with masks and a costume, lean and sleek, that would be worn under the Eskimo dress, removed and disposed of at the end of the enchantment with a momentary darkening of the stage and more intense beating of the drum. There should be a marked difference in the movement once Anatou has been changed into a wolf.)

ACT II, SCENE 2

STORYTELLER:

All that winter Anatou lived with the animals enjoying the forest. She made friends with the beaver, fox and ermine. She forgot she had ever been Anatou, the Fair One — an Eskimo. Then one morning she woke up to a spring sun. It warmed the air and touched her fur.

(Spring in the forest. Early dawn. ANATOU wakes, stretches,

451

and smells the air with curiosity.)

ANATOU: Whorlberries. That's what I smell. And sunlight! Even the forest can't shut it out. *(She puts a paw down on a patch of melting snow.)* Beaver! Fox! Wake up. The snow's melting. *(They enter.)*

FOX: Did you have to wake me up and tell me that? It happens every spring.

ANATOU *(With growing excitement)*: But there are at least a thousand things to see and smell and hear. Come on. I'll race you through the forest and we'll explore the other side.

BEAVER *(Slowly):* What do you mean by the other side? We've never gone beyond the edge.

ANATOU: Oh, that was all right in the winter time. But now it's Spring. I want to leave the forest today, see what else there is.

FOX *(Sharply):* No, Anatou.

BEAVER: I thought you liked it here in the forest.

ANATOU: Of course I do, but ... *(Reluctant to speak of it)* ... But last night I had a strange dream. I can't remember it now. But it was something out there. There's something I have to see.

BEAVER: Outside the forest?

FOX: Don't go there, Anatou.

ANATOU: Why not?

FOX: Don't go or you'll be sorry

ANATOU: I just want to look. It's a beautiful day. I want to run in the sunlight and explore.

FOX: If you leave, the Wood God will be furious.

ANATOU: The Wood God? Why? I'll be back tonight, I promise. What's there to be afraid of.

FOX *(Quietly):* Danger.

BEAVER: Danger.

ANATOU: Maybe there's something dangerous for little animals like you, but I'm strong. I've got sharp teeth and claws. *(Boasting)* Nothing can hurt me.

FOX: You're a fool!

ANATOU *(Angry):* Wait and see. I'll be back without a scratch on me. I'm not afraid like the rest of you.

BEAVER: Listen to her! We'll let her go if she wants to.

FOX: For the last time. We're warning you. Don't go. There'll be trouble if you do.

ANATOU: I must go. I don't know why, but I must. Don't try to stop me.

FOX: Remember, we warned you!

BEAVER: You wouldn't listen.

ANATOU: I can't help it. It's something inside. *(Lights fade, animals exit. Forest scrim rises and ANATOU mimes her journey through the forest. She stops at the edge. The hilltops are brown, and there are black willow twigs with new buds)* Willow trees! And sunlight everywhere. Wood God, what a beautiful world outside your forest. *(Her journey continues in dance movement. The lights fade to indicate twilight. She stops worn-out.)* Loons on the water. It's so peaceful here. *(Enjoying it)* I'm all alone in the world. *(She prepares to settle down when lights begin to come up on a summer village tent and we hear the sharp sound of an Eskimo dog howling. ANATOU peers at the tent and moves in cautiously, closer and closer. The tent should be a movable unit that glides on. As Anatou gets closer, we hear the sound of Eskimo singing or chanting. ANATOU realizes what it is and cries out.)* Eskimos! Wood God! Wood God! Wood God! I'd forgotten. *(As she watches, KIVIOG and TARTO cross stage to tent.)* Tarto. And he still has the charm I gave him. He still has it.

KIVIOG: Tarto, we'll never have to worry with you as a hunter. All the pots of the village will boil this spring. Aja, since

Anatou left, there's been plenty to eat.

TARTO: There'd be enough for her, too, if she were here.

KIVIOG: Forget about her Tarto.
(They go inside.)

ANATOU *(Creeping closer):* Look at them eating, laughing and singing. "Let her die in the snow." That's what they said. I'll show them. I'm strong now. I'll get even. If it's the last thing I do, I'll get even. *(She moves nearer the tent and sees a piece of meat outside.)* I'll take some back to the forest. *(But the dogs hear her and they start howling. The singing stops and a villager runs out with his bow and arrow. ANATOU sees him and runs, but not before he shoots an arrow at her. ANATOU falls and the man disappears into the tent. ANATOU is hurt but gets up, limping to the side of the tent.)* That one! That one used to call me names. He hurt my mother and father. *(In pain)* I'm remembering. His arrow cut through my heart! *(VILLAGER comes out to check whether the animal is dead or not and he carries another weapon. He looks about.)* He'll kill me! Unless ... *(ANATOU springs. There is a short struggle and the man falls without a sound.)* Who is stronger now, Eskimo? Who's stronger now? *(ANATOU leaves. Curtain)*

ACT II, SCENE 3

In the forest. Anatou goes toward Fox. Fox retreats. Anatou approaches Beaver. He moves away in fear.

WOOD GOD: You must leave man alone.

ANATOU: He did not leave me alone. Why should I?

WOOD GOD: Man has a bow, harpoons, knives, spears. You will see, Anatou. He will hunt you out. Stay away! Do not hurt another human.

ANATOU: But he wounded me.

FOX: You shouldn't have gone near his tent.

454

BEAVER: You don't deserve to stay in the forest with us.

ANATOU: But the wound hurt. *(Softly)* And then ... I saw his face. I remembered. I remembered everything before then!

WOOD GOD: That wound will heal, Anatou. But will this new wound heal? Your hatred is more chilling than the ice caves near the sea. It will grow if you don't kill it now, Anatou. It will grow and freeze your heart.

FOX: You are a disgrace to the animals.

BEAVER: Animals kill because they must eat.

FOX: They must survive.

WOOD GOD: It's the law of the forest. But you, Anatou, killed out of hate. Men do that, not the animals!

ANATOU *(with awful realization):* Wood God ... when I saw him, and I saw the tent, and I remembered how they made me leave the village, and the arrow pierced me ... I felt something ... something I had forgotten. I had to get even!

WOOD GOD *(Sternly):* Live in peace with man, Anatou, or leave the forest forever. *(He sweeps off with the animals. Curtain)*

ACT II, SCENE 4

The interior of a snow house. Drums are beating. Three village hunters are assembled in a circle. In the distance there is the piercing cry of a wolf. They shudder.

KIVIOG *(Arises):* We must try again. The wolf must be stopped.

ATATA: Never was a wolf spirit so hungry for men's souls.

VILLAGER 2: Hunter after hunter has gone and not returned. What can we do?

ATATA: Aja! But what good is a bow and arrow?

VILLAGER 2: What good are knives if we live in terror in our own houses?

KIVIOG: The great North is no longer safe. We mustn't let the wolf escape this time. Since Spring, he has not let us alone. At night he always disappears into the forest ... where no Eskimo ever goes.

VILLAGER 2: Even if it does go into the forest, we must find it and put an end to this.

ATATA: But if we go into the forest, we'll be trapped.

KIVIOG: We are trapped in our own homes now!

ALL: Aja! Aja!

ATATA: Never has there been a wolf like this. Its howl makes the fire die and the seal-oil lamp tremble.

VILLAGER 2: We must hunt till we find it.

ATATA: We have lost many good hunters.

VILLAGER 2: They have all failed.

KIVIOG: But we must find it.

TARTO *(Has been sitting there all the time unnoticed by the others.):* I have hunted before. Let me go, Father.

KIVIOG: Tarto! This is a council for our best hunters. Go outside. You should not be here. You're too young.

VILLAGER 2: He is so small that we don't notice him. It's all right, Kiviog.

ATATA: Perhaps he is so small that he could creep upon the wolf and he wouldn't notice him either. *(They all laugh.)*

TARTO: Please, Father. Please, I'm strong.

KIVOG: No. We go too far. You will be tired.

TARTO: I won't. Wait and see.

KIVIOG: The men of Little Whale River are going to the forest, Tarto. It's dangerous.

TARTO: Then I will find the wolf's hiding place.

VILLAGER 2: He is swift, Kiviog. His eyes are sharp. He is as good a hunter as the men. If he wishes, let him come.

(KIVIOG thinks, then nods to TARTO. TARTO beams.)

KIVIOG: We must cover the great North and not stop till the snow is free of the wolf's tracks.

VILLAGERS: Aja! Aja!

VILLAGER 2: We must hunt towards the great plains.

KIVIOG: And hunt towards the forest.

ATATA: And by the caves along the sea.

KIVIOG: We've no time to waste. Harness the dogs!
(Drums increase. Men leave to get dog teams and begin the hunt. Interior fades)

ACT III, SCENE I

The forest. There is snow on the ground and a rock unit has been added left center. There is a group of tangled trees that have been blown down in the winter near right center. Anatou sleepily comes from behind the rock. She sniffs the air casually, then her body tenses.

ANATOU *(Calling with increasing alarm):* Wood God! Wood God! Wood God! I smell danger.
(BEAVER and FOX appear.)

FOX: The hunters are here.

BEAVER: The hunters.

ANATOU: But the Eskimos are afraid of the forest. Why do they come here?

FOX: They hunt the wolf.

BEAVER: They hunt you.

FOX: Anatou.

WOOD GOD *(Entering):* I warned you, Anatou. You have hurt too many of them. They are angry, angry enough to enter the forest and to hunt you out.

457

ANATOU: I'm frightened, Wood God. Please help me.

WOOD GOD: You hate and so you killed. You deliberately disobeyed me after I first sheltered you. I cannot protect you now.

ANATOU: Was I wrong to defend myself, Wood God, to wound when I was wounded?

WOOD GOD: You've been cruel, Anatou, and hate is like a disease spreading through your heart. If you strike an Eskimo, how does the Beaver know that you won't strike him, too, when he sleeps in the night?

ANATOU: No! I'd never do that. You know that, Wood God.

WOOD GOD: How do I know? I only see what you do. That speaks for itself.

ANATOU *(Ashamed):* I won't leave the forest again, Wood God. I have been wrong.'

WOOD GOD *(Angry):* It's too late for that, Anatou. The hunters are here.

FOX: They're coming closer.

BEAVER: Closer.

ANATOU *(Panicked):* Wood God, what should I do?

WOOD GOD *(Harshly):* Replace the hunters you made them lose. Erase the terror you've caused them. Anatou, even the animals have been frightened of you.

ANATOU: But I didn't mean them. They've been good to me. I didn't want to hurt the animals.

WOOD GOD *(Watching her intently):* If you cannot live in peace with man, Anatou, then one day you will have to face his bow and arrow. There is no law of the forest that can protect you from that time.

ANATOU: Wood God, why didn't you warn me? Why didn't you stop me? I have worn a coat of thick hate — so thick it stopped my feeling or seeing anything else.

WOOD GOD: We tried, Anatou, but before you weren't ready to hear our words.

ANATOU: I am now, Wood God. Please, please, animals.

FOX: Hurry, Anatou. They are closer.

ANATOU: What should I do?

WOOD GOD: Run, Anatou. There is no time. If the hunters find you.

ANATOU: I know.

WOOD GOD: But remember this if you are truly sorry, if you know what understanding means, if you can show me your heart is empty of all its dark hate and cruelty, no matter what happens, your spirit will not die. It will live forever and teach others. Remember that.

ANATOU: Thank you, Wood God.

WOOD GOD: Now run, Anatou.

ANIMALS: Run, Anatou, run.
(*ANATOU exits across the stage. Village hunters enter. They are frightened. Suddenly a wind comes up.*)

VILLAGER 2: Aja! The wind is alive.

ATATA: Let's leave. No Eskimo should be here.

KIVIOG: No! We have promised our village.

TARTO: We cannot return 'til the wolf is found.

KIVIOG: Look! His tracks are here,

VILLAGER 2: Follow them!

KIVIOG: Sh-h-h-h. Fresh tracks. Quickly, carefully.
(*There is silence as they begin the serious search.*)

ANIMALS (*Whispering*): Hurry, Anatou. Hurry.
(*ANATOU streaks across the stage. They see her.*)

VILLAGER 1: Follow it! Follow it!
(*They rush off left. TARTO, who is behind them, gets trapped in the fallen trees; his bow and arrow fly to the side. TARTO*)

tries to escape, but is caught fast.)

TARTO: I can't get out! *(Trying to free himself)* I'm trapped!
(There is deathly silence around him.) Where did they go?
I can't even hear them. *(Shouting)* Father! Father, come
back. Hurry! *(Sees his bow and arrow, but he can't reach
it. ANATOU runs on right. She stumbles on bow and arrow
and in so doing kicks it to other side. TARTO is terrified.
He whispers horrified.)* The wolf. What'll I do? *(He tries to
struggle out, but he can't. ANATOU comes closer. TARTO is
wearing the charm she gave him. She half turns away.)*

ANATOU: It's Tarto! I've got to help him.
*(ANATOU moves in. TARTO thinks she is going to attack
him. He becomes more and more terrified.)*

TARTO: No! No! Father! Help! Help!
*(He covers his face instinctively, afraid to watch, but then
forces himself to look. She pushes with all her might and
finally the pressure is released and TARTO is out of the trap.
He is amazed and does not understand what happened. As
soon as Tarto is free, Anatou starts to run, but is too late. Just
as she is passing the rock unit, we hear the whiz of an arrow
and ANATOU falls behind the rock unit.)* No! He set me free.
Don't kill him. He set me free.

(KIVIOG, ATATA and VILLAGER 2 rush in.)

KIVIOG: Tarto, what happened?

TARTO: I got trapped over there in the logs ... and then the wolf
... he set me free.

KIVIOG: What?

TARTO: The wolf, Father, the wolf. That's the truth. He pulled
the log away so I could get out. I thought he was going to kill
me.

KIVIOG: Where is your bow and arrow?

TARTO: There! I couldn't reach them. But Father, he saved my
life. He pushed the log away.

460

ATATA: The forest is alive with things we can't understand.

KIVIOG: Where is he now?

TARTO: The arrow hit near the rock ... but ... *(They look. She is not there.)* He's not there. Where did he go?

ATATA: It may be a trick.

VILLAGER 2 *(Advancing cautiously):* Here's a fresh footprint.

ATATA: Watch out. *(They move cautiously.)*

TARTO *(With a cry):* It's ... *(Turns to KIVIOG)* Anatou. It's Anatou, Father. We've hurt her. *(They all stare amazed by the sight of the girl. TARTO kneels down by the rock unit. ANATOU's spirit appears above. This can be done by seeing her through a scrim on a higher level so that she looks the same but paler, as though in a dream)*

ANATOU: Tarto ... don't cry.

TARTO *(To himself):* Anatou. You were my best friend. *(To her)* I didn't mean to hurt you. Do you understand. We didn't mean ... *(He can't say it. TARTO tries to hold back the anguish inside.)*

ANATOU: I do, Tarto, I do. Oh, Wood God, they can't hear me.

TARTO: She could have killed me, Father, but she didn't. She saved my life instead.

VILLAGER 2: Aja. She was brave.

KIVIOG: Braver than all the hunters of Little Whale River. None of us would have done what she did. *(He puts his hand on TARTO's shoulder, but he can't say what he'd like to.)*

VILLAGER 2: But why did she run into the forest?

TARTO: Don't you see? She had no place else to go. We chased her here. *(This is the most painful of all)* Anatou, even I chased you away.

KIVIOG: We would not speak or smile at the different one, remember. Our silence was worse than a hundred harpoons.

TARTO: Will she forgive me, Father?

461

KIVIOG: The spirits of the dead know our hearts, Tarto. You cannot keep a secret from them.

TARTO: But will she forgive me?

KIVIOG: We are all to blame.

TARTO: But I want to know! I have to know! She saved me, Father, and then the hunters shot an arrow when she finished.

KIVIOG: She had a bigger heart than you or I, Tarto, but if she is angry we'll be trapped by the snow and the wind and lose our way. No Eskimo should ever enter the realm of the forest. If she forgives us our way will be safe.
(They prepare to leave.)

ANATOU: Wood God! Please let me help them.

WOOD GOD *(Pleased):* 'Til the end of the forest and then I will guide them.

ANATOU: Do they understand, Wood God? How will they remember?

WOOD GOD: Tarto will tell your story tonight, the first time, and they will tell it for many nights. They will remember, for someone will always tell the story of Anatou, the Fair One.

VILLAGER *(Goes over slowly and picks up the arrow, holds it thoughtfully.):* I shot it! I killed her!

KIVIOG: No, we all killed her. But when? Today or long ago?

END

STEP ON A CRACK

by
Suzan Zeder

On August 13, 1978, the Poncho Theatre of Seattle (out of which the Seattle Children's Theatre later grew) performed *Step on a Crack* at the national conference of the American Theatre Association in New Orleans, Louisiana. The audience for this production, consisting of theatre artists and educators from around the country, gave the production an enthusiastic standing ovation; and, over the subsequent days of the conference, the play generated significant conversation among those who attended. This well-received production introduced Suzan Zeder's work to a national audience; and this play, as well as other plays by Zeder (particularly *Wiley and the Hairy Man*), became among the most popular plays presented throughout the next decades.

In *Step on a Crack* Zeder dramatizes the story of Ellie, a lifelike character struggling with problems typical of a ten-year-old girl. The action of the play revolves not around external, melodramatic conflicts, but rather around the touching and humorous insecurities of the young protagonist. With realism, touches of fantasy, and theatrical sophistication, Zeder offered audiences of the time a vision of a "real" child on the stage, situated within a "real" world. This stood in marked contrast to the romanticized and stereotypical characterizations typical of children's theatre throughout the previous decades; and producers of the time eagerly embraced this play both for its theatrical substance and the way in which it offered an open and honest conversation with young audiences.

Step on a Crack begins with Ellie chanting a variation of a well-known children's rhyme:

Step on a crack . . . break your mother's back.

Step on a crack . . . break your mother's back.

Step on a crack . . . break your *stepmother's* back.

The rhyme both introduces the conflict of the play and sets the stage for the playful spirit that characterizes the world of the play. According to Voice (Ellie's alter ego), "Ellie Murphy used to be a perfectly good little girl"—that is until her life changed when her widowed father remarried, and a stepmother entered Ellie's life. Because Ellie sees Lucille, her new stepmother, as a threat to her own relationship with her father, she refuses to accommodate this change and retreats into a comfortable fantasy world, peopled by two imaginary friends: Lana (an aspiring movie actress) and Frizbee, a clown-like mischief maker. Together they play out a series of comical situations that comment on Ellie's real world situation. In one vignette, Ellie sees herself as the abused "Cinderella," and her imaginary friends support her fully in the charade. The climax of this episode comes when Ellie directs her own funeral, "where everybody is real sorry for all of the mean things they ever did to you."

As her stepmother attempts conciliation, and as her father becomes increasingly inept at managing the situation, Ellie tries to run away. When this does not work out, she returns home to discover that she is indeed loved, and she is able to face her problems directly and discard her fantasy life.

As the synopsis suggests, the play rather quickly and easily "solves" a difficult and complex problem, but the light tone of the piece accommodates these obvious plot machinations. Zeder presents a serious idea, one that was (and is) relevant to the many young people struggling with changing family structures. Zeder does not dwell on the sentimental: the fantasy scenes examine the situation with humor, and the many dimensions of Ellie's character (she is alternately loveable and insecure, obnoxious and angry) allow us to see her more as a lifelike girl, complicit in the action, rather than a passive victim of circumstances.

The play shifts rapidly back and forth between the "real" world and Ellie's fantasy world, wherein we see the situations from her perspective. Characters move freely from one world to the other, as even her father and stepmother become a part of Ellie's fantasies. This structure provides a pleasant variety to the typical exposition-complication-denouement form. The messy room, knock-knock jokes, imaginary friends, and dress-up games, add playful childhood resonances to Ellie's characterization that reinforce the truthfulness and the spirit of fun of Ellie's world.

Over twenty-five years after its premier, *Step on a Crack* remains popular with producers and audiences throughout the country. Examined from a contemorary perspective, the play presents narrow and traditional constructions of gender and parenthood, replete with stereotypical dialogue and action. Yet the vibrancy and theatricality of the character, Ellie, supersedes these dated cultural constructions to make the play resonate with today's audiences. At the time of its premiere, *Step on a Crack,* assumed a prominent place in a generation of children's plays that reflected a newfound respect for the intelligence and artistic discrimination of young audiences.

Suzan Zeder is the first holder of an endowed chair in Theatre For Youth/Playwriting at the University of Texas at Austin. Her plays have been performed in all fifty states, Canada, Great Britain, Japan, Australia, Germany, Israel and New Zealand; and they have been published in Great Britain, Germany and Japan. *Step on a Crack, Wiley and the Hairy Man, In A Room Somewhere,* and *The Death and Life of Sherlock Holmes* are regularly performed by professional and university theatres throughout the country. *Doors* and *Mother Hicks* were produced at the Kennedy Center in Washington, D.C., which also co-commissioned *Do Not Go Gentle.* In 1990 Anchorage Press published *Wish in one Hand and Spit in the Other*, an anthology of her nine published plays. *The Taste of Sunrise: Tuc's Story*, premiered at Seattle Children's Theatre in September of 1996. Professor Zeder is the three-time winner of the Distinguished Play Award given by the American Alliance of Theatre and Education. In the spring of 1996, Professor Zeder was inducted into the College of Fellows of the American Theatre in Washington, D.C.

STEP ON A CRACK

by
Suzan Zeder

STEP ON A CRACK is also
available as an individual play script from the publisher
Optional music composed by John Engerman
is also available from the publisher
Anchorage Press Plays, Inc.
ISBN 0-87602-207-7

Licensing for Production
Productions of this play are encouraged, and those who wish to present it may
seek the necessary permission by contacting:
Anchorage Press Plays, Inc, P.O. Box 2901, Louisville, KY 40201-2901, USA,
or via the internet: www.applays.com .
Licensing for production includes gaining clearance for performance, paying
the performance royalty fees, use of authorized play scripts and proper
crediting of the title, author, composer (if a musical), and publisher in printed
materials associated with the production.

FOREWORD

I offer this play to you with a profound respect for the complexity of childhood. As a writer, I have tried to confront the child within myself as honestly as possible in order to bring you a child of this moment. A funny, crazy, wildly imaginative child who arms herself with a full-blown fantasy life to fight her way through real life problems. Ellie's difficulty adjusting to her new stepmother is as classic as Cinderella and as timely as tomorrow.

I have been deeply gratified by audience reaction to this play. I remember one day after a matinee performance a child and a young woman sat quietly together in the empty lobby of the theatre. After a few moments the child turned to the woman and said, "That could have been about us." "Yes," the woman replied, "Do you want to talk about it?" The child thought for a moment and finally said, "Okay. Let's go home!"

Perhaps I might offer a bit of advice to potential producers and directors of this play. If a child actress with sufficient maturity, skill, and depth can be found, by all means cast her. But do not let this be a limitation. I have seen this play work equally well with a young adult in this role. Perhaps you might consider a college student with a bit of training behind her. I have even seen an impressive performance by a high school student.

If an adult actress is used I would urge her to spend some time with children; to notice how they move; to listen to the patterns of their laughter; to watch them closely in the whirlwind of temper tantrums, in joyous flights of fantasy, and in quiet moments of frustration and despair. All of these things are part of Ellie. It is my sincere wish that Ellie be played as a real child and not as an adult comment on childhood.

Above all, please have fun with this script... I have!

— *Suzan Zeder*

STEP ON A CRACK

Characters

ELLIE MURPHY: A ten year old girl.

MAX MURPHY:
Her father, about thirty-seven.

LUCILLE MURPHY:
Her stepmother, about thirty-five.

LANA: Ellie's imaginary friend.

FRIZBEE: An imaginary friend.

VOICE: Ellie's alter-ego.

Setting

THE PRESENT.

ELLIE'S HOUSE, A BOWLING ALLEY,

THE STREETS

The premiere production of STEP ON A CRACK, was presented on March 14, 1974, at Southern Methodist University, Dallas, Texas, with the following cast:

ELLIE...Martha LaFollette

LUCILLE ....Mary Jo Lutticken

MAX ....Ron DeLucia

LANA...Jackie Ezzell

FRISBEE..John Rainone

VOICE..Jennifer Glenn

The production was directed by Susan Pearson.

Set Design by ....John Tillotson

Costume Design by... Nina Vail

Faculty Advisor..Charley Helfert

The main playing space consists of two areas: Ellie's bedroom and a living room. A free standing door separates the two areas. The set should be little more than a brightly colored framework. Each space has a ladder which is hung with the various costumes and props used throughout the play.

Ellie's room is the larger of the two spaces. It is outlandishly decorated with old pieces of junk, flags, banners, old clothes etc. which have been rescued by Ellie from her father's junk yard. The room is a mess, strewn with piles of clothes and junk. Up center is a larger box marked TOYZ. At the far side of the room there is a stool surrounded by a simple frame. This frame indicates a mirror. This is Voice's area. Voice never moves from this spot until the very end of the play. It would be helpful to have a microphone and P.A. speaker system here. Voice will make all of the sound effects during the play.

The living room, Max and Lucille's space, is conspicuously neat. A coffee table and a few chairs indicate this area.

At Rise: Ellie, Max, Lucille, and Voice are onstage. Max holds one end of a jumprope, the other end is tied to the set. Voice sits on the stool. LUCILLE sits in the living room area. Ellie jumps as Max turns the rope for her. She jumps for a few seconds to establish a rhythm.

MAX: Cinderella ... Dressed in yeller ... Went downtown to meet her feller. Cinderella ... Dressed in yeller ... Went downtown to meet her feller. *(MAX continues to chant and ELLIE to jump as LUCILLE speaks.)*

LUCILLE: Grace, Grace ... dressed in lace ... Went upstairs to wash her face. Grace, Grace ... Dressed in lace ... Went upstairs to wash her face.

VOICE: *(Joins in)* Step on a Crack ... Break your mother's back. Step on a crack ... Break your mother's back. Step on a Crack ... Break your mother's back!
(ELLIE jumps out of the rope and hops four times firmly.)

ELLIE: CRACK! CRACK! CRACK! CRACK! Step on a crack, break your STEPMOTHER's back!

VOICE: Red Light! *(All freeze.)* Ellie Murphy used to be a perfectly good little girl. Green Light! *(All come to life for a second. MAX and ELLIE take a few steps toward each other.)* Red Light! *(All freeze.)* Her mom died when Ellie was just four years old, and everybody felt so sorry for her. They said "Oh you poor little girl." And they brought her extra helpings of cake and lots of presents. Ellie lived with her Pop, Max Murphy, boss of Murphy's Wrecking and Salvage Company. Green Light!
(During the next few lines MAX and ELLIE play a game.)

ELLIE: Not it!

MAX: Knock, knock ...

ELLIE: Who's there?

MAX: Banana.

ELLIE: Banana who?

MAX: Knock, knock ...

ELLIE: Who's there?

MAX: Banana.

ELLIE: Banana who?

MAX: Knock, knock ...

ELLIE: Who's there?

MAX: Orange.

ELLIE: Orange who?

MAX: Orange you glad I didn't say banana?

VOICE: Red Light! *(All freeze.)* They played tag and went bowling; they ate T.V. dinners and practiced baseball for six years and they were very happy. Green Light!
(ELLIE and MAX mime practicing baseball.)

MAX: Listen Midget, if I told you once I told you a million times, you gotta keep your eye on the ball. *(He throws an*

473

imaginary baseball; ELLIE hits it and MAX follows the ball with his eyes and sees LUCILLE.)

MAX: Fantastic!

VOICE: Red Light! *(All freeze.)* About two months ago Ellie went to camp and Pop met a pretty lady who taught music. Green Light!
(ELLIE and MAX hug goodbye. ELLIE moves up her ladder and scratches her bottom, she mimes writing.)

ELLIE: Dear Pop, Today we went camping in the woods and guess where I got poison ivy?
(MAX moves over to LUCILLE.)

MAX: *(shyly)* Hi, my name is Max, Max Murphy.

LUCILLE: Pleased to meet you Max, I'm Lucille.

VOICE: Red Light!
(All freeze.)

VOICE: And Pop liked Lucille and Lucille liked Pop. Green Light!
(ELLIE puts a blindfold over her eyes.)

ELLIE: Dear Pop, I can't go swimming today cause I got pink eye.

VOICE: Ellie came back from camp and everything in her whole life was different.
(ELLIE, MAX, and LUCILLE play blind man's bluff.)

ELLIE: 5, 4, 3, 2, 1 ... Ready or not here I come.

MAX: We're over here.

ELLIE: Where? Am I getting warmer?

MAX: Naw, you're a mile off.

ELLIE: Am I getting warmer?

VOICE: Red Light! *(All freeze.)* Pop and Lucille got married. Green Light!
(MAX and LUCILLE move into wedding positions. They mime an exchange of rings and kiss.)

ELLIE: I said am I getting warmer? Hey Pop where did you ...

(ELLIE takes off the blindfold and sees them kissing. She claps her hand over her eyes and giggles.)

VOICE: Red Light! *(All freeze.)* Everything was different. Lucille cooked well balanced meals with vegetables. She kept the house neat and sewed buttons on all Ellie's clothing. Pop liked Lucille a lot, he wanted Ellie to like her too but somewhere deep inside Ellie's head this little voice kept saying ... Look how pretty she is ...

ELLIE: Look how pretty she is.

VOICE: Look how neat she is ...

ELLIE: Look how neat she is.

VOICE: Pop likes her much better than he likes you.

ELLIE: No!

VOICE: Oh yes he does! *(ELLIE turns away.)* Ellie Murphy used to be a perfectly good little girl. Green Light!

(MAX exits. ELLIE moves into her room and picks up a Whammo paddleball. LUCILLE moves into the living room area and sets up a music stand and practices singing scales. She has a beautiful voice.)

ELLIE: *(Hitting the paddle-ball)* 235, 236, 237, 238, 239, 240, 241, 242, 243, 244, 245, 246 ... *(ELLIE misses, sighs, and starts again.)* 1,2,3,4,5,6,7,8,9,10,11,12,13,14 *(and starts again. ELLIE misses, sighs.)* 1, 2, 3, 4, 5, 6, 7, 8, 9, 10, 11 ... *(ELLIE misses.)* I'll never make 300! 1, 2, 3, 4, 5, 6 ... *(ELLIE misses. She crosses to the mirror. VOICE mimes her gestures.)* If I could make 300 I'd be famous. I'd be the world's champion. I'd be rich and famous and everyone in the whole world would come up to me and ... How de do? Yes, it was very difficult, but I just kept practicing and practicing. No, it wasn't easy.
(LUCILLE sings louder.)

VOICE: Considering all the racket SHE was making.

ELLIE: Considering all the racket SHE was making.

VOICE: How could anyone expect to concentrate with all that toot toot de doot?

ELLIE: How could anyone expect to concentrate with all that toot toot de doot.

VOICE: What does she think this is Grand Opree or something?

(ELLIE clutches her throat and mimics LUCILLE, she warbles off-key.)

ELLIE: Laaaaa ... Laaaaaaa, Laaaaaaa, Laaaaaaa

(LUCILLE hears her and stops.)

LUCILLE: Ellinor? Did you call me?

ELLIE: No.

(LUCILLE resumes the scales. ELLIE gets an idea. She crosses to the toy box and pulls out a weird assortment of junk; a couple of old hats, a black cloak, a deflated inner tube, silver shoes, and a set of Dracula fangs. ELLIE dresses herself and makes a couple of menacing passes at the mirror. VOICE mimics her action. ELLIE sneaks out of the room and up behind LUCILLE.)

ELLIE: I am Count Dracula and I have come to suck your blood!

LUCILLE: *(Startled)* Oh my!

ELLIE: Did I scare you?

LUCILLE: You startled me.

ELLIE: What are you doing anyway?

LUCILLE: I am just running through a few scales.

ELLIE: Do you have to?

LUCILLE: Well, yes. The voice is just like any other instrument, you have to practice every day.

ELLIE: You call that MUSIC? All that toot toot de doot?

LUCILLE: Well, scales aren't exactly music but ...

ELLIE: *(Singing very off-key)* "Everybody was Kung Fu

Fighting." Uh. ..uh ... uh ... uh ... hu!**

LUCILLE: Well, ummm that's very nice but ...

ELLIE: *(Lying on her back with feet in the air.)* "I've got tears in my ears from lying on my back crying out my eyes over you."**

LUCILLE: Ellinor, what in the world are you wearing?

ELLIE: Pretty neat huh? I got this stuff from Pop, it's from the yard. He said I could keep it. You should go down there, he's got some great stuff.

LUCILLE: Oh Ellinor, you have such a nice room and so many lovely toys. Why do you keep bringing home all this junk?

ELLIE: This isn't junk! It's perfectly good stuff!

LUCILLE: But people have thrown it away.

ELLIE: That doesn't mean it isn't any good! How would you like to be thrown away?

LUCILLE: When I was your age I had a collection of dolls from all over the world. I used to make clothes for them and make up stories about them. You know I still have those dolls. I gave them to my brother for his children, maybe I could write to him and we could ...

ELLIE: Dolls! Ugghhh! I like this stuff better. Besides most of it isn't mine. Most of this belongs to Lana and Frizbee.

LUCILLE: Oh?

ELLIE: This tire is for Frizbee's motorcycle and these hats and beautiful shoes are for Lana. She's a movie star and she needs these things in her work.

LUCILLE: I thought you told me she was a Roller Derby Queen.

ELLIE: She's both! Oh, the Dracula fangs ... they're mine.

LUCILLE: Just put them away when you are through. Have you finished cleaning up your room yet?

* * These songs should be constantly changed to songs that are currently popular.

ELLIE: Ohhh I have been busy.

LUCILLE: You promised to do it before your father came home.

ELLIE: Pop doesn't care. He never used to make me clean up my room.

LUCILLE: Look, why don't I give you a hand. Together we can do it in no time.

ELLIE: No way! You'll just make me throw stuff out.
(ELLIE walks back to her room and stands in her doorway.)

ELLIE: Nobody gets in my room without a pass!
(She slams the door. LUCILLE sighs and turns back to her music.)

VOICE: Red Light! *(All freeze.)*

VOICE: She doesn't like you.
(ELLIE is drawn to the mirror.)

ELLIE and VOICE: Pick up your room you messy little girl. Why don't you play with dolls like normal children? You're freaky and you like junk. You could have such a lovely room if it wasn't such a mess.

VOICE: She could never like a messy little girl like you. Green Light!
(LUCILLE resumes her scales. ELLIE listens for a second and begins to mimic her. ELLIE leaps to the top of the toy box and warbles in a high squeaky voice. FRISBEE pops up from under a pile of dirty clothes.)

FRIZBEE: Bravo! Bravo! What a beautiful voice you have! You sing like an angel! You sing like a bird, only better. I kiss your hand. May I have your autograph?

ELLIE: Why certainly young man! *(ELLIE scribbles on his back)* "To Frizbee from Ellie, the world's greatest opera singer."

FRIZBEE: I will treasure this forever. Here this is for you!
(FRIZBEE pulls a flower from nowhere and presents it to ELLIE .)

LANA: *(Her voice comes from the toy box.)* Everybody out of my way.

(*ELLIE jumps off the box, the lid flies open and LANA pops out.*)

LANA: Ellie Murphy, the great opera singer, do you have anything to say to our viewers at home?

ELLIE: How de do.

LANA: How did you get to be such a great opera singer?

ELLIE: Oh it was very difficult. The voice is just like any other instrument you have to practice every day.

(*FRIZBEE presents her with a bowling pin.*)

FRIZBEE: Ellie Murphy I am pleased and proud to present you with this singer of the year award.

ELLIE: Dear friends, I thank you and I have only one thing to say, I deserved it. I practiced every day ...

(*LUCILLE starts to sing a beautiful melody. ELLIE moves toward the mirror.*)

ELLIE: I practiced until my throat was sore from singing and ...

VOICE: Red Light! (*All freeze.*)

VOICE: You'll never be as good as Lucille.
(*VOICE snatches the pin away from her.*)

VOICE: She's a much better singer than you are. Green Light!

ELLIE: (*Grabs for the pin*) This is MY prize and I deserve it!
(*They struggle with the pin*)

ELLIE: (*To LANA and FRIZBEE.*) Hey you guys!
(*They rush to her aid. The pin is tossed in the air and FRIZBEE catches it.*)

FRIZBEE: Ellie Murphy I am pleased and proud to present you with this singer of the year award.

ELLIE: Thank you for my prize. It is neat!
(*There is the sound of thunderous applause. LUCILLE crosses to ELLIE's door and knocks. The applause stops instantly.*)

479

LUCILLE: Ellinor?
(LANA and FRIZBEE freeze.)

ELLIE: Who goes there?

LUCILLE: May I come in?

ELLIE: What's the password?

LUCILLE: Please?

ELLIE: *(Peeking out)* Have you got a pass?
(LUCILLE enters and looks around.)

LUCILLE: Who were you talking to?

ELLIE: Lana and Frizbee.

LUCILLE: *(Playing along)* OH! Are they still here?
(FRIZBEE pops his head up and makes a rude sound, then disappears into the box.)

ELLIE: Sure, Frizbee just did a raspberry.

LUCILLE: Oh?
(LANA crosses in front of LUCILLE making ugly faces at her.)

ELLIE: And Lana's making faces ... like this and this and this ...
(LANA goes into the toy box. LUCILLE crosses to the middle of the room crouches down and speaks into empty air.)

LUCILLE: Were you two helping Ellie clean up her room?

ELLIE: Lucille, they're not here. They went into the toy box.

LUCILLE: *(Playing along a bit too much)* Oh I see. Do they live in the toy box?

ELLIE: *(Nonplussed)* It's too small to live in there. They just sit there sometimes.

LUCILLE: Oh. Please Ellie, let me help you. We'll have this place cleaned up in no time. Now where does this go?

ELLIE: No deal! You throw out too much!
(ELLIE starts putting things away.)

LUCILLE: Oh, Ellinor, you've lost another button. I just sewed that one on too.

ELLIE: It's a scientific fact that some people are allergic to buttons. *(ELLIE looks hard at LUCILLE.)* Hey, Lucille, how old are you?

LUCILLE: *(A bit taken aback)* Uhhh, well, I'm thirty-five.

ELLIE: *(Very serious)* Boy that's old.

LUCILLE: Well, it's not that old.

ELLIE: Do you use a lot of make-up?

LUCILLE: I use some.

ELLIE: A lot? Do you put that goopy stuff on your eyes to make them look big?

LUCILLE: Would you like me to show you about make-up?

ELLIE: Uhhhgg. NO! Make-up is for girlies and OLD people.

LUCILLE: Come on Ellinor, let's get this room done before your father gets home.

(MAX enters with a football helmet and a feather duster for ELLIE.)

MAX: Anybody home?

ELLIE: Too late!

(ELLIE runs to greet him and jumps into his arms. He gives her the helmet and duster, as LUCILLE enters ELLIE hides them behind her back and sneaks them into her room.)

MAX: Hey Midget.

ELLIE: Neato. Thanks.
(LUCILLE approaches to hug him.)

LUCILLE : Hello dear, you're early.

MAX: Be careful, I'm a mess. I gotta wash up.
(LUCILLE gets him a rag. He wipes his hands and then kisses her. He sits down to take off his boots. ELLIE enters with his house shoes.)

MAX: Hey Ellie, what's the matter with your shirt?

481

(MAX points to an imaginary spot on her shirt. ELLIE looks down and MAX tweaks her nose.)

MAX: Ha! Hah! Gotcha! Can't have your nose back. Not till you answer three knock knocks ... Let's see ... Knock, knock ...

ELLIE: *(With her nose still held.)* Who's there?

MAX: Dwain.

ELLIE: Dwain who?

MAX: Dwain the bathtub I'm dwouning.

ELLIE: Hey, I got one. Knock, knock.

MAX: Who's there?

ELLIE: DeGaulle.

MAX: Degaulle who?

ELLIE: *(Crossing her eyes)* De-gaulle-f ball hit me in the head and dats why I talk dis way.

MAX: Ohhhh.

ELLIE: Oh I got another one Pop. Knock, knock ...

LUCILLE: *(Jumping in)* Who's there?

(ELLIE shoots her a nasty look and turns away.)

ELLIE: Nobody.

LUCILLE: *(Puzzled)* Nobody who?

ELLIE: *(Insolently)* Just nobody that's all!
(MAX and LUCILLE exchange a look.)

MAX: I've still got your nose.

ELLIE: *(Back in the game)* Give it back you Bozo.

MAX: Nope you gotta get it.
(MAX pretends to hold her nose just out of reach. ELLIE jumps for it. MAX tosses it to LUCILLE.)

MAX: Here Lucille, catch!
(LUCILLE, confused, misses it.)

LUCILLE: Huh? Oh I'm sorry.

(The game is over and ELLIE scowls.)

ELLIE: Pop, do I have to clean up my room? Can I get you a beer? Can I watch T.V.? Do I have to throw out all my good stuff?

MAX: Whoa! What's going on?

ELLIE: Can I watch T.V.?

MAX: Sure.

LUCILLE: Max, I have been trying to get her to clean up her room for days.

MAX: Awww it's Friday afternoon.

LUCILLE: Max.

MAX: Clean up your room Ellie.

ELLIE: Awww Pop, you never used to make me.

MAX: Sorry Midget. This ship's got a new captain.

ELLIE: Awww Pop!

MAX: Do what your mother says.

ELLIE: *(Under her breath)* She is not my real mother.

MAX: What did you say?

ELLIE: Nothing.

MAX: Hey, maybe later we'll do something fun.

ELLIE: Can we go bowling?

MAX: Maybe.

ELLIE: Oh please, oh please, oh please! We used to go all the time. Pop and me, we were practically professional bowlers. We were practicing to go on Family Bowl-O-Rama, on T.V.

MAX: Clean up your room and we'll talk about bowling later. *(ELLIE trudges into her room. MAX sits down and LUCILLE massages his back.)*

LUCILLE: You're early.

MAX: Yep, and I have a surprise for you.

LUCILLE: For me, Max? What is it?

MAX: You gotta guess. It's something we've been talking about. *(ELLIE interrupts. She is wearing a long black cape, a tall hat and a scarf. She holds a piece of metal pipe.)*

ELLIE: Ta Dah! Presenting the Great Mysterioso! You will see that I have nothing up my sleeve. See this pipe? See this scarf? Here hold this hat lady. *(ELLIE hands the hat to LUCILLE.)* Now I take this scarf, just an ordinary everyday magic scarf, and I put it over this piece of pipe. Now you both will blow on it.
(MAX and LUCILLE blow on the scarf.)

ELLIE: I say some magic words. OOOOOBLEEEDOOOO OBBBBBLEEEDAY ZOOOOOBLEEDA! Zap! Zap! Zap! *(ELLIE flips the pipe over her shoulder, it lands with a loud crash. She grabs the hat and places the scarf in it.)* Presto! No more pipe! Ta Dah!
(ELLIE displays the empty scarf. MAX and LUCILLE clap.)

MAX: I thought you went to ...

ELLIE: I found this stuff while I was cleaning. Pretty neat huh?

LUCILLE: That was very nice Ellie.

MAX: Ellie, Lucille and I are talking.

ELLIE : What about?

MAX: ELLIE!

ELLIE: I'm going. I'm going.
(ELLIE goes back to her room. MAX takes some folders out of his pocket.)

MAX: Do you remember that travel agent I said I was going to talk to?

LUCILLE: Oh Max, do you mean you did it?

MAX: Did I talk to him? Ta Dah! Little lady, you and I are going on a honeymoon. We are going to Hawaii.

LUCILLE: Hawaii? Oh Max!

484

MAX: Just look at this, "American Express twenty-one day excursion to Honolulu and the islands." That's our honeymoon, that is if you want to go.

LUCILLE: Want to? I have always wanted to go to those places. But can we? I mean should we? Right now?

MAX: Why not? I've been saving for a trip and I think I can take about three weeks off. Now's as good a time as ever.

LUCILLE: I'm not sure we ought to leave Ellie right now.

MAX: She'll be fine. I can get someone to stay with her and after all she's in school. There is this lady, Mrs. Dougan, she used to stay with Ellie when I'd go on hunting trips. I'll call her tomorrow.

LUCILLE: I just don't want her to think that we are running off and leaving her.

MAX: Don't worry, I'll talk to her.

LUCILLE: Right away ... that is if you are serious.

MAX: You bet I'm serious. I got all this stuff didn't I? Look at some of these tour deals. You get everything: air fare, meals, hotel, an air conditioned bus ...

LUCILLE: Oh look at that sun, and all that sand. What a beautiful beach.
(ELLIE enters clutching T.V. Guide.)

ELLIE: Guess what! Midnight Spook-a-thon has a double feature tonight! *The Curse of Frankenstein* and the *Return of the Mummy's Hand!* Isn't that neat? Can I watch it Pop?

MAX: *(Hiding the folders)* Uhhh Sure, why not.

LUCILLE: What time does it come on?

ELLIE: *(Nonchalantly)* Oh early.

LUCILLE: What time?

ELLIE: *(Quickly)* Eleven-thirty.

LUCILLE: That's awfully late.

ELLIE: Tomorrow's Saturday. And besides Pop said I could.

LUCILLE: We'll see.

ELLIE: You always say that when you mean no. What are you guys doing?

MAX: We're talking.

ELLIE: *(Seeing the folders)* What's this?
(LUCILLE starts to show them to her and MAX snatches them away.)

MAX: Papers, papers of mine. Ellie is your room cleaned up yet?

ELLIE: No! Gee whiz! I'm going. I'm going!
(ELLIE crosses back to her room.)

LUCILLE: Max, why didn't you talk to her?

MAX: Oh I don't know, I just hate it when she yells.

LUCILLE: Yells? I thought you said it was going to be alright.

MAX: It is! I just have to kind of talk to her about it ... when she's in a good mood.

LUCILLE: If you really think it is going to upset her, let's not do it now. We can always go later.

MAX: I said I was going to talk to her and I will ...
(MAX crosses to ELLIE's room. LUCILLE follows slightly behind.)

MAX: Ellie ... uhhh

ELLIE: I'm not finished yet but I'm cleaning!

MAX: Looks like you are doing a good job here. Want any help?

ELLIE: Huh?
(ELLIE finds the duster and dusts everything and then starts dusting MAX.)

MAX: Ellie, umm Lucille and I ... uhhh we were thinking that it might be a good idea if ... if ... we went ... bowling! Tonight!

ELLIE: Hey, neato!

MAX: After you clean up your room.

ELLIE: I'll hurry. I'll hurry.

(MAX leaves the room with LUCILLE shaking her head.)

LUCILLE: Why didn't you tell her?

MAX: Let's wait until we know exactly when we're going.

LUCILLE: I don't want her to think that we are sneaking around behind her back.

MAX: I'll tell her. I just want to pick my own time.
(ELLIE starts out the door.)

VOICE: Red Light! *(ELLIE freezes.)*

VOICE: Something fishy's going on. They don't want you around. They're trying to get rid of you ... Green Light.
(ELLIE stares into the mirror.)

MAX: So that's your surprise. How do you like it?

LUCILLE: Oh Max!
(LUCILLE hugs him. ELLIE enters.)

ELLIE: Ahem!

MAX: What do you want?

ELLIE: I just came to get a shovel.

LUCILLE: What do you need a shovel for?

ELLIE: I'm cleaning! I'm cleaning!
(MAX turns her around and marches her back into the room.)

LUCILLE: Please Max! *(They all enter the room.)*

MAX: Ellie, I want to talk to you ..... *(ELLIE shines his shoes.)*
ELLIE! *(ELLIE looks up at him and gives him a goofy look.)*
I just want to tell you .... I tell you what! If you clean up your room right now then we'll all go get ice cream or something!

LUCILLE: *(Exasperated)* I have to stop at the market anyway.
I'll go make a list.
(LUCILLE exits.)

MAX: And now once and for all ... listen here tough guy ... you is gonna clean up that room. Okay?

ELLIE: *(Tough guy.)* Oh Yeah? Who is gonna make me?

487

MAX: I am Louie, cause I am da tough cop in dis town. Now you is gonna get in dat cell and you is gonna clean it up, or else I is gonna throw you in solitary ... see? *(They tussle for a moment, MAX pulls her cap over her eyes.)* An I don't want to see you outta there till you is done.
(MAX shuts the door and exits.)

ELLIE: Darn! Lately this place is really getting like a prison.

VOICE: Red Light! She keeps you locked up like some kind of prisoner.

ELLIE: Yeah! A prison with walls and bars and chains. A dungeon with cold stones and bread and water and rats. Solitary confinement ... The walls are closing in. You gotta let me out ... You gotta let me out ...

VOICE: Green Light!
(Suddenly the toy lid flips open and a shovel full of dirt comes flying out. A shovel appears and on the other end of the shovel is LANA.)

LANA: Hi yah, Sweetie!

ELLIE: Lana!

LANA: Who else? You think we wuz gonna let you take a bum rap? We dug this tunnel t'bust you outta here.

ELLIE: We?

LANA: Frizbee and me! Right Frizbee? Frizbee? He was right behind me in the tunnel. He must be here someplace. *(They look for FRIZBEE. LANA looks in the toy chest and slams the lid.)*

LANA: Oh no!

ELLIE: What?

LANA: Don't look!

ELLIE: Why not?

LANA: Cave in! The tunnel's caved in.

ELLIE: Oh NO!

LANA: The whole thing ... Squash!

ELLIE: Poor Frizbee!

LANA: What are we gonna do?

ELLIE: There is only one thing we can do!

LANA: Yeah?

ELLIE: Blast!

LANA: Blast Boss?

ELLIE: It's the only way. You get the dynamite and I'll get the fuse. (*They gather together junk to make a blasting box, fuse and plunger.*) First you gotta make the box. Then you gotta put the dynamite in and then stick your fingers in your ears, and count down 10,9,8,7,6,5,4,3,2, ...1 BARRROOOOOOOM. (*VOICE makes the sound of the explosion. The lid flies open, a puff of smoke comes out. FRIZBEE's arms and legs hang out of the box.*)

FRIZBEE: (Weakly) Hey you guys ...
(*LANA and ELLIE rush to FRIZBEE and lift him out of the toy chest.*)

LANA: Are you alright?

FRIZBEE: Sure.

ELLIE: The tunnel collapsed on you.

FRIZBEE: I thought it got dark all of a sudden.

ELLIE: Okay. Youse guys we gotta blow this joint.
(*FRIZBEE pulls a handkerchief out of costume and blows his nose, as he pulls another handkerchief comes out and a whole string of handkerchiefs follow to FRIZBEE'S amazement.*)

ELLIE: Great idea Frizbee. Here Lana you take one end and go first, I'll hold this, and Frizbee, you bring up the rear. Goodbye cruel cell. (*LANA and ELLIE dive into the box.*)

FRIZBEE: Goodbye cruel ceeeeeeee...
(*FRIZBEE is pulled in after them. LUCILLE enters wearing*

489

a police hat and badge.)

LUCILLE: Calling all cars. Calling all cars. This is the warden speaking! Ellie-the-mess-Murphy has just escaped from solitary confinement. She is messy and extremely dangerous. After her? After her!
(There is a chase. LANA and ELLIE crawl under the bed, and around the stage. LUCILLE crouches behind the bed.)

LANA: We made it!

ELLIE: Free at last.

LANA: Wow that was close. *(LUCILLE appears.)*

LUCILLE: Have you cleaned up your room yet?

ELLIE and LANA: EEEK!

(There is a short chase. LUCILLE lassos ELLIE and LANA with the scarfs and drags them over to one side of the stage where she crouches down and voice makes the sound of a car. LUCILLE mimes driving the paddy wagon. FRIZBEE finally makes it out of the tunnel, sees what's going on, disappears for a second and reappears wearing the football helmet. VOICE makes the sound of a siren. FRIZBEE mimes riding a motorcycle. LUCILLE puts on the brakes. FRIZBEE gets off the motorcycle, pulls an imaginary pad out of his pocket, licks an imaginary pencil.)

FRIZBEE: Okay girlie, where's the fire?

LUCILLE: I'm sorry officer, I ... just wanted her to clean up her...

FRIZBEE: Let me see your license. I'm gonna give you a ticket.

LUCILLE: But officer I ...

FRIZBEE: But first I'm gonna give you a ... tickle.
(FRIZBEE tickles LUCILLE, she laughs helplessly, LANA and ELLIE escape.)

LUCILLE: You can't do that!

FRIZBEE: Oh yeah? I just did!

ELLIE: To the hideout!

490

(LUCILLE chases them off. ELLIE, LANA and FRIZBEE race back to ELLIE's room. They overturn the benches to make a barricade. ELLIE rifles through the toy chest throwing junk everywhere. They put on guns and helmets.)

ELLIE: Get the ammo and take cover.

VOICE: Come out with your hands up.

ELLIE: Let 'em have it.

(Imaginary battle takes place. They throw things all over the room. FRIZBEE uses a toilet paper roll like a grenade. ELLIE clutches a grease gun like a tommy gun. All make sounds. LUCILLE enters dressed in regular street clothes. She is not part of the fantasy.)

LUCILLE: *(Approaching the door)* Ellinor, are you ready?

ELLIE: You'll never take us copper!
(LUCILLE opens the door. All sound effects stop. LANA and FRIZBEE freeze. The room is totally destroyed. ELLIE pretends to be oiling the bed.)

LUCILLE: *(Dumbfounded)* Ellinor.

ELLIE: I ... I ... I ... uh, was just cleaning my room.

LUCILLE: Ellinor.

ELLIE: I didn't do it. Lana threw the grenade.

LANA: I did not!

LUCILLE: I certainly hope you don't mean to tell me that Lana and Frizbee made all this mess.

ELLIE: What are you hoping I'll tell you?

LUCILLE: Oh Ellinor.

ELLIE: They made most of it.

FRIZBEE: We did not!

LUCILLE: Are they supposed to be here now?

ELLIE: *(Gesturing with grease gun)* They're right over ...

LUCILLE: Ellinor, that's a grease gun ..... don't .....

491

(ELLIE squeezes a glob of grease on the floor.)

VOICE: Glop!

ELLIE: Uh oh!

LUCILLE: The carpet! A brand new carpet! Grease is the worst possible stain. Oh my lord.

ELLIE: I thought it was empty.

LUCILLE: Now which is it, hot water or cold? ... Oh my lord.

(LUCILLE rushes off to get a rag.)

LANA: Uhhhh so long Boss.

FRIZBEE: Be seeing you around.

ELLIE: Where are you going?

LANA: I just remembered something I gotta do.

FRIZBEE: Yeah and I gotta do it with her ... Whatever it is .....
(They exit into the box. LUCILLE enters and rubs frantically at the spot.)

LUCILLE: It just gets worse and worse ... It's ruined. A brand new carpet.

ELLIE: Well, I'm your brand new kid.

LUCILLE: Ellinor I knew something like this would happen. This is the last time you bring junk into your room. Oh it just gets bigger and bigger.

(MAX enters, and rushes to help.)

MAX: What in the world .....

LUCILLE: Oh Max, Ellinor spilled grease on the carpet.

ELLIE: I didn't mean to.

LUCILLE: The more I rub the worse it gets.

ELLIE: It's not my fault.

MAX: Did you try cold water?

LUCILLE: No, it's hot water for grease.

ELLIE: Hey listen, I don't mind that spot.

MAX: No, I'm sure it's cold water.

ELLIE: Honest, I like that spot just the way it is.

LUCILLE: Max, it's hot water for grease and cold water for blood stains and ink.

MAX: I've got this stuff in my car.

LUCILLE: Oh it's no use!

ELLIE: *(Shouting)* Would you leave it alone! I like that spot. *(They both stop and stare at her.)* This is MY room.

LUCILLE: But it is a brand new carpet.

ELLIE: BIG DEAL.

MAX: Ellie, don't talk that way to your mother.

ELLIE: She is not my real mother. *(Stiff pause)* *(To LUCILLE)* You'll never be my REAL mother.

LUCILLE: *(Angry but even)* You know, Ellie. You're absolutely right. *(Pause, Covering.)* Well if we are going to the market I better get my coat.
(LUCILLE exits. MAX is angry and very depressed.)

MAX: That was nice ... that was really nice.

ELLIE: It's not my fault.

MAX: You hurt her feelings.

ELLIE: I have feelings too you know. Just because you're a kid doesn't mean you're junk!

MAX: Come off it Ellie.

ELLIE: That spot is almost out.

MAX: *(Really down)* Yeah!

ELLIE: Maybe we could put something over it.

MAX: Yeah.

ELLIE: With a sign that says "Don't look here."

MAX: *(With a slight laugh)* Sure.

493

ELLIE: *(Trying to get him out of his mood.)* Knock, knock.

MAX: Not now, Ellie.

ELLIE: Let's wrestle.

MAX: Uh uh! You're getting too big for me.

ELLIE: Do you think I'm too fat?

MAX: You? Naw you're fine.

ELLIE: Hey Pop, do you remember the time we went camping and you drove all afternoon to get out of the woods? It was dark when we pitched the tent and we heard all those funny sounds and you said it was MONSTERS. Then in the morning we found out we were in somebody's front lawn.

MAX: *(Responding a bit)* I knew where we were all the time.

ELLIE: Or when we went to the Super Bowl and I got cold, and you said yell something in your megaphone.

MAX: Yeah, and you yelled "I'm cold and I want to go home." *(They both laugh.)*

ELLIE: *(Tentatively.)* Hey Pop, tell me about my real mother.

MAX: How come you want to hear about her all the time these days?
(ELLIE sits at his feet and rests against his knees.)

ELLIE: I just do. Hey do you remember the time it was my birthday and you brought Mom home from the hospital, and I didn't know she was coming that time? I remember I was already in bed and you guys wanted to surprise me. She just came into my room, kissed me goodnight and tucked me in, just like it was any other night.

MAX: *(Moved)* How could you remember that? You were just four years old.

ELLIE: I just remember.

MAX: Your mother was a wonderful person and I loved her very much.

ELLIE: As much as you ... like Lucille?

494

MAX: Ellie.

ELLIE: Was she pretty?

MAX: She was beautiful.

ELLIE: Do I look like her?

MAX: Naw, you look more like me, you mug.

ELLIE: *(Suddenly angry)* Why does everything have to change?

MAX: Hey.

ELLIE: How come Lucille is always so neat and everything? I bet she never even burps.

MAX: She does.

ELLIE: HUH!

MAX: I heard her once.

ELLIE: Do you think I'd look cute with make-up on?

MAX: You? You're just a kid.

ELLIE: But Lucille wears make-up. Lot's of it.

MAX: Well she's grown up.

ELLIE: Hey do you know how old she is?

MAX: Sure. Thirty-five.

ELLIE: How come you married such an old one?

MAX: That's not old.

ELLIE: Huh!

MAX: Why I am older than that myself.

ELLIE: You are??

MAX: Ellie, you know how you get to go to camp in the summer. You get to go away all by yourself.

ELLIE: Yeah but I'm not going any more.

MAX: You're not?

ELLIE: Nope, look what happened the last time I went. You and Lucille got to be good friends, then as soon as I get back you get married. Who knows if I go away again I might get back and find out you moved to Alaska.

MAX: We wouldn't do that.

ELLIE: You might.

MAX: Ellie, kids can't always go where parents go. Sometimes parents go away all by themselves.

ELLIE: How come ever since you got married I am such a kid. You never used to say I was a kid. We did everything together. Now all I hear is, "Kids can't do this," "Kids can't do that," "Kids have to go to bed at eight-thirty." "Kids have to clean up their rooms." Why does everything have to change?

MAX: Nothing's changed. I still love you the same. Now there's just two of us who love you.

ELLIE: HUH!

MAX: I just wish you'd try a little harder to .....

ELLIE: To like Lucille? Why should I? She doesn't like me. She likes cute little girls who play with dollies.

MAX: Well she got herself a messy little mug that likes junk. (*ELLIE pulls away.*)

MAX: I'm just kidding. She likes you fine the way you are.

ELLIE: Oh yeah, well I don't like her.

MAX: Why not?

(*LUCILLE enters and overhears the following.*)

ELLIE: Cause ... Cause ... Cause she's a wicked stepmother ..... (*ELLIE giggles in spite of herself. MAX is really angry.*)

MAX: That's not funny!

ELLIE: You shout at me all the time!

MAX: (*Shouting*) I'm not shouting!

LUCILLE: (*Breaking it up*) Is everybody ready to go?

MAX: Ellie get your coat.

ELLIE: I'm not going.

MAX: Get your coat. We are going for ice cream!

ELLIE: *(Pouting)* I don't want any.

MAX: Okay. Lucille let's go. Ellie you can just stay at home and clean up your room.

LUCILLE: Max ...

MAX: I said let's go!

ELLIE: See if I care.

(They leave the room. ELLIE pouts.)

LUCILLE: Was it about the trip?

MAX: What?

LUCILLE: Were you two arguing about the trip?

MAX: Are you kidding. I didn't even get that far.

LUCILLE: Let's just forget it.

MAX: What?

LUCILLE: Forget the whole thing!

MAX: Oh no, I need this trip. We need it; we have got to have some time for US.

LUCILLE: If you want to go, then let's talk to her and we'll go. If not, let's just forget it!

MAX: Let me work this out in my own way.

LUCILLE: Why does everything have to be a game or a joke? Max, it really isn't fair to Ellie or me. Why can't we just talk?

MAX: This isn't easy for her.

LUCILLE: Well, it isn't easy for me either; and frankly, Max, I have just about had it.

MAX: Lucille ...

LUCILLE: If we are ever going to be a family, we've got to be able to talk ...

MAX: Not now! You're angry, she's angry. Let's go to the

market, calm down, and we'll talk when we get home. *(They exit.)*

ELLIE: Hey, wait a minute ... Wait, I changed my mind. I want to go. *(They have gone. ELLIE turns back.)*

VOICE: Red Light! It's all her fault! She didn't want you to go. SHE made it so you couldn't go.
(ELLIE is drawn to the mirror.)

ELLIE and VOICE: Pick up your toys. Make your bed. Do what we say or you won't be fed.

ELLIE: I'll never be pretty. Ugly face, ugly hair and squinty little eyes. If I had my real mother I'd be pretty.

VOICE: You'll never be as pretty as Lucille. Green Light!

ELLIE: They dress me in rags. They make me work all day.

VOICE: Ugly Ellie.

ELLIE: Ugly Ellie, Ugly Ellie ... *(ELLIE sits on the bed and pulls her cap over her face dejectedly.)*

FRIZBEE: *(Inside the toy box)* Cinderelli, Cinderelli Cinderelli, *(Lid to the box opens and out pops FRIZBEE wearing Mickey Mouse ears and singing the Walt Disney song.)*

FRIZBEE: Cinderelli, Cinderelli, Cinderelli, Cinderelli ...

ELLIE: What are you supposed to be?

FRIZBEE: I am just a little Mouse. Who lives inside this great big house. Oh Cinderelli kind and dear, I see what's been going on right here. Your wicked stepmother cruel and mean, Makes you wash and wax and clean. Now she's gone to the ice cream ball, And left you here with nothing at all.

ELLIE: Dear little Mouse you've seen everything?

FRIZBEE: Oh Yes! Everything and more.
Ever since your stepmother came to stay,
I have seen you slave all day.
She gives you crusts of bread to eat.
She pinches your elbows and stamps on your feet.
She gives you rags and paper towels to wear.

498

She calls you names and tangles your hair.

ELLIE: But what are we to do? I want to go to the ball but I have nothing to wear, my hair is dull, dull, dull, and my face is blah!

LANA: *(From the toy box)* Perhaps there's something I can do. *(Toy box opens again we see LANA's feet waving in the air. ELLIE and FRIZBEE pull her out, she is outlandishly dressed in a gold lame dress, blond wig, tiara, and silvery shoes.)*

LANA: I am your fairy godmother and I have come to make you a star. We have much to do, after all stars are made not born.

ELLIE: Are you going to do a spell?

LANA: Oh no, spells are old fashioned. Today we have something much better ... money!
(LANA throws a fist-full of money in the air.)

LANA: First we need a dress.

ELLIE: Hey, I got an idea. Come with me .....
(ELLIE leads them out of her room to LUCILLE's ladder where she gets an elaborate party dress.)

LANA: Perfect!

FRIZBEE: But that's Lucille's.

LANA: Not anymore. We just bought it. *(LANA spears a bill on the hanger and helps ELLIE on with the dress over her clothes.)* And now the hair! Give her something that simply screams glamour.
(FRIZBEE becomes the hairdresser.)

FRIZBEE: Would Madame care for a flip?
(FRIZBEE does a flip.)

LANA: The hair you dolt!
(LANA clobbers him. FRIZBEE makes an elaborate production of messing up ELLIE's hair.)

LANA: Make-up!

(FRIZBEE slaps make-up on ELLIE and shows her how to blot her lipstick by smacking her lips. He gets carried away

499

with the smacking and gives LANA a big kiss.)

LANA: Oh gross! *(LANA clobbers him.)*

LANA: And now the coach.
(FRIZBEE puts on the football helmet and jumps around being a coach.)

LANA: THE CARRIAGE!!
(FRIZBEE gets a broomstick horse.)

LANA: And last but not least ... your public!
(LANA throws a fist full of money in the air and there is tumultuous cheering.)

(ELLIE, FRIZBEE and LANA exit in procession. A fanfare is heard. FRIZBEE enters with a roll of paper towels which he rolls out like a red carpet. He stands at attention at the end of the carpet. LANA swirls on and down the carpet, she curtsies to FRIZBEE.)

VOICE: Ladies and gentlemen, the Prince.
(MAX enters dressed in a frock coat over his regular clothes. He bows and stands at the end of the "carpet.")

VOICE: And now ladies and gentlemen, the moment we have all been waiting for, the star of stage, screen and television ... the Princess Cinderelli!
(Music plays the Sleeping Beauty Waltz, ELLIE enters, a spot light catches her, she sweeps down the carpet to MAX who bows. They dance.)

LANA: *(As they waltz by her)* Remember darling, your contract is up at midnight.
(VOICE begins to bang on a pot with a spoon, twelve times in all. On the stroke of twelve LUCILLE appears, sweeps down the "carpet." MAX turns and bows to her and dances off with her leaving ELLIE.)

ELLIE: Hey wait a minute, what do you think you're doing?
(LANA and FRIZBEE Exit.)

ELLIE: Hey, I'm supposed to be the Princess around here. Hey, I'm Cinderelli! Come back. Alright see if I care. I don't need any stupid old prince. I can have a good time all by myself. *(ELLIE sings and dances all by herself. Music out. ELLIE, obviously upset, dances faster and faster. MAX and LUCILLE enter with groceries. They stop at her door and watch. MAX bursts out laughing. LUCILLE elbows him. ELLIE stops, mortified at being caught.)*

ELLIE: Well what are you staring at?

MAX: What is this, Halloween?

ELLIE: What's so funny?

LUCILLE: I think you look very pretty.

ELLIE: *(Defensively.)* Well I wasn't trying to look pretty! I was trying to look dumb and funny, like this ... and this ... and this ... *(ELLIE makes faces.)* Since I can't be pretty I might as well be funny and dumb. *(ELLIE capers around wildly until she stubs her toe.)*

ELLIE: Owwwwwwww!

LUCILLE: What's the matter?

ELLIE: I stubbed my dumb toe.
(ELLIE sits and buries her head in her hands. MAX starts to go to her. LUCILLE stops him by shoving her sack of groceries into his arms.)

LUCILLE: Max, will you put these in the kitchen for me?
(MAX gives her a look, she waves him away and he exits. LUCILLE goes to ELLIE and helps her out of the dress.)

LUCILLE: You okay?
(ELLIE pulls away and sits on the bed. She shrugs.)

LUCILLE: Ellinor, if I asked you to help me with something would you do it?

ELLIE: I didn't clean up my room.

LUCILLE: So I see, but that's not what I am talking about. I want you to help me with something else.

ELLIE: Huh! I don't see what I could help you do.

501

LUCILLE: *(Tentatively)* Well, I never had any children ... and lots of times I'm not too sure what mothers are supposed to do. So I wanted you to help me.

ELLIE: How should I know I never really had a mother, not one I remember real well.

LUCILLE: Well, maybe we could help each other. *(ELLIE shrugs.)* You see, my mother was very strict. She made me pick up my room and practice my voice every day and I loved her.

ELLIE: She was your real mother.

LUCILLE: Yes.

ELLIE: That makes a difference. You have to love your real mother and your real kids.

LUCILLE: But you can choose to love your stepchildren.

ELLIE: But nobody can make you.

LUCILLE: *(Pause.)* That's right.

ELLIE: Well I can tell you a couple of things mothers shouldn't do. They shouldn't try to make their kids different from the way they are. Like if the kid is messy, they shouldn't try to make them be neat. And mothers shouldn't make their kids go to bed at eight-thirty, especially when there's good movies on T.V.

LUCILLE: But what if the mother wants the child to be healthy and she thinks the child should get some sleep?

ELLIE: Who's supposed to be doing the helping around here, you or me?

LUCILLE: Sorry.

ELLIE: Mothers should love their kids no matter what. Even if the kid is funny and dumb and looks like a gorilla; mothers should make them think they are beautiful.

LUCILLE: But what if the ... kid won't let the mother ...

ELLIE: Mothers gotta go first! That's the rules.

LUCILLE: Ellie ... I ...

ELLIE: *(Turning away)* What's for supper?

LUCILLE: Huh?

ELLIE: I'm getting hungry. What's for supper?

LUCILLE: I thought I'd make a beef stroganoff.

ELLIE: What's that?

LUCILLE: It's little slices of beef with sour cream and ...

ELLIE: SOUR CREAM! UHHHHHH! Mothers should never make their kids eat SOUR CREAM!
(*ELLIE clutches her throat.*)

LUCILLE: *(Laughing)* You should try it.

ELLIE: I know, Why don't I make dinner tonight? I used to do that all the time. Pop and I had this really neat game we'd play. First we'd cook up a whole bunch of T.V. dinners and then we'd put on blindfolds and try to guess what we were eating.

MAX: *(Entering)* Did I hear somebody mention food?

LUCILLE: 1 just had a great idea! Why don't we eat out tonight?

ELLIE: Knock knock ...

MAX: Who's there?

ELLIE: Uda.

MAX: Uda who?

ELLIE: *(Singing)* "You deserve a break today" .....

MAX: *(Joining in)* ... "So go on and get away to MacDonalds."**
(*MAX encourages LUCILLE to join in.*)

LUCILLE: But I don't know the words.

ELLIE: It's simple. But you can't sing it in that toot toot de doot voice. You gotta do it like this ...
(*ELLIE belts it out.*)

**This jingle should be constantly updated to any popular theme song of a fast food chain.

ELLIE: "You deserve a break today. So go on and get away to MacDonalds."

LUCILLE: *(Belting)* Like this? "You deserve a break today. So go on and get away to MacDonalds."
(They all join in on the last line.)

ELLIE: Not bad, for a beginner.

MAX: Let's go.

LUCILLE: Wait a minute, I have to put the meat in the freezer.
(LUCILLE exits.)

MAX: Hey Ellie, after supper how about a little ...
(MAX mimes bowling.)

ELLIE: Great! Just you and me, like the old days?

MAX: Ellie?

ELLIE: Oh I bet Lucille doesn't even know how to bowl. I bet she thinks it is a dirty smelly sport.

MAX: Oh, come on.

ELLIE: Oh, I guess she can come.

MAX: If she doesn't know you'll have to teach her.

ELLIE: Yeah, I could. Cause if there is one thing I do know it is bowling.
(LUCILLE enters.)

MAX: Lucille, would you like to go bowling after supper?

LUCILLE: Oh Max, I was hoping we could all come back here and TALK.

MAX: *(Ignoring the hint)* Oh yeah, yeah. We can do that afterward.

LUCILLE: Maybe just you two should go. I've never bowled before and I wouldn't want to slow you down.

MAX: Baloney! There's nothing to it. We'll show you. Right Midget?
(ELLIE shrugs and MAX elbows her.)

504

ELLIE: Sure, sure, it just takes practice, to get good that is. I'll show you.

MAX: Let's go. *(They start out.)*

ELLIE: Wait a sec, let me get my shoes.

MAX: We'll meet you in the car.

(MAX and LUCILLE exit. ELLIE gets her bowling shoes from under the bed and starts out.)

VOICE: Red Light! *(ELLIE freezes.)* You aren't going to fall for all that stuff are you?

ELLIE: Huh?

VOICE: All that "Help me be a mother" stuff?

ELLIE: Well

VOICE: Stepmothers always say that ... to soften you up. They don't really mean that. And now she's going bowling with you. And after you teach her you know what will happen? She and Pop will go and leave you home ... alone. Green Light!

MAX: *(Off stage)* Come on Ellie!
(ELLIE hesitates and exits. By minor adjustments in the set it switches to the bowling alley. The sound of balls rolling and pins falling can be heard through the next scene. As soon as the scene is shifted ELLIE, MAX and LUCILLE enter. ELLIE munches a bag of french fries, they cross to benches set up to indicate their alley. MAX sets up a score sheet, changes his shoes. All bowling should be mimed.) Why don't we take a couple of practice shots? Will you show Lucille how to hold the ball while I get squared away?

ELLIE: *(Licking her fingers)* Okay, first you get a ball ...
(ELLIE points, LUCILLE looks a bit apprehensive but she gets a ball.)

MAX: *(Under his breath)* Ellie, I want you to be nice.

ELLIE: *(Slaps on a huge smile)* I am being nice ... SEE? Now you hold the ball like this with three fingers ... That's good

... very very good! And you look right at that center pin and bring your hand straight back ... like this and you just swing through ... See?

LUCILLE: *(Gamely)* Sure I think so...

ELLIE: Well go ahead ... Try one.
(LUCILLE follows all ELLIE's instructions but the unexpected weight of the ball throws her off balance. Finally she manages to bowl one ball but very badly. There is the sound of a gutter ball.)

ELLIE: *(Much too nice)* Good! VERY GOOD Lucille. (*ELLIE smirks.*)

MAX: Lucille, that's called a gutterball, and it's not good. Ellie I'll show her. Why don't you take your turn?

ELLIE: Can I have a Coke?

LUCILLE: You just finished dinner.

ELLIE: Pop?

MAX: Yeah sure, here's fifteen cents.

(ELLIE walks away a few steps. MAX moves over to LUCILLE and shows her how to hold the ball, very cozily. ELLIE returns.)

ELLIE: AHEM! I believe it is MY turn.
(ELLIE takes a ball and goes through a very elaborate warm-up.)

MAX: *(Quietly)* Now you see you just bring the ball straight back and ...

LUCILLE: Where is the aiming?

(ELLIE bowls just as LUCILLE is talking, she slips a little and is thrown off. There is the sound of a few pins falling.)

ELLIE: No fair! No fair! You're not supposed to talk! You threw me off!

MAX: *(Writing down the score)* Uhhh, three! A little to the left.

ELLIE: That's not fair.

MAX: Oh go on, you've still got another ball.

ELLIE: This time NO talking. (*ELLIE bowls. All pins fall.*)

MAX: Fantastic.

LUCILLE: Nice aiming, Ellinor. That was a good shot wasn't it dear?

ELLIE: *(Cocky)* You bet. That's what they call a spare. It is just about the best you can do. Of course it takes hours and hours of practice.

MAX: Nice one Midget! Okay Lucille, it's all yours. Just relax and concentrate.
(*LUCILLE starts into the backswing.*)

ELLIE: Hold IT!
(*LUCILLE stops clumsily.*)

LUCILLE: This is the foul line. If you step over it nothing counts. ... I was just trying to help! (*LUCILLE bowls, very awkwardly. Sound of ball rolling very slowly.*)

ELLIE: *(Watching the ball.)* Don't expect too much, not right at first. After all there is only one thing better than a spare and that's a ... (*Sound of pins falling domino effect. ELLIE's face contorts in utter amazement.*) A STRIKE?????

MAX: Fantastic!

LUCILLE: Is that good?

MAX: You bet it is!

ELLIE: I think I'm going to be sick!

LUCILLE: What does that little X mean up there?

ELLIE: *(Nasty)* It means a strike!

MAX: Not bad, old lady, not bad at all.
(*ELLIE starts coughing real jokey.}*

LUCILLE: Beginner's luck.

MAX: Let's see. My turn now. (*ELLIE coughs.*) What's the matter with you?

ELLIE: I don't feel so good.

MAX: Well lie down for a minute.

ELLIE: I don't exactly feel like bowling.
(MAX shoots her a look which silences her. MAX picks up the ball and lines up the shot, very machismo. Just as he bowls ELLIE coughs and throws him off. He gets a gutterball.)

MAX: Ellie!

ELLIE: *(Innocently)* Sorry.

LUCILLE: What's the matter Ellinor?

MAX: Nothing's the matter. She's just got a bad case of fakeitus that's all!

ELLIE: By the way, Lucille, that's called a gutterball, it's not good.

MAX: Now, no more talking, noisemaking, sneezing, coughing or anything. *(MAX lines up the shot and ELLIE yawns.)* One more noise out of you and it's out to the car.
(MAX takes his time lining up the shot, ELLIE picks up her Coke can which she opens just as he bowls. The can explodes in a spray of Coke. MAX tosses his ball over several lanes. He is furious.)

ELLIE: Ooops!

MAX: ELLIE!

LUCILLE: Good Lord it is all over everything!

ELLIE: I couldn't help it.

MAX: You did that on purpose 'cause you're a rotten sport.

ELLIE: I did not.

MAX : Out to the car!

ELLIE: POP!

MAX: I said out to the car!

LUCILLE: Dear!

MAX: I am not going to have her wreck our game just because

she's a lousy sport.

LUCILLE: Let's go home.

MAX: WHAT?

LUCILLE: I don't really care about bowling.

MAX: Well I do. Ellie out to the car. I said it and I meant it.

LUCILLE: You can't send her out there to wait in a dark parking lot.

MAX: Oh yes I can. We are going to finish this game, and Ellie is going to wait for us out in the car. If there is one thing I can't stand it is a rotten sport.

LUCILLE: I will not permit you to send that child out there alone.

MAX: It's just out to the car, do you want me to hire a babysitter?

ELLIE: *(Embarrassed)* Pop!

LUCILLE: Max, keep your voice down. We'll settle this when we get home.

MAX: Are you telling me how to discipline my kid?

LUCILLE: You? You're a fine one to talk about discipline. Why you're a bigger kid than she is. Why we should all be sitting at home right now having a family discussion. But Oh no! We have to get ice cream. We all have to go bowling first ... all because you can't even talk to your own child ...

MAX: *(Impulsive)* Oh you don't think I can tell her ...

(MAX crosses to ELLIE. LUCILLE tries to stop him.)

LUCILLE: Max, not here and not now ... Let's go home.

MAX: *(To ELLIE)* Ellie, we are going to Hawaii! *(To LUCILLE)* There! Now are you satisfied?
(LUCILLE is horrified. MAX realizes instantly that he has really blown it.)

LUCILLE: Oh MAX!

ELLIE: What are you guys talking about?

MAX: *(Fighting his way out)* Uhhh, Ellie, we are going away ... We're going to Hawaii.

ELLIE: HAWAII?

MAX: Yeah, for about three weeks.

ELLIE: Neato! Do I get to get out of school?

MAX: No Ellie, just Lucille and I are going. I was gonna tell you all about it when we got home tonight, well now you know.

ELLIE: What ... What about me?

MAX: Well you kind of like Mrs. Dougan and I thought maybe she'd come and ...

ELLIE: You are going away and leaving me.

LUCILLE: Ellie ...

ELLIE: *(Getting mad)* So that's what all that sneaking around was about! So that's what all those papers and secret stuff was about. You guys are going away and leaving me.

LUCILLE: Ellinor, that's not ...

ELLIE: *(Turns on her)* And YOU! All that "Help me be a mother," stuff! That was just to soften me up. Well I'll tell you one thing mothers shouldn't do, mothers shouldn't lie to their kids about all that love stuff and then dump them.

MAX: Ellie, stop shouting.

ELLIE: I should have known. I should have known you didn't really like me. You just wanted to have POP all to yourself. Well go ahead! See if I care!

MAX: Ellie, we are going home. Take off your shoes and wait for me in the car.

ELLIE: You can't just throw me out like the trash you know.

MAX: ELLIE OUT TO THE CAR!
(ELLIE starts to run out. MAX stops her.)

MAX: Ellie, your shoes!
(ELLIE, furious, takes off her shoes and throws them at him and runs out. LUCILLE looks at MAX for a minute.)

LUCILLE: Well you certainly handled that one well.

MAX: Lay off! Oh I'm sorry, I didn't mean for this to happen.

LUCILLE: I should hope not. Max, discipline isn't something you turn off and on like hot water.

MAX: I know.

LUCILLE: *(Taking off her shoes and exiting.)* We were just beginning. After two months we were just beginning. *(LUCILLE exits. MAX sits for a minute. He picks up the score sheet and crumples it. He starts out when LUCILLE enters at a run.)*

LUCILLE: Max, she isn't there! She's gone!

MAX: What?

LUCILLE: She's run away. She left this note on the windshield. *(LUCILLE hands MAX a note.)*

MAX: *(Reading)* "You win Lucille."

LUCILLE: *(Panicking)* Where could she have gone?

MAX: Anywhere! Let's go, she can't have gotten too far. *(LUCILLE sees ELLIE's shoes.)*

LUCILLE: Oh Max, she hasn't even got her shoes on.

MAX: Come on. *(MAX and LUCILLE exit. Weird sounds begin, the recorded voices of LANA and FRIZBEE and VOICE are heard chanting "Run away." The following scene is a mixture of fantasy and reality. A sound collage of voices and scarey music form the background.)*

VOICE, LANA and FRIZBEE: Run away ... Run away ... Run away ... Run away ... *(ELLIE enters at a run. LANA and FRIZBEE enter also but they appear as strange menacing figures, such as a stop sign that is knocked over, a staggering drunk, a car that nearly runs ELLIE down.)*

VOICE, LANA and FRIZBEE: Run away. Run away. Run away. Run away. There's a fact you've got to face ...

Run away. Run away.
That she's taken your place ...
Run away. Run away.

VOICE, LANA and FRIZBEE: *(Recorded)* And there's nothing you can do ... Run away, Run away. Cause he loves her more than you ... Run away, Run away.

ELLIE: I'll show you. Boy will you be sorry! I'm never going home.
(A cat yeowls and LUCILLE appears dressed in a long black cloak.)

LUCILLE: *(Recorded)* Mirror, mirror, on the wall, who's the fairest of them all?

ELLIE: I am, you wicked old stepmother!
(ELLIE runs into FRIZBEE who holds a newspaper in front of his face.)

FRIZBEE: Go home little girl.

ELLIE: I'm never going home. I'll find some new parents.
(ELLIE runs over to LANA who is wearing a farmer's hat and mimes churning butter.) Will you adopt a poor orphan child?

LANA: *(Malevolently)* My lands, who is this child?

ELLIE: I am just a poor orphan with no father or mother.

FRIZBEE: *(Also wearing a farmer's hat.)* I see the mark of the princess Cinderelli upon her cheek. We will adopt you.

ELLIE: I am not a princess, I'm just Ellie, Ellie Murphy.

FRIZBEE: Well, if you are not the princess then get lost. *(ELLIE staggers away from them.)*

ELLIE: I'm not scared. I'm not scared. I'm not scared. Oh, my feet are so cold. *(MAX enters slowly with his back to the audience. He wears a raincoat with a hood. LUCILLE enters with her back to the audience, she too wears a long coat.)* Pop! Is that you Pop? Hey!

MAX: *(Still with his back to her)* I beg your pardon?

512

ELLIE: Pop! It's me, Ellie.

MAX: I'm sorry but I don't believe I know you.

ELLIE: Pop, It's me, your daughter! Ellie!

MAX: Who?

ELLIE: Hey Lucille! It's me, Ellie.

LUCILLE: *(Still with her back to her)* I beg your pardon?

ELLIE: Look at me! It's Ellie!

LUCILLE: I don't believe I know you. *(Slowly they turn to look at her. They wear half-masks which are transparent.)* Do you know this child?

MAX: No, I'm sorry little girl.

LUCILLE: Come dear, we have a plane to catch.

MAX: Oh yes, we mustn't be late.

LUCILLE: *(As they exit)* What a strange little girl.

ELLIE: Don't you know me? I'm your child!
(Strange music and recorded voices begin again. LANA and FRIZBEE step in and out of the shadows moving in slow motion.)

VOICE, LANA and FRIZBEE: *(Recorded)* You're alone ... You're alone.

LANA: *(Like a cat yeowl)* Hi ya Sweetie ...

VOICE, LANA and FRIZBEE: *(Recorded)* Can't go home ... Can't go home...

ELLIE: Doesn't anybody know me?

LANA: Hi ya Boss ...

ELLIE: I'm not the Boss. I'm ...

VOICE, LANA and FRIZBEE: *(Recorded)* You're alone ... You're alone.

FRIZBEE: Singer of the year ...

ELLIE: I don't want to be ...

VOICE, LANA and FIZBEE: Got no home ... Got no home ...

ELLIE: I don't want to be an orphan.

VOICE, LANA and FRIZBEE: You're alone ... You're alone ... All alone ... All alone...

ELLIE: I just want to go home.
> (*ELLIE runs around the stage, as she does the scene is shifted back to her house. ELLIE enters the living room area and looks around.*)

ELLIE: I'm home! Hey Pop? Lucille? I'm home. I don't want to be an orphan. Pop? LUCILLE?

> (*ELLIE sighs and goes into her room. She throws herself down on her bed and falls into a deep sleep.*)

> (*Soft music begins, a lullabye played on a music box. ELLIE dreams and in her dream MAX and LUCILLE enter wearing dressing gowns. LANA and FRIZBEE enter. They carry windchimes which tinkle softly. During this scene the words must tumble and flow like a waterfall, nothing frightening. It is a soft and gentle dream.*)

LUCILLE: Shhhh. Don't wake the baby ...

FRIZBEE: What a beautiful baby ...

LANA: What a good baby ...

MAX: Daddy's beautiful baby girl.

ELLIE: *(Recorded)* I never had a mother, not one I remember real well.

LANA: Sleep ...

FRIZBEE: ... Dream.

ELLIE: *(Recorded)* Mother? Mother? Where are you? It's dark. I'm scared.
> (*LUCILLE billows a soft coverlet and covers ELLIE.*)

LUCILLE: Shall I tell you a story? Shall I sing you a song?

ELLIE: *(Recorded)* I can't see myself. I'm messy. I'm mean.

LANA: Sleep ...

FRIZBEE: ... Dream.

MAX: Daddy's pretty Ellie.

ELLIE: *(Recorded)* Mother tell me a story. Mother sing me a
song.
(LUCILLE begins to hum softly.)

LANA: Sleep ...

FRIZBEE: ... Dream.

ELLIE: Can you be my mother?

LUCILLE: Sleep ...

ELLIE: Please be my mother.

MAX: ...Dream.

ELLIE: I want to have a mother!

LANA: Shhh. Don't wake the child.

FRIZBEE: What a beautiful child.

MAX: Daddy's beautiful girl.

LUCILLE: Pretty Ellie ...

MAX and LUCILLE: *(Recorded)* Pretty Ellie ... Pretty Ellie ...
Pretty Ellie ... Pretty Ellie.
*(All exit slowly as the recorded music and sound continue
for a moment. ELLIE tosses and turns on the bed. The dream
fades and the house returns to normal. MAX enters the house
dressed as he was at the bowling alley. He is upset and in a
hurry.)*

MAX: I know I have a recent photograph around here
somewhere. Lucille you call the police, say you want to
report a missing person.
(LUCILLE enters.)

LUCILLE: I just don't understand how she could have gotten so
far so quickly. Oh Max, what are we going to do?

MAX: I know we had some pictures taken at Woolworths right
before she left for camp. Where did I put them?

LUCILLE: She's been gone two hours. Anything could have happened.

MAX: Take it easy. We'll find her. She's probably just hiding in a restaurant or something. You call the police. I'll go back to the bowling alley.

LUCILLE: I can't help feeling this is all my fault.

MAX: Maybe they are in her room. Call the police. (*MAX enters ELLIE's room. He stops dead when he sees her asleep. He is unable to speak for a second and sighs in relief.*)

MAX: (*Very calmly*) Lucille. (*LUCILLE crosses to him. He points to the sleeping figure. LUCILLE crouches by the bed.*)

LUCILLE: Thank God.

MAX: Let's let her sleep. She must be exhausted. (*They leave the room and close the door behind them.*)

LUCILLE: She must have walked all this way.

MAX: She must have run.

LUCILLE: (*Still slightly hysterical*) Thank God she's alright. Anything could have happened to her. I don't know what 1 would have done if ...
(*ELLIE wakes up, sits and listens.*)

MAX: Hey, calm down. Everything is alright now.

LUCILLE: She could have been killed. What if she'd gotten hit by a car?

MAX: (*Firmly*) Lucille, it is all over now. Take it easy. She's home. I'll get something to relax you, just a minute.
(*MAX exits. ELLIE gets out of bed and starts toward the door.*)

VOICE: Red Light! (*ELLIE freezes.*) Where are you going?

ELLIE: Out there.

VOICE: Why?

ELLIE: To tell them I'm ...

VOICE: You could have been killed and it's all HER fault. She almost got rid of you once and for all.

ELLIE: But she really sounded worried.

VOICE: You aren't going to fall for that stuff again are you? She just said that so Pop wouldn't be mad at her. She's trying to get rid of you.

ELLIE: Aww that's dumb.

VOICE: You could have been killed and she'd live happily ever after with Pop. That's how wicked stepmothers are you know.

ELLIE: But ...

VOICE: You could have been killed. Green Light!
(*MAX enters with a drink for LUCILLE.*)

MAX: Here, this will calm you down. Everything is going to be alright.

LUCILLE: Thanks. I've been thinking, Max, maybe I should go away.

MAX: What?

LUCILLE: Maybe I should just let you and Ellie work things out alone. I kept hoping it was just a matter of time ... that gradually she would come to accept me.

MAX: You're just upset.

LUCILLE: I care for both of you too much to see you destroy what you had together. Maybe I should just leave for a while.

MAX: That's crazy. We are a family now and we are going to work through this thing, all of us, together. Your leaving isn't going to help.

LUCILLE: I don't know.

MAX: Well, I do.

LUCILLE: She must have loved her real mother very much to hate me so.

MAX: She doesn't hate you. She's just mixed up right now. It's late and we are tired. Let's talk about this in the morning.

LUCILLE: No, I really think it would be better for me to leave you two alone for a while to work things out any way you can.

MAX: Let's go to bed.
(MAX exits, LUCILLE picks up the note ELLIE left on the windshield and reads.)

LUCILLE: "You win, Lucille." *(She looks towards ELLIE's room.)* No, Ellie, YOU win. *(She exits.)*

(ELLIE is disturbed and she starts out the door after them.)

ELLIE: Hey you guys ...

VOICE: Red Light!
(ELLIE freezes.)

VOICE: Congratulations! You won!

ELLIE: But she's leaving.

VOICE: That's what you wanted isn't it? Now you and Pop can go back to having things the way they used to be.

ELLIE: Yeah but ...

VOICE: After all, she wanted to get rid of you. She wanted you to get killed, and then you could have had a funeral.

ELLIE: A funeral?

VOICE: Yeah a funeral. At funerals everybody is real sorry for all the means things they ever did to you. Everybody just sits around and says nice things about you and they cry and cry and cry. *(FRIZBEE starts to sniffle.)*

ELLIE: What about Pop?

VOICE: He cries the loudest of all. *(FRIZBEE bursts into sobs.)*

ELLIE: What am I supposed to do?

VOICE: Well, first you gotta have a coffin. *(LANA and FRIZBEE move the toy box forward for the coffin.)*

VOICE: You just lie there.

ELLIE: Suppose I want to see what's going on.

VOICE: No, you gotta just lie there.

ELLIE: That sounds stupid. Hey, I got an idea. Why don't you lie there and be me in the coffin.

VOICE: No, I stay right here.

ELLIE: Get in that coffin!

VOICE: Okay ... Okay ... Green Light!
(VOICE lies on the box and ELLIE takes charge of the microphone.)

ELLIE: Okay ladies and gentlemen. Let's get this show on the road. Ellie Murphy's funeral ... Take one!
(LANA and FRIZBEE clap their hands like a claque board.)

ELLIE: Now the parade starts over there. I want a black horse with a plume.
(FRIZBEE puts a plume on his head and neighs.)

ELLIE: Fantastic! I want music, drums sad and slow! That's right. *(LANA wearing a long black veil falls into a procession behind FRIZBEE and they both wail.)*

ELLIE: Now start with the nice things.

LANA: She was so young and so beautiful.

ELLIE: Cut! Lana, honey, more tears ... that's right cry, cry, cry. Now throw yourself over the coffin. Preacher that's your cue.
(FRIZBEE becomes the preacher.)

FRIZBEE: Poor Ellie Murphy! Why didn't I tell her how cute she was and what nice straight teeth she had.

ELLIE: Come on preacher, nicer things!

FRIZBEE: Poor Ellie Murphy. Why didn't I tell her how pretty she was, what a good voice she had. She was the best bowler I ever saw!

ELLIE: Pop! You're on! *(MAX enters wearing pajamas and a high silk hat, and black arm bands.)*

MAX: I'm sorry Ellie.

ELLIE: More feeling Pop!

MAX: I'M SORRY ELLIE!!!! How could I have been so blind? I never needed anyone but you. Now my life is empty, bleak, bland ...

ELLIE: From the bottom of your heart, Pop!

MAX: What a fool I have been and now it is too late!!!

ELLIE: And now for the final touch! Lucille enters up right, rubbing her hand and laughing.
(*ELLIE indicates up right. Nothing happens.*)

ELLIE: I said, the grand finale ...
(*LUCILLE enters up right, rubbing her hands and laughing. ELLIE indicates up right again and LUCILLE enters up left. She wears a coat and carries a suitcase.*)

LUCILLE: I have been thinking, Max, maybe I should go away.

ELLIE: No, CUT! Lucille enters up right, rubbing her hands and laughing.

LUCILLE: Maybe I should let you and Ellie work things out alone.

ELLIE: I said, up right!

LUCILLE: I kept hoping that it was just a matter of time.

ELLIE: Cut! Cut! You are not supposed to be saying that!

LUCILLE: I kept hoping that gradually she would come to accept me.

ELLIE: You are supposed to be glad that I'm dead.

LUCILLE: I care for you both too much to see you destroy what you had together. Maybe I should just leave.

ELLIE: You are not supposed to be saying that!

LUCILLE: She must have loved her real mother very much to hate me so. So I'm leaving.

ELLIE: Hey wait, Lucille.

LUCILLE: No Ellie, YOU win.

ELLIE: Wait I didn't mean for it to go this far.

VOICE: Red Light! (*ELLIE freezes.*) Don't call her back. You've won! Now things will be the way they always have been.

ELLIE: Why don't you shut up! You are supposed to be dead! I want a mother and she's a perfectly good one.

VOICE: But she's a wicked step ...

ELLIE: RED LIGHT! (*VOICE freezes.*)

ELLIE: Lana, Frizbee, take that thing away. Green Light! (*LANA and FRIZBEE move like puppets. They move voice back to the stool and move the toy box back into its place.*) Now get in. (*ELLIE helps them both into the toy box. She closes the lid and sits on the box for a second.*) Lucille! Lucille! Come back! (*ELLIE moves back into bed as LUCILLE and MAX enter her room. They both wear the dressing gowns seen in the dream scene.*)

MAX: (*Entering first*) Ellie? What's the matter?

ELLIE: Where is Lucille?

LUCILLE: (*Entering*) Right here. What's the matter?

ELLIE: (*Relieved*) Oh ... uhhh, nothing. I must have had a bad dream.

MAX: Do you want to tell me about it?

ELLIE: I don't think you'd like it.

MAX: Is it alright now?

ELLIE: Yeah. I guess so.

MAX: Well, goodnight Midget.
(*MAX kisses her on the forehead.*)

ELLIE: Goodnight Pop.
(*MAX and LUCILLE turn to leave.*)

ELLIE: Uhhh Lucille?
(*MAX stays in the doorway and LUCILLE crosses to her.*)

LUCILLE: Yes?

ELLIE: I'm ... sorry I ran away.

LUCILLE: So am I.

ELLIE: Well, I'm back now.

LUCILLE: I'm glad.

ELLIE: So am I.
(Pause)

ELLIE: Uhhh Lucille, I'm cold.

LUCILLE: Well no wonder, you kicked your covers off.
*(LUCILLE billows the covers over her and tucks her in.
ELLIE smiles.)*

ELLIE: Uhh. Lucille, knock, knock ...

LUCILLE: Who's there?

ELLIE: Sticker.

LUCILLE: Sticker who?

ELLIE: Sticker-ound for a while, okay?

LUCILLE: Okay. Goodnight Ellie. Sleep well.
(LUCILLE moves away a few steps and crouches.)

LUCILLE: Goodnight Lana. Goodnight Frizbee.

ELLIE: Uhhh Lucille, they're not here.

LUCILLE: Oh.
(LUCILLE crosses to MAX and turns back.)

LUCILLE: Goodnight Ellie.

ELLIE: *(Pulling the covers up and turning over.)* See ya in
the morning.

BLACK OUT

THE ARKANSAW BEAR

by
Aurand Harris

This play changed the perception many people had about the place of serious ideas in dramatic literature for children. Prior to the 1980s, the repertoire of plays for children in this country included so few serious plays that, over the years, children's theatre became synonymous with light superficial dramas. Plays like *The Birthday of the Infanta* and *The Ice Wolf* certainly belie that stereotype; but, serious children's plays, were never as widely produced as the more escapist and fantasy dramas. Paradoxically, many of the popular children's plays of the first decades of the century, particularly the ubiquitous fairytale dramas, present ostensibly serious threats to their protagonists; but their fantasy-world protagonists and heightened melodramatic forms distract the audience from personalizing the seriousness of the situations.

The mid-century trend toward more realistic children's plays challenged this protectionist ethos by placing lifelike children in lifelike situations and thus inviting artists to more fully present the cares and concerns of young people. In *The Arkansaw Bear* Aurand Harris utilizes many of the elements found in more traditional children's plays (such as animal characters and fantasy action), but the play confronts directly the hurt, confusion, and fear experienced by the protagonist, Tish, when she is told that her grandfather is about to die.

The opening scene of the play quickly places the audience in the midst of the conflict. Tish, alone on stage, talks to her Mother and her aunt, characters we hear but do not see. When they tell Tish that her grandfather is about to die, Tish tries to visit him, but she is prevented from entering his room. She is thus isolated in her fear and loneliness. She does not understand death, and she particularly does not understand why her grandfather has to die. With minimal exposition, Harris outlines the problem: not that the grandfather has to die, but that Tish must come to some understanding of his death.

Tish escapes to her favorite tree, where she initiates the ensuing action through a wish to Star Bright (a character representing the first star visible that night), asking her to answer the question of why her grandfather must die. Star Bright does not answer the question directly, but instead conjures a fantasy world of circus characters who play out an answer to the "riddle of life." Tish's situation is specifically mirrored in the metaphorical action of Dancing Bear, who, accepting the inevitability of his own death, passes on his dances to Little Bear.

Through her fantasized participation in this fable, Tish comes to realize that she, like Little Bear, is a "chip off the old block," and she will carry on where her grandfather left off. She realizes that although her grandfather has to die, much of him lives on in her. Armed with this new perspective, she breaks out of the fantasy and returns home to say good-bye to her grandfather.

The play includes two separate but related stories. The first shows Tish's interaction with her family; the second tells of the Dancing Bear's quest to understand the meaning of life. This latter story comprises the major portion of the play—a factor that essentially sidelines the protagonist for the majority of the action. While this can present staging difficulties as the audience shifts attention to the Dancing Bear story, the two worlds effectively merge in Tish's realization of her own part in the circle of life.

Harris confronts the issue of death directly, and offers an explicit answer to the riddle of life. While not subtle in his metaphors, he also does not shy away from the fact that death is a part of the lives of young people; and he offers a theatrical world to help young spectators find some meaning in the experience, and to understand that they are not alone in the feelings of fear and loneliness when confronted with the idea of death.

The play begins in the real world and ends in the real world, with a sad but affirmative and realistic denouement. Harris does not offer magic to avert death, but rather presents a child who comes to some understanding about death and grows considerably in the process. When Tish is pushed aside by her grieving Mother at the beginning of the play, and she is left alone to deal with her sadness and fear, the play reminds the audience just how seriously children process the events of the world around them. *The Arkansaw*

Bear shows a profound respect for children as it acknowledges this depth of feeling, and it offers young people an imaginative theatrical journey through issues that touch them deeply.

Aurand Harris (1915-1996) was born in Jamesport, Missouri, on July 4, 1915. He attended the University of Kansas City (AB 1936), Northwestern University (MA 1939), and Columbia University. He worked for many years as a teacher at Grace Church School in New York, in addition to serving short terms as playwright-in-residence at several universities throughout the country. He was a recipient of the Chorpenning Cup from the Children's Theatre Association of America in 1967, in honor of his work as a playwright for young audiences.

Throughout the later decades of the twentieth century Harris was the most prolific and most-produced playwright for children in this country. His plays range from original works, such as *The Arkansaw Bear*, to adaptations of traditional stories, such as *The Brave Little Tailor*. Harris died in New York City in 1996.

A more complete summary of Harris's life and work can be found in *Six Plays for Children by Aurand Harris*, with biography and play analysis by Coleman Jennings (Austin TX: University of Texas Press, 1977).

THE
ARKANSAW BEAR

by
Aurand Harris

Copyright ©1980
Aurand Harris
Anchorage Press, Inc.
Anchorage Press Plays, Inc.

528

THE ARKANSAW BEAR

Characters

TISH

STAR BRIGHT

MIME

WORLD'S GREATEST DANCING BEAR

GREAT RINGMASTER

LITTLE BEAR

VOICES: MOTHER

              AUNT ELLEN

              ANNOUNCER

Setting

THE PRESENT. SOMEWHERE IN ARKANSAS.

(As the house lights dim, there is a glow or light on the front curtain. Over a loud speaker a man's whistling of "0 Susannah" is heard. The curtains open. TISH walks into a large spot of warm light at L. The whistling dims out. TISH is a little girl and carries some hand-picked flowers. She listens to the voices, heard over a loud speaker, and reacts to them as if MOTHER and AUNT ELLEN were on each side of her, downstage.)

TISH: I've come to see Grandpa.

MOTHER'S VOICE: No, dear. No. You can't go in.

TISH: But Mother — —

MOTHER'S VOICE: No, Tish! You can't see Grandpa now.

TISH: I picked him some flowers. These are Grandpa's favorites.

AUNT ELLEN'S VOICE: *(She is TISH's great aunt, elderly, gentle and emotional)* Quiet, child.

TISH: But Aunt Ellen — —

AUNT ELLEN'S VOICE: The doctor is here.

TISH: The doctor?

MOTHER'S VOICE: Tish, dear.

TISH: Yes, Mother?

MOTHER'S VOICE: Grandpa had a turn for the worse. His heart — —

AUNT ELLEN'S VOICE: Oh, it's the end.
(Cries quietly)

TISH: The end?

AUNT ELLEN'S VOICE: The doctor said ... no hope.
(TISH reacts)

MOTHER'S VOICE: Don't cry, Aunt Ellen.

TISH: Is Grandpa going ... to die?

AUNT ELLEN'S VOICE: Yes.

TISH: No! He can't.

MOTHER'S VOICE: We all have to die, dear.

TISH: I know. But not Grandpa. *(Start to move)*

MOTHER'S VOICE: Stop. You can't go in.

TISH: Why can't he live forever!

AUNT ELLEN'S VOICE: You're too young to understand. To full of life.

TISH: I have to tell him there's a circus coming. I saw a poster with a bear.

MOTHER'S VOICE: It doesn't matter now.

TISH: Yes, it does! Do something!

MOTHER'S VOICE: *(Firmly)* We've done all we can.

TISH: But not enough! I ... I didn't do enough!

AUNT ELLEN'S VOICE: Quiet. Quiet.

TISH: *(Softly)* Yes, if I'd been quiet so he could sleep. And — Oh! Once when I was mad, I said ... I wish he was dead. I didn't mean it, Grandpa. I didn't mean it.

MOTHER'S VOICE: Hush, dear. It's not your fault. Grandpa loved you.

TISH: Then why is he ... leaving me? *(Pulls away as if being held)*

TISH: Oh, let me go!

MOTHER'S VOICE: *(Sharply, becoming edgy with emotion)* Yes. Go put the flowers in some water.

TISH: He liked the pink ones. Now ... he'll never see them. Oh, why ... why does Grandpa have to die?

MOTHER'S VOICE: *(Sternly, trying to control and cover her grief)* Run along, dear. Run along.

AUNT ELLEN'S VOICE: Keep away. Away from his door. Away ... away. *(The voices of MOTHER and AUNT ELLEN overlap and mix together, as they keep repeating, "Run along," "Away," "Run . . . run," "Away . . . away," "Run," "Away."*

"Run . . . away; run . . . away." They build to a climax in a choral chant, "Run . . . away.)

TISH: I will. I'll run away. Up the hill ... to my tree ... my tree. *(She runs, circling to the tree which is at R. and on which the lights come up. The circle of light on the first scene dims out, and the chanting of the voices stop. TISH stands alone by her tree in the soft light of evening. She brushes back a tear, shakes her head, and throws the flowers on the ground.*

She sinks low the ground by the tree, hugs her knees, and looks up. She sees the first star, which is out of sight. Quickly she gets up, points to the star and chants)

Star light, star bright,
First star I see tonight,
I wish I may, I wish I might,
Have the wish I wish tonight.

I wish ... I wish ... Oh, Grandpa ... why? *(Goes back to tree)* Why do you have to die?
(There is star music, tinkling with bells. From above, a small swing starts descending. Magic star light spots on it. STAR BRIGHT stands on the swing, which stops in mid-air. Music dims out)

STAR BRIGHT: Repeat, please.

TISH: I wish ... I wish ...

STAR BRIGHT: I know you are wishing: That's why I'm here. But WHAT? Repeat please.

TISH: *(Sees and goes near him)* Who are you?

STAR BRIGHT: *(Slowly and proudly)* I am the first star out tonight! *(Happily)* I did it! I did it! I did it again! *(Excitedly)* First star ... first star ... first star out tonight! *(To TISH)* It's the early star, you know, who gets the wish. What is yours? Repeat, please.

TISH: Can you make a wish come true?

STAR BRIGHT: I've been making wishes come true for a thousand years.

TISH: A thousand years! You're older than Grandpa.

STAR BRIGHT: *(Sits on swing)* Old? Oh, no. I'll twinkle for another thousand years.

TISH: And then?

STAR BRIGHT: *(Cheerfully)* Then my light will go out.

TISH: Like Grandpa.

STAR BRIGHT: But there will be a new star. It's the great pattern...

TISH: I'll never have another Grandpa.

STAR BRIGHT: ... the great circle of life. In every ending there is a new beginning.

TISH: *(Fully realizing it)* I'll never see Grandpa again. I'll never hear him whistle.
(Begins to whistle "O Susannah")

STAR BRIGHT: Your wish? What is your wish?

TISH: I wish ... I wish Grandpa could live a thousand years!

STAR BRIGHT: *(Startled)* What? Repeat, please!

TISH: *(Excited)* I wish he'd never die. Nobody would ever die! Everyone live forever!

STAR BRIGHT: Oh, no, no. no! Think what a mixed up world it would be!

TISH: *(Speaks intently)* I wish ... I wish I knew why ... why Grandpa has to die.

STAR BRIGHT: That is not a quick one-two-buckle-my shoe wish. No. That is a think-and-show-it, then you-know-it, come-true wish.

TISH: Please.

STAR BRIGHT: *(With anticipated excitement)* Close your eyes. Whisper the words again. Open your eyes. And your wish will begin.
(TISH closes her eyes. STAR BRIGHT claps his hands, then motions. There are music and beautiful lights. STAR BRIGHT

is delighted with the effect.) Very good! Repeat, please. *(He claps and waves his hand. Again there are music and beautiful lights.)* Excellent! Thank you!

(The swing with STAR BRIGHT is pulled up and out of sight. The full stage is seen, lighted brightly and in soft colors. Never is the stage dark, eerie, or frightening. It is TISH's fantasy. There are the large tree at R. and open space with beautiful sky.

MIME appears at R. He is a showman, a magician and an accomplished mime who never speaks. He wears a long coat with many colorful patch pockets. He is NOT in white face, but his face is natural, friendly and expressive. He enters cautiously, carrying a traveling box, which he sets down at C. On the side the audience sees, is painted the word, BEAR. On the other side is painted the word, DANCING. He beckons off R. The World's Greatest Dancing BEAR enters R. He is a star performer, amusing, vain and loveable like a teddy bear. He does NOT wear an animal mask, nor is the actor's face painted, frightening or grotesque, with animal make up. He wears his traveling hat. He hurries in, worried and out of breath.)

BEAR: I must stop and get my breath. *(Pants heavily)* My heart is pounding. *(Looks about)* Are we safe? *(Frightened)* I don't see him. I don't hear him. Yes, we have out run him. *(Motions and MIME places box for BEAR to sit)* Where ... where in this wide whirling wonderful world ... do you think we are? Switzerland? *(MIME makes pointed mountain with his wrist, runs his fingers up and down the "mountain," then shakes his head.)* You are right. No mountains. England? *(MIME opens and holds up imaginary umbrella, holds hand out to feel the rain, shakes his head.)* You are right. No rain. India? *(MIME leans over, swings one arm for a trunk, then other for his tail and walks.)* No elephants.

TISH: Excuse me. *(They freeze. She comes to them.)* I can tell you where you are. You are in Arkansas.

BEAR: Quick! Disguise. Hide.

(He and MIME hurry to R. MIME quickly takes from one of his pockets a pair of dark glasses and gives them to Bear who puts them on; then stands beside BEAR to hide him.)

TISH: *(Recites with pride)* Arkansas was the 25th state to be admitted to the union. It is the 27th in size, and the state flower is apple blossom.

BEAR: Who is it? *(Mime pantomines a girl)* A girl? *(Mime pantomimes a small girl)* A little girl? Tell her to go away. To run away.
(MIME pantomimes to TISH. BEAR hides behind tree.)

TISH: I have. I have run away. Have you run away, too? *(MIME nods)* Why? *(MIME looks frightened off R. then puts finger to lips)* Who are you? *(MIME takes a card from a pocket and presents it to her. She reads)* "A Mime." You never speak. *(MIME shakes his head, and "walks" in one spot and tips his hat.)* "A Magician." You do tricks! *(MIME pulls handkerchief from sleeve)* "Friend." You give help. *(MIME touches handkerchief under her eyes)* Thank you. I was crying because my Grandpa ... he's going to ... *(BEAR, without glasses steps out from behind the tree, does a loud tap dance step and poses. MIME turns the traveling box around and with a flourish points to the word painted on the side of the box. TISH reads it with amazement.)* Dancing. *(MIME turns box around again. She reads)* Bear. *(MIME motions to Bear who steps forward.)* I've never met a bear. I've never seen a DANCING bear.

BEAR: *(To MIME)* Should I? *(MIME nods)* Shall I? *(MIME nods)* I will! My Spanish hat. *(MIME jumps with joy and gets hat from box. BEAR motions to TISH who sits on the ground.)* Be seated, please. *(MIME holds up handmirror, which he takes from a pocket, holds it up for BEAR to look at himself, and fixes the hat.)* To the right ... to the right ... Ah, just right! *(MIME motions and a spot light comes on. An announcer's voice is heard over a loud speaker.)*

ANNOUNCER'S: Ladies and Gentlemen: Presenting in his spectacular special, Spanish dance, the World's famous, the

World's favorite, the World's Greatest Dancing Bear!

BEAR: *(Mime motions and Spanish music is heard. Bear steps into the spotlight. He dances with professional perfection a Spanish dance, but he does not finish. At a climactic moment, he stops, holds his hand against his heart and speaks with short breaths.)* Stop the music. *(MIME motions. Music stops.)* Dim the light. *(MIME motions. Spot dims out.)*

TISH: What is it?

BEAR: *(Breathing heavily.)* He is near. He is coming.

TISH: Who?

BEAR: He is almost here. Hide. I must hide. He must not find me. *(MIME points to tree.)* Yes, the tree. Hurry! *(MIME helps BEAR to tree.)*

TISH: Who? Who is coming?

BEAR: The box. Cover the box. *(He disappears behind the tree. MIME sits on traveling box. BEAR's head appears.)* Talk. *(MIME mime-talks with hands and face.)* Louder! *(Bear's head disappears. MIME motions for TISH to talk.)*

TISH: Talk? What about?

BEAR: *(Head appears)* Arkansas. *(Head disappears)*

TISH: *(Recites nervously)* Arkansas has mineral springs, natural caves, and ... and ... diamond mines. *(Looks off R. and whispers frightened)* I don't hear anyone. I don't see anyone. *(MIME motions for her to talk.)* Arkansas was first known as the state of many bears. *(Looks and whispers mysteriously)* There isn't anyone. Nothing. Just quiet, nothing. Who is he running away from?
(MIME motions "Sh," then runs L. to R. and looks, then motions for BEAR to come out.)

BEAR: *(Comes from behind tree)* He didn't find me. I escaped ... this time. *(Pleased, but short of breath)* My traveling hat. We must go on.
(MIME takes Spanish hat and gives BEAR traveling hat.)

536

TISH: Where? Where will you go?

BEAR: *(Looks off R. afraid)* I must keep ahead of him.

TISH: Ahead of who? Who!

BEAR: *(Cautiously)* Never speak his name aloud. *(Looks around)* He may be listening, and come at once. *(MIME gives him hat)* Oh, my poor hat. You and I have traveled together for many a mile and many a year. We are both beginning to look a little weary. *(Puts hat on)*

TISH: Grandpa has an old hat.

BEAR: Perhaps, if it had a new feather. Yes! A bright new feather!

TISH: I think your hat is very stylish.

BEAR: *(Pleased)* You do?

TISH: And very becoming.

BEAR: *(Flattered)* Thank   you: You are a very charming little girl. What is your name?

TISH: Tish.

BEAR: Tish-sh-sh! That is not a name. That is a whistle. Ti-sh-sh-sh!

TISH: It's short for Leticia. It was my Grandmother's name.

BEAR: Leticia. Ah, that is a name with beauty.

TISH: Grandpa calls me "Little Leticia."

BEAR: I shall call you ... *(Rolling the "R")* Princess Leticia.

TISH: Princess?

BEAR: All my friends are important. Kings and Queens ... Command performances for Ambassadors and Presidents ... *(To MIME)* The velvet box, please. *(MIME takes from a pocket a small box)* I will show you my medals, my honors.

TISH: My Grandpa won a medal.

BEAR: Ah?

TISH: He was the best turkey caller in Arkansas.

BEAR: Turkey caller?

TISH: He won first prize!

BEAR: (To MIME) Pin them on me so she can see. And so that I can remember ... once again ... all my glories.
(Royal music begins and continues during the scene. MIME puts ribbons and jeweled medals on BEAR as VOICE announces each decoration. Two are pinned on. One is on a ribbon which is fastened around BEAR's neck.)

ANNOUNCER'S VOICE: The Queen's highest honor, the Royal Medallion.

BEAR: I danced in the Great Hall. It was the Queen's birthday party.

ANNOUNCER'S VOICE: The Diamond Crescent of the East.

BEAR: Fifteen encores. Fifteen encores and they still applauded.

ANNOUNCER'S VOICE: The Royal Ribbon of Honor for Distinguished Service.

BEAR: It was during the war. I danced for the soldiers.

ANNOUNCER'S VOICE: And today, a new decoration. Her Royal Highness, Princess Leticia presents, in honor of her Grandfather, the highest award in the State of Arkansas — the Turkey Feather.
(MIME takes a bright feather from a pocket and gives it to TISH. BEAR parades to her, with a few dance steps, and she puts the feather in his hat. Royal music stops.)

BEAR: Thank you. A party! We will celebrate my new honor! *(To Mime)* Food and festivities! Honey bread! *(MIME nods)* Thick with honey spread! *(MIME nods twice, then makes magic motions toward BEAR. Suddenly MIME turns and points to LETICIA. She puts out her hand which, magically, holds a honey bun.)*

TISH: *(Delighted)* O-o-oh! It looks delicious.

BEAR: *(MIME turns and points to BEAR who puts out his hand which, also magically, holds a colorful honey bun.)* A-a-ah! It

538

IS delicious. *(BEAR puts finger in it, then licks finger. MIME raises his hand.)* Yes, give us a toast. *(BEAR and TISH hold honey buns up. MIME pantomimes "A toast ... " holds up his hand; "to the winner ... " clasps his hands and shakes them high in the air; "of the turkey feather," walks like a turkey, bobbing his head, then MIME pulls out an imaginary feather from his hip.)* Thank you.

TISH: What did he say?

BEAR: You didn't listen.

TISH: How can I hear when he doesn't speak?

BEAR: You listen with your eyes, and then YOU say the words. Listen. He will repeat the toast.

TISH: *(Mime pantomimes the toast again. She watches and speaks aloud.)* "A toast ... to the winner ... of the turkey feather!"

BEAR: Thank you. Now entertainment! *(To MIME)* You tell us a story. *(To TISH)* You listen and say the words.

TISH: Me?

BEAR: And I will eat!
(Wiggles with excitement and sits on box.)

TISH: *(MIME pantomimes a story which TISH, watching him, repeats in words.)* "Once there was ... a princess ... a beautiful princess!"

BEAR: Named *(Sings it)* Leticia. *(Takes a bite)*

TISH: "One day ... in the woods ... she met ... *(Doubtful)* ... a cat?" *(MIME shakes his head. Mimes again)* A ... goosey-gander? *(MIME shakes his head. Mimes again.)* A ... bear!

BEAR: The World's Greatest Dancing Bear!
(Seated, he makes his own vocal music and dances with his feet.)

TISH: "Under a spreading tree ... they had a party ... with honey bread, thick with honey spread."

BEAR: (Licks his five fingers, one on each word) Yum ... yum ...

TO ... the ... last ... crumb.
(Licks his hand and picks and eats crumbs from his lap).

TISH: "Now honey bread, thick with honey spread ... made the
bear very ... sleepy. He yawned." *(BEAR follows action of the
story and goes to sleep.)* " ... gave a little sigh ... and took
a little nap." *(BEAR snores)* He's asleep. Who ... who is he
running away from? *(MIME goes to sleeping BEAR, puts
his fingers to his lips then mimes.)* "The World's Greatest
Dancing Bear ... is old and tired ... and his heart ... is tired."
(Herself) Like Grandpa. *(Speaking for Mime)* "He is running
away from ... " Who? "Someone is coming to take him away
... forever." Does that mean if he's caught, he will die?
(Mime nods) Is he running away ... from death? *(MIME nods)*
Oh! I'll help him. Yes, I'll help him. *(Faint music of calliope
is heard, BEAR stirs)* He's waking up.

BEAR: *(Slowly wakes up)* Music ... the calliope ... circus music
of the Great Center ring! *(Rises)* The Ringmaster is coming!

TISH: *(To MIME)* Death?
(Mime nods)

BEAR: He is near. I hear the music.

TISH: I don't hear it. *(To MIME)* Do you?
(MIME shakes his head)

BEAR: Only I can hear him. Only I can see him. He is coming
for me. Quick! We must go.

TISH: Yes, I'll help you.

BEAR: This way. Hurry! *(MIME carries box. Led by BEAR they
start L. but stop when the music becomes louder.)* No! No!
The music is here. Quick! Turn! Run the other way. *(They
rush to R. and are stopped by music becoming louder.)* No!
The music is coming from here. It is all around us! Here!
There! Look! *(He points off R.)*

TISH: What?

BEAR: The Great Ringmaster. He is there! He is coming ... for
me!

540

(RINGMASTER enters slowly from R. He wears an ornate ringmaster's jacket, boots and a tall hat. He has a friendly face, a pleasant voice, but walks and speaks with authority. He stops. Music stops.)

Quick! Hide me! Hide me! *(BEAR runs L. TISH and MIME follow. He quickly hides behind them when (key stop. Bear peeks over TISH's shoulder.)* Tell him to go away.

TISH: I can't see him. Where is he?

BEAR: There.
(Hides)

TISH: *(Bravely speaks, facing front talking into space.)* Excuse me ... sir. This is my secret place ... by the big tree. You must leave at once. Go away. Now. *(Whispers to BEAR)* Did he go?

BEAR: *(Peeks) No. (Hides)*

RINGMASTER: *(Distinctly and with authority)* I have come for the Dancing Bear. I have come to take him to the Great Center Ring.

BEAR: Tell him he has made a mistake.

TISH: Excuse me ... sir. You have made a mistake.

RINGMASTER: *(Opens book)* No. It is written plainly in the book. The date is today. The name ... is the Dancing Bear.

BEAR: *(Who was hidden by MIME at the side, now steps into view, wearing boxing gloves and a sport cap.)* You HAVE made a mistake. I am a BOXING BEAR: *(MIME blows a whistle and continues to blow it, as BEAR shadow boxes, comically, with a few dance steps and kicks thrown in. He ends in a heroic pose.)* Goodbye.

RINGMASTER: A boxing bear? *(Looks in book)* There has never been a mistake.

TISH: *(Whispers)* Have you tricked him? Outwitted him?

BEAR: *(Nods, then calls loudly)* Yes. Training time. On your mark; get set; ready — talleyho!

541

(Starts jogging off R.)

RINGMASTER: *(Reads)* The book says: His father, born in Russia, a dancing bear.

BEAR: *(Stops, indignant)* Correct that. He was Russia's most honored dancing bear.

RINGMASTER: His mother, born in Spain, also a dancing bear,

BEAR: She was the prima ballerina bear of all Spain!

RINGMASTER: He, only son –

BEAR: Is the World's Greatest Dancing Bear!

RINGMASTER: Then you are the one I have come for!

BEAR: Yes!

RINGMASTER: Then we will have no more tricks or games. *(BEAR realizes he has revealed himself.)* Come. Take my hand. *(BEAR always reacts with fear to the RINGMASTER's white gloved hand.)* I will show you the way to the Great Center Ring.

BEAR: No! No!

TISH: What is he saying?

BEAR: He is going to take me away.

RINGMASTER: Come. You must. And it is easier if you go quietly.

BEAR: No! I will not go with you. I will fight!
(Holds up boxing gloves)

TISH: Fight him! I'll help you!

BEAR: I have fought all my life. Battled my way to the top. Look at my medals. I will fight to the end.

RINGMASTER: This, my friend, is the end.

BEAR: No! No! Not for me. Not yet! Stay away! I have new dances to do.

BEAR: No! No. *(Savagely)* I will claw! I will eat! I will crush! I will kill! Kill to live! *(Violently throws boxing gloves away)*

To live! To live!

RINGMASTER: Everyone shouts when he is frightened of the dark.

BEAR: I WILL NOT DIE!

RINGMASTER: You have no choice.

BEAR: But ... why? Why me? ME!

RINGMASTER: You are like all the others. Everyone thinks HE will live forever. Come.

BEAR: No! What did I do wrong? What can I do now? To stop it!

RINGMASTER: Death comes to all. It has never been IF you will die. The only question has been WHEN you will die. Now you know.

BEAR: *(Runs)* I will run, I will hide.

RINGMASTER: *(With authority)* You cannot escape from death.

BEAR: *(Bargaining desperately)* More time. Give me more time. I have so much to do.

RINGMASTER: *(Slightly annoyed)* There is always that which is left undone.

BEAR: I don't know how ... to die. I need to rehearse.

RINGMASTER: No one has to rehearse. It is very simple ... very easy. *(Holds out hand)* Come. It is growing late.

BEAR: No! *(Desperate for any excuse)* I must write my memories! Tell the world the glories of my life. My life ... *(Pause. TISHand MIME rush to him as he falters, place box and help him sit.)* it is almost over. And what was it? A few medals that will be lost. There must be more to life. Give me time. Time to find the answer.

TISH: *(Kneeling by him, pleads into space.)* Please ... let him live.

RINGMASTER: Your life is over. Today is the day.

BEAR: But my day is not over. *(To TISH)* The day is not ended, is it?

TISH: Give him to the END of the day!

BEAR: Yes! To the end. Oh, you are a very smart little girl!

RINGMASTER: Well ... *(Looks in his book)*

TISH: What did he say?

BEAR: He's looking in his book.

RINGMASTER: The day you are to die is written plainly. But not the hour.

BEAR: Then give me the full day.

TISH: Please.

BEAR: YES!

TISH: Can you live?

BEAR: YES! Oh, let me shout to the world! I AM ALIVE! *(To MIME)* Give me my brightest, my happiest hat! *(To RINGMASTER, who has gone)* Oh, thank you ... thank you ... He is gone ... for a while. *(To TISH)* Oh, let me touch you. Let me feel the warmth ... the life in you. There is so much yet to do! And so little time. My life ... it went too fast. I didn't stop to listen ... I didn't stop to see. *(MIME waves clown hat in front of BEAR)* Oh, yes! I will be the clown! *(Puts hat on. To TISH)* Come. Dance with me! And we will make the world spin round and round with joy!

TISH: Grandpa taught me how to whistle and how to dance a jig. *(Quickly she whistles "O Susannah," and does a little jig, looking at her feet.)*

BEAR: No, no, no. To dance is a great honor. Hold your head high. *(He follows his own instructions)* And first you smile to the right ... then you smile to the left ... and you bow to the center ... and then ... begin.
(MIME motions. A spotlight comes on BEAR. Music is heard. BEAR does a short, charming soft-shoe dance. Spotlight and music dim out. TISH applauds. BEAR sits on box which MIME places for him. BEAR is happy, but breathless.)

TISH: Oh, how wonderful!

544

BEAR: Thank you.

TISH: You're better than Grandpa! He can only do a little jig.

BEAR: But he taught you?

TISH: Yes.

BEAR: And he taught you how to whistle?

TISH: Yes.

BEAR: *(Rises)* If I could teach my dances to someone ... if someone could carry on the fame of my family ... All my hats ... there will be no one to wear my hats. They, too, will be put in a box and forgotten. Tell me, are you like your Grandfather?

TISH: Daddy says I'm a chip off the old block.

BEAR: You are a part of him. And you will carry on for him in life. *(Excited)* Yes! Yes, that is the answer to the riddle.

TISH: What riddle?

BEAR: The riddle of life. I must leave my dances! They will be a part of me that will live on! But who? Where! How!

TISH: Make a wish!

BEAR: A wish?

TISH: On the first star you see. And it will come true. It will. It will!

BEAR: *(Wanting to believe)* You are sure it will? *(TISH nods. To MIME)* Do you believe it will? *(MIME nods)* I could try.

TISH: Quick!

BEAR: Of course I don't believe in superstitions. But I did get up on the right side of the bed. *(MIME nods)* I did find a four leaf clover, *(MIME nods)* And I haven't sneezed once. *(MIME shakes his head)* Yes, luck is with me today! So let me knock on wood — three times — and I will do it! *(MIME takes off hat. BEAR knocks on MIME's head three times, with sound effects.)* What do I say?

TISH: Point to the first star you see.

BEAR: *(Looks about, then points.)* There! I see a bright twinkling one.

TISH: Say, "Star light, star bright ... "

BEAR: *(To MIME)* The rabbit's foot! This wish must come true. *(Looks up)* "Star light, star bright."

TISH: "First star I see tonight."

BEAR: "First star I see tonight." *(Takes rabbit's foot from MIME and rubs it vigorously)* Oh, bring me luck. Make my wish come true.

TISH: "I wish I may, I wish I might ... "

BEAR: "I wish I may, I wish I might" Oh, it won't work. It's nothing but a nursery rhyme.

TISH: "Have the wish I wish tonight." Say it. Say it!

BEAR: "Have the wish I wish tonight." *(Pause)* Nothing. Nothing. I told you so.

TISH: Look. Look! It's beginning to happen.

STAR BRIGHT: *(Star music and lights begin as STAR BRIGHT enters on swing. He is joyously happy.)* Tonight I'm blinking. Tonight I'm winking. Wishes are flying past. Wishes are coming quick and fast! I'm twinkling bright and RIGHT tonight! *(Laughs)* Your wish, please.

BEAR: *(Lost in happy memories)* Look. It is like the circus. The trapeze high in a tent of blue ... the music of the band ...

(MIME motions. Soft band music of the circus is heard. Colorful lights play on the backdrop.)

the acrobats; the jugglers tossing, catching bouncing balls ... *(MIME pantomimes juggling)*

the delicious smell of popcorn ... the dance on the high wire...

(TISH holds up an imaginary umbrella and walks on an imaginary tight rope)

the sweet taste of pink lemonade ... Oh, the beauty, the wonder of life. Let me look at it. The happiness of living ...

Oh, let me feel it. The joy of being alive! Let me keep it. Let me hold it forever. *(Holds out his arms to embrace it all)*

STAR BRIGHT: *(Clasps his hands. Music and circus scene stops.)* Your wish. Your wish. Repeat, please.

BEAR: *(Confused, he is led by MIME to STAR.)* I wish to leave a foot print.

STAR BRIGHT: *(Puzzled)* Repeat, please.

TISH: The answer to the riddle.

BEAR: *(Intently)* I wish to leave with someone my dances so that I ... so that they ... will be remembered.

STAR BRIGHT: That is a wish I hear every night ... every night. A wish to shine on earth ... and leave behind a trace ... to learn, to earn the grace ... of immortality. Of your wish, half I can do. The other half is left for you. But quick! You must start. Because all wishes on a star must be done before the star is over shadowed by the sun. *(He claps his hands. Magic music and lights begin.)*

One, two;
Sunset red;
Midnight blue;
The wish you wish
I give to you.
(Magic lights and music end as STAR BRIGHT exits up and out of sight. From off L. LITTLE BEAR is heard singing. All look to L. LITTLE BEAR enters finishing his song to the tune of "Turkey in the Straw." He is a small cub, wearing country overalls and a little turned-up straw hat. Over his shoulder he carries a small fishing pole.)

LITTLE BEAR: *(Sings)*
Turkey in the straw, haw, haw, haw;
Turkey in the hay, hay, hay, hay;
Bait the hook, give the line a swish;
Jumpin' jiggers, I caught a fish.

TISH: A little bear.

BEAR: *(Little Bear does a few dance steps of joy, and continues walking and singing)* A little dancing bear.

(To MIME) Meet him. Greet him. Make him welcome. *(To TISH)* Quick, the handmirror. *(TISH holds mirror which MIME gives her and BEAR preens. MIME hurries to LITTLE BEAR and pantomimes a big and friendly greeting. LITTLE BEAR, as if it were a game, happily imitates every movement of the MIME. It ends with both shaking hands. Then LITTLE BEAR gives a friendly goodbye wave and starts off R. singing)*

Stop him! *(MIME rushes in front of LITTLE BEAER and turns him around.)* I am ready to be presented. *(MIME, with a flourish, presents BEAR.)*

LITTLE BEAR: Howdy-do to you.

BEAR: You have come from my WISHING on a star.

LITTLE BEAR: Huh uh. I've come from my FISHING in the river.

BEAR: Oh, my little one, I am going to give you the treasure of my life. Bestow on you all my gifts.

LITTLE BEAR: I could use a new fishing pole.

BEAR: I am going to teach you all my dances. You will wear all my hats. Oh-ho! I have never felt so alive in my life! *(He gives a joyous whoop and jumps and clicks his heels. LITTLE BEAR is bewildered. BEAR, with the eyes of a dancing master, looks LITTLE BEAR over.)* Yes, you have a good build. Good stance. Relaxed torso. *(Taps LITTLE BEAR's waist. LITTLE BEAR wiggles and giggles from the tickling.)* Legs sturdy, Up! Leg up. Up! *(LITTLE BEAR cautiously lifts leg.)* Up! Up! *(BEAR raises LITTLE BEAR's leg high.)*

LITTLE BEAR: Whoa!

BEAR: Point, Point!

LITTLE BEAR: *(Points with finger)* Point where?

BEAR: *(Holding LITTLE BEAR's foot high)* Point your foot. Ah, feet too stiff ... too stiff. *(Lets leg down. LITTLE BEAR stands in profile, stomach pushed out.)* Stomach flat! *(Taps stomach. LITTLE BEAR pulls stomach in, but pushes hips out.)* Rear push in! *(Smacks LITTLE BEAR on the bottom. Little Bear pulls hips in, and turns facing audience.)* Stretch ... up ... up! *(Pulls LITTLE BEAR up who tries to stretch. His face is tense.)* Relax. *(Pats LITTLE BEAR on forehead. LITTLE BEAR slowly sinks to the ground. BEAR lifts him up.)* Smile. *(LITTLE BEAR forces a tortured smile.)* Walk! Walk! *(LITTLE BEAR starts walking stiffly.)*

TISH: Will he be a good dancer?

BEAR: He will be magnificent! *(Puts arm out and stops LITTLE BEAR's escape)* He will be — ME! My rehearsal hat. My father's Russian dancing hat! *(He dances a few steps of a Russian dance, and shouts a few Russian words.)* To the dressing room. *(He continues the dance steps and shouting as he exits at R. MIME, with traveling box follows him, imitating the dance steps.)*

LITTLE BEAR: Who ... who is he?

TISH: He is the greatest dancing bear in the world.

LITTLE BEAR: Oh!

TISH: And ... he's going to die.

LITTLE BEAR: Oh.

TISH: My Grandpa is going to die and I don't know what to do.

LITTLE BEAR: Up in the hills, I've seen a lot of them die.

TISH: You have?

LITTLE BEAR: Old ones, little ones, and big ones, too. And there ain't nothing you can do about it. 'Cause as sure as you're born, you're sure of dying.

TISH: It's sad.

LITTLE BEAR: Course it's sad.

TISH: It's frightening.

LITTLE BEAR: *(Thinking it out)* No. It ain't dyin' that you're afraid of. It's the not knowin' what comes AFTER you die. That's what scares you.

TISH: *(Tearfully)* I'll never see Grandpa again.

LITTLE BEAR: *(With gentle understanding)* You go on. You have yourself a good cry. It'll help you to give him up. And you got to. *(With emphasis)* You got to let him go.

TISH: No.

LITTLE BEAR: You have to! 'Cause he gone ... forever.

TISH: You don't know what it's like to have your Grandpa die.

LITTLE BEAR: Yes, I do. My Grandpa died last winter. And my Papa ... I saw a hunter shoot my Papa.

TISH: *(Shocked)* Shoot your Papa! Oh, what did you do?

LITTLE BEAR: First, I cried. Yes, I cried, and then I started hatin' and I kicked and clawed 'cause I felt all alone.

TISH: *(Nods)* All by yourself.

LITTLE BEAR: Then my Mama said, "You have to go on living, so ... do your best. Give yourself to the livin'. 'Cause that's the best way to say goodbye to your Pa." So I made my peace.

TISH: Your peace?

LITTLE BEAR: Inside myself. Oh, it don't mean I understand about dyin'. I don't. But you do go on living. The next day. The next year. So if you love your Grandpa like I loved my Papa ...

TISH: Oh, I do. How?

LITTLE BEAR: Tell him goodbye ... by giving your most to the living. I'm wanting to do something ... something big ... just for Papa.

BEAR: *(Off)* All is ready!

TISH: Please, dance with him. He needs you.

LITTLE BEAR: Well, I like to help folks.

TISH: You said, "Give to the living."

LITTLE BEAR: And I do like the dance!

TISH: *(Excited with a new idea)* This is the big thing you can do for your Papa.

LITTLE BEAR: For Papa?

TISH: *(Points with her hand as she visualizes it)* Your name will be in lights. You will be the NEW World's Greatest Dancing Bear!

BEAR: *(BEAR and MIME enter, BEAR wearing his Russian Cossack hat)* Let the flags fly! Let the band play! *(To LITTLE BEAR)* We will start with a simple waltz. My mother's famous skating waltz. One, two, three; one, two, three ... *(He dances, continuing during the next speeches)*

LITTLE BEAR: *(Tries to do the step, then stops)* No. I'm just a country bear, with no schoolin'.

TISH: You will be the famous ... "Arkansas Bear!"
(Urges him on)

LITTLE BEAR: Arkansas. I ain't right sure how to spell Arkansas. *(He moves in one spot to the beat of the music, wanting to dance, but afraid)*

TISH: Like it sounds. A — R — — K — A — N— — —

LITTLE BEAR: *(Shouts, eager to dance)* S — A — W! *(With a burst of energy he follows BEAR and dances with joy, counting loudly and happily.)* One! Two! Three! One! Two! Three! I'm doing it!
(The first chime of midnight is heard, loud and distinct. The other chimes follow slowly. MIME runs to BEAR, motions for him to listen.)

TISH: What is it?

BEAR: The chimes are striking twelve.

LITTLE BEAR: It's the end of the day. Midnight.

BEAR: No! No! Not yet! I have not taught you my dances. Stop the clock!

551

TISH: Run! Hide! Before he comes back!

BEAR: Where?

LITTLE BEAR: In the caves! In the hills!

TISH: Hurry! *(TISH and LITTLE BEAR help BEAR. MIME carries box. All start toward back. Soft calliope music is heard. RINGMASTER enters R.)*

RINGMASTER: Twelve. *(They stop)* Your day is ended. Your time is up. I will take you to the Great Center Ring.

BEAR: No. No!

TISH: Is he here?

BEAR: Yes, he has come for me. *(Comes down stage. Backs off towards L.)* Stop him.

RINGMASTER: There is no way to stop death.

TISH: I know a way. *(Grabs MIME and points up toward star)* You! Make a wish on the first star you see. Say, *(Shouts)*
Star light, star bright,
First star I see tonight ...
(MIME quickly points and looks up, rapidly miming the words of the rhyme)

STAR BRIGHT: *(Off)* Louder, please.

RINGMASTER: Come. *(Holds out his hand and slowly crosses toward BEAR at far L.)*

TISH: *(MIME pantomimes, repeating with larger gestures, while TISH says the words.)*
I wish I may, I wish I might,
Have the wish I wish tonight.

STAR BRIGHT: *(Quickly descends into view)* Wish quickly chanted. Wish quickly granted.

TISH: *(MIME pantomimes her words)* Stop death! *(With a sound effect of a roll on a cymbal, STAR BRIGHT points at RINGMASTER, who has advanced almost to BEAR. RINGMASTER stops in a walking position.)* Make him go away! *(A roll on acymbal is heard, as STAR BRIGHT makes*

552

a circle with his hand. RINGMASTER slowly turns around.)
LOCK HIM UP IN THE TREE!
(Another roll on the cymbal)

STAR BRIGHT: Walk to the tree. *(RINGMASTER slowly walks to a tree.)* Your home it will be ... for a time. *(RINGMASTER stops. STAR BRIGHT points to tree again. There is a roll on a cymbal as the trunk slowly opens.)* It is open wide ... to welcome you. Step inside. *(RINGMASTER faces tree and slowly steps inside the tree trunk, and turns and faces audience.)* Let it enfold and hold you ... for a time. *(Waves his hand. There is a last roll on a cymbal. The tree trunk slowly closes shut.)* Locked, blocked, and enclosed! *(He laughs)*

BEAR: *(To TISH)* You did it! You stopped death!

TISH: *(She and BEAR shout together, while MIME jumps with joy and blows whistle.)* We did it!

BEAR: We did it!

STAR BRIGHT: *(Claps his hands)* Remember ... soon will come the morning sun, and then ... Remember that is when ... all wishes become ... undone.
(Star music and light begin as he ascends out of sight, and then stop)

BEAR: *(Their joy changes to concern)* It is true! Time is short! Quick. I must teach the little one — *(Looks about. LITTLE BEAR has, unnoticed, slipped away when RINGMASTER appeared.)* Where is he?

TISH: Little Bear!
(Pause. There is no answer.)

BEAR: Little Bear, come back!

TISH: *(She and MIME run looking for him)* Little Bear?

BEAR: He was frightened ... *(Looks at tree)* of death. He is gone. And with him all my hopes are gone.
(He slumps, wearily)

TISH: *(Concerned, rushes to him)* You must rest, like Grandpa.

553

BEAR: Your Grandfather has you. *(Amused)* A chip off the old block, eh? *(She nods)* You gave him happiness in life ... peace in death.

TISH: Are you all right?

BEAR: I am old, and weary and tired. And I am going to die.

TISH: No. We stopped death.

BEAR: But only for a brief time. Death, they say is a clock. Every minute our lives are ticking away. Now ... soon ... my clock will stop.

TISH: No.

BEAR: When I was young like you, I wondered, "Where did I come from?" And now when I am old, I wonder, "Where am I going?" *(MIME looks and listens off R. then runs to them and excitedly mimes that LITTLE BEAR is coming.)* What is it? *(MIME pantomimes more)* Who? Where? *(MIME points to R. All watch as LITTLE BEAR enters)* You have come back.

LITTLE BEAR: I left my fishing pole.

BEAR: Have no fear. Death is locked in the tree.
(LITTLE BEAR reacts with fright at tree)

TISH: You have come back to help.

LITTLE BEAR: I come back to learn all your fancy dancin'.

TISH: *(Runs to LITTLE BEAR and hugs him)* Oh, you are the best, the sweetest, the most wonderful little bear in the world! *(LITTLE BEAR is embarrassed.)*

BEAR: Yes! Quick! We must begin the lesson. There is so little time and so much to learn. *(Looks frightened off R. To MIME)* Stand watch. Yes, watch for the first rays of the sun! *(MIME stands at R. anxiously looking off. TISH sits on box. BEAR motions to LITTLE BEAR.)* Come! Come! Attention! I will teach you all I know. *(Takes position)* First, you smile to the right. *(BEAR does the action with the words. LITTLE BEAR watches and tries to do the action.)* You smile to the left. You bow to the center. And then ... begin ... to dance. We will

554

start with my father's famous Russian dance. Master this and all else will be easy. *(To MIME)* How many more minutes? *(MIME holds up ten fingers)* Ten! Position. Position! *(LITTLE BEAR imitates him)* Listen to the beat ... the beat ... *(Taps foot)*

LITTLE BEAR: Beat what?

BEAR: Your feet! Your feet! The beat ... the beat ... *(Taps foot. LITTLE BEAR slowly and timidly taps beat)* Too slow. Too slow. *(LITTLE BEAR pivots in a circle, weight on one foot while tapping fast with the other foot.)* Too fast. Too fast. *(LITTLE BEAR does it right.)* Ah! Ah! Ah! Good! Good!

LITTLE BEAR: I'm doing it right!

BEAR: *(Shows him next Russian step)* The first step. Hop, hop, hop, switch, hop. *(LITTLE BEAR tries, awkward at first, then better.)* Hop, hop, hop, switch, hop. Yes, hop, hop, hop, switch, hop. Yes! Yes! *(Shows him next step)* Deep knee, hop. *(LITTLE BEAR shakes his head)* Try. Try. *(LITTLE BEAR tries deep knee bends with a hop.)* Deep knee, hop. Lower. Lower. *(LITTLE BEAR puts hands on floor in front of him and does a step. He smiles at the audience at the easiness of it.)* No, no, no! No hands! *(Lifts LITTLE BEAR up. LITTLE BEAR continues to kick his feet.)* The next step. The finale. *(Shows step)* Turn, two, up, two. Turn, two, up, two.

LITTLE BEAR: Oh, my!

BEAR: Turn, two, up, two. *(LITTLE BEAR tries.)* Turn, two, up, two. Faster. Faster.

LITTLE BEAR: *(Falls)* I can't do it. I can't do it.

BEAR: You will. You must do it. I must leave my dances with you.

TISH: Try, please, Please, try.

LITTLE BEAR: Well ...
(Gets up)

BEAR: Again. Again. Ready. Turn, two, up, two. *(Bear keeps repeating the count, and LITTLE BEAR does the step better and better, until he is perfect — and happy.)* He did it! He did it!

TISH: He did it!

LITTLE BEAR: I did it!

BEAR: *(To MIME)* How many minutes are left? *(MIME holds up eight fingers)* Eight minutes. Time is running out. Quick. The polka. The dance of the people. Music! *(MIME motions. Music is heard. Bear dances a few steps. LITTLE BEAR quickly follows him and masters them. Music stops. BEAR breathes heavily.)* How many more minutes? *(MIME holds up seven fingers)* Only seven minutes left! Hurry. My famous tarentella. *(MIME motions and music is heard. BEAR does a few steps. LITTLE BEAR again quickly does them and they dance together. Music stops. BEAR pants for breath. MIME runs to him and holds up six fingers.)* Six minutes. And at the end take your bow. The first bow. *(Bear bows, short of breath)* The second bow. *(BEAR bows, pauses, then with trembling voice he speaks with emotion, knowing it is his last bow.)* And the last and final bow.

TISH: More, more! Encore! Encore! *(BEAR slumps to the floor. She rushes to him.)* He's fallen. *(She and MIME cradle BEAR on either side)* Are you all right?

BEAR: *(Stirs, weakly)* How ... many more minutes ... do I have left? *(MIME holds up five fingers)* My little one, you will do my dances, you will carry on for me?

LITTLE BEAR: Yes. Yes.

BEAR: Take my father's hat ... and it was HIS father's hat ...

LITTLE BEAR: No, you must wear it.

BEAR: I will not need it where I am going. I have taken my last bow.

TISH: No. *(Buries her head on his shoulder)*

BEAR: Ah, tears can be beautiful. But there is no need to cry. I am content. I was a part of what went before and I will be a part of what is yet to come. That is the answer to the riddle of life. *(Weakly)* How many more minutes? *(MIME holds up two fingers)* Two. Bring me my traveling hat. I will wear it on my last journey. *(LITTLE BEAR gets traveling hat from box, as MIME and TISH help BEAR to stand)* I must look my best when I enter the Great Center Ring. *(MIME puts hat on BEAR, who smiles at TISH)* Does it look stylish?

TISH: Yes.

BEAR: Is it becoming? *(She nods)* Then I am ready. *(Gently pushes TISH and MIME away)* No. This journey I must go alone. *(Extends hand to MIME)* Goodbye, good friend. Thank you for everything. And sometimes when the band plays ... think of an old bear. *(MIME motions for BEAR to wait. MIME quickly gets a pink balloon on a string from the side and holds it out to BEAR)* Yes, I remember when once we said, "Life is like a bright balloon." Hold it tight. Hold it tight. Because ... once you let it go ... it floats away forever. *(Breathless)* How many more minutes? *(MIME holds up one finger. BEAR turns to TISH.)* I have one last request. When the end comes ... when I enter the Great Center Ring ... I want music. I want you to whistle the tune your Grandfather taught you.

TISH: "O Susannah."

BEAR: *(Nods and smiles)* You will find that when you whistle you cannot cry at the same time. *(A rooster is heard crowing)* Listen.

LITTLE BEAR: It's a rooster crowin'. It's almost mornin'.

TISH: The sun is up. The stars are fading away.

STAR BRIGHT: *(Star music is heard as STAR BRIGHT descends into view. He speaks softly.)* Announcing: the first ray of sun is peeping out. Warning: all wishes end as the sun begins. The new day is starting, the old departing. That is the great pattern ... The circle of life. Tomorrow is today. *(He points at the tree, and claps his hands. The tree trunk opens.)* And the night and the stars fade away ... fade away.
(There is star music as STAR BRIGHT disappears. Soft

calliope music is heard which continues during the scene.)

RINGMASTER: *(Steps out from tree trunk. He speaks with authority.)* There is no more time. The book is closed.

BEAR: Poets tell us death is but a sleep, but who can tell me what I will dream?

RINGMASTER: *(Walks slowly to BEAR)* Take my hand.

BEAR: Tell me, tell me what is death?

RINGMASTER: When there is no answer, you do not ask the question. Come.

BEAR: Yes, I am ready. *(To LITTLE BEAR)* My little one ... I give you my feather ... and you ... give joy ... to the world. *(Gives turkey feather to LITTLE BEAR. He whispers.)* Let the balloon go.
(RINGMASTER holds out his hand, which BEAR takes. Together they walk off L. slowly. MIME lets the balloon go. He, TISH and LITTLE BEAR watch as it floats up and out of sight. At the same time the calliope music builds in volume. There is a second of silence. Then the ANNOUNCER's voice is heard, loud and distinctly.)

ANNOUNCER'S VOICE: Ladies and gentlemen: presenting for your pleasure and entertainment, the new dancing bear, the world's famous, the world's favorite, the world's greatest — The Arkansaw Bear!
(During the announcement, MIME points to LITTLE BEAR. LITTLE BEAR looks frightened, amazed and pleased. MIME holds up mirror and LITTLE BEAR puts feather in his hat. MIME motions for LITTLE BEAR to step forward, then motions a circle of light on the floor. Spotlight comes on and LITTLE BEAR steps into the light.)

BEAR'S VOICE: *(Over the loud speaker, Bear's voice is heard. He speaks softly and with emotion. LITTLE BEAR follows his instructions.)* You smile to the right ... smile to the left ... bow to the center ... and then begin to dance! *(Music begins, lively "Turkey in the Straw." LITTLE BEAR begins his dance.)* My dances ... your dances ... and make the world spin round and round with joy.

(LITTLE BEAR dances with fun, excitement, and joy, a wonderful short dance. During this TISH exits, and MIME exits with box. At the end of the dance, LITTLE BEAR bows as the audience applauds, and exits at L., peeks out and waves again. Spotlight goes out. Fantasy music is heard and a soft night light illuminates the tree. TISH is leaning against it. She looks up, sighs, picks up the flowers, and slowly circles back to the downstage area of the first scene, which becomes light as the tree area dims out. Fantasy music also fades out. MOTHER's and AUNT ELLEN's voices are heard, and TISH answers as if they were standing on each side of her downstage.)

MOTHER'S VOICE: *(Worried)* Tish? Tish, is that you?

TISH: Yes, mother.

MOTHER'S VOICE: Where have you been?

TISH: I went up the hill to my tree. I want to see Grandpa.

AUNT ELLEN'S VOICE: He's dead ... dead.
(Cries)

TISH: *(Trying to be brave)* Dead. Tears can be beautiful, Aunt Ellen. But you have to give him up. Let the balloon go.

AUNT ELLEN'S VOICE: What?

TISH: *(Trying to keep back her tears)* I know everyone ... everything has a time to die ... and it's sad. But Grandpa knew the answer to the riddle.

AUNT ELLEN'S VOICE: The riddle?

TISH: He left his footprint. He left a chip off the old block.

MOTHER'S VOICE: What, dear? What did he leave?

TISH: Me! And I want to do something ... something big for Grandpa. Because that's the best way to say goodbye. *(Softly)* Let me give him his flowers ... the pink ones.

MOTHER'S VOICE: *(Positive, and with a mother's love and authority)*

All right, dear. Come along. We'll go together and see Grandpa. *(TISH starts L., and begins to whistle)* What are you doing?

TISH: Whistling ... for the bear ... and for Grandpa. Because it helps ... when you are afraid and in the dark. And ... when you whistle, you can't cry. *(Whispers)* Goodbye, Grandpa, I ... I love you.
(TISH exits L., bravely trying to control her crying. At the same time, lights slowly come up so the full stage is seen. The light on TISH's area dims out. The stage is bright with soft beautiful colors. The lone whistling of "O Susannah," the same as at the beginning of the play, is heard. There is a moment of a final picture — the living tree standing, as it has through the years, against a beautiful endless sky. The whistling continues as the curtains close.)

JACK AND THE WONDER BEANS

adapted by
Larry Snipes

from the book by
James Still

musical selections
and original lyrics by
Mike Norderer

additional lyrics by
Vivian Robin Snipes

This play represents a form of theatre for young people, participation theatre, which, in its ideal, offers young audiences meaningful participatory experiences within the context of the fictive world of a play. Participation theatre for young audiences occupies a unique niche in the development of the field. Created, in part, because of the acknowledgement that young children do not always make a clear separation between reality and the imaginary world presented on stage, this movement sought to channel the overt physical and vocal excitement sometimes evoked from an otherwise passive child audience into more formalized participatory experiences.

Barrie's *Peter Pan* includes one of the most familiar instances of audience participation: when Peter solicits help from the audience to save Tinkerbell. Yet this play also suggests some of the difficulties inherent in the participation form. This request to help Tinkerbell, made directly to the audience, is the only solicitation for participation in the play, and it thus stands out as a stylistic inconsistency that threatens to undermine the fragile illusory reality of the piece. Such examples remind us that, while young audiences may freely offer vocal responses, participation plays carry with them unique aesthetic issues.

Throughout the last century, many theorists and practitioners in the adult theatre (Brecht, Artaud, Grotowski, and Schechner, for example) attacked the conventions of illusory theatre, consciously seeking to break down the physical and psychic distance between actor and audience. While each of these theatre artists operated in and for explicit political ideologies, each sought to make the theatre experience *immediate*, and the audience members more than mere spectators. The movement of participation theatre for young people shares these aims, if not the larger political agendas.

British playwright Brian Way, who wrote scores of participation plays, has been the most prolific writer of this theatre form, which, in this country, reached its height in popularity during the 1970s and 1980s. While Way's plays have not been produced widely across this country, they illustrate the diverse spectrum of the movement.

Way's plays range from simplistic works that ask the spectators to make sounds to move the characters (*The Mirrorman*), to plays that solicit more sophisticated intellectual participation when the audience must act as a jury reacting to a morally ambiguous and difficult situation (*On Trial*).

Given the goals of participation theatre for young audiences, the plays differ markedly in form and content from other plays in the repertoire, and performances of the plays necessitate careful preparation by the performers, both for their roles and their work with the young audiences. *Jack and the Wonder Beans* illustrates well the issues involved in this work.

Snipes wrote *Jack and the Wonder Beans* to be presented in an open area, preferably a "black box" theatre wherein the actors can perform on the same physical level as the audience. In this play, as in most participation plays, the desired setting has the audience sitting on the floor, in a three-quarter or full arena arrangement. Production notes underscore the importance of the actors helping seat the young audience members as they enter the space, so they can develop an easy, nonthreatening relationship with them. This same physical arrangement also necessarily limits the audience in size so that all audience members are seated close to the action.

Like many participation plays, *Jack and the Wonder Beans* offers explicit storytelling, as well as simple songs, with which the actors ask the audience to sing along. Through the lyrics the audience members receive their "participation" instructions. Thereby, from the audience's entrance into the playing space, through the opening song, the "rules" of this theatrical adventure are revealed to them, as they are told implicitly and explicitly that this will not be a "regular" theatregoing experience. The play openly solicits audience involvement, but the actors must control the parameters of the involvement so that the play moves forward appropriately; and the young audience members, if well-prepared, enjoy not just a play, but a unique storytelling experience.

The ensuing play presents a version of the "Jack and the Beanstalk" story, with some twists driven by Jack's sense of adventure; yet, the essence of this play rests not in the play, but in the entire experience offered to the audience. The audience participation ranges from general sounds and actions, to children assuming the role of the cow and the hen. Because of this range, audience members can enjoy the broad ensemble participation, as well as delight in seeing someone they know placed as an important part of the action.

Over the last century, scores of children's plays have been written that include gratuitous and distracting kinds of audience "participation" (chase scenes that run through the audience, characters asking the audience to help them find a hidden character, etc.); but only a few writers have approached this form seriously by considering the totality of the participatory experience for the child. *Jack and the Wonder Beans*, like most participation plays, works best for younger audiences, those most willing to lose themselves in the "fun" of the moment. The dialogue and the action of the play, while seemingly simplistic from dramatic standards, appropriately reveal a singular, unambiguous action, suitable for this activity.

Participation plays do not fit easily into the accepted canon of dramatic literature for children, primarily because the design for the child's experience extends well beyond the play itself. *Jack and the Wonder Beans* offers a delightful example of this unique form of theatre for young audiences.

Larry Snipes has served as Lexington Children's Theatre's (LCT) Producing Director since 1979. After completing his MA in theatre for young audiences at Alabama's University of Montevallo, he worked for two years as a professional actor and director in the Washington, D.C. area. He has directed more than sixty productions for LCT and performed in many others.

Under his leadership, Lexington Children's Theatre has grown from a small community arts organization to Lexington's only professional theatre company.

His adaptation of Kentucky author James Still's *Jack and the Wonder Beans* has been performed at theatres across the country. This play remains Lexington Children's Theatre's most popular production. A participatory version of *The Fisherman and His Wife*, adapted by Mr. Snipes and his wife, Vivian, was recently published by New Plays for Children. Additionally he has adapted several unpublished scripts for LCT's touring company including: *The Legend of John Henry*, *Pecos Bill and Sluefoot Sue*, and *Tales of Edgar Allan Poe*. Mr. Snipes is currently working on a new adaptation, *Cows Don't Fly and Other Known Facts*, based on the work of Kentucky children's author and illustrator, Paul Brett Johnson.

JACK AND THE WONDER BEANS

adapted by
Larry Snipes

from the book by
James Still

musical selections
and original lyrics by
Mike Norderer

additional lyrics by
Vivian Robin Snipes

JACK AND THE WONDER BEANS was originally produced in February 1991 at Lexington Children's Theatre. The original production was directed by Vivian Robin Snipes with the following cast.

JACK .... Joe Gatton

STORYTELLER/MUSICIAN .... Roy Guill

MAM, CHICKEN LADY,
and the HIGH TALL GIANT WOMAN .... Evelyn Blythe

CARPENTER, GYPSY, GIANT ....Larry Snipes

For
Erica & Casey
and the "wonder" in their eyes.

JACK AND THE WONDER BEANS

Characters

STORYTELLER

JACK

HIS MAM

A CARPENTER

THE CHICKEN LADY

THE GYPSY

THE HIGH TALL GIANT WOMAN

THE HIGH TALL GIANT

Setting

TIME:
WAY BACK YONDER

PLACE:
IN, AROUND AND ABOVE WOLFPEN CREEK

ALL:	*(MELODY #1)*
	Set yourself down and put on a grin
	Set yourself down and put on a grin
	Jack and the Wonder Beans soon begins
	Wack Fa La Diddle all day
STORY:	**We're going to spin a tale for you**
& JACK:	**'Bout a boy,**
& MAM:	**his mam,**
& GIANT:	**and giants too**
ALL:	**You decide if you think it's true**
	Wack Fa La Diddle all day
STORY:	**Listen up good you girls and boys**
ALL:	**Keep your eyes on me/him, I'm Roy!**
ALL:	**I'll need your help to make some noise**
	Wack Fa La Diddle all day
STORY:	**If I make a sound,**
	make it back
STORY:	**If I make a motion,**
STORY:	**give it a whack**
ALL:	**We'll sing another song,**
	and you'll catch the knack
	Wack Fa La Diddle all day
	(MELODY #2)

(ALL SING EXCEPT THE STORYTELLER WHO ENCOURAGES THE AUDIENCE TO PARTICIPATE DURING THE SONG.)

The wind it blows on Wolfpen Creek
(WIND NOISES)

Dillum Dow Dillum
The rain comes down with snow and sleet
(RAIN NOISES)

> Dillum Dow
> Flowers bloom in the summertime
> *(FLOWERS BLOOM IN AUDIENCE)*
>
> > We hear bees buzz but that don't rhyme
> > *(BEES BUZZ)*
> >
> > Cuttle Dee Cuttle Dow Dillum Dow Day
> >
> > *(MELODY #1*
> > *This verse is sung by the STORYTELLER and the*
> > *REMAINDER OF THE CAST encourages the audience*
> > *to join in for the next verse.)*
> >
> > > There's a song to sing
> > > in the middle of the show
> > > I'll teach how the words do go
> > > Then you can sing along I know
> > > Wack Fa La Diddle all day

STORY: *(Sings)* **Night falls by and the beanstalk grown**
    (Spoken) Now you try it.

KIDS: *(Sung)*   **Night falls by and the beanstalk grows**

STORY: *(Spoken)* Same words again, only higher.

KIDS: *(Sung)*   **Night falls by and the beanstalk grows**

STORY: *(Spoken)* Now listen ...
    (Sings)   **The beanstalk grows 'til the rooster crows**
    (Spoken) Now you try it.

KIDS: *(Sung)*   **The beanstalk grows 'til the rooster crows**

STORY: *(Spoken)* You know the last line, sing it with me

KIDS: *(Sung)*   **Wack Fa La Diddle all day**

STORY: *(Spoken)* Now lets try the whole thing

ALL: *(Sing)*   **Night falls by and the beanstalk grows**
    Night falls by and the beanstalk grows
    The beanstalk grows 'til the rooster crows
    Wack Fa La Diddle all day

COMPANY: *(Spoken)* Good job! Well done! etc.

(All exit except STORYTELLER.)

STORY: **Listen and watch throughout our play**
There's more for you to do today
Than you can imagine or I can say
Wack Fa La Diddle all day

If you keep your bottoms right on the ground
We'll all be ready for Jack to come 'round
To hear the tale of the beans he found
Wack Fa La Diddle all day

Way back yonder there was a widow woman *(She enters.)*

WIDOW: H'lo!

STORY: and her son Jack

JACK: *(He enters.)* Howdy!

STORY: and they were as poor as Job's turkey. The way some tell it, their homeseat was here on Wolfpen Creek.

JACK & WIDOW: Or around about.

STORY: Well, all Jack and his Mam had was their home root, a cow and a patch of land.
(STORYTELLER exits to get volunteer for the cow.)

WIDOW: Jack, it's gettin' late. Go on out, fetch in the cow and bring in a pail of milk afore it gets dark.

JACK: Yes, mam. Cow! Cow! Now where is that torn fool cow any how? Have you seen a cow. She's about this high and brown and white all over.

(During the above a child is prepared to play the cow. The STORYTELLER explains that the cow should moo every time she hears the word "cow.")

Well, I'll be. There you are. Come on, come on in here cow. *(Moo)* *(He leads the COW in a circle around the bucket.)* Now Mam says I'm to fetch her a bucket of milk. *(He picks up the full bucket.)* That's good cow. *(Moo)* Now let's get you all settled in for the night, cow. *(The COW is left with the STORYTELLER for security.)*

574

WIDOW: That's a good cow. *(Moo)*

STORY: Now, they had the cow *(Moo)* and the patch of land. They lived on ...

JACK: garden sass.

WIDOW: and crumble-in!

JACK: Made of plain bread! Thank you, mam.

WIDOW: And milk!

JACK: Thank you, mam. That'll be just dandy.

STORY: Now, hit come a rough winter. *(As set up in the opening song the STORYTELLER solicits help from the children to make sound effects for the cold winter.)* The wind howled about the hills and the valleys.

(MELODY #2)

WIDOW: **Winter howled about them hills**

JACK & WIDOW:

> **Dillum Dow Dillum**
> **Winter howled about them hills**
> **Dillum Dow**

(During the song JACK returns to the cow and repeats the circle to fill the bucket with more milk.)

JACK: That's a good cow. *(Moo)*

STORY: The rain and sleet fell on the tin roofs.

WIDOW: **The rain and sleet came down so cold**

JACK& WIDOW:

> **Wolfpen Creek froze up I'm told**
> **Cuttle Dee Cuttle Dow Dillum Dow Day**

STORY: And then the snow drifted down and all was silent quiet.

JACK: Mam, it's cold as doorknobs.

WIDOW: Here, boy, eat some of this corn seed.

JACK: But, mam, what about the ...

WIDOW: I know. I held it back to plant the sass patch next spring, but it's all we got. You eat, hit'll warm you up some.

JACK: Yes, mam

STORY: And come spring the flowers bloomed all across the mountain.

(MELODY #2)

WIDOW: **Winter finally went away**

JACK & WIDOW:

> **Dillum Dow Dillum**
> **The rain and sleet did not stay**
> **Dillum Dow**

JACK: Well I'll be.

STORY: Birds sang, and bees buzzed throughout the valley.

WIDOW: **Winter finally went away**

JACK & WIDOW:

> **Springtime sun warmed up the day**
> **Cuttle Dee Cuttle Dow Dillum Dow Day**

STORY: The sun smiled down and all who saw it were awed by it's beauty.

WIDOW: My soul, Jack, what a lovely day. Now you run along and milk the cow *(Moo).*

JACK: Yes, mam. *(JACK returns to the cow for more milk.)*

STORY: But that spring ... *(JACK walks the COW in a circle.)*

JACK: Easy now. That's a good cow. *(Moo)*

STORY: ... the cow *(Moo)* went dry.

JACK: dry as a hat.

WIDOW: Dry as a hat!

JACK: Yes, mam. Not a drop.

WIDOW: Nothing to do, but take and sell that cow *(Moo)* so we will have money for bread.

576

JACK: But, mam, sell this ol' cow. *(Moo)* She's been a good cow *(Moo)* all these years.

WIDOW: I know son, but we've nothing else to do. Now go on Jack.

JACK: Yes, mam.
(JACK prepares the cow and MAM clears the area of props for the next scene during the following.)

(MELODY #3)

STORY: **Shady grove on Wolfpen Creek**
Shady grove my darlin
Shady grove on Wolfpen Creek
Bound for the shady grove

Jack went out to milk the cow
JACK: **No milk there was had**
Jack went home to tell his mam

STORY: **Jack was feeling sad**

WIDOW: **Jack go out and sell the cow**
Sell the cow I said
Bring a little money home
So we can buy some bread

STORY: **Shady grove on Wolfpen Creek**
Shady grove my darlin
Shady grove on Wolfpen Creek
Bound for the shady grove

STORY: So Jack hung a sign betwix the cow's *(Moo)* horns ...

WIDOW: *(As he hangs the sign on the cow)* Lady ... cow *(Moo)* ... for ... sale

JACK: Anybody.

WIDOW: Anybody.

JACK: There. *(JACK and COW travel around the audience.)*

STORY: He went up the road and down the road, through brush and saw-briar, aiming for to sell the critter.

(MELODY #3)

**Shady grove on Wolfpen Creek
Shady grove my darlin
Shady grove on Wolfpen Creek
Bound for the shady grove**

But dry cows *(Moo)* are hard numbers to unload. And she was all hide and bones. A walking shikepoke. Yet he had bids.
(Enter a CARPENTER. He spills his tool box of wooden folk toys which JACK plays with as he helps pick them up.)

JACK: H'lo!

MAN: Why, H'io there, Jack

JACK: Let me help you with that.

MAN: Thank you kindly.

JACK: It's my pleasure.

MAN: Jack, you're a long way from home. What brings you to these parts?

JACK: My Mam sent me out to sell the cow. *(Moo)*
(He shows the MAN the sign.)

MAN: *(Reading)* Lady cow *(Moo)* for sale.

JACK: Anybody.

MAN: Anybody. *(Looking over cow)* Hmmmmmmmmmmm. Scrawny cow. *(Moo)*

JACK: But she is nice mannered. How much would you give me for her?

MAN: Hmmmmmmmmmmmmmmm. Would you took a busted up hammer with one ear gone?

JACK: *(Thinks it over)* No.

MAN: Boy, that cow *(Moo)* ain't nothing but a bag of bones.

JACK: Yes sir, that's true, but she's real nice and she don't eat much.

578

MAN: Reckon she's gone dry.

JACK: Yes sir, but she is a likable ol' heifer.

MAN: I'll swap ye for my gee-haw whimmy diddle.

JACK: Now, no.

MAN: Are you sure?

JACK: Not even for a gee-haw whimmy diddle.

MAN: Well, I'll be. *(MAN exits. JACK continues.)*

STORY: So Jack ambled on down the road a bit further.

> *(MELODY #3)*
> **Shady grove on Wolfpen Creek**
> **Shady grove my darlin**
> **Shady grove on Wolfpen Creek**
> **Bound for the shady grove**
>
> **Jack went out to sell his cow**
> **Up the road a bit**
> **Came upon some chickens and**
> **A woman who said ...**

WOMAN: *(Feeding her chickens [the audience])* Here, chick, chick, chick, chick. Here chick, chick, chick, chick.

JACK: Would ya like me to help with that?

WOMAN: It ain't the feedin' I need help with, it's the gatherin'. Every time I say, "Hen, Lay!" sittin' right there in their nests, all these chickens flap their wings and lay an egg.

JACK: They do?

JACK: They do! Watch, I'll show ya. Get ready Chickens. "Hen, Lay!"
(When the WOMAN, says, "Hen, Lay" the children will begin to respond to her directions. JACK and the WOMAN should encourage this with improvised dialogue like: "Look at the size of that egg! or "Look at all the eggs!" "Thank you, chickens" is the stop control said whenever JACK and the WOMAN are ready.)

WOMAN: Thank you, chickens!

JACK: Thank you, chickens!

WOMAN: Thank you.

JACK: I've never seen anything like that before. Do it again.

WOMAN: You try it.

WOMAN: They'll flap their wings and lay an egg even if I say, "Hen, Lay!"?

WOMAN: From right where they are.

JACK: Hen, Lay! *(The students will repeat their actions and JACK and the WOMAN begin to gather the eggs.)*

WOMAN: Thank you, chickens!

JACK: Thank you, chickens!

WOMAN: And thank you, son. What's your name, child?

JACK: Jack.

WOMAN: Might scrawny cow *(Moo)* you got there, Jack.

JACK: Yes, but she is nice. Dry, but nice.

WOMAN: What you doing out this here way with a dry cow? *(Moo) (JACK shows her the sign.)* Lady cow *(Moo)* for sale.

JACK: Anybody.

WOMAN: Anybody.

JACK: My mam sent me out to sell the cow *(Moo)* so we could buy some bread.

WOMAN: Would you take a poke for catching snipe fer that bag o' bones?

JACK: Now, no. Not a poke, not a hammer, not even a GEE-HAW WHIMMY-DIDDLE! No. You can't eat airy a one of them.

WOMAN: Well, I'll be.

JACK: Would you swap for one of them laying hens?

WOMAN: Now, no. Not for a cow as dry as a hat. But I'll tell

580

you this. One of my chickens has wandered off and gotten herself lost. If' n you find her you can keep her.

JACK: Well, I'll be. Thank you M'am. Good day to ye.

WOMAN: Good day, son.
(GYPSY appears at the end of the aisle to see the end of the above and watches as JACK travels around the audience again.)

STORY: So off he went up the road and down the road aiming for to sell the critter.

(MELODY #3)

Shady grove on Wolfpen Creek
Shady grove my darlin
Shady grove on Wolfpen Creek
Bound for the shady grove

Jack went down the grove a piece
To sell a cow that day
Ran into a Gypsy man
This is what he say ...

GYPSY: *(Reads the sign)* Lady cow *(Moo)* for sale ... Anybody.

JACK: Anybody. *(Attempting to avoid the GYPSY JACK leads COW around behind the mountain drop.)* Come on cow *(Moo),* you just can't be too careful these days. *(JACK continues to talk to the COW as he goes. The GYPSY crosses to the other side to meet them when they re-enter the playing area.)* Now, that's better. Here we go ... *(He sees the GYPSY again and crosses to the center of the playing area.)* UH, OH!

GYPSY: Hmmmmmm. I'll give three beans for the cow. *(Moo)*

JACK: Beans! Three beans?

GYPSY: Not regular beans. WONDER BEANS!

JACK: Wonder Beans?

GYPSY: Wonder beans!

JACK: What are wonder beans?

GYPSY: Sow them and they will feed you your life tee-total.

JACK: Tee-total?

GYPSY: ... your life tee-total!

JACK: Hit looks like I'm a'bein' tooken.

GYPSY: Now, no, Jack. You're no simpleton.

JACK: To get ahead of me you'd have to have long ears and a bushy tail. *(The GYPSY holds the bag of wonder beans up in front of JACK.)* Now I know you can't buy wonder beans any day of the week.

GYPSY: Not just one, but three wonder beans!

JACK: Well, three beans beat nothing. Seeds for the sass patch.

GYPSY: So we swap?

JACK: Did Jack? We swap. *(A handshake seals the deal.)* Goodbye, ol' cow. *(Moo)*

GYPSY: Come on cow. *(Moo)*

JACK: Goodbye, ol' cow. *(The GYPSY exits with the COW and helps the volunteer back to her/his seat. JACK retraces his path home.)* Beans. Beans! Won't my Mam be proud. And not just one neither. Not one, not two, but three beans! Three beans that'll feed us our lives tee-total! *(During this travel time, the STORYTELLER resets for JACK'S home.)*

(MELODY #3)

STORY: **Shady grove on Wolfpen Creek**
Shady grove my darlin
Shady grove on Wolfpen Creek
Bound for the shady grove

The cow was sold for Wonder Beans
Three was all he had
Jack was proud of the trade he made
But the widow Mam was ...

WIDOW: *(Entering)* Here Jack comes home, with ...

JACK: No money!

582

WIDOW: And no cow!

JACK: No nothing except three beans.

WIDOW: Three beans? Fewer beans than fingers on a hand!

JACK: WONDER BEANS!

WIDOW: Wonder beans! Well, I never!

JACK: We plant them, and they'll feed us, our lives tee-total.

WIDOW: Tee-Total?

WIDOW: Did his mam throw a conniption! She sizzled like a red-hot horseshoe in the cooling tub.

WIDOW: *(Sizzle)* Upon my word and deed and honor, you couldn't be trusted to pack slops to a sick bear!

STORY: And she took and throwed the seeds away.

WIDOW: You don't know beans!

STORY: Jack quick pulled the kivers over his head so as not to hear worse.

WIDOW: Wonder beans! I never heerd such foolishness. And now we're left with nothin' to eat. I don't see how that son of mine could give our cow away for a handful of beans. How could I have raised such a fool. *(WIDOW exits.)*

STORY: Night fell. Tired and hungry Jack soon collapsed with the sleepies. Now while Jack was sleepin' an odd thing happened ... those beans set in a growin'.
(The STORYTELLER removes the beanstalk from one of the boxes and helps it grow under and around JACK finally attaching it to the Mountain backdrop during the following song.)

> *(MELODY #1)*
>
> **Now we sing the song**
> **in the middle of the show**
> **You will sing along I know**
> **A song to make the beanstalk grow**
> **Whack Fa La Diddle all day**

Night falls by and the beanstalk grows
Night falls by and the beanstalk grows
The beanstalk grows till the rooster crows
Whack Fa La Diddle all day

Night falls by and the beanstalk grows
Night falls by and the beanstalk grows
The beanstalk grows till the rooster crows
Whack Fa La Diddle all day

STORY: That vine grew, a creepin' and a crawlin' over, under and through anything in it's path. But, did Jack wake up? Now, no.

Night falls by and the beanstalk grows
Night falls by and the beanstalk grows
The beanstalk grows till the rooster crows
Whack Fa La Diddle all day.

Now that vine grew up and up and up, until it touched the sky. And come mornin' Jack he heered something rustlin' outside the window. *(STORYTELLER begins beanstalk rustle participation by rubbing hands together.)* But did that wake him up? Now, no. Soon ALL the leaves set to rustling. *(We give the students a moment to rustle while the STORYTELLER looks expectantly at JACK.)* He cracked his eyes. *(JACK stretches on his 'bed', STORYTELLER encourages the children to rustle louder.)* He saw something looked just like ...

JACK: ... bean vines!

STORY: Right!
(This is the cut off for the participation. An implied thank you is helpful.)

JACK: Right as a rabbit foot. They are bean vines! The beans have come up! Look at that, all twisted together into a stalk as thick as a blacksmith's arm. An' that stalk goes up and up and up ...

STORY: The stalk reached above the window, above the eaves, the roof,

JACK: and up into the sky.
(JACK begins to dust his hands and prepares to climb. He climbs until reaching the top of the mountain backdrop in time for whoo ... wheee.)

STORY: You know Jack. Independent as a hog on ice.

JACK: Ready ...

STORY: ... for anything. He made to climb the beanstalk to see where it went.

JACK: Did Jack. Up and up.

STORY: Up and up

JACK: and up. WHOO ..... WHEEE!
(JACK climbs down the back of the mountain backdrop and crosses behind. During this action the STORYTELLER has begun to set for the land of the giants.)

STORY: And directly he came to where the stalk leaned against a path.

JACK: *(Enters the playing area and steps out onto path)* A path, I'll go where it goes.

STORY: Did Jack. He went up the path and the countryside all around him was unlike anything he'd ever seen.

JACK: I'm not rightly certain that I recognize this place.
(As for earlier participation, the STORYTELLER encourages the children to help out with sounds that fit the narration.)

STORY: Everything was bigger than he was used to. The flowers, the buzzin' of the bees. *(BEES buzz.)*

JACK: 'Bout the only thing that reminds me of home is the breeze blowin'. *(WIND blows.)*

STORY: But that breeze blew a might stronger than it did on Wolfpen Creek. *(WIND sounds increase.)*

JACK: I sure wish this wind was blowin t'other direction to speed me on my journey.

STORY: And don't you know that's what happened.

JACK: Well I'll be, that wind seems to do whatever I tell it. Stop wind. It did! Wind blow me over yonder. Now wind, blow me down this path so I see where it goes.
(JACK works with the wind using it to move around the playing area and behind the audience giving the STORYTELLER time to set for the giants house and steps.)

STORY: Directly he ran smack dab into ...

JACK: Steps! Stop wind. Thank you, wind. These steps go up and up and up ...

STORY: He made to climb those steps.

JACK: Did Jack. Up and up. A castle house. Hit has the biggest door I ever seen.

STORY: Jack banged on the biggest thickest door ever and a woman opened it. A high tall giant woman. Of a size she could put Jack in her apron pocket. Said Jack, cocky as they come ...
(HIGH TALL GIANT WOMAN [HTGW] enters.)

JACK: Where's the master of this house place - - your old man?

HTGW: He hain't come in yet, and woe when he does. He eats tadwhackers the likes of you boiled ...

JACK: Boiled?

HTGW: ... fried ...

JACK: Fried?

HTGW: or baked in a pie.

JACK: Pie!

HTGW: Any which way when he's hungry.

JACK: Old sister, I'm hungry myself.

HTGW: Well, come on in.

JACK: What's a-cooking?

HTGW: Crumble-in. I'll fetch you a bowl.
(She brings JACK a large bowl of crumble-in. As he eats she begins to size him up in relation to pots, etc.)

(JACK finishes the first bowl.)

HTGW: Here, let me get you another.
(She brings JACK another bowl.)

JACK: Thank you.

HTGW: You, look like you could use another bowl. Are you still hungry?

JACK: Well, yes'um. Me and my mam, we're all out of food. But this Gypsy gave me three ...

HTGW: Here, have another bowl ...

STORY: Well, the giant woman tried to fatten him up. She thought she would eat Jack herself. She'd make a stew.

HTGW: A Jack stew. Seasoned with dill. *(Returning her attention to JACK.)* Just three bowls, wouldn't you like another ...
(Singing softly)

> *(MELODY #1)*
> **Fatten up Jack and bile him in stew**
> **Fatten up Jack and bile him in stew**
> **Giant likes to eat tadwhackers like you**
> **Wack Fa La Diddle all day**

STORY: Scarce had he finished when in walked a giant seventeen feet tall.
(GIANT enters in aisle.)

GIANT: Fee, fie, chew tobacco, I smell the toes of a tadwhacker.

STORY: With feet like cornsleds, hands like hams,

HTGW: You hide in here, quick.
(Grabbing JACK and shoving him into the oven, out of sight.)

STORY: Fingernails to match bucket lids, and the meanest eye ever beheld in this earthly world.

GIANT: Fee, fie, chew tobacco, I smell the toes of a tadwhacker.

HTGW: *(To GIANT)* You're smelling the crumbs in your beard.

GIANT: Humn?

HTGW: From the two tadwhackers you wolfed down for

breakfast.

GIANT: Humn. Smells fresh.

HTGW: Never you mind.

(MELODY #1)

GIANT: **Smells like a tadwhacker**

HTGW: **- - Never you mind**

GIANT: **Smells like a tadwhacker**

HTGW: **- - Never you mind**

BOTH: **Tadwhacker stew is going to be mine**
Wack Fa La Diddle all day

STORY: Even a giant knows when a woman says something
that's it. He set himself down, fetched out a flax sack of gold
money and began to count.

GIANT: One, two, three, four, ...

HTGW: I've got scrubbin' to do.

GIANT: eight, nine, ten, ...

STORY: His wife she got busy polishing her kettle pot. She was
making readies for a Jack stew.

HTGW: Sprinkled with dill.

GIANT: 17,18,19,20, ...

HTGW: **Fatten up Jack and bile him in stew, etc.**
(She begins to sing and continues throughout.)

(JACK peeks out of his hiding place to watch.)

GIANT: 28, 29, 30, ...

STORY: Counting beyond thirty-three will make a torn-body
drowsy.

GIANT: 33, 34, 35, ... *(Getting drowsy)*

STORY: Beyond ninety-nine hit's worse.

GIANT: 98, 99, 100, 101, ... *(Sleepier)*

STORY: By two hundred and twenty-two you're bedazed.

GIANT: 222, 223, 224, ... *(Almost completely out of it.)*

STORY: Messing with figures always made the giant sleepy, and the more he counted the dozier he got.

GIANT: 250, 251, ... *(He falls asleep.) (Snores)*

STORY: Jack caught his chance when the high tall woman stuck her head in the kettle to rub a spot clean.

HTGW: Now, that spot just won't clean up.
(She puts her head in the kettle.)

STORY: (As *narration continues, JACK executes the action.)* He jumped out of the oven. He grabbed the sack of gold and took off like Snider's hound.

JACK: Headin' for the beanstalk. *(His path is blocked accidentally by the HTGW. He returns to hide behind the GIANT.)*

STORY: And nobody was in knowance of it.

GIANT: *(Snores loud enough to wake himself up.)* Unh ...

HTGW: If all ye aim to do is sleep, get yerself up and go on to bed.

GIANT: Grumble *(Starts off. Notices he doesn't have his gold.)* What happened to my gold?

HTGW: Never you mind, just get yerself off to bed.

GIANT: Oh I reckon hit'l turn up. *(Exit)*

HTGW: Sure it will, now get on with ye. *(After he's gone)* Now, for a Jack stew. *(Opens oven and discovers JACK is missing.)* You little tadwhacker, where did you get off to? *(She looks around to no avail.)* You little scoundrel. *(JACK returns to the oven.)* You mighta escaped this time. But if'n you ever show your face around these parts again, hit'l be Jack stew for sure. *(She exits.)*

STORY: She's gone son.
(JACK comes out of the oven and sneaks out. He sings the following song as he retraces his path to the beanstalk and the STORYTELLER resets for the mam's house.)

JACK: **Jack be nimble Jack be quick**
Run down the stalk much faster
The Giant's wife ain't gonna eat
Stew made with tadwhacker

                   Jack runs like a rabbit. He's
goin' straight home to his mammy
Holdin' hard to a bag of gold
He hopes will make her happy

(From the top of the Beanstalk.) Will you look down there? I do believe I can see our home-seat. I wonder where Mam is? Reckon I'd best climb down. *(He does so.)* Will my mam be glad to see this here bag of gold! I'll just take a little peek. Woo-whee! That's a passel! How many is a passel, anyway? If two is a pair, three is a few and four is a batch I wonder how many it takes to make a passel. I'll just find out. One, two three, four, ...

STORY: And Jack he set to countin'.

JACK: five, six, seven, ...

STORY: Just like that giant.

JACK: eight, nine, ten, ...

STORY: And he began to get drowsy ...

JACK: 'leven, twelve, ...

STORY: Just like the giant. And bless his heart ... He didn't make it past

JACK: fifteen, ...

STORY: Until he collapsed with the sleepies.

JACK: *(Snores)*
    (STORYTELLER gets another cow during the following.)

WIDOW: Jack? Jack? Where could that child have got to? Why, Jack? Wake up child!

JACK: Mam! Mam! Look what I got!

WIDOW: Jack, where have you been?

JACK: I climbed the beanstalk an took this bag of gold from a giant who lives up there. He has the meanest eye you ever seen.

WIDOW: Now, Jack! I ain't never heard such a tall tale.

JACK: But, it's true mam. Just look at all this gold.
(He shows her the bag.)

WIDOW: That sure is one big bag of gold son.

JACK: Yes mam, and with it we can get all kinds of things ...

WIDOW: Now hold on there. This bag says that the gold come from the (Fill county or town name) Savings Bank. That means it belongs to our friends and neighbors. It's only rightful to return it.

JACK: But mam!

WIDOW: No buts about it. You go and return it right now!

JACK: Yes'um.

STORY: Now the (Fill county or town name) Savings Bank was so pleased to get the bag of gold back that they gave Jack five gold pieces as a reward. Now with some gold of their own, Jack and his mam bought another cow ...

WIDOW: with ribbons for her horns.
(While MAM sits for a spell on the porch and fixes ribbons for the cow's horns, JACK walks the cow in a circle to "milk" her. He is looking at the sky and not very happy about being here.)
(MELODY #2)

JACK & WIDOW:

> **Simple life is right with Mam**
> **Dillum Dow Dillum**
> **Cows milk goes with bread and jam**
> **Dillum Dow**

WIDOW: *(JACK looks at the sky as he hands her the full bucket.)*
That's a good cow!

591

STORY: They planted the ...

JACK & WIDOW: *(She points to the sass patch JACK goes.)*

> **Simple life is right with Mam**
> **Plant the seeds for food to can**
> **Cuttle Dee Cuttle Dow Dillum Dow Day**

STORY: They lived in ease.

WIDOW: *(As she ties the ribbons on the cow's horns.)* Jack, come an set a spell on the porch. Let your feet hang over the banisters.

STORY: That was all they had to do. And I reckon you'd say they were satisfied ...

WIDOW: tee-totally!

STORY: Not Jack. As the saying goes, he hadn't got his barrel full.

> *(MELODY #2)*

> **Jack thought there was more to do**
> **Dillum Dow Dillum**
> **Jack's adventures were not through**
> **Dillum Dow**
>
> *(JACK fiddles with the beanstalk from the sass patch; his focus is on the sky.)*

WIDOW: Jack, come on and sit a spell.
> *(JACK goes to sit by MAM but is directly beneath or beside the beanstalk. He fidgets enough to knock MAM and the cow off the bench by the end of the song.)*

STORY: **Jack thought there was more to do**
> **Up in the sky where the beanstalk grew**
> **Cuttle Dee Cuttle Dow Dillum Dow Day**

WIDOW: You'll wear yourself out with all that fidgeting. Come on, cow. *(Moo) (She takes the cow and exits.)*

JACK: Not me, mam. I can't just sit.

STORY: And besides his curiosity was stinging him. *(JACK gets nearer to the beanstalk.)* So one fine clever day Jack took his

foot in his hand and gave it another crack. He clambered up the beanstalk. Up and up and up.
(He does. Repeat the same process as the first time.)

JACK: Jack did.

STORY: And directly he came to where the stalk leaned against the path.

JACK: *(Steps out onto path)* I hear the buzzin of the bees. *(BEES buzz.)* I see the big flowers and here's the path. The only thing different is there ain't no breeze.

STORY: And we know that breeze blows stronger here than it does on Wolfpen Creek.
(Repeat travel as in the first participatory section.)

JACK: Wind, speed me along my journey. Now wind, I need to go this a way. Thank ye. Now that a way, wind. Thank ye kindly, wind. Now take me down the path that takes me to the ... Steps! Stop wind. Thank you, wind.

STORY: So once more Jack climbed up the steps.

JACK: Did Jack. Up and up.
(Use the following section if needed to cover costume change.)

STORY: Now that high tall woman must have had her head down deep in a kettle pot 'cuz she didn't answer that door. So Jack he ran 'round to the back door.
(Pick up here if HTGW is ready.)

JACK: Did Jack.

STORY: And he climbed up those steps.

JACK: Jack did. Up and up.

STORY: And he commenced a 'knockin on the door. And there was the high tall woman.
(HTGW enters.)

HTGW: Jack, I'm right proud to see you.

STORY: He'd not sidestep her stew this time.

JACK: Old sister, I'm hungry.

HTGW: Jack, come on in you little tadwhacker.

JACK: What's cooking?

HTGW: Crumble-in of course. How about a bowl?

STORY: Well, she feed him five bowls. She'd fatten him plump.

(MELODY #1)

HTGW: **Fatten up Jack and bile him in stew**
Fatten up Jack and bile him in stew
Giant likes to eat tadwhackers like you
Wack Fa La Diddle all day

(GIANT enters.)

GIANT: Fee, fie, pickle cracker
I smell the toes of a tadwhacker

HTGW: Quick Jack, here comes my husband, hide in here.

STORY: The high tall giant woman clapped a skillet over him. A
skillet the size to fry a whole beef.
(GIANT enters.)

GIANT: (Sniffing and snorting) Fee, fie, pickle cracker.
I smell the toes of a tadwhacker.

HTGW: You're smelling your upper lip.

GIANT: Hmmn.

HTGW: The grease from the couple you gobbled for breakfast.

GIANT: **Smells like a tadwhacker**

HTGW: **--Never you mind**

GIANT: **Smells like a tadwhacker**

HTGW: **--Never you mind**

BOTH: **Tadwhacker stew is going to be mine**
Wack Fa La Diddle all day

STORY: Even a giant with feet like cornsleds understands you
can't out-argue a woman. So he hushed on that.

GIANT: Old wife, bring me my little banty hen that lays

594

golden eggs.

STORY: Even a woman big enough to tuck a boy in her apron pocket knows that when a man speaks he's spoken. So she brought the hen. *(STORYTELLER recruits a volunteer hen from the audience. The hen is instructed to flap his/her wings and make chicken noises every time someone says "Hen, lay." While STORYTELLER is working with hen GIANT and HTGW cover.)*

HTGW: *(As she begins her search she brings the GIANT a bowl of crumble-in.)*

GIANT: Crumble-in, I wanted tadwhacker!

HTGW: Jest you eat your crumble-in and be happy.
(The HTGW taps the fry pan lid. JACK peeks out.)

HTGW: Jack stew. You won't get away this time tadwhacker.

GIANT: TADWHACKER?

HTGW: No tadwhacker, just crumble-in.
(When the hen is ready the HTGW goes to get her and bring her in to the GIANT.)

GIANT: Hey, Hen, come on in here, ... etc. Are you ready Hen? hen, lay. *(Braaack)*

STORY: The hen did.

GIANT: One gold egg. Hen, lay. *(Braack)*
(GIANT continues to command and count.)

STORY: And another and another every time he said lay.

GIANT: Hen, lay. *(Braack)* Four gold eggs.

JACK: Well I'll be.

GIANT: Hen, lay. *(Braack)*

JACK: *(Peeking out from under the frying pan.)* That must be the lost hen that lady told me about. The High Tall Giant must have stolen that little chicken just like he stole that bag of gold!

GIANT: Five gold eggs. *(Braack)*

JACK: She told me I could keep her if I found her.

STORY: The giant counted. And here he was messing with figures again. And he got sleepy.

GIANT: *(Yawn)* Hen, lay. *(Braack.)*

STORY: The high tall woman got out her kettle pot and began to polish it,

GIANT: Eight gold eggs.

HTGW: *(As she begins to polish her stew pot. Under her breath.)* Jack stew. Stew with dill. *(She sings her song and continues throughout.)*

> **Fatten up Jack and bile him in stew,**
> **Fatten up Jack and bile him in stew**
> **Giant likes to eat tadwhackers like you**
> **Whack Fa la diddle all day**

STORY: The banty hen kept laying.

GIANT: Hen, lay! *(Braaack)*

STORY: The giant kept tallying.

GIANT: *(Yawn)* Ten gold eggs, Hen, lay. *(Braack)*

STORY: And fairly soon the giant was nodding. *(He does.)* And snoring. *(He does.)* And the woman had her head so deep in the kettle she couldn't hear thunder.

HTGW: *(Sings with her head in the pot)*

JACK: Now's my chance.

STORY: He threw off the skillet. *(Crash.)* It made a racket that would of woke seven sleepers. The Giant cracked his eyelids. *(Both GIANTS look up. JACK hides beside the GIANT so the FEMALE GIANT can't see him. She starts looking knowing something is amiss.)*

GIANT: Hmmmn. Huh? *(He falls asleep again.)*

STORY: And Jack grabbed the little hen.

HEN: Braaack!

JACK: Quiet, hen! *(Braack!)*

GIANTS: *(HTGW sees him. GIANT wakes.)* What?

HTGW: Hold on there tadwhacker!

GIANT: A tadwhacker!

STORY: And he lit out for the beanstalk.
(His path is blocked by the STORY TELLER.)

HTGW: I need you for stew!

GIANT: You wait'll I get my hands on you ...

HTGW: You keep your hands off him. He's my stew! Stew with dill. You would eat the meat and leave me the gristle ...

GIANT: Out of the way! He's got my hen.

JACK: My hen. That chicken lady said if'n I found it I could keep it. Come on hen, lets skedaddle!
(GIANTS surround JACK but he and the hen escape between them and hide in the flowers.)

GIANT: Ole Wife, fetch me a poke for catchin' a tadwhacker.

HTGW: A tadwhacker poke, you bet! *(HTGW exits.)*

STORY: And did Jack skedaddle! You could of shot marbles on his shirttail.
(GIANT starts after JACK and discovers his hiding place.)

GIANT: You better look out Tadwhacker, I'm gonna eat you!
(JACK and the hen begin to retrace the path back to the beanstalk. The GIANT follows.) Come back here!

JACK: Come on hen, that old giant is shaving my heels. Wind? I need your help. *(The GIANT continues in pursuit delayed several times as the WIND blows on him in various directions to protect JACK.)* I need you to blow and slow down the giant, just long enough for me to get down the beanstalk. Now, wind. Blow! *(JACK sends the hen to wait with the STORYTELLER who has set up the playing area for Jack's home.)* That's it, Blow! *(The wind process continues until JACK is at the top of the beanstalk.)* Harder!
(He begins his descent.)

GIANT: I'll come right down that there beanstalk, don't you

think I won't. You best watch yourself tadwhacker!

STORY: Jack came down the stalk in a shower of leaves and a hail of beans and the wind didn't let the giant ketch up with him.

JACK: Mam! Mam! Fetch the ax!
(WIDOW enters.)

WIDOW: Hallo, Jack. Come here and set a spell.

JACK: Hallo, Mam. Fetch the Ax! Please.

WIDOW: Slow down there son. There ain't no hurry.

GIANT: *(At the edge of mountain drop)* Fee, fie, chew tobacco, I'm gonna eat me a young tadwhacker!

JACK: Hurry, Mam. The Giant is right behind me.

GIANT: *(Behind the scenery)* Fee, fie, pickle, cracker, I'm gonna eat YOU tadwhacker!

WIDOW: Well, I never.

JACK: Mam! Hurry!

STORY: Jack's mam fetched a double-bitted ax which could cut coming and going.

GIANT: Hold on there tadwhacker! You, put down that ax.

JACK & STORY: All right!

STORY: Jack cut down that beanstalk with a single blow.
(As JACK cuts the beanstalk it drops leaving the GIANT hanging with nowhere to go. He falls.)

And that was the end of the seventeen-foot giant with feet as big as cornsleds and fingernails to match bucket lids and the meanest eye in the world earthly.
(STORYTELLER gets another cow.)

WIDOW: Merciful heavens Jack, what was all that ruckus about.

JACK: Nothing mam, just this little old banty hen.

WIDOW: A banty hen. Well I never!

JACK: That's for sure, mam. You never saw a banty hen like

this'un. Just you watch. Hen, lay! *(Braack)*

STORY: And an odd thing! On earth the little hen would lay only common brown eggs.

JACK: Regular eggs. Just plain regular eggs.

WIDOW: Well, Jack what did you expect. Gold eggs.

STORY: Ay, no matter. Jack had his barrel full enough. And he bought a second cow. *(Mooo)*

WIDOW: with ribbons to her horns. A pretty cow, *(Mooo)*

JACK: One to come fresh while the other was dry.

STORY: They lived on banty eggs and garden sass and crumble-in thereinafter.

JACK: And no body could rightly say Jack didn't know beans.

STORY: Now, no.

(MELODY #4)

ALL: **Thank you all for comin'**
To see the Tale of Jack
We hope to tell another tale
Next time we come back

The Tale you saw of Jack
and the Wonder Beans is True

GIANT: **My Favorite Dish is Stew made**
with Tadwhackers like you!

ALL: **Now, put your hands together**
and clap with all your friends
The play about the Wonder beans
Has now come to the END!

PRODUCTION NOTES-JACK AND THE WONDER BEANS

THE PLAYING AREA: The original production was staged in a rectangular playing area with a mountain background at one end and an aisle on each remaining side. The playing area was delineated by a very low split-rail fence which separated the seating area from the playing area. The audience was seated on the floor on all three sides. Our mountain background was painted on 3/4" plywood which provided the support for Jack to ascend into the sky as he climbed the beanstalk.

THE MUSIC: The music, which consisted of traditional folk melodies, was all played live on a guitar. An autoharp or dulcimer would also be a good choice.

THE PARTICIPATION: Since the production involves both on-stage as well as off-stage participation, it is important that the cast be available to help seat the audience. We found that doing so provided the actors and audience members an opportunity to develop the needed lines of communication before the show started. A very informal atmosphere where the children can ask questions and talk directly to the performers is encouraged. This arrangement also allowed the cast to identify likely participants.

Gender? Our experience was that both boys and girls easily played the cow or the hen, but when the first cow is being played by a boy, it is best not to refer to it as a "lady cow," "ol' cow" works well. We always shifted the personal pronouns to fit the gender of the participants as needed.

THE GIANTS: The most difficult production problem to overcome was the size difference between Jack and the Giants. We chose to increase the Giants height through the use of dry wall stilts. We worked on 18"- 20" stilts which provided plenty of height difference, especially when you remember that the audience is sitting on the floor looking up at someone well over seven feet tall. I encourage you to look for your own solution to this problem, but I assure your there is nothing like the reaction when the audience first saw the "High Tall Giant Woman."

600

THE
YELLOW BOAT

by
David Saar

Plays for children written throughout the last century reflect the various contexts out of which they grew. All manner of social, political, educational, and/or artistic influences inform each playwright and ultimately impact every play written. Just as the social work agendas of the early part of the century shaped the plays of the field in particular ways, the growing influence of professional theatre artists on the field offers yet another example of influence on the development of the literature. A prominent recurring theme found in any interrogation of the contexts of new play development centers on a given society's concept of children and childhood. From this perspective comes the question: What is appropriate for children? How should the form and content of children's plays address and be of service to the vulnerability of children? This, in turn, leads directly to issues of appropriate content for plays for young audiences.

As noted previously in this anthology, serious plays, from *The Birthday of the Infanta* to *The Arkansaw Bear*, have occupied an important place in the development of dramatic literature for children. Plays such as these have challenged the pervasive idea that children's theatre should consist only of escapist entertainment. Yet, no single serious play has exerted as much influence on the contemporary field as that of David Saar's *The Yellow Boat*. Amidst a sparse tradition of serious work in the field, Saar's play bravely introduced the subject of AIDS to child audiences at a time when even many adult communities still could not address the subject in a rational manner.

The Yellow Boat is not about AIDS; rather it is a play about a young boy, Benjamin, who, through a blood transfusion, acquires AIDS and ultimately dies from the disease. But even mentioning the name of this disease in the context of children's theatre at the time this play premiered provoked a swirl of contesting social, educational, and political agendas. Saar met the challenge of this debate by creating a captivating play, which has subsequently become an important and often-produced part of the contemporary repertoire.

The Yellow Boat follows Benjamin's journey, through the prejudices of neighbors and schools, the indignities of medical procedures, to his inevitable death, all while celebrating the resilient spirit of this young protagonist. The play also depicts the effect of Benjamin's journey on his family, his friends, and the medical community with whom he comes in contact. Saar employs a fluid, theatrical style, to move the action through various locales. A yellow boat, featured prominently in a story important to the young protagonist, serves as the dominant scenic element for the play.

This play stands out not just because it introduces the subject of AIDS, but because it features a protagonist who dies at the end of the play. But Saar does not present capricious melodrama, where "bad guys" win over the "good guys." Benjamin's death is presented as a sad but logical reality, both in the world of the play and consistent with the outside world the play mirrors. Through following Benjamin's journey, young audience members are allowed to acknowledge their own fears about death, and, even more importantly, they are offered joy and hope through the spirit embodied in Benjamin's journey.

By the early 1980s, the professional community had begun to support an increasing and much needed diversification of the repertoire of plays for children in terms of forms and styles of production. Because of its success as a play and apart from any controversies the subject may have engendered, *The Yellow Boat,* which premiered in 1993, opened new horizons for theatre artists to deal with difficult subjects important to young people.

David Saar is the founder and Artistic Director of Childsplay, Inc., a professional theatre for young audiences, located in Tempe, AZ. He has directed and taught for Childsplay since the company was formed in 1977. Saar has served on the roster of the Arizona Artist-in-Education program for nine years, has been an adjunct faculty member for the Department of Theatre at Arizona State University (ASU), and he has worked for the Mesa School District as a drama curriculum specialist. He is a former board member of the U.S. Branch of the International Children's Theatre Association (ASSITEJ), and he is a member of the American Alliance for Theatre and Education and the Arizona Theatre Association. In 1989 he received the Governor's Arts Award for his contributions to the arts in Arizona. In 1991 he received the national Winifred Ward Dare to Dream Fellowship; and in 1993 he received the Phoenix Futures Forum Dream Weavers Vision Award. In 2002 he received the first Notable Achievement Award from the Herberger College of Fine Arts at ASU. He also currently serves as a site reporter for the National Endowment for the Arts.

THE
YELLOW BOAT

by
David Saar

THE YELLOW BOAT is also
available as an individual play script from the publisher
Anchorage Press Plays, Inc.
ISBN 0-87602-352-9

Licensing for Production
Productions of this play are encouraged, and those who wish to present it may
seek the necessary permission by contacting:
Anchorage Press Plays, Inc, P.O. Box 2901, Louisville, KY 40201-2901, USA,
or via the internet: www.applays.com .
Licensing for production includes gaining clearance for performance, paying
the performance royalty fees, use of authorized play scripts and proper
crediting of the title, author, composer (if a musical), and publisher in printed
materials associated with the production.

Characters

BENJAMIN

MOTHER

FATHER

A CHORUS of 4 actors:

> ACTORS #1 AND #2: MALE
>
> ACTORS #3 AND #4: FEMALE.

They will play the following roles:

> CHORUS
>
> SCHOOL CHILDREN
>
> SCHOOL TEACHERS
>
> PARENTS
>
> SCHOOL ADMINISTRATORS
>
> KIDS
>
> EDDY
>
> JOY
>
> DOCTORS

For
Sonja and Benjamin

PLAYWRIGHT'S NOTE:

In the early drafts of the play, the Chorus parts were called "T.P.'s" - shorthand for "Transformational Potential." While their names have changed, they continue to serve this purpose in the play. They play all the above roles, but can also be used, for example, to "create drawing" - or anything else the director might want to use to tell the story.

Time is fluid in the play and should be approached cinematically rather than realistically. We can and will move forward, back, and across time. "Time shift' means just that - a cinematic shift to another moment.

The drawings that Benjamin describes in various monologues can be "drawn" in the air or on a blank piece of paper with a prop crayon.

The boat mentioned in some stage directions refers to a set piece used in the Tempe and Seattle productions, a small, movable Yellow Boat that was manipulated to become an ambulance, a bed, etc. There are many scenic solutions; this is provided as just one example.

The Yellow Boat was first presented by Childsplay, Inc. at the Tempe Performing Arts Center, Tempe, Arizona in October, 1993. It was directed by Carol North. The dramaturg was Suzan Zeder; associate dramaturg, Judy Matetzschk. Scenic design by Greg Lucas, lighting design by Amarante Lucero, costumes by Susan Johnson-Hood. Original music composed and performed by Alan Ruch. The cast was as follows:

BENJAMIN..Jon Gentry
MOTHER... Ellen Benton
FATHER... Dwayne Hartford
JOY .... Debra K. Stevens
EDDY/CHORUS #1................................D. Scott Withers
CHORUS #2.. Alec Call
CHORUS #3..Alejandra Garcia
CHORUS #4..Helen Hayes

A touring version of *The Yellow Boat* was first presented in February, 1994, by The Metro Theater Company, St. Louis, MO. It was directed by Jim Hancock. The dramaturg was Suzan Zeder; associate dramaturg, Judy Matetzschk. Scenic design by Nicholas Kryah, lights designed by Jack Brown, costume design by Clyde Ruffin, original music composed and performed by Al Fischer. The cast was as follows:

BENJAMIN.. Jennifer Makuch
MOTHER ....Grace Adellen
FATHER..Nicholas Kryah
JOY.. Gina Ojile
EDDY/CHORUS #1.......................................Eddie Webb
CHORUS #2..Al Fischer

A STUDY GUIDE IS AVAILABLE FROM
CHILDSPLAY, INC.
P.O. BOX 517
TEMPE, AZ 85281

A set of greeting cards, featuring eight of Benjamin's drawings is available from the Hemophilia Association, Inc., Phoenix, AZ. The proceeds from the sale of these cards will benefit its services to men, women and children affected by hemophilia and HIV/AIDS. To purchase cards, please contact Hemophilia Association: (602)955-3947.

(Soft light, sound swirl. The time is past, present, future. Lights come up on a BOY who will become BENJAMIN playing with a toy boat.)

BOY: It began ... 10-9-8-7-6-5-4-3-2-1: Blast-off! *(Vocalized sounds of rocket launching.)* Beep, beep, beep, beep ...

CHORUS #1 - #4, MOTHER and FATHER: It began before the beginning ...
(The BOY's play holds stage alone for a moment, and then others, the characters who will become the parents DOCTORS, and community members become part of the playing space. Their voices overlap, and build.)

#1: This is a story about ...

#3: This story is about ...

#4: Not an ordinary story ...

#2: It happened ...

#3: Did it happen?

FATHER: How could it happen?

#4: This is a story about ...

#3: This story is about ...

FATHER: Not an ordinary story ...

MOTHER: It happened ...

#2: Did it happen?

ALL: It happened.
(The BOY looks around at this gathering for the first time.)

BOY: This is a story about ... me.
(From the perimeter of the playing space the other characters begin to vocalize different parental labels.)

MOTHER: Mother ...

FATHER: Father ...

#4: Momma ...

#2: Pappa ...

#3: Mommy ...

FATHER: Daddy ...

#1: My Old Man ...

BOY: It began before the beginning with a sort of choosing ...
*(Choral voices continue to offer up a variety of "parental
choices" from which the BOY will make his selection.)*

MOTHER: Mommy's here.

#1: You're getting so big.

#3: What did you do in school today?

#2: Brush your teeth.

FATHER: Way to go! I'm so proud of you.

#4: Do I have to stop this car?

FATHER: That's my boy.

MOTHER: Sweet dreams.

BOY: Mom? Dad?
*(BOY shifts his focus to FATHER and MOTHER. The scene
"shifts" to a more realistic style.)*

FATHER: You're what!?! Are you sure?

MOTHER: I'm sure.

FATHER: Positive? You're sure? Whoooh ... ! This is great! It's
really great, isn't it?

MOTHER: I've never felt so happy; ...

FATHER: Can you feel him yet?

MOTHER: No, but I know he's there.

FATHER: 'He.' We both said, 'he'!

MOTHER: I know.

FATHER: What does ... <u>he</u> feel like?

MOTHER: He feels like himself.

BOY: *(The BOY points to MOTHER and FATHER.)* You will be
my Mom. And you, my Dad. This is a story about us. And it

takes ...
(The CHORUS begins a vocalized list of "time choices"
which overlap and build. The "choices" may be repeated if
desired.)

#4: Forty-eight years, sixty-seven years, fourteen years, three
years ...

#2: Ninety-six years, seventy-nine years, sixty-seven years,
thirty-two years ...

#3: Eleven months, five months, seven months, three months ...

#1: Fourteen days, four days, twenty-three days, nine days...
(He stops the time swirl with his announcement.)

BOY: It takes: eight years, four months, twenty-nine days ...
That's enough!
(This launches a "birth dance" with MOTHER, FATHER and
BENJAMIN. As BENJAMIN names each color, CHORUS
members swirl colored silks into the air, transforming the
playing space into a swirl of color.)
I see ... red.
I hear ... blue.
I feel ... purple.
I taste ... green.
I ... choose ... yellow.
(MOTHER gives birth to a small yellow doll that "becomes"
the baby BENJAMIN. MOTHER and FATHER use the doll as
baby while the actor playing BENJAMIN voices and reacts
for him.)

FATHER: It's a boy!

MOTHER: A boy.

BENJAMIN: My birthday. April 19, 1979.
(The CHORUS form a cradle of ribbons in which the doll
BENJAMIN is rocked, and become various DOCTORS, and
friends.)

#2 and #4: Congratulations!

#4: Yes, it's a boy. That I'm sure of.

613

#2: Yup, a boy.

#3: Ooohhhhhh! He's so little. I keep forgetting how little they always are.

#1: Now don't wait too long to have a brother or sister for this one ...

#3: Is'm's Mumsy's and Dadsy's little itsy bitsy ... ooh, look, he's smiling at me!

FATHER: I think it's gas ...
(The ribbon cradle breaks away, and the parents are in another space.)

MOTHER: A beautiful boy.

FATHER: Seven pounds, six ounces.

MOTHER: His fingers are right, and his toes are on ... The nurse says he's the most beautiful child she's ever seen.

FATHER: She says that to everyone.

MOTHER: Still, today ... I went down to the nursery ...

FATHER: ... just to check out the competition?

MOTHER and FATHER: She's right.

FATHER: So what's his name ... ?

MOTHER: His eyelashes are the longest ... and his little fingers, look ...

FATHER: The nurse says they'll hold him for ransom if we don't give him a name.

MOTHER: He's small, and wise, and ... mine.

FATHER: And mine.
(Mom gives baby to Dad, who doesn't quite know what to do with him.)

MOTHER: That's it!

FATHER: What?

MOTHER: His name. "Benjamin."

FATHER: Benjamin?

MOTHER: It works in lots of languages. Translate: Ben ...

FATHER: "Son."

MOTHER: Ja ...

FATHER: "Yes."

MOTHER: Min ...

FATHER: "Mine."

(FATHER cuddles his son and parents simultaneously translate his new name.)

MOTHER: Son. Yes, he's mine!   FATHER: Ben. Ja. Min.!
(BENJAMIN begins a fussy cry, Dad gives doll back to Mom. They move to another space. "Busen lull" underscoring begins.)

BENJAMIN: Once upon a time, there was a Mom, a Dad, and a little, teeny baby ...

FATHER: Welcome, Benjamin.

BENJAMIN: And a song!

MOTHER: This is a story my Mother used to tell to me every night before I went to sleep. It's about boats, and sails, and ... It takes place in a harbor ...

FATHER: far, far away ...
(The actor BENJAMIN "claims" the doll BENJAMIN and the MOTHER holds both in her arms to tell the story. From this point until doll BENJAMIN "grows up" to actor BENJAMIN, the doll is manipulated by the actor.)

MOTHER: Now inside this harbor there were three boats. A red one. A blue one. And a yellow one. They all sailed far out to the sea, and the red one came back, and the blue one came back; but the yellow boat? The yellow boat sailed straight up to the sun.
(Singing.)
Busen lull, cook the kettle full,
There sailed three boats from the harbor,
The first was so blue,

>The second so red,
>The third was the color of the sun.

MOTHER and FATHER:
>Busen lull, cook the kettle full,
>There sailed three boats from the harbor,
>The blue carried hope,
>The red carried faith,
>The yellow filled itself with love.

FATHER: **I sail the blue boat**

MOTHER: **The red one's for me ...**

(The lullaby has almost put him to sleep.)

BENJAMIN: **I am the yellow boat.**
(He falls asleep. The music resolves. Parents "pull away" from the baby to work.)

MOTHER and FATHER: Work time!

MOTHER: **I'll weave you a sail ...**

FATHER: **I'll write you a world ...**

BENJAMIN: *(Sleepily)* I'll do it myself!
(FATHER and MOTHER separate to their individual work spaces. MOTHER weaves some of the colored silk ribbons, FATHER works on a new story. The CHORUS are used to help create these work environments or assist in the creation of the work itself - they are "transformational potential." Each parent works to rhythms which weave together and separate. The intention of this movement/ music beat is to show the parents at work, and the baby BENJAMIN discovering that he has the power to interrupt that work. Use the following choral litany to underscore the scene - or figure out another way to do it!)

#3 & #4: Shuttle, Beat. Shuttle, Beat. Shuttle, Beat. Shuttle, Beat. *(Repeat.)*

#1 & #2: Comma, Dot. Comma, Word. Comma, Dot. Comma, Word. *(Repeat.)*

616

(BENJAMIN awakes, and watches the surrounding activity, perhaps joining in, or getting in the way, and then, tired of no one paying attention to him, starts to cry. Both parents come running, BENJAMIN gives them his most charming smile.)

FATHER: What's wrong?

MOTHER: Oh, you're okay.

FATHER: Now, where was I ... ?
(They return to work, and after a short time BENJAMIN begins to cry, again.)

MOTHER: *(Not wanting to interrupt her weaving.)* Mamma's right here. *(To FATHER)* Can you see what he needs?

FATHER: Yeah, sure.
(He tries to ignore the crying for a beat, so BENJAMIN intensifies his efforts.)

FATHER: Okay, here's the scoop   I'll write the story, and you color it! *(FATHER hands BENJAMIN a crayon, and the actor BENJAMIN manipulates it for the doll. Rhythm starts. FATHER returns to writing, and the story gets the interest of the CHORUS.)* Now, once upon a time ...

#1, #2, #3, #4: Hmmmmm?

FATHER: Once upon a time ..:
        In a ... land-kind-of-place,
        Where the palm trees grew ...
        And the sky was painted ...

BENJAMIN: *(He chooses.)* Blue!

FATHER: Blue?

BENJAMIN: Blue.
        (A bluesy kind of music is heard, the stage turns blue, and the CHORUS illustrates the color in movement as BENJAMIN colors.)

#1, #2, #3, #4: Cool, cooler, coolest, blue, Smooth, soothing, blues ...

FATHER: That's exactly what I mean. And the trees are painted...

BENJAMIN: *(Holding up another crayon.)* Green.
(Change in sound as he colors, the stage turns green and the CHORUS explores "green" in movement.)

#1, #2, #3, #4: It's a mean kind of green, like a scream in a dream, Like a ...

BENJAMIN: Ghost ... on Halloween ...
(They all read in Béla Lugosi style.)

FATHER: No that isn't what! mean. Those trees are ...

BENJAMIN: Red. And they're dead.
(Blackout)

FATHER and MOTHER: Hey!

FATHER: What's going on here?

MOTHER: What happened to the lights?

FATHER: I don't know. Maybe it's ... Or the ... ? Or maybe it's a kid?!?
(Lights up and Dad finds the CHORUS in shaped positions representing the wall drawings that BENJAMIN has created. He is in their midst, happily drawing with the crayon. Dad takes the crayon from him.)

MOTHER: What?

FATHER: Well, I gave him some crayons and, ... uhhhh, he got a little carried away and scribbled across the wall and the light switch.

MOTHER: Is he alright?

FATHER: He's fine, but the wall's a goner.
(She crosses over and looks at the damage.)

MOTHER: Oh Benjamin ... *(Then looks more closely at the wall, assessing ...)* Oh ... !
(FATHER joins her.)

FATHER: Oh ... ? Oh ... ! Look at the ...

MOTHER: And the ...

FATHER: Not to mention the ...

618

FATHER and MOTHER: *(Appreciative)* Oh ... , Benjamin ...

MOTHER: That's a very nice drawing ... , but it would be so much nicer on a piece of paper ... *(She hands him a sheet of paper. With her finger she defines the space of the paper.)* Here. Draw here. You can draw from here to here, and from here to here. *(MOTHER helps BENJAMIN draw a long line on the paper.)* A nice, long line that connects from here to here, and from here to here.

BENJAMIN: Line?

MOTHER: Line.
(BENJAMIN takes the crayon and draws a line.)

BENJAMIN: Line.

MOTHER: Lovely!
(MOTHER returns to her work. BENJAMIN begins to explore the concept.)

BENJAMIN: Line! Here. Line here. Here. Line here. Here. Line here: Line!
(BENJAMIN draws a long line right off the paper. Suddenly discovering another dimension, he abandons the paper and moves into the third and fourth dimension, moving through space as he explores "line." The CHORUS illustrates his "line exploration" with colored elastics which they manipulate to create visible lines and shapes in space.)

BENJAMIN: Line!

#4: S-p-i-r-al.

BENJAMIN: Line!

#2: Straight!

BENJAMIN: Line.

#1: An-gle?

BENJAMIN: Line!

#3: Curving ....

BENJAMIN: Line!

#4: Squiggle!

BENJAMIN: Line!

> *(BENJAMIN is delighted by his line drawings and his explorations grow bolder and bolder. Finally FATHER notices, and calls to MOTHER.)*

FATHER: Look, look what he's doing!

MOTHER: Those aren't just scribbles, those are shapes!

BENJAMIN: Shapes?

MOTHER and FATHER: Shapes!

> *(A music and movement section follows. As BENJAMIN draws, the CHORUS illustrates with the elastics and his parents help by naming the shapes.)*

MOTHER and FATHER: Square, triangle ... There's a circle ...

BENJAMIN: Circle? Wavy circle.

> *(The circle becomes so.)*

MOTHER: Lines and shapes for a ...

MOTHER and FATHER: Picture!

BENJAMIN: Picture of ... a tree! *(#1 and #3 use yellow and orange elastics to make a tree.)* A heart. *(#2 and #4 use the blue and green elastics to make a heart shape that "beats.")* A bow and arrow. *(#1 makes the bow with yellow elastic; #3 Makes the arrow with the orange elastic which is "shot" through the heart, pulling the bow and #1 with it.)* Lines and shapes and colors make a picture ... of a house with about a million rooms. *(#1-4 form an abstract shape with the elastics that has lots of room shapes.)* Roof top, mountain top ... *(The house is transformed to a mountain.)* Lines for a picture of a yellow sun, *(The mountain is transformed into a sun.)*

BENJAMIN: Lines for a boat. Yeah! A yellow boat! *(The elastics are formed into the shape of a small sail boat. BENJAMIN jumps onto the boat, and beckons his parents, all the while drawing with the crayon.)* Come on board!

> *(Mom and Dad come aboard. BENJAMIN finishes by drawing the round sun in the air above the boat.)*

BENJAMIN: Yellow Boat sailing ... , sailing ... , sailing ... , to the sun! Stop! *(The boat "disappears," and the CHORUS moves upstage.)*

New Drawing. Benjamin's Body! *(BENJAMIN picks up the paper he was drawing on earlier, and begins to draw again. MOTHER and FATHER are seated on the boat with the doll. BENJAMIN begins to draw the story as the parents live it.)*

Here's a picture of Mom, and she's singing to me. *(The MOTHER and the CHORUS begins to hum "Busen lull" softly in a minor key.)* Then she sees something funny. *(BENJAMIN "draws" a bruise.)*

MOTHER: Look at this bruise. It seems to hurt him if I touch it.

FATHER: So don't touch it.

MOTHER: What caused it?

FATHER: It's just a bruise. Stop worrying.

BENJAMIN: I cry. (He does.) Loud. Lots! They worry! *(He cries more.)*

MOTHER: He keeps crying, just keeps on crying ...

FATHER: I'll change him.

MOTHER: He doesn't need changing.

FATHER: Colic?

MOTHER: Four nights straight? Something hurts! *(BENJAMIN cries more.)*

FATHER: Teeth? *(Very loud crying. Both react.)*

MOTHER: Something's wrong!

MOTHER and FATHER: Call the Doctor! *(The boat piece becomes the ambulance. BENJAMIN draws as he tells.)*

BENJAMIN: I'm going to the hospital in an ambulance. Just me ... and Mom, and Dad. Big Siren! Cars scoot out of the way ... Fast. Neat! Then ... Doctors!

621

(DOCTORS enter with clip boards, and whisk the baby away from the parents. They are robotic, clinical; the parents are left waiting outside, overhearing what is being said.)

DOCTOR #1: Hematocrit every two hours.

MOTHER: What? What does that mean?

DOCTOR #3: Two pints whole blood, ...

FATHER: What's wrong?

DOCTOR #1: ... and a CAT Scan.

FATHER: What are you testing?

DOCTOR #2: Wait here, please. Just a few more tests ...

BENJAMIN: More checks.
(DOCTORS move to continue exam.)

DOCTOR #1: Left pupil, three millimeters: right pupil, four millimeters. Note.

DOCTOR #3: Check.

DOCTOR #1: Charted?

DOCTOR #4: Check.

DOCTOR #1: Irregular.

DOCTOR #3: Highly irregular.

DOCTOR #1: I don't understand all this bleeding.
(DOCTORS #1 - #3 cross to BENJAMIN. He tears a piece of his drawing paper, and hands it to one. Each "reads" the test result, each says "Hmmm?," and passes it to the next. The last to receive it is DOCTOR #2.)

BENJAMIN: Then they figure it out.
(DOCTOR #2 announces to the parents.)

DOCTOR #1: Blood tests confirm that your son has ... Classic hemophilia, Type A.

MOTHER: What does that mean?

BENJAMIN: It means my blood isn't like everyone else's. It's missing the "Stop Bleeding Stuff." So, when I get a cut or bump inside, it doesn't stop bleeding. It just keeps dribbling and drabbling ... like a leaky faucet.

FATHER: What do we do?

DOCTOR #1: We'll begin the infusion procedure immediately. Check the weight and order up ... one hundred and sixty units of Factor 8.

MOTHER: What?

DOCTOR #1: Factors.

FATHER: What does that do?
(#1 and #3 swirl multiple red ribbons into the air, the separate blood sources that are then "mixed" to create the factor.)

BENJAMIN: It's this really great stuff that works like a bunch of plugs to stop the bleeding. It's really strong because lots of people's blood gets mixed up to make it.

MOTHER: Where does it come from?

DOCTOR #1: From thousands of blood donors. Excuse me. We have to infuse him with the factor!
(The infusion process is set up with a long length of knotted ribbons. This is the Factor 8 which is infused into the dolls body. Two CHORUS members control the ribbon movement in such a way that it looks like the stream of red is being infused into the doll's body. One DOCTOR holds the doll, another holds the syringe and guides the blood line into the doll.)

BENJAMIN: *(As he draws it.)* The first time they poke me, I cry. Poke! Owww. *(The DOCTOR with the syringe "pokes" the doll, searching for a vein. Actor BENJAMIN "cries out" "Owww" with each attempt.)* Poke! Owwww ...

DOCTOR #1: Once more.

BENJAMIN: Poke! Owww ... Poke!

DOCTOR #1: Bull's eye!
(The infusion process begins. The parents speak from the

waiting room.)

MOTHER: He's stopped crying.

FATHER: Is everything alright?

DOCTOR #1: Everything is under control.

FATHER: How often will he need to go through this?

DOCTOR #1: Whenever he has a bleed. Each patient is different.

MOTHER: Is it safe?

DOCTOR #1: What?

MOTHER: That ... Factor?

DOCTOR #1: Factor Eight is completely safe. Almost finished.
Done.

FATHER: Are you sure he'll be okay?

DOCTOR #1: He can do anything any other child can, with just a
few precautions. Trust me. He'll have a normal life.
*(The "baby" is returned to the parents. All except the family
exit.)*

MOTHER: A "normal life." What's that supposed to mean?
*(Music may underscore this scene, which effects the time
transition from babyhood to young boyhood. The other
purpose of the scene is to show the parents <u>attempting</u> to
"protect" their young hemophiliac — and his energy and
zest for living making this clearly impossible.)*

BENJAMIN: I'll show you,
*(He moves to his parents, who are holding the doll, cuddling.
He tries to pull the baby away from them so he can explore
— MOTHER and FATHER resist, wanting him to stay
"safely" with them.)*

MOTHER: You stay with Mommy.
*(He tricks them into releasing the doll, and then manipulates
the doll/puppet to show "himself" growing up — learning
to crawl, to stand, to fall (which <u>really</u> worries the parents),
to walk. The following lines are interspersed with this
movement exploration.)*

624

MOTHER: Look what he's doing?

FATHER: Hold his hand.
(He leaps in pure joy and runs!)

BENJAMIN: Can't catch me.

MOTHER: *(Coaxing him back onto the boat.)* Benjamin. All aboard the Yellow Boat.
(BENJAMIN swims to the boat, climbs up and shakes himself off and fishes for a beat or two, then jumps off, swimming again.)

FATHER: All ashore, who's goin' ashore! Set sail for destinations unknown.
(BENJAMIN begins to climb a pole. Then runs to the top of the ramp.)

BENJAMIN: Mom, Dad, look at me.

MOTHER: We see you!
(In this moment the actor BENJAMIN replaces the doll BENJAMIN - - he is a young boy.)

FATHER: Good going, partner

MOTHER: You are getting so big.

BENJAMIN: Let's play ... on the boat. *(Music begins again, they all come on board.)* Come on Dad! Let's explore. All aboard the Yellow Boat. Bound for destinations unknown. Cargo aboard? We each get to take one favorite thing. I'll take a Happy Meal.

FATHER: I'll take a pizza ...

FATHER and BENJAMIN: With Hollandaise sauce.

MOTHER: I'll just take both of you *(BENJAMIN and FATHER indicate that this is a lame choice)* ... and a bunch of white and yellow daisies.

BENJAMIN: That's where we'll go. To Flower Island!   Hoist the sails!

FATHER and MOTHER: Aye, aye, Captain.

BENJAMIN: Hoist the anchor!

FATHER and MOTHER: Aye, Aye, Captain.

BENJAMIN: Set sail for Flower Island.
Okay, we're there. The best flowers are always found at the top of Glacier Mountain, so that's where I'll go.
(He shimmies up a pole, and falls.)

FATHER: Are you alright?

MOTHER: I think it's swelling.

BENJAMIN: Darn. I think I need a shot! Just when Tyrannosaurus Rex was gonna attack us.

FATHER: Tell T. Rex to take a coffee break, and we'll get back to him later. Deal?

BENJAMIN: Deal.

MOTHER and FATHER: Hospital time.
(They move to the hospital and the infusion procedure is set up.)

BENJAMIN: It hurts, but I don't cry. Much. *(The infusion procedure is set up by the doctors and nurses. It takes numerous attempts before they are successful. DOCTOR #2 attempts a "poke.")* Owwwww!

FATHER: Easy partner ...

DOCTOR #2: (To BENJAMIN) Now remember, watch this tube. When it fills with blood we'll stop all this poking! (Poke.)

BENJAMIN: Owwwwww!

FATHER: (Giving him crayons, as a diversion.) Look! Crayons!

DOCTOR #2: (To BENJAMIN) When you see the tube red, we ...

BENJAMIN: I'll color it red!
(They divert him.)

FATHER: Look, draw here on this paper ...

MOTHER: Use the red crayon, color what you feel!

626

BENJAMIN: *(He begins to use the crayon as a vehicle for "escape.")* Red! Red ... ? Red ... !

DOCTOR #2: One more try. *(Poke.)*

BENJAMIN: Owwww!

MOTHER: Benjamin, <u>use</u> the red crayon; color it out.

DOCTOR #2: Hold real still ...

BENJAMIN: Just do it! The red train is waiting for the signal.

FATHER: What's the signal, partner?

BENJAMIN: "Poke." That's the signal.

ALL: Poke, poke, poke!

DOCTOR #2: Bull's eye!
(With the "bulls-eye!", BENJAMIN pulls away from the infusion action and launches into the story, drawing it three-dimensionally in the space around the continuing infusion scene.)

BENJAMIN: Red. Train! Color it in. Takes the factor way inside to my knee. Factor Eight! Looks like ... <u>bathtub plugs!</u> The Red Train picks up speed, climbs all the way to my knee. Then ... all the bathtub plugs spill out, and <u>that</u> stops the bleeding! *(He "signs" his name at the bottom of the drawing, and then moves back into the infusion scene.)* Ben ... ja ... min. Ta da! The End. Now that's a good drawing! *(The infusion ends.)*

DOCTOR #2: Good job, partner. You held still just the way you should.

BENJAMIN: I know. But next time <u>you</u> should do better than four pokes!
(The DOCTOR gives him a big sucker, and the medical staff exit.)

BENJAMIN: Let's go back to the glacier and look for some jewels.

MOTHER: Let's go back and look for some bed.

627

BENJAMIN: Awwww Mom ...

FATHER: *(Imitating ...)* Awwww Mom ... Okay, three seconds of sulk time. *(They all sulk while Dad counts to three.)* Now, time for bed. No ifs, ands or buts.

BENJAMIN: You said "BUTT": You're not supposed to say "BUTT," huh Mom? You said so.

FATHER: Then how about keister? And how about bed?

ALL THREE: And brush your teeth.
    (He races off.)

MOTHER: Slowdown. Take it easy on that knee.

BENJAMIN: Can I have a glass of water?

MOTHER: Time for bed.

BENJAMIN: Time ... for a story?

FATHER: Time for bed.

BENJAMIN: I won't be able to sleep if I don't know how the story ends.

FATHER: Okay. You want to know how the rest goes, right?

BENJAMIN: Right. After we fall off the cliff and are hanging by our ankles from the bungee cords ...

FATHER: Well, the ropes stretch and stretch, like ...

FATHER and BENJAMIN: ... limp spaghetti!

BENJAMIN: And we fall into a giant vat of poison!

FATHER: Nooo. We fall into a giant, soft, feather bed ...

MOTHER: ... and drift slowly off to sleep ...
    (MOTHER and FATHER, thinking they are finished, turn to exit.)

BENJAMIN: That's against the rules!

FATHER: What rules?

BENJAMIN: The rules! If you <u>start</u> a story on the Yellow Boat, you have to finish it on the Yellow Boat!

MOTHER: Are you sure?

BENJAMIN: I made them up!

FATHER: I forgot, I forgot. So sue me! Okay. We roll off the feather bed ...

BENJAMIN: Into a giant vat of acid!!!

FATHER: Rule number two. Don't interrupt! We roll off the bed, down the hill, and onto our boats. I'm blue ...

MOTHER: I'm yellow, you're red ...

BENJAMIN: Nuh, uh. I'm yellow.

FATHER: You sure?

BENJAMIN: I'm sure. <u>I'm</u> the Yellow Boat.

FATHER: (Revising) Okay. So the blue one sails back ...

MOTHER: And the red one sails back ...

BENJAMIN: But the Yellow Boat sails up ...

MOTHER and BENJAMIN: Up ...

MOTHER and FATHER and BENJAMIN: Up ... to the Sun!

BENJAMIN: That was awfully short!

FATHER: I know. But Union Story Time is over, and that's all you get in the off hours!

MOTHER: Good night!

BENJAMIN: Time for a hug?
(As they hug together.)

MOTHER and FATHER: Love you.

BENJAMIN: Love you too. But tomorrow can I play with some kids?

MOTHER and FATHER: We'll see.

BENJAMIN: Does that mean no?

FATHER: It means we'll see.

BENJAMIN: Next day!

ALL KIDS: Tag!

KID#1: (Tagging Kid #3) You're it!
(A game of tag erupts. MOTHER hovers protectively near BENJAMIN. The game swirls around them, until everyone has been "it" except BENJAMIN. He is tagged.

MOTHER: Oh Benjamin, be careful!
(BENJAMIN tags MOTHER and runs away to join the other kids. MOTHER runs after the kids, tags one, and the game continues until BENJAMIN is tagged again.)

BENJAMIN: Pig-Pile!!!
(A pile-up of all the kids with BENJAMIN at the bottom. The worried parents make their way towards the pile and pull the kid bodies off of what they are sure is a smashed and bleeding child.)

MOTHER: Are you all right?

BENJAMIN: I'm fine!

MOTHER: Promise me you'll be more careful ...

BENJAMIN: Mom. I won!
(BENJAMIN returns to the group to continue playing a king of the mountain game.)

FATHER: I think it's time for school.

MOTHER: Is he ready?

FATHER: Look at him.

MOTHER: *(She can't bear to watch his rough housing.)* Are we ready?

FATHER: Hang in there, Mom. We'll find the right school.

MOTHER: Where? How?

FATHER: Hey, this is America. We shop!
(The CHORUS quickly set up "options" for the family to choose.)

BENJAMIN: Mom, Dad? Come on over here.
(Coach #2 enters with "students," using his whistle often,

to put the kids through their paces. The first whistle, they snap to attention, at the second whistle, they begin to sprint in place. Kids #1 and #4 are clearly the best jocks; #3 and BENJAMIN have more of a struggle to keep up.)

COACH #1: Sports! That's what's important. Competition, Challenge. Be the best, the best!

#2 and #3: Whoof, Whoof, Whoof, Whoof.

COACH #1: *(He whistles again, they stop running, Second whistle, they start jumping jacks.)* Firm body, firm mind.

MOTHER: Our son has hemophilia so he may need to take it a little easy on some things.
(He whistles them to a stop, then on the second whistle, they begin toe touches.)

COACH #1: He is kind of puny, isn't he? Don't worry about a thing; few months on the field? We'll work out that "nemo" thing.

FATHER: Thanks. But no thanks.

COACH #1: Okay, one more lap ... (Whistle) ... move it, move it, move it!
(They all jog off, and transform into another school: the Montessori School from Hell.)

BENJAMIN: Here!

TEACHER #3: *(The children run amuck.)* We have no rules. We need no rules. Children should be free. Free to explore, free to find their own limits. Our job is to gently remind them of ... consequences. Excuse me.
(During her speech, her shoelaces have been tied together, and Jessica #4 has started to pound on an imaginary Aaron. The other kids gather around the body. Teacher #3 hops over to Jessica and grabs her.)

TEACHER #3: Jessica, put down that crowbar, and why don't you think about how Aaron might be feeling right now ...

MOTHER and FATHER: Keep looking.
(They move to another area.)

631

BENJAMIN: Mom, Dad! Over here.

(Teacher #2 and Kids #1, #3, #4, and EDDY # I enter with "Me dolls" and create another school scene. The parents meet Teacher #2 and he introduces the parents and BENJAMIN to the class. The parents stay to watch the class as BENJAMIN joins in.)

TEACHER: Come and join us. Class, this is Benjamin. *(The kids immediately "react" to the newcomer, checking him out. The teacher sees this and adopts a strategy to help break the ice.)* Today's assignment is "Me drawings"

KID #3: What's that?

TEACHER #2: Drawings of You.

EDDY #1: Of Me?

TEACHER: (Pointing to each kid, and including BENJAMIN.) Yes. You. And you, and you ...

KIDS #1, #2, #4, BENJAMIN: And you and you and you! Me drawings!

KID #2: I'm brown.

KID #3: I'm pink.

BENJAMIN: I'm yellow.

EDDY: I'm green.

KID #4: Yucko.

BENJAMIN: No, that's cool.

KID #4: It is? Oh.

(The kids draw about themselves, using soft dolls that can "become" them in the later community rejection scene.)

BENJAMIN: Any shape we want?

TEACHER: Any shape you are.

EDDY: Any color we like?

TEACHER: Any color you feel.

BENJAMIN: I feel purple. I see red. I hear blue. I taste green. I

632

am ... having a good time here. Mom, Dad? *(Shows them his drawing.)* You can go, now.
(Mom and Dad leave scene area.)

TEACHER: Benjamin, will you share your drawing with us?

BENJAMIN: This is my blue stomach, and my checkerboard high tops, and my yellow hat, and these are my bones, and they're dancing inside my body.

KID #4: Gross.

EDDY: Cool!

BENJAMIN: And this is my knee where I had a bleed, and ...

KID #3: I don't see any blood.

BENJAMIN: No, it's on the inside. See, it bleeds on the inside, here and here, and gets all red and hot and squishy ...

KID #4: Gross.

EDDY: Cool!

BENJAMIN: Then I go to the doctor.

TEACHER: What happens at the doctor, Benjamin?

BENJAMIN: I get a shot of Factor 8, and the bleed stops, and then I get a sucker.

EDDY, KID #3, KID #4: *(The kids voice approval, and freeze.)* Yeah!

FATHER: *(To teacher)* His hemophilia isn't a problem for you?

TEACHER: Problem? It's an opportunity. Welcome to our community.
(Adults exit. Time Shift. Playtime.)

BENJAMIN, EDDY, KID #3, KID #4: Recess!

KID #3: So what do you want to do?

KID #4: I don't know, what do you want to do?

KID #3: I don't know.

BENJAMIN: I have an idea. We can go on the Yellow Boat. C'mon Eddy.

KID #4: Boats are boring.

BENJAMIN: This is a Yellow Boat!

EDDY: And it can fly!

KID #4: Really?

EDDY: Really.

KID #4: Cool.

BENJAMIN: Here, I'll draw it for you.

KID #4: Drawing? Drawing's boring.

BENJAMIN: Not this way. I'll draw it so you can do it! C'mon aboard. Here's the deck, and here's the mast. *(#1 has become a kid, and he is hiding, waiting to be pulled up into the action of BENJAMIN's story. He becomes the mast.)* Load cargo, now.
(BENJAMIN continues drawing as the kids begin to do so.)

KID #3: Are we going or what?
(Music begins to support this change to fantasy storytelling.)

BENJAMIN: Okay, hoist the sails, hoist the anchor. You're supposed to say: "Aye, aye, Captain."

ALL the KIDS: Aye, aye, Captain! *(They begin to sail.)*

KID #3: Can I steer?

BENJAMIN: Nope, only the Captain gets to steer. I stand right here and draw, and steer.

KID #3: I want to be captain!

BENJAMIN: Then draw your own boat.

KID #3: I can't draw as good as you!

BENJAMIN: I know. You can be helper. She gets to steer if the Captain gets tired.

KID #3: Does that ever happen?

BENJAMIN: Nope.
(Music changes to indicate approaching storm.)

KID #1: Storm up ahead!

634

BENJAMIN: We can fly! Start special hydraulic-powered flyers.
(BENJAMIN draws as kids become a flying Yellow Boat, complete with sound effects. They begin to fly, Kid #3 grabs the crayon from BENJAMIN and draws in the air.)

KID #3: Land ho.

BENJAMIN: How do you know?

KID #3: I just drew it!

BENJAMIN: I'm the captain!

EDDY: Don't be so bossy.

BENJAMIN: I'm not. Land ho!

KID #4: Where are we?

BENJAMIN: Ask her. She's drawing it.
(The scene shifts to a Fantasy Island.)

KID #3: Uh, it's an island. There are palm trees, and monkeys.
(BENJAMIN climbs a pole as a monkey, but falls.)

EDDY: Benjamin, you all right?

BENJAMIN: I'm fine.
(They continue.)

KID #3: And there's a cave there. *(#2 and #4 make a cave as she draws it.)* It's the home of ... a king? A Giant King of the ... *(Searching for a name.)*

BENJAMIN: Svengalese.

KID #3: Yeah! The Giant King of the Svengalese.
(When the kids look up, they see that #2 and #4 have transformed themselves into the King, and he is indeed, evil and vicious. A little too so!)

BENJAMIN: No, not the Giant King. Erasers! *(They all erase it as the Giant falls apart and reforms. To Kid #3)* You have to be careful around here. *(He takes the crayon and continues. He whispers with EDDY, and EDDY's finger becomes the midgetized king. They have played this game before, and BENJAMIN is clearly the director.)* Now, we have stumbled upon the magical castle of the teeny-tiny midgetized King of the Svengalese. *(EDDY slowly reveals his index finger with crown and grass skirt: The King.)* He's friendly. He speaks in Svengalese. Luckily, I know it.

EDDY-KING: *(10 seconds of gibberish.)*

KID #3: What did he say?

BENJAMIN: Hello.

EDDY-KING: *(Gibberish)*

BENJAMIN: "You strangers are welcome here, and have come just in time."

KING: *(Gibberish, is overlapped with translation.)*

KID #4: Why just in time?

BENJAMIN: Why just in time? *(Eddy/King pantomimes a volcano erupting, and then BENJAMIN communicates the emergency.)* The volcano is erupting, and you must save my people. Quick, take us on your boat, and let's get out of here! *(BENJAMIN draws #1 into The Erupting Volcano as kids run around in terror.)*

EDDY: How do we save all the Svengalese?

BENJAMIN: Erase the volcano. *(They do, and the Volcano melts, turning back into EDDY.)* Draw more boats.
(KIDS sail away, saving the Svengalese.)

BENJAMIN: Land ho!

EDDY: Safe!
(The Boat vanishes as the game ends.)

KID #4: That was fun. Let's do it again tomorrow.

EDDY: I think she likes you.

BENJAMIN: Yuck. *(The KIDS exit and BENJAMIN takes out a huge piece of paper to make a new drawing. The previous play has triggered a bleed, but drawing a new adventure is more important than that right now.)* This is going to be a big one. This is a map to help the Svengalese, and their friendly

King <u>know</u> where to find ... their Enemy! That Big Guy.
(MOTHER enters.)

MOTHER: What are you doing?

BENJAMIN: I'm drawing. His castle sits high on top of a cliff,
so to get there, first you have to climb all these ladders of ...
bones. Cat bones ... yea!
*(As he draws, he enters into the action of his picture enough
so that MOTHER notices that he is limping slightly.)*

MOTHER: How's your knee?

BENJAMIN: Oh ... fine. The Big Guy's hiding way up here, in
this tower ...
*(As he shows the path that will be taken on the paper, his
movement betrays the knee-bleed he's trying to ignore.)*

MOTHER: Are you limping?

BENJAMIN: Mom! Now, the King has to go through these traps
and mazes ...

MOTHER: Let me see it. *(She examines his knee.)* Can you
straighten it? *(It hurts.)*

BENJAMIN: Mom!

MOTHER: I'll call the hospital.

BENJAMIN: I don't have time for that; I'm working on this
map ...

MOTHER: You can take it along.

BENJAMIN: It's too big for the car! It's a whole castle!!!

MOTHER: Then just take one room.

BENJAMIN: Oh. Okay, I'll take ... the torture room!

MOTHER: Of course.

BENJAMIN: I'll need lots of red for the blood ... *(MOTHER and
BENJAMIN shift location, and the infusion procedure begins,
set up as before. He draws throughout the procedure. During
this infusion we see the red "blood" tinged with another
colored contaminant: the HIV virus. BENJAMIN continues*

637

his monologue as he draws.) When you open this door, the skeleton is waiting with buckets of poison ... lemonade. Drink it, you turn into ... a ghost! So, don't drink it! But if you step here, you fall through the floor of the torture room. Ahhhhhhhhh ... Splat!

MOTHER: *(Returning.)* They're all done. You can finish that up at home. *(They return home. Sound underscores the following.#2, #3, and #4 tear and fold the large piece of drawing paper into "newspapers," or the scene can be staged to include some other medias.)*

BENJAMIN: *(He begins to draw on his "Me Doll.")* New drawing. Benjamin's Body. Everything looks the same. Outside.
(CHORUS [#2, #3, #4] moves and announce the following headlines. There is a sense of this information moving into, invading, the personal space of the family. The parents do not react directly to the announcements, but are affected by their sense.)

#3: Doctors alarmed by mystery illness.

#4: Disease approaching epidemic proportions.

MOTHER: I've just got this feeling ...

FATHER: You worry too much,
(CHORUS moves and announces:)

#2: Immune deficiency linked to infant deaths.

MOTHER: Doctor says his weight is down, and he's a little anemic.

FATHER: Maybe it's a growth spurt?

BENJAMIN: Inside. Almost the same. Except my stomach.
(CHORUS moves and announces:)

#3: Transmitted by the exchange of body fluids ...

#2: Rate of infection up among at-risk populations.

FATHER: Maybe it's the flu, everybody in his class has an upset stomach and diarrhea.

638

MOTHER: But he's had it over a week.
(CHORUS moves and announces:)

#3: Officials insist blood supply is 100% safe!

#4: 83-year-old Grandmother dies of AIDS?

#2: Cause of infection unknown.

BENJAMIN: And my head turns tired. And my legs turn tired.
And my fingers ... even my drawing is tired.

FATHER: He's going to be all right!

MOTHER: How do you know that?

FATHER: I don't know that. I hope that.
*(BENJAMIN begins to make "spots" on the "Me Doll," and
gradually on himself. The CHORUS begins a litany of states.)*

#2: Cases of AIDS reported in California

#4: New York.

#3: Florida.

MOTHER: Something's wrong, I just know it. It's like a spark
has gone out of him ...

#2: Indiana.

MOTHER: Don't you think he should be tested?

#4: Pennsylvania.

#3: Arizona.

FATHER: Tested for what?

#4: Illinois. Michigan.

#3: Texas. Tennessee.
(DOCTOR #1 enters.)

DOCTOR #1: We checked first with the ELISA ...

MOTHER: Tested for everything!

DOCTOR #1: ... and the Western Blot Test.

MOTHER: You know ... EVERYTHING!

DOCTOR #1: Your son ... has tested ... positive for the AIDS

virus. I'm very sorry. We'll do <u>everything</u> that we can.
(He exits.)

MOTHER: I just knew it. What are we going to do?

FATHER: I don't know. We'll ... just do, I guess.

MOTHER: How do we tell him?

FATHER: The right words will come.
(The parents move to BENJAMIN.)

FATHER: Uh, Benjamin, we need to talk.

BENJAMIN: About what?

MOTHER and FATHER: Well, ...

MOTHER: Well, about some things that ... we're thinking about,
and ...

BENJAMIN: About your meeting with the doctor, yesterday?

MOTHER: Yes.

FATHER: You know he's been giving you lots of tests, to see if
there's any reason why you've been more tired lately.
And one of the tests ...

MOTHER: He did a couple of special tests. And he found
something in your blood that shouldn't be there.

FATHER: A bug; a kind of bug — a virus.

BENJAMIN: AIDS?

FATHER: How do you know ... ?

BENJAMIN: TV.

MOTHER: No. Not AIDS. Not AIDS ... But they found a little bit
of the virus that can lead to the disease.

FATHER: They'll do a lot more tests; they want to make you feel
better!

BENJAMIN: How did I get it?

FATHER: Some of the blood that makes the factor must have had
some of the virus in it.

BENJAMIN: Does everybody who gets a shot get AIDS?

FATHER: No. And not everyone who gets a transfusion will get it.

BENJAMIN: Will I be alright?

FATHER: Yes.

MOTHER: I promise you.

FATHER: We're right here.
(BENJAMIN moves away from his parents to assimilate the news.)

FATHER: We're going to get some answers! *(The parents move to where DOCTOR #2 has entered. The following scenes should swirl around the space as the parents try to get some control of the situation.)* What about this AZT?

DOCTOR #2: It looks promising.

FATHER: When can we start it?

DOCTOR #2: We can't. It's not available for children.

MOTHER: When will it be available?

DOCTOR #2: I don't know.
(They move away from this DOCTOR over to where the HEALER #4 has entered.)

MOTHER: Let's just try this.

HEALER #4: Two quarts of clover tea daily, and wear this crystal.

FATHER: Will that help?

HEALER #4: I don't know.
(They whirl up stage to where DOCTOR #1 has entered.)

FATHER: What do we call it?

DOCTOR #1: Well, it's not AIDS.

FATHER: No?

DOCTOR #1: Technically. He has the virus, but none of the diseases that the government posts as markers.

MOTHER: He has the disease? But not the disease.

DOCTOR #1: Technically.

FATHER: Which is it?

MOTHER: Yes or no?

DOCTOR #1: Yes and no.

FATHER: What do we do?
(The DOCTORS' words swirl around the parents.)

DOCTOR #1: I don't know ... appointment, next week; Wednesday, nine-thirty.

DOCTOR #2: I don't know.

HEALER #3: Appointment, Friday at one.

DOCTOR #1: I don't know.

DOCTOR #2: Appointment on Thursday, three o'clock.

HEALER #3: I don't know.

DOCTOR and HEALER: I don't know, I don't know, I don't know...
(This builds to their exit, leaving MOTHER and FATHER totally bewildered. BENJAMIN jumps up.)

BENJAMIN: Nobody knows anything, except me, and all I know is that no one knows anything!

FATHER: *(To MOTHER)* It's going to be alright ... but we're going to need help on this one. We've got a lot of friends.
*(The community parents [#1, #2, #3 and #4] enter, and gather their "children," the Me Dolls that were last seen in the recess scene. They greet Mom and Dad.
BENJAMIN returns to drawing on his Me Doll.)*

FATHER: Thank you all for coming on such short notice. We need to ask for some help. Lots of help, actually.
(Community response overlaps:)

#4: Sure, anything.

#1: Anything at all.

#3: Whatever we can do to help, just ask.

#2: Hey, what are friends for?

FATHER: Benjamin has tested ... positive ... for the AIDS virus. *(There is a moment of total silence. Then slightly overlapping response.)*

#1 and #3: Oh.

#4: Sorry.

#2: How did he ... ?

MOTHER: (To break the silence.) There is so much about this that we don't know right now ...

FATHER: We need your help! *(Community parents, without wanting to appear so, slowly begin to pull their children away from the family, all the while voicing their support.)*

#3: Sure, anything. Anything at all.

#2: Whatever we can do to help.

#3: Just ask.

FATHER: The best thing we can do is just to keep things as normal as possible.

MOTHER: What he needs, what we need, is to try to have a normal life.

#1: *(Backing away)* Hey, what are friends for?

FATHER: So, how about we take all the kids to Ghostbusters, Friday night? *(#1 unfurls a large sheet of plastic, which slowly forms a plastic barrier between BENJAMIN and everyone else. His Me Doll tries to "contact" other Me Dolls through the plastic wall, but their parents pull them away.)*

#4: Anything.

#3: Anything at all.

FATHER: Saturday afternoon?

#1: Anything at all.

FATHER: Sunday?

#1: Anything.

MOTHER: The pool is open, we could take the kids swimming?

#3: Whatever we can do,

#1: ... just ask,

MOTHER: We're going camping this weekend; how about ...

#4: Just ask.

#1: Just ask.

MOTHER: A sleep over?

#3: Just ask.

#4: Just ask.

#1: Just ask.

MOTHER: I AM asking!
  (Time shift.)

BENJAMIN: Today is my birthday and I'm seven, and I'm having a party.
  (EDDY enters with a box wrapped in paper with a long ribbon. He and BENJAMIN are in separate spaces, divided by the plastic wall.)

EDDY: This is so great. He'll never guess what this is 'til it pops out in his face.

EDDY's MOTHER (#4): Eddy, what are you doing?

EDDY: Finishing up my present for Benjamin.
  (He tries to tie the bow.)

EDDY's MOTHER: Finish up quickly, and I'll drop it off on my way to the grocery store.

BENJAMIN: I'm having pie instead of cake, 'cause I don't like cake, and it's MY birthday.

EDDY: You can just drop <u>me</u> off for the party ...

644

EDDY's MOTHER: I can't do that. I'm sorry Eddy, but you can't go to that party!

EDDY: But he's my best friend.

EDDY's MOTHER: I know this is hard, but ...

EDDY: But I have to go ...

EDDY's MOTHER: Don't argue with me! I'll drop the present off this afternoon. I know what's best for you.
(They exit.)

BENJAMIN: No one's coming? Not even Eddy?
(Time shift. TEACHER enters.)

TEACHER (#2): The board met last night. I'm afraid Benjamin won't be able to attend school here anymore.

MOTHER: What?

TEACHER: We're just not set up to handle this sort of thing.

FATHER: The doctors are positive that he's safe in school and with some simple precautions, everyone else is safe as well.

TEACHER: The board is comfortable with its decision. He'll have to leave.

MOTHER: When?

TEACHER: Immediately.

MOTHER: Can he stay to the end of the week?

TEACHER: Immediately!

MOTHER: Just another day?

TEACHER: I'll see ... if I can help you find a tutor ...
(He exits. Time shift.)

BENJAMIN: Why can't I go to school?

MOTHER: I don't know.

BENJAMIN: Why won't anyone come to play with me?

FATHER: We're here to play with you.

MOTHER: What would you like to play?

BENJAMIN: Nothing.

(He takes out a wide black marker, and slowly draws an outline of himself on the plastic, in silence. As he is doing this body drawing, the parents are isolated in their own spaces, but try to "contact" him, and each other, with the following lines. He shuts them out.)

MOTHER: Benjamin. Would you like some juice?

FATHER: It's like he's slipped away ...

MOTHER: How about a sandwich?

FATHER: Or a Happy Meal. You've got to eat something, so you can get better.

MOTHER: Slipped away. On his own boat ... on his own sea.

FATHER: He doesn't speak. He doesn't eat.

MOTHER: Benjamin?

FATHER: He spends day after day curled up on the sofa ...

MOTHER: Just picking his arm.

FATHER: Benjamin.

MOTHER: Picking. Like a little monkey.

FATHER: Benjamin.

MOTHER: Benjamin.

(BENJAMIN crosses out his image. He drops the marker. He has stopped drawing. DOCTOR #2 enters.)

DOCTOR #1: His white blood count is dangerously low. We need to admit him to the hospital immediately.

(The scene shifts to the hospital. The sound support for the hospital should be constant; hum, buzz, beep, at varying volumes for each scene. It can also be used to help mark time shifts. By adding a sheet and pillow, the boat becomes a hospital bed. BENJAMIN is given a hospital gown, and moved to the bed. The parents move through long hallways, answering questions.)

DOCTOR #4: Name?

FATHER: Benjamin.

DOCTOR #4: Spell that please.

FATHER: B-E-N-J-A-M-I-N.

DOCTOR #4: Number?

FATHER: 516-43-8645

DOCTOR #2: Name?

MOTHER: Benjamin.

DOCTOR #4: Spell that please.

MOTHER: B-E-N-J-A-M-I-N.

DOCTOR #2: Number?

MOTHER: 516-43-8645.

DOCTOR #1: Name?

MOTHER and FATHER: Benjamin.

DOCTOR #1: Spell that please.

MOTHER and FATHER: B-E-N-J-A-M-I-N.

DOCTOR #1: Number?

MOTHER and FATHER: 516-43-8645.

> (As BENJAMIN is put in the bed, DOCTORS repeat these
> requests. MOTHER and FATHER continue to answer, and
> then stop. BENJAMIN, in the bed, looks around, and registers
> with a look that he feels completely alone. Silence for a beat.
>
> JOY [#3] enters, carrying her backpack. As soon as he hears
> her approach he turns away. She pulls a kazoo out and
> tootles a greeting. There is no response. She tries again; no
> response. She tootles "bye, bye." and then leaves the kazoo
> near his feet at the end of the bed. JOY exits, but watches for
> a moment in the doorway. BENJAMIN is tempted to check
> out what she has left, but just as he is reaching for it, three
> DOCTORS enter.)

DOCTOR #2: Good morning.

DOCTOR #4: ... afternoon.

DOCTOR #1: ... evening.

ALL DOCTORS: And how are we feeling today? Hmmmm?
(Short pause for response.)

DOCTOR #2: Patient ...

DOCTOR #4: Not responding.

DOCTOR #1: Check.

DOCTOR #2: Vital signs, Q-2 times 4.

DOCTOR #4: Check.

FATHER: It's like another country.

MOTHER: White walls, white floors, white sound ...

DOCTOR #2: NPO, 48 hours.

DOCTOR #1: Charted.

DOCTOR #4: Check.
(The DOCTORS retreat; as they exit one removes the kazoo as if it had no place here.)

FATHER: Stainless steel, hard edges ...

MOTHER: Not a single soft thing in this whole place.
(The parents move toward the room, but are intercepted by the swoop of the DOCTORS.)

DOCTOR #2: Caution! Blood Precautions!

DOCTOR #4: Oxygen in use!

DOCTOR #1: Gowns, masks, gloves suggested!

MOTHER: I'm his Mother!
(All DOCTORS snap on their gloves.)

MOTHER: I hate that sound! Benjamin ...
(Time Shift. The parents and DOCTORS move to the bed. One doctor has a length of plastic tubing for a medical test.)

DOCTOR #2: We'll need samples,

DOCTOR #4: ... specimens,

DOCTOR #1: ... statistics!

ALL DOCTORS: Check!

MOTHER: Benjamin, these doctors need to do some tests ...
    (BENJAMIN turns away, shutting them all out.)

FATHER: Help us with this ... they need you to swallow this little
    plastic tube ...

DOCTOR #1: We need a sample ...

FATHER: We need your help, sport ...

DOCTOR #2: Please cough,

DOCTOR #4: Open your mouth,

DOCTOR #1: Just relax ...

ALL DOCTORS: Breathe.

DOCTOR #2: Cough.

DOCTOR #4: Open.

DOCTOR #1: Relax.

ALL DOCTORS: Breathe.

DOCTOR #2: Cough.

DOCTOR #4: Open.

DOCTOR #1: Relax.

ALL DOCTORS: Breathe.

BENJAMIN: Leave me alone. Just leave me alone!

DOCTOR #2: Please step out into the hall?
    *(Parents and DOCTOR #2 move to one side. DOCTORS #1
    and #4 move away, consulting their charts.)*

DOCTOR #2: We're doing our best. He's maintaining ...

DOCTOR #4: maintaining ...

DOCTOR #1: maintaining ...

FATHER: Tell me what we're fighting? AIDS, depression, what?

DOCTOR #2: All of it.

DOCTORS #1 & #4: All of it.

(DOCTORS move away and continue to consult their charts and each other. MOTHER and FATHER stay to the side as JOY approaches the room a second time. She is wearing a necklace of whistles and kazoos.)

JOY: *(She tootles him a "hello" on several different whistles and/ or kazoos. BENJAMIN "shuts her out", both physically and with an angry sound.)* Okay, okay. I'll come back later. *(Takes three steps away, and returns. Kazoo flourish.)* It's later. *(He turns his back to her.)* Tell you what. Whenever you want me to disappear, just flick your hand, like this. *(She demonstrates with small hand flick of dismissal.)* I'm gone. History.

(BENJAMIN flicks his hand. She withdraws. Then returns.)

JOY: I'm back, *(BENJAMIN flicks his hand.)* I'm gone. *(Kazoo "good-bye." She exits.)*

(Time shift. Three DOCTORS enter to bedside.)

DOCTOR #2: Good morning.

DOCTOR #3: ... afternoon.

DOCTOR #1: ... evening.

ALL DOCTORS: And how are we feeling today? Hmmmm? *(DOCTOR #1 goes to parents. DOCTORS #2 and #3 repeat the following lines, but become increasingly more "human" in their delivery; a "time shift" that indicates a change in attitude towards this patient.)*

DOCTOR #2 and #3: And how are we feeling today? Hmmmm? And how are we feeling today? Hmmmm?

MOTHER: Why is nothing working? You keep testing and poking and prodding; there's <u>no</u> change.

FATHER: He's pulling further and further away.

DOCTOR #1: We're doing everything we know. Everything we can ... We'll keep trying! *(He moves to join the other doctors.)*

(To other doctors as they exit.) Let's take another look at those X-rays.
(JOY moves to parents.)

JOY: Hi. I'm Joy, the Child Life Specialist on this wing.

MOTHER: Another doctor?

JOY: Not exactly. The doctors work with the sick parts: my specialty is the well parts.

FATHER: What?

JOY: My work is play.

FATHER: There's not much of that around here.

JOY: I'll try to change that. I'm here to work with Benjamin to try to make some sense out of this place.

FATHER: Good luck!

MOTHER: He won't eat, he won't talk ... He won't even draw.

JOY: Is that something he likes to do? Drawing?

MOTHER: He used to draw all the time.

FATHER: He's just not Benjamin if he's not drawing.

JOY: That's good to know. Why don't you two get a cup of coffee?

MOTHER: We should stay ...

JOY: *(She pulls a crayon from her pack.)* Just let me have a look for a well part.

FATHER: Come on.
(They exit. JOY approaches BENJAMIN.)

JOY: *(She enters, heralding her arrival on a slide whistle. He flicks his hand to dismiss her. She withdraws then returns, this time with a train whistle. He flicks her away. She withdraws then returns with a duck call. BENJAMIN almost flicks. Then changes his mind. There is a moment of "small victory" for JOY.)* You don't need to talk. I can just sit here with you. *(She sits, and pulls a small cloth doll and set of markers out of her backpack.)* I have some work to do. I want to make this doll for a boy here in the hospital. He hates being here, what with the shots and the medicines ... ? But this doll needs a name ... Can you think of a good name?

BENJAMIN: No.

JOY: No is an excellent name! Now, No has to have a lot of tests, and maybe even an operation. Can you tell him anything he needs to know?

BENJAMIN: No.

JOY: Okay. But No needs some hair, what color should it be? *(No response.)* Brown? Nah. Purple! *(This odd choice tweaks just the smallest bit of interest in BENJAMIN. He watches as JOY colors the hair.)* How about his eyes? *(She holds out some crayons between she and BENJAMIN, and after some hesitation, BENJAMIN chooses an orange one.)* Orange.

BENJAMIN: Except when he cries. His tears are red.

JOY: Red tears ... ! And his mouth?
(She colors as he chooses.)

BENJAMIN: Mad green.

JOY: And his eye brows are ... ?

BENJAMIN: Yellow. Scared yellow.

JOY: So, his mouth is mad, and his eyes are scared, and his red tears are so very sad. And he feels ... ?

BENJAMIN: Alone.

JOY: Isn't it amazing how you can have so many people in and out of here, and still feel so all alone? *(She finished up the coloring.)* TAHDAH!! *(Or the kazoo equivalent)* *(BENJAMIN looks over at the drawing on the doll, and makes a sound of some disapproval ...)*

BENJAMIN: EEUUuwwwww!

JOY: So I'm not good at faces ... you want to try?

BENJAMIN: No. *(He turns away again.)*

JOY: Okay. I have to go. Maybe No can come back tomorrow?

(He shrugs "Maybe ..." She leaves the whistle necklace on his bed and exits.)
(Time shift.)

BENJAMIN: *(Remembering, and punctuating the speech with various whistles.)* And she comes back tomorrow. And the next tomorrow. And the next. She lets me talk when I want to, and she doesn't make me say "I'm fine" if I don't feel like it. She tells me about hospital things, so I know what's going on ...
(Time shift. DOCTOR #1 is speaking to the parents.)

DOCTOR #1: I've ordered up an endoscopy ... a stomach test. We'll set it up for the morning.
(JOY enters, with an armful of medical equipment: an endoscope, plastic tubing, a flash light, an elastic string, a No doll with surgical mask and cap. As part of her setup, she presents each piece to BENJAMIN without directly doing so. He watches, but doesn't want to be seen doing so. The parents also enter, and JOY involves them in her Magical Medical Circus. She introduces the event with a kazoo fanfare.)

JOY: Good evening ladies and gentlemen, and welcome to the Magical Medical Circus — a really big show in a really small space, hastily assembled for you today. Thank-you. Featuring No, the daredevil artiste! He's here to show you how a stomach test works. Thank-you, No. He will use this ... *(She shows the elastic string.)* ... and this ... *(She pulls out a flashlight and beckons to MOTHER.)* *(Speaking as NO:)* Hey, pretty lady, come over here. *(MOTHER comes over and NO hands her a flash light.)* *(As NO:)* Thank you. *(As JOY:)* And he will use this. *(She presents the endoscope. At this scary sight BENJAMIN turns away, but JOY quickly wins him back with NO.)* Quiet please, the artiste prepares. *(She puts NO through traditional actor warm-up techniques, then explains the procedure in circus terms.)* He's going to fly up to a highwire stretched from here ... *(She stretches an elastic string over BENJAMIN.)* ... to ... here. Could you hold this, please? *(She offers it to BENJAMIN, who finally decides to take it. He holds it in the air, making a tightrope line for NO.)* Thanks!

(As NO:) It's time for Stomach Bungee jumping! I will descend to your stomach, fetch a sample with this ... *(Showing him the light and tube at the end of the scope.)* ... and then "sproing" back to my starting position, unscathed, untouched, unharmed. Watch! *(NO is unable to jump all the way up to the elastic line with the weight of the scope, so after a few attempts, he gets an idea:)* AAHhhh, wait. *(JOY blows up a rubber glove like a balloon and attaches it to NO.)*

(As NO:) Lights! *(Mom turns on the flash light as a follow spot.)* *(As NO:)* Drum roll, please! *(Dad does, at the foot of the bed. NO floats up to the elastic wire, walks down the wire, and prepares to descend.)* *(As NO:)* Attach bungee! Uno, Duo, Tre ... BUNGEEE! *(NO, with elastic end at his foot, descends to BENJAMIN's stomach, and bounces back up.)* *(As NO:)* Safe! Stomach test complete! *(BENJAMIN lets the line snap free, so NO crashes to the floor.)* Thank you No! *(The parents clap then exit.)*

BENJAMIN: What's No going to do with it?

JOY: With what?

BENJAMIN: With that stomach stuff.

JOY: The doctors need to look at it.

BENJAMIN: Yuck.

JOY: So they can figure out the right medicines.

BENJAMIN: Will it hurt?

JOY: Just 'til No stops bouncing. So: Are you ready to help them?

BENJAMIN: Maybe ...
(He holds out his hand for her to shake; when she tries to do so he fakes her out, and quite enjoys his little victory.

654

She exits.)

(Time shift.)

(Remembering.) Then one night, as a surprise, she sticks glow-in-the-dark stars on the ceiling over my bed, and another day, she paints a picture right on my window, so when the sun shines through it in the afternoon, it turns the white wall into colors.
(Time shift. MOTHER enters to tuck him in, and EDDY enters.)

MOTHER: Benjamin? Look who's here.

BENJAMIN: Eddy!!!
(They both silently indicate to Mom that they'd like her to leave.)

MOTHER: I'll leave you two alone.
(She exits. There is an awkward silence.)

BENJAMIN: Eddy ...

EDDY: *(Indicating the bed control panel.)* So. What's all this stuff?

BENJAMIN: This is my remote control for my very own TV, and this makes my bed go up and down ...

EDDY: Cool.

BENJAMIN: And see this tube stuck in my chest?

EDDY: Wooah!

BENJAMIN: It's for medicine, so the doctors don't have to keep giving me shots. If I had a couple of bolts, I'd look just like Frankenstein.

EDDY: I could bring you some.

BENJAMIN: Some what?

EDDY: Some Frankenstein bolts.

BENJAMIN: Could you?

EDDY: They stick right to your head.

BENJAMIN: No way!

EDDY: Way!

BENJAMIN: That'd really surprise the doctors.

EDDY: Yeah! So what's it like to be in here?

BENJAMIN: It's okay. But they never leave you alone.

EDDY: Like my Mom?

BENJAMIN: Worse than your Mom.

EDDY: Oh, no! Does it hurt?

BENJAMIN: Yeah.

EDDY: Do you cry?

BENJAMIN: No. Sometimes.

EDDY: Yeah.

BENJAMIN: Were you scared to come see me?

EDDY: No. A little.

BENJAMIN: Why? I'm just me.

EDDY: Yeah, but I never knew anyone, who ... you know ...

BENJAMIN: Was sick ... ? Had AIDS?

EDDY: Yeah.

BENJAMIN: You can't catch it just by sitting next to me. It's not like cooties.

EDDY: I know that. I didn't know if you'd be mad at me.

BENJAMIN: Why didn't you come to my birthday?

EDDY: My Mom said no.

BENJAMIN: So why'd she let you come now?

EDDY: I dunno. She read a bunch of stuff, we all talked about it, and she changed her mind. You want to draw or something?

BENJAMIN: I'm a little tired ...

EDDY: I'd better go then; they said I shouldn't stay too long.

BENJAMIN: I'm glad you came.

EDDY: Yeah.

BENJAMIN: Will you come back?

EDDY: I said I'd bring the bolts, didn't I?
(They high five, EDDY exits.)
(Time shift. JOY and DOCTOR #2 enter. JOY carries an X-Ray, and backpack, the DOCTOR consults his chart.)

JOY: Good morning

BENJAMIN: ... afternoon,

DOCTOR #4: Evening!

JOY: And how are we feeling today ...

BENJAMIN, JOY and DOCTOR #4: Hmmmmmm???

BENJAMIN: Eddy came to visit!

JOY: How did it go?

BENJAMIN: He's still my best friend. And he's bringing me ... it's a surprise.

JOY: Did you have a good night?

BENJAMIN: No...

JOY: What happened?

BENJAMIN: More bleeding.

DOCTOR #4: That explains this new plan.

BENJAMIN: More tests?

DOCTOR #4: We're going to do an exploratory surgery, so we can take a look at what's going on in there.

BENJAMIN: I'm tired of all the looking; I'm ready for some finding.

JOY: They'll have an easier time if you'll help them.

BENJAMIN: What else are they going to do to me?

JOY: Remember when you drank that Barium stuff yesterday?

BENJAMIN: Yuckli!

JOY: And they took an X-Ray of your insides? Well here it is! *(She shows him an X-Ray film.)*

BENJAMIN: *(Examining the picture.)* That's me?

JOY: Yep.

BENJAMIN: Inside?

JOY: Yep.

BENJAMIN: Well that's a pretty crummy picture. It's all gray. Gray is not what it feels like.

DOCTOR #4: Then how does it feel?

BENJAMIN: Not gray.

JOY: Tell me.

BENJAMIN: This, down here ... ? (Indicating stomach.) It feels ... it feels like ... I can't tell you ...

JOY: Keep trying ...

BENJAMIN: When it hurts the worst, like last night? It's like ... like slow red spikes of hurt ... *(Indicating on himself.)* Here and here.

JOY: *(Indicating the X-Ray, then his stomach.)* This part here, is a picture of that part there.

BENJAMIN: Well it's not the right colors.

JOY: *(Holding out the crayons.)* You want to make it the right colors?

BENJAMIN: *(Tempted but not buying it yet.)* No. You can.

JOY: Okay, but you have to tell me how.

BENJAMIN: *(He indicates on himself. She colors the X-Ray.)* This is blue. It's fine, but orange is getting closer ... burning orange. And farther down, that's where it really hurts; sharp pains like ... pins dripping acid, purple and green. That's where it's dark, hurting, red. Red. Red. RED!!! *(The coloring is interrupted by the entrance of DOCTORS #1 & s#2.)*

DOCTOR #1: Good morning ...

DOCTOR #2: ... afternoon ...

DOCTOR #1: ... evening ...

DOCTOR#1 & #2: And how are we feeling today, hmmmm?

BENJAMIN: Red.

DOCTOR #1: I beg your pardon?

JOY: He feels red.

DOCTOR #1: That's nice ...

BENJAMIN: And here is black-and-blue, where <u>he</u> poked me yesterday.

DOCTOR #2: I needed those samples to help us prepare for exploratory surgery.

BENJAMIN: You're an explorer?

DOCTOR #2: Well, I guess so ...

DOCTOR #4: We're exploring ways to make you feel better.

BENJAMIN: You're awfully white. Why so white?

DOCTOR #1: Doctors always wear white.

BENJAMIN: Explorers don't wear white. White's boring.

JOY: Benjamin, why don't you tell the doctors about the pain?

BENJAMIN: I can't.

DOCTOR #4: It would help us if you could.

BENJAMIN: It hurts all over.

DOCTOR #1: Where?

BENJAMIN: Some places more than others.

DOCTOR #2: When?

BENJAMIN: Sometimes, all the time, I don't know ...

DOCTOR #1: How?

BENJAMIN: It doesn't have words, it just feels! I can't tell them!

JOY: You could show them. *(Holding out the X-Ray film.)* This could be a map. Color it to help them find the hurt!
(She holds out a crayon. BENJAMIN hesitates for a moment, then seizes it.)

BENJAMIN: A map? *(He takes the X-Ray from her.)* I'm good at maps. New Drawing! *(Everybody freezes in position as BENJAMIN takes up the crayon and holds it aloft.)* Journey to the Center of My Guts!
(The DOCTORS and JOY are transformed into a small band of explorers, checking supplies prior to departure on an expedition.)

JOY: Equipment check. What do we need?

DOCTOR #2: Antibiotic.

DOCTOR #4: Hypodermic.

DOCTOR #1: Antiseptic.

BENJAMIN: Ick. Get Well Medicine. And a bazooka!

ALL DOCTORS: Bazooka?

JOY: Bazooka!

BENJAMIN: Command Central over to Field Team One. Do you read me?

JOY: Roger, Captain. How do we get in?

BENJAMIN: Through my mouth. I'll leave it open so you can see better. *(BENJAMIN draws his mouth with big circles, as the DOCTORS climb over the boat, starting into his body. The progress through the body should be supported with as much movement, lighting and sound support as can be mustered.)* First stop? My lungs. *(They enter a whoosh world.)* Air world, feels blue ...

DOCTOR #4: This side is clear. No problems. Let's check the other lobe ...

BENJAMIN: Here grayer, tighter ...

DOCTOR #4: Definite congestion. I'll order up respiratory therapy.

660

BENJAMIN: Now find the hurt. Into the blood. *(They are swept along through the bloodstream.)* In one side of my heart. It's blue, 'cause I've got a strong heart - - and out the other.

DOCTOR #2: Past the liver:

BENJAMIN: Gross. I hate liver, it's green! Be careful.

JOY: Where are we?

BENJAMIN: In my guts. That's where it hurts.

DOCTOR #1: Looks like the small intestine.

BENJAMIN: Entering danger zone. But you're not there yet, keep going ...

DOCTOR #1: Farther?

BENJAMIN: Farther. Go farther. Feel the fire ...

DOCTOR #2: Signs of infection ahead ...

BENJAMIN: Dark red! Scorch arrows. Shooting fire.
(The attack begins. BENJAMIN becomes the general of the battle.)

JOY: What's happening?

BENJAMIN: Bad guys, attack! Guys with purple jack hammers, over there! Red-orange flame throwers over there! Blue grenades, exploding into flaming yellow over here!

DOCTOR #1: I had no idea it was this bad.

DOCTOR #4: It's EVERYWHERE!

JOY: What do we do?

BENJAMIN: Try the bazooka!

JOY: Good idea.

DOCTOR #1: Try a little Tagamet.

DOCTOR #2: Maybe some Bactrum.

BENJAMIN: Let 'em have it! *(They fire a medical Bazooka.)* It isn't working.

DOCTOR #2: We've got to get out of here.

DOCTOR #4: We need reinforcements.

JOY: Command Central, request exit instructions.

BENJAMIN: You've got two choices: up to the lungs or down to my ...

JOY and DOCTORS: Head for the lungs!

BENJAMIN: I'll cough you out!
(He does so and they return to the hospital room, in exactly the same positions they held before beginning the Body Tour.)

JOY: Now, that's an excellent map!

DOCTOR #4: I'll order up respiratory therapy to start Q - 4.

DOCTOR #1: I'll need some new X-Rays, Benjamin.

DOCTOR #2: Now we're ready for surgery. Thanks for your help, Command Central.
(DOCTORS salute and exit.)

JOY: You look tired. You want to rest for a bit?

BENJAMIN: Yeah.
(She takes the X-Ray from him.)

JOY: So, that's what it feels like. You sure are good at drawing.

BENJAMIN: Yeah. But I wish we could just erase it.

JOY: Erase what?

BENJAMIN: The hurt.

JOY: Me too. I'll see you tomorrow.
(She hands him several pieces of drawing paper to go with his crayon, which he accepts. She offers her hand to shake with him — and then fakes him out. JOY exits. DOCTOR #2 brings in something to represent an IV pump and hooks it up to the bed. DOCTOR #4 brings in another.)

DOCTOR #2: Command Central? New defense weapons.
(They exit.)

BENJAMIN: After surgery, I get a little better. Everybody smiles. Dad figures out how to put plastic lizards into old IV bags, so

it looks like I'm getting lizard medicine. *(FATHER does so.)* Then, I get worse. No more smiles.
(Voices of DOCTORS as they move in and out of the room, checking.)

DOCTOR #1: Colostomy complete, but he's bleeding into the abdomen now.

BENJAMIN: There are about a million machines in my room now, like robots standing guard round my bed.

DOCTOR #2: His white blood count is dropping.

BENJAMIN: I hear machines and voices all night long; whispering to me ...
(The night takes over, with MOTHER and FATHER on either side of the bed: a vigil. The monitors and machines whir and thrum and beep softly.)

FATHER: Four A.M. Peacetime.

MOTHER: Time to grab a slice of silence.

FATHER: Smooth brow, soft fingers, gentle breath. Almost normal.

MOTHER: So peaceful you can forget. Almost.

FATHER: Machines. *(Indicating medical machinery.)* Pumping food, pumping medicine, pumping blood ... pumping hope?

MOTHER: And the sound. Like horses. Like galloping horses of hope in the night. I'm afraid of losing those horses.

FATHER: *(Trying to offer comfort and strength, for them both.)*
Busen lull, cook the kettle full,
There sailed three boats from the harbor.
The blue carried hope,
The red carried faith,
The yellow filled itself with love.
(Time shift.)

BENJAMIN: Mom! Dad! Look. Come look!

MOTHER: What is it?

FATHER: What's wrong?

BENJAMIN: Look at the moon. Just look at the moon!

MOTHER: I've never seen it so ...

BENJAMIN: It's so big ...

MOTHER: So close.

FATHER: So bright.
(They climb into bed with him.)

MOTHER: If I could be Queen of the World and have anything that I wanted ...

FATHER: If I could be King of the World, and have anything I wanted ...

BENJAMIN: I've never seen it so ...

MOTHER: It's so big ...

FATHER: So close.

BOTH: So bright.
(BENJAMIN interrupts ...)

BENJAMIN: Dad, What's it like to die?

FATHER: What?

BENJAMIN: What will it feel like when I die?

FATHER: I ... don't know.

BENJAMIN: Will it hurt?

FATHER: I don't kn ... Probably. Some.
(Pause.)

MOTHER: I don't think more than now.

BENJAMIN: Where will I go?

FATHER: I don't know.

MOTHER: But it will be a new adventure.

BENJAMIN: Will you put me in a box?

MOTHER: What?

BENJAMIN: Will you put me in a box? You know, what's left?

FATHER: What do you want us to do?

BENJAMIN: I really want to be home again.

MOTHER: Then that's what we'll do.

BENJAMIN: Love you.

MOTHER and FATHER: Love you too.

BENJAMIN: And I'll always be your boy.

MOTHER and FATHER: Always.
(BENJAMIN falls asleep, MOTHER and FATHER tuck him in, then exit. DOCTORS' voices come from outside the room.)

DOCTOR #2: Orders?

DOCTOR #4: 800 units, packed red cells.

DOCTOR #2: Have you seen the latest liver results?

DOCTOR #4: Any change?

DOCTOR #2: Not for the better.
(Time shift. EDDY enters, wakes up BENJAMIN.)

EDDY: Hey, Benjamin. I got the bolts. See? I got some for me too ...

BENJAMIN: Wow. Thanks Eddy. They're great.

EDDY: Don't you want to put them on?

BENJAMIN: *(He is tired, but he puts one on.)* Sure.
(They do Frankenstein impersonations, but BENJAMIN is weak and starts to cough, scaring EDDY. Silence, as he looks around the room.)

EDDY: Wow, you've got a lot more stuff here now.

BENJAMIN: Yeah.

EDDY: What's it all for?

BENJAMIN: So I can get better.

EDDY: Is it working?

BENJAMIN: I dunno ...

EDDY: Really?

BENJAMIN: Really.

EDDY: Will you get better?

BENJAMIN: *(Shrugs "I don t know.")*

EDDY: Are you going to ... *(BENJAMIN shrugs his shoulders, "yeah, maybe.")* I never knew anyone that was ... well, you know ... going to ...

BENJAMIN: Die?

EDDY: Yeah.

BENJAMIN: Well, now you do.

EDDY: Do your folks know?

BENJAMIN: Yeah, I think so.

EDDY: What's it feel like? To know?

BENJAMIN: Better than not knowing.

EDDY: I'm glad you're still my friend.

BENJAMIN: Me too.

EDDY: Benjamin. Can I have some of your Legos?

BENJAMIN: Sure. But not the castle.

EDDY: Deal. *(DOCTOR enters to check the machines.)* I'd better go. Will I see you later?

BENJAMIN: Sure. Sometime. Bye.
    (They do a very gentle high-five, EDDY exits.)

    (Time shift. DOCTORS hook up another IV pump, then exit. BENJAMIN begins drawing, narrating as he draws.)

BENJAMIN: This is a yellow brick road, leading from the gangplank of my boat, all along a long, long,
    (JOY enters.)

JOY and BENJAMIN: long, long ...

BENJAMIN: ... rock wall. I walk and I walk, and my knee doesn't hurt a bit, and when I come to a gate, I meet a gardener. That's him. He tells me that the gate is locked, but I can squeeze through the bars if I want to. Because on the other side is ... *(He draws a rainbow shape on the paper.)*

JOY: What do you see?

BENJAMIN: See? Here. That is for Momma and Pappa. But later. You'll know.
(He continues drawing, she exits. DOCTORS begin to move in and out of the room constantly. There is an escalating sense of crisis.)

BENJAMIN: Then I get worse. Everybody carries worry into the room and sadness out.

DOCTOR #2: Tuberculosis present, but we don't know the strain.

BENJAMIN: The oxygen tube in my nose makes it so I can whistle, and I could never whistle before! My heart starts doing a tap dance ...

DOCTOR #1: Heart fibrillation! Get me an EKG!
(The DOCTORS hook up another IV pump.)

BENJAMIN: So they hook up a little TV with a blue squiggle and no commercials! And then I get worse, and everyone gets real serious. *(He quietly looks around the room.)* I sure hope heaven's not all white. 'Cause that would really be boring. It should look like this ... *(He draws.)*
(Sounds increase.)

DOCTOR #2: Gradual enlargement of his heart muscle ...

DOCTOR #1: Liver functions, way off ...

DOCTOR #2: I'll up his oxygen level.

DOCTOR #4: *(Moving to the parents.)* It's like a brush fire. You stamp out sparks in one place, it flares up in another.

BENJAMIN: They put a red light on my finger, just like E.T.

DOCTOR #2: Internal bleeding is out of control.

BENJAMIN: Phone home! Phone home!

DOCTOR #4: It's just a matter of time. I'm so sorry.

BENJAMIN: The body part just can't keep up with the rest of me. So I tell it to let go. But I'm not alone. *(Parents, JOY* and *DOCTOR enter and move to bed.*) Almost time for the Yellow Boat to set sail.

FATHER: We'll all sail together ...

MOTHER: I'll hoist the sails, Joy can do the anchor ...

BENJAMIN: No. This time I have to go by myself.

MOTHER: Is there anything you want?

BENJAMIN: Just be here close. And a Dr. Pepper.
   (BENJAMIN's breathing becomes increasingly labored.)

FATHER: Reach up and tickle the ceiling stars ... makes it easier to breathe.
   (BENJAMIN reaches for the sky, and then "releases" into the arms of his parents. Time stops. After a beat, the DOCTORS slowly unhook the IV lines and BENJAMIN slowly pulls away from the bed, on his way someplace else. The focus of the others in the room remains on the body left behind. BENJAMIN watches the scene he has just left as JOY steps forward and hands a drawing to the parents.)

BENJAMIN: *(He colors the space with his words.)*
   I see red.
   I hear blue.
   I feel purple.
   I taste green.
   (Music underscores the last drawing, as the words and lights and images take us all to the "inside of a rainbow.")

   Last Drawing. The Captain decides that it's time for the Yellow Boat to set sail. I sail on the path the sun makes on the water. Then, the boat shoots up, straight up to the sun. *(He signs the final picture.)* B-E-N-J-A-M-I-N.
   (He jumps onto the boat, which is slowly surrounded by the unfurling rays of the sun. He has set sail. Musical resolution. Blackout.)

TOMATO PLANT GIRL

A play for young audiences

by
Wesley Middleton

"Foreigner: Anyone who looks acts speaks appears or suggests themselves to be in any way different from the glorious ways of the virtuous people of Heretown!"

With a protagonist named Little Girl, her antagonist, Bossy Best Friend, and a human/plant character ("a tomato spirit") called Tomato Plant Girl, Wesley Middleton creates a fantastic yet altogether real story of the sensitivity, vulnerability, and, yes, even cruelty, of young people. Middleton sets her play in "Heretown, a small American town where foreigners are suspicious and rules are important." There, Little Girl struggles to maintain a friendship with Bossy Best Friend; yet, in doing so, Little Girl risks losing her own identity to her alleged friend. Middleton employs a broad theatrical style in picturing the interaction of young people, and her depiction of the rituals and games of childhood adds rich texture to the play. In the play, the game, "Mother May I," used as an instrument of power, reveals the insecurities of both the tormentor (herself tormented by her Mother) and the object of that torment.

The story unfolds through exploration of metaphors specific to a girl's world, such as Barbie doll rituals; but the action resonates beyond a specific gender in its exploration of bullying, insecurity, and conformity. All audience members empathize with Little Girl in her journey with Tomato Plant Girl toward finding her own, nonconforming self, comfortable in her own world.

Neither a fairy tale nor dramatic realism, *Tomato Plant Girl*, resists classification and belies stereotypes. The simple tale, presents a world of and for young children, yet Middleton tells the tale with sophisticated theatricality. Consistent with the best of the newest generation of plays for children, *Tomato Plant Girl* offers a multilayered dialogue for young people concerning ideas about which they care very much.

Like much of the contemporary dramatic literature for children, the needs and audiences of the professional theatres influenced the aesthetics of "The Tomato Plant Girl." Specifically, the scenic and technical requirements and the small cast make the play suitable for tours to non-theatre settings, such as schools, which comprise the majority of audiences for many theatres.

Given the play's simple requirements, it also can easily be performed in a simplistic manner. But the necessary ambiguities within the text, the importance of subtext in performance, and the deceptively complex characters and action, demand deft and skillful performance and direction—all to the play's credit. As is detailed in the chronology of the play's development, Middleton developed *Tomato Plant Girl* with support from both a university play writing program and two professional theatres. Such play development resources figure prominently in the increased sophistication of this new generation of plays for young people.

Wesley Middleton is a playwright, teacher, and arts manager living in Seattle. She received her MFA in Playwriting from the University of Texas at Austin in 1996, where she studied with Suzan Zeder. Her plays for young audiences include *Tomato Plant Girl*, *Degas' Little Dancer* (both available through Dramatic Publishing), *Egypt on the Mother Road*, and *Emperor, Incorporated*, a collaboration with composer and co-lyricist Michael Keck, commissioned by the Children's Theatre Company of Sioux Falls. *Tomato Plant Girl* has been produced by theatre companies around the U.S. and was recently translated into Dutch. In Seattle, Ms. Middleton's work has been seen in Theatre Babylon's 9 Holes, 14/48: the world's quickest fringe festival, the Seattle Fringe Festival, and 12 Minutes Max.

TOMATO PLANT GIRL

A play for young audiences

by
Wesley Middleton

674

For performance of any songs, music and recordings mentioned in the play which are in copyright, the permission of the copyright owners must be obtained or other songs and recordings in the public domain substituted. The play printed in this anthology is not to be used as an acting script. All inquiries regarding performance rights should be adressed to Dramatic Publishing, 311 Washington St., Woodstock, IL 60098. Phone: (815) 338-7170. Fax: (815)338-8981

THE DRAMATIC PUBLISHING COMPANY of Woodstock, Illinois

Tomato Plant Girl was originally produced and premiered by Metro Theater Company, St. Louis, Mo., Carol North, Producing Director, and Idaho Theatre for Youth, Boise, Idaho, Pamela Sterling, Artistic Director with major support from the Theatre for Youth Endowment at the University of Texas at Austin.

Metro Theater Company, Fall 1998

Bossy Best Friend .... Carlyn Armintrout
Little Girl .... Monica Holeczy
Tomato Plant Girl..Kate Frank
The Facilitator .... Eddie Webb
(role specific to Metro Theater Company production)

Director ....Carol North
Assistant Director/Music Director .... Christopher Gurr
Composer ....Al Fisher
Costume Designer... Clyde Ruffin
Set Designer .... Nicholas Kryah and Jennifer Cassidy
Props .... Jennifer Cassidy
Dramaturg ....Suzan Zeder
Associate Dramaturg..................................... Tamara Goldbogen

Idaho Theatre for Youth, Spring 1999

Bossy Best Friend .... Karen Wennstrom
Little Girl .... Leonda Clendenen
Tomato Plant Girl...Sara Bruner

Director .... Pamela Sterling
Production Manager...Monica Coburn
Composer/Music Director..................................... Michael Keck
Costume Designer...Anne Hoste
Set Designer ....Dean Panttaja
Dramaturg .... Tamara Goldbogen

676

TOMATO PLANT GIRL

Characters (may be expanded with "stagehand" roles)

LITTLE GIRL:
A small girl, about 10 years old. Recently moved to Heretown from Thereville. Loves books and tomatoes.

BOSSY BEST FRIEND:
Older, richer and girlier than Little Girl. Has always lived in Heretown. Loves Barbies and clothes.

TOMATO PLANT GIRL:
A tomato spirit who appears in Heretown in the shape of a girl. Does not understand Heretown's rules.

VOICE OF BOSSY BEST FRIEND'S MOTHER

Setting

HERETOWN, A SMALL AMERICAN TOWN WHERE FOREIGNERS ARE SUSPICIOUS AND RULES ARE IMPORTANT. SUMMERTIME.

Set requirements: Simple tourable set, props.
Approximate running time: 60 minutes

SCENE 1

SETTING: *The action takes place in a makeshift garden. The garden is a fenced vacant lot on a small-town residential street. It belongs to LITTLE GIRL and BOSSY BEST FRIEND. Mostly BOSSY BEST FRIEND. There are two tomato plants in the garden. One is dry and wilted. A sign beside it says: "DO NOT TOUCH!" The other is healthy and green, with a single young tomato.*

AT RISE: *We hear the sound of quick, rhythmic ticking. BOSSY BEST FRIEND enters. Everything matches on BOSSY BEST FRIEND: her cute summer dress, the big bow in her hair, her bag. She carries a parasol to shade her from the sun. BOSSY BEST FRIEND looks around the garden. Takes a deep breath. Smiles. Consults her big plastic watch.*

BOSSY BEST FRIEND: Four fifty-eight and thirty seconds.
(She straightens her bow; looks back at her watch.)

Four fifty-eight and forty-eight seconds.
Four fifty-eight and forty-nine seconds.
(She looks off, then back at her watch.)
Four fifty-eight and fifty-two seconds. Fifty-three. Fifty-four. Fifty—
(LITTLE GIRL runs in, excited and anxious. She wears overall shorts, a T-shirt and a hat. She carries a big book, Tales of Tomatoes, with a tomato on the cover.)

LITTLE GIRL: Five? Is it five o'clock?
(BOSSY BEST FRIEND holds out her watch, points at it, then hides it, fast. She's lying.)

BOSSY BEST FRIEND: And 10 seconds. You're late!

LITTLE GIRL: I was reading!

BOSSY BEST FRIEND: You're late.

LITTLE GIRL: About tomatoes! *(Holding out the book)* Grandma gave it to me. When she was alive.

BOSSY BEST FRIEND: Poor dear. Put it out of your mind.
(BOSSY BEST FRIEND tries to take the book. LITTLE GIRL

678

holds on.)

LITTLE GIRL: We could read to the plants!

BOSSY BEST FRIEND: It is not time to read! Give me the book
now, Booknose. Please.
*(LITTLE GIRL lets BOSSY BEST FRIEND take the book.
BOSSY BEST FRIEND puts it with her things.)*

LITTLE GIRL: Grandma used to read to me.

BOSSY BEST FRIEND: Well, maybe you'll meet my grandma
someday.

LITTLE GIRL: Really?

BOSSY BEST FRIEND: If you're a very good friend. We'll see.
Now hurry. We're late for your favorite game! *(BOSSY BEST
FRIEND smiles and claps twice.)* Mother May I! *(LITTLE
GIRL, who does like this game, walks several paces away
from BOSSY BEST FRIEND and turns to face her.)* Ready?
Good. Two queenly curtsies.

LITTLE GIRL: Mother may I?

BOSSY BEST FRIEND: Yes you may. *(LITTLE GIRL curtsies
twice.)* Lovely! Three ballerina twirls.

LITTLE GIRL: Mother may I?

BOSSY BEST FRIEND: Yes you may. *(LITTLE GIRL does three
twirls.)* Gorgeous! Five giant steps.

LITTLE GIRL: Mother may I?

BOSSY BEST FRIEND: Yes you may. *(LITTLE GIRL starts
giant-stepping toward BOSSY BEST FRIEND.)* Backward.
*(LITTLE GIRL freezes mid-step, then steps backward with the
same foot, almost losing her balance. She does the five steps.)*
Now hop eight times on your lefthand foot. Forward. Hurry
up!

LITTLE GIRL: Mother may I?

BOSSY BEST FRIEND: Yes you may. *(LITTLE GIRL starts to
hop. BOSSY BEST FRIEND interrupts.)* Now stand on your
tippy tiptoes and eat dirt! *(LITTLE GIRL quickly picks up*

some dirt, stands on tiptoe, and starts to bring the dirt to her lips.) Ha! Quit, silly girl! We don't eat dirt!

LITTLE GIRL *(freezes):* I forgot.

BOSSY BEST FRIEND: Poor Booknose. Still — you did very well. You get a gold star! *(BOSSY BEST FRIEND takes a big gold star from her pocket and sticks it on LITTLE GIRL's forehead.)* Ta-da!
(They do a very proper "buddy" handshake.)

BOSSY BEST FRIEND, LITTLE GIRL: Best friends forever — Number One!
(LITTLE GIRL smiles proudly and curtsies, removing her hat. As she does, she feels the sun on her face and hair.)

LITTLE GIRL: Mmmm. *(She closes her eyes, stretches upward, breathes.)* The sun!

BOSSY BEST FRIEND: Booknose! Careful! The ultraviolent rays!

LITTLE GIRL: But —

BOSSY BEST FRIEND: Sunburn is wrong! Put on your hat! *(LITTLE GIRL puts on her hat.)* Now. What time is it?

LITTLE GIRL: Book time!

BOSSY BEST FRIEND: No —

LITTLE GIRL: Tomato plant time!

BOSSY BEST FRIEND: No. Not five-fifteen. What time is it?

LITTLE GIRL: Barbie.
(BOSSY BEST FRIEND smiles, snaps her fingers once. LITTLE GIRL gets in place for the game. BOSSY BEST FRIEND takes out two Barbies. One wears a fancy dress. The other wears a plain dress and has bad hair. BOSSY BEST FRIEND hands the latter Barbie to LITTLE GIRL.)

BOSSY BEST FRIEND: You're this one.

LITTLE GIRL: I know.
(BOSSY BEST FRIEND and LITTLE GIRL place their Barbies in stiff standing positions.)

BOSSY BEST FRIEND: One-two-three!
(Both speak, in quick rhythm, as their Barbies.)

BOSSY BEST FRIEND: Dena!

LITTLE GIRL: Lena! *(The Barbies cheek-kiss loudly, three times. Rhythm: "Dena! Lena! Kiss kiss kiss!")* How are you?

BOSSY BEST FRIEND: Just grand!

LITTLE GIRL: And your job?

BOSSY BEST FRIEND: Unsurpassed!

LITTLE GIRL: And your boyfriends?

BOSSY BEST FRIEND: Ooh la!

LITTLE GIRL: You look lovely.

BOSSY BEST FRIEND: Can't hear you!

LITTLE GIRL: Just lovely.

BOSSY BEST FRIEND: Why thanks. Are you wearing that dress to my party tonight?

LITTLE GIRL: Of course.

BOSSY BEST FRIEND: But it's ugly!

LITTLE GIRL: Oh. Then I'll wear — a satin ball gown with rose petticoats!

BOSSY BEST FRIEND: You can't have a new dress!

LITTLE GIRL *(as herself)*: But I've got a gold star!

BOSSY BEST FRIEND *(as her Barbie)*: Guess all the young beaus will be looking at me!

LITTLE GIRL: Beaus?

BOSSY BEST FRIEND: Young beaus. At the party! The boys!

LITTLE GIRL: Oh.

BOSSY BEST FRIEND: You're jealous!

LITTLE GIRL *(matter of fact)*: I'm not.

BOSSY BEST FRIEND: Yes you are.

LITTLE GIRL *(as before)*: No. You can go. I'll read.
(LITTLE GIRL reaches for her book. BOSSY BEST FRIEND stops her, snatches her Barbie.)

BOSSY BEST FRIEND *(as herself)*: Your Barbie loves parties and would die for a beau. Your Barbie wants what my Barbie wants but my Barbie can have it and your Barbie can't. That's the game! Now what do you say?

LITTLE GIRL: I'm sorry.

BOSSY BEST FRIEND: What time is it?

LITTLE GIRL: Tomato plant —

BOSSY BEST FRIEND: NO!! *(BOSSY BEST FRIEND composes herself to lecture.)* Booknose: who were you three months ago? *(LITTLE GIRL starts to speak.)* You were no one. You were the new girl, just moved here from Thereville. Always alone — reading, walking, talking to plants ... till I found you and told you: you need a friend. I taught you not to act like a *(lowers her voice)* foreigner.
(LITTLE GIRL gasps at the word. BOSSY BEST FRIEND points to LITTLE GIRL; LITTLE GIRL recites the definition with military precision.)

LITTLE GIRL: Foreigner: Anyone who looks acts speaks appears seems or suggests themselves to be in any way different from the glorious ways of the virtuous people of Heretown!

BOSSY BEST FRIEND: You're lucky I've taught you. Don't forget to play right. You're this one. *(She holds out LITTLE GIRL's Barbie. LITTLE GIRL looks at her, doesn't take it.)* What?

LITTLE GIRL *(matter of fact)*: It's tomato plant time.

BOSSY BEST FRIEND: You're this one!

LITTLE GIRL: It's time! It's past five-fifteen!

(Reluctantly, BOSSY BEST FRIEND checks her watch.)

BOSSY BEST FRIEND *(annoyed)*: All right. No Barbie. *(BOSSY*

BEST FRIEND puts the Barbies in the bag.) You'll do better next time. Now —

LITTLE GIRL: Now for the glorious harvest! Hurrah!
(LITTLE GIRL starts to run toward her planter.)

BOSSY BEST FRIEND: Hold your little ponies. *(LITTLE GIRL stops.)* We go at the same time. Remember? *(Slowly, the two turn together toward the garden plots and walk toward them. They stand in front of their respective garden plots. Both gasp.)* Oh! This can't be right!

LITTLE GIRL: Wow. Velvet green leaves and flowers of gold! Look! Come look.

BOSSY BEST FRIEND *(approaches the plant)*: Well, Little Girl. What a beautiful plant. Look at mine.

LITTLE GIRL: Oh! It's — um, it's —

BOSSY BEST FRIEND: Dead. It's dead. It's all your fault.

LITTLE GIRL: My fault?

BOSSY BEST FRIEND *(mocking her)*: "Put it in the sun!"

LITTLE GIRL: Sun's good for them!

BOSSY BEST FRIEND: It's withered!

LITTLE GIRL: Did you water it?

BOSSY BEST FRIEND: What?

LITTLE GIRL: Plants need water!

BOSSY BEST FRIEND: Since when?

LITTLE GIRL: I told you!

BOSSY BEST FRIEND: You don't water yours.

LITTLE GIRL: I do.
(BOSSY BEST FRIEND is shocked. LITTLE GIRL realizes she said the wrong thing.)

BOSSY BEST FRIEND: You've been coming in secret to water your plant?

LITTLE GIRL: To make sure it lived.

683

BOSSY BEST FRIEND: And make sure mine died!

LITTLE GIRL: No!

BOSSY BEST FRIEND: You didn't water my plant.

LITTLE GIRL: You said never touch it! You said "DO NOT TOUCH!"

BOSSY BEST FRIEND: Give me your plant.

LITTLE GIRL *(shocked)*: I couldn't!

BOSSY BEST FRIEND: If I had a gorgeous green plant, Little Girl, and yours was wilted and withered and dead, I'd give you my plant if you wanted it. *(LITTLE GIRL says nothing.)* Little Girl?

LITTLE GIRL: I wouldn't want that.

BOSSY BEST FRIEND: But I would do it — because I'm your friend. Just like you're mine. You are my friend. Aren't you?

LITTLE GIRL: Yes. I'm your *friend*.

BOSSY BEST FRIEND: So give me your plant! *(LITTLE GIRL wrings her hands.)* Little Girl — *please*?

LITTLE GIRL: The plant is precious.

BOSSY BEST FRIEND: The plant will be fine.

LITTLE GIRL: Will you water it?

BOSSY BEST FRIEND: Little Girl: I'm your friend! What's more important? Me or the plant?
(LITTLE GIRL looks at the plant. BOSSY BEST FRIEND glares at her. LITTLE GIRL gives in.)

LITTLE GIRL: When we move it, we have to be careful. OK?

BOSSY BEST FRIEND: Good, Little Girl! You did the right thing. *(BOSSY BEST FRIEND pats LITTLE GIRL on the shoulder. Then smiles at the plant.)* Now, tomato plant: this won't hurt a bit. We'll just move you to my pretty side of the garden. We'll do that right now. Together.
(BOSSY BEST FRIEND looks at LITTLE GIRL. LITTLE GIRL helps, reluctantly. BOSSY BEST FRIEND points to

LITTLE GIRL's plant. LITTLE GIRL carefully uproots it. BOSSY BEST FRIEND plucks up the dead plant from her own planter and pitches it over her shoulder, out of the garden — preferably offstage. [It must be offstage by the start of Scene 2.] Then she takes LITTLE GIRL's plant from her, and crudely replants it in her own planter.)

LITTLE GIRL: Careful!

BOSSY BEST FRIEND: All done! *(LITTLE GIRL hovers, worried, over the plant. BOSSY BEST FRIEND stands in front of it, moving her out of the way. She smiles at LITTLE GIRL.)* Thank you for your beautiful gift.

LITTLE GIRL: Gift?

BOSSY BEST FRIEND: Of course. You gave it to me.

LITTLE GIRL *(confused)*: But you made me—

BOSSY BEST FRIEND *(gives LITTLE GIRL her book.)*: Okay, Booknose. That's all for today. *(Sweetly)* Here's your book. Time to go read! *(LITTLE GIRL takes the book, looks back at the plant. BOSSY BEST FRIEND moves her off.)* Toodle-oo! See you tomorrow! Bye-bye! *(LITTLE GIRL goes, looking back at the plant. BOSSY BEST FRIEND preens and admires the plant.)* Mm-hm. Mm-hm. Mm-hm. Ooh, lovely plant! Now you're all mine!
(BOSSY BEST FRIEND blows her plant a kiss, then exits.)

SCENE 2

(The next day. LITTLE GIRL runs onstage with a watering can. She checks to make sure BOSSY BEST FRIEND isn't there, then rushes to the plant.)

LITTLE GIRL: Oh, poor plant! You're thirsty!
(LITTLE GIRL raises the watering can, about to water the plant. The sound of quick, rhythmic ticking. LITTLE GIRL freezes. BOSSY BEST FRIEND enters, carrying her bag.)

BOSSY BEST FRIEND: You're early! It's four fifty-nine.

685

(BOSSY BEST FRIEND puts her hand out for the watering can, clears her throat. LITTLE GIRL hands it over.) Thank you.

LITTLE GIRL: The plant —

BOSSY BEST FRIEND: The plant is fine.

LITTLE GIRL: It's unhappy!

BOSSY BEST FRIEND: I watered it.

LITTLE GIRL: When?

BOSSY BEST FRIEND: Last night.

LITTLE GIRL: Are you sure?

BOSSY BEST FRIEND *(points at her watch)*: Oh my. Look at the time! Come on, Little Girl: your favorite game! *(BOSSY BEST FRIEND claps twice. LITTLE GIRL steps into position for the start of Mother May I. She does not stop looking at the plant.)*

BOSSY BEST FRIEND: Ready? Good. Five helicopter twirls.

LITTLE GIRL: Mother may I?

BOSSY BEST FRIEND: Yes you may. *(LITTLE GIRL starts doing big twirls toward the plant.)* This way! Stop! Start over! *(LITTLE GIRL stops. BOSSY BEST FRIEND glares, then claps twice.)* Now. Three teeny-tiny baby steps.

LITTLE GIRL: Mother may I?

BOSSY BEST FRIEND: Yes you may. *(LITTLE GIRL does the steps, bigger than usual, moving toward the plant.)* Booknose! *(BOSSY BEST FRIEND stands between LITTLE GIRL and the plant.)* No more game. Barbie time. *(BOSSY BEST FRIEND snaps her fingers once. She takes the Barbies from the bag and holds out the one with bad hair.)* You're this one.

LITTLE GIRL: I know.

BOSSY BEST FRIEND: One — two — three! *(As Barbies.)* Dena!

LITTLE GIRL: Lena! *(Kiss-kiss-kiss.)* How are you?

BOSSY BEST FRIEND *(as an adjective)*: Ladeda!

LITTLE GIRL: And your job?

BOSSY BEST FRIEND: Tip-top.

LITTLE GIRL: And your plant?

BOSSY BEST FRIEND: My what?

LITTLE GIRL: Your tomato plant!
  (BOSSY BEST FRIEND grabs LITTLE GIRL's Barbie.)

BOSSY BEST FRIEND *(as herself)*: NO! That's not it! That is
  not how we play! Dumb tomato plant girl. Dumb like a plant!
  *(Tears start down LITTLE GIRL's cheeks. She turns away to
  hide them.)* Are you crying?

LITTLE GIRL: No.

BOSSY BEST FRIEND *(wipes a tear off LITTLE GIRL's cheek)*:
  Yes you are. Only foreigners cry! *(She hands LITTLE GIRL
  a hanky.)* Here. Hurry up. Don't let anyone see! *(LITTLE
  GIRL dries her tears. BOSSY BEST FRIEND grabs the hanky
  back.)* And don't be a worry wart. My plant will be fine. Of
  course, it will miss me when I go away —

LITTLE GIRL: You're going away?

BOSSY BEST FRIEND: To my grandma's.

LITTLE GIRL *(wistful)*: Oh.

BOSSY BEST FRIEND *(gloating)*: Back-to-school shopping! It
  could take a week.

LITTLE GIRL: But the plant —

BOSSY BEST FRIEND: Will miss me. But it will be fine.

LITTLE GIRL: I'll take care of it.

BOSSY BEST FRIEND: No.

LITTLE GIRL: But you can't —

BOSSY BEST FRIEND: Little Girl: I can do what I like! I can
  water the plant or leave it be. I can pick the fruit, I can preen

687

the vine, I can perfume the flowers — I can pluck off a leaf!

(BOSSY BEST FRIEND *(plucks off a leaf, crumples it, and tosses it into the air.)*: It's my plant! It lives for me! *(LITTLE GIRL gasps, in shock, and covers her mouth with her hands.)* What climbed up your nostril? *(LITTLE GIRL, mouth still covered, makes a noise of distress.)* Little Girl —
(Sound of quick, rhythmic ticking. BOSSY BEST FRIEND's MOTHER calls from offstage. BOSSY BEST FRIEND jumps and freezes.)

BOSSY BEST FRIEND'S MOTHER: *(recorded; snooty, agitated)*: Dar—ling!

LITTLE GIRL: Your Mother.

BOSSY BEST FRIEND: Shut up! *(To MOTHER, nervous.)* Yes ma'am!

BOSSY BEST FRIEND'S MOTHER *(off)*: Grandma's waiting!

BOSSY BEST FRIEND *(gathers her things)*: Yes ma'am! *(To LITTLE GIRL.)* I'll be back.

BOSSY BEST FRIEND'S MOTHER *(off)*: Darling!

BOSSY BEST FRIEND *(To MOTHER.)*: Yes ma'am! *(To LITTLE GIRL.)* And don't you forget —

BOSSY BEST FRIEND'S MOTHER *(off)*: You're late!

BOSSY BEST FRIEND: If you touch my new plant —

BOSSY BEST FRIEND'S MOTHER *(off):* If you're late for Grandma —

BOSSY BEST FRIEND: I'll rip up your book and feed it to my poodle!

BOSSY BEST FRIEND'S MOTHER *(off):* I'll melt down those Barbies and serve them for dinner.

BOSSY BEST FRIEND & MOTHER: We wouldn't want that to happen.

BOSSY BEST FRIEND *(to MOTHER)*: I'm coming!

BOSSY BEST FRIEND'S MOTHER *(off)*: Hurry up!

BOSSY BEST FRIEND *(to LITTLE GIRL)*: Be good!

BOSSY BEST FRIEND & MOTHER: Now do as I say, dearie. Or else! *(BOSSY BEST FRIEND runs off. LITTLE GIRL watches her go, then explodes.)*

LITTLE GIRL: Oooh wicked badness meanmeanmean tomato-hating leaf-killing evil rudeness jerk! *(LITTLE GIRL claps her hand over her mouth. She can't believe what she just said. Then she kneels near the tomato plant.)* Oh plant — I won't let you suffer. I'll replant you on my good side of the garden. *(LITTLE GIRL closes her eyes.)* Okay. *(LITTLE GIRL puts her hands around the stem. To the plant.)* Ready? *(To herself.)* Ready. One — two — three. *(LITTLE GIRL begins to pull up the plant. But the root system has grown. It is yards and yards long. Endless.)* All these roots! *(LITTLE GIRL keeps pulling up roots. A low, vibrating sound — the Earthsoil Hum — fills the garden. LITTLE GIRL looks around, a bit scared.)* What's that noise? *(The roots start coming more slowly. Something heavy is attached to the roots, moving upward with them, through the soil.)* What's that?
(LITTLE GIRL pulls harder. The ends of the roots emerge, clutched in two small hands. Arms and shoulders follow —) Ohh — *(Then a face: the face of TOMATO PLANT GIRL. She is messy, dirt-covered. Her eyes are closed. She is totally new to her body.)* WHOA! *(Stunned, LITTLE GIRL lets go of the roots, reeling backward. TOMATO PLANT GIRL opens her eyes, lets go of the roots, and opens her mouth; she spits out dirt and a burst of sound. [The words should not sound like words.])*

TOMATO PLANT GIRL: Ooohtomatomeanmeanmeansufferleaf plantreadyonetworoot!
(TOMATO PLANT GIRL and LITTLE GIRL are both startled by the sound. LITTLE GIRL gasps. TOMATO PLANT GIRL slowly moves her head till she sees LITTLE GIRL. TOMATO PLANT GIRL looks at her and bursts into laughter. After some hesitation, LITTLE GIRL, still nervous, starts laughing

too. TOMATO PLANT GIRL laughs so hard that she cries.
Then she actually starts to cry. She looks at the strange world
around her and big red tears roll down her cheeks.)

LITTLE GIRL: Don't cry. Only foreigners cry! Stop! Stop!
Don't let anyone see! *(TOMATO PLANT GIRL doesn't*
stop. Anxious, LITTLE GIRL hesitates, then gathers resolve.
LITTLE GIRL wipes a tear from TOMATO PLANT GIRL's
cheek. She steps back and looks at the tear.) Red! *(LITTLE*
GIRL looks at TOMATO PLANT GIRL. Very cautiously, she
tastes the tear. With wonder.) Tomato.
(TOMATO PLANT GIRL picks up a handful of dirt, then
hums and lets it fall through her fingers. She is calling
the Earthsoil Hum. The Earthsoil Hum returns. TOMATO
PLANT GIRL welcomes the hum with a gesture, closes
her eyes and hums with it.) What is it? What's that sound?
(TOMATO PLANT GIRL keeps humming, eyes closed.
LITTLE GIRL covers her ears, steps away from TOMATO
PLANT GIRL.) I'm sure you're very nice and from a very
nice place, and I'd like to welcome you and show you
around, but I can't. *(TOMATO PLANT GIRL keeps humming,*
eyes closed.) So — I'm sure you have to go, and when I
get back, you'll be gone. And I'll replant the plant, and
everything will be fine. *(The Earthsoil Hum fades. TOMATO*
PLANT GIRL opens her eyes. Looks at LITTLE GIRL.) I have
to go now. It's dinner time. Mom-Dad-table-TV! Nice to
meet you. Have a good trip! Goodbye!
(LITTLE GIRL rushes off. TOMATO PLANT GIRL emerges
fully from the earth. She moves and makes sounds as she
discovers her new body. She tastes some of the garden dirt:
it's too dry. As she spits it out, she discovers her tongue. She
realizes she is thirsty. TOMATO PLANT GIRL looks at the
sky. Then, with purposeful gestures, she calls on the rain
[It does not come.] TOMATO PLANT GIRL continues this
movement until LITTLE GIRL approaches.)

SCENE 3

(The same night. About an hour later. The uprooted tomato plant from Scene 2 and its long roots are in a pile on the ground. LITTLE GIRL approaches the garden. She carries a watering can and flowerpot. She's nervous.)

LITTLE GIRL *(continuous, as she enters)*: Is she here is she here is she here is she here is she here is she here? *(At the sound of the voice, TOMATO PLANT GIRL hides. LITTLE GIRL looks, quickly, for TOMATO PLANT GIRL. Doesn't see her.)* Ha! She's not here! *(LITTLE GIRL approaches the dead plant.)* She's not here and now I can help my poor plant! Look, plant — look what I've got! It's Mom's best topsoil! With minerals! Yum! *(LITTLE GIRL attempts to replant the dead plant. She reaches into the flowerpot for topsoil, sprinkling it on the roots. TOMATO PLANT GIRL emerges from hiding and begins to eat topsoil from the pot, unseen by LITTLE GIRL.)* See? It'll put you in tip-top shape. My best friend will come back, and she'll be so happy — *(LITTLE GIRL reaches back into the flowerpot and accidentally touches TOMATO PLANT GIRL's hand. She shrieks. She doesn't look at TOMATO PLANT GIRL.)* Go away. You're not here! *(TOMATO PLANT GIRL eats another handful of dirt, looks intently at LITTLE GIRL. Slowly, LITTLE GIRL turns to look at TOMATO PLANT GIRL.)* Hey! Hey! *No!* We don't eat *dirt!*

TOMATO PLANT GIRL: Dirrrrrrtt.
(TOMATO PLANT GIRL eats noisily and happily. LITTLE GIRL grabs the flowerpot.)

LITTLE GIRL: Don't do that! Dumb tomato plant girl! *(LITTLE GIRL stops, hearing herself. To herself:)* Tomato Plant Girl. *(TOMATO PLANT GIRL looks at LITTLE GIRL, confused. LITTLE GIRL picks up the flowerpot, starts to pace.)* I need to line things up in my brain.
(TOMATO PLANT GIRL follows her, tugs on the flowerpot.)

TOMATO PLANT GIRL: *Mm.*

LITTLE GIRL: What?

691

TOMATO PLANT GIRL: *Mmm.* Dirrt.

LITTLE GIRL *(showing her it's empty)*: No. No more. You ate it! *(TOMATO PLANT GIRL moans.)* Sorry.

TOMATO PLANT GIRL: "Sorry."

LITTLE GIRL *(pointing to herself)*: "I'm sorry." *(TOMATO PLANT GIRL points at LITTLE GIRL, as if "Sorry" is her name.)*

TOMATO PLANT GIRL: Sorry.

LITTLE GIRL: No. Sorry. It means — I should have done something, but I didn't. Or I shouldn't have, but I did. *(TOMATO PLANT GIRL looks puzzled.)* It's important. *(Pointing to herself again.)* "I'm sorry." It's *important. Big!* *(LITTLE GIRL does a "big" movement. TOMATO PLANT GIRL mirrors it, laughs.)*

TOMATO PLANT GIRL: BIG! *(TOMATO PLANT GIRL points at LITTLE GIRL, makes the "big" movement.)* BIG SORR-RRY!

LITTLE GIRL: *Shhh*!

TOMATO PLANT GIRL: "SHHH!"

LITTLE GIRL: *Shhh.*
(In "SHHH!" TOMATO PLANT GIRL hears the sound of water. She begins to do her rain-calling movement, now directed at LITTLE GIRL.)

TOMATO PLANT GIRL: Shhhhhh.

LITTLE GIRL: What? What — you want a shower? Not at my house — my shower's clean! My parents work hard and our house is neat. You eat dirt and you dress upside-down! *(TOMATO PLANT GIRL continues the motion, but opens her mouth and tilts her face to the sky.)* What? What? Oh! *(Pointing to her mouth.)* Drink!

TOMATO PLANT GIRL: Drrrink!

LITTLE GIRL: Drink. *(LITTLE GIRL holds up the watering can and pours water into TOMATO PLANT GIRL's mouth.)* You were thirsty. *(LITTLE GIRL suddenly remembers the [dead] plant.)* Oh! Thirsty! *(LITTLE GIRL rushes to the plant, pours water on it.)* Here, poor plant — *(TOMATO PLANT GIRL follows, tugs on the watering can, points to herself.)*

TOMATO PLANT GIRL: Drink.

LITTLE GIRL: No! It's for the plant! *(LITTLE GIRL pours the rest of the water on the plant. TOMATO PLANT GIRL moans and shakes her head, confused.)* Lots of things went backwards and I need to fix them up. *(LITTLE GIRL kneels next to the plant.)* I need to replant these roots — all these roots —
(LITTLE GIRL pushes the rest of the roots underground, covering them with soil. TOMATO PLANT GIRL grabs a root and looks at LITTLE GIRL.)

TOMATO PLANT GIRL: Root.

LITTLE GIRL *(puts the root back)*: Root. There. In place. Ready, plant? One, two, three! *(LITTLE GIRL tries to stand the plant up. The plant flops over. LITTLE GIRL tries again. To the plant:)* Plant! PLANT! Come on. You're not dead. You're not dead.
(TOMATO PLANT GIRL points to the plant. She is matter-of-fact.)

TOMATO PLANT GIRL: Dead.

LITTLE GIRL *(knowing it's true)*: Not dead.

TOMATO PLANT GIRL *(as before)*: Dead.
(TOMATO PLANT GIRL holds a handful of dirt out to LITTLE GIRL. LITTLE GIRL looks at TOMATO PLANT GIRL. Then at the plant.)

LITTLE GIRL *(slowly accepting it)*: Dead.
(LITTLE GIRL takes the dirt. She helps TOMATO PLANT GIRL bury the plant. They are silent for a moment. The Earthsoil Hum returns. TOMATO PLANT GIRL hears it. As before, she gestures to acknowledge its presence, then hums with it. LITTLE GIRL covers her ears.)

LITTLE GIRL: That hum—

TOMATO PLANT GIRL: Humm.
(LITTLE GIRL cautiously uncovers her ears for a moment, then covers them.)

LITTLE GIRL: It's from down in the earth!

TOMATO PLANT GIRL: Errth.

LITTLE GIRL: Earth ... hum. *(The Earthsoil Hum fades. LITTLE GIRL slowly uncovers her ears. She looks at the buried plant.)* My grandma said, when plants die, they go back to the earth and feed other plants. So they might go away, but they're not really gone.
(LITTLE GIRL looks at TOMATO PLANT GIRL. TOMATO PLANT GIRL looks at LITTLE GIRL.)

TOMATO PLANT GIRL *(agreeing)*: Errth. *(LITTLE GIRL smiles. Then TOMATO PLANT GIRL motions to the watering can and flowerpot.)* Dirrt ... drrink.

LITTLE GIRL: You eat a lot!

TOMATO PLANT GIRL *(a hungry noise)*: Mmm.

LITTLE GIRL: You need to learn some things.
(TOMATO PLANT GIRL holds the flowerpot and watering can out to LITTLE GIRL.)

TOMATO PLANT GIRL: Dirt drink.

LITTLE GIRL: If you're going to stay here —

TOMATO PLANT GIRL: DIRT! DRINK!

LITTLE GIRL: Okay! *(LITTLE GIRL takes the flowerpot and watering can.)* But you have to learn how to play.

TOMATO PLANT GIRL *(confused)*: Mmm?

LITTLE GIRL: Mother May I. I'll teach you tomorrow. Here. At tomato plant time! Five-fifteen.
(LITTLE GIRL goes.)

TOMATO PLANT GIRL *(calling LITTLE GIRL's "name")*: Sorry? Sorr-rry! Dirt…drink.

694

(TOMATO PLANT GIRL turns back to the garden. She stands and does her rain-calling gesture.)

SCENE 4

(The next day. TOMATO PLANT GIRL sits, holding her belly. She moans. LITTLE GIRL enters with the flowerpot and watering can.)

LITTLE GIRL: Tomato Plant Girl? It's time for a game! *(TOMATO PLANT GIRL rushes to the flowerpot and watering can.)* Hey! Wait. *(LITTLE GIRL holds the flowerpot and watering can in the air so TOMATO PLANT GIRL cannot reach them.)* First you learn to play. Then: dirt and drink. Okay. Mother may I! *(LITTLE GIRL claps twice.)* Ready? Good. Three queenly curtsies! Watch. *(LITTLE GIRL begins to demonstrate.)* One — two — *(TOMATO PLANT GIRL rushes to the flowerpot, grabs it, eats a handful of dirt.)* No no wait! You have to play right! *(LITTLE GIRL grabs the flowerpot back. TOMATO PLANT GIRL makes a frustrated noise.)* You didn't say "Mother may I!" Start over. Say "Mother may I!"

TOMATO PLANT GIRL: Mmm — mthrrrr — *(TOMATO PLANT GIRL spits out the word, laughs at the sound. LITTLE GIRL creates a hand gesture to represent the words.)*

LITTLE GIRL: Here. *"Mother may I!"* *(LITTLE GIRL does the gesture. TOMATO PLANT GIRL repeats it.)* Good! Now — *(TOMATO PLANT GIRL, repeating the "Mother may I" gesture, moves toward the dirt and drink, with no curtsies.)*

TOMATO PLANT GIRL: Mthrr mthrr mthrr —

LITTLE GIRL: No! Curtsy curtsy curtsy! *(TOMATO PLANT GIRL stops and does one slow curtsy to LITTLE GIRL.)*

TOMATO PLANT GIRL: Crrrtze.

LITTLE GIRL *(giving in)*: You'll do better next time.

695

(LITTLE GIRL gives TOMATO PLANT GIRL a handful of dirt. TOMATO PLANT GIRL eats avidly. LITTLE GIRL pours water into TOMATO PLANT GIRL's mouth. TOMATO PLANT GIRL, after drinking her fill, holds onto a big mouthful of water, so she can share a trick with LITTLE GIRL.)

LITTLE GIRL: Next is ballerina twirl. It's difficult. *(LITTLE GIRL gets into position for the twirl.)* You start like this. Watch carefully. *(Gleefully, TOMATO PLANT GIRL spits a spray of water in the air. It sprinkles down on her and on LITTLE GIRL.)* Hey!

TOMATO PLANT GIRL: Mmmm. Currt-ze!
(TOMATO PLANT GIRL does her own big curtsy of joy.)

LITTLE GIRL: That's not the *game!*
(On "game," LITTLE GIRL makes an emphatic gesture. TOMATO PLANT GIRL repeats the gesture.)

TOMATO PLANT GIRL *(liking the sound)*: Gaaame.

LITTLE GIRL: "Game." It has rules. It's very specific.
(TOMATO PLANT GIRL begins to repeat the "game" gesture, transforming it each time, creating her own game, inviting LITTLE GIRL to join her.)

TOMATO PLANT GIRL *(continuous)*: Gamegamegame—

LITTLE GIRL: One person tells the other: do something. The other asks permission: "Mother may I." Then — What are you doing?

TOMATO PLANT GIRL *(shows LITTLE GIRL the gesture)*: Gaaaame.
(Warily, LITTLE GIRL watches TOMATO PLANT GIRL and mirrors her gesture. Note: While it should appear to be improvised, the following action is "very specific." It is important that the audience see LITTLE GIRL and TOMATO PLANT GIRL mirroring each other, paying attention to each other's movements, and transforming gestures together.)

TOMATO PLANT GIRL, LITTLE GIRL: *Gaaame.*

LITTLE GIRL: Right. A game has rules.
(TOMATO PLANT GIRL moves into a new gesture, an exaggeration of LITTLE GIRL's gesture from the line, "A game has rules.")

TOMATO PLANT GIRL: Gaame…ruulz!
(LITTLE GIRL is surprised to see herself in TOMATO PLANT GIRL's gesture. She laughs, then transforms the gesture into a new one.)

LITTLE GIRL: Gameruulz!
(Facing each other, they do LITTLE GIRL's gesture together.)

LITTLE GIRL, TOMATO PLANT GIRL: Gameruulz! *(They transform LITTLE GIRL's gesture to create a new gesture together.)* Gaameruulz!

LITTLE GIRL: We made a new game!
(TOMATO PLANT GIRL motions for LITTLE GIRL to stay put. Then she picks up the flowerpot and watering can and moves to where LITTLE GIRL stood during the Mother May I game. TOMATO PLANT GIRL begins to reward LITTLE GIRL. She holds out a handful of dirt.)

TOMATO PLANT GIRL: Dirrrt! *(LITTLE GIRL politely refuses. TOMATO PLANT GIRL eats the dirt, then holds up the watering can.)* Drrink.
(Cautiously, LITTLE GIRL opens her mouth. TOMATO PLANT GIRL pours water in LITTLE GIRL's mouth. LITTLE GIRL gets a mouthful of water. She looks impishly at TOMATO PLANT GIRL. She spits the water up in the air — just for a second. LITTLE GIRL takes the watering can and starts to give TOMATO PLANT GIRL a drink. TOMATO PLANT GIRL leads LITTLE GIRL to LITTLE GIRL's side of the garden, where her plant once grew, and stands with her arms outstretched. LITTLE GIRL "waters" TOMATO PLANT GIRL. TOMATO PLANT GIRL starts to grow. The Earthsoil Hum returns. Again, TOMATO PLANT GIRL acknowledges it with a gesture.)

LITTLE GIRL: The Earth hum! *(As before, LITTLE GIRL covers*

her ears. TOMATO PLANT GIRL, still turning, begins to grow bigger, redder, greener.) Tomato Plant Girl—you're growing! *(LITTLE GIRL removes her hands from her ears and watches the process, amazed.)* Wow!
(TOMATO PLANT GIRL makes one full turn, then yawns and settles to the ground, asleep. LITTLE GIRL sits watching her, intrigued. The sound of quick, rhythmic ticking. LITTLE GIRL looks around, nervous. A pink plastic postcard drops from the sky. LITTLE GIRL jumps, then catches the postcard and silently reads.)

VOICE OF BOSSY BEST FRIEND *(off):* Dear Booknose — Hope you're not too lonely. Don't worry, dear; I miss you too. I'll be back in two days, three hours, and forty-five minutes. In the meantime, be good and keep your hands off my plant!
(LITTLE GIRL looks at TOMATO PLANT GIRL, and at BOSSY BEST FRIEND's side of the garden.)

LITTLE GIRL *(panicked):* "Keep your hands off my plant —" Oh no! *(LITTLE GIRL paces, remembering.)* I should have, but I didn't ... I shouldn't have, but I did ... "Do as I say — or else!" Oh no! *(LITTLE GIRL takes a deep breath. Thinks for a moment. Looks at TOMATO PLANT GIRL. Makes a decision. Then picks up the postcard, flowerpot, and watering can. She turns back to the sleeping TOMATO PLANT GIRL.)* Don't go away! I'll be back! I'll be back.
(LITTLE GIRL exits, quickly.)

SCENE 5

(The next day. TOMATO PLANT GIRL wakes, stretches slowly, then stands with her eyes closed, her arms reaching up and her face tilted into the sun. She touches her cheeks lightly with her fingertips, making light kissing sounds. She plays with new sounds to describe the feel of the sun:)

TOMATO PLANT GIRL: Firrre— kissss!
(LITTLE GIRL rushes in, carrying the flowerpot, the

watering can, and her book, Tales of Tomatoes.)

LITTLE GIRL: Tomato Plant Girl — *(Seeing TOMATO PLANT GIRL in the sun.)* Hey! Hey careful! *(LITTLE GIRL stands in front of TOMATO PLANT GIRL, blocking the sun. TOMATO PLANT GIRL tries to move around her. LITTLE GIRL doesn't let her.)* The ultraviolent rays! Sunburn is *wrong.*

TOMATO PLANT GIRL *(reaches for the flowerpot and watering can)*: Drink. Dirt!

LITTLE GIRL: Okay! *(LITTLE GIRL gives TOMATO PLANT GIRL dirt and water. TOMATO PLANT GIRL eats and drinks quickly, avidly.)* Tomato Plant Girl: this is important!

TOMATO PLANT GIRL *(satisfied)*: Ahhh.
(TOMATO PLANT GIRL tilts her head back to the sun. To herself.) Firrre—

LITTLE GIRL: Listen! You're going to be my best friend!

TOMATO PLANT GIRL *(to herself)*: kisss…

LITTLE GIRL: You're going to come home and live with me! We'll go to school and play games every day — and no one will know you're a *(lowers her voice)* — foreigner. See? *(TOMATO PLANT GIRL looks down at herself, looks back at LITTLE GIRL.)* Come on! I'll show you my house! Let's go!

TOMATO PLANT GIRL *(not moving)*: Root. I.

LITTLE GIRL: You can wash, and dress, and eat normal food — and borrow my books! I'll teach you to read! *(LITTLE GIRL holds out the book.)* I'll teach you to be like a real normal girl so you can be my best friend and be happy!

TOMATO PLANT GIRL *(looks at LITTLE GIRL, shakes her head)*: Grow.

LITTLE GIRL *(tries not to cry)*: My best friend's coming back, and she's going to be angry! If you're not my best friend, I'll be all alone!
(TOMATO PLANT GIRL looks at LITTLE GIRL, picks up a handful of dirt, shows it to her.)

TOMATO PLANT GIRL: *Grow I.*

LITTLE GIRL *(hurt)*: Fine then! You grow!
(Hurt, LITTLE GIRL turns away from TOMATO PLANT GIRL. She opens her book, tries to read. TOMATO PLANT GIRL knows something is wrong.)

TOMATO PLANT GIRL: Sorry…

LITTLE GIRL: What?

TOMATO PLANT GIRL: Sor-ry! *(TOMATO PLANT GIRL tugs on the book.)* Mmm.

LITTLE GIRL *(still hurt)*: It's just a book.

TOMATO PLANT GIRL *(points at the cover)*: Red. *(She makes the "BIG" gesture.)* TOMATO! *(LITTLE GIRL smiles in spite of herself.)* TO-MA-TO! *(TOMATO PLANT GIRL sweeps the book out of LITTLE GIRL's hands, dances with it.)* TOMATO!

LITTLE GIRL: HEY! That's my book! *(LITTLE GIRL takes the book back.)* I'm glad you like it — but you can say "please."

TOMATO PLANT GIRL: Plse.

LITTLE GIRL: It means, "If it pleases you." *(LITTLE GIRL holds out the book.)* Say you want this book. But the book is mine; it's precious to me. So I need you to ask and say "please." *(TOMATO PLANT GIRL points at the book, naming it "Please.")*

TOMATO PLANT GIRL: Please!

LITTLE GIRL: No … *(LITTLE GIRL decides to demonstrate.)* Here. Hold it. Just for a second. *(Carefully, LITTLE GIRL hands TOMATO PLANT GIRL the book. TOMATO PLANT GIRL holds the book carefully, watching LITTLE GIRL. LITTLE GIRL points at the book.)* Book. *(LITTLE GIRL pretends to admire the book.)* Mmm! *(LITTLE GIRL gestures toward the book, asking permission.)* Please? *(TOMATO PLANT GIRL hands LITTLE GIRL the book.)* Yes! That's right!
(Excited, TOMATO PLANT GIRL does a sped-up, auto-

700

version of the previous actions.)

TOMATO PLANT GIRL: Book—Mmm! *Please*? *(Skeptical, LITTLE GIRL holds the book out to TOMATO PLANT GIRL. TOMATO PLANT GIRL grabs onto it.)* Yezatsright!

LITTLE GIRL *(takes the book back)*: If you say "please" but you don't really mean it, then it's just like you're grabbing the book. But if you say "please" and you really *do* mean it, then I have a choice. I can give you the book.
(TOMATO PLANT GIRL looks at LITTLE GIRL. Motions to the book.)

TOMATO PLANT GIRL: Please?

LITTLE GIRL: Yes! *(LITTLE GIRL hands TOMATO PLANT GIRL the book.)* Thank you for asking!
(TOMATO PLANT GIRL gently touches the page, then lifts and turns it. She sees something.)

TOMATO PLANT GIRL: Ahh—firre!
(TOMATO PLANT GIRL buries her head in the book. LITTLE GIRL reaches toward the book.

LITTLE GIRL: Fire? Let me see! *(TOMATO PLANT GIRL looks at LITTLE GIRL.)* Please? *(TOMATO PLANT GIRL shows LITTLE GIRL the picture.)* Oh! That's the sun! *(LITTLE GIRL points at the sky.)* Remember, I told you — it's dangerous!

TOMATO PLANT GIRL *(points at the sky)*: Firrrekisss!
(TOMATO PLANT GIRL tilts her face to the sky. Then she remembers the book and carefully hands it back to LITTLE GIRL before stretching into the sun, as before.) Mmm.
(Intrigued but still concerned, LITTLE GIRL moves between TOMATO PLANT GIRL and the sun.)

LITTLE GIRL: The sun is ultraviolent.

TOMATO PLANT GIRL: *(calling LITTLE GIRL by her name)* Sorry.
(TOMATO PLANT GIRL moves around LITTLE GIRL, back

*into the sun. Then she has an idea. She turns back to LITTLE
GIRL. She points to the spot next to her.)* Root you. Please.
*(LITTLE GIRL, wary, moves toward TOMATO PLANT GIRL.
TOMATO PLANT GIRL shares her "Firekiss" gestures with
LITTLE GIRL: she stretches into the sun, then does the sun-
kissing gesture and sound.)* Fiire kiss.

LITTLE GIRL *(watching TOMATO PLANT GIRL)*: Firekiss.
(Slowly, LITTLE GIRL tilts her head into the sun.) Mmm.
(LITTLE GIRL does the sun-kissing gesture and sound.)

TOMATO PLANT GIRL: Mmm!

LITTLE GIRL: Firekiss!
*(LITTLE GIRL takes off her hat. They stand there for a
moment, side by side. They speak separately, but at the same
time:)*

LITTLE GIRL, TOMATO PLANT GIRL: Fiirre…kisss!
*(Sound of quick, rhythmic ticking. LITTLE GIRL jumps.
BOSSY BEST FRIEND calls from offstage.)*

BOSSY BEST FRIEND *(offstage)*: Hello-o! I'm back! Who
missed me?

LITTLE GIRL: Oh no!
*(LITTLE GIRL looks around, panicked. TOMATO PLANT
GIRL thinks it's a game, mirrors her.)*

TOMATO PLANT GIRL: Oh no!

LITTLE GIRL: Tomato Plant Girl! Over here!
*(LITTLE GIRL crouches down. TOMATO PLANT GIRL
crouches down too. LITTLE GIRL hands the book to
TOMATO PLANT GIRL, then stands in front of her,
attempting to block her from view. BOSSY BEST FRIEND
sails in like a queen. She wears fancy new clothes and carries
her bag. She makes a big show of closing her eyes and
breathing in the air of the garden.)*

BOSSY BEST FRIEND: Ahh. Lovely to be back.
*(BOSSY BEST FRIEND opens her eyes. LITTLE GIRL waves
with forced enthusiasm, still trying to hide TOMATO PLANT*

702

GIRL.)

LITTLE GIRL: Hello. Hi!

BOSSY BEST FRIEND: I'm early. I know. I was worried, poor dear. You've been here all alone — *(BOSSY BEST FRIEND sees her plant is gone.)* Where's my plant? Did you let it die?

LITTLE GIRL: You said not to touch it!

BOSSY BEST FRIEND: You should have known better! *(TOMATO PLANT GIRL, still hidden, points at a picture in the book.)*

TOMATO PLANT GIRL: RED! *(BOSSY BEST FRIEND hears the sound; LITTLE GIRL tries to distract her and block TOMATO PLANT GIRL.)*

LITTLE GIRL *(loudly)*: Yes! You're right! I'm very sorry! *(BOSSY BEST FRIEND moves LITTLE GIRL aside. Shocked, she stares at TOMATO PLANT GIRL)*

BOSSY BEST FRIEND: Who's that thing.

LITTLE GIRL: She's new.

BOSSY BEST FRIEND: She's *repulsive*.

LITTLE GIRL: She's nice.

BOSSY BEST FRIEND: She's got that dumb book. *(TOMATO PLANT GIRL stares, fascinated, at BOSSY BEST FRIEND. LITTLE GIRL tries to take the book from TOMATO PLANT GIRL, who holds on.)*

LITTLE GIRL: Tomato Plant Girl —

BOSSY BEST FRIEND: "Tomato Plant Girl"?

LITTLE GIRL: — please give me the book! *(TOMATO PLANT GIRL lets LITTLE GIRL have the book. Still watching TOMATO PLANT GIRL, BOSSY BEST FRIEND sweeps the book away from LITTLE GIRL.)*

BOSSY BEST FRIEND: Thank you. *(BOSSY BEST FRIEND puts the book in her bag. LITTLE GIRL watches, upset, but says nothing. BOSSY BEST*

FRIEND *clears her throat, suddenly very polite.)* Excuse me, you grimy strange girl. You're in my garden. I'd like to know who you are.
(BOSSY BEST FRIEND summons TOMATO PLANT GIRL with a wave. TOMATO PLANT GIRL moves toward her, intrigued, imitating the wave.)

LITTLE GIRL: There's nothing wrong with her. She's new.
(BOSSY BEST FRIEND walks slowly around TOMATO PLANT GIRL, inspecting her at a slight distance.)

BOSSY BEST FRIEND: Mmm-hmm—mmm-hmm—mmm-hmm. *(TOMATO PLANT GIRL notices the bow on BOSSY BEST FRIEND's dress. She becomes entranced. She tugs at and unties it, makes a sound of delight. BOSSY BEST FRIEND gasps, whirls around. TOMATO PLANT GIRL looks at her, innocent. LITTLE GIRL starts to laugh. BOSSY BEST FRIEND turns back to LITTLE GIRL, furious.) Booknose —* *(LITTLE GIRL stands at attention.)* Come here. *(BOSSY BEST FRIEND motions for LITTLE GIRL to stand behind her and tie the bow. She does, but sneaks a look at TOMATO PLANT GIRL. TOMATO PLANT GIRL stands up close, facing BOSSY BEST FRIEND, and stares at her.)* You're dirty.

TOMATO PLANT GIRL *(gleeful)*: DIRRT!
(BOSSY BEST FRIEND stamps her foot, turns to LITTLE GIRL, points at her watch.)

BOSSY BEST FRIEND: It's five-o-five. Barbie time. Now.
(BOSSY BEST FRIEND snaps her fingers once, then points for LITTLE GIRL to set up the game. She does. BOSSY BEST FRIEND holds out LITTLE GIRL's Barbie. TOMATO PLANT GIRL stands between them and watches, fascinated.) You're this one.

LITTLE GIRL: I know.

BOSSY BEST FRIEND: One — two — *(To TOMATO PLANT GIRL.)* Move away, please!

TOMATO PLANT GIRL *(recognizing the word)*: Please!

LITTLE GIRL *(to BOSSY BEST FRIEND)*: She can watch.

BOSSY BEST FRIEND *(glaring)*: *One. Two. Three.*
(LITTLE GIRL is quiet. During the next lines, TOMATO PLANT GIRL hovers over BOSSY BEST FRIEND's shoulder, moving her head with the rhythm of the words. LITTLE GIRL plays with one eye on TOMATO PLANT GIRL.)

BOSSY BEST FRIEND: Dena!

LITTLE GIRL: Lena! *(Three loud, fakey kisses.)* How are you?

BOSSY BEST FRIEND: Terrific.

LITTLE GIRL: And your job?

BOSSY BEST FRIEND: Perfecto.

LITTLE GIRL: And your boyfriends?

BOSSY BEST FRIEND: Too fine.

LITTLE GIRL: You look —

TOMATO PLANT GIRL: HA!
(TOMATO PLANT GIRL plucks the Barbie from BOSSY BEST FRIEND's hand. She shakes the Barbie around until its hair is big and messy. Then she puts the Barbie's feet in her mouth. BOSSY BEST FRIEND grabs the Barbie and points it at TOMATO PLANT GIRL.)

BOSSY BEST FRIEND: *You stop that and say sorry!*

TOMATO PLANT GIRL *(to LITTLE GIRL)*: Sorry?

LITTLE GIRL: Never mind. It's okay. *(LITTLE GIRL starts to show TOMATO PLANT GIRL how to hold Barbie.)* Here. Watch. *(BOSSY BEST FRIEND takes LITTLE GIRL's Barbie from her hand and moves her aside.)*

BOSSY BEST FRIEND: Excuse me. Thank you. *(BOSSY BEST FRIEND stands next to TOMATO PLANT GIRL and smiles, holding up LITTLE GIRL's Barbie.)* This is how we play with Barbie. Like this. Feet. Head. *(Smoothing the hair.)* Hair. In place. Then: arrange Barbie.
(BOSSY BEST FRIEND puts the Barbie's arms in a proper position. She hands it to TOMATO PLANT GIRL. LITTLE

*GIRL watches. TOMATO PLANT GIRL holds the Barbie
right side up, pats her hair, then starts to move her into an
odd position.)*

LITTLE GIRL *(correcting her)*: No, like this —
(BOSSY BEST FRIEND glares at LITTLE GIRL.)

BOSSY BEST FRIEND *(to TOMATO PLANT GIRL)*: You're
such a fast learner. That's lovely. *(BOSSY BEST FRIEND
takes the Barbie and hands it back to TOMATO PLANT
GIRL. LITTLE GIRL watches, frustrated.)* Now. One-two-
three. *(As her own Barbie.)* Dena! *(Pointing at TOMATO
PLANT GIRL's Barbie.)* Lena!

TOMATO PLANT GIRL: LEEENA!

BOSSY BEST FRIEND *(as herself)*: Beautiful. Now —

TOMATO PLANT GIRL: LEENA LEENA —

LITTLE GIRL *(starting to join her)*: LEENA —

BOSSY BEST FRIEND *(to LITTLE GIRL)*: Stop! *(To TOMATO
PLANT GIRL.)* Lena. That's right. *(BOSSY BEST FRIEND
takes the Barbie and keeps it away from TOMATO PLANT
GIRL.)* Now watch. One-two-three. *(BOSSY BEST FRIEND
demonstrates with both Barbies.)* Dena! Lena! *(Kiss-kiss-
kiss.)* How are you? Just *terrific.* And your job? Perfecto. And
your boyfriends? Too —
*(TOMATO PLANT GIRL picks up a stick from the ground
and holds it up proudly between the Barbies, as if it is a doll.
This is her way of playing.)*

TOMATO PLANT GIRL: *Stick!*

BOSSY BEST FRIEND: Stop it! *(Handing LITTLE GIRL her
Barbie.)* Tell her to stop.

TOMATO PLANT GIRL *(as Stick, to the other Barbies)*: *Stick*
Bar-bieee! Stick I!
*(TOMATO PLANT GIRL kisses LITTLE GIRL's Barbie on
the cheek.)*

LITTLE GIRL *(as her Barbie)*: Oh! Hello Stick!
(TOMATO PLANT GIRL repeats "Stick" over and over,

moving around BOSSY BEST FRIEND and LITTLE GIRL.)

BOSSY BEST FRIEND *(to LITTLE GIRL)*: Stop playing like that! *(As her Barbie.)* Now listen, Stick —

TOMATO PLANT GIRL *(to LITTLE GIRL)*: Terrrriffic! Stick I!

LITTLE GIRL *(as her Barbie)*: Perfecto! Too fine!

BOSSY BEST FRIEND *(to LITTLE GIRL):* You're doing it wrong! *(BOSSY BEST FRIEND takes LITTLE GIRL's Barbie and blocks TOMATO PLANT GIRL's way.)* Stop playing with her! I'm your friend!

LITTLE GIRL: She's my friend too!

BOSSY BEST FRIEND: *I'm* your friend.

LITTLE GIRL *(matter-of-fact)*: And she's my—

BOSSY BEST FRIEND: Dumb Booknose. Dumb *foreigner* girl! *(LITTLE GIRL freezes.)*

TOMATO PLANT GIRL *(in LITTLE GIRL's face)*: Stick!!

LITTLE GIRL *(to TOMATO PLANT GIRL)*: STOP. Stop that now. *(LITTLE GIRL grabs Stick Barbie out of TOMATO PLANT GIRL's hand. TOMATO PLANT GIRL makes an indignant noise.)* This is *not* how we play. It's loud and dangerous. *Now sit over there and calm down. Right now. (Cornered, TOMATO PLANT GIRL bites LITTLE GIRL's pointing finger in self-defense, then runs off. Shocked.)* Ow! Tomato Plant Girl — wait!
(LITTLE GIRL starts to go after TOMATO PLANT GIRL. BOSSY BEST FRIEND blocks her way.)

BOSSY BEST FRIEND: Don't.

LITTLE GIRL: But I —

BOSSY BEST FRIEND: You did the right thing. *(Holding up LITTLE GIRL's Barbie.)* You're this one. *(LITTLE GIRL doesn't take it.)* You're *this* one.
(LITTLE GIRL makes a decision. She takes her Barbie, looks at BOSSY BEST FRIEND.)

LITTLE GIRL: I know.

BOSSY BEST FRIEND: One — two —three! *(BOSSY BEST FRIEND speaks as her Barbie.)* Dena!
(LITTLE GIRL plays, ignoring BOSSY BEST FRIEND's game.)

LITTLE GIRL: *Root!*

BOSSY BEST FRIEND: Don't I look stunning?

LITTLE GIRL: *Dirrrt.*

BOSSY BEST FRIEND: My job is divine!

LITTLE GIRL: *Fiire—*

BOSSY BEST FRIEND *(furious)*: That's a horrible dress!

LITTLE GIRL: *—kissssun!*
(BOSSY BEST FRIEND grabs LITTLE GIRL's Barbie.)

BOSSY BEST FRIEND: Your Barbie wants what my Barbie wants but my Barbie can have it and your Barbie —

LITTLE GIRL: No!

BOSSY BEST FRIEND: That's the game.

LITTLE GIRL: *Your* game.

BOSSY BEST FRIEND: Our game!

LITTLE GIRL: Your game. I don't like it. *(BOSSY BEST FRIEND starts to speak. LITTLE GIRL steps forward.)* And I didn't like you taking my book or making me give you your plant!

BOSSY BEST FRIEND: *Making* you?

LITTLE GIRL: Yes!

BOSSY BEST FRIEND: I said "please"!

LITTLE GIRL: You didn't mean it!

BOSSY BEST FRIEND: Fine. Never mind. We'll play Mother May I.
(BOSSY BEST FRIEND claps twice. LITTLE GIRL picks up the stick.)

LITTLE GIRL: *Stick!*

708

(LITTLE GIRL spins and plays with the stick.)

BOSSY BEST FRIEND: Put it down.

LITTLE GIRL *(still playing)*: No.

BOSSY BEST FRIEND *(grabs hold of the stick)*: Little Girl: I'm your friend!

LITTLE GIRL *(matter-of-fact)*: No. *(LITTLE GIRL lets go of the stick.)* You're not.

BOSSY BEST FRIEND: Booknose: be careful. Your other friend's gone.

LITTLE GIRL *(uncertain)*: Then — I'll play alone.

BOSSY BEST FRIEND *(scornful)*: You'll play *alone?*

LITTLE GIRL *(more confident):* I'll play alone. *(BOSSY BEST FRIEND drops the stick on the ground. She picks up her Barbies and bag and turns to go.)* Wait—

BOSSY BEST FRIEND *(turns back, expectant)*: Yes?

LITTLE GIRL: My book. *(Respectfully.)* Please.
(Crushed, BOSSY BEST FRIEND glares at LITTLE GIRL. BOSSY BEST FRIEND takes the book from her bag and holds it high in the air.)

BOSSY BEST FRIEND: Dumb boring foreigner book! *(BOSSY BEST FRIEND drops the book. LITTLE GIRL catches it.)* Have fun alone!
(BOSSY BEST FRIEND turns on her heel and exits. LITTLE GIRL hugs the book.)

LITTLE GIRL *(to herself)*: I'll play alone. *(Pause. LITTLE GIRL looks around her, uncertain.)* Alone. *(Calling.)* Tomato Plant Girl? *(LITTLE GIRL takes a deep breath and closes her eyes, gathering courage.)* I'll play alone.
(LITTLE GIRL breathes deep, eyes closed, hugging the book.

TOMATO PLANT GIRL enters. She is fully grown: a red, round tomato. But she is still hurt and wary of LITTLE GIRL. She approaches LITTLE GIRL and gently taps her shoulder.

LITTLE GIRL jumps, looks at TOMATO PLANT GIRL.)

LITTLE GIRL: Tomato Plant Girl! Wow! Look at you!

TOMATO PLANT GIRL: Grow I.

(Pause. They look at each other, then away. They start to speak at the same time.)

LITTLE GIRL *(an apology)*: I'm sorry.

TOMATO PLANT GIRL *(LITTLE GIRL's name)*: Sorry —
(They laugh for a moment.)

LITTLE GIRL: I should have, but I didn't. I shouldn't have, but I did.
(TOMATO PLANT GIRL points at LITTLE GIRL, imitating her reprimand.)

TOMATO PLANT GIRL: Sitoverthere! SitoverthereNOW!

LITTLE GIRL: I didn't know what to do.
(TOMATO PLANT GIRL imitates BOSSY BEST FRIEND yelling "Foreigner!" at LITTLE GIRL.)

TOMATO PLANT GIRL: "Forrner!"
(TOMATO PLANT GIRL imitates LITTLE GIRL gasping in shock.)

LITTLE GIRL: I *like* being a foreigner! That's why I like you. That's why I'm your friend.

TOMATO PLANT GIRL *(unsure of the meaning)*: Frrrend.

LITTLE GIRL: Someone who … knows who you are. And likes you. All of you. *(Pause.)* Are you still my friend?
(TOMATO PLANT GIRL takes LITTLE GIRL's hand and kisses the finger she bit earlier.)

TOMATO PLANT GIRL: Frrrend.
(LITTLE GIRL starts to cry and laugh at the same time. TOMATO PLANT GIRL starts to cry/laugh too. TOMATO PLANT GIRL lifts her index finger and reaches out toward LITTLE GIRL's face. LITTLE GIRL slowly does the same. At

710

the same moment, each wipes a tear from the other's cheek. LITTLE GIRL tastes TOMATO PLANT GIRL's tear.)

LITTLE GIRL: Friend.
(TOMATO PLANT GIRL tastes LITTLE GIRL's tear.)

TOMATO PLANT GIRL: Friend.
(They stand facing each other a moment.)

LITTLE GIRL: Tomato Plant Girl —

TOMATO PLANT GIRL: Grow I.

LITTLE GIRL: I know.

TOMATO PLANT GIRL: Errth.

LITTLE GIRL *(remembering)*: Plants go back to the earth … to feed other plants. *(To TOMATO PLANT GIRL.)* You have to go back, don't you?

TOMATO PLANT GIRL *(affirming)*: Errth.

LITTLE GIRL *(holds out her book to TOMATO PLANT GIRL)*: Here. I want you to have it.

TOMATO PLANT GIRL *(takes the book)*: Red!

LITTLE GIRL: It's a gift.

TOMATO PLANT GIRL: Gifft. *(Thanking her.)* Tomato. *(TOMATO PLANT GIRL hugs the book, accepting it. She motions to LITTLE GIRL.)* Root you. Please. *(TOMATO PLANT GIRL scoops up handfuls of dirt from LITTLE GIRL's side of the garden. She begins to hum as she sprinkles the dirt onto LITTLE GIRL.)* Grow you. Gift.
(LITTLE GIRL smiles, rubs the dirt on her hands and face.)

LITTLE GIRL: Gift. *(The Earthsoil Hum returns.)* The Earth hum! *(LITTLE GIRL acknowledges the Earthsoil Hum with TOMATO PLANT GIRL's gesture. TOMATO PLANT GIRL joins her in the gesture and the hum. They continue to hum, transforming the gesture, once, then twice. The second time, they join hands. They spin in a circle, facing each other.)*Tom atosweetleafplantreadyonetwo! *(LITTLE GIRL drops a hand. They hold on by one.)* Velvet green and flower-sun gold! In

711

root, in heart, in sun — alone! *(LITTLE GIRL lets TOMATO PLANT GIRL go. TOMATO PLANT GIRL spins off and folds back into the earth at the same spot where she emerged. LITTLE GIRL stops spinning.)* Alone. I'll play alone. *(LITTLE GIRL looks at the place where TOMATO PLANT GIRL disappeared. She picks up two handfuls of earth and sprinkles it over the spot. Then she stretches up and spins, breathing out. She reaches up and lets the earth fall through her fingers.)* Gift I. Grow I. Grow I. *(In the place where TOMATO PLANT GIRL folded into the earth, a new tomato plant springs up, healthy and green, with a single red tomato.)*

END OF PLAY

THE
HIGHEST HEAVEN

A full-length play

by
José Cruz González

Through most of the last century the repertoire of plays for young audiences in this country represented a singular, narrow, western European perspective of theatre, both in subject matter and style. The early twentieth century settlement house drama programs aggressively employed drama and theatre programs, often specifically in service to homogenizing the diverse audiences under a so-called "American" perspective. As organizations such as the Junior League continued the tradition of children's theatre as social work throughout the first half of the century, this Eurocentric approach solidified the children's theatre field around a canon of simplistic, moralistic fairy plays, presenting the stories and reinforcing the values of the debutantes who produced the plays.

Primarily through the support of the professional theatres in the 1960s and 1970s, playwrights gradually wrenched children's theatre from the social work agendas of the earlier decades; and the professional producers slowly—very slowly—began to introduce characters and stories on their stages that reflect the cultural diversity of the audiences in their theatres. In addition, new, ongoing, play development programs, such as New Visions/ New Voices, sponsored by the Kennedy Center for the Performing Arts, in Washington, D.C., specifically and aggressively looked to enhancing diversity in the field. Many professional theatres also created play development programs devoted to expanding the cultural diversity of the field. This has resulted in the support and development of a growing body of significant plays that speak from and to many different cultural perspectives. The plays of José Cruz González figure prominently in this development.

González first developed *The Highest Heaven* at Childsplay, Inc., a professional theatre, in Tempe, AZ, and then later at New Visions/New Voices. The play offers a theatrically fluid tale of a search for "home," compounded by the pressures and realities of geo-political borders and cultural longings. Set during the time of the Depression, the play relates the troubled journey of a young Latino, Hurácon, who, expelled from his home in the United States, struggles to return. Each scene of the journey opens with

714

a projected title—written in English and Spanish—presented to the audience. With this Brechtian device, González introduces the idea of Monarch Butterflies, a metaphor he employs throughout the play to reinforce the fragile beauty of life and Hurácon's determination to complete his journey despite the many obstacles in his way.

González employs an almost bare stage approach to telling the poetic tale. With five actors, some playing multiple characters, the action moves quickly from scene to scene, and the technique easily accommodates multiple and diverse locations. Through the use of vivid cultural symbols, including Negro spirituals, and customs and artifacts from Day of the Dead celebrations, González situates the action in a spiritual as well as a physical realm.

With *The Highest Heaven,* González probes questions of identity that call to question Hurácon's struggles against myriad cultural, physical, and political borders. Such sophisticated cultural interrogations in a play for young audiences stand as a tribute to the growing diversity in the field as well as the increasing sophistication in the dramaturgy of the field throughout the last decade.

José Cruz González's plays include *The Red Forest, September Shoes, Always Running, Two Donuts, Salt & Pepper, The Highest Heaven, La Posada, Calabasas Street, Harvest Moon* and *Mariachi Quixote.* In 2004 *Lily Plants a Garden* premiered at the Mark Taper Forum P.L.A.Y. program, *Fast and Loose* at Actors Theatre of Louisville, *Rip Van Winkle in Lost Hills* with Cornerstone Theater Company and *Earth Songs* with Metro Theater. Mr. González has written for *PAZ*, produced by Discovery Kids for The Learning Channel. Mr. González was a recipient of a 1997 NEA/TCG Theatre Residency Program for Playwrights and in 1985 was an NEA Director Fellow. He is a graduate of the University of California, Irvine. He teaches theatre at California State University at Los Angeles and is a member of The Dramatists Guild of America, ASSITEJ/USA, and is an Associate Artist with Cornerstone Theater Company.

THE
HIGHEST HEAVEN

A full-length play

by
José Cruz González

THE HIGHEST HEAVEN

For performance of any songs, music and recordings mentioned in the play
which are in copyright, the permission of the copyright owners must be
obtained or other songs and recordings in the public domain substituted.

The play printed in this anthology is not to be used as an acting script.
All inquiries regarding performance rights should be adressed to
Dramatic Publishing, 311 Washington St., Woodstock, IL 60098.
Phone: (815) 338-7170. Fax: (815)338-8981

THE DRAMATIC PUBLISHING COMPANY of Woodstock, Illinois

"When we are really honest with ourselves we must admit that our lives are all that really belong to us. So, it is how we use our lives that determines what kind of men we are. It is my deepest belief that only by giving our lives do we find life."
—César Chávez

"La necesidad desconoce fronteras."
"Necessity knows no borders."
—Mexican American Proverb

"Butterflies
Flying Like the Breeze
Sucking Nectar Quietly
Colors Everywhere"
—Kelsey Miguel González, Age 9

"If you haven't forgiven yourself something,
how can you forgive others?"
—Dolores Huerta

THE HIGHEST HEAVEN

The Highest Heaven premiered with Childsplay, Inc., in association with Borderlands Theater in January 1999 at the Tucson Center for the Performing Arts and February 1999 at the Tempe Performing Arts Center, Tempe, Arizona.

CAST

Huracán	STEVEN PENA
Kika/Wife	ALEJANDRA GARCIA
El Negro	ELLEN BENTON
Doña Elena	DEBRA K. STEVENS
Moises, Police Official, Addict, Undertaker-Barber, Husband	JON GENTRY

PRODUCTION STAFF

Director	DAVID SAAR
Scenic Design	GRO JOHRE
Costume Design	CONNIE FURR
Lighting Design	AMARANTE LUCERO
Music Composition/ Sound Design	RICK ARECCO & ALLEN LEA
Dramaturg	GRAHAM WHITEHEAD
Properties	DARREN GOAD
Technical Director	KENNETH P. LAGER JR.
Stage Manager	MARIE KRUEGER-JONES

Originally developed at Childsplay, Inc. with support from the NEA/ TCG Theatre Residency Program for Playwrights.

The Highest Heaven was workshopped in 1996 at the New Visions/New Voices Program, The Kennedy Center, Washington, D.C.

Special thanks: David Saar, Debra K. Stevens, Graham Whitehead, Rosemary Walsh, Childsplay, NEA/TCG, The Kennedy Center's New Visions/New Voices Program, John McCluggage, Mary Hall Surface, Susan Mason, Palabras, the San Jose Repertory, CSULA, Isaiah Sanders, Lucille Oliver, Alejandra Garcia Iñiguez, and my family.

The Highest Heaven received its second production with the Center Theatre Group/Mark Taper Forum's P.L.A.Y., Los Angeles, Calif., February 7-March 4, 2000.

CAST

Doña Elena, Kika, Wife .... CHRISTINE DEAVER
Moises, Police Official, Addict,
Undertaker-Barber .... DAVID FURUMOTO
Huracán .... OMAR GOMEZ
El Negro .... RICKE V. HOWELL

PRODUCTION STAFF AND CREW

Director .... DIANE RODRIGUEZ
Set Design .... EDWARD E. HAYNES JR.
Costume Design .... INGRID FERRIN
Lighting Design .... JOSE LOPEZ
Musical Director/Sound Design .... DAVE OSSMANN
Casting .... AMY LIEBERMAN
Production Stage Manager .... BOBBY DELUCA
Stage Manager .... VANESSA J. NOON
Coordinating Producer .... DOLORES CHAVEZ
Artistic Supervisor .... COREY MADDEN
Master Electrician .... EFRAIN MORALES
Production Assistant .... ROBERT BOYD
Crew Head/Audio Engineer .... JAMES WITHERALL
Tour Coordinator .... KIMIKO L. BRODER

Characters

HURACÁN: a 12-year-old Latino boy.

EL NEGRO:
a Black man in his 50s. Worn like the earth,he is troubled by his past. Caretaker of the monarch butterflies

KIKA:
Huracán's Mother. A memory.
(May also play the WIFE)

DOÑA ELENA:
a dark-skinned Mexican widow.
Old, possessive, petty and disturbed.

MOISES, THE POLICE OFFICIAL, THE ADDICT, THE UNDERTAKER-BARBER and the HUSBAND:
may be played by one actor. A fool. Related to Doña Elena.

BUTTERFLY EFFECT: *Both productions incorporated a small fan which was rigged below the stage. A small hole was cut on the stage floor to allow the actor to remove the cut piece and release the butterfly confetti over the fan allowing the butterflies to float high into the air. The floating butterflies seen throughout the play were rigged on long poles and manipulated by actors.*

MUSIC: *The Negro spirituals used in the play are believed to be in public domain. They are: O, Sit Down Servant, Somebody's Calling My Name, Couldn't Hear Nobody Pray, Roll, Jordan, Roll. Music is available at the back of the published playbook.*

SCENE 1

SETTING: *The 1930s when America was in the middle of the Depression. During that period thousands of Mexican nationals, as well as Americans of Mexican descent were repatriated to Mexico with or without their consent. The setting takes place in various locales and should only be suggestive. Title projections are optional. SOUND: A Negro spiritual is heard. Several monarch butterflies appear fluttering over the stage. Their wings glow, revealing deep vibrant colors.*

AT RISE: *"The Great Depression. October 1931. The monarch butterfly begins his journey.—La gran Depresión. Octubre 1931. La mariposa monarca comienza su viaje venturoso." SOUND: A train station. It is chaotic. Noisy. Dusty. Lights rise on a young Latino boy named HURACÁN holding a suitcase. He is scared and alone. KIKA, Huracán's Mother appears.*

KIKA: *Huracán!*

HURACAN: What is it, 'Amá?

KIKA: Grab your things.

HURACAN: But why?

KIKA: They're taking us away.

HURACAN: Who is?

KIKA: Men with guns and badges!

HURACAN: Where are we going?

KIKA: They're taking us away on a train to Mexico!

HURACAN: But why?

KIKA: I don't know! Where's your Father?

HURACAN: *'Apá* was right behind us.

KIKA: I've got to find him. Stay here.

HURACAN: Can't I go with you?

KIKA: I'll be right back. Everything is going to be fine.

HURACAN: How do you know?

KIKA: I just do. *(SOUND: Another train whistle blast is heard. HURACAN sits on a suitcase.)* Remember, when you're scared God's watching.
(KIKA exits. EL NEGRO, an old black man, appears.)

EL NEGRO (to HURACAN): Boy?

HURACAN: Huh?

EL NEGRO: That suitcase belongs to me.

HURACAN: My *'amá* told me to wait here.

EL NEGRO: You're sittin' on it.

HURACAN: That's what she said.

EL NEGRO: What are you lookin' at?

HURACAN: You must be *San Martin de Porres.*

EL NEGRO: Who?

HURACAN: The patron saint of the defenseless. Have you come to answer my prayer?

EL NEGRO: I ain't *San Martin.*

HURACAN: But he's black like you. Am I in heaven?

EL NEGRO: You ain't dead and I ain't no saint! This is *Misas,* Mexico, boy. Don't you know where you at?

HURACAN: No, my *'amá* said to stay here.

EL NEGRO: They all gone, boy. You're on your own. *Andale,* I got a train to catch. (HURACAN watches as EL NEGRO picks up his suitcase and waits for the train. Then …) I can't do it. I can't get on. (EL NEGRO exits as the train leaves.)

HURACAN *(yelling). 'Amá!*

SCENE 2

"Far from home a small caterpillar searches for food.—Lejos de su casa una pequeña oruga busca comida." November. El dia de los muertos — The Day of the Dead. A cemetery. A remembrance for the dead. Like a Diego Rivera painting shawled women kneel whispering prayers before the graves of their dead. Candles burn, fresh cempasúchil [marigolds] flowers adorn, candy skulls and bread lie out on plates inviting the lost souls to partake. A wealthy woman, DONA ELENA, dressed in black, and her servant, MOISES, enter. DONA ELENA stands before her husband's tomb.

DONA ELENA: Help me down, *Moises.*

MOISES: *Sí, Doña Elena.*

DONA ELENA: Bring me his basket.

MOISES: Here it is, *Doña Elena.*

DONA ELENA *(kneels at a grave): Porfirio,* my dear sweet dead husband, I bring you wine from your vineyard, bread from your bakery and meat from your rancho. *(To MOISES.)* What are you looking at, *Indio*?

MOISES: Nothing, *Doña Elena.*

DONA ELENA: Turn your back and cover your ears. This

conversation doesn't concern you.

MOISES: *Sí, Doña Elena.*
(He turns his back and covers his ears.)

DONA ELENA: I'm afraid I don't trust your unwanted son,
Porfirio. You created him but he's nothing like you. None of
those "cousins" are. There's the banker, the bread maker, the
harlot, the nun, the police official, the addict and this Indio
half-breed. Your infidelities have cost me dearly, Querido.
I spit on you. *(She spits and then crosses herself.)* But I
remember you, husband, as a faithful wife should on the Day
of the Dead. I want all of those "cousins" to know how loyal
I am. *(Pause.)* It gets me things.
(HURACAN enters and crosses to DONA ELENA.)

HURACAN: *Señora*, may I have a piece of sweetbread?

DONA ELENA: No, you may not. This food belongs to me and
my dead husband.

HURACAN: But I'm hungry.

DONA ELENA: Begging won't do you any good. I gave at
church. *Moises?!*

HURACAN: Please, I haven't eaten all day.

DONA ELENA: I don't care! *Moises?!*
(She hits MOISES with her cane. He uncovers his ears.)

MOISES: *Ay! Doña Elena?*

DONA ELENA: What are you doing?

MOISES: Talking to the spirits, *Doña.*

DONA ELENA: Crazy Indio. Help me up. Go away, you
wretched boy.

MOISES: You heard the *Señora*. Go!

HURACAN: But I'm dizzy from hunger.

DONA ELENA *(tempting him)*: Then take the bread.

MOISES: *Doña?*

DONA ELENA: Be my guest.

HURACAN: Thank you, *Señora.* *(HURACAN reaches for the sweetbread and DONA ELENA hits him with her cane.)* Ouch!

DONA ELENA: Stupid boy. I said, "no" the first time. Now do you understand? My possessions are not to be touched. Not! Not! Not! *(HURACAN hides.)* Moises, you should be more attentive.

MOISES: *Sí, Doña Elena.*

DONA ELENA: I tire of this country's filth, its lack of culture and mostly of its poor. My dead husband and I started with nothing. We became quite successful and respected. Why must we carry the poor on our backs?

MOISES: I don't know ...
(DONA ELENA hits MOISES with her cane.)

DONA ELENA: I wasn't speaking to you. If only you had lived, *Querido.* We would have been rid of *El Negro* by now. Taken what's ours. Everyone would fear us. But you died too soon. Once again, leaving me to clean up your mess. *El Negro* is like a cancer. How I hate him. But I'll find a way. Find his weakness. Then strike. *(To MOISES.)* Why hasn't *Don Porfirio's* tomb been cleaned? I'm ashamed at how dirty it looks. There's dust everywhere. One can never be clean in this godforsaken country. Take me home!
(DONA ELENA and MOISES exit, HURACAN begins to eat as incense burns and prayers are whispered. MOISES reenters.)

MOISES: The dead must be respected, *muchacho.* Leave an offering.

HURACAN: Huh?
(MOISES places some coins on the tombstone.)

MOISES: If *Doña Elena* catches you we'll both be in trouble. Serious trouble. *(MOISES begins collecting food from other tombs and placing it on Don Porfirio's tomb.)* She's going to tell my cousin, the police official, and he'll come looking for you. You better leave now. You can't stay here. She does hateful things to people, especially children.

HURACAN: Have you seen my *'amá?* I lost her at the train station.

MOISES: No, I'm sorry, I haven't. But what do you expect? The whole station was a disaster. It's been like that all month. People everywhere. Screaming and crying. It makes no sense. And now everyone's gone.

HURACAN: Do you know where the train went?

MOISES: Maybe south. I'm not sure.

HURACAN: But I have to find my *'amá.*

MOISES: You can't go back there. Not even into town. *Doña Elena* has spies everywhere.

HURACAN: Please help me.

MOISES: There's nothing I can do. If Doña Elena knew I was talking to you …

HURACAN: I want my *'amá.*
   (SOUND: A coyote's howl is heard off in the distance.)

MOISES: Perhaps you can go into the forest.

HURACAN: Forest?

MOISES: That's where *El Negro* lives. Nobody ever goes there. Everyone's afraid of him, but not me. I'll go find him for you. But if *Doña Elena* finds out I helped you …

HURACAN: I won't say a word.

MOISES: Good. Here, take this blanket. It'll be cold tonight. It's all I can give you. And remember my cousin will be looking for you.

HURACAN: Who?

MOISES: The police official.
   (MOISES exits. HURACAN wraps himself in the blanket. A moment later he pushes everything off the tomb in anger.)

HURACAN: Why is this happening to me?! Where are you, *'Amá?*

("The small caterpillar remembers his past. — La oruga pequeña recuerda su pasado." El valle — The valley appears. A barn sits on the edge of a green field and the valley is filled with blue sky. KIKA, Huracán's Mother, enters carrying a laundry basket.)

KIKA: *Huracán*, you've got chores!

HURACAN: But I'm hungry, *'Amá*.

KIKA: There's plenty of time to eat later.

HURACAN: I hate chores, *'Amá*. Why can't we have a maid like in the movies?

KIKA: *Andale!*
(She takes the bread away and hands HURACAN a coffee can. He begins to feed the imaginary chickens.)

HURACAN: It's so hopeless. Things only get messy again.

KIKA: If everyone went around thinking like that nothing would ever get done. Laundry would never get washed. Rooms would never get cleaned. Your socks and *chonies* would never get starched and ironed.

HURACAN: It would be my kind of heaven.

KIKA: Well, heaven wouldn't be very clean now, would it? God would be very unhappy. Angels flying with filthy wings? *Imposible*.
(SOUND: A train whistle is heard off in the distance.)

HURACAN: The train's on time!

KIKA: I hate how it rumbles past our home. There's dust everywhere. My heaven is going to be a place without railroads and trains or specks of dirt anywhere. Your Father promised he'd be back now. We live in the United States where everything's on time except for him. *(A little worried.)* Where can he be?

HURACAN: Maybe he's buying something.

KIKA: He won't go into town. It isn't safe. People are being sent away. So, you stay near me.

HURACAN: Do you know what's today, *'Amá?*

KIKA: It's Tuesday.

HURACAN: Yeah, but it's not just any Tuesday. There's something special about this Tuesday. Remember?

KIKA: No.

HURACAN: *'Amá.*

KIKA: Of course I remember! You're growing so quickly. You'll never be eleven again.
(She kisses him on the cheek.)

HURACAN: So?

KIKA: So?

HURACAN: So, is there anything I should open now, *'Amá?*

KIKA: Ay, *Huracán*, can't you wait to celebrate tonight?

HURACAN: No!

KIKA: You're just like your father. *Imposible. (She gives HURACAN a small gift wrapped in burlap.)* Happy Birthday, *Huracán!*
(HURACAN immediately opens it. It is a glass jar with a monarch butterfly.)

HURACAN: It's a butterfly!

KIKA: It's not just any butterfly, *Huracán*. It's a *monarca*. A king butterfly.

HURACAN: What am I supposed to do with it?

KIKA: Make a wish and then let it go.

HURACAN: But I want to keep it.

KIKA: It isn't for you to keep.

HURACAN: But what kind of gift is that, if I can't keep it?

KIKA: You're suppose to make a wish. Then let it go, and your wish will come true.

HURACAN: Will my butterfly ever come back?

KIKA: No, but one of his children might. And when he returns, *Huracán*, there'll be thousands of monarchs with him dancing like leaves in the wind. They'll stop here to rest their weary wings and quench their thirsty mouths. When they do we'll dampen the earth with fresh water.

HURACAN: Why?

KIKA: So the flowers will be strong to feed these *mariposas* their sweet nectar. It's a glimpse at God's heart.

HURACAN: God's heart?

KIKA: It's a blessing, *mijo*.

HURACAN: How come you know so much about things?

KIKA: Not everything comes out of a book, *Huracán*. Who taught you to tell time by reading the sun?

HURACAN: You did.

KIKA: Who taught you to eat cactus without pricking yourself?

HURACAN: You.

KIKA: There are many ways to learn and they don't all come from a book. The earth has secrets. If you watch and listen closely she'll share them with you.

HURACAN *(closing his eyes)*: Okay. Done. Time to go, *mariposa*. Fly! *(HURACAN opens the jar and releases the butterfly. The monarch butterfly flutters off into the blue sky. SOUND: A siren is heard. KIKA sees something off in the distance.)* What is it, *'Amá?*

KIKA: Oh, no, they're coming this way!

HURACAN: Who is?

KIKA: Men with guns and badges!

HURACAN: Why?

KIKA: There's no time to explain. We have to go!

HURACAN: But my butterfly king. I've got to save him!

KIKA: No, *Huracán*, there isn't time!

732

HURACAN: He won't make it by himself!

KIKA: *Huracán!*
(A dust storm arrives. A moment later HURACAN struggles to awaken from his nightmare. DONA ELENA enters standing over him.)

DONA ELENA: Wake up! Wake up, you!

HURACAN: *'Amá?*

DONA ELENA: How dare you call me your Mother! I'm nobody's Mother! You little thief, you've taken food from my dead husband!
(She begins beating him with her cane.)

HURACAN: No! Stop hitting me!

DONA ELENA: I'll teach you never to steal from the dead! *Toma!*
(EL NEGRO enters and crosses to DONA ELENA taking away her cane.)

EL NEGRO: Leave the boy alone!

DONA ELENA: How dare you interfere, *Negro!*

EL NEGRO: What's he done?

DONA ELENA: He's a thief!

HURACAN: I was hungry.

DONA ELENA *(grabs HURACAN by the ear)*: Do you know what I do to horrible little children?

HURACAN: Ouch!

EL NEGRO: Leave the boy alone!

DONA ELENA: Give me back my cane, *Negro!* *(EL NEGRO holds the cane up as if to strike her. She releases HURACAN.)* How dare you try to strike me!

EL NEGRO: I ain't yet, but I might. Get up, boy.

DONA ELENA: I promise you'll pay for this insult!

EL NEGRO: Get in line.

DONA ELENA: Crazy old *gringo*, Protector of the butterflies and now children too? Saint *El Negro*, is it?

EL NEGRO: This ain't got nothin' to do with saints.

DONA ELENA: That's right, *Negro*. How can I forget? There's unfinished business between you and me.

EL NEGRO: The boy's got nothin' to do with it.

DONA ELENA: I'll see you dead yet.

EL NEGRO: Them mountain spirits got powerful magic.

DONA ELENA: How frightening. But it's a matter of time. I have it and you don't.

EL NEGRO: You ain't won yet.

DONA ELENA: When I do I'll dance on your grave.

EL NEGRO: I ain't afraid of you. Everybody knows it. People laughin' at you 'cause you ain't got rid of me yet.

DONA ELENA *(to EL NEGRO)*: Just wait! *(EL NEGRO lets out a loud howl. To HURACAN:)* Your selfishness will cost you too, boy, mark my words! *Ay! Oficial?! Oficial?! (She exits.)*

EL NEGRO: You better go. She'll be back soon.

HURACAN: Which way did my *'amá's* train go?

EL NEGRO: That old spider has no compassion in her.

HURACAN: Will it come back?

EL NEGRO: *Andale!* Go!
(EL NEGRO exits quickly. HURACAN grabs as much bread as he can as the POLICE OFFICIAL races in. He is the same actor who plays MOISES: The POLICE OFFICIAL wears a mustache, a uniform and holds a revolver in one hand and a lantern in the other.)

POLICE OFFICIAL *(frightened)*: *Negro?* *(No answer.)* Oh, thank God. *(HURACAN tries to exit.)* Who's there?

HURACAN *(freezing)*: ...

POLICE OFFICIA:. Is that you, beggar boy? What have you done to *Doña Elena?* She's erupted like a volcano spewing curses at everyone. No one will sleep tonight. Beggar boy?

HURACAN: … *(HURACAN covers himself with the blanket. The POLICE OFFICIAL shines the light toward HURACAN.)*

POLICE OFFICIAL: Oh, forgive me, *Señora?* Or is *Señor?*

HURACAN: ...

POLICE OFFICIAL: *Ah, Señor! (HURACAN nods his head "Yes." From beneath HURACAN's blanket a piece of sweetbread falls to the ground. The POLICE OFFICIAL picks it up.* Suddenly:) What are you doing with *Don Porfirio's* sweetbread?! *(HURACAN accidentally drops more bread onto the ground.) Ay!* It can't be? Can it? *Don Porfirio?* Is that you?

HURACAN *(dropping his voice)*: *Sí.*

POLICE OFFICIAL: Sí! Of course it's you! It's the Day of the Dead. Are you well, Father?

HURACAN *(dropping his voice)*: No.

POLICE OFFICIAL *(to himself)*: No! You fool, how can he be well? He's dead! *(To HURACAN.)* I'm not use to talking to the dead, Father. Um, did you happen to see a beggar boy come this way?

HURACAN *(dropping his voice):* No.
(HURACAN begins to walk away as the bread he collected keeps falling to the ground.)

POLICE OFFICIAL: Wait! *(HURACAN freezes.)* You dropped this, Father. *(He hands HURACAN all the sweetbread.)*

HURACAN: *Gracias.*

POLICE OFFICIAL: *No hay de que.* Forgive me for disturbing your meal, FATHER. I mean no harm.

HURACAN: Boo!

POLICE OFFICIAL: *Ay! (The POLICE OFFICIAL exits out quickly. HURACAN exits the other way.)*

SCENE 3

"Butterfly sanctuary. Deep within the forest. The caterpillar finds a home.—Santuario de las mariposas. Un bosque, la oruga encuentra un hogar." EL NEGRO sits by a fire. He opens his suitcase. It glows from within. He senses something wrong. EL NEGRO closes his suitcase and picks up a large stick.

EL NEGRO *(calling out)*: Who's out there?

HURACAN: …

EL NEGRO: *Doña Elena?*

HURACAN: No.

EL NEGRO: Is that you, boy?

HURACAN: Yes.

EL NEGRO: How long you been there watchin'?

HURACAN: Forever.

EL NEGRO: What's your business?

HURACAN: I'm hungry. May I have something to eat?

EL NEGRO: I don't take freeloaders. What's you got to trade?

HURACAN: I can work for my food.

EL NEGRO *(laughing)*: You mean you gonna pull your own weight like a man? With them skinny arms?

HURACAN: What's wrong with my arms?

EL NEGRO: They skinny!
    (EL NEGRO coughs.)

HURACAN: Stop laughing at me! I don't need your help, old man! I can do this all by myself!

EL NEGRO: Then go! No one stoppin' you!

HURACAN: Okay, I'm goin'!
    (HURACAN stops.)

EL NEGRO: Well, I'm waitin'!

HURACAN: I'm real hungry!

EL NEGRO (*throws HURACAN some food*): Eat, boy. Then go!
(*Singing.*)
> **O, sit down, servant, sit down;**
> **O, sit down, servant...**

HURACAN: Why did that old woman beat me?

EL NEGRO: You probably had it comin'.

HURACAN: I didn't do nothing to her.

EL NEGRO: 'Cept steal her food.

HURACAN: I was hungry.

EL NEGRO: She's a nasty old crow. Dangerous too. Her name
is *Doña Elena*. Wealthiest woman in town. Owns everything
'cept these woods and she wants them too.

HURACAN: Why?

EL NEGRO: 'Cause she gotta possess everythin' there is. Take
my soul if she could. Cut them trees down and sell it as
lumber.

HURACAN: She called you a crazy gringo. Are you?

EL NEGRO: I can howl at the moon and make it disappear.

HURACAN: No, you can't. (*EL NEGRO howls. And the moon
disappears.*) How'd you do that?

EL NEGRO: That's a secret.

HURACAN: It's a stupid trick.

EL NEGRO: Ain't no trick. That's coyote talk. Where you from,
boy?

HURACAN: ... (*HURACAN crosses his arms.*)

EL NEGRO: Oh, so now you ain't talkin'?

HURACAN: ...

EL NEGRO: I bet you must be from California.

HURACAN: How do you know that?

EL NEGRO: 'Cause that attitude of yours is as big as that state. Gots to be California.

HURACAN: So what if I am?

EL NEGRO: That means you and me from Gringoland. You a long ways from home.

HURACAN: Me and my *'amá* got sent here.
(SOUND: A train is heard rolling through the night. A boxcar interior appears. KIKA enters. HURACAN joins her.)

KIKA: Huracán!

HURACAN: I'm right here, *'Amá.*

KIKA: Stay where I can see you.

HURACAN: Okay. Where's *'Apá?*

KIKA: He must be on another boxcar.
(She begins to cry softly.)

HURACAN: Are you crying, *'Amá?*

KIKA: No, my eyes are just tired. Go to sleep.
(Pause.)

HURACAN: Have you ever been on a train before, *'Amá?*

KIKA: No.

HURACAN: It's one of the most best things you can do. I mean, look out there?

KIKA: There's nothing to see.

HURACAN: The moon's out, *'Amá.* The earth has secrets. If you watch and listen she'll share them with you, remember? Look at the white clouds glow. You can see the shapes of family faces. See? There's *Nana Licha* ...

KIKA: You're right.

HURACAN: And *Tia Lupe.*

KIKA: And there's our *primo, Conejo.*

HURACAN & KIKA *(placing their fingers on their head and*

making rabbit ears): Rabbit cousin!

HURACAN: Riding a train isn't so bad, is it, *'Amá?*

KIKA: I guess not. Say a prayer to *San Martin.* (Sadly.) Happy twelfth birthday, *Huracán.*
(The boxcar fades away. HURACAN joins EL NEGRO.)

EL NEGRO: You got "Repatriated."
(He hands HURACAN some more food.)

HURACAN: What's that mean?

EL NEGRO: It means *los norte gringos* don't want you in their stinking country. That's why they sent you away.

HURACAN: But why would they send me here? Mexico isn't my country.

EL NEGRO: They in a "Depression." Country's broke.

HURACAN: I broke nothing.

EL NEGRO: Depression's made people crazy. Plenty of trains been comin' through *Misas* lately. Lots of folk. Steppin' outta them boxcars. Carryin' what they own. Old men, women and children all lookin' like they come outta the Bible. Like them Israelites leavin' Egypt. Searchin' for the Promised Land. 'Cept this ain't Egypt and they ain't got Moses.

HURACAN: Will you help me find my *'amá?*

EL NEGRO: Ain't my business. You got to learn to help yourself. Understand? But you best wait 'til *Doña Elena* forgets about you 'fore you go into town.
(EL NEGRO prepares to sleep near the fire. Sings.)
> **O, sit down, servant, sit down;**
> **Sit down and rest a little while.**

You snore?

HURACAN: No.

EL NEGRO: Good. You can sleep here tonight. But tomorrow you go.
(EL NEGRO lies down to sleep. So does HURACAN.)

739

HURACAN: *Señor?*

EL NEGRO: What?

HURACAN: Do you have anything else to eat?

SCENE 4

"The caterpillar becomes a chrysalis changing form and color.—La oruga se transforma en una crisálida, cambiando de forma y color." At the train station. SOUND: Voices from EL NEGRO's haunting past are heard. EL NEGRO stands holding his suitcase and a train ticket.

EL NEGRO: I can't do it. I can't get on. *(Pause.)* Yeah. Made them *Indios* a promise. Somebody's gotta look after them monarchs.
(He tears up the ticket. He coughs. The train departs. He exits as HURACAN rushes in picking up the torn pieces. He looks at it. SOUND: A train is heard. KIKA appears as a memory.)

KIKA: *Huracán!*
(She crosses to him.)

HURACAN: '*Amá?*

KIKA: Hold this.
(She places a handful of earth onto HURACAN's palm.)

HURACAN: What is it?

KIKA: Smell it!

HURACAN: Why?

KIKA: Do as I say!

HURACAN *(smells it)*. It's just dirt.

KIKA: It's more than that! Taste it!

HURACAN: No, '*Amá!*

KIKA: Do as I tell you!

HURACAN *(tastes the earth)*. Aagghh…

KIKA: This soil is from the valley you come from. You mustn't ever forget

HURACAN: I won't.
(He cleans his mouth.)

KIKA: You've tasted it. It's in your body now. Our valley will always be your home. No matter what happens. Remember. Promise me.

HURACAN: Okay, I promise. *(KIKA begins to back away.)* Where are you going, 'Amá?

KIKA: To look for your 'apá. Stay here.

HURACAN: Can't I go with you?

KIKA: I'll be right back. Everything is going to be fine.

HURACAN: How do you know?

KIKA: I just do.
(Lights fade.)

SCENE 5

"Walking among the sleeping monarchs.—Caminando entre las mariposas monarcas dormidas." The sun whispers in the night. EL NEGRO holds a dead butterfly in his palm.

EL NEGRO: *Mariposa*, you've traveled such a long way only to die. Was it worth it? (He buries the butterfly. He hears something off in the distance. He picks up his stick.) Who's out there?

HURACAN: …

EL NEGRO: Boy?

HURACAN: Yes.
(HURACAN enters.)

EL NEGRO: Why do you keep followin' me?

741

HURACAN: I don't like to be alone.

EL NEGRO: Come here. *(HURACAN comes closer.)* Closer. *(HURACAN crosses cautiously towards EL NEGRO.)* You don't spy on people 'cause they're gonna think you're a snake. And you know what happens to snakes?

HURACAN: They get hit?

EL NEGRO: They ain't got friends.
(EL NEGRO puts the stick down.)

HURACAN: Oh ...

EL NEGRO: Sit down. *(HURACAN sits on EL NEGRO's suitcase.)* Not there! That's my baggage!

HURACAN: What's in it?

EL NEGRO: Ghosts! You wanna see?

HURACAN *(afraid)*: Uh-uh!!

EL NEGRO: Them cousins are afraid of it too. Got powerful magic. *Doña Elena* lookin' to take it from me. But she can't 'cause I won't let her. Nobody comes near it. Understand?

HURACAN: I won't touch it.

EL NEGRO: Good. I suppose you want somethin' to eat?

HURACAN: I'll work for it.

EL NEGRO: You gonna pull your own weight?

HURACAN: I will.

EL NEGRO: There ain't gonna be no complainin'.

HURACAN: Okay.

EL NEGRO: I like my peace.
(They sit and eat.)

HURACAN: Why do you live here?
(EL NEGRO shoots him a look. Pause. He hands EL NEGRO some sweetbread.)

EL NEGRO: Where'd you get this?

HURACAN: I stole it.

EL NEGRO: Ain't right for a boy to steal.

HURACAN: Ain't right I'm in Mexico! Ain't right I've been beaten! Ain't right my *'amá's* gone!

EL NEGRO: Now, hold on there. All I'm sayin' is, it ain't right. That's all. A man's gotta do what he's gotta do.

HURACAN: Well, I'm doin' it!

EL NEGRO: You in a nasty mood. Man's gotta have himself a sense of humor. Be able to laugh at his self. It helps cut the pain, boy. Understand? It's good bread. Hard, but good. *(HURACAN shrugs his shoulders.)* Look up in them trees.

HURACAN: What are they?

EL NEGRO: Them's monarchs.

HURACAN: Monarch butterflies? What are they doing up there?

EL NEGRO: It's where they live. This here is *Santuario de las Mariposas.*

HURACAN: Is this where they come to?

EL NEGRO: Every year.

HURACAN: I wonder which one is mine?

EL NEGRO: What?

HURACAN: Why are they bunched together like that in the trees?

EL NEGRO: Maybe to keep warm. Maybe for protection.

HURACAN: There must be millions of them.

EL NEGRO: Wait 'til the sun warms them. It's a beautiful sight when they dance in the air. The *Indios* believe that the souls of the dead are carried up to heaven on the backs of butterflies. You think it's true? *(HURACAN shrugs his shoulders.)* I want to believe. Believe in somethin'.

HURACAN: I want to be eleven again.

EL NEGRO: Pretty soon their children will come out of them cocoons, dry their wings in the warm sun and start flyin' home.

HURACAN: I want to be in my home and my *'amá* waiting there for me. It's not fair! Why did this happen to me! I want everything back the way it was! I want to wake up in my bed ...

EL NEGRO: Listen here, boy ...

HURACAN: I hate Mexico!

EL NEGRO: There once was a butterfly who wanted to be a caterpillar. Yeah. You see, them seasons started changin' and lots of them monarchs got to dyin'. So the butterfly asked the great Creator to change him back to a caterpillar. The great Creator told him he was gonna give the butterfly a gift but he had to stay a butterfly. "You gonna carry the souls of the dead humans up to heaven. And your children and your children's children too." "But I want to be caterpillar again," said the monarch. "Let them other butterflies fly to heaven." Well, that butterfly got his wish and became a caterpillar once more. He was so happy he began dancin' 'cept he slipped off a leaf and landed right into a black spider's web. Bam! Never knew what hit him.

HURACAN: Why are you telling me this?

EL NEGRO: You can never go back. Our lives are measured by moments. And them moments change your life forever. Sometimes you gotta grow up sooner than you want. Gotta move on. Fact of life.

HURACAN: No! I don't want to be here!

EL NEGRO: This is all you got!

HURACAN: I don't want to be like you!

EL NEGRO: All you got is me!

HURACAN: No!

EL NEGRO: Your mama ain't comin' back!

HURACAN: I did what she told me! I waited for her!

EL NEGRO: Get it through your head!

744

HURACAN: Why didn't she come back for me?

EL NEGRO: Maybe she tried! Maybe the train never stopped!
Maybe —

HURACAN: Why didn't she come back?
*(HURACAN cries. EL NEGRO reaches out to comfort the boy
but stops himself.)*

EL NEGRO: You a *cabezon!* And lazy too!

HURACAN: What are you talking about?

EL NEGRO: Where's my wood? Said you was gonna get me
some. Man's gotta keep his word.

HURACAN: I ain't a man!

EL NEGRO: Well, I'm treatin' you like one. *(Starts coughing.)*
Get use to it.

HURACAN: That's blood.

EL NEGRO: Ain't nothin'! Now go get me my wood!

SCENE 6

*"The Black Widow spider spins her web.—La Viuda Negra
hila su telaraña." DONA ELENA sits near her husband's
tomb. She takes out a cigar.*

DONA ELENA: From the grave you do me no good, *Porfirio.*
Between all those cousins they can't capture one small boy
and a howling old man. Why are they all so afraid of him?
Stupid superstitious nincompoops. Magic spells, prayers and
potions are the poor's only answer to reality. I need someone
with intelligence, discretion and resourcefulness. Someone
desperate. Someone with needs. Someone with a bad habit.
*(THE ADDICT appears. He lights DONA ELENA's cigar. He
is the same actor who played the POLICE OFFICIAL.)*

THE ADDICT: You sent for me, *Doña Elena.*

DONA ELENA: I have work for you.

THE ADDICT: How wonderful it is to see you.

DONA ELENA: Be quiet. I want you to do a job for me. It must be done quickly and quietly.

THE ADDICT: What is it you ask?

DONA ELENA: Find a way to get *El Negro* and that boy off the mountain.

THE ADDICT: This will be very difficult. The land belongs to the *Indios*. *El Negro* is their friend. Besides he beats everyone who goes up there with a big stick.

DONA ELENA: I don't care how you do it! Just find a way. I won't be made a fool of. I hate that black man.

THE ADDICT: But you're Black.

DONA ELENA: No, I'm not. I'm Spanish.

THE ADDICT: You're part Black.

DONA ELENA: I'm Spanish I tell you!

THE ADDICT: But you're …

DONA ELENA: Shut up, *idiota! (She hits THE ADDICT with her cane.)* Now, find a way to get *El Negro* off my mountain! I want that land and that suitcase. They should belong to me.

THE ADDICT: What's in it?

DONA ELENA: It's not your concern. Something valuable only to me. Just bring it.

THE ADDICT: Revenge does have its price, *Doña.*

DONA ELENA: I see you have your father's knack for business and his addiction.

THE ADDICT: We all have our crosses to bear.

(DONA ELENA hands THE ADDICT money. They exit.)

SCENE 7

"Within the chrysalis a metamorphosis begins.—Dentro de la crisálida comienza una metamorfosis." HURACAN *and* EL NEGRO *sit by a campfire.* HURACAN *has grown out of his old clothes. He eats quickly.*

EL NEGRO: Slow down! You gonna get yourself sick!

HURACAN: But I'm hungry.

EL NEGRO: You're like them monarch caterpillars. They eat everythin' in sight. They called *orugas*. That's what you are. An *oruga!*

HURACAN: I ain't no *oruga!*

EL NEGRO: Well, you eat like one! You been growin' out of them clothes and eatin' everything in sight for the last few months. Pretty soon you gonna be growin' hair in places you never thought you could!

HURACAN: No, I'm not!

EL NEGRO: Voice is gonna drop. Face gonna get bumpy and you gonna have thoughts about them females.

HURACAN: Is that wrong?

EL NEGRO: Ain't nothin' wrong with it. It's nature's way of makin' you a man. Like them *orugas* becomin' monarchs.

HURACAN: I'm startin' to forget things.

EL NEGRO: What things?

HURACAN: My *'amá's* voice. My *'amá's* face.

EL NEGRO: Come spring them monarchs gonna leave. Under them milkweed plants they're growin' big. Changin' form. Preparin' themselves for the trip home. You think it's true them monarchs carry the souls of them dead humans to heaven?

HURACAN: I don't know. *(Two butterflies fall to the ground*

747

fighting.) Why do the monarchs fight like that?

EL NEGRO: You ever been in love?

HURACAN: I love my Mother.

EL NEGRO: That's not the same kind of love. See that male monarch is courtin' the female. They catch each other in the air and fall to the ground. Now, he'll try to woo her. And if she wants him she'll close her wings and he'll carry her to the tops of them trees and ...
(The monarchs fly away. EL NEGRO begins laughing.)

HURACAN *(disgusted)*: Ugghhh...

EL NEGRO: One day you gonna be just like this male. And hairy too!

HURACAN *(embarrassed)*: Ugghhh ...

EL NEGRO: Fact of life.

HURACAN: I wanna go home. Look for my *'amá* and *'apá.*

EL NEGRO: When I first come here, this was the only place I could stay. Now, it's the only place I wanna stay. This here is sacred land. Nature's church.

HURACAN: Don't you got any family?

EL NEGRO: Them monarchs are my family now.

HURACAN: There's no one?

EL NEGRO: No.
(SOUND: A train whistle is heard off in the distance.)

HURACAN: How come you always got that suitcase with you?

EL NEGRO: I told you. Me and that suitcase ain't your business.

HURACAN: You walk to the station. I see you.

EL NEGRO: Why you gotta do that?

HURACAN: Do what?

EL NEGRO: Get in my business?

HURACAN: 'Cause you wanna leave without me.

EL NEGRO: I'm still here, ain't I?

HURACAN: I see you standin' there, but you don't get on the train. What's stoppin' you?

EL NEGRO: Listen here, every man has got to have a code to guide him through life. A system of rules to live by. I call them my "Don'ts." "Don't let anybody know your business. Don't walk away from a fight. Don't borrow money if you can't pay it back and don't mess with people 'cause they might mess you up." These been my guiding principles through life. You best learn it!

HURACAN: Then how do I get home?

EL NEGRO: Home?

HURACAN: What'da I gotta do?

EL NEGRO: You got a train ticket?

HURACAN: No!

EL NEGRO: You got any money?

HURACAN: No!

EL NEGRO: Then you outta luck!
    (EL NEGRO coughs.)

HURACAN: You coughing up blood again.

EL NEGRO: 'Cause it's a curse.

HURACAN: Was it *Doña Elena?*

EL NEGRO: It was long before her. Another lifetime. Things I wish I could change but can't.
    (Singing.)
> **Hush, hush,**
> **Somebody's calling my name,**
> **Hush, hush,**
> **Somebody's calling my name,**

HURACAN: Did you do something bad?

EL NEGRO: Ain't no one gonna forgive what I done.

HURACAN: You can't go back, can you?

EL NEGRO *(singing)*:
O, my Lord,
O, my Lord,
What shall I do?

HURACAN: Guardin' them monarchs is your penance, ain't it?

SCENE 8

"The dreams of butterflies.—Los sueños de las mariposas."
Dawn. SOUND: Voices from EL NEGRO's past are
heard once again. HURACAN and EL NEGRO sleep by a
smoldering fire. THE ADDICT sneaks in quietly. He opens
his knife.

EL NEGRO *(in his sleep)*: Snake eye starin' at me. Don't! Ain't
gettin onboard. No! Ain't afraid of no man. Beast. Night.
Snake eye. No! *(THE ADDICT picks up EL NEGRO's*
suitcase and opens it with his knife. The suitcase glows. He
smiles. HURACAN awakens seeing THE ADDICT.)

EL NEGRO *(in his sleep)*: Ain't my time. No! Stay away.

THE ADDICT *(startled, mocking EL NEGRO)*: *El Diablo*, huh!
(He crosses to finish EL NEGRO off. HURACAN howls,
throwing his blanket over THE ADDICT. Frightened:) El
Diablo! (THE ADDICT drops the suitcase and runs off.)

HURACAN: Wake up, old man!

EL NEGRO: What is it?

HURACAN: Are you all right?

EL NEGRO: What's goin' on?

HURACAN: Somebody tried takin' your suitcase, but I scared
him away. Just like you show me.
(HURACAN howls.)

EL NEGRO: Was it one of them cousins?

HURACAN: I think so.

EL NEGRO: That old crow is gettin' desperate. Ain't no tellin' what she'll do. You better be careful.

HURACAN: They can't catch me. I'm too fast. I'm a coyote! *(HURACAN howls. EL NEGRO starts to cough.)* You're coughin' up more blood.

EL NEGRO: I got consumption. Tuberculosis.

HURACAN: Is it bad?

EL NEGRO: Ain't good.

HURACAN: Are you gonna die?

EL NEGRO: Hell no!

HURACAN: I'm just askin'.

EL NEGRO: I ain't dead yet. So don't you try buryin' me 'fore my time. I gots too much fight in me yet. (He coughs again.) Bring that blanket here! And put some more wood on that fire!

HURACAN: Okay!
(He picks up the blanket, and throws it at EL NEGRO.)

SCENE 9

"The spider captures her prey. —La araña atrapa a su victima." The police station walls are filled with massive cracks as if a great weight rests on them. HURACAN's hands are tied and he is dragged in by the POLICE OFFICIAL: The POLICE OFFICIAL is the same actor who plays THE ADDICT. He is eating some chocolate candy.

POLICE OFFICIAL: Come here, boy! You're one of those *deportados*, aren't you? Thousands have been coming through town. It hasn't been this busy since *Pancho Villa* and the entire revolution rode through!
(DONA ELENA enters.)

POLICE OFFICIAL: *Doña Elena*, good morning. I found the beggar boy! I found him wandering around looking at girls.

751

DONA ELENA: Shut up! You dishonor your father. Look at you. Stay out of the sun. And lose some weight.

POLICE OFFICIAL: *Sí, Doña.*

DONA ELENA: Beggar boy, stealing from the dead and assaulting me on a holy day has its consequences.

HURACAN: That was a long time ago.

DONA ELENA: Eleven months. Twelve days. Six hours. Thirty-one seconds. I've burned you into my memory. One of my husband's sons is the town judge. He'll throw you in jail. I could see to it!

HURACAN: I don't want to go to jail.

POLICE OFFICIAL: But you're already in jail!

DONA ELENA: Shut up! Turn around and cover your ears! This conversation doesn't concern you!

POLICE OFFICIAL: *Sí, Doña Elena. (The POLICE OFFICIAL turns around and covers his ears.)* Tell me, why does *El Negro* hate me?

HURACAN: …

DONA ELENA: We used to be friends.

HURACAN: …

DONA ELENA: You know, when *El Negro* came to *Misas* we offered him a job. He took our money and betrayed us. My poor husband went to his grave because he was so heartbroken. He left me all alone just like you.

HURACAN: May I go now?

DONA ELENA: You poor boy. By yourself without a mother. How terrifying it must be.

HURACAN: I can take care of myself.

DONA ELENA: Of course you can. If you were my child I would never have left you. I couldn't live with myself.

HURACAN: Well, maybe my *'amá* tried.

DONA ELENA: Maybe ...

HURACAN: And maybe she's still looking for me.

DONA ELENA: Maybe, but if she really loved you, don't you think she would have found you by now?

HURACAN: …

DONA ELENA: But look how you've survived? You've triumphed over adversity. I admire that quality. It's sadly lacking in this town. You and I are very similar. We'll fight to survive.

HURACAN: It's not easy.

DONA ELENA: No one can appreciate the sacrifice but us. (She caresses his face.) Would you like a piece of candy?

HURACAN: Okay.

DONA ELENA: *Oficial! (The POLICE OFFICIAL doesn't hear her.) Oficial!! (He still doesn't hear her.) Oficial!!! (DONA ELENA strikes the POLICE OFFICIAL: He uncovers his ears and turns around.)*

POLICE OFFICIAL: Ouch!! *Sí, Doña Elena?*

DONA ELENA: Why do these *tontos* all torment me?

POLICE OFFICIAL: I'm sorry, *Doña.*

DONA ELENA: Be quiet and give me a piece of chocolate.

POLICE OFFICIAL: But it's my last piece.

DONA ELENA: Give it to me! *(She reaches out and takes the candy from the POLICE OFFICIAL: To HURACAN:)* Ay, Pobrecito. *(HURACAN begins eating the chocolate candy.)* Is it good?

HURACAN: Ah huh.

DONA ELENA: Tell me, does *El Negro* ever talk about leaving?

HURACAN: Sometimes. I tell him he should go back home with me, but then he talks about his ghosts.

POLICE OFFICIAL: Ghosts? What ghosts?

HURACAN: They're in his suitcase. I'm not supposed to touch it.

DONA ELENA: His ghosts are a great burden. His soul riddled with pain. You see, he has a very dark secret.

HURACAN: What secret?

DONA ELENA: Hasn't he told you?

HURACAN: No.

DONA ELENA: It's in his suitcase. He's never without it. Tell me, do you miss your home?

HURACAN: Yes.

DONA ELENA: Your *'amá* could be there waiting for you, do you think? I bet she would be so happy to see you. I could help you, you know?

HURACAN: Help me?

DONA ELENA: Look what I've got for you.
(She holds up a train pass.)

HURACAN: What is it?

DONA ELENA: A train ticket.

HURACAN: For me?

DONA ELENA: Yes. Just think, you could be with your *'amá. El Negro* at peace with himself.

POLICE OFFICIAL: And you'll have the suitcase!

DONA ELENA: Shut up, *idiota! (The POLICE OFFICIAL covers his ears. To HURACAN:)* All you have to do is bring *El Negro's* suitcase to me. Just pick it up and walk away. It's so simple. What do you say?
(HURACAN holds out his bound hands. DONA ELENA hits the POLICE OFFICIAL.)

POLICE OFFICIAL: Ouch!

DONA ELENA: Untie him. *(The POLICE OFFICIAL unties HURACAN's hands.)* Would you like another piece of candy?
(She smiles.)

SCENE 10

"The monarch chooses. — La monarca hace su decision."
Santuario de las mariposas. SOUND: A coyote's howl is
heard off in the distance. HURACAN enters. The forest casts
dark shadows.

HURACAN: Old man? *(Pause.)* Are you here? *(HURACAN*
picks up the suitcase. SOUND: A distant train is heard. EL
NEGRO enters wrapped in a blanket and carrying some
wood. He appears frail. HURACAN doesn't see him. EL
NEGRO watches as HURACAN stands there deciding what to
do. HURACAN places the suitcase back.) I can't do it. I can't.

EL NEGRO: She put you up to it?

HURACAN: …

EL NEGRO: Why didn't you take it?

HURACAN: What's in it?

EL NEGRO: My life. *Doña Elena* thinks I still got her money,
but I don't. I give it away to them *Indios* long ago, 'cause
they was starvin'. I ruined her plans. Now, you too. She ain't
gonna be too happy 'bout this.

HURACAN: I won't go back into town.

EL NEGRO: Won't matter. She'll find you.

HURACAN: I ain't afraid of her.

EL NEGRO: But you should be. There's no tellin' what she's
gonna do now. It's time for you to go.

HURACAN: Go where?

EL NEGRO: Anyplace, but here.

HURACAN: I can't leave you.

EL NEGRO: Don't you see? It ain't safe. I can't protect you no
more.

HURACAN: Then come back with me!

EL NEGRO: I can't.

HURACAN: Why not?

EL NEGRO: I can't go back.

HURACAN: I ain't leavin' you.

EL NEGRO: Pack your things and go!

HURACAN: We's friends!

EL NEGRO: I ain't your friend! Don't wanna be your friend!
Ain't never had a friend. You just in the way.

HURACAN: No, I'm not!

EL NEGRO: And I'm through carrying you! So go!

HURACAN *(crying)*. But we's friends!

EL NEGRO: Get outta here! Get!
(HURACAN exits.)

SCENE 11

*"The spider attacks.—La araña ataca." DONA ELENA and
the UNDERTAKER-BARBER enter. The UNDERTAKER-
BARBER is played by the same actor who plays the POLICE
OFFICIAL: He carries a shovel. They surprise EL NEGRO.*

DONA ELENA: *Viejo Negro!*

EL NEGRO: So the black widow spider's finally come?

DONA ELENA: Is that how you treat an old friend, *Negro?*

EL NEGRO: What do you want?

DONA ELENA: Perhaps the Undertaker-Barber could help you
understand what I want? I finally found someone who isn't
afraid of you. He even brought his own shovel!

UNDERTAKER-BARBER: Agghhh!
*(The UNDERTAKER-BARBER lunges at EL NEGRO holding
the shovel to his throat. HURACAN runs in.)*

HURACAN: Let him go!

DONA ELENA: You don't give orders here. I do!

756

(She hits HURACAN with her cane.)

HURACAN: Ouch!

DONA ELENA: We had a deal, *Cucaracha*, and you betrayed me. You should've left while you had the chance. Now you'll never see your Mother. (She tears up the train ticket.) She'll wander the earth like *La Llorona* crying and tearing out her hair! *"Mijo! Mijo!" (To EL NEGRO.)* And you, *Negro*, we offered you a job, respect, wealth and you refused!

EL NEGRO: You wanted me to burn this forest!

HURACAN: He wouldn't do that!

DONA ELENA: He's done far worse!

EL NEGRO *(to DONA ELENA)*: I ain't that man no more!

DONA ELENA: Tell him, *Negro!* Tell him the truth why you can't go back to your own country. No matter how many times you've tried getting on board a train, you can't. Tell him why you're so afraid.

HURACAN: He ain't afraid of nothin'!

DONA ELENA: Then let me enlighten you, *Cucaracha.* Your patron saint of butterflies is a wanted man. A dead man. His ghosts are there waiting him.

EL NEGRO: Don't you say nothin'!

DONA ELENA: He won't tell you his terrible dark secret.

HURACAN: It don't matter!

DONA ELENA: But it does. He set a house on fire in your country.

EL NEGRO: Don't you believe her!

DONA ELENA *(mocking him)*: He had been wronged. Mistreated. His pride demanded revenge so he burned it to the ground. But in that house children were sleeping.

HURACAN: Children?

EL NEGRO: She ain't tellin' you everythin'!

DONA ELENA: Five little angels tucked away in their beds.

EL NEGRO: I was after the man who done me wrong!

DONA ELENA: He drenched the whole house with gasoline.

EL NEGRO: He stole my land. Burned my crops!

DONA ELENA: Lit a match and the whole house went up in flames. They couldn't get out. Only their cries got out. Calling for their mommy.

HURACAN: Is it true?

DONA ELENA: Tell him!

EL NEGRO: They wasn't supposed to be there!

HURACAN: How could you do that?

EL NEGRO: They wasn't supposed to be there!

DONA ELENA: Those little angels went to heaven and *El Diablo* ran away.

EL NEGRO: I ain't that man no more.
(He coughs up blood.)

DONA ELENA: Oh, how it breaks my heart to see you so disappointed, *Cucaracha*. But revenge tastes sweetest when sprinkled with tears.

UNDERTAKER-BARBER: We're going to be rich!

DONA ELENA: Shut up! *(To HURACAN.)* Get me that suitcase, boy!

HURACAN: No!

EL NEGRO: Do as she says.

HURACAN: It ain't right. It belongs to you.

EL NEGRO: I don't want it no more. Too many ghosts.

UNDERTAKER-BARBER *(to DONA ELENA)*: Ghosts?

HURACAN: Yeah, ghosts ... *(HURACAN crosses to pick up the suitcase.)* And devils too!
(He suddenly throws the suitcase at the UNDERTAKER-BARBER scaring him away. HURACAN howls.)

758

UNDERTAKER-BARBER: *Ay, que susto! El Diablo!*

DONA ELENA: Come back, *idiota!*
(The UNDERTAKER-BARBER runs off. HURACAN chases after him. DONA ELENA picks up the shovel.)

DONA ELENA: Coward! Just like your Father! I should've done this myself long ago!

EL NEGRO: Whatcha doin'?

DONA ELENA: Taking what belongs to me! I'll have it all!
(She scoops up hot coals from the fire.)

EL NEGRO: No, you can't do that!

DONA ELENA: Watch me!
(She throws the hot coals onto the trees.)

EL NEGRO: You settin' the trees on fire!

DONA ELENA: No one cheats me!

EL NEGRO: The whole forest is gonna burn!

HURACAN *(entering)*: No!
(HURACAN charges DONA ELENA trying to stop her but she holds the shovel threateningly.)

DONA ELENA: Not so fast, *amigito!*

EL NEGRO *(weakened)*: I gotta save them monarchs!
(He tries to stomp out the fire with a blanket.)

DONA ELENA: You selfish boy! You had your chance! *(She picks up the suitcase, but HURACAN grabs it at the same time. They fight for it.)* Let go! It belongs to me!

HURACAN: No, it don't!

DONA ELENA: Let go before we all die! *(SOUND: A tree is heard exploding, startling DONA ELENA. She drops the suitcase. Exiting.) Ay!* Go ahead and burn *El Negro.* Burn like those children! I'll see you in hell!
(EL NEGRO howls.)

EL NEGRO: Wake up, *mariposas!*

(HURACAN joins EL NEGRO howling.)

HURACAN: Fly *mariposas!* Fly!

EL NEGRO: Get up and fly away! Fly!
(SOUND: Another tree explodes.)

HURACAN: We got to get out of here!

EL NEGRO: No, leave me!

HURACAN: We gotta go! Now!
(He leads EL NEGRO out as the flames engulf the forest.)

SCENE 12

"A chrysalis splits open and a new monarch emerges. —La crisálida se abre y brota una nueva mariposa monarca." La frontera — Somewhere near the American border. A full moon. And two shadows appear.

HURACAN *(singing):*
> **Couldn't hear nobody pray**
> **Couldn't hear nobody pray...**

EL NEGRO: Come on, old man!

HURACAN & EL NEGRO *(singing):*
> **Oh, I'm just a way down yonder by myself**
> **And I couldn't hear nobody pray.**
(EL NEGRO falls to his knees. His breathing is labored.)

EL NEGRO: We in the states now. We through walkin'.

HURACAN: I thought there'd be fences, walls, men with guns and badges.

EL NEGRO: Not when we walk across. Gonna travel first class.

HURACAN *(proudly)*: I still got your suitcase.

EL NEGRO: I was hopin' you'd leave it. *(SOUND: A train whistle.)* There's our ride.

HURACAN: We ain't got no tickets.

EL NEGRO: Don't need none. We gonna ride hobo style. Now

listen here, we got to be careful of them yard bulls.

HURACAN: Yard bulls?

EL NEGRO: They don't take to freeloaders on their trains. If they come chasin' after you, you run like hell. Them yard bulls carry guns and sticks. They ain't gonna ask questions.

HURACAN: When do we go?

EL NEGRO: What's you in such a hurry for?

HURACAN: I wanna get home. Find my *'amá* and my *'apá*.

EL NEGRO: We ain't goin' nowhere 'til that train moves. Hoboin' is about waitin'. Waitin' for the right moment. When that highball signals that's when we go. Gonna have to run fast and hard. Somewhere between the hog and crummy we gotta find ourselves an empty car.

HURACAN: Hog and crummy?

EL NEGRO: Hog's the locomotive. Crummy's the caboose. Highball is the whistle signalin' the train's leavin'. Do I gotta tell you everythin'?

HURACAN: Do you think them butterflies made it out?

EL NEGRO: Them monarchs got special magic. They fragile but they got a will to survive. They gonna be all right.

HURACAN: Like us?

EL NEGRO: That's right.

HURACAN: Them children ...

EL NEGRO: What children? ... Oh ... I never meant to hurt them children but I did. I carry their cries wherever I go. And there ain't day that goes by but I don't wish it was me in that house instead of them. I'm sorry, boy. I'm sorry for all the bad I done.

HURACAN: You think them children went to heaven?

EL NEGRO: I don't know.

HURACAN: I bet they did.

EL NEGRO: How do you figure?

HURACAN: Well, them monarch butterflies could've carried their souls up to heaven. And if they in heaven then their souls must be angels.

EL NEGRO: Angels?

HURACAN: And if they's angels then they can forgive.

EL NEGRO: Why would they forgive me?

HURACAN: 'Cause your butterflies carried them there.

EL NEGRO: You really believe that? *(SOUND: A train whistle is heard. EL NEGRO coughs.)* It's time for you to go!

HURACAN: Ain't you comin'?

EL NEGRO: I'll only hold you up. Go!

HURACAN: I ain't leavin' without you!

EL NEGRO: You gonna miss your train!

HURACAN: I ain't leavin' you!

EL NEGRO: Why you gotta argue with me?

HURACAN: 'Cause you a *cabezon!*

EL NEGRO: *Cabezon?*

HURACAN: That's right!

EL NEGRO: Wait 'til I get my hands on you!

HURACAN: Gotta catch me first, *cabezon! Cabezon!*
(EL NEGRO chases after HURACAN: They exit.)

SCENE 13

"The monarchs search for home. —Las mariposas monarcas buscan su hogar." Lights flicker as the train rumbles through the desert. HURACAN and EL NEGRO are in a boxcar. EL NEGRO lies on the floor. His breathing is heavy. HURACAN holds the suitcase. EL NEGRO inhales the night air.

HURACAN: What are you doing, old man?

EL NEGRO: It smells sweet, don't it?

HURACAN: What does?

EL NEGRO: Gringoland.
(He coughs. HURACAN inhales the air.)

HURACAN: We ridin' through the night, hobo style.

EL NEGRO: There ain't no borders for butterflies.

HURACAN & EL NEGRO: We's butterflies.

HURACAN: How much longer is it gonna take?

EL NEGRO: If we lucky. Couple more days.
(Something stirs in the boxcar. HURACAN picks up a stick.)

HURACAN: Who's there?

EL NEGRO: Be careful.
(TWO HOBOES step out of the shadows, It is a husband and wife. They are the same actors who played KIKA and MOISES.)

HUSBAND. Forgive us, *Señores,* we mean you no harm. My wife and I are hungry. Do you have anything to eat?

HURACAN: We got plenty. *(EL NEGRO starts to laugh.)* What's you laughing at, old man?

EL NEGRO: You a walkin' grocery store! You'll never go hungry.

HURACAN: That's right, I've learned.
(He gives the HUSBAND and WIFE some food.)

WIFE. Thank you. *(HURACAN stares at the WIFE for a moment.)* What is it?

HURACAN: You remind me of someone.

WIFE. Who?

HURACAN: Someone I once knew.
(EL NEGRO coughs deeply. The WIFE touches EL NEGRO's face.)

HUSBAND. *El Señor* looks very ill.

HURACAN: He's gonna be all right.

WIFE. He has a fever.

HURACAN: No, he's just tired. That's all.
   (The HUSBAND takes his blanket and places it on EL NEGRO.)

EL NEGRO: My lungs feel like they on fire. *(To the HUSBAND.)* Who are you?

HUSBAND. My name is *Gabriel*. This is my wife, *Esperanza*.

WIFE. *Hola.*

EL NEGRO *(to HUSBAND)*. I seen you before. You from *Misas?*

HUSBAND. Oh, no, but I have lots of cousins there. We're heading north like you.

WIFE. Back to our home. We were sent away.

EL NEGRO: What's you got there?

HUSBAND. It's my *guitarra*. I can play something for you? Would *el Señor* like to hear something?

EL NEGRO: Play me somethin' sweet.
   (The HUSBAND plays his guitar softly. A monarch butterfly gently floats into the boxcar and lands on HURACAN's hand.)

HURACAN: Where did you come from, little fella? Lookin' for a free ride, huh? Hobo butterfly. You can rest here all you want. *(EL NEGRO coughs.)* We almost home.

SCENE 14

"The monarch butterfly returns.—La mariposa monarca regresa." HURACAN enters carrying EL NEGRO.

EL NEGRO: Gotta catch my breath.

HURACAN *(singing)*.
> **Roll, Jordan, roll; roll, Jordan, roll—**

EL NEGRO: Put me down.

HURACAN *(singing)*.
> **I want to go to heaven when I die,**
> **To hear ole' Jordan roll.**

EL NEGRO: Please.

HURACAN: All right. But just for a while.
(He places EL NEGRO on the ground.)

EL NEGRO: How come you in such a hurry?

HURACAN: I just am.

EL NEGRO: What's so special about today?

HURACAN: It's my birthday. I'll never be twelve again.
(El valle—The valley. A barn sitting on the edge of a green field appears.)

HURACAN *(discovering)*. We're here. Home. *(He searches.)*
'Amá? 'Apá? 'Amá?

EL NEGRO: They ain't here?

HURACAN: 'Amá? 'Apá?

EL NEGRO: I'm sorry, boy.

HURACAN: Maybe they waitin' somewhere else for me.

EL NEGRO: Maybe …

HURACAN: Maybe I gotta just keep lookin'.

EL NEGRO: Maybe.
(He coughs deeply.)

HURACAN *(panicked)*. I can't do this alone. You gotta help me!

EL NEGRO: You gonna be fine, boy.

HURACAN: How do you know?

EL NEGRO: 'Cause I just do.

HURACAN: That's what my *'amá* once said and she never came

765

back. *(EL NEGRO coughs deeply.)* Don't you quit on me, old man!

EL NEGRO *(proudly)*: My name's Benjamin Price.
(HURACAN opens EL NEGRO's hand and places some dirt in it.)

HURACAN: This is dirt, Benjamin Price. You hold it tight. This is gonna be our home.

EL NEGRO: Home.
(Coughs deeply.)

HURACAN: Promise me you ain't gonna give up?

EL NEGRO: Do you see them?

HURACAN: See what?

EL NEGRO: Them monarchs!

HURACAN *(looks around, but there are no monarchs).* I don't see anythin'.

EL NEGRO: Sure you do.

HURACAN: Where are they?

EL NEGRO: They all around you. Do you think they comin' for me?

HURACAN: "Don't walk away from a fight!" Remember your code!

EL NEGRO: So this is where they come to?

HURACAN: "Man's gotta pull his own weight!"

EL NEGRO: Look at them, circlin' all around me!

HURACAN: Get angry and fight!

EL NEGRO: There must be thousands of 'em.

HURACAN: Fight.

EL NEGRO: Ain't that a beautiful sight?

HURACAN: Please don't leave me!

EL NEGRO: Don't you see 'em? Don't you see 'em, son?

(Coughs deeply.)

HURACAN: Yeah, I see 'em. Maybe we gotta feed them hungry butterflies, huh?

EL NEGRO: I can feel them lifting me up!

HURACAN: Dampen the earth with fresh water so the flowers will be strong.

EL NEGRO: They carryin' me up over the trees.

HURACAN: Feed them *mariposas* sweet nectar.

EL NEGRO: Up mountains. Past clouds.

HURACAN: A glimpse at God's heart.

EL NEGRO: To the highest heaven.

HURACAN: Fly! Benjamin Price. Fly!

EL NEGRO *(laughs)*. It tickles…
    (He dies.)

HURACAN: Benjamin Price?
    (SOUND: The Negro spiritual heard at the opening of the play is introduced once again. HURACAN covers EL NEGRO with a blanket. He crosses to EL NEGRO's suitcase and opens it. It glows brightly. He smiles as hundreds of monarch butterflies emerge from it fluttering everywhere. HURACAN closes the suitcase. He picks it up and looks off into the horizon.)

HURACAN: I can do it. I can do it.
    ("The journey begins.—El viaje venturoso comienza.")

END OF PLAY

GLOSSARY

Andale: Go on!

'Amá: Mother.

Amigito: Little friend.

'Apá: Father

Ay, que susto!: Oh, what fright!

Cabezon: Knucklehead, hardheaded.

Chocolate: Chocolate candy.

Cucaracha: Cockroach.

Conejo: Rabbit.

Dia de los muertos: Day of the Dead: A holiday which blends the pre-Hispanic Aztec beliefs honoring the dead with the Catholic Church's All Saints' and All Souls' Days (November 1 and 2).

Deportados: Those who are deported.

El Diablo: The Devil.

Gringo: A North American citizen.

Guitarra: Guitar.

Idiota: Idiot.

Imposible: Impossible.

Indio: Indian.

La Llorona: The Weeping Woman. A legend having this ghostly woman wandering along canals and rivers crying for her missing children. Told to frighten children into behaving.

Mariposa: Butterfly.

Mijo: My son.

Monarca: Monarch butterfly.

Muchacho: Boy.

Nana: Grandmother.

No hay de que: You're welcome; don't mention it.

Oruga: Caterpillar.

Pobrecito: Poor little one.

Primo: Cousin.

Querido: My love.

Santuario de las Mariposas: Butterfly Sanctuary

Señor: Mister, Gentleman.

Señora: Madam, Lady.

Sí: Yes.

Tia: Aunt.

Toma: Here.

Tontos: Dummies.

Viejo Negro: Old Black Man.

THE
WRESTLING SEASON

A play

by
Laurie Brooks

Matt:
"I don't want to be hated for something I'm not."

Kori:
"Imagine what it would be like to be hated for what you are."

The Wrestling Season premiered at the Coterie Theatre in Kansas City, MO in January 2000. The play quickly generated wide interest across the theatre community; and, in November 2000, the script was published in *American Theatre* magazine, the journal serving nonprofit professional theatre artists across the country.

In the play, Brooks probes deeply into the intense emotional world of adolescent sexual identity, peer relations, and personal conflicts. She creates an innovative form that theatrically incorporates the metaphors of competitive high school wrestling to frame the action; and with this style she theatrically highlights the tensions between the characters. Issues of homosexuality and homophobic reactions, stirred by rumor and innuendo, constitute some of the more vivid elements of the play, but the core of the action rests in the varied identity conflicts addressed by all the major characters. Brooks sums this up through a refrain offered several times throughout the play by various characters: "You think you know me but you don't."

Brooks includes a "Post Performance Forum" with the play, to enhance the audience experience. While she notes that the play can be performed on its own, the Forum builds on the emotions and ideas generated by the play by moving the audience members from passive spectators to participants in a discourse of these ideas. This allows the spectators to extend their personal and private reactions to a more public sphere, and thus to grapple with these difficult ideas within the context of the sometimes conflicting perspectives of their peers (other members of the audience).

Like any good play, *The Wrestling Season* plays well to a wide range of audiences; but, in contrast to most of the plays in this anthology, it presents adolescent characters embroiled in issues particularly relevant to adolescents. Few theatres perform plays written specifically for this age group, as this segment of theatre audiences seems caught between TYA companies who work primarily for children, and regional theatres who program for adult audiences. As the field has diversified over the last decade, several playwrights, with Brooks prominent among them, have sought to create plays that resonate truthfully with young adults. This, in turn, has had a significant effect on the culture of theatre for young audiences, as an increasing number of professional theatres are now seriously working to serve this age group.

From most perspectives it appears a long developmental journey over the one hundred years from *The Little Princess* to *The Wrestling Season;* but each play reflects the theatrical sensibilities and cultural resonances of their respective times. Where *The Little Princess* offered young people, from a singular, authoritative perspective, a melodramatic model of proper Victorian behavior, *The Wrestling Season* consciously explores the multiple moral conflicts students confront in the tumultuous high school culture. While Burnett assumed a relatively passive audience, seeking entertainment divorced from their everyday lives, Brooks assumes an inquisitive audience, interested in interrogating the realities presented on the stage. Both the play and the Forum that follows it honor that audience in not offering simple answers to the difficult questions posed.

The Wrestling Season reflects the theatrical sophistication of that new generation of plays for young audiences nurtured in the professional theatres. Within a fluid, theatrical form, Brooks explores personal issues lived by contemporary young people, and she explores them without melodrama, didacticism, or happy endings. She also presents these ideas and situations with frankness rarely seen in even the contemporary dramatic literature for young people.

Laurie Brooks is currently a Professor and Playwright–in–Residence at New York University's Program in Educational Theatre, and Playwright–in–Residence at The Coterie Theatre in Kansas City, MO. She also serves as a site reporter for The National Endowment for the Arts. Brooks is a member of The Dramatists Guild.

Brooks's *Lies and Deceptions Quartet* for young adults includes *The Wrestling Season*, *Deadly Weapons* (which was nominated for a Leon Rabin Award for best new play in Dallas, 2002), *The Tangled Web* (which received an AT&T: Firststage Award from Theatre Communications Group), and *Everyday Heroes* (which was commissioned and premiered at The Kennedy Center Imagination Celebration and Salt Lake City in conjunction with the 2002 Winter Olympic Games). Other award-winning plays include *Selkie*, *Devon's Hurt*, *The Match Girl's Gift*, *Franklin's Apprentice*, and *A Laura Ingalls Wilder Christmas*.

Brooks's plays for young audiences have been commissioned, developed and produced at Graffiti Theatre Company, Cork, Ireland; The Coterie Theatre, Kansas City, MO; The Kennedy Center; Indiana Repertory Theatre; Seattle Children's Theatre; Stage One: The Louisville Children's Theatre; Nashville Children's Theatre; Dallas Children's Theater; Arden Theatre in Philadelphia; and The Provincetown Playhouse in New York.

She has received two AATE Distinguished Play Awards and the 2003 Charlotte Chorpenning Cup for a distinguished body of work for young people.

THE
WRESTLING SEASON

A play

by
Laurie Brooks

775

THE WRESTLING SEASON

THE DRAMATIC PUBLISHING COMPANY of Woodstock, Illinois

777

For Joanna
Brave and Beautiful
and
For Jeff Church
Who made the play and the playwright stronger

ACKNOWLEDGMENTS

For support and nourishment, my love and appreciation to Jeff Church, Leigh Miller, the fabulous UMKC cast, Brooke, Joette and the entire Coterie Theatre family, The Children's Theatre Foundation of America, John Shorter, Manhasset High School Theatre Department, Peter Guastella, Manhasset High School wrestling coach, Phillip John Kinen and the Shawnee Mission High School Theatre Department, The Kennedy Center's New Visions/New Voices 1998, Mary Hall Surface, Lowell Swortzell and the New York University Program in Educational Theatre's Summer Reading Series at The Provincetown Playhouse 1999, clinical psychologist Sidney Horowitz, novelist John Irving, and especially my daughters, Joanna, Liz and Stephanie.

The Wrestling Season was developed at The Kennedy Center's 1998 New Visions/New Voices: A Forum for New Works in Progress for Young Audiences, and the New York University Program in Educational Theatre's Summer Reading Series at The Provincetown Playhouse, 1999.

The Wrestling Season was featured at New Visions 2000/One Theatre World, a National Festival of Theatre for Young people and Families at The Kennedy Center, Washington, D.C.

Laurie Brooks was the recipient of a 1999 Aurand Harris grant to The Coterie for *The Wrestling Season*, awarded by The Children's Theatre Foundation of America.

The Wrestling Season was developed and featured at the 1998 New Visions/New Voices: A Forum for New Plays-in-Progress for Young Audiences, at The John F. Kennedy Center in Washington, D.C., May 1998. The production was directed by Jeff Church. It was commissioned by The Coterie Theatre, Kansas City, Missouri.

CAST

Jolt	TOM COSTELLO
Willy	REGGIE HARRIS
Luke	ANDREAS KRAEMER
Matt	LAFONTAINE ELITE OLIVER
Melanie	BONNIE WAGGONER
Heather	JODY FLADER
Nicole	RISA GREEN
Kori	MEGAN GILBRIDE
Referee	MATT SAWYER

THE WRESTLING SEASON

PRODUCTION STAFF

DEREK E. GORDON..................... Vice President for Education, Executive Producer

KIM PETER KOVAC .... Program Manager, Youth and Family Programs, New Visions/New Voices Producer

DIEDRE KELLY LAVRAKAS ..Production Operations Manager NV/NV Casting Director/Production Manager

JOHN "SCOOTER" KRATTENMAKER .... Stage Manager

In 1999, *The Wrestling Season* was further developed at New York University, School of Education, Department of Music and Performing Arts Professions Program in Educational Theatre and presented at Staged Readings of New Plays for Young Audiences, The Provincetown Playhouse, New York, N.Y. The production was directed by Jeff Church and included the following artists:

CAST

Matt .... SHANNON GANNON
Luke .... JOHN JEFFREY MARTIN
Willy.. GERARD T. SCOTT
Jolt.. DENNIS WALTERS
Heather .... LAUREN O'BRIEN
Nicole .... MARIA ELENA LOPEZ-FRANK
Melanie .... SIDNEY AUSTIN
Kori .... AMANDA RAFUSE
Referee .... JIM GROLLMAN
Stage Directions .... DANA LEVIN

PRODUCTION STAFF

Producer .... JEFF KENNEDY
Stage Manager .... JOHN DEL GAUDIO
Lighting Design ....JASON LIVINGSTON
Production Supervisor...........................LOWELL SWORTZELL

The Wrestling Season's world premiere was at The Coterie Theatre,
Kansas City, Missouri, January 2000. The production was directed
by Jeff Church and included the following artists:

CAST

Referee .... ANTHONY GUEST
Luke ....JOSHUA F. DECKER
Kori .... MELANNA D. GRAY
Melanie ....BETH GUEST
Nicole... ALICIA JENKINS-EWING
Matt..DAVID MCNAMARA
Jolt...JUDSON MORGAN
Heather...AMANDA RAFUSE
Willy... MATT RAMSEY

PRODUCTION STAFF

Associate Director/Wrestling Coach..................LEIGH MILLER
Set and Costume Design/Properties.........................ELIZA CAIN
Lighting Design .... ART KENT
Sound Design...DAVID KIEHL
Production Stage Manager.....................BROOKE SCHEPPNER
Scenic Construction .... DAN ESLINGER

PLAYWRIGHT'S NOTES:

The action of the play is seamless, moving from one scene to another unencumbered by sets and costume changes. Much will be left to the audience's imagination. The ensemble functions as a chorus when they are not in the playing space, responding to the action onstage as a group, in pairs and individually. All eight young people wear wrestling singlets and wrestling shoes throughout the play.

Movement in the scenes suggests wrestling moves, holds and escapes. When the stage directions read, "Ensemble shifts," they form new physical arrangements to underscore the action.

Wrestling weight classes in the play can be adjusted according to the actors' approximate size and current high school wrestling rules.

The referee is an integral part of the play throughout, moving about the mat as if each scene is a wrestling match.

Entrances and exits on and off the mat should be used to further define relationships between the characters.

The action between Matt and Melanie on page 45 is an act of sexual agression, but it is not rape.

THE WRESTLING SEASON

Characters

MATT: 17 years old

KORI: 17 years old

MELANIE: 17, "Cherry" Garcia

LUKE: 17, Matt's best friend

HEATHER: Jolt's girlfriend

JOLT: 17, wrestler

WILLY: 17, about the same size as Matt

NICOLE: 17, Heather's friend

REFEREE:
wears black and white referee
uniform and carries a whistle

Setting

A BARE STAGE. STANDARD-ISSUE WRESTLING

MAT AT CENTER.

(Lights. All nine characters are grouped on the mat.
ENSEMBLE FUNCTIONS AS A CHORUS.)

ALL *(except REFEREE)*: I will remember always that fair play,
moral obligation and ethics are a part of winning and losing,
that graciousness and humility should always characterize a
winner and that pride and honor do not desert a good loser.
(The ensemble explodes out into the space. They remain
present throughout the play, watching and commenting on the
action.)

HEATHER: You think you know the way it is.

JOLT: You think you know the score.

NICOLE: You think you're so smart.

KORI: You think you've got me figured out.

WILLY: You think you've got me pegged. Pinned.

MELANIE: You think you know me, but you don't.

LUKE: How can you know me?

MATT: I'm not even sure I know myself.
(REF blows whistle. MATT, LUKE, JOLT and WILLY warm
up. REF blows whistle, indicates MATT and LUKE: They
take positions and the practice match begins. The ensemble
yells, "Take him down!" "Push him! Push him!" and "Go!
Go! Go!" Each wrestler struggles to take the other down.
MATT flips LUKE onto his back. REF signals two points.
LUKE tries to escape. MATT pins him. REF counts "One,
two ..." slaps the mat to signal a pin. Buzzer.)

MATT: And now I'd like to thank all the little people who have
helped me to attain my goals.

LUKE: Save it for the media.

MATT: I'd like to thank my mom for believing in me, my coach
for kicking my butt ...

LUKE: I think I'm gonna be sick.

MATT: ... and last but not least, my buddy Luke, inspiration and
guiding force.

LUKE: Next time you'll beg for mercy.

MATT: In your dreams.

LUKE: I wrestle slicker than you any day.

MATT: You won't have to worry about outsmarting me this year.

LUKE: I never worry about outsmarting you.

MATT: I mean, I won't be a threat at 171. I talked to Coach this morning. I'm gonna weigh in at 160 this season.

LUKE: You're kiddin'.

MATT: Dead serious.

LUKE: You're gonna be unstoppable at 160.

MATT: Yeah. It was Mom's idea.

LUKE: She wants that scholarship more than you do.

MATT: Nobody wants it more than I do. Here's the plan. Drop weight to 160, train like a madman for that slot, kick ass in the wrestle-offs, win the divisionals, then the regional championship, then the state finals. One. Two. Three.

LUKE: Easy as that?

MATT: I didn't say it'd be easy.

LUKE: Good, because you gotta pass pre-calc to stay on the team.

MATT: Thanks, Mom.

LUKE: You're gonna need major help to pull up that pre-calc grade.

MATT: You got me through Algebra III, didn't you?

LUKE: Yeah, that was a minor miracle.

MATT: If I can keep my concentration, I'll be home free. Like Coach says …

LUKE: … don't need to be the best, you just gotta win.

MATT: One match at a time.

LUKE: And pass pre-calc.

MATT: Yeah. I'm counting on you for that.

LUKE: And lose the weight and keep it off.
  (MATT wrestles LUKE.)

MATT: Wait a minute. Is this encouragement?

LUKE: This is realism.

MATT: I'll do whatever it takes, okay? I'll do extra workouts. I'll
  visualize my goals. I'll fast and meditate like those demented
  monks over in Tibet. I want this.

LUKE: Quarter finals weren't good enough for you, huh?

MATT: I've gotta go all the way this year if I want a scholarship.
  This is my future we're talking about here.

LUKE: You forgot one minor detail. If you drop down to the 160
  slot, you gotta get past Willy in the wrestle-offs. He's good.

MATT: Yeah, but he's not slick. I'll out-maneuver him. I learned
  to kick your butt, didn't I?

LUKE: Yeah. Only because I taught you all my moves in old man
  Gebhardt's garage.

MATT: The sacred training ground. Seems like a hundred years
  ago.

LUKE: Yeah. Remember how we drilled those reversals?

MATT: I remember how scrawny you were.

LUKE: Oh, yeah?

MATT: Yeah.

LUKE: Scrawny? I don't think so.
  *(LUKE wrestles MATT. Buzzer. Ensemble shifts. REF blows
  whistle, indicates MATT and LUKE.)*

MATT: Come on. We're gonna be late.

LUKE: Late for what?

MATT: I told you about ten times. My mom's expecting you for
  dinner.

LUKE: Power bars and yogurt? I'm not hungry.

MATT: Will you lighten up? What's going on with you lately?

LUKE: Nothing.

MATT: I'm pretty sure it's not nothing.

LUKE: I've got a paper due on Monday and that lab report's killing me.

MATT: You work too hard, my friend. You need to have some fun. *(LUKE sobs silently.)* Hey. Come on, man. Come on. It can't be that bad.

LUKE: How would you know how bad it is.

MATT: 'Cause I'm the best friend you got in the world?

LUKE: You don't have a clue, okay?

MATT: So enlighten me.

LUKE: You wouldn't understand.

MATT: If you're trying to insult me, you've succeeded.

LUKE: I'm not trying to insult you.

MATT: What, then? Did I do something?

LUKE: It's not you. It's me. Just forget it. Let's go.

MATT: No. I'm not going to forget it. Whatever this is, it's really got to you. Tell me.

LUKE: You know how you got this plan? You can see your whole year in front of you.

MATT: Yeah ...

LUKE: You got your whole future figured out.

MATT: Yeah …

LUKE: Well, I don't have anything figured out. I don't have a plan.

MATT: You don't need a plan. You're ten times smarter than I am. You can have your pick of schools next year and scholarships, too. You're ugly, but looks aren't everything. You've got it all, man.

LUKE: You don't know.

MATT: I know everything there is to know about you and some
things you don't even know about yourself.
(REF blows whistle, indicates LUKE in spotlight.)

LUKE: You think you know me, but you don't.
(REF blows whistle twice to resume scene. Ensemble shifts.)

MATT: I know. It's some girl, right?

LUKE: No.

MATT: Is it the team? Are you worried about the wrestle-offs?

LUKE: No. Jolt'll probably kick my butt.

MATT: Maybe not. We'll train together. In Gebhardt's garage,
like the old days.

LUKE: It doesn't matter. Nothing really matters now.

MATT: Hey. Don't say that. It'll be all right. (Reaches out to
LUKE: LUKE grabs MATT, hugs him.) It's okay. Whatever
it is, it'll be all right.
(Buzzer. REF blows whistle, indicates JOLT and WILLY.)

JOLT: They're mighty friendly.

WILLY: Too friendly, if you ask me.

JOLT: I didn't ask you.

WILLY: Too bad. Guess you don't want to hear the news about
Mr. Can't Do Wrong and his sidekick.

JOLT: What news?

WILLY: I don't think I heard you ask me.

JOLT: I heard he's after your wrestling slot, if that's what you
mean. Coach said he's dropping weight to the 160 slot.
Trouble for you.

WILLY: I can take him.

JOLT: Yeah, you and who else? He's tough. And look how he's
muscled up since last year.

WILLY: Do I look worried?

JOLT: You should be.

WILLY: He's nothin' but an ass-kisser.

JOLT: Yeah, he's on Coach's A-list, all right.

WILLY: If Coach only knew.

JOLT: Knew what?

WILLY: Was that a question?

JOLT: All right. What about Mr. Can't Do Wrong and his sidekick?

WILLY: I know the truth about those perverts.

JOLT: What truth?

WILLY: They're too sweet for their own good, if you know what I mean. They got it bad for each other.

JOLT: Yeah?

WILLY: It's so obvious.

JOLT: Yeah. How can you tell?

WILLY: Can't you?

JOLT: Sure I can. I can always tell. But do you have any proof?

WILLY: Yeah. I do.

JOLT: You've got proof?

WILLY: Yeah.

JOLT: Right. You're so full of it.

WILLY: I saw them. In the locker room. They were all over each other.

JOLT: What were they doing?

WILLY: What do you think? *(REF blows whistle, signals #20, says, "Unsportsmanlike Conduct.")* It was disgusting. *(REF indicates HEATHER and NICOLE, who join WILLY and JOLT on the mat.)*

HEATHER: What was disgusting?

WILLY: You don't wanna know.

NICOLE: I do.

HEATHER: I do, too.

JOLT: I'll tell you later tonight when we're alone.

HEATHER: My parents'll be home tonight.

JOLT: Then I'll meet you at the library.

HEATHER: Eight o'clock. Reference.

JOLT: I got somethin' you can refer to.

NICOLE: Would somebody please tell me what was disgusting?

WILLY: Come here. I'll show you.

NICOLE: Uh-uh. I don't wanna know that bad.

WILLY: Come on. Just a little closer.

NICOLE: Tell me from a distance, okay?

WILLY: That takes all the fun out of it.

NICOLE: For you, maybe.
    (JOLT and HEATHER whisper together.)

WILLY: You're hurting my feelings.

NICOLE: You'll get over it.

HEATHER *(to JOLT)*. You're kidding!

JOLT: Do I look like I'm kidding?

HEATHER: I never would have thought that. Never!

JOLT: It's true. Willy's got proof.

HEATHER: Oh, my God.

JOLT: Willy saw them together.

NICOLE: Saw who?

HEATHER: You mean together together?

WILLY: Yeah. Well … sort of.

HEATHER: Well, either you saw them or you didn't.

JOLT: I told you. He saw them. In the locker room.

791

HEATHER: Oh, my God!

NICOLE: Saw who?

HEATHER: Well, it makes perfect sense if you think of it. They're always together.

NICOLE: If you don't tell me this instant who you're talking about, I'm going to scream.

HEATHER: Matt and Luke, of course.

NICOLE: Matt and Luke?

HEATHER: That's why Matt doesn't have a girl.

WILLY: Who'd have him?

NICOLE: I would. But he's not interested in me.

HEATHER: That's what I mean. That's the point.

NICOLE: He's always hanging out with Luke.

HEATHER: And Kori. Why else would he hang out with those two?

NICOLE: What do you mean?

HEATHER: Well, Kori's not exactly Miss America. All that chopped-off hair and those weird hanging things she calls jewelry.

NICOLE: Yeah, she's scary.

HEATHER: She must shop at the junkyard.

NICOLE: And you know her and food.

HEATHER: Have you ever seen her at a dessert table?
    (REF blows whistle, indicates KORI in spotlight.)

KORI: You think you know me, but you don't.
    (REF blows whistle twice to resume action. Ensemble shifts.)

NICOLE: So what about Matt and Luke?

HEATHER: God, Nicki, do we have to draw you a picture?

WILLY: Those guys give me the creeps.

NICOLE: What guys?

JOLT: Especially Mr. Can't Do Wrong. I'm glad you're wrestling him.

WILLY: Yeah, but you gotta wrestle Luke.

NICOLE: Matt and Luke what?

HEATHER: Come on, Nicki, I'll tell you all about it.
(Buzzer. Ensemble shifts, whispering to one another. MATT jumps rope double time. REF blows whistle, indicates MATT and LUKE. LUKE sees MATT, turns to leave.)

MATT: Hey, wait.

LUKE: What?

MATT: I'm down to 162. Two pounds to go.

LUKE: Your mom's not coping too well. She called me.

MATT: What did she say?

LUKE: She's worried you're killing yourself. She wanted me to tell her what to do to get you to eat.

MATT: What'd you say?

LUKE: I told her to get off your back about scholarships.

MATT: Right. You said that.

LUKE: I didn't but I should have. I gotta go.

MATT: I thought you were gonna work out. Isn't that why you came in here?

LUKE: I forgot something.

MATT: What? *(LUKE picks up a towel at the edge of the mat.)* That's what you forgot? A towel?

LUKE: No.

MATT: What then?

LUKE: What is this — twenty questions? I don't have to answer to you.

MATT: You can stop the act now because I know.

LUKE: Know what?

MATT: What do you think?

LUKE: I've gotta go.

MATT: You can't stand to be in the same room with me, can you?

LUKE: What are you talking about?

MATT: It's not my fault.

LUKE: I know that.

MATT: Then why are you avoiding me?

LUKE: I'm not avoiding you.

MATT: Oh, no? I came to pick you up this morning and you'd already left. You managed to get to pre-calc late and leave early.

LUKE: They wrote faggot on my locker.
(Silence.)

MATT: Do you know who did it?

LUKE: I've got a pretty good idea.

MATT: Doesn't take a rocket scientist to figure it out.

LUKE: It won't come off.

MATT: Willy better watch himself in the wrestle-offs, 'cause I'm gonna hurt him for this.

LUKE: I gotta go.

MATT: You gonna help me study tonight for that pre-calc test?

LUKE: I can't.

MATT: I thought you said you'd help me.

LUKE: I'm not responsible for your grades. I've got my own studying to do.

MATT: Liar. This thing's got to you worse than me. We gotta stick together, man, or they'll win. That's what this is all about. Wrestling. One slot per weight class. They want our slots, man.

LUKE: No, that's what this is about for you.

MATT: You bet. It's wrestling season.

LUKE: The whole world is about you and wrestling.

MATT: Right now, yeah.

LUKE: I'm outta here.

MATT *(grabs LUKE)*. Luke, wait.

LUKE: Get off me.
(MATT makes an elaborate gesture of letting go of LUKE's arm.)

MATT: You think it's true, don't you? You believe it. *(LUKE laughs.)* It's not funny. You think I want you like that? Is that what you think of me?

LUKE: You? It's all about you, isn't it? Whatever it takes to get what you want.
(REF blows whistle, signals #10, says, "Potentially Dangerous." LUKE throws the towel, exits off mat. MATT jumps rope. Ensemble stares at MATT, whispers. Someone points. There is laughter. JOLT gives out with a long, slow, wolf whistle.)

MATT: Okay. I'm gay. Is that what you want to hear?
(Ensemble shifts. MATT jumps rope. REF indicates KORI and MATT.)

KORI: You don't have to shout. We can all hear you.

MATT: Don't start, Kori. I don't want to talk about it.

KORI: Okay.

MATT: I gotta stay focused. I can't let them get to me. Not even Luke.

KORI: Okay.

MATT: They stare at me like I'm some kind of freak.

KORI: Who?

MATT: Everyone. They stare at me and then look away real fast when I see them. Like they're waiting for me to do something.

KORI: I thought you didn't want to talk about it.

MATT: It's like I've done something wrong, but I don't know what it is.

KORI: It's not about what you have or haven't done.

MATT: Even Coach treated me different today, like … I don't know, like I was someone else. I wanted to kill somebody.

KORI: You guys don't get it, do you? You're entertainment, that's all. So what if you are gay?

MATT: I'm not gay. And neither is Luke.

KORI: What if you were? What's the big deal? You're the same person either way, aren't you?
(HEATHER and NICOLE shift.)

HEATHER: Well, it figures. They're always together. And Luke's kind of … *(Flops her wrist)* Well, you know.

NICOLE: Heather!

HEATHER: Well, it's the truth.

NICOLE: That's not very nice.

HEATHER: Nice? How boring can you get?

KORI *(to HEATHER)*: It's too bad you have no life. I guess you have to make up stories about everyone else's just to have something to talk about.

HEATHER: Kori, you wouldn't recognize a life if it jumped up and bit you.

NICOLE: Ooooo.

HEATHER: Don't pay any attention to her, Nicki, she's a non-person.
(HEATHER and NICOLE shift.)

KORI: Heather and her minions. It's a power thing. Makes her the main attraction and she knows it.

MATT: But everyone believes her.

KORI: It's too much fun not to believe her.

MATT: I gotta do something. I can't stand it. I can't concentrate.

KORI: Well, you could kill Heather. I'll assist you on that one.

MATT: Yeah, let's smother her with her hair.

KORI: I was kidding, Matt. Just let it go. That's what I do when they talk about me. *(She imitates.)* "Hey, Kori's parents are drug addicts. They did so much acid in the Sixties their brains are fried. I heard she wears thong underwear. I heard she never changes her underwear. I heard she doesn't wear any underwear." Remember when they said I stripped at a party and danced buck-naked for everybody there.

MATT: I knew that wasn't true. I was there.

KORI: What about that time in ninth grade that money was missing and everyone accused me of taking it.

MATT: That was bad, but it's not the same. It's not personal.

KORI: I took being labeled a thief personal.

MATT: I hear them talking in my head. Whole conversations. That's what gets me. I know what they're thinking.

KORI: Because you've thought the same thing about somebody else, right?

MATT: Wrong.

KORI: Come on. You hate the whole idea of being gay.

MATT: I'm glad I'm not.

KORI: Because that makes you better?

MATT: I didn't say that.

KORI: You feel sorry for them? Is that it?

MATT: Whose side are you on, anyway?

KORI: Nobody's side. I'm sick of everybody judging everybody else. It's like some big courtroom and everyone thinks they can decide what's okay and what's not.

MATT: I'm not judging anybody.

KORI: Yes, you are. You don't even realize it.

MATT: Look. I don't care who's gay and who isn't.

KORI: As long as it's not you.

MATT: I don't want to be hated for something I'm not.

KORI: Imagine what it would be like to be hated for what you are.

(REF blows whistle, signals #19, says, "Two points." Ensemble shifts.)

MATT: I'm gonna do a double workout today, double steam room, then jog home.

KORI: Maybe you ought to give them something else to talk about.

MATT: Like what?

KORI: You could hook up with somebody. Then they'd know you like girls.

MATT: I hang around you, don't I?

KORI: And I've loved you since kindergarten. But we're friends. That's all. You need to get hooked up with somebody. Connected. Nobody talked about you when you were with what's her name.

MATT: Sandy.

KORI: Yeah. That's her.

MATT: She was okay.

KORI: If you're a Neanderthal.

MATT: You don't have to rub it in.

KORI: Look, if you were dating someone, they'd have something new to focus on and they'd forget the old stuff, that's all.

MATT: Wait a minute.

KORI: Every now and then I have a decent suggestion. And there must be some girl you're hot for, if you're not hot for Luke.

MATT: Melanie Garcia.

KORI: Melanie?

MATT: Yeah, it's perfect.

KORI: I know you think she's hot. You only said it about a
hundred times.

MATT: That'd take care of the rumors. She's slept with every
jock in the school. "Cherry" Garcia.
(REF blows whistle, indicates MELANIE in spotlight.)

MELANIE: You think you know me, but you don't.
(REF blows whistle twice to resume. Ensemble shifts.)

KORI: Don't call her "Cherry." I like her. She's always nice to
me.

MATT: She's nice to everyone.

KORI: You think she'll go out with you? You're not exactly her
type.

MATT: What do you mean by that?

KORI: Well, look at the guys she's dated, most notably your
nemesis, Willy. He's like a walking testosterone ad. Want me
to ask her if she's interested in you?

MATT: No, thanks. I can get my own dates.

KORI: Right. That's why you've had so many this year.

MATT: What's that supposed to mean?

KORI: My. Aren't we defensive. I didn't mean anything.

MATT: I've got other priorities.

KORI: Yeah. Wrestling. Wrestling and, oh yeah, I almost forgot,
wrestling.

MATT: This year's my year, Kori. I don't wanna blow it.

KORI: You mean your mom'll kill you.

MATT: That, too.

KORI: So don't ask Melanie out. We'll think of something else.
Hey, where you going?

MATT: I've gotta study pre-calc.

KORI: Eat something, will you? You look terrible. And tell Luke

799

to call me, okay?

MATT: I can't. Every time I see him, he runs in the opposite direction.

KORI: This isn't good. I don't like this at all.

MATT: He thinks it's true. What they're saying about me. It's not true, Kori. It's not.

KORI: Okay. Okay. Who are you trying to convince?
(Buzzer. KORI exits off the mat. MATT does a series of push-ups, then spits into a can. He is dizzy, stumbles, drops. Ensemble reacts. LUKE helps MATT. MATT revives. Ensemble whispers. MATT and LUKE move away from each other.)

MATT: I'm all right. I can handle this. I know what to do.
(REF blows whistle, signals #12, says, "Caution." Ensemble continues whispering. REF repeats signal and command. Ensemble shifts. REF blows whistle, indicates MELANIE.)

MELANIE: Are you sure you're all right?

MATT: Yeah. Probably just dehydrated. You know, drying out before the wrestle-offs. Gotta make weight at 160.

MELANIE: Want some gum?

MATT: Is it sugarless?

MELANIE: Of course.

MATT: Thanks.

MELANIE: You guys are worse than the cheerleaders about your weight.

MATT: We gotta qualify.

MELANIE: What did you want to talk to me about? *(Pause.)* You said you wanted to talk to me.

MATT: I really like that … what you're wearing.

MELANIE: My shirt?

MATT: Yeah. Your shirt. You look good.

MELANIE: Thanks. It's kind of new.

MATT: Yeah. I never saw it before.

MELANIE: That's because it's new.

MATT: You want to do something Friday night?

MELANIE: With you?

MATT: Yeah, with me.

MELANIE: Are you asking me out?

MATT: Sounds like that to me. How about it?

MELANIE: Okay, I guess.

MATT: You don't sound very enthusiastic.

MELANIE: I'm just surprised, that's all.

MATT: Because …

MELANIE: I don't know. We don't run with the same crowd.

MATT: Look. If you don't want to go, that's okay. It was probably a bad idea anyway.

MELANIE: It's not a bad idea. I'd like to go out with you. I just never thought you'd ask me.
(REF blows whistle, indicates MATT and MELANIE: They assume the neutral position to wrestle. REF blows whistle to begin. MATT and MELANIE thumb wrestle.

REF stops thumb wrestling, blows whistle to begin again. MATT and MELANIE assume wrestling stance. MATT tickles MELANIE: REF blows whistle, signals #7, says, "Out of Bounds."

REF blows whistle. MATT and MELANIE assume the position again. They wrestle, then melt into each other and slow dance. REF, amused, gently separates them, raises their hands in the air, says, "Tie."

JOLT wrestles WILLY onto the mat.)

JOLT: You're looking mighty happy today.

WILLY: Who, me?

JOLT: Yeah, you.

WILLY: Luke was really rattled at practice yesterday.

JOLT: He lost it completely.

WILLY: He didn't have a prayer.

JOLT: It was solid, no doubt about it.

WILLY: Like taking candy from a baby.

JOLT: I wouldn't say that, but you were good, real good.

WILLY: Did you see Melanie watching me?

JOLT: Yeah. She took it in all right.

WILLY: She wants me back, I can tell.

HEATHER: You guys make me sick. Should we tell them, Nicki?

NICOLE: Yeah. Tell them.

HEATHER: I don't know. I hate to burst their bubble.

NICOLE: Yeah, but it's not fair not to tell. You have to.
    (MATT and MELANIE whisper and laugh as if at a private joke.)

WILLY: What's this about?

HEATHER: Melanie, of course.

WILLY: What about Melanie?

HEATHER: I don't think she's coming to practice to see you, Willy.

NICOLE: I don't think so, either.

HEATHER: I saw her coming out of the movies Friday night with someone else.

NICOLE: This is unbelievable. It's so good.

WILLY: Who?

HEATHER: A certain wrestler named Matt.

JOLT: What? What would Melanie be doing with a loser like him.

HEATHER: I don't know, but … she was wearing his jacket.

NICOLE: Maybe she was cold.

HEATHER: Maybe she was hot.

WILLY: For him?

JOLT: He was probably on his way to meet Luke.

WILLY: Yeah. They must have met there by accident. Did you see them go in together?

HEATHER: No, but that doesn't explain why I saw them walking together after practice yesterday.

NICOLE: It's true. I was with her.
(MATT and MELANIE cross in view of the others. MELANIE tackles MATT: He responds playfully. Ensemble shifts.)

JOLT: Wait. You think she's been coming to practice to see him?

WILLY: Yeah, right. Never happen.

JOLT: Melanie wouldn't be dating a loser like him. Besides, he's not her type.

NICOLE: Maybe they're madly, passionately in love like the poets. You know, platonic love, like in the movies.

HEATHER: You're scaring me, Nicole.

NICOLE: Well, it's possible.

HEATHER: No, it isn't.

WILLY: He's a jerk.

HEATHER: Maybe you're not the stud you thought you were, Wilbur.

NICOLE: Yeah. Some Romeo you are, Wilbur.

HEATHER: Lose your girl to Matt and Luke.

WILLY: Shut up, Heather.

JOLT: She's got it for you, man, don't worry.

WILLY: Yeah. I broke up with her, remember?

HEATHER: We'll see.

NICOLE: Yeah. We'll see.

(*Buzzer. WILLY and JOLT, NICOLE and HEATHER off the mat. REF blows whistle, indicates MATT and MELANIE.*)

MATT: You coming to practice again today?

MELANIE: Wouldn't miss it.

MATT: I like having you there.

MELANIE: Me and all the other wrestling groupies, huh?

MATT: I don't even see them.

MELANIE: You're too busy staring down Willy.

MATT: That's right. You coming over tonight after practice? I guarantee my mom'll ask you to stay for dinner. She likes you.

MELANIE: Will you eat something?

MATT: Right. I can eat if I do a double workout and sit in the steam room for an hour.

MELANIE: I can't believe I'm going out with a wrestler. Let's break up and then get back together when wrestling season's over.

MATT: If you want to.

MELANIE: Do you want to?

MATT: Do you?

MELANIE: I asked you first.

MATT: Not a chance.

MELANIE: I worry about you, though. Pushing yourself too far.

MATT: You sound like my Mother.

MELANIE: I wouldn't want to do that.

MATT: You don't look like my Mother.

MELANIE: That's good.

MATT: You don't smell like my Mother, either.

MELANIE: That's good, too.

(MATT play wrestles MELANIE: She wrestles him back.
MATT playfully pins her.)

MATT: You're pretty strong.

MELANIE: For a girl?

MATT: For anyone. Will you come over tonight?

MELANIE: Okay. And if you eat something, I'll work out with
   you after dinner.

MATT: You're amazing, you know that? Different than I thought
   you'd be.

MELANIE: How different?

MATT: I don't know. You just are.

MELANIE: So are you.

MATT: Good different or bad different?

MELANIE: Good different. I thought maybe you'd be like Willy.

MATT: Whoa. Stop right there.

MELANIE: You're not like Willy.

MATT: Say that again.

MELANIE: You're not like Willy. I don't think the two of us ever
   really did have a conversation.

MATT: Maybe you were too busy to talk.

MELANIE: What do you mean by that?

MATT: Nothing. Forget it. I don't care about what you did
   before.

MELANIE: What I did before?

MATT: You know, with Willy and those other guys.

MELANIE: You forgive me.

MATT: Yeah.

MELANIE: For sleeping with Willy and those other guys.

MATT: Yeah.

MELANIE: How do you know who I slept with?

MATT: You and Willy were famous. Legend.

MELANIE: You shouldn't believe what everyone says. Not all of it's true.
(Buzzer. REF blows whistle, signals #2, says, "Warning" directly to HEATHER, as she crosses onto the mat. REF indicates NICOLE and MELANIE: HEATHER paints MELANIE's toenails.)

NICOLE: I can't believe you're dating a wrestler.

MELANIE: I know. I know.

NICOLE: You're crazy.

MELANIE: Heather's dating a wrestler.

NICOLE: That's different. Heather and Jolt are practically married.

HEATHER: Don't say that too loud. My mom might hear you. I like this shade on you, Mel.

MELANIE: Plum Raisin. It's kind of dark.

NICOLE: It's sexy. You said you'd never go out with another wrestler as long as you lived. Remember?

MELANIE: I know, but that was before Matt.

NICOLE: Oooo.

HEATHER: What's he like?

MELANIE: I don't know. He's kind of shy.

HEATHER: Jolt doesn't have a shy bone in his body.

NICOLE: Yeah, Jolt's not exactly the shy type.

MELANIE: Yesterday, after wrestling practice, Matt and I walked over to his house and his mom asked me to stay for dinner. We actually sat down at the dining room table and ate together. Then me and Matt went for a long walk and talked until really late.

NICOLE: That sounds kind of boring, Mel.

MELANIE: It wasn't.

NICOLE: Oooo.

HEATHER: Do you know what Jolt did yesterday? He bought me one of those skimpy, underwear things. All lace.

NICOLE: No!

HEATHER: Yeah, can you believe it? We were up in my room and one thing led to another, you know…

NICOLE: Oh, my God!

HEATHER: … and my mom was right downstairs in the kitchen!

NICOLE: I can't believe it.

HEATHER: I was so afraid we'd get caught, but that made it even more fun.

NICOLE: I want a boyfriend just like that. It's so romantic. *(Pause.)* But I don't think I'm ready to be sexually active.

HEATHER: God, Nicki, you sound like you're reading from a textbook.

NICOLE: Well, I don't know how else to put it. I don't want the first time to be with just anyone. Maybe there's something wrong with me, but I'm kind of scared.

HEATHER: You would be.

MELANIE: You didn't meet the right guy yet, that's all.

NICOLE: You really think so?

HEATHER: Or else you're horribly repressed and probably frigid.

NICOLE: Shut up, Heather. My mom says wait, don't hurry. You'll know when it's the right time.

HEATHER: You listen to your mom?

MELANIE: I think you're smart, Nicole. Take your time.

HEATHER: Well, she doesn't want to become a member of the over eighteen club. You don't have much more time left, Nicki. Maybe you could be the president.

NICOLE: If you tell anybody, I'll die.

HEATHER: I won't tell anybody. But you better hurry up.

NICOLE: All the good guys are taken. Like Matt.

HEATHER: I'm kinda surprised you like him, Mel. I wouldn't think he was your type.

MELANIE: Yeah. It's kind of weird. He does this thing when I talk to him. He listens.

HEATHER: What?

NICOLE: That's so romantic. I want my boyfriend to listen to me.

HEATHER: Jolt loves me. He can't keep his hands off me. And he's jealous. I think it's so cute that he's jealous. As if I'd even look at another guy. Is Matt the jealous type?

MELANIE: Matt? He doesn't seem jealous. He's different.

NICOLE: Yeah, he's nice.

MELANIE: It's like … he's my friend.

NICOLE: I want my boyfriend to be my friend.

HEATHER: That's not what she means, Nicki. Go ahead, Mel.

MELANIE: Never mind. It's nothing.

HEATHER: No, tell me, what is it?

MELANIE: Well, don't tell anyone, okay?

NICOLE: Scout's honor.

HEATHER: What is it?

MELANIE: You know how guys try to see how far they can get before you stop them? Matt…well, he hasn't really done that. *(Knowing look between HEATHER and NICOLE.)*

NICOLE: Maybe he doesn't feel good from losing all that weight.

HEATHER: That's stupid. Jolt says that wrestling season makes them all so horny they can hardly stand it.

MELANIE: It's like he's being careful, cautious for some reason.

HEATHER: Maybe.

NICOLE: Why don't you ask him?

HEATHER: She can't do that. That's stupid. You don't ask a guy something like that.

MELANIE: I kind of like it, in a way. One less thing to worry about.

HEATHER: There might be another reason.

MELANIE: What?

HEATHER: Maybe what they say about Matt and Luke is true.

NICOLE: Hey, that would explain it.

MELANIE: Why would he be going out with me if he's gay?

NICOLE: Yeah. That doesn't make any sense.

HEATHER: Unless he didn't want anyone to know. Then dating Melanie would be … well, excuse me for saying so, Mel … the perfect decoy.

NICOLE: Yeah, maybe he's just dating Mel so that people will think he's not gay.

HEATHER: That's really low. Drop him, Melanie. Don't let him use you like that.

MELANIE: That can't be true.

HEATHER: How else can you explain it?

NICOLE: Yeah. Why doesn't he act normal towards you?

MELANIE: Maybe he's just not a sex fiend.

HEATHER: Come on. That's not normal for a guy.

MELANIE: You're right about that.

NICOLE: Why don't you ask him?

HEATHER: I told you. That's stupid. You can't just come out and ask a guy a question like that.

NICOLE: Why not?

HEATHER: Get a boyfriend of your own before you wither up and die of old age.

NICOLE: I told you. All the good ones are taken.

HEATHER: Maybe you could have Matt after Melanie dumps him.

NICOLE: I still think he's cute, even if he is gay.

HEATHER: You would.

(Buzzer. REF blows whistle, indicates JOLT and HEATHER to take the neutral position to start match. They circle, then engage, then embrace on the mat. REF blows whistle, signals #17, says, "Illegal Hold." JOLT and HEATHER pay no attention. REF repeats signal, "Illegal Hold." JOLT and HEATHER continue their embrace. REF indicates JOLT, signals #8, says, "Wrestler in Control.")

HEATHER: Jolt, take it easy. My mom'll be home any minute.

JOLT: Let's go upstairs.

HEATHER: I told you. My mom's on her way home.

JOLT: Please, I love you so much it hurts. Please.

HEATHER: Not now.

JOLT: Where you goin'? Come back here.

HEATHER: You're too dangerous.

JOLT: Come over here.

HEATHER: What time is it?

JOLT: You're killin' me. Take a knife and cut me. Go ahead. Put me out of my misery.

HEATHER: You don't act like you're suffering.

JOLT: I feel like I'm gonna explode, okay? Like I'm in a vise and you're squeezing it.

HEATHER: Me, squeeze it?

JOLT: Go ahead. I'm yours.

HEATHER: No. My mom's coming any minute and I know you.

JOLT: Who, me? I didn't do anything. Well, nothing you didn't want me to do.

HEATHER: That's all you ever want to do. Hey, I know something you'd like to know.

JOLT: Let's not talk, okay?

HEATHER: You never want to talk.

JOLT: Sure I do. Just not right now.

HEATHER: It's about a certain wrestler dating Mel.

JOLT: Not him. I hate that guy.

HEATHER: You're gonna love it.

JOLT: Whatever it is it won't make up for practice today.

HEATHER: What happened?

JOLT: He's down to 160, so it's me and Luke.

HEATHER: Oh, no.

JOLT: Oh, yes. I can't stand to touch that freak.

HEATHER: Well, do you want to hear what I heard or not?

JOLT: I'm gonna destroy him in the wrestle-offs.

HEATHER: I don't know about that. He pinned you twice last week in practice.

JOLT: Whose side are you on?

HEATHER: It's the truth. I was there.

JOLT: I'll get him rattled. I'll psych him out. I won't let him find an opening.

HEATHER: Don't worry. You'll take him.

JOLT: What if I don't?

HEATHER: Then you'll lose. It's not the end of the world.

JOLT: What are you talking about? Losing to one of those guys… it's humiliating.

HEATHER: I'll still love you, even if you lose.

JOLT: I won't lose. I can't.

HEATHER: Do you want to know what I heard, or not?

JOLT: I'll go low for the takedown and nail him before he can figure out what hit him.

HEATHER: Jolt. You are so annoying. You never listen to me.

JOLT: Okay. Tell me.

HEATHER: You have to promise you won't tell anybody or Melanie'll kill me.

JOLT: Okay.

HEATHER: Mel told me Matt hasn't even tried anything with her. Like he's just going out with her to impress everybody. They've never made out, got anywhere, done anything.

JOLT: He probably can't — unless he's with Luke.
(REF blows whistle, indicates MATT in spotlight.)

MATT: You think you know me, but you don't.
(Ensemble shifts position. REF blows whistle twice to resume.)

HEATHER: For a while I thought we were wrong about Matt, but now … well, there's no doubt in my mind.

JOLT: Why are we wasting time talking about those guys? Come here.
(They embrace. A door opens and slams. HEATHER and JOLT break apart, adjusting their clothes and hair. REF poses as MOM.)

HEATHER: Hi, Mom.

JOLT: Yeah. Hi, Mrs. Huntley. Want a hand with those groceries?
(Buzzer. REF signals #6, says, "No Control."

REF blows whistle, indicates MATT and WILLY to take positions. REF whistles to begin practice match. Ensemble cheers. REF blows whistle. The match begins. The two wrestlers circle, then engage. The remaining wrestling sequences are accompanied by loud, ugly music. Wrestling begins in real time, then becomes slow motion, then real time again. Ensemble response matches wrestling time. WILLY gains the advantage and takes MATT down. REF signals #19, says, "Two Points."

Buzzer. End of first period. REF confers with WILLY, blows whistle. MATT assumes the defensive position. WILLY crouches behind him, in the offensive position. REF blows whistle. Second round begins. The two wrestlers struggle. MATT manages to get out from under WILLY, and REF signals #15, says, "Reversal.")

WILLY: What? That was illegal! You touch me like that, I'll take your head off!

MATT: What's your problem? That was a legal move.
(REF blows whistle, signals, says, "Restart.")

WILLY: Even if you wrestle dirty, I can still whip your ass.

MATT: You're crazy. I didn't do anything to you.
(REF blows whistle, signals, repeats, "Restart.")

WILLY: No way. I'm not wrestling him. I don't want him touching me.
(WILLY off the mat. Ensemble whispers, points at MATT: MATT turns to REF for help.)

MATT: Tell them. That wasn't illegal.
(REF blows whistle, raises MATT's hand, says, "Forfeit.")

WILLY: You keep your hands off me. I know about you. What you are.
(ENSEMBLE FUNCTIONS AS A CHORUS.)

HEATHER: Melanie told us.

JOLT: Melanie told everybody.

NICOLE: Everybody.

WILLY: Everybody knows about you now.
(MATT removes his headgear, throws it. Ensemble whispers, points.)

LUKE: Matt, wait.

MATT: Stay away from me, man. Just stay away.

(LUKE moves away from MATT. REF blows whistle, signals #11, says, "Stalemate." Buzzer. REF blows whistle, indicates KORI and LUKE.)

KORI: How'd you do on the history test?

LUKE: Ninety-three.

KORI: Not bad. Beats my pathetic eighty-nine.

LUKE: Yeah.

KORI: Wanna talk about it?

LUKE: What's the point?

KORI: I don't know. You might feel better.

LUKE: He doesn't get it, Kori. He doesn't have a clue.

KORI: He's too busy achieving his goals.

LUKE: Yeah. One match at a time.

KORI: You should talk to him.

LUKE: And say what? It's not that easy, Kori.

KORI: You got that right. (Pause.) Wouldn't it be great if everyone could just tell each other how they feel. I wish I …

LUKE: What?

KORI: Never mind.

LUKE: Kori?

KORI: Yeah?

LUKE: Sometimes I do think about … I don't know. Don't tell Matt.

KORI: I won't.

LUKE: I don't know if … I don't know what it means.

KORI: Me neither. (Pause.) Luke?

LUKE: What?

KORI: Sometimes I think about you.
(Buzzer. Ensemble shifts. REF blows whistle, indicates MATT and MELANIE: MELANIE curls herself around MATT. He

814

withdraws.)

MELANIE: What's wrong?

MATT: Everything.

MELANIE: You want to talk about it?

MATT: No. *(Pause)* Yes. *(Pause)* No.

MELANIE: How was practice?

MATT: Bad.

MELANIE: You worried about the wrestle-offs?

MATT: You could say that.

MELANIE: You gonna go for the takedown?

MATT: I don't know. I'm better at defense.

MELANIE: I've watched you. I think you can take him.

MATT: I'm not so sure. I'm not sure of anything anymore.

MELANIE: I know you can beat Willy.

MATT: I don't want to talk about it.

MELANIE: Okay, let's not talk about wrestling. I just want to be here with you. *(Pause)* Matt?

MATT: What?

MELANIE: Come sit with me. *(He sits. They wait. She caresses him. MATT grabs her.)* Hey, what's your hurry? *(He takes her down on the mat.)* Matt, you're hurting me.

MATT: Am I?

MELANIE: What's the matter?

MATT: Nothing.

MELANIE: Why are you acting like this?

MATT: Isn't this what you wanted?

MELANIE: Matt, stop it. *(He does not stop. He pins her.)* Stop it, Matt! Stop it!

MATT: Isn't this what you wanted?

MELANIE: Matt, no! Please! Not like this.

MATT: You told Willy I couldn't, didn't you? *(He presses himself against her until he makes his point.)* Now do you think I can? Do you? Do you?

MELANIE: Yes. Yes. Please. Let me go. *(MATT releases her. She is crying.)* What's the matter with you?

MATT: What's the matter with you?

MELANIE: I haven't even talked to Willy. And even if I did that doesn't give you the right to …to …

MATT: I thought that's what you wanted, what you did with those other guys.

MELANIE: What I did? How would you know what I did? *(Ensemble whispers in the background.)* Those guys … everyone who talks about me, they don't know me. They don't know how I feel. I never slept with anyone, Matt. No one. Not even Willy. *(She laughs through her tears.)* It's funny, isn't it? I never even wanted to be with anyone like that … except you.

MATT: Right. You expect me to believe that?

MELANIE: You can believe what you want.

MATT: Tell me what to believe.

MELANIE: I don't care anymore.
(Ensemble is silent.)

MATT: Melanie …

MELANIE: Don't touch me.

MATT: Why didn't you say something? Why did you let everybody believe you were a …
(He hesitates.)

MELANIE: Say it. Go ahead. Say it. Slut. It's an ugly word.

MATT: How could you take all the lies about you?

MELANIE: How could I take it? I liked it. I wanted them to talk about me, all right? Nobody talked about me before. No one even knew I existed. Now guys brag about me to their friends. A lot of guys want to go out with me now. Would you have asked me out if my nickname wasn't "Cherry" Garcia? Would you? Would you? *(Silence.)* I thought so.

MATT: Melanie … I'm sorry.

MELANIE: Forget it. Why should you be any different.

MATT: Melanie, wait.

MELANIE: Finally, I meet someone who makes me feel good, like I'm special. But you know what, I made you up, you're not real. You're just like all the rest of them.
(REF blows whistle, signals #15, says, "Reversal." MELANIE joins ensemble. KORI crosses onto mat.)

KORI: Guess you blew that big time.

MATT: Don't rub it in.

KORI: She'll probably never speak to you again.

MATT: Probably.

KORI: What are you gonna do?

MATT: Beat Willy in the wrestle-offs.

KORI: I mean about Melanie.

MATT: Beat Willy in the wrestle-offs.
(Buzzer. Lights dim to dappled night. Ensemble seems to disappear in darkness. LUKE enters the space. He becomes aware he is not alone. The first blow knocks him to the ground.)

LUKE: What … *(He shields his face.)* No, don't.
(He is overpowered and pummeled in the face and body. We do not see the attackers. We experience the assault through LUKE's face and body movement. REF blows whistle, signals #21, says, "Flagrant Misconduct." LUKE crawls off the mat and exits. Restore lights. Ensemble re-emerges. REF blows whistle, indicates MATT and KORI.)

KORI: How was the weigh-in?

MATT: No problem. A piece of cake.

KORI: I see Melanie.

MATT: Where?

KORI: Don't strain yourself. She's over there.

MATT: You seen Luke?

KORI: No. Not today. I don't think he came to school.

MATT: I can't believe it. The day of the wrestle-offs.

KORI: He called me last night. He sounded pretty bad.

MATT: What did he say?

KORI: I can't tell you. Luke made me promise not to say anything.

MATT: Then why did you bring it up?

KORI: Because I'm worried. I don't like it that he didn't come to school. And where is he now?

MATT: He won't miss the wrestle-offs.

KORI: I called his house. He's not there and his mom doesn't know where he is. She's worried, too.

MATT: What time is it?

KORI: Ten after three.

MATT: It's just warm-up. The match won't start until four. He'll be here.

KORI: Matt, have you ever known Luke to miss a warm-up? I'm really worried.

MATT: Did you check the locker room?

KORI: Now, how am I going to do that?

MATT: Wait here. I'll go.
    (REF indicates MATT, JOLT and WILLY.)

WILLY: Well, look who's here.

JOLT: Yeah, Mr. Can't Do Wrong.

WILLY: Who you looking for?

JOLT: Yeah, you looking for your buddy Luke?

MATT: Kiss my ass.

WILLY: I bet he is looking for Luke.

MATT: I'm not looking for anyone.

JOLT: Let me see. Luke.

WILLY: Yeah, Luke. You remember, the 171 pounder you used to wrestle.

MATT: What do you mean, used to wrestle?

WILLY: I heard he quit the team.

JOLT: Probably scared of the wrestle-offs.

WILLY: Coach said he won't be wrestling today. Guess that's a forfeit.

JOLT: Too bad. I was looking forward to a public humiliation.

WILLY: Or two.

MATT: You'd like that, wouldn't you?

JOLT: I would.

WILLY: Sounds good to me.

MATT: Where is he?

JOLT: Thought you weren't looking for him.

WILLY: And I don't see him anywhere, do you?

MATT: Where is he?

JOLT: If I knew, do you think I'd tell you?

MATT (controls his rage): Thanks. You reminded me of something I almost forgot.

WILLY: Glad to oblige.

JOLT: Yeah. Always happy to be helpful.
(REF blows whistle, signals #2, says, "Time Out." Dappled light. REF leads LUKE onto the mat, wearing warm-up jacket. MATT puts on his warm-up jacket.)

MATT: God, it's cold. How long you been here?

LUKE: Since last night.

MATT: You spent the night in Gebhardt's garage? You're lucky you didn't freeze to death.

LUKE: I worked out. That helped. Old man Gebhardt nearly caught me.

MATT: Was it that stupid dog barking?

LUKE: Yeah. Gebhardt came out here with his flashlight to check. Good thing he's blind as a bat or he'd have found me for sure.

MATT: You could have come to my house. *(Silence.)* I heard you quit the team.

LUKE: Yeah. I told Coach I couldn't make the wrestle-offs.

MATT: You told him you couldn't make it? This isn't a tea party. Are you crazy?

LUKE: That's it. You've found me out. I'm crazy. So I quit.

MATT: That's not what I mean. Why'd you do it?

LUKE: I just did, that's all.

MATT: Tell me what the hell's going on. Why did you quit the team?

LUKE: Go to the wrestle-offs. You're gonna be late.

MATT: I don't have time for games, Luke.

LUKE: Then go.

MATT: You can rot here for all I care. *(MATT begins to leave, then stops.)* Wait a minute. Not this time. You're pretty slick, Luke, but I'm not going without you. *(He goes to LUKE: LUKE pulls off his hood. Light falls on LUKE's bloodied face.)* Aw, God, Luke. Who did this to you?

LUKE: There were two of them.

MATT: Two of them?

LUKE: They were wearing masks. I don't know for sure. It might have been them.

MATT: Why didn't you tell me?

LUKE: I didn't want to make things worse than they already are.

MATT: You should have told me.

LUKE: So you could do what?

MATT: Beat them both to a bloody pulp. One at a time.

LUKE: That's what I thought.

MATT: What do you expect me to do?

LUKE: Go to the wrestle-offs and pin Willy.

MATT: And leave you here? No way.

LUKE: I'll be okay.

MATT: I'm not leaving you here.

LUKE: You'd be better off if you did.

MATT: What's that supposed to mean?

LUKE: Do you think all this would have happened if we weren't friends?

MATT: This isn't your fault. It could have happened to anybody.

LUKE: But it happened to me.

MATT: So?

LUKE: Don't you know why? They got me pegged. Pinned. Figured out. I'm a freak. And everybody knows it.

MATT: You're not a freak. They don't even know you.

LUKE: Maybe they do. Maybe they know something I don't.

MATT: They don't know anything.

LUKE: What if it's true about me? Have you ever thought about that?

MATT: No, I haven't.

LUKE: Well, maybe you should.

MATT (*prowls*): Listen to me. I know you. The rest of it doesn't matter. Not to me. *(Silence.)* It's freezing in here.

LUKE: Sorry I deserted you on the pre-calc test.

MATT: That's okay. I passed anyway.

LUKE: I thought if I stayed away it would be better.

MATT: You gonna hide out here for the rest of your life?

LUKE: No.

MATT: Good. Because I'm sick of freezing my butt off talking to you. Let's get you cleaned up. We don't have much time.

LUKE: I'm scared.

MATT: I know. It got to me, too. But Jolt and Willy reminded me who the good guys are. Come on. I'm not taking no for an answer. Get up.

LUKE: You're worse than your mom. You're a maniac.

MATT: That's right. Let's go.

LUKE: I'm not sure I can win.

MATT: I'm not either. But if you don't try then they win for sure. *(Holds out his hand to LUKE, helps him to his feet.)* If Jolt kills you, I'll donate your body to science.
(Buzzer. REF signals #19, says, "Two Points." Restore lights. MATT helps LUKE off the mat. JOLT and LUKE put on headgear, warm up for match.)

ENSEMBLE *(cheer).*

> Tick, tick, tick, tick, tick, tick, tick.
> Hold up, wait a minute, put a little boom in it,
> Boom, dynamite,
> Boom, boom, dynamite
> Boom, dynamite,
> Boom, boom.
> When you mess with dynamite,
> It goes like this …
> Tick, tick, tick, tick, tick, tick, tick, tick … BOOM!
> *(REF blows whistle, indicates JOLT and LUKE to take positions for the match. REF blows whistle. Wrestlers*

shake hands. REF checks LUKE's face, blows whistle to start match. Music and real time, slow motion, real time as suggested before. JOLT shoots low and takes LUKE down. JOLT struggles to pin LUKE but LUKE twists out of JOLT's grip and escapes. Buzzer. End of first period. REF signals #19, says, "Two Points."

REF blows whistle, indicates LUKE, who takes the defensive position. JOLT kneels behind him. REF blows whistle to begin second period. JOLT tries to flip LUKE onto his back. They struggle. LUKE gains control. JOLT works himself out of bounds. REF blows whistle, signals #7, says, "Out of Bounds."

REF blows whistle, JOLT takes the defensive position, LUKE on top. JOLT rolls LUKE, gains control. The two wrestlers strain against each other. REF lies down on the mat to watch for the pin.)

ENSEMBLE. Ten…nine…eight…seven…six…
(REF shouts: "One, two," slaps the mat. Buzzer. LUKE is defeated. JOLT jumps to his feet. Ensemble cheers. LUKE lies on the mat, then gets to his feet. REF blows whistle, indicates wrestlers shake hands. LUKE and JOLT touch hands. REF holds JOLT's hand in the air, indicating a win. Ensemble cheers. LUKE removes headgear and is comforted by KORI.)

ENSEMBLE (cheer).
> Don't mess, don't mess,
> Don't mess with the best,
> 'Cause the best don't mess.
> Don't fool, don't fool,
> Don't fool with the cool,
> 'Cause the cool don't fool.
> To the east, to the west,
> Willy is the best, best, best!

(REF blows whistle, indicates MATT and WILLY. They take the starting position, staring each other down.)

823

WILLY: You ready for this?

MATT: Ready? No, I'd say eager describes it better.
(REF signals wrestlers shake hands. REF blows whistle to start match. Wrestlers lock arms, competing for the takedown. Each endeavors to gain control but they are evenly matched. WILLY takes MATT down. REF signals #19, says, "Two Points." MATT tries to escape but WILLY flips him on his back, forcing his shoulders onto the mat. WILLY gets MATT in a painful scissor hold. The crowd cheers, anticipating a pin. MATT gains control, flips WILLY onto his back. REF signals one point for the escape. Ensemble cheers, as MATT pushes WILLY closer and closer to the mat. The ref counts: "One, two," and slaps the mat, indicating a pin. Buzzer.)

ENSEMBLE (cheer):

Hey, Matt, what's your cry?
V-I-C-T-O-R-Y! Go-o-o, Matt!
(WILLY gets up, barely containing his fury. REF signals wrestlers to shake hands. MATT holds out his hand and WILLY grazes it. REF blows whistle, raises MATT's arm to indicate victory. Ensemble cheers.)

JOLT: This isn't over yet. One down. One to go.

MATT: We could settle this right now.

WILLY: Sounds like a good idea to me.

LUKE: Let's go, Matt.

MATT: Move out of the way. You're in no shape to get in the middle of this.

JOLT: Haven't you had enough?

LUKE: Matt, this is what he wants.

MATT: No, it's what I want.

LUKE: If you do this you'll be disqualified. Willy'll step into your slot.

MATT: I don't care.

LUKE: I do.

MATT: Move out of the way, Luke.

JOLT: Yeah, move out of the way, Luke.

LUKE: Remember what you said to me? We gotta stick together or they'll win. I'm not moving. You'll have to go through me to get to him.

JOLT: I'd like to see that.

LUKE: You won here today. *(Pause.)* And so did I.

KORI: Luke's right. They're not worth the hassle.

LUKE: Let's go.

JOLT: Guess you two have better things to do than fight, huh?

MATT *(grabs JOLT in a choke hold)*. Look at him. Look at him! Do you know the guts it took for him to show up here? If you ever lay a hand on my friend again, I'll stick you to the mat so hard you'll never get up.
(REF blows whistle, thinks, signals #8, says, "Wrestler in Control." MATT releases JOLT.)

JOLT: We didn't do it, man. I don't know who nailed your friend, but it wasn't us.
(Ensemble shifts. REF indicates MELANIE and KORI.)

MELANIE: Guess you're gonna celebrate tonight, huh?

KORI: Yeah. I guess so. (Pause.) You wanna join us?

MELANIE: No, thanks.

KORI: I'm sorry about you and Matt.

MELANIE: It's not your fault.

KORI: I'm sorry anyway. Did he hurt you?

MELANIE: He told you what happened?

KORI: He's really upset about it. Are you okay?

MELANIE: Yeah. No. I thought he really cared about me. That's a joke, huh? Someone like Matt caring for someone like me?

KORI: It's not a joke.

MELANIE: Yes, it is. It's the joke of the century. And I set it up. I let them talk about me that way. Melanie's hot. She'll go for it. He thought that's what I wanted. I deserved what I got.

KORI: No, you didn't. You didn't deserve to be the target of Matt's insane determination. Nobody deserves that.

MELANIE: I only wanted him to … *(KORI reaches for her, she recoils.)* You want to hear the real irony of it? I would have given him anything if he'd asked me.

KORI: Melanie?

MELANIE: Yeah?

KORI: I thought you two were good for each other. I really did.

MELANIE: Guess we were both wrong about that.

KORI: Maybe you should talk to him?

MELANIE: I wish I could just disappear.
    (Silence.)

KORI: Hey, I'm going to a poetry reading tomorrow at The Barn.

MELANIE: Oh, yeah. I heard you go there a lot.

KORI: There'll be some cool people there. Want to come along?

MELANIE: I better not. I've gotta work. You know.

KORI: Yeah, I know. Maybe some other time.

MELANIE: Yeah. Sure.
    (REF blows whistle, indicates KORI and MELANIE in spotlight.)

KORI & MELANIE: You think you know me, but you don't.
    (Ensemble shifts. REF whistles twice to resume, indicates MATT and MELANIE.)

MATT: I did it, Melanie. I won.

MELANIE: Congratulations.

MATT: Melanie, wait.

MELANIE: Don't. My friends are waiting.

MATT: They're not your friends. *(Pause.)* I'll call you, okay?

MELANIE: I probably won't be home.

MATT: I want to talk to you, Melanie. I want to explain.

WILLY: Come on, Mel. We're getting old waiting for you.

MELANIE: I'm coming.

MATT: You're going with him?

MELANIE: Yeah.

MATT: I can't believe it. You don't even like him.

MELANIE: So what?

MATT: Melanie, give me a chance.

MELANIE: Why should I?

MATT: Because he doesn't care about you. You're just a trophy to him.

MELANIE: And you? What do you care about?

MATT: I don't know.

MELANIE: At least with Willy I know what to expect.

MATT: That's not what I meant. Melanie. I care about you. *(He reaches for her. She recoils.)* Please. Don't write me off. I know I went about this all wrong. I want to start over. I want to make it right.

HEATHER: Come on, Mel, we're waiting.

MELANIE: Heather thinks I should press charges.

MATT: What? Press charges for what? Nothing happened.

MELANIE: Nothing happened? Maybe not for you.

MATT: That's not what I meant. I shouldn't have been so rough, but I was angry. I made a mistake. I'm sorry.

MELANIE: I wish I could believe that.

MATT: Believe it. Don't press charges. Don't do that to me. Please, Melanie.

WILLY: We're leaving without you, Mel.

MATT: What are you going to do?

MELANIE: I don't know.

MATT: Don't go with him, Melanie. Let's talk this over. Please. *(MATT extends his hand. MELANIE hesitates, then takes it, drops it, joins WILLY: MATT remains alone on the mat. REF blows whistle, signals #15, says, "Reversal." REF indicates HEATHER and JOLT.)*

HEATHER: Hey, my parents aren't home tonight. We could have a little celebration at my house.

JOLT: I can't. I promised the guys I'd party with them tonight. You know, wrestling buddies.

HEATHER: Oh, well, that's okay, I guess. I'll ask Nicki to sleep over. See ya tomorrow?

JOLT: Yeah, sure, baby. *(REF indicates NICOLE.)*

NICOLE: Psst! Heather!

HEATHER: What?

NICOLE: Oh, God, I don't know how to tell you this. You'll die.

HEATHER: Don't be so melodramatic, Nicki. Just tell me.

NICOLE: I can't.

HEATHER: If you don't tell me, I'll strangle you right here in front of everybody.

NICOLE: You're going out with Jolt tonight, aren't you?

HEATHER: As a matter of fact, no. Why?

NICOLE: Oh, God.

HEATHER: Nicki, give it up.

NICOLE: Liz and Anne Marie are meeting Jolt at the diner.

HEATHER: What?

NICOLE: Oh, God … I can't tell you.

HEATHER: Tell me!

NICOLE: I heard that Liz can't wait anymore to tell him that she's …

828

(NICOLE whispers to HEATHER.)

HEATHER: Shut up.

NICOLE: What?

HEATHER: I said shut up. You must have heard wrong.

NICOLE: But she said …

HEATHER: Jolt loves me. He hasn't slept with Liz or anyone else.
(REF blows whistle, indicates JOLT in spotlight.)

JOLT: You think you know me, but you don't.
(REF whistles twice to resume. Ensemble shifts.)

NICOLE: Okay. Okay. But I know what I heard.

HEATHER: No, you don't.

NICOLE: Yes, I do.

HEATHER: No, you don't.

NICOLE: Well, I guess I could have heard wrong.

HEATHER: That's right.
(Buzzer. REF signals #1, says, "End of Match." Ensemble is grouped at center of mat.)

REFEREE. Because sportsmanship always takes priority over winning, and because losing is a lesson which must be learned early in life…
(ENSEMBLE FUNCTIONS AS A CHORUS.)

ALL *(except REFEREE)*. I will remember always that fair play, moral obligation and ethics are a part of winning and losing, that graciousness and humility should always characterize a winner and that pride and honor do not desert a good loser.
(Ensemble speaks directly to the audience.)

HEATHER: You think you know the way it is.

JOLT: You think you know the score.

NICOLE: You think you're so smart.

KORI: You think you've got me figured out.

WILLY: You think you've got me pegged. Pinned.

MELANIE: You think you know me, but you don't.

LUKE: How can you know me?

ENSEMBLE *(except REFEREE)*. I'm not even sure I know myself.
(Ensemble stands facing the audience as lights fade slowly to ...)

BLACKOUT—END PLAY

POST PERFORMANCE FORUM
DESIGNED BY LAURIE BROOKS

If the theatre decides to employ the forum, there is no curtain call directly following the performance. Instead, following the final blackout, the audience is greeted by the facilitator, who introduces himself and invites them to participate in a brief post-performance experience. The forum can be as long as an hour or as short as twenty minutes. The facilitator then takes audience members through five steps that encourage them to travel deeper into the issues, emotions, and characters in the play. The play may be performed with or without the forum. The audience experience is enhanced by the forum, but the play stands on its own.

PART I. AGREE AND DISAGREE STATEMENTS:

As the Facilitator reads each statement, audience members are asked to stand in support if they agree or remain seated in protest if they disagree. This all-group opening exercise provides safe expression of audience opinions and strong visual images regarding character actions in the play.

1. Melanie should get back together with Matt.

2. Jolt is lying when he says that he and Willy aren't the ones who beat up Luke.

3. Rumors can be hurtful but they usually don't cause any lasting damage.

4. Kori's suggestion that Matt hook up with someone to help dispel the rumors was ill-advised.

5. Even though he stands by Luke, Matt is still homophobic.

6. Most people believe rumors without making the effort to discover the truth.

7. The pressure to succeed that Matt feels in the play is mostly self-generated.

8. Heather got what she deserves at the end of the play.

PART II. RANKING

Facilitator invites the characters from the play to join the proceedings.

After the characters are introduced, audience members rank their behavior in the play from most objectionable to least objectionable. Facilitator places the characters in a line from most objectionable behavior to least objectionable according to audience ranking, providing a visual reference.

Facilitator then calls on individual audience members to adjust the rankings according to their personal opinions. Facilitator will re-adjust the characters in the lineup, asking volunteers to share their reasons for ranking the characters as indicated. This affords the opportunity for awareness of differing opinions.

PART III. GROUP RESPONSE

Characters respond to audience ranking. Taking turns, the group speaks about their actions and motivations in the play. These brief speeches may be rehearsed, improvised or a combination of both. They may take the form of an apology, thoughts about what audience members have said, or defending their actions in the play. It is important that this segment not become didactic, but that the characters speak from their personal points of view. Now the audience has new information about the characters. One character does not speak but is withheld for closure.

PART IV. REFLECTION

Audience members are asked to share sentences or phrases of comfort, advice, affirmation or counsel to the characters in the play. In this portion of the forum, the facilitator stands back, allowing participants to negotiate this segment themselves. Audience members stand, one at a time, offer brief thoughts, then sit, taking turns until all who choose to participate have had an opportunity to speak. The characters are silent throughout, listening.

832

PART V. CLOSURE

The character who did not speak earlier now brings the workshop to a close with thoughts about his or her actions and motivations in the play, or perhaps some commentary about what the audience members have said. It is important to end this closing step on a positive note.

The facilitator thanks audience members and the characters for their participation, encouraging applause for themselves and the actors. Curtain call.

END OF FORUM

FACILITATOR'S GUIDE

After the actors exit, the facilitator greets the audience and invites them to participate in the forum. It is crucial that the facilitator not make any judgments, positive or negative, regarding audience responses in the forum. He/She remains neutral throughout.

SAMPLE DIALOGUE:

FACILITATOR: Good afternoon, and welcome to *The Wrestling Season.* I'd like to invite you now to participate in a unique theatre forum where we'll ask you to share some of your opinions and thoughts about the issues raised in the play.

PART I. AGREE AND DISAGREE STATEMENTS

This step should move quickly. No discussion. If someone wants to speak, ask him/her to hold the question/comment for later.

Sample Dialogue:

FACILITATOR. I'm going to read a series of statements about some of the actions in the play and I want you to stand in support if you agree or stay seated in protest if you disagree.

Facilitator thanks the audience for their participation after each statement, asking them to sit down before beginning the next. Facilitator may offer neutral comments on audience response.

Sample Dialogue:

FACILITATOR. That looks fairly unanimous to me.
or: I think that's about half and half.

NOTE: In the premiere production, the referee took on the role of facilitator, so in this description the pronoun "he" will be used for simplicity. However, facilitating this forum is equally effective done by a woman.

PART II. RANKING

The facilitator brings the actors back into the space, never referring to them as actors but, rather, calling them "the characters" or "the group." He asks them to introduce themselves and, in character, the actors state their names. Facilitator then explains that he will determine the ranking of the characters by the volume of a "yes" response as each character's name is called. Again, no discussion at this point. This is still information gathering.

Sample Dialogue:

FACILITATOR. When I point to someone in the group you'll help me determine how to rank their behavior from most objectionable to least objectionable by the volume of your yeses. Did you object to Nicole's behavior?

After all the characters have been named, the facilitator brings onstage four or five characters, placing them in order based on the strongest responses on objectionable behavior. He then reverses the process, asking the audience to rank the four or five characters based on behavior that meets with their approval.

FACILITATOR. Did you approve of Kori's behavior?

The facilitator states he has attempted to best represent the majority viewpoint regarding the characters' behavior. He now calls upon several audience members with differing opinions to re-rank the group, stating their reasons.

FACILITATOR. This is how I think you, the audience, has ranked the group. But some of you may feel differently about the ranking. Who would like to stand and give us your re-ranking and reasons why?

Remaining in character, the group of actors rearrange themselves to represent the new rankings.

PART III. GROUP RESPONSE

Sample Dialogue:

FACILITATOR. Now I'm going to give the group a chance to respond to your ranking them in this order.

One at a time, the characters speak. (As noted above, the characters speak about their actions and motivations in the play. These brief speeches may be rehearsed, improvised or a combination of both. They may take the form of an apology, thoughts about what audience members have said or defending their actions in the play.)

Sample Dialogue:

NICOLE. I just want to say that regardless of anyone's behavior, I don't think that Heather deserved what she got. No one deserves that. (Audience response.) Do any of you deserve that?

WILLY. I want to take responsibility for my actions and I think everyone up here should do the same.

MELANIE. I know people make mistakes and I know that it was a mistake that allowed the rumors about me, but people don't have to believe them.

JOLT. I see now what you guys are talking about. When you say stuff it means something to someone else. It's a bigger deal to them than it is to you. But I think it's really sad that some of you say you can't forgive. I mean, I'm really sorry about what I did to Heather and I just hope she can forgive me.

PART IV. REFLECTION

After stating the guidelines, the facilitator will step into the background during this portion of the workshop. He asks audience members not to raise their hands but to negotiate their responses by simply standing and taking turns. The facilitator allows many comments, allowing the reflection to build over the course of ten minutes or more. Sensing a wrap-up moment, the facilitator waits for someone to make an especially cogent or pointed comment and stops the action.

The facilitator lays out these guidelines for the participants.

1. No name-calling. If someone breaks this rule, don't let it go by. Stop the action and ask the participants what they think of that behavior. They will self-patrol the action. The facilitator models appropriate language.

2. No cursing. Facilitator responds as above.

3. Use "I" messages. "You" is accusatory and puts everyone on the defensive. This rule offers a message to young people about effective communication.

Sample Dialogue:

FACILITATOR. Just like at school, there'll be no cursing or name-calling. Can we agree on that? *(Audience response.)*

I'm not sure about that response. Can we agree to no cursing and no name-calling? *(Audience response — more enthusiastic.)* Thank you. It's important to start with the word "I," like I think or I feel…and follow that with your phrase or sentence to someone in the group.

After comments are complete, the facilitator thanks the audience and states he would like to conclude the forum. At this time, the actor who has not spoken now says s/he would like to speak.

PART V. CLOSURE

The final character speaks. Which character closes the workshop may be determined before the proceedings.

Sample Dialogue:

KORI. You know what, it doesn't matter if Jolt and Willy did or didn't do it. They still caused it. They created an atmosphere of hate that made it possible for someone to think it was okay to go after Luke. Look at that locker! That word hit him harder than the fists, whoever they belonged to. Matt, I had no right to suggest that you ask Melanie out just to stop the rumors. If I had known that something like this would happen, I never would have said such a dumb thing. But hindsight is 20/20, isn't it?

The Facilitator ends the forum:

FACILITATOR. Thank you, audience, for your great participation today. I want to take a moment now to introduce you to *(names the intervention specialist or counselor in attendance)* who has more information for you and your teachers on the way out. And now, give yourselves and the cast of *The Wrestling Season* a big hand.

Comments from Jeff Church, Producing Artistic Director, The Coterie Theatre, Kansas City, Missouri, about his experience directing The Wrestling Season.

• An actual wrestling coach is vital. If you should be lucky enough to find someone who can be at every rehearsal and has theatre experience, you'll be even better off. The best scenario, we found, was to give the company a vocabulary of wrestling movements they could draw upon throughout the staging of the play. We kept much of the action low to the mat and played against traditional or realistic "high school hallway" staging.

• Using wrestling singlets for all, no matter what vocal reaction the audience has in the beginning, is worth it overall.

• Peppered throughout the play is: "You think you know me, but you don't." These worked best when the characters spoke directly to the other characters instead of direct address — yet, the referee's spoken explanation of his signals worked best given to the audience.

• Laurie's play being an anti-model, the logical extension of this played out in rehearsal when the characters with the most deplorable behavior became fully justified in their own minds — and filling their actions with dimension became important. *(The villains weren't villains, and the victims weren't played as victims.)*

• In the post performance forum, you'll want a series of test audiences throughout rehearsals for the referee and the group. Waiting for previews to begin the forum would have been a mistake. We found the forum was very much an ongoing process, and we were adjusting and refining it throughout the run.

• The audience may finally realize that the ranking section of the forum ironically puts them in the position of judging the characters — and we found people having strong feelings about this to be okay. The referee is simply there to allow them to air their feelings, not to teach or justify the forum.

Laurie Brooks' plays for young audiences have been widely produced at theatres and festivals across the United States, Ireland and the United Kingdom. Awards include a John Gassner Playwriting Award from the New England Theatre Conference for Imaginary Friends, the Bonderman/IUPUI Youth Theatre Playwriting Award and the Distinguished Play Award from the American Alliance for Theatre and Education for Selkie, the first Aurand Harris Playwriting Award from the New England Theatre Conference for Devon's Hurt and The Kennedy Center's New Visions/New Voices for Imaginary Friends, Selkie and The Wrestling Season, also the recipient of an Aurand Harris grant from The Children's Theatre Foundation of America. Commissioned plays also include Deadly Weapons (Graffiti Theatre, Cork, Ireland), The Match Girl's Gift: A Christmas Story (Nashville Children's Theatre), and Franklin's Apprentice (Stage One: The Louisville Children's Theatre). Anthologized plays include Selkie in Theatre for Young Audiences: Twenty Great Plays for Children (St. Martin's Press, 1998) and The Match Girl's Gift in The Twelve Plays of Christmas (Applause, 1999). Brooks teaches playwriting at New York University and lives with her three daughters, Joanna, Elizabeth and Stephanie.

BIBLIOGRAPHY OF ANTHOLOGIES OF PLAYS FOR YOUNG AUDIENCES

The following bibliography samples the authors, subject matter, and publishers active in the field in this country. I have arranged the material chronologically so that readers might better observe trends. The entries were checked in the Arizona State University Library catalogue for accuracy. I list authors' and editors' names as they appear in these records (based on the Library of Congress Name Authorization Files, not as they appear on many of the title pages) so that scholars can better locate other works by these authors. Many of these books had multiple editions, but the Child Drama Collection copy is listed. Some are one edition of an annual series.

At the end I include a short list of bibliographies of plays for young audiences.

I want to express a special thank you to the Child Drama Collection donors for placing these valuable historical books in a site accessible to scholars from all over the world.

— Katherine Krzys, Curator, Child Drama Collection

— Hayden Library, Arizona State University

1700s

Stearns, Charles. *Dramatic Dialogues for the Use of Schools.* Leominster, MA: John Prentiss & Co., 1798.

1800s

Baker, George M. *Amateur Dramas for Parlor Theatricals, Evening Entertainments, and School Exhibitions.* Boston: Lee & Shepard, 1867.

Bell, Florence Eveleen Eleanore Olliffe, Lady. *Fairy Tale Plays and How to Act Them.* London/New York: Longmans Green and Co., 1899.

Genlis, Stephanie Felicite, Comtesse de. *The Juvenile Theatre: Containing the Best Dramatic Productions of the Celebrated Madam de Genlis: Translated from the French by a Friend to Youth.* New York: Printed for the translator by D. and G. Bruce, 1897.

Dugan, Caro Atherton. *The King's Jester, and Other Short Plays for Small Stages.* Boston/New York: Houghton, Mifflin, 1899.

Fowle, William B. *Parlor Dramas, or, Dramatic Scenes: For Home Amusement.* Boston: Samuel F. Nichols, 1856.

Freiligrath-Kroeker, Kate. *Alice Thro' the Looking-Glass and Other Fairy Plays for Children.* New York: G. P. Putnam's Sons, 1883.

Frost, S. Annie. *Amateur Theatricals and Fairy-Tale Dramas: A Collection of Original Plays, Expressly Designed for Drawing-Room Performance.* New York: Dick & Fitzgerald, 1868.

More, Hannah. *Sacred Dramas, Chiefly Intended for Young Persons: The Subjects Taken from the Bible: To Which Are Added Reflections of King Hezekiah; Sensibility, a Poem; and Search After Happiness.* Newark, NJ: W. Tuttle & Co., 1806.

1900-1909

Chapman, John Jay. *Four Plays for Children. New York: Moffat, Yard & Co., 1908.*

Mackay, Constance D'Arcy. *The House of the Heart and Other Plays for Children: Designed for Use in the Schools.* New York: H. Holt and Co., 1909.

Stevenson, Augusta. *Children's Classics in Dramatic Form: Book Three. Boston/New York:* Houghton Mifflin Co., 1908.

Anderson, Isabel. *Everyboy and Other Plays for Children.* New York: Shakespeare Press, 1914.

Briscoe, Margaret Sutton, et. al. *Harper's Book of Little Plays: Selected for Home and School Entertainments.* New York/London: Harper & Brothers, 1910.

Chapman, John Jay. *Neptune's Isle and Other Plays for Children.* New York: Moffat, Yard and Co., 1911.

Dunsany, Edward John Moreton Drax Plunkett, Baron [Lord]. *Plays of Gods and Men.* Boston: John W. Luce & Co., 1917. *The First Flag and Other Patriotic Plays and Exercises, For Children from Eight to Fifteen Years.* Boston/New York/etc.: Educational Pub. Co., 1917.

Irish, Marie. *Little People's Plays for Children and Young People.* Chicago: T. S. Denison, 1913.

Mackay, Constance D'Arcy. *Patriotic Plays and Pageants for Young People.* New York: H. Holt and Co., 1912.

Mackay, Constance D'Arcy. *The Silver Thread and Other Folk Plays for Young People: Arranged for Use in the Grammar Grades.* New York: H. Holt and Co., [c1910].

Lütkenhaus, Anna M., ed. *Plays for School Children.* New York: Century, 1915.

Skinner, Eleanor L., and Ada M. Skinner. *Children's Plays.* New York: D. Appleton, 1918.

Walker, Stuart. *Portmanteau Plays.* Edited by Edward Hale Bierstadt. 2nd ed. rev. Cincinnati: Stewart & Kidd Co., 1917.

Walker, Stuart. *More Portmanteau Plays.* Edited by Edward Hale Bierstadt. Cincinnati: Stewart & Kidd Co., 1919.

1920-1929

Benton, Rita. *The Star-Child and Other Plays.* Illustrated by photographs of actual performances by children. New York: Writers Pub. Co., 1921.

Brooks, Charles S. *Frightful Plays!* New York: Harcourt, Brace and Co., 1922. *Dickon Goes to the Fair and Other Plays. From the Drama League's Prize Contest.* New York: George H. Doran Co., 1927.

Edland, Elisabeth. *The Children's King and Other Plays for Children, with Chapters on Dramatizing with Children.* New York: Abingdon Press, 1928.

Farrar, John Chipman. *The Magic Sea Shell and Other Plays for Children.* New York: George H. Doran Co., 1923.

Folmsbee, Beulah. *Guki the Moon Boy and Other Plays.* New York: Harcourt, Brace & Co., 1928.

Frank, Florence Kiper. *Three Plays for a Children's Theatre.* New York: H. Vinal, 1926.

Fyleman, Rose. *Eight Little Plays for Children.* New York: George H. Doran Co., 1925.

Garnett, Louise Ayres. *Three to Make Ready: Hilltop, Muffins, The Pig Prince: Three Plays for Young People.* The Drama League Junior Play Series. New York: George H. Doran Co., 1923.

Goldsmith, Sophie L., adapter. *Wonder Clock Plays: Adapted for Children from Howard Pyle's* The Wonder Clock. New York/London: Harper & Bros., 1925.

Hubbard, Eleanore. *Citizenship Plays: A Dramatic Reader for Upper Grades.* Chicago/New York/Boston: B. H. Sanborn & Co., 1922.

Jagendorf, M. A. *Fairyland and Footlights: Five Children's Plays.* New York: Bretano's, 1925.

843

Jagendorf, M. A. *Pantomimes for the Children's Theatre*. New York: Brentano's, 1926.

Knickerbocker, Edwin Van B., ed. *Plays for Classroom Interpretation*. New York: H. Holt, 1921.

Lord, Katharine. *Plays for School and Camp*. Boston: Little, Brown and Co., 1922.

Moses, Montrose Jonas, ed. *A Treasury of Plays for Children*. Boston: Little, Brown & Co., 1921.

Moses, Montrose Jonas, ed. *Another Treasury of Plays for Children*. Boston: Little, Brown and Co., 1926.

Riley, Alice C. D. *Ten Minutes by the Clock and Three Other Plays for Out-Door and In-Door Production*. New York: George H. Doran Co., 1923.

Taylert, Gertrude Ermatinger, and Martina B. Rodney. *Three Splendid Plays for Junior High*. Franklin, OH: Eldridge Entertainment House, 1927.

Taylor, Katharine, and Henry Copley Greene. *The Shady Hill Play Book*. New York: Macmillan Co., 1928.

Thomas, Charles Swain, ed. *Atlantic Book of Junior Plays*. Boston: Little, Brown and Co., 1924.

1930-1939

Berman, Sadye A. *Plays for the Schoolroom: Safety, Character, Holiday*. New York: Samuel French, 1936.

Ceppi, Marc. *Twelve French Plays for Schools: A Conversational Reader*. Boston: Heath, 1936.

Coit, Dorothy. *Kai Khosru and Other Plays for Children, As Produced by the King-Coit Children's Theatre*. New York: Theatre Arts Inc., 1934.

Dean, Alexander, comp. and ed. *Seven to Seventeen: Plays for School and Camp: Twenty-One New Plays for Boys and Girls, Printed for the First Time.* New York/Los Angeles/London: Samuel French, 1931.

Field, Rachel. *Patchwork Plays.* Garden City, NY: Doubleday, Doran & Co., 1930.

Hofer, Mari Ruef. *Festival and Civic Plays from Greek and Roman Tales.* Educational PlayBook Series. Rev. ed. Chicago: Beckley-Cardy, 1931.

Housman, Louise and Edward T. Koehler. *Footlights Up! Practical Plays for Boys and Girls.* New York/London: Harper & Bros., 1935.

Johnson, Theodore, ed. *Easy Plays for Teen Age Girls.* Boston: Baker's Plays, 1938.

Knox, Jessie A., ed. *Plays with a Purpose: A Group of Short Sketches for Presentation by Home Economics Students.* New York: Lakeside Pub. Co., 1930.

Major, Clare Tree. *Playing Theatre: Six Plays for Children.* New York/London: Oxford University Press, 1930.

Moses, Montrose Jonas, ed. *Ring Up the Curtain! A Collection of Plays for Children.* Boston: Little, Brown & Co., 1932.

Robbins, Estelle Harriet. *A Comedy of the Woods (Animated Botany): Presenting Three Separate Plays Entitled: Mother Earth's Children, Jacks's Sermon, The Adventurous Tulip.* Los Angeles: Grafton Pub. Corp., 1930.

1940-1949

Henry, Robert David and James M. Lynch. *History Makers: Eight Radio Plays Designed to Teach the Fundamentals of Broadcasting and an Appreciation of American History: Adaptable for Classroom Use.* Evanston, IL: Row, Peterson, 1941.

845

Mayorga, Margaret, ed. *The World's a Stage: Short Plays for Juniors.* New York/Los Angeles/etc.: Samuel French, 1943.

Robinson, Marvin G. *From Story to Stage: Eleven Miniature Dramatizations of Well Known Stories by Famous Authors.* Boston/ Los Angeles: Baker's Plays, 1946.

Watson, Katherine Williams, comp. *Radio Plays for Children.* New York: H. W. Wilson, 1947.

1950-1959

Goulding, Dorothy Jane. *The Master Cat, and Other Plays.* Chicago: Coach House Press, 1955.

Gross, Edwin A. and Nathalie Gross. *Teen Theater: A Guide to Play Production and Six Royalty- Free Plays.* New York: McGraw-Hill, 1953.

Kamerman, Sylvia E., ed. *Children's Plays from Favorite Stories: Royalty-Free Dramatizations of Fables, Fairy Tales, Folk Tales, and Legends.* Boston: Plays, Inc. 1959.

MacAlvay, Nora Tully, and Virginia Lee Comer, comp and eds. *First Performance: Plays for the Junior High School Age.* New York: Harcourt, Brace, 1952.

McCaslin, Nellie. *More Legends in Action: Ten Plays of Ten Lands.* Evanston, IL: Row, Peterson, 1950

Miller, Madge. *Miniature Plays: Volume I: Written for The Pittsburgh Miniature Theatre.* Anchorage, KY: Children's Theatre Press, 1954.

Wallerstein, James S. *Adventure: Five Plays for Youth.* New York: Bellamy Press, 1956.

1960-1969:

Birner, William B., comp. *Twenty Plays for Young People: A Collection of Plays for Children.* Anchorage, KY: Anchorage Press, 1967.

Jarvis, Sally Melcher. *Fried Onions and Marshmallows: And Other Little Plays for Young People.* New York: Parents' Magazine Press, 1968.

McCaslin, Nellie. *Pioneers in Petticoats: Dramatized Tales and Legends of Heroic American Women.* Evanston, IL: Row, Peterson, 1960.

Preston, Carol. *A Trilogy of Christmas Plays for Children.* Music selected by John Langstaff. New York: Harcourt, Brace & World, 1967.

Year 'Round Plays: A Grade Teacher Publication: Primary. Darien, CT: Teachers Publishing Corp., 1960.

1970-1979

Chorpenning, Charlotte B. *Three Plays of Adventure: The Adventures of Tom Sawyer, Radio Rescue, The Magic Horn* (with Anne Nicholson). Chicago: Coach House Press, 1972.

Cullum, Albert. *Aesop in the Afternoon.* New York: Citation Press, 1972.

Donahue, John Clark. *The Cookie Jar and Other Plays.* Ed. Linda Walsh Jenkins. Minneapolis: University of Minnesota Press, 1975.

Donahue, John Clark, and Linda Walsh Jenkins, eds. *Five Plays from the Children's Theatre Company of Minneapolis.* Minneapolis: University of Minnesota Press, 1975.

Harris, Aurand. *Six Plays for Children.* Biography and play analyses by Coleman A. Jennings. Austin: University of Texas Press, 1977.

Jonson, Marian. *Timblewit and Other Plays.* London: J. G. Miller/Chicago: Coach House Press, 1973.

Korty, Carol. *Plays from African Folktales.* Boston: Baker's Plays, 1975.

Korty, Carol. *Silly Soup: Ten Zany Plays with Songs and Ideas for Making Them Your Own.* Music by Mary Lynn Solot. New York: Charles Scribner, 1977.

Lifton, Betty Jean, ed. *Contemporary Children's Theater.* New York: Equinox, 1974.

Martin, Judith. *Christmas All Over the Place: Four Contemporary Christmas Plays from the Paper Bag Players.* Music by Donald Ashwander. New Orleans: Anchorage Press, 1977.

Moe, Christian, and Darwin Reid Payne, eds. *Six New Plays for Children.* Carbondale: Southern Illinois University Press, 1971.

Morton, Miriam, trans. and ed. *Russian Plays for Young Audiences: Five Contemporary Selections.* Foreword by Natalya Sats. Rowayton, CT: New Plays Books, 1977.

Scripts. Vol. 1, no. 10, Children, October 1972. New York: New York Shakespeare Festival Public Theater, 1972.

Swortzell, Lowell, ed. *All the World's a Stage: Modern Plays for Young People.* New York: Delacorte Press, 1972.

Zipes, Jack, ed. and trans. *Political Plays for Children: The Grips Theater of Berlin.* St. Louis: Telos Press, 1976.

1980-1989

Chirinian, Helane. *Let's Pretend: Short Plays Parents and Children Can Do Together.* Los Angeles: Price/Stern/Sloan, 1987.

Jennings, Coleman A., and Aurand Harris, eds. *Plays Children Love: A Treasury of Contemporary and Classic Plays for Children.* Garden City, NY: Doubleday, 1981.

Jennings, Coleman A., and Aurand Harris, eds. *Plays Children Love: Volume II: A Treasury of Contemporary and Classic Plays for Children.* New York: St. Martin's Press, 1988.

Jennings, Coleman A. and Gretta Berghammer, eds. *Theatre for Youth: Twelve Plays with Mature Themes.* Austin, TX: University of Texas Press, 1986.

Martin, Judith. *Everybody, Everybody: A Collection from the Paper Bag Players.* Music by Donald Ashwander. New York: Elsevier/Nelson Books, 1981.

Swortzell, Lowell, ed. *Six Plays for Young People from the Federal Theatre Project (1936-1939): An Introductory Analysis and Six Representative Plays.* New York: Greenwood Press, 1986.

Ustinov, Lev. *Fairy Tales for Theater.* Woodstock, IL: Dramatic Publishing Co., 1989.

Whitton, Patricia, ed. *Six Adventure Theatre Plays: A Celebration of the Plays and Playwrights of the Adventure Theatre, Montgomery County, Maryland.* Rowayton, CT: New Plays Inc., 1987.

1990-1999:

Averill, Ric. *The Princess and the Pea, No TV, and Other Plays: Four Short Plays for Children.* Woodstock, IL: Dramatic Publishing, 1999.

Bush, Max. *Plays for Young Audiences: Featuring the Emerald Circle and Other Plays by Max Bush*. Ed. Roger Ellis. Colorado Springs, CO: Meriwether Pub., 1995.

Enciso, Pilar, and Lauro Olmo. *Three Lion Plays for Children* (cover title). Estreno Collection of Contemporary Spanish Plays. Trans. Carys Evans-Corrales. University Park, PA: ESTRENO, 1997.

Jennings, Coleman A., ed. *Theatre for Young Audiences: 20 Great Plays for Children*. New York: St. Martin's Press, 1998.

Jennings, Coleman A., ed. *Eight Plays for Children: The New Generation Play Project*. Austin: University of Texas Press, 1999.

Kamerman, Sylvia E. *Plays of Black Americans: The Black Experience in America, Dramatized for Young People*. New expanded ed. Boston: Plays, 1994.

Levy, Jonathan, comp. *The Gymnasium of the Imagination: A Collection of Children's Plays in English, 1780-1860*. New York: Greenwood Press, 1992.

Martin, Judith. *Out of the Bag: The Paper Bag Players Book of Plays*. New York: Hyperion Books for Children, 1997.

Rosenberg, Joe, ed. *Aplauso! Hispanic Children's Theater*. Houston: Arte Publico Press, 1995.

Smith, Marisa, ed. *Seattle Children's Theatre: Six Plays for Young Audiences. Vol. 1*. Young Actor Series. Lyme, NH: Smith and Kraus, 1997.

Surface, Mary Hall. *Most Valuable Player and Four Other All-Star Plays for Middle and High School Audiences*. Young Actors Series. Lyme, NH: Smith and Kraus, 1999.

Swortzell, Lowell, ed. *Around the World in 21 Plays: Theatre for Young Audiences*. New York: Applause, 1997.

Swortzell, Lowell. *The Theatre of Aurand Harris: America's Most Produced Playwright for Young Audiences, His Career, His Theories, His Plays: Including Fifteen Complete Plays by Aurand Harris.* New Orleans: Anchorage Press, 1996.

Zeder, Suzan. *Wish in One Hand, Spit in the Other: A Collection of Plays by Suzan Zeder.* Edited with introduction and critical essays by Susan Pearson-Davis. New Orleans: Anchorage Press, 1990

2000

Frockt, Deborah Lynn, ed. *Seattle Children's Theatre: Six Plays for Young Audiences.* Vol. 2. Young Actor Series. Hanover, NH: Smith and Kraus, 2000

Kraus, Joanna H. *Women of Courage: Five Plays by Joanna H. Kraus.* Ed. Janet E. Rubin. Woodstock, IL: Dramatic Publishing, 2000.

BIBLIOGRAPHIES

Award-Winning Plays from the Playwrights Network of the American Alliance for Theatre and Education. Features the plays that have won or participated in the AATE Distinguished Play Award, the AATE Unpublished Play Reading Project Award, the IUPUI/Bonderman Playwriting Symposium and the Kennedy Center's New Visions/New Voices. [Tempe, AZ: American Alliance for Theatre & Education, 1999.]

The Best Available Project. ASSITEJ/USA. Vol. 1 (1989)-vol. 3 (1990).

Hammood, Emily, ed. *Annotated Bibliography of Opera/Music Theatre Works for Young and Family Audiences, 1978-1998: Opera for Children to Perform, Operas for Adults to Perform, Opera for Children and Adults to Perform.* 1st ed. [Pleasant Grove, AL]:

Opera for Youth, Inc., 1995.

Kreider, Barbara. *Index to Children's Plays in Collections.* Metuchen, NJ: Scarecrow Press, 1972.

Levy, Jonathan and Martha Mahard. "Preliminary Checklist of Early Printed Children's Plays in English, 1780-1855." In *Performing Arts Resources: Topical Bibliographies of the American Theatre.* Vol. 12. New York: Theatre Library Association, 1987.

Levy, Jonathan and Floraine Kay. "Checklist of Plays in English from 1856-1919." On the Child Drama website at www.asu.edu/lib/speccoll/drama/playindx.htm

Oglebay, Kate, comp. *Plays for Children: A Selected List. Compiled for the New York Drama League and the Inter-Theatre-Arts, Inc.* New York: H. W. Wilson Co.; London: Grafton & Co., 1922.

Outstanding Plays for Young Audiences: International Bibliography. ASSITEJ/USA.Vol. 1 (1984)-vol. 7 (2002).

Plays for High Schools and Colleges. Compiled by a joint committee, National Council of Teachers of English and The Drama League of America. Chicago: National Council of Teachers of English, 1923.

Subject Index to Children's Plays. Compiled by a subcommittee of the A.L.A. Board on Library Service to Children and Young People. Chicago: American Library Association, 1940.

Van Tassel, Wesley. *Children's Theatre: A Selected and Annotated Bibliography.* [Washington, DC]: Children's Theatre Association, 1975.